A DOONESBURY BOO

Tee Time in Berzerkistan

BY G. B. TRUDEAU

Andrews McMeel
Publishing, LLC

Kansas City • Sydney • London

DOONESBURY is distributed internationally by Universal Press Syndicate.

Tee Time in Berzerkistan copyright © 2009 by G. B. Trudeau. All rights reserved. Printed in the United States of America. No part of this book may be used or reproduced in any manner whatsoever without written permission except in the case of reprints in the context of reviews. For information, write Andrews McMeel Publishing, LLC, an Andrews McMeel Universal company, 1130 Walnut Street, Kansas City, Missouri 64106.

09 10 11 12 13 BAM 10 9 8 7 6 5 4 3 2 1

ISBN-13: 978-0-7407-7357-0
ISBN-10: 0-7407-7357-7

Library of Congress Control Number: 2009922833

www.andrewsmcmeel.com

DOONESBURY may be viewed on the Internet at
www.doonesbury.com and www.GoComics.com.

"I think playing golf during a war just sends the wrong signal."

—George W. Bush

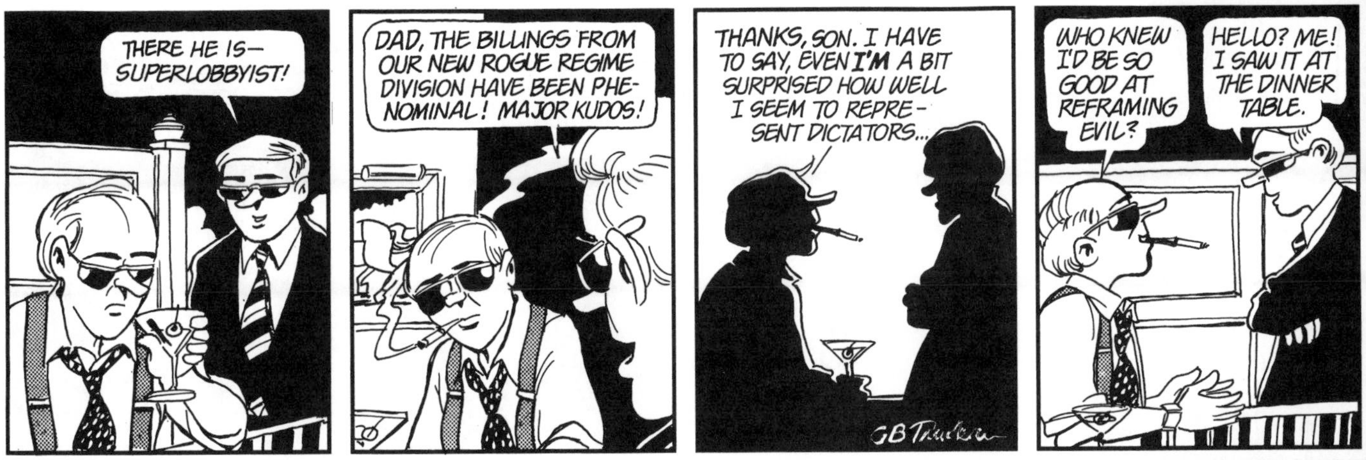
THERE HE IS—SUPERLOBBYIST!
DAD, THE BILLINGS FROM OUR NEW ROGUE REGIME DIVISION HAVE BEEN PHENOMINAL! MAJOR KUDOS!
THANKS, SON. I HAVE TO SAY, EVEN I'M A BIT SURPRISED HOW WELL I SEEM TO REPRESENT DICTATORS...
WHO KNEW I'D BE SO GOOD AT REFRAMING EVIL?
HELLO? ME! I SAW IT AT THE DINNER TABLE.

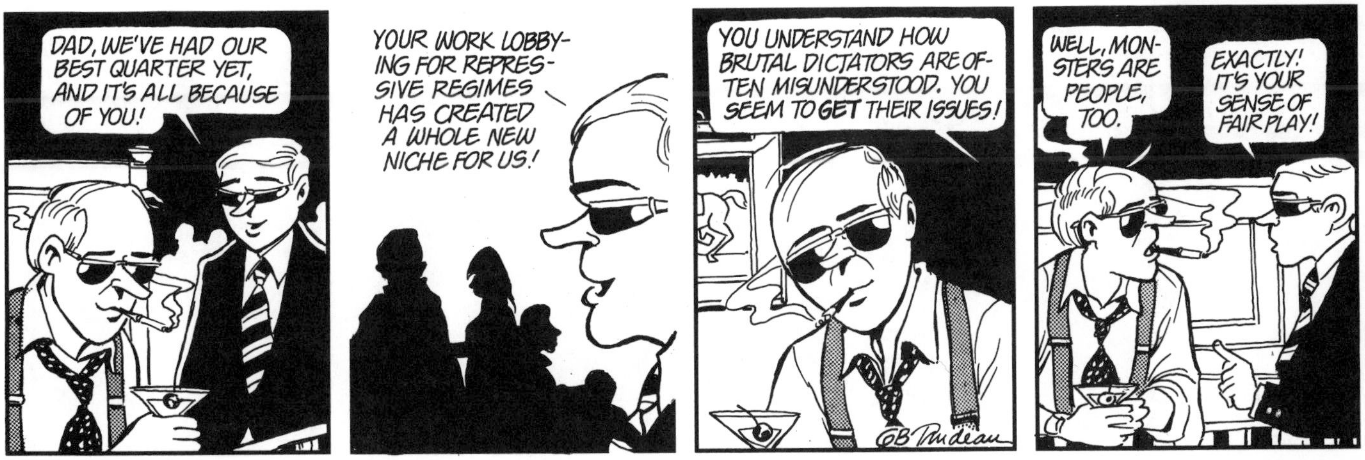
DAD, WE'VE HAD OUR BEST QUARTER YET, AND IT'S ALL BECAUSE OF YOU!
YOUR WORK LOBBYING FOR REPRESSIVE REGIMES HAS CREATED A WHOLE NEW NICHE FOR US!
YOU UNDERSTAND HOW BRUTAL DICTATORS ARE OFTEN MISUNDERSTOOD. YOU SEEM TO GET THEIR ISSUES!
WELL, MONSTERS ARE PEOPLE, TOO.
EXACTLY! IT'S YOUR SENSE OF FAIR PLAY!

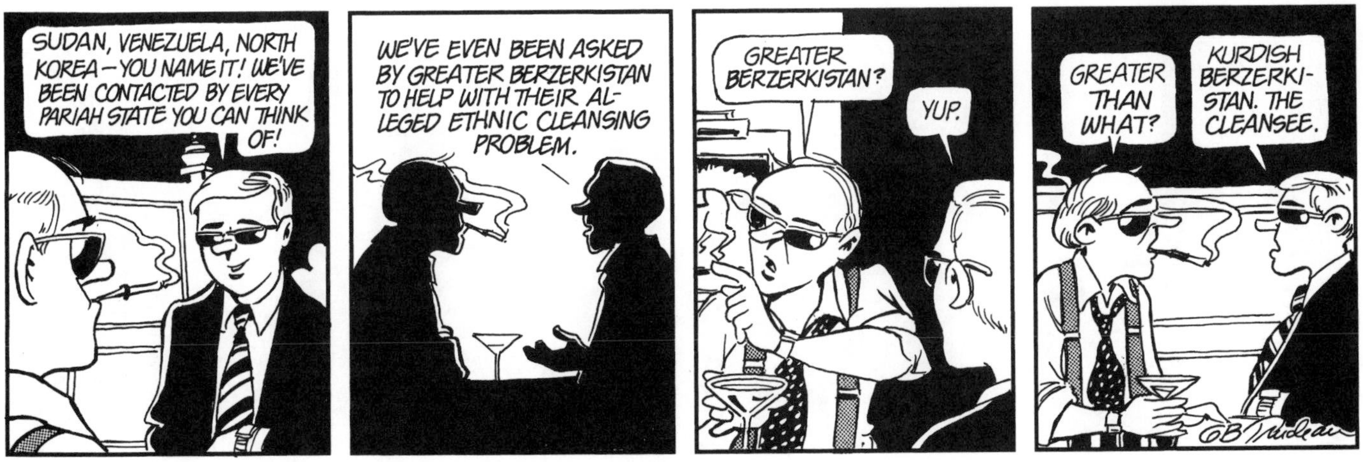
SUDAN, VENEZUELA, NORTH KOREA—YOU NAME IT! WE'VE BEEN CONTACTED BY EVERY PARIAH STATE YOU CAN THINK OF!
WE'VE EVEN BEEN ASKED BY GREATER BERZERKISTAN TO HELP WITH THEIR ALLEGED ETHNIC CLEANSING PROBLEM.
GREATER BERZERKISTAN?
YUP.
GREATER THAN WHAT?
KURDISH BERZERKISTAN. THE CLEANSEE.

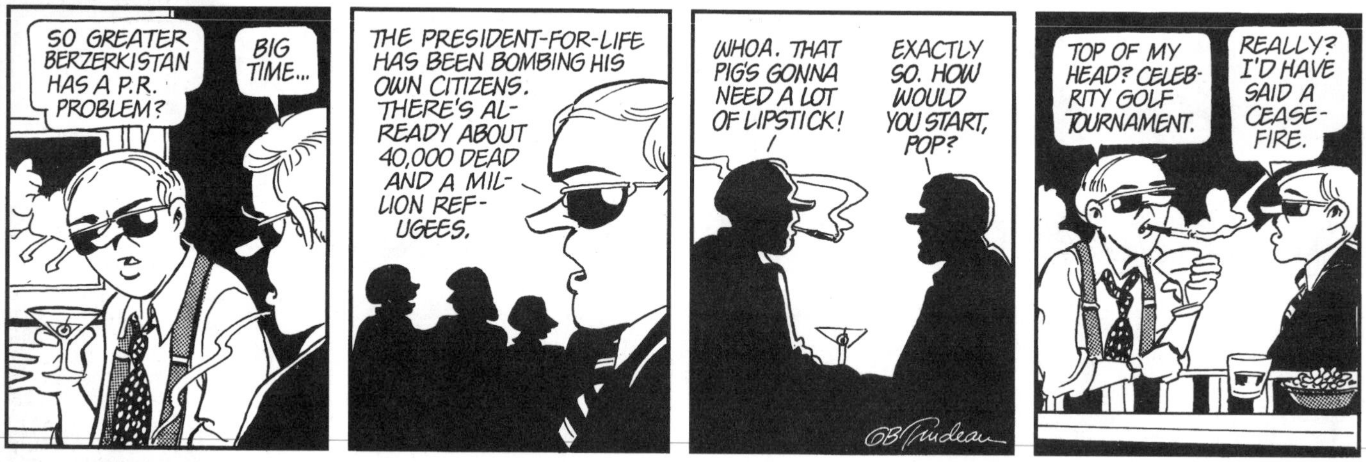
SO GREATER BERZERKISTAN HAS A P.R. PROBLEM?
BIG TIME...
THE PRESIDENT-FOR-LIFE HAS BEEN BOMBING HIS OWN CITIZENS. THERE'S AL-READY ABOUT 40,000 DEAD AND A MIL-LION REF-UGEES.
WHOA. THAT PIG'S GONNA NEED A LOT OF LIPSTICK!
EXACTLY SO. HOW WOULD YOU START, POP?
TOP OF MY HEAD? CELEB-RITY GOLF TOURNAMENT.
REALLY? I'D HAVE SAID A CEASE-FIRE.
GB Trudeau

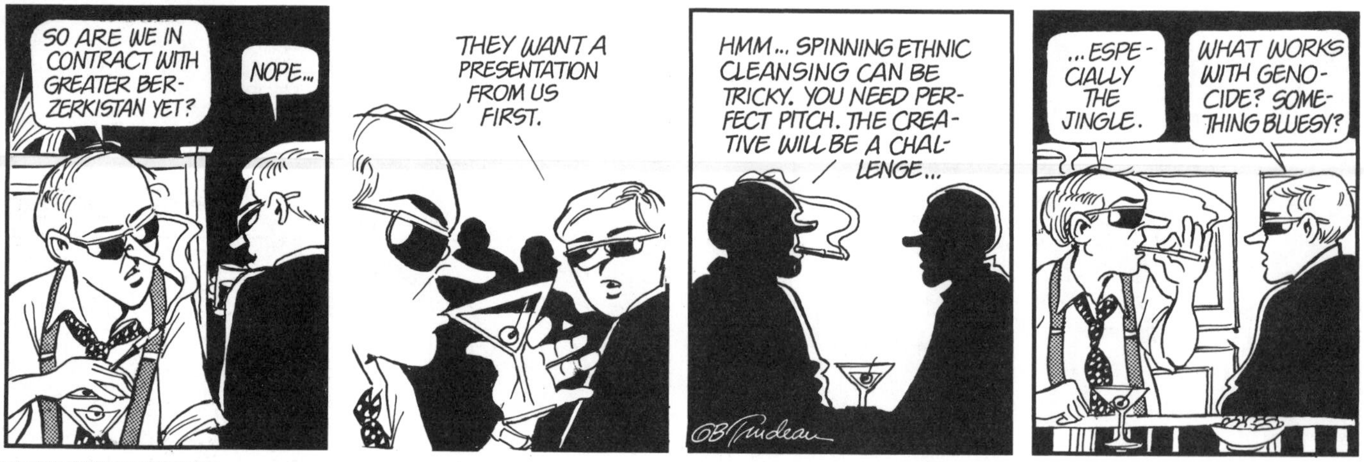
SO ARE WE IN CONTRACT WITH GREATER BER-ZERKISTAN YET?
NOPE...
THEY WANT A PRESENTATION FROM US FIRST.
HMM... SPINNING ETHNIC CLEANSING CAN BE TRICKY. YOU NEED PER-FECT PITCH. THE CREA-TIVE WILL BE A CHAL-LENGE...
...ESPE-CIALLY THE JINGLE.
WHAT WORKS WITH GENO-CIDE? SOME-THING BLUESY?
GB Trudeau

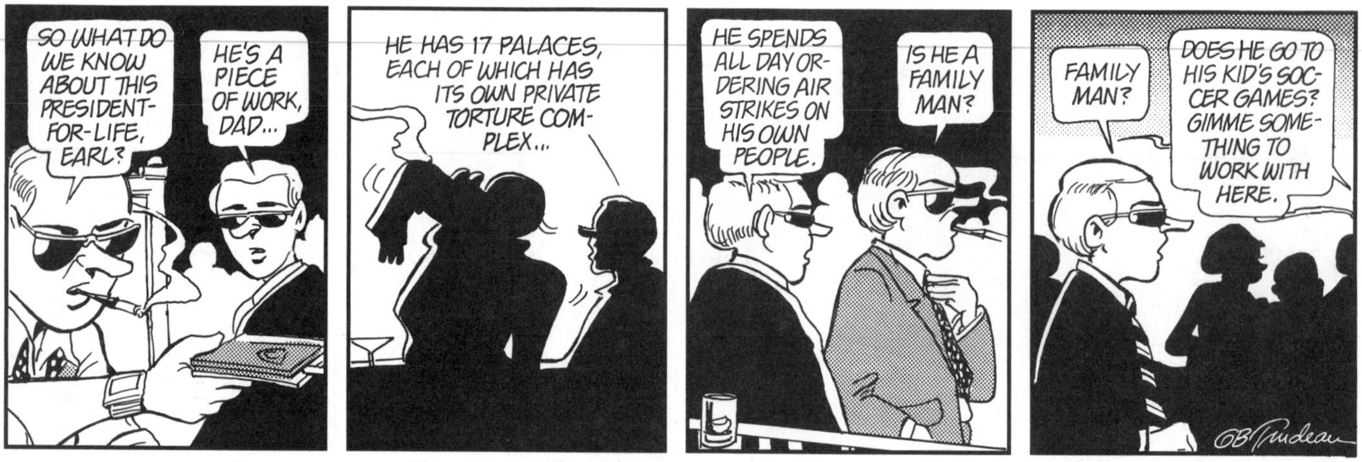
SO WHAT DO WE KNOW ABOUT THIS PRESIDENT-FOR-LIFE, EARL?
HE'S A PIECE OF WORK, DAD...
HE HAS 17 PALACES, EACH OF WHICH HAS ITS OWN PRIVATE TORTURE COM-PLEX...
HE SPENDS ALL DAY OR-DERING AIR STRIKES ON HIS OWN PEOPLE.
IS HE A FAMILY MAN?
FAMILY MAN?
DOES HE GO TO HIS KID'S SOC-CER GAMES? GIMME SOME-THING TO WORK WITH HERE.
GB Trudeau

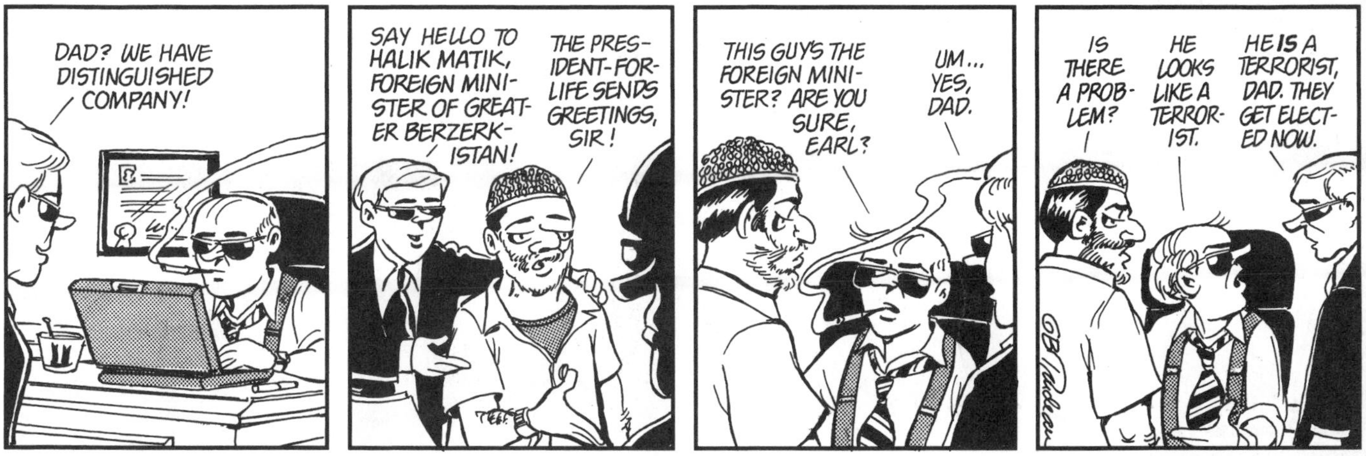
DAD? WE HAVE DISTINGUISHED COMPANY!
SAY HELLO TO HALIK MATIK, FOREIGN MINISTER OF GREATER BERZERKISTAN!
THE PRESIDENT-FOR-LIFE SENDS GREETINGS, SIR!
THIS GUY'S THE FOREIGN MINISTER? ARE YOU SURE, EARL?
UM... YES, DAD.
IS THERE A PROBLEM?
HE LOOKS LIKE A TERRORIST.
HE **IS** A TERRORIST, DAD. THEY GET ELECTED NOW.

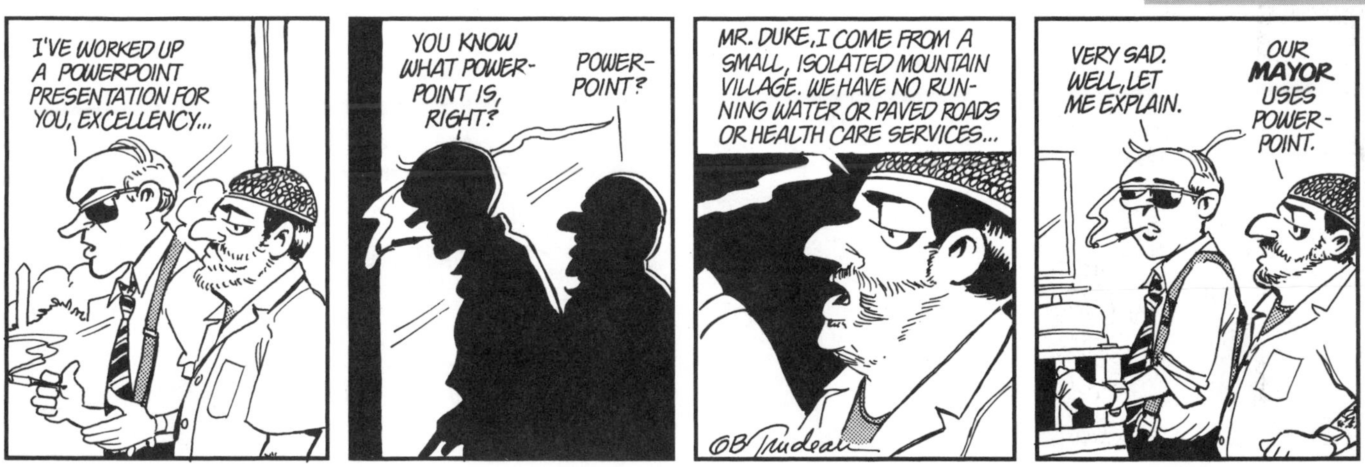
I'VE WORKED UP A POWERPOINT PRESENTATION FOR YOU, EXCELLENCY...
YOU KNOW WHAT POWERPOINT IS, RIGHT?
POWERPOINT?
MR. DUKE, I COME FROM A SMALL, ISOLATED MOUNTAIN VILLAGE. WE HAVE NO RUNNING WATER OR PAVED ROADS OR HEALTH CARE SERVICES...
VERY SAD. WELL, LET ME EXPLAIN.
OUR **MAYOR** USES POWERPOINT.

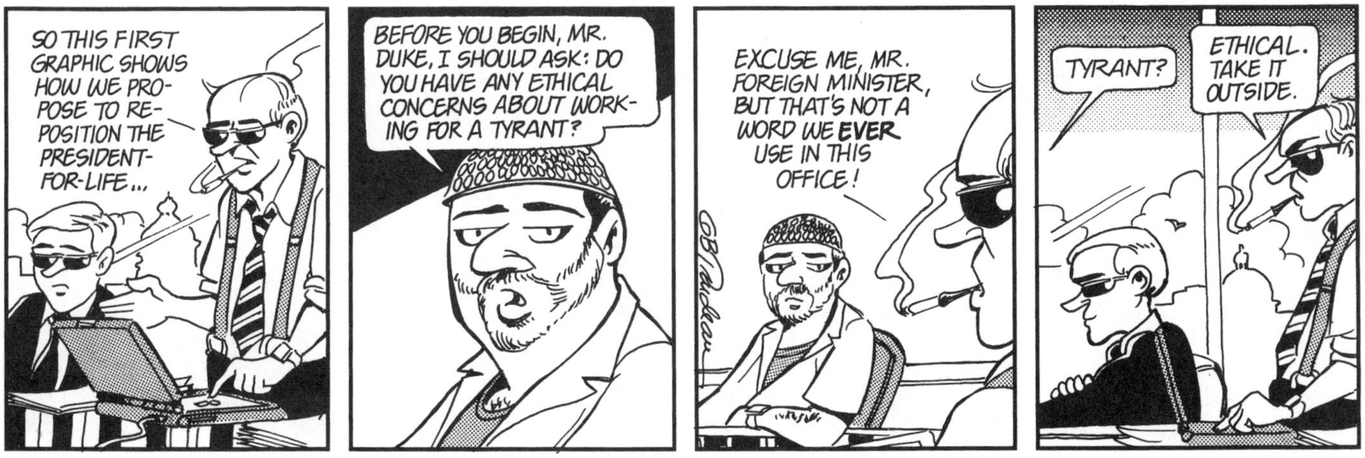
SO THIS FIRST GRAPHIC SHOWS HOW WE PROPOSE TO REPOSITION THE PRESIDENT-FOR-LIFE...
BEFORE YOU BEGIN, MR. DUKE, I SHOULD ASK: DO YOU HAVE ANY ETHICAL CONCERNS ABOUT WORKING FOR A TYRANT?
EXCUSE ME, MR. FOREIGN MINISTER, BUT THAT'S NOT A WORD WE **EVER** USE IN THIS OFFICE!
TYRANT?
ETHICAL. TAKE IT OUTSIDE.

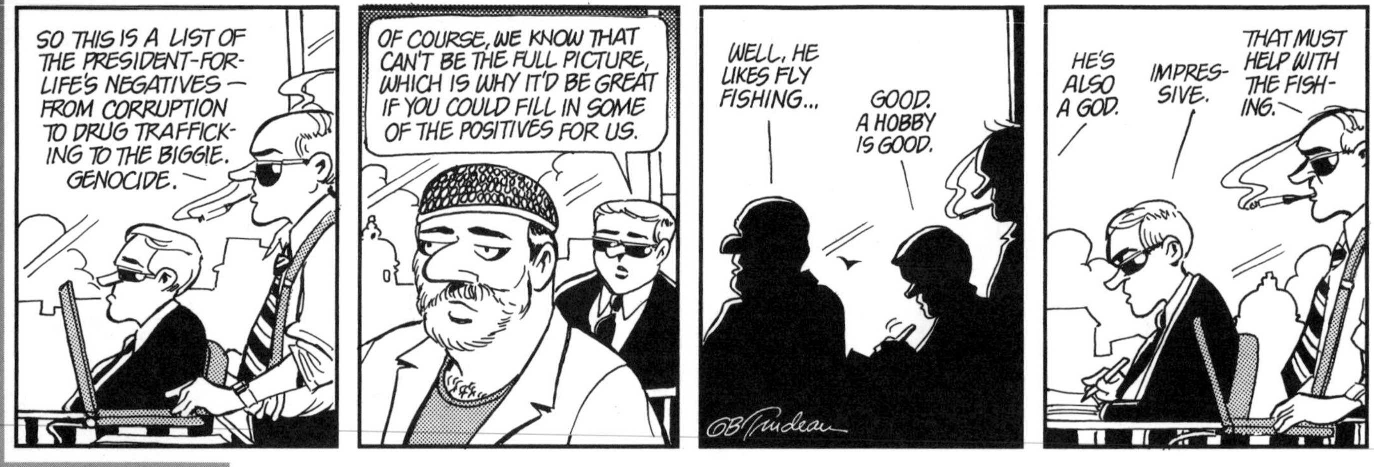
SO THIS IS A LIST OF THE PRESIDENT-FOR-LIFE'S NEGATIVES — FROM CORRUPTION TO DRUG TRAFFICKING TO THE BIGGIE. GENOCIDE.
OF COURSE, WE KNOW THAT CAN'T BE THE FULL PICTURE, WHICH IS WHY IT'D BE GREAT IF YOU COULD FILL IN SOME OF THE POSITIVES FOR US.
WELL, HE LIKES FLY FISHING...
GOOD. A HOBBY IS GOOD.
©B Trudeau
HE'S ALSO A GOD.
IMPRESSIVE.
THAT MUST HELP WITH THE FISHING.

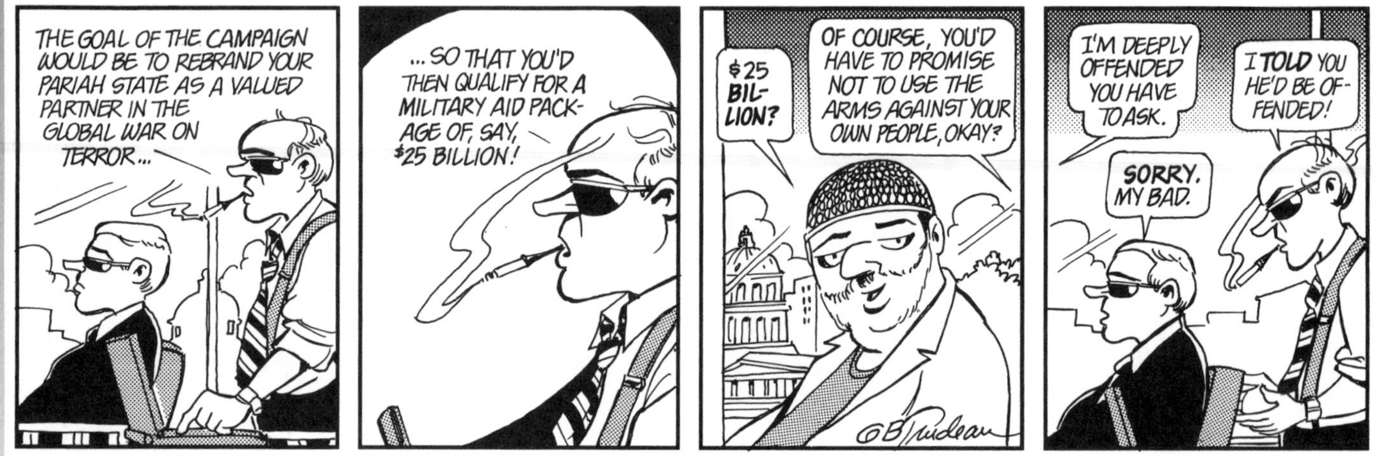
THE GOAL OF THE CAMPAIGN WOULD BE TO REBRAND YOUR PARIAH STATE AS A VALUED PARTNER IN THE GLOBAL WAR ON TERROR...
...SO THAT YOU'D THEN QUALIFY FOR A MILITARY AID PACKAGE OF, SAY, $25 BILLION!
$25 BILLION?
OF COURSE, YOU'D HAVE TO PROMISE NOT TO USE THE ARMS AGAINST YOUR OWN PEOPLE, OKAY?
©B Trudeau
I'M DEEPLY OFFENDED YOU HAVE TO ASK.
I TOLD YOU HE'D BE OFFENDED!
SORRY. MY BAD.

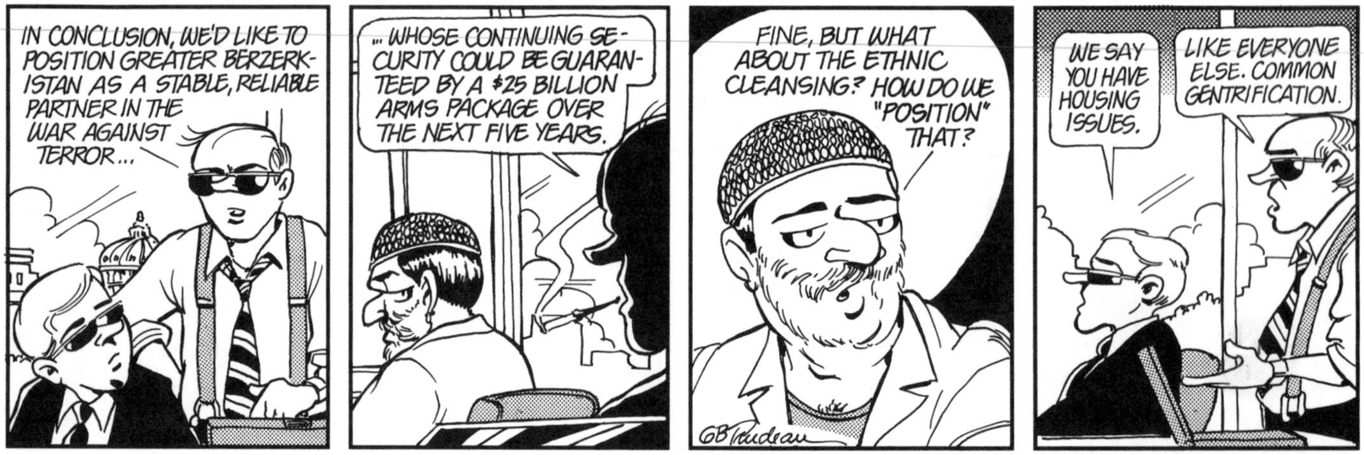
IN CONCLUSION, WE'D LIKE TO POSITION GREATER BERZERKISTAN AS A STABLE, RELIABLE PARTNER IN THE WAR AGAINST TERROR...
...WHOSE CONTINUING SECURITY COULD BE GUARANTEED BY A $25 BILLION ARMS PACKAGE OVER THE NEXT FIVE YEARS.
FINE, BUT WHAT ABOUT THE ETHNIC CLEANSING? HOW DO WE "POSITION" THAT?
©B Trudeau
WE SAY YOU HAVE HOUSING ISSUES.
LIKE EVERYONE ELSE. COMMON GENTRIFICATION.

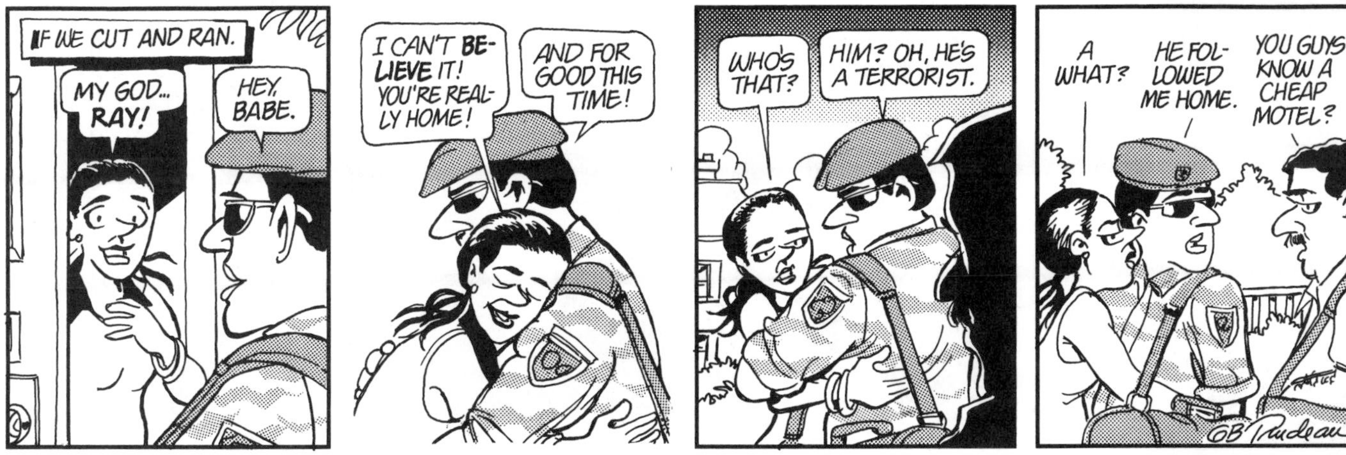
IF WE CUT AND RAN.
MY GOD... RAY!
HEY, BABE.
I CAN'T BELIEVE IT! YOU'RE REALLY HOME!
AND FOR GOOD THIS TIME!
WHO'S THAT?
HIM? OH, HE'S A TERRORIST.
A WHAT?
HE FOLLOWED ME HOME.
YOU GUYS KNOW A CHEAP MOTEL?

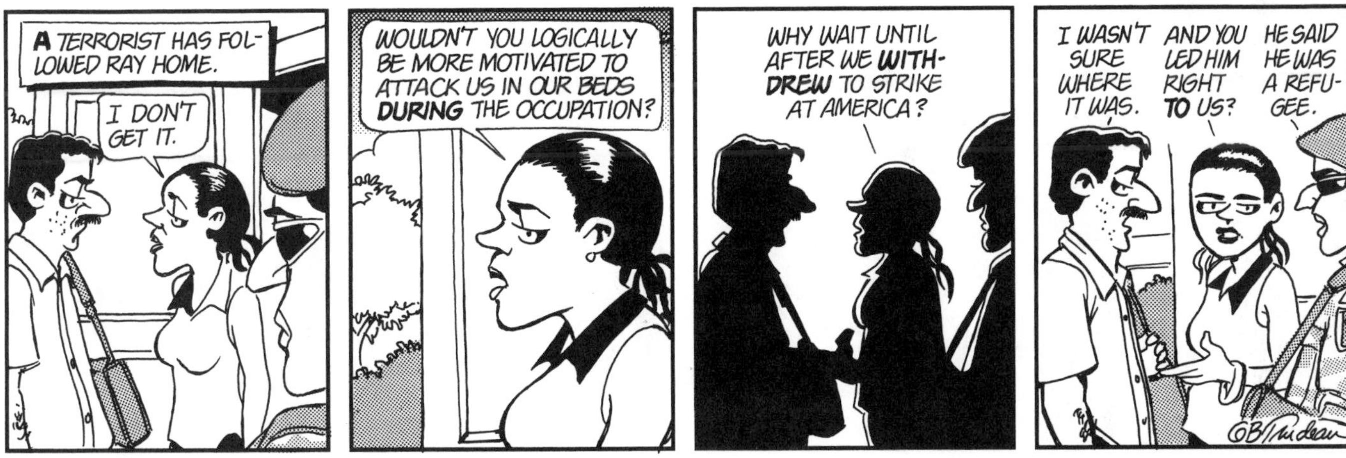
A TERRORIST HAS FOLLOWED RAY HOME.
I DON'T GET IT.
WOULDN'T YOU LOGICALLY BE MORE MOTIVATED TO ATTACK US IN OUR BEDS DURING THE OCCUPATION?
WHY WAIT UNTIL AFTER WE WITHDREW TO STRIKE AT AMERICA?
I WASN'T SURE WHERE IT WAS.
AND YOU LED HIM RIGHT TO US?
HE SAID HE WAS A REFUGEE.

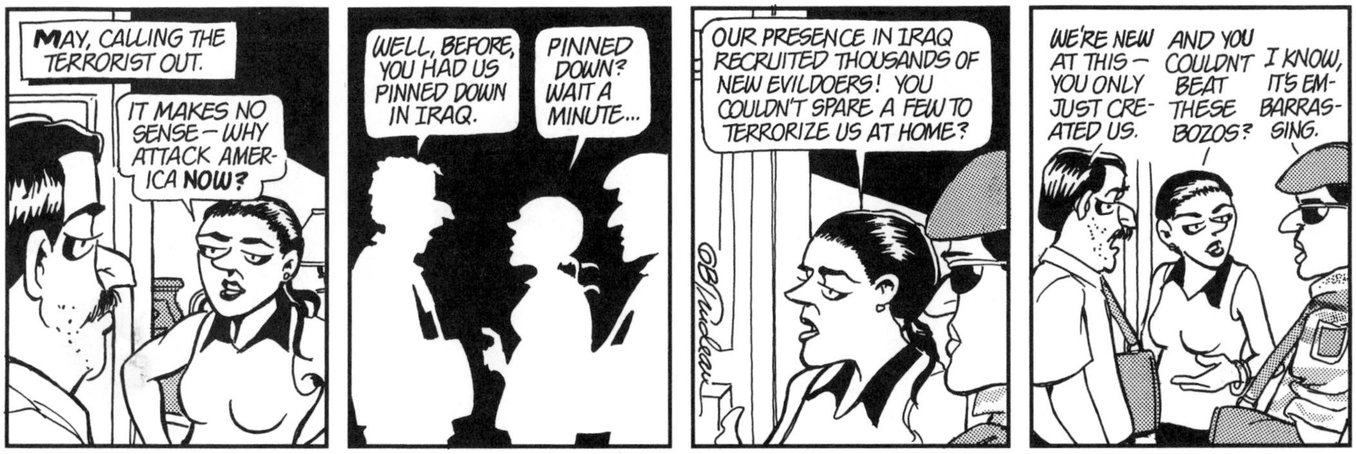
MAY, CALLING THE TERRORIST OUT.
IT MAKES NO SENSE—WHY ATTACK AMERICA NOW?
WELL, BEFORE, YOU HAD US PINNED DOWN IN IRAQ.
PINNED DOWN? WAIT A MINUTE...
OUR PRESENCE IN IRAQ RECRUITED THOUSANDS OF NEW EVILDOERS! YOU COULDN'T SPARE A FEW TO TERRORIZE US AT HOME?
WE'RE NEW AT THIS—YOU ONLY JUST CREATED US.
AND YOU COULDN'T BEAT THESE BOZOS?
I KNOW, IT'S EMBARRASSING.

WELL, I SHOULD BE GOING—TIME TO WAGE JIHAD.
GOOD LUCK WITH THAT. NO OFFENSE, BUT YOU'RE A PROFILER'S DREAM.
YOU ARE COMMENTING ON MY APPEARANCE, YES?
YES.
AND YET YOU YOURSELF DRESS AS A PROSTITUTE.
EXCUSE ME?
HE SOUNDS LIKE YOUR MOTHER.

I MUST BE GOING. COULD YOU GIVE ME A HEAD START BEFORE YOU CALL HOMELAND SECURITY?
NO.
NO?
NO—AND YOU SHOULD HAVE THOUGHT OF THAT BEFORE FOLLOWING ME HOME.
OKAY, BE LIKE THAT. DEATH TO YOU BOTH!
YOU, TOO.
OH...WHERE'S THE NEAREST UNGUARDED WEAPONS DEPOT?
SORRY. THIS AIN'T LIKE HOME.
TRY A GUN SHOW.

RAY, I CAN'T BELIEVE YOU LET A TERRORIST FOLLOW YOU HOME!
HEY, I'M AS NONPLUSSED AS YOU! HOW'D SOMEONE WHO LOOKS LIKE THAT EVER GET PAST IMMIGRATION?
GOOD QUESTION...
DID HE TELL YOU HIS NAME?
SKIPPY JEFFERSON.

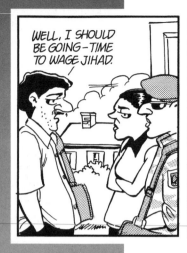

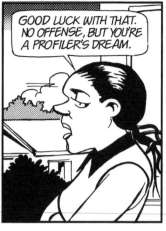

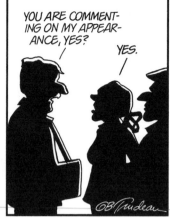

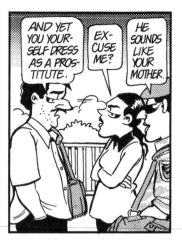

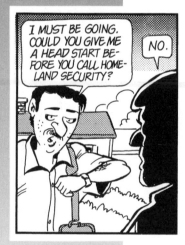

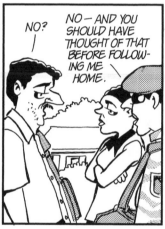

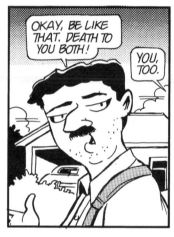

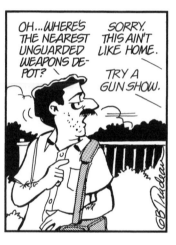

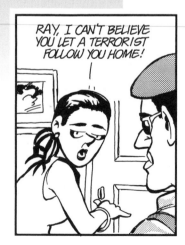

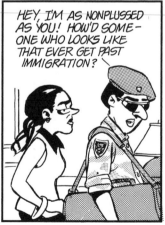

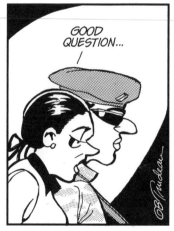

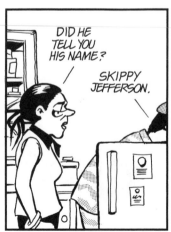

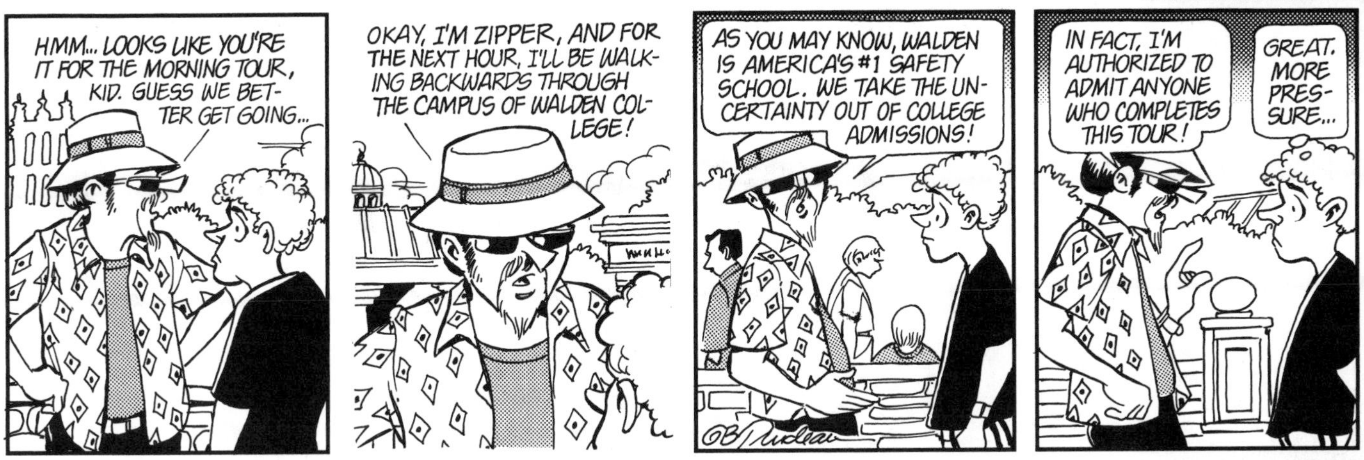
HMM... LOOKS LIKE YOU'RE IT FOR THE MORNING TOUR, KID. GUESS WE BETTER GET GOING...
OKAY, I'M ZIPPER, AND FOR THE NEXT HOUR, I'LL BE WALKING BACKWARDS THROUGH THE CAMPUS OF WALDEN COLLEGE!
AS YOU MAY KNOW, WALDEN IS AMERICA'S #1 SAFETY SCHOOL. WE TAKE THE UNCERTAINTY OUT OF COLLEGE ADMISSIONS!
IN FACT, I'M AUTHORIZED TO ADMIT ANYONE WHO COMPLETES THIS TOUR!
GREAT. MORE PRESSURE...

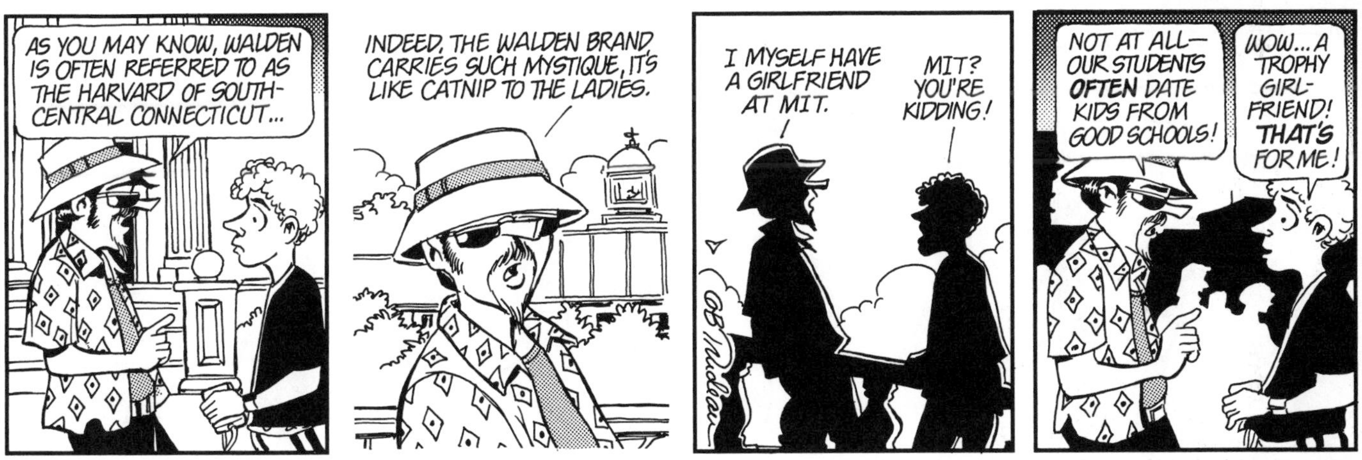
AS YOU MAY KNOW, WALDEN IS OFTEN REFERRED TO AS THE HARVARD OF SOUTH-CENTRAL CONNECTICUT...
INDEED, THE WALDEN BRAND CARRIES SUCH MYSTIQUE, IT'S LIKE CATNIP TO THE LADIES.
I MYSELF HAVE A GIRLFRIEND AT MIT.
MIT? YOU'RE KIDDING!
NOT AT ALL— OUR STUDENTS **OFTEN** DATE KIDS FROM GOOD SCHOOLS!
WOW... A TROPHY GIRLFRIEND! **THAT'S** FOR ME!

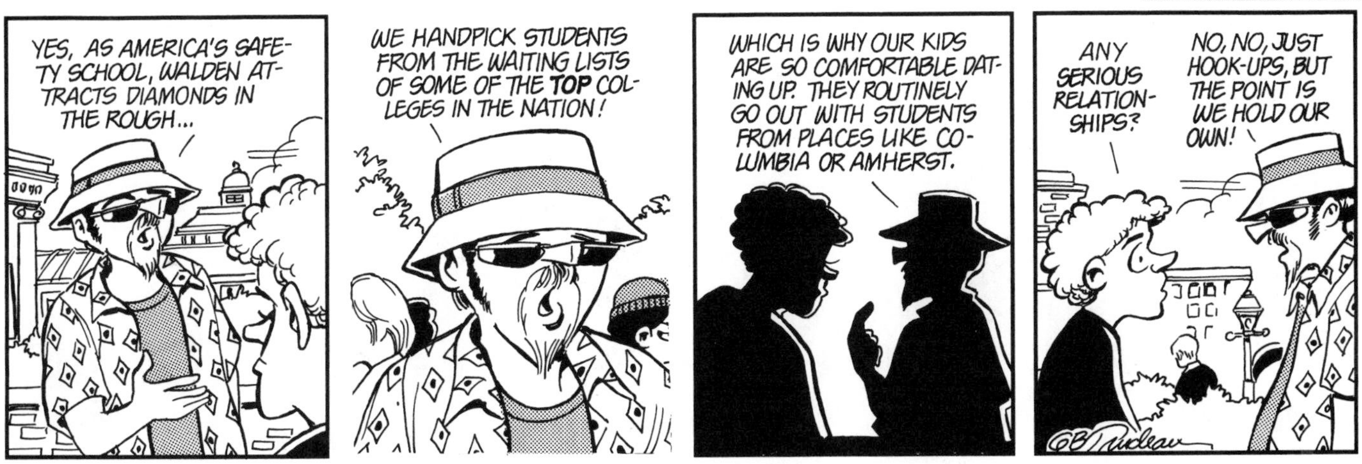
YES, AS AMERICA'S SAFETY SCHOOL, WALDEN ATTRACTS DIAMONDS IN THE ROUGH...
WE HANDPICK STUDENTS FROM THE WAITING LISTS OF SOME OF THE **TOP** COLLEGES IN THE NATION!
WHICH IS WHY OUR KIDS ARE SO COMFORTABLE DATING UP. THEY ROUTINELY GO OUT WITH STUDENTS FROM PLACES LIKE COLUMBIA OR AMHERST.
ANY SERIOUS RELATIONSHIPS?
NO, NO, JUST HOOK-UPS, BUT THE POINT IS WE HOLD OUR OWN!

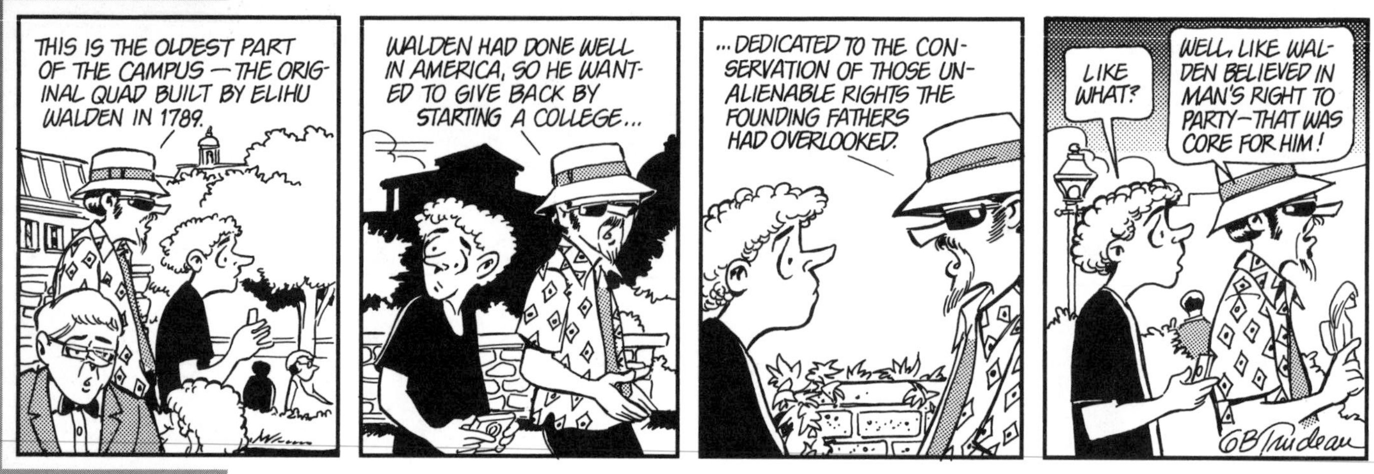
THIS IS THE OLDEST PART OF THE CAMPUS — THE ORIGINAL QUAD BUILT BY ELIHU WALDEN IN 1789.
WALDEN HAD DONE WELL IN AMERICA, SO HE WANTED TO GIVE BACK BY STARTING A COLLEGE...
...DEDICATED TO THE CONSERVATION OF THOSE UNALIENABLE RIGHTS THE FOUNDING FATHERS HAD OVERLOOKED.
LIKE WHAT?
WELL, LIKE WALDEN BELIEVED IN MAN'S RIGHT TO PARTY—THAT WAS CORE FOR HIM!
GB Trudeau

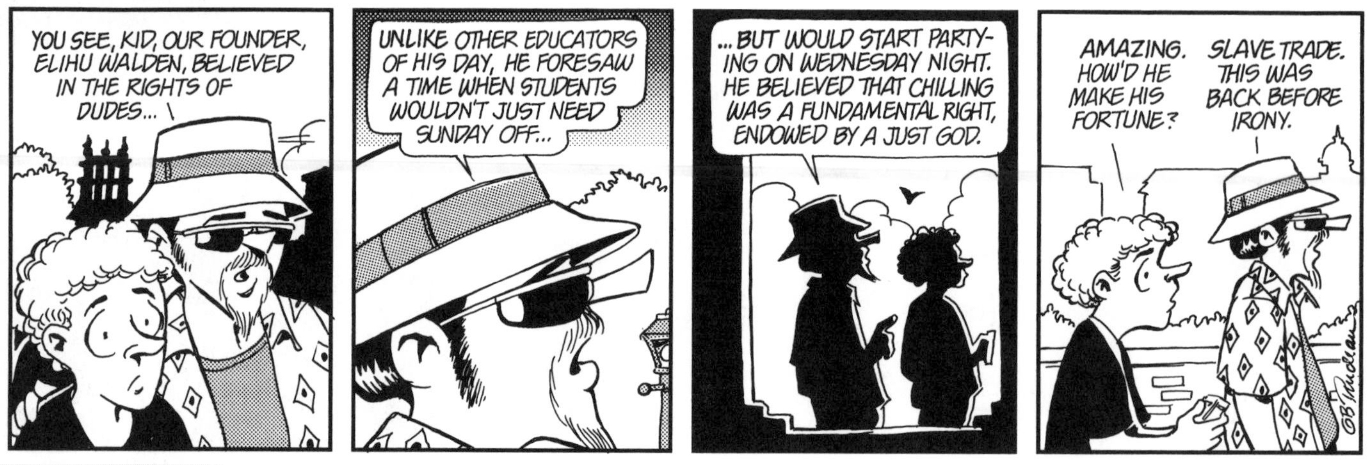
YOU SEE, KID, OUR FOUNDER, ELIHU WALDEN, BELIEVED IN THE RIGHTS OF DUDES...
UNLIKE OTHER EDUCATORS OF HIS DAY, HE FORESAW A TIME WHEN STUDENTS WOULDN'T JUST NEED SUNDAY OFF...
...BUT WOULD START PARTYING ON WEDNESDAY NIGHT. HE BELIEVED THAT CHILLING WAS A FUNDAMENTAL RIGHT, ENDOWED BY A JUST GOD.
AMAZING. HOW'D HE MAKE HIS FORTUNE?
SLAVE TRADE. THIS WAS BACK BEFORE IRONY.
©B Trudeau

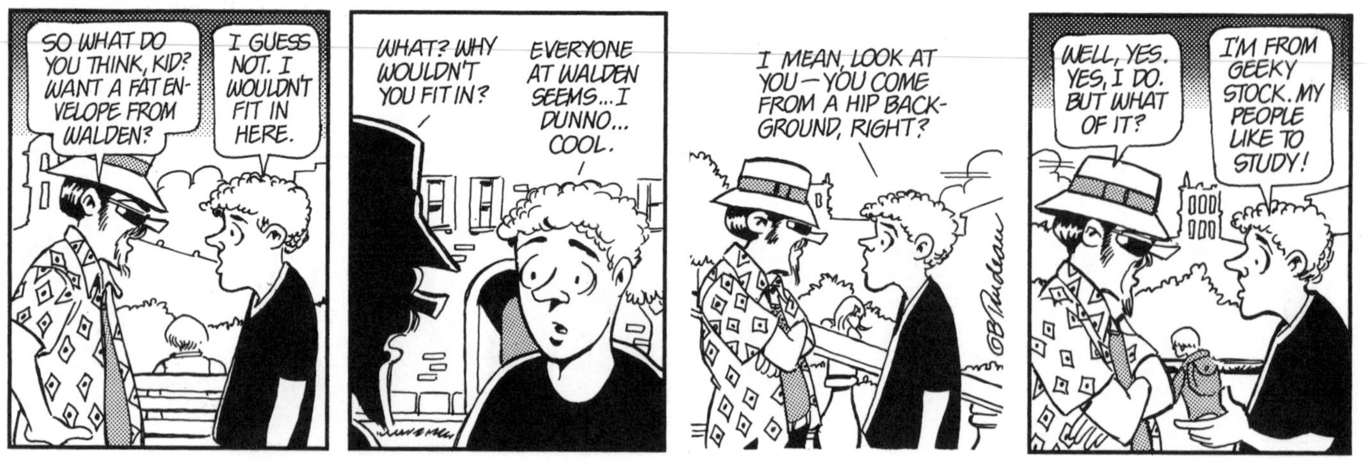
SO WHAT DO YOU THINK, KID? WANT A FAT ENVELOPE FROM WALDEN?
I GUESS NOT. I WOULDN'T FIT IN HERE.
WHAT? WHY WOULDN'T YOU FIT IN?
EVERYONE AT WALDEN SEEMS... I DUNNO... COOL.
I MEAN, LOOK AT YOU—YOU COME FROM A HIP BACKGROUND, RIGHT?
WELL, YES. YES, I DO. BUT WHAT OF IT?
I'M FROM GEEKY STOCK. MY PEOPLE LIKE TO STUDY!
©B Trudeau

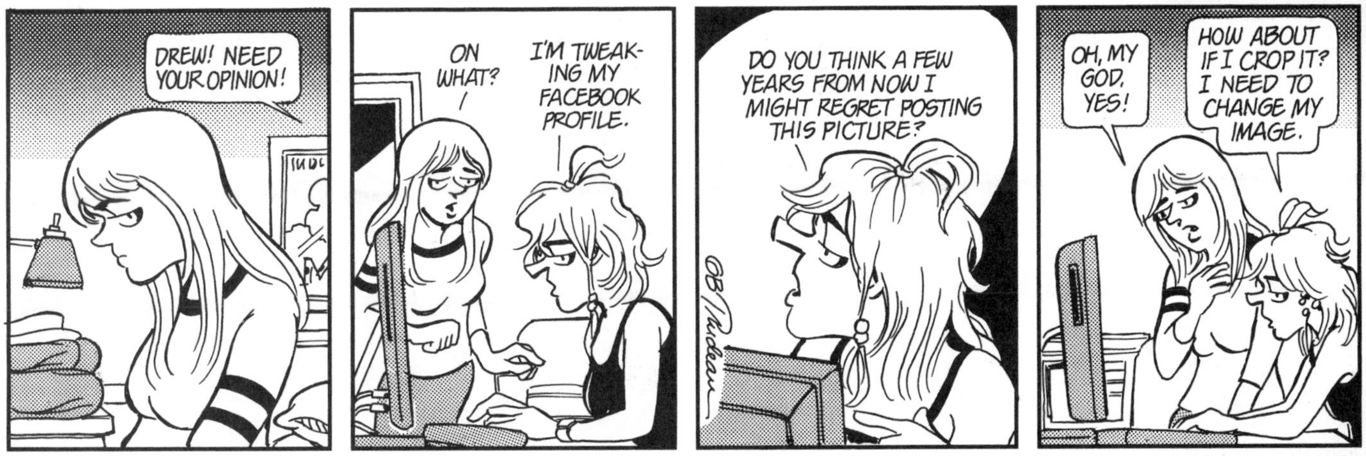
DREW! NEED YOUR OPINION!
ON WHAT?
I'M TWEAKING MY FACEBOOK PROFILE.
DO YOU THINK A FEW YEARS FROM NOW I MIGHT REGRET POSTING THIS PICTURE?
OH, MY GOD, YES!
HOW ABOUT IF I CROP IT? I NEED TO CHANGE MY IMAGE.

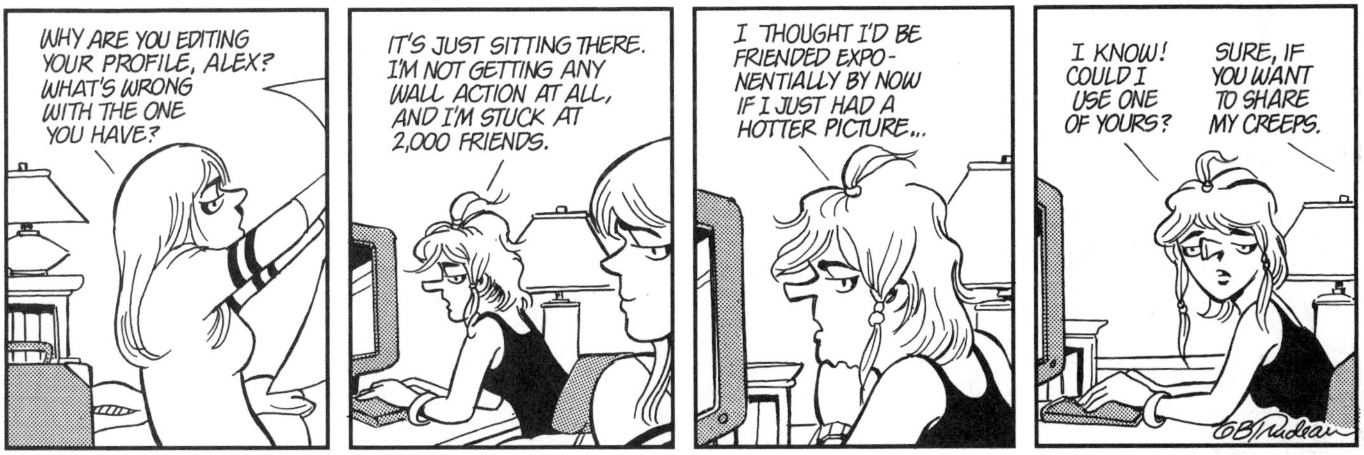
WHY ARE YOU EDITING YOUR PROFILE, ALEX? WHAT'S WRONG WITH THE ONE YOU HAVE?
IT'S JUST SITTING THERE. I'M NOT GETTING ANY WALL ACTION AT ALL, AND I'M STUCK AT 2,000 FRIENDS.
I THOUGHT I'D BE FRIENDED EXPONENTIALLY BY NOW IF I JUST HAD A HOTTER PICTURE...
I KNOW! COULD I USE ONE OF YOURS?
SURE, IF YOU WANT TO SHARE MY CREEPS.

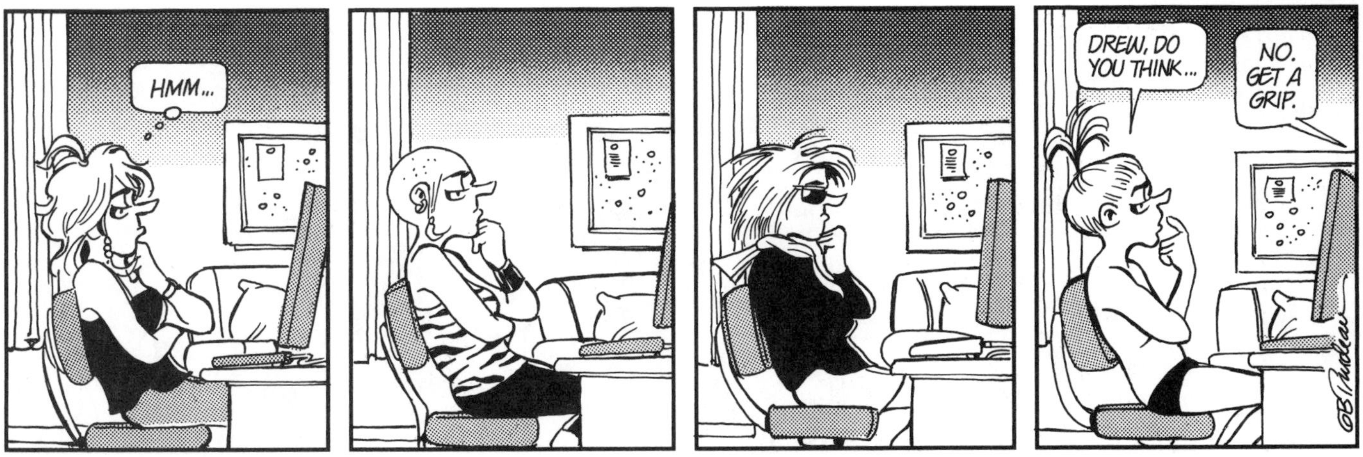
HMM...
DREW, DO YOU THINK...
NO. GET A GRIP.

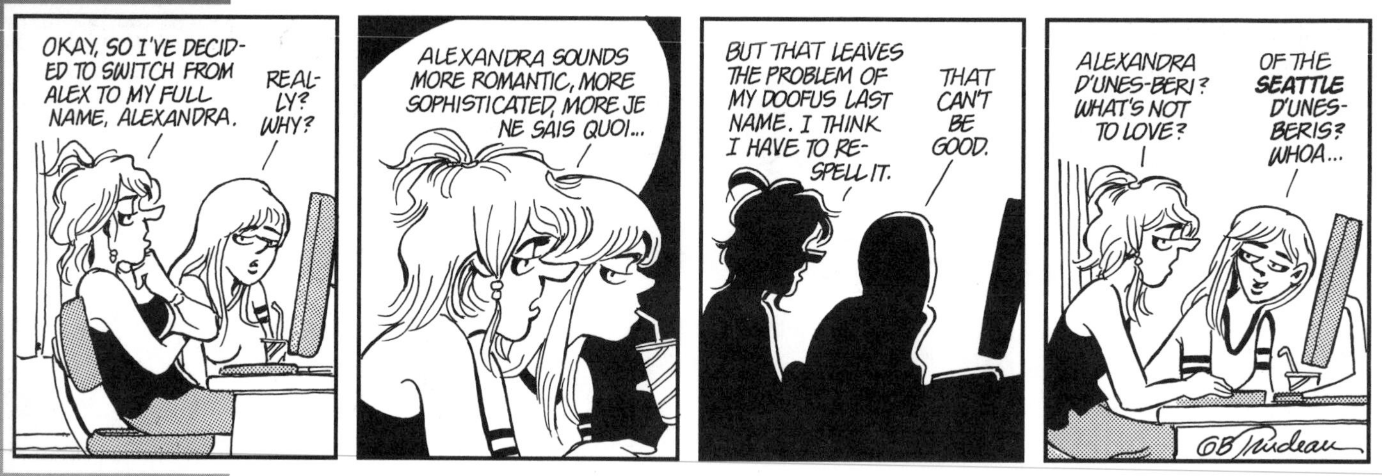
OKAY, SO I'VE DECIDED TO SWITCH FROM ALEX TO MY FULL NAME, ALEXANDRA.
REALLY? WHY?
ALEXANDRA SOUNDS MORE ROMANTIC, MORE SOPHISTICATED, MORE JE NE SAIS QUOI...
BUT THAT LEAVES THE PROBLEM OF MY DOOFUS LAST NAME. I THINK I HAVE TO RE-SPELL IT.
THAT CAN'T BE GOOD.
ALEXANDRA D'UNES-BERI? WHAT'S NOT TO LOVE?
OF THE **SEATTLE** D'UNES-BERIS? WHOA...
GB Trudeau

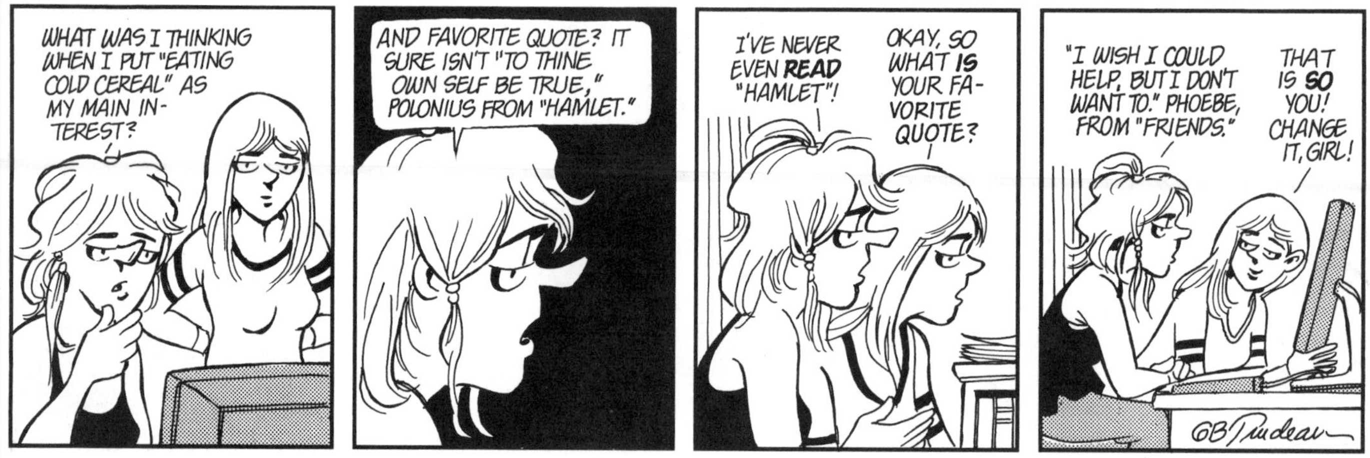
WHAT WAS I THINKING WHEN I PUT "EATING COLD CEREAL" AS MY MAIN INTEREST?
AND FAVORITE QUOTE? IT SURE ISN'T "TO THINE OWN SELF BE TRUE," POLONIUS FROM "HAMLET."
I'VE NEVER EVEN **READ** "HAMLET"!
OKAY, SO WHAT **IS** YOUR FAVORITE QUOTE?
"I WISH I COULD HELP, BUT I DON'T WANT TO." PHOEBE, FROM "FRIENDS."
THAT IS **SO** YOU! CHANGE IT, GIRL!
GB Trudeau

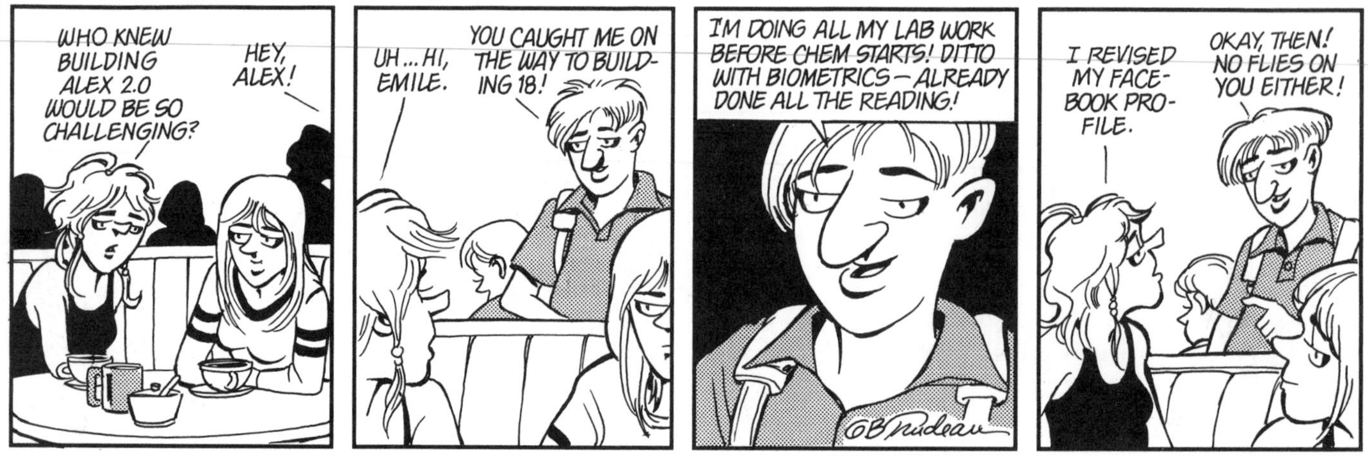
WHO KNEW BUILDING ALEX 2.0 WOULD BE SO CHALLENGING?
HEY, ALEX!
UH... HI, EMILE.
YOU CAUGHT ME ON THE WAY TO BUILDING 18!
I'M DOING ALL MY LAB WORK BEFORE CHEM STARTS! DITTO WITH BIOMETRICS — ALREADY DONE ALL THE READING!
GB Trudeau
I REVISED MY FACEBOOK PROFILE.
OKAY, THEN! NO FLIES ON YOU EITHER!

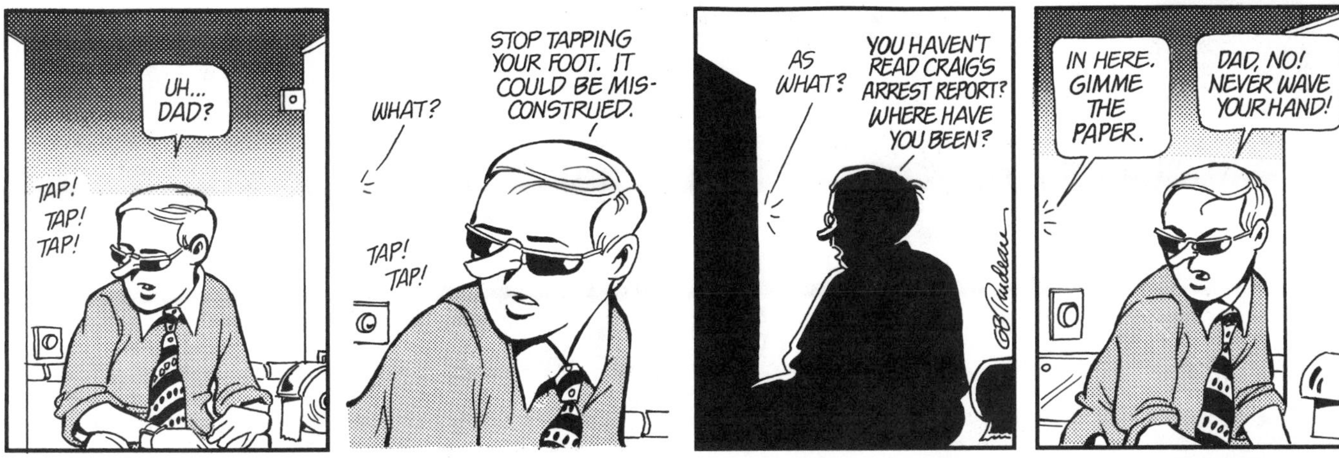
UH... DAD?
TAP! TAP! TAP!
WHAT?
TAP! TAP!
STOP TAPPING YOUR FOOT. IT COULD BE MIS-CONSTRUED.
AS WHAT?
YOU HAVEN'T READ CRAIG'S ARREST REPORT? WHERE HAVE YOU BEEN?
IN HERE. GIMME THE PAPER.
DAD, NO! NEVER WAVE YOUR HAND!

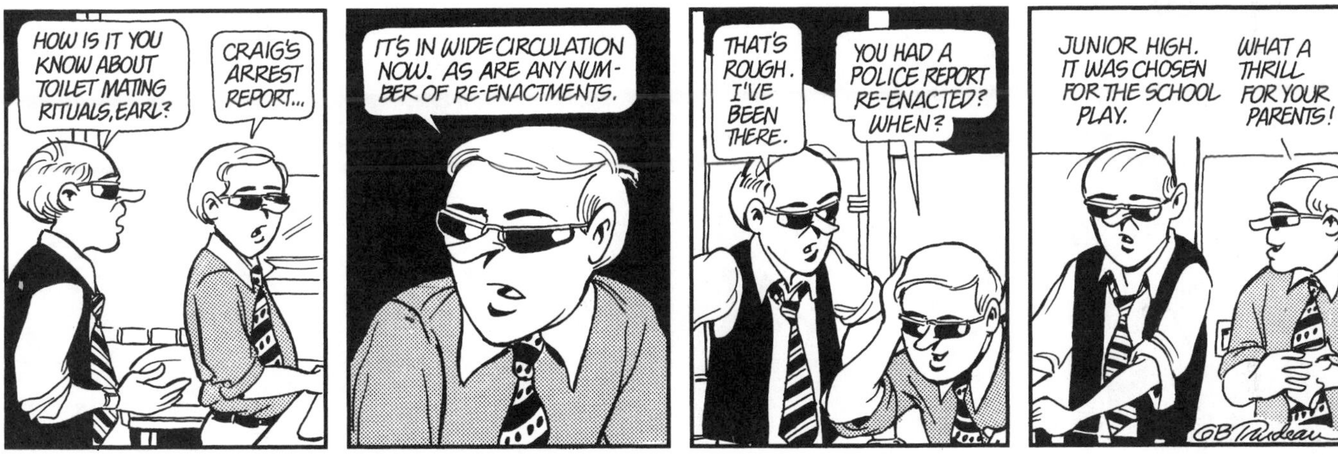
HOW IS IT YOU KNOW ABOUT TOILET MATING RITUALS, EARL?
CRAIG'S ARREST REPORT...
IT'S IN WIDE CIRCULATION NOW. AS ARE ANY NUMBER OF RE-ENACTMENTS.
THAT'S ROUGH. I'VE BEEN THERE.
YOU HAD A POLICE REPORT RE-ENACTED? WHEN?
JUNIOR HIGH. IT WAS CHOSEN FOR THE SCHOOL PLAY.
WHAT A THRILL FOR YOUR PARENTS!

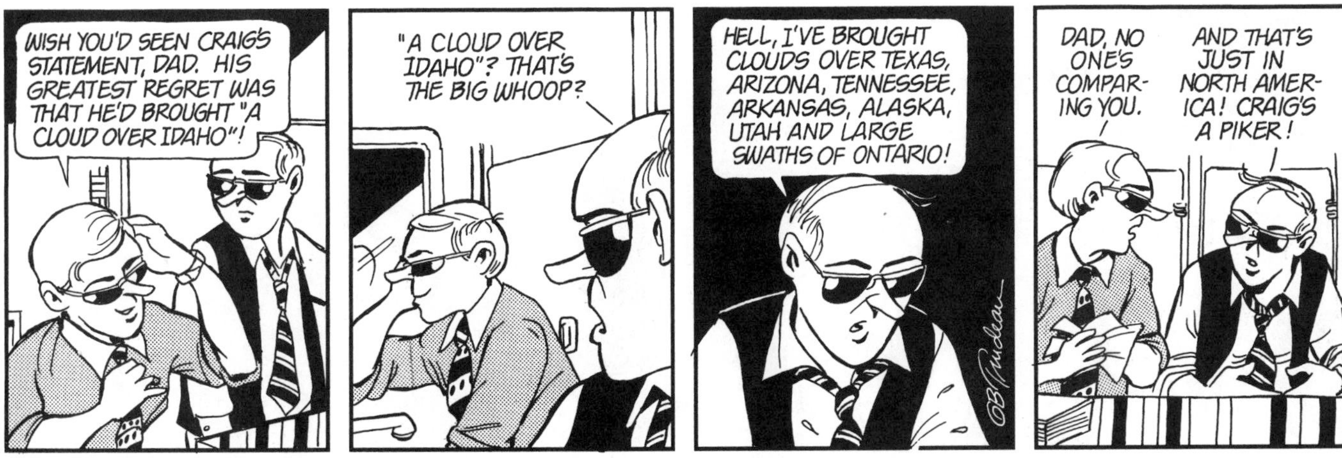
WISH YOU'D SEEN CRAIG'S STATEMENT, DAD. HIS GREATEST REGRET WAS THAT HE'D BROUGHT "A CLOUD OVER IDAHO"!
"A CLOUD OVER IDAHO"? THAT'S THE BIG WHOOP?
HELL, I'VE BROUGHT CLOUDS OVER TEXAS, ARIZONA, TENNESSEE, ARKANSAS, ALASKA, UTAH AND LARGE SWATHS OF ONTARIO!
DAD, NO ONE'S COMPARING YOU.
AND THAT'S JUST IN NORTH AMERICA! CRAIG'S A PIKER!

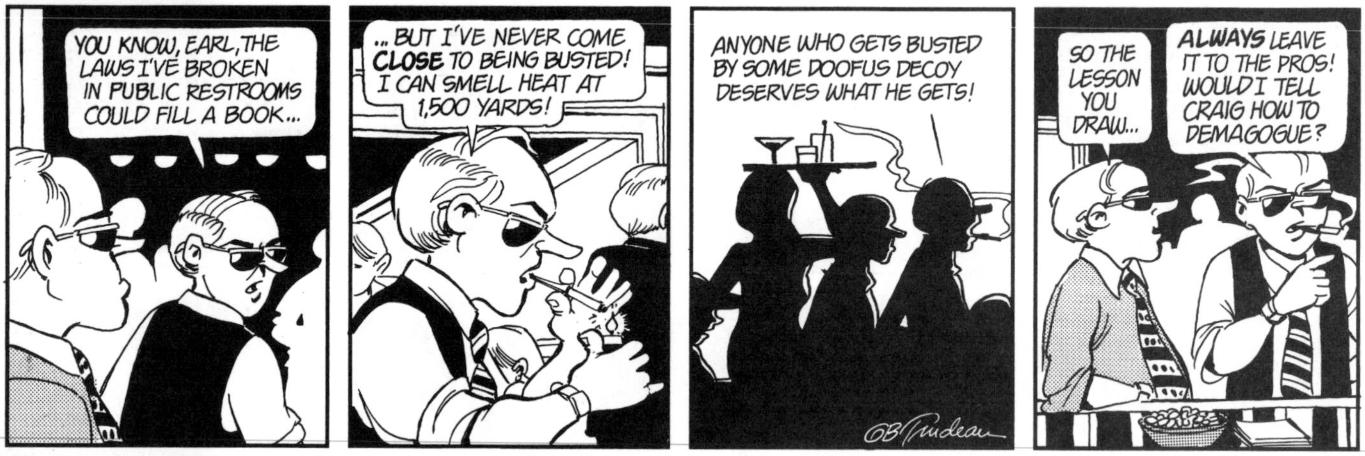
YOU KNOW, EARL, THE LAWS I'VE BROKEN IN PUBLIC RESTROOMS COULD FILL A BOOK...
... BUT I'VE NEVER COME CLOSE TO BEING BUSTED! I CAN SMELL HEAT AT 1,500 YARDS!
ANYONE WHO GETS BUSTED BY SOME DOOFUS DECOY DESERVES WHAT HE GETS!
©B Trudeau
SO THE LESSON YOU DRAW...
ALWAYS LEAVE IT TO THE PROS! WOULD I TELL CRAIG HOW TO DEMAGOGUE?

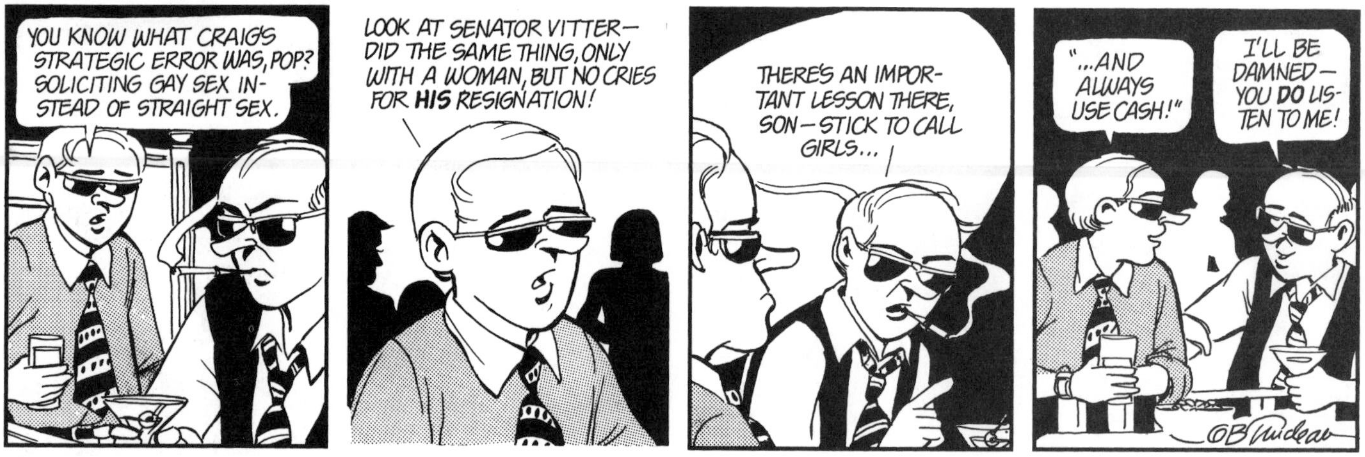
YOU KNOW WHAT CRAIG'S STRATEGIC ERROR WAS, POP? SOLICITING GAY SEX INSTEAD OF STRAIGHT SEX.
LOOK AT SENATOR VITTER—DID THE SAME THING, ONLY WITH A WOMAN, BUT NO CRIES FOR HIS RESIGNATION!
THERE'S AN IMPORTANT LESSON THERE, SON—STICK TO CALL GIRLS...
"...AND ALWAYS USE CASH!"
I'LL BE DAMNED—YOU DO LISTEN TO ME!
©B Trudeau

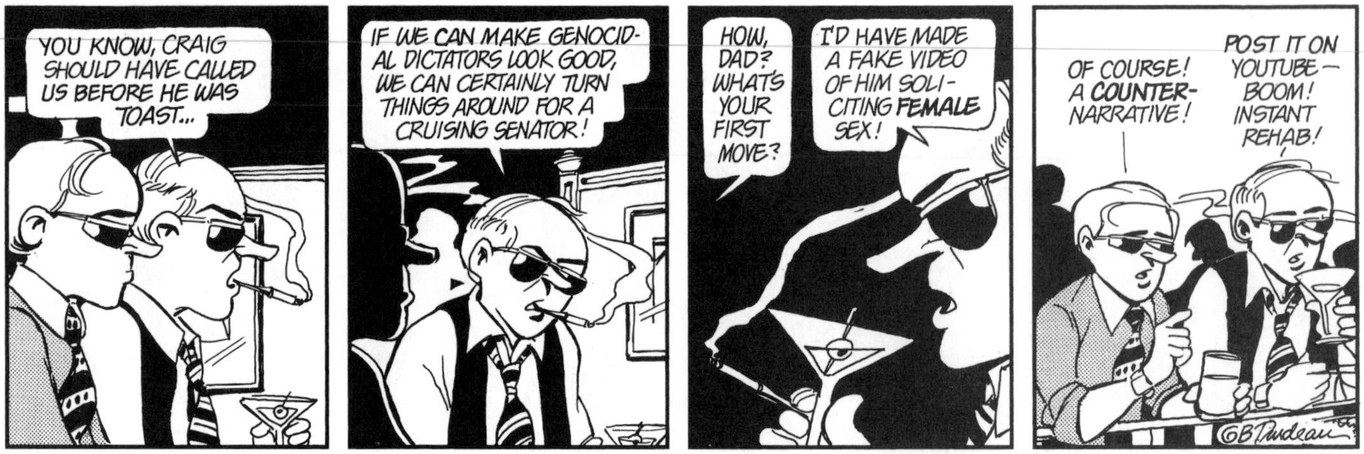
YOU KNOW, CRAIG SHOULD HAVE CALLED US BEFORE HE WAS TOAST...
IF WE CAN MAKE GENOCIDAL DICTATORS LOOK GOOD, WE CAN CERTAINLY TURN THINGS AROUND FOR A CRUISING SENATOR!
HOW, DAD? WHAT'S YOUR FIRST MOVE?
I'D HAVE MADE A FAKE VIDEO OF HIM SOLICITING FEMALE SEX!
OF COURSE! A COUNTER-NARRATIVE!
POST IT ON YOUTUBE—BOOM! INSTANT REHAB!
©B Trudeau

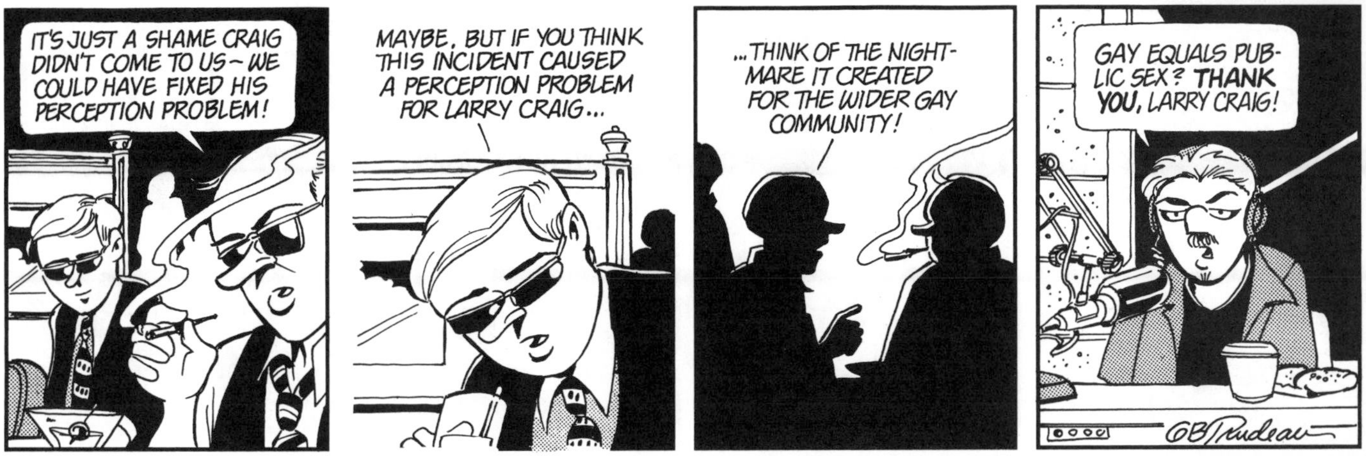
IT'S JUST A SHAME CRAIG DIDN'T COME TO US~WE COULD HAVE FIXED HIS PERCEPTION PROBLEM!
MAYBE, BUT IF YOU THINK THIS INCIDENT CAUSED A PERCEPTION PROBLEM FOR LARRY CRAIG...
...THINK OF THE NIGHTMARE IT CREATED FOR THE WIDER GAY COMMUNITY!
GAY EQUALS PUBLIC SEX? THANK YOU, LARRY CRAIG!
GBTrudeau

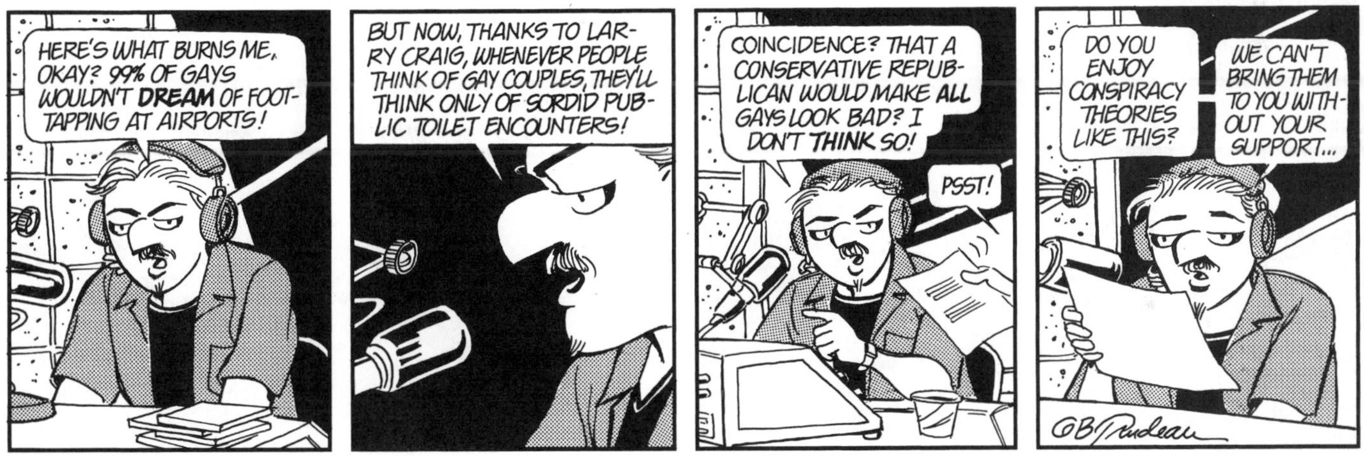
HERE'S WHAT BURNS ME, OKAY? 99% OF GAYS WOULDN'T DREAM OF FOOT-TAPPING AT AIRPORTS!
BUT NOW, THANKS TO LARRY CRAIG, WHENEVER PEOPLE THINK OF GAY COUPLES, THEY'LL THINK ONLY OF SORDID PUBLIC TOILET ENCOUNTERS!
COINCIDENCE? THAT A CONSERVATIVE REPUBLICAN WOULD MAKE ALL GAYS LOOK BAD? I DON'T THINK SO!
PSST!
DO YOU ENJOY CONSPIRACY THEORIES LIKE THIS?
WE CAN'T BRING THEM TO YOU WITHOUT YOUR SUPPORT...
GBTrudeau

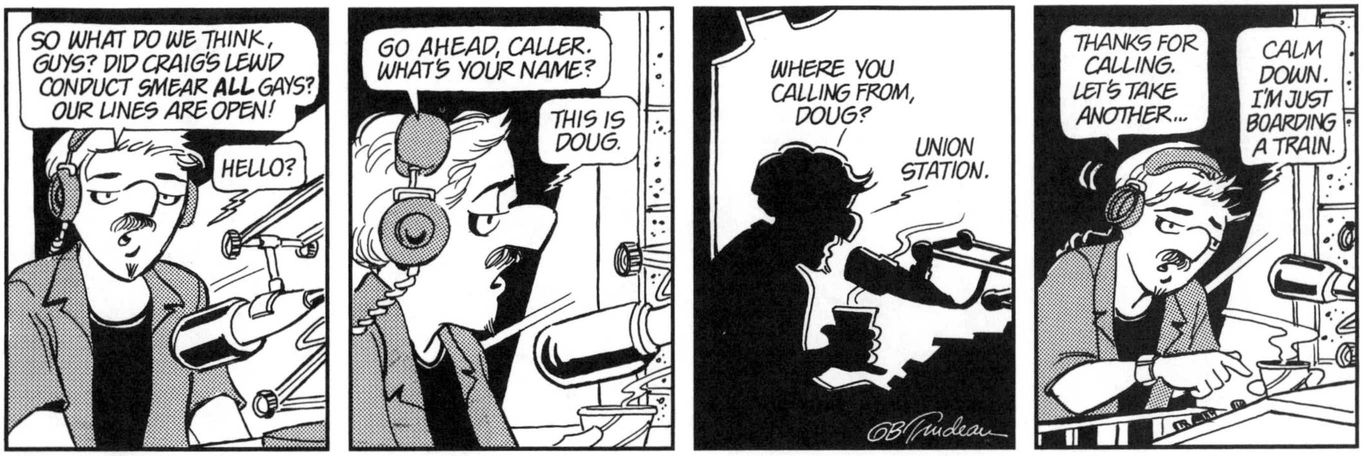
SO WHAT DO WE THINK, GUYS? DID CRAIG'S LEWD CONDUCT SMEAR ALL GAYS? OUR LINES ARE OPEN!
HELLO?
GO AHEAD, CALLER. WHAT'S YOUR NAME?
THIS IS DOUG.
WHERE YOU CALLING FROM, DOUG?
UNION STATION.
THANKS FOR CALLING. LET'S TAKE ANOTHER...
CALM DOWN. I'M JUST BOARDING A TRAIN.
GBTrudeau

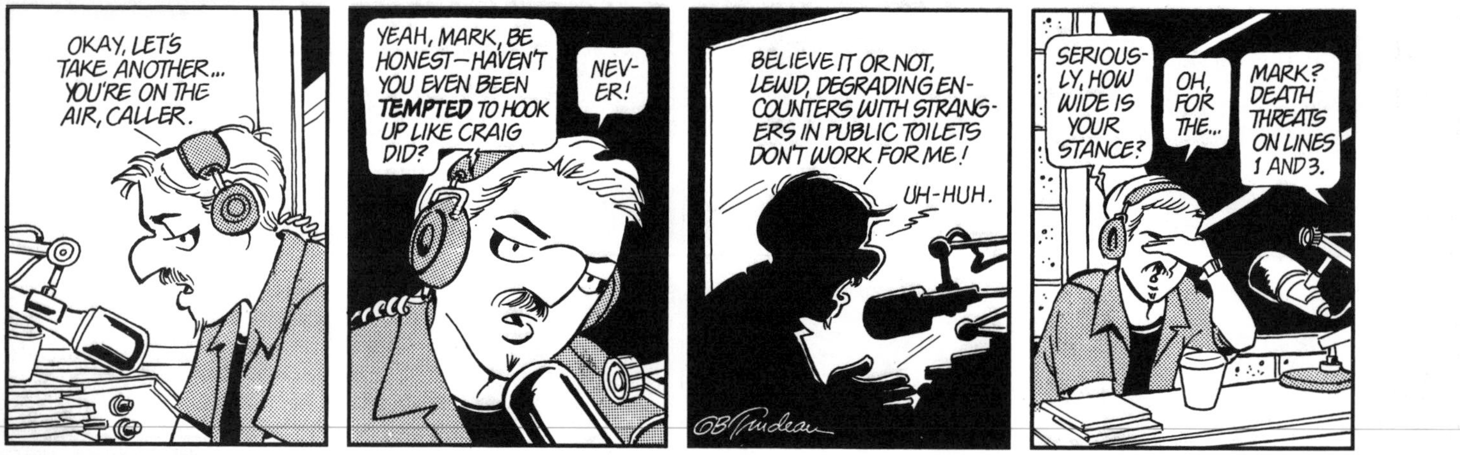
OKAY, LET'S TAKE ANOTHER... YOU'RE ON THE AIR, CALLER.
YEAH, MARK, BE HONEST—HAVEN'T YOU EVEN BEEN **TEMPTED** TO HOOK UP LIKE CRAIG DID?
NEVER!
BELIEVE IT OR NOT, LEWD, DEGRADING ENCOUNTERS WITH STRANGERS IN PUBLIC TOILETS DON'T WORK FOR ME!
UH-HUH.
SERIOUSLY, HOW WIDE IS YOUR STANCE?
OH, FOR THE...
MARK? DEATH THREATS ON LINES 1 AND 3.
©B Trudeau

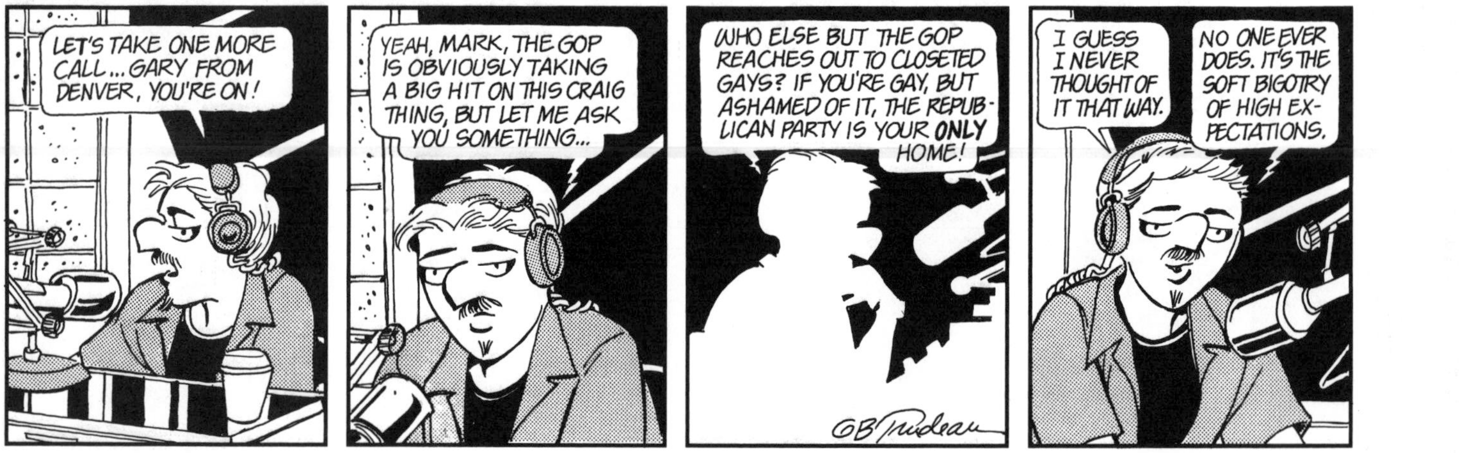
LET'S TAKE ONE MORE CALL... GARY FROM DENVER, YOU'RE ON!
YEAH, MARK, THE GOP IS OBVIOUSLY TAKING A BIG HIT ON THIS CRAIG THING, BUT LET ME ASK YOU SOMETHING...
WHO ELSE BUT THE GOP REACHES OUT TO CLOSETED GAYS? IF YOU'RE GAY, BUT ASHAMED OF IT, THE REPUBLICAN PARTY IS YOUR **ONLY** HOME!
I GUESS I NEVER THOUGHT OF IT THAT WAY.
NO ONE EVER DOES. IT'S THE SOFT BIGOTRY OF HIGH EXPECTATIONS.
©B Trudeau

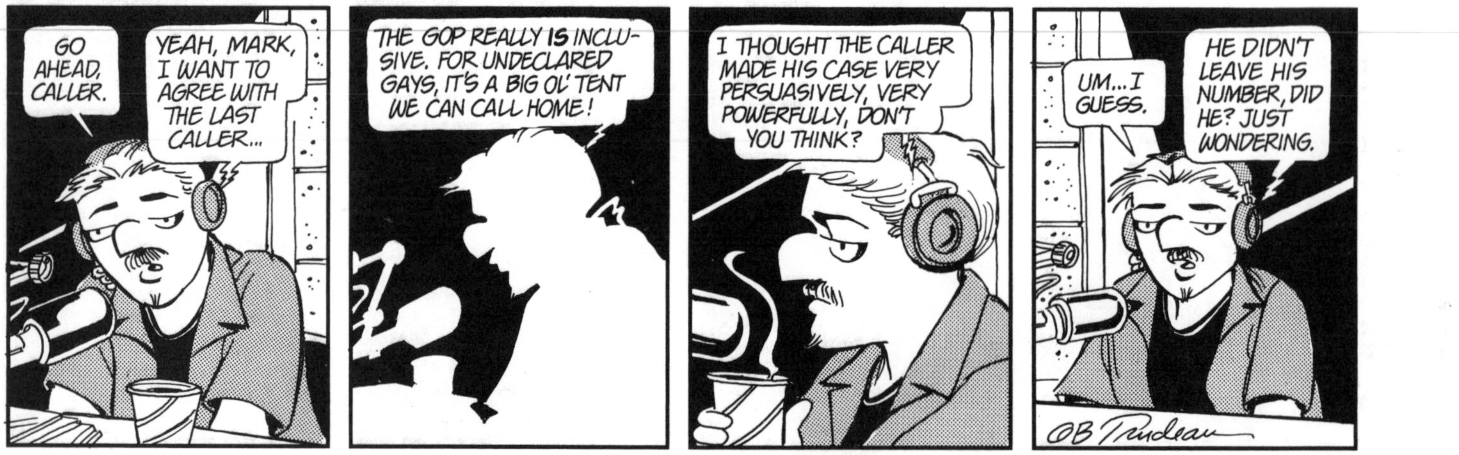
GO AHEAD, CALLER.
YEAH, MARK, I WANT TO AGREE WITH THE LAST CALLER...
THE GOP REALLY **IS** INCLUSIVE. FOR UNDECLARED GAYS, IT'S A BIG OL' TENT WE CAN CALL HOME!
I THOUGHT THE CALLER MADE HIS CASE VERY PERSUASIVELY, VERY POWERFULLY, DON'T YOU THINK?
UM... I GUESS.
HE DIDN'T LEAVE HIS NUMBER, DID HE? JUST WONDERING.
©B Trudeau

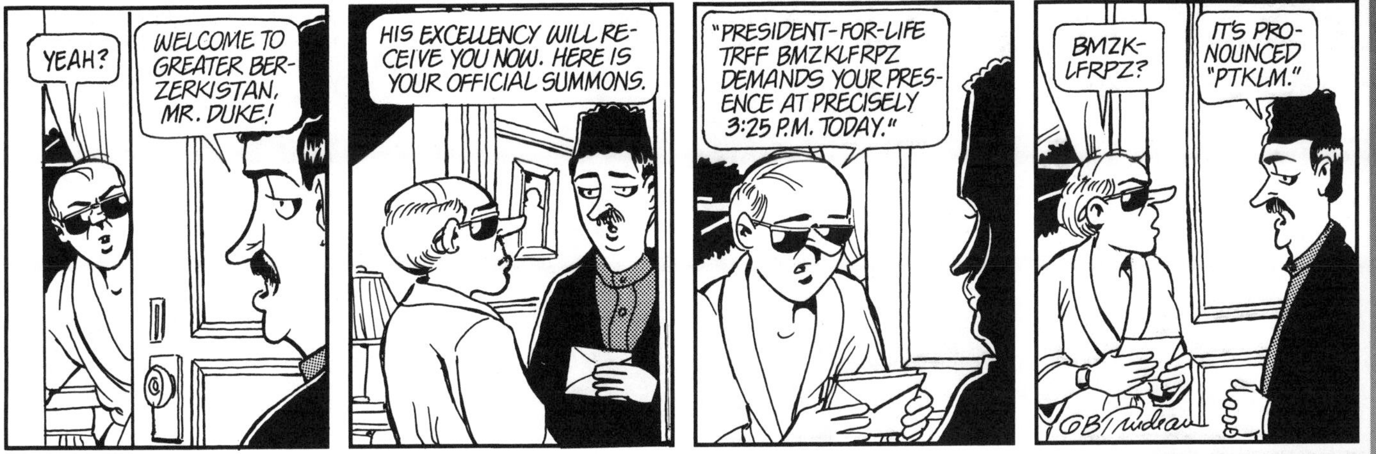
YEAH?
WELCOME TO GREATER BERZERKISTAN, MR. DUKE!
HIS EXCELLENCY WILL RECEIVE YOU NOW. HERE IS YOUR OFFICIAL SUMMONS.
"PRESIDENT-FOR-LIFE TRFF BMZKLFRPZ DEMANDS YOUR PRESENCE AT PRECISELY 3:25 P.M. TODAY."
BMZKLFRPZ?
IT'S PRONOUNCED "PTKLM."

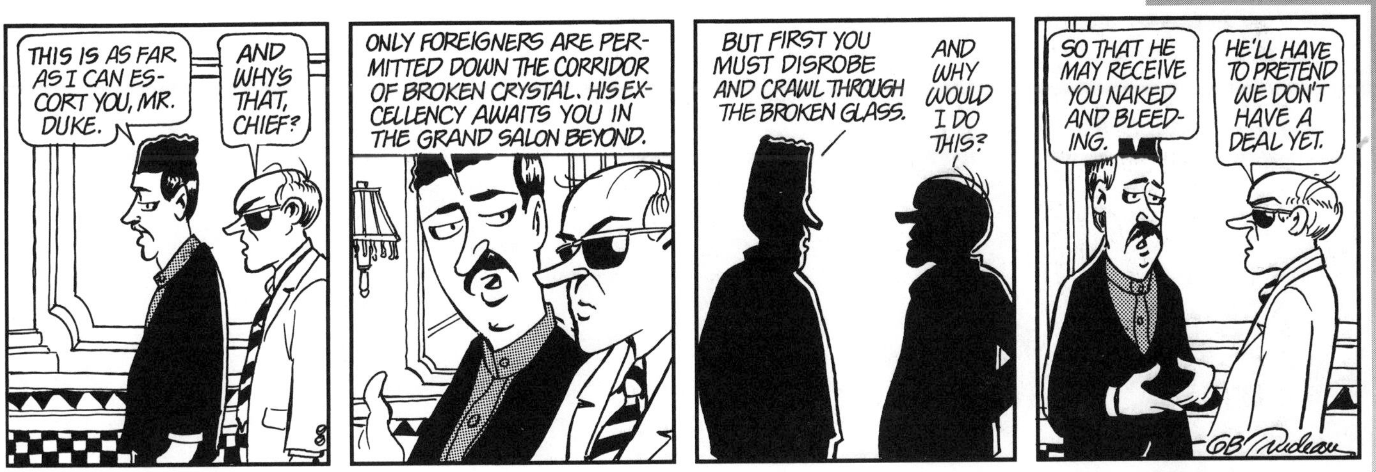
THIS IS AS FAR AS I CAN ESCORT YOU, MR. DUKE.
AND WHY'S THAT, CHIEF?
ONLY FOREIGNERS ARE PERMITTED DOWN THE CORRIDOR OF BROKEN CRYSTAL. HIS EXCELLENCY AWAITS YOU IN THE GRAND SALON BEYOND.
BUT FIRST YOU MUST DISROBE AND CRAWL THROUGH THE BROKEN GLASS.
AND WHY WOULD I DO THIS?
SO THAT HE MAY RECEIVE YOU NAKED AND BLEEDING.
HE'LL HAVE TO PRETEND WE DON'T HAVE A DEAL YET.

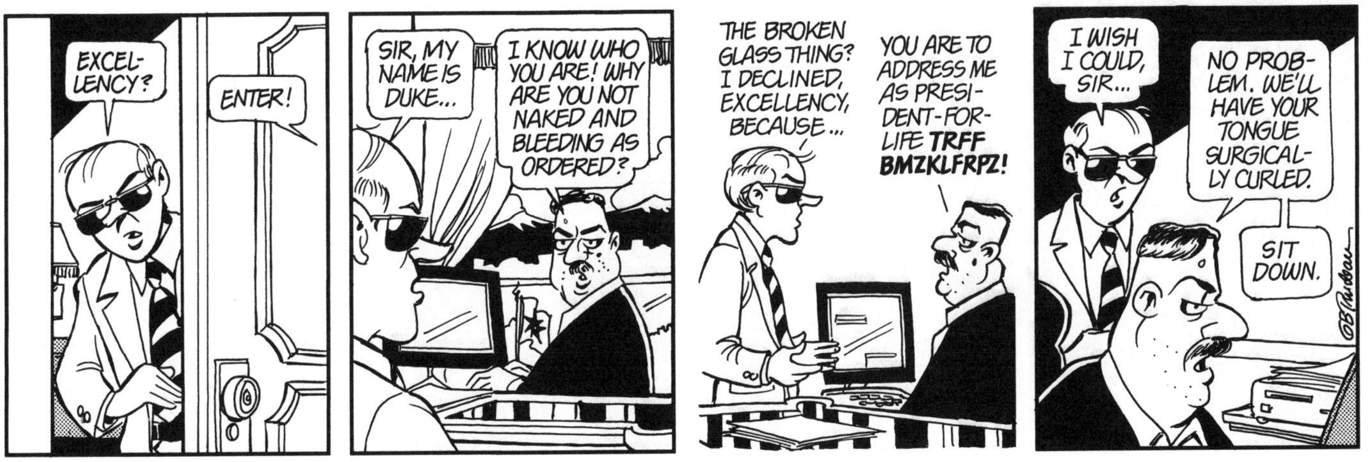
EXCELLENCY?
ENTER!
SIR, MY NAME IS DUKE...
I KNOW WHO YOU ARE! WHY ARE YOU NOT NAKED AND BLEEDING AS ORDERED?
THE BROKEN GLASS THING? I DECLINED, EXCELLENCY, BECAUSE...
YOU ARE TO ADDRESS ME AS PRESIDENT-FOR-LIFE TRFF BMZKLFRPZ!
I WISH I COULD, SIR...
NO PROBLEM. WE'LL HAVE YOUR TONGUE SURGICALLY CURLED.
SIT DOWN.

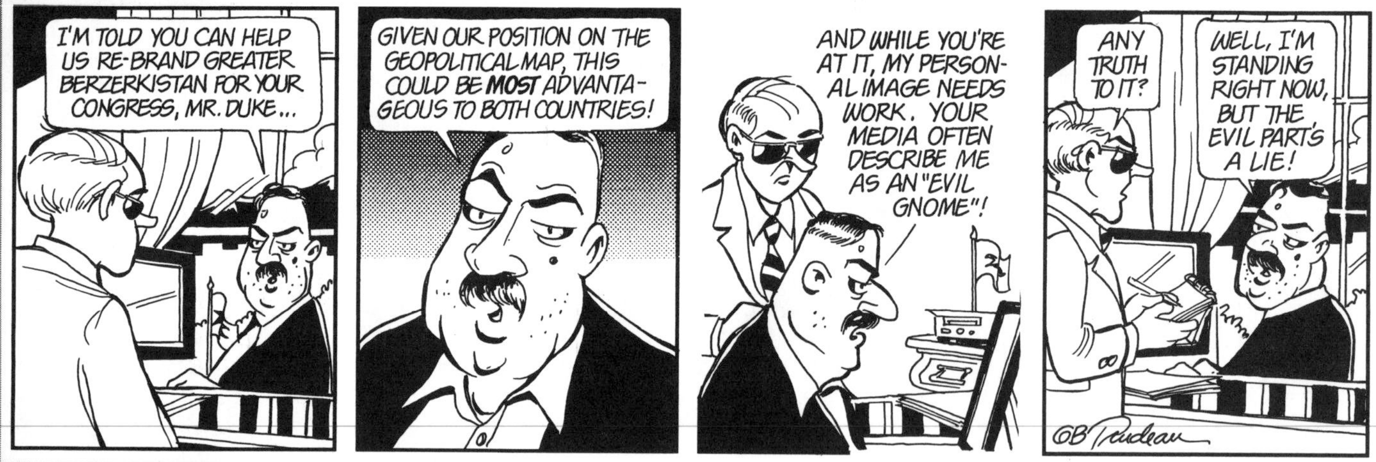
I'M TOLD YOU CAN HELP US RE-BRAND GREATER BERZERKISTAN FOR YOUR CONGRESS, MR. DUKE...
GIVEN OUR POSITION ON THE GEOPOLITICAL MAP, THIS COULD BE **MOST** ADVANTAGEOUS TO BOTH COUNTRIES!
AND WHILE YOU'RE AT IT, MY PERSONAL IMAGE NEEDS WORK. YOUR MEDIA OFTEN DESCRIBE ME AS AN "EVIL GNOME"!
ANY TRUTH TO IT?
WELL, I'M STANDING RIGHT NOW, BUT THE EVIL PART'S A LIE!
©B Trudeau

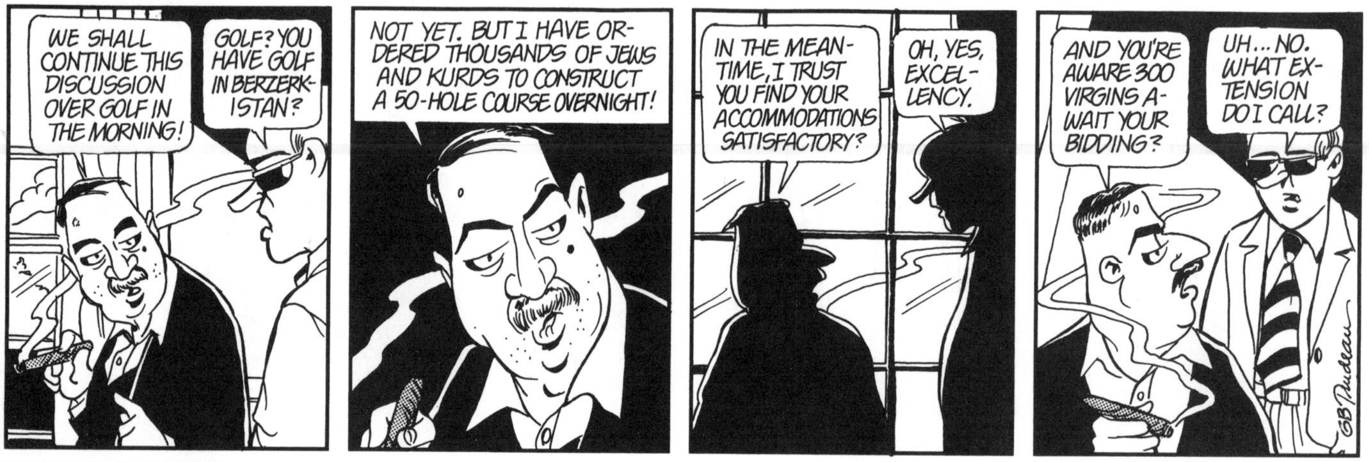
WE SHALL CONTINUE THIS DISCUSSION OVER GOLF IN THE MORNING!
GOLF? YOU HAVE GOLF IN BERZERKISTAN?
NOT YET. BUT I HAVE ORDERED THOUSANDS OF JEWS AND KURDS TO CONSTRUCT A 50-HOLE COURSE OVERNIGHT!
IN THE MEANTIME, I TRUST YOU FIND YOUR ACCOMMODATIONS SATISFACTORY?
OH, YES, EXCELLENCY.
AND YOU'RE AWARE 300 VIRGINS AWAIT YOUR BIDDING?
UH... NO. WHAT EXTENSION DO I CALL?
©B Trudeau

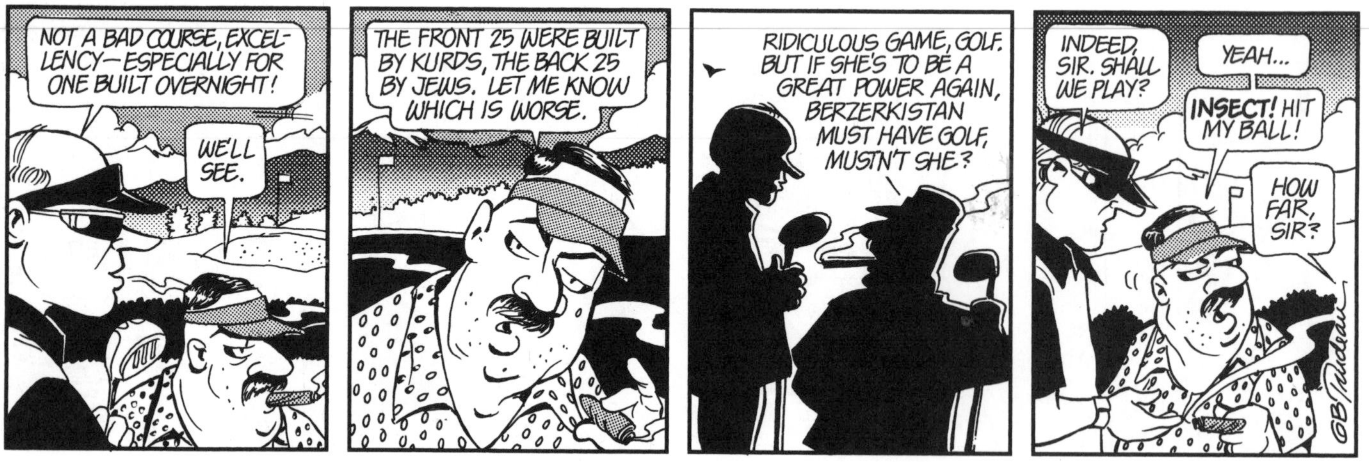
NOT A BAD COURSE, EXCELLENCY—ESPECIALLY FOR ONE BUILT OVERNIGHT!
WE'LL SEE.
THE FRONT 25 WERE BUILT BY KURDS, THE BACK 25 BY JEWS. LET ME KNOW WHICH IS WORSE.
RIDICULOUS GAME, GOLF. BUT IF SHE'S TO BE A GREAT POWER AGAIN, BERZERKISTAN MUST HAVE GOLF, MUSTN'T SHE?
INDEED, SIR. SHALL WE PLAY?
YEAH...
INSECT! HIT MY BALL!
HOW FAR, SIR?
©B Trudeau

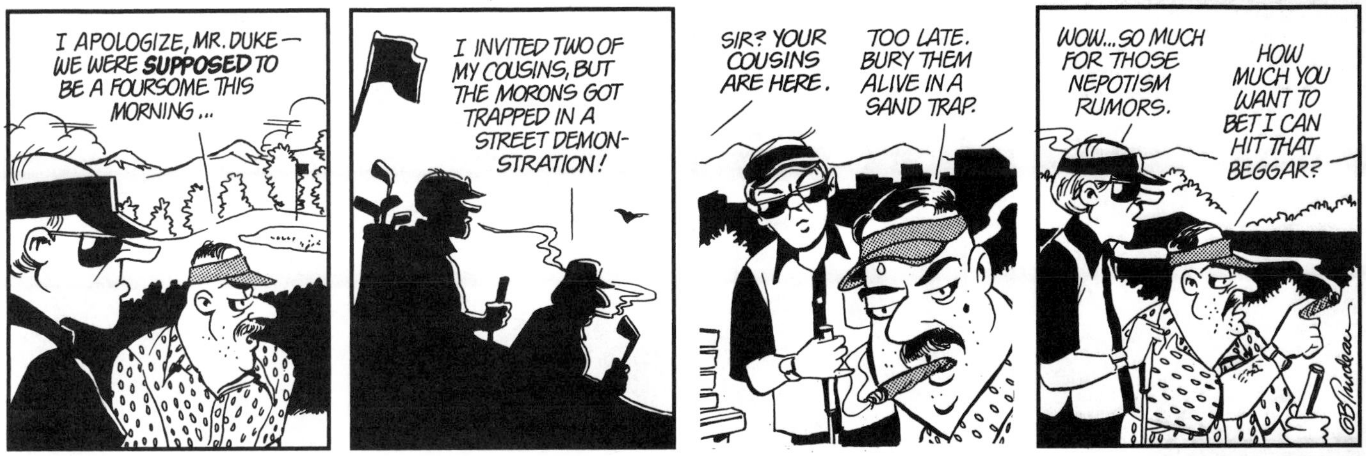
I APOLOGIZE, MR. DUKE — WE WERE **SUPPOSED** TO BE A FOURSOME THIS MORNING...
I INVITED TWO OF MY COUSINS, BUT THE MORONS GOT TRAPPED IN A STREET DEMONSTRATION!
SIR? YOUR COUSINS ARE HERE.
TOO LATE. BURY THEM ALIVE IN A SAND TRAP.
WOW... SO MUCH FOR THOSE NEPOTISM RUMORS.
HOW MUCH YOU WANT TO BET I CAN HIT THAT BEGGAR?
GB Trudeau

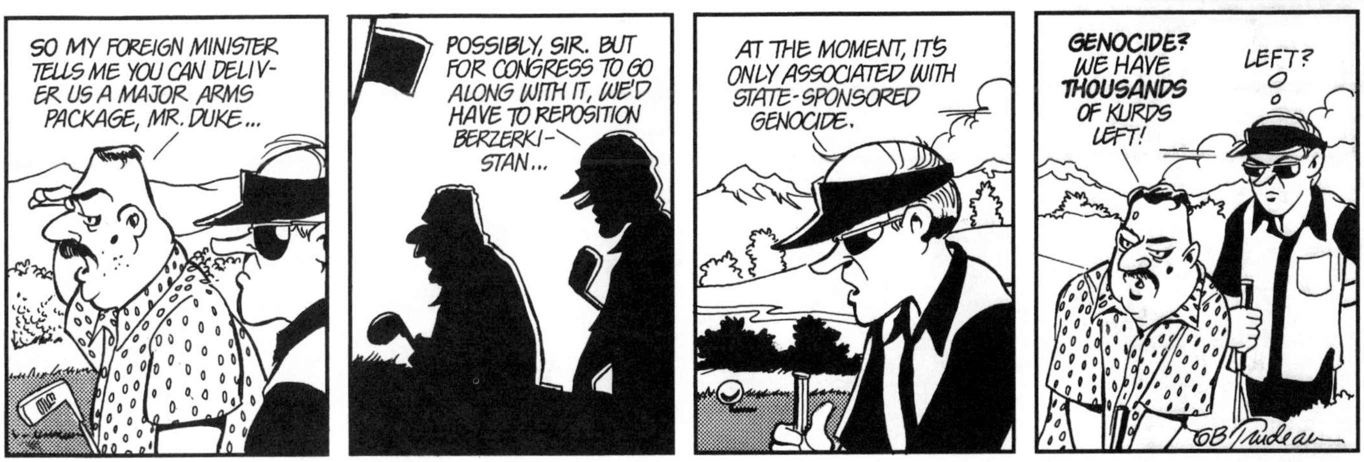
SO MY FOREIGN MINISTER TELLS ME YOU CAN DELIVER US A MAJOR ARMS PACKAGE, MR. DUKE...
POSSIBLY, SIR. BUT FOR CONGRESS TO GO ALONG WITH IT, WE'D HAVE TO REPOSITION BERZERKISTAN...
AT THE MOMENT, IT'S ONLY ASSOCIATED WITH STATE-SPONSORED GENOCIDE.
GENOCIDE? WE HAVE **THOUSANDS** OF KURDS LEFT!
LEFT?
GB Trudeau

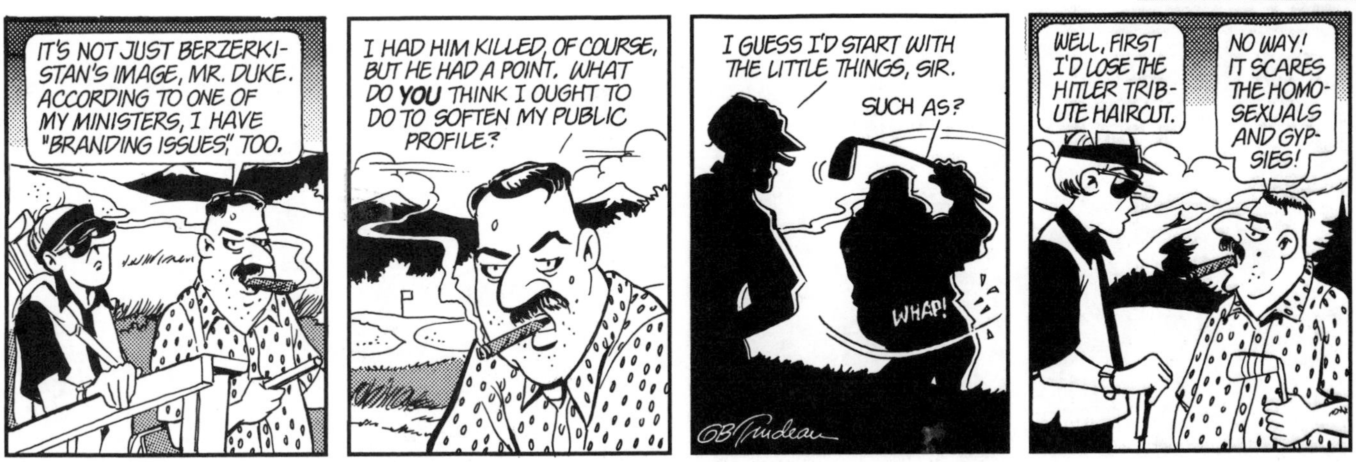
IT'S NOT JUST BERZERKISTAN'S IMAGE, MR. DUKE. ACCORDING TO ONE OF MY MINISTERS, I HAVE "BRANDING ISSUES," TOO.
I HAD HIM KILLED, OF COURSE, BUT HE HAD A POINT. WHAT DO **YOU** THINK I OUGHT TO DO TO SOFTEN MY PUBLIC PROFILE?
I GUESS I'D START WITH THE LITTLE THINGS, SIR.
SUCH AS?
WHAP!
GB Trudeau
WELL, FIRST I'D LOSE THE HITLER TRIBUTE HAIRCUT.
NO WAY! IT SCARES THE HOMOSEXUALS AND GYPSIES!

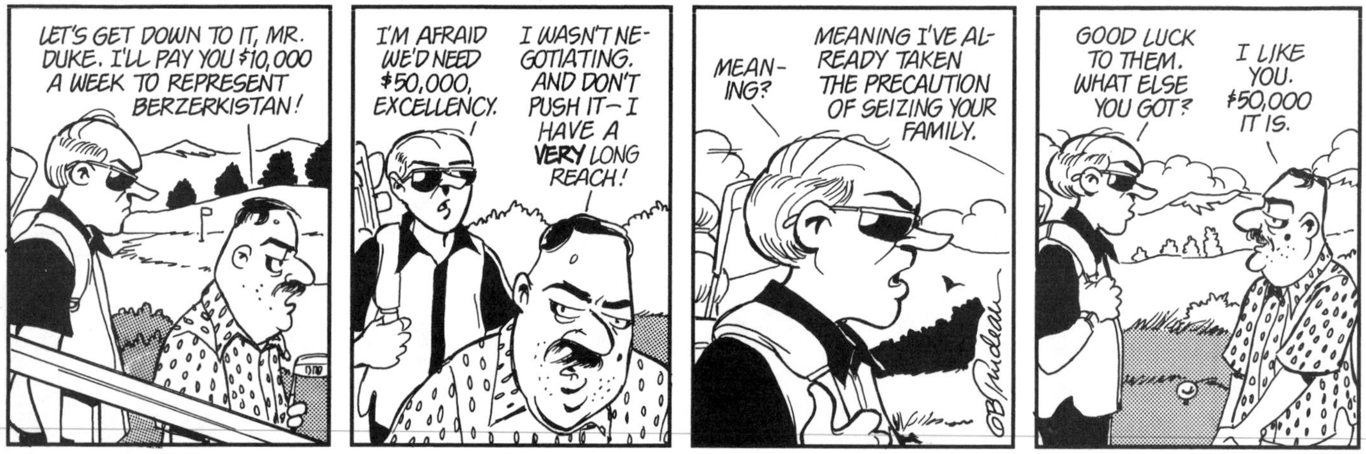
LET'S GET DOWN TO IT, MR. DUKE. I'LL PAY YOU $10,000 A WEEK TO REPRESENT BERZERKISTAN!
I'M AFRAID WE'D NEED $50,000, EXCELLENCY.
I WASN'T NEGOTIATING. AND DON'T PUSH IT— I HAVE A VERY LONG REACH!
MEANING?
MEANING I'VE ALREADY TAKEN THE PRECAUTION OF SEIZING YOUR FAMILY.
GOOD LUCK TO THEM. WHAT ELSE YOU GOT?
I LIKE YOU. $50,000 IT IS.

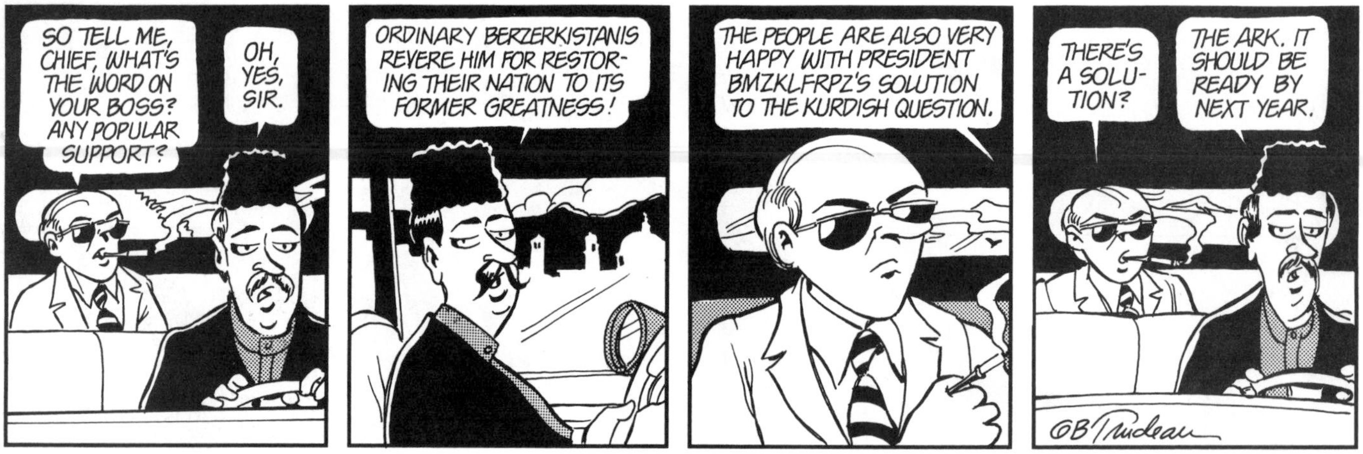
SO TELL ME, CHIEF, WHAT'S THE WORD ON YOUR BOSS? ANY POPULAR SUPPORT?
OH, YES, SIR.
ORDINARY BERZERKISTANIS REVERE HIM FOR RESTORING THEIR NATION TO ITS FORMER GREATNESS!
THE PEOPLE ARE ALSO VERY HAPPY WITH PRESIDENT BMZKLFRPZ'S SOLUTION TO THE KURDISH QUESTION.
THERE'S A SOLUTION?
THE ARK. IT SHOULD BE READY BY NEXT YEAR.

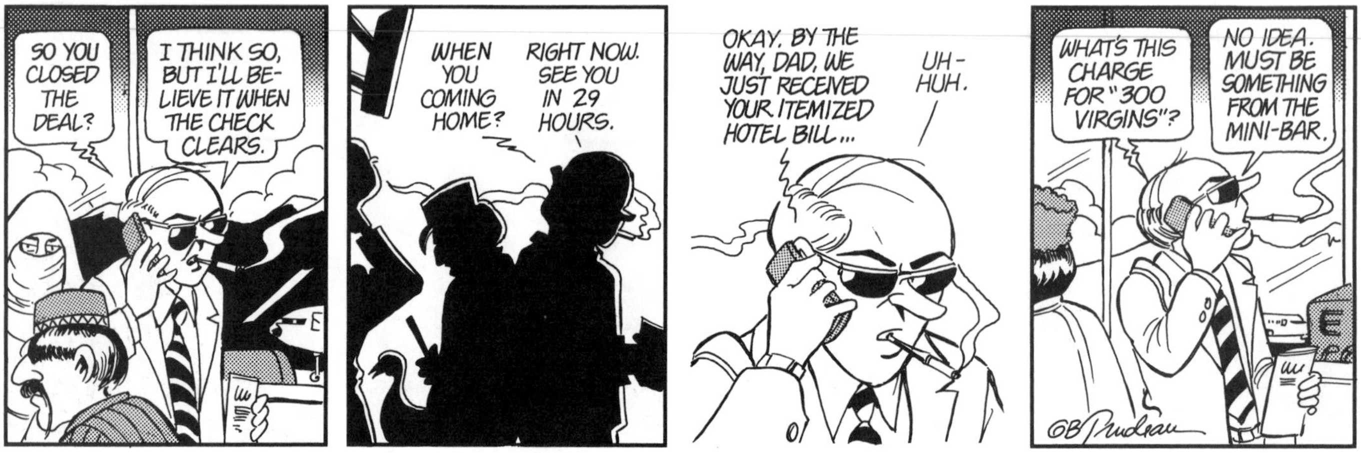
SO YOU CLOSED THE DEAL?
I THINK SO, BUT I'LL BELIEVE IT WHEN THE CHECK CLEARS.
WHEN YOU COMING HOME?
RIGHT NOW. SEE YOU IN 29 HOURS.
OKAY. BY THE WAY, DAD, WE JUST RECEIVED YOUR ITEMIZED HOTEL BILL...
UH-HUH.
WHAT'S THIS CHARGE FOR "300 VIRGINS"?
NO IDEA. MUST BE SOMETHING FROM THE MINI-BAR.

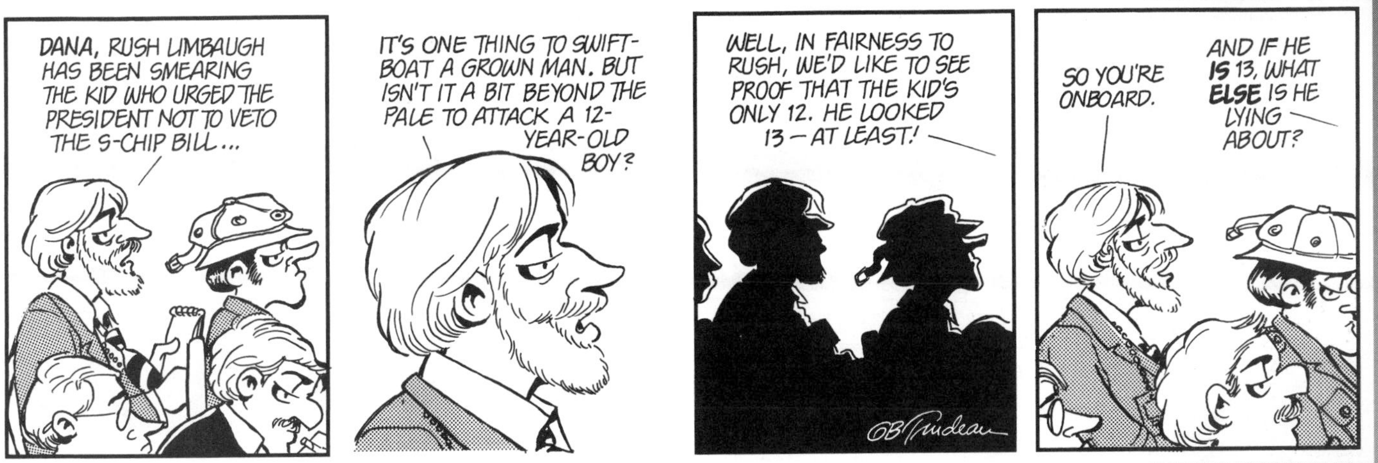
DANA, RUSH LIMBAUGH HAS BEEN SMEARING THE KID WHO URGED THE PRESIDENT NOT TO VETO THE S-CHIP BILL ...
IT'S ONE THING TO SWIFT-BOAT A GROWN MAN. BUT ISN'T IT A BIT BEYOND THE PALE TO ATTACK A 12-YEAR-OLD BOY?
WELL, IN FAIRNESS TO RUSH, WE'D LIKE TO SEE PROOF THAT THE KID'S ONLY 12. HE LOOKED 13 — AT LEAST!
SO YOU'RE ONBOARD.
AND IF HE **IS** 13, WHAT **ELSE** IS HE LYING ABOUT?
©B Trudeau

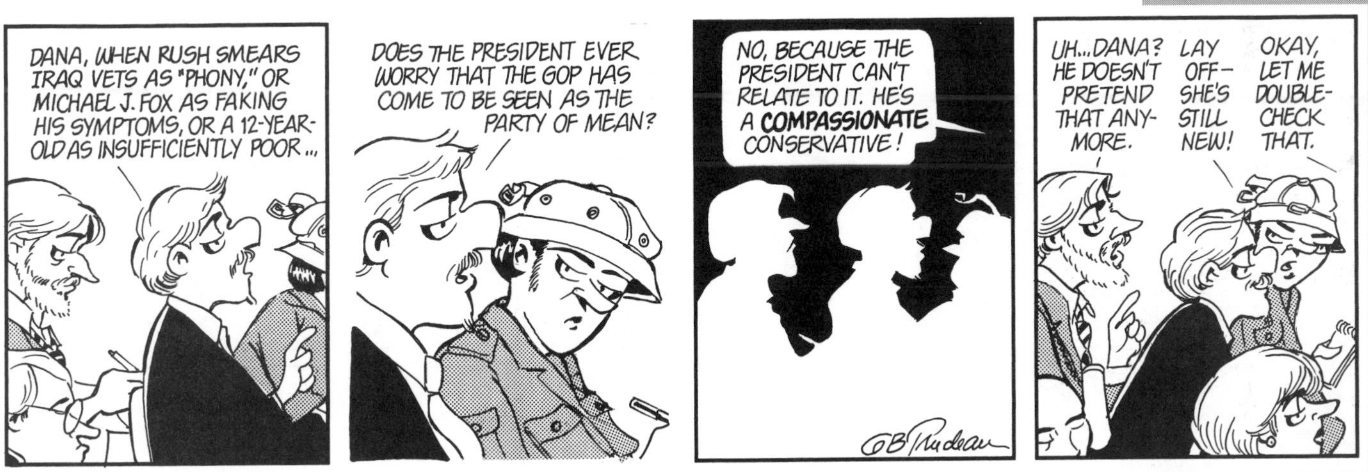
DANA, WHEN RUSH SMEARS IRAQ VETS AS "PHONY," OR MICHAEL J. FOX AS FAKING HIS SYMPTOMS, OR A 12-YEAR-OLD AS INSUFFICIENTLY POOR ...
DOES THE PRESIDENT EVER WORRY THAT THE GOP HAS COME TO BE SEEN AS THE PARTY OF MEAN?
NO, BECAUSE THE PRESIDENT CAN'T RELATE TO IT. HE'S A **COMPASSIONATE** CONSERVATIVE!
UH...DANA? HE DOESN'T PRETEND THAT ANY-MORE.
LAY OFF-SHE'S STILL NEW!
OKAY, LET ME DOUBLE-CHECK THAT.
©B Trudeau

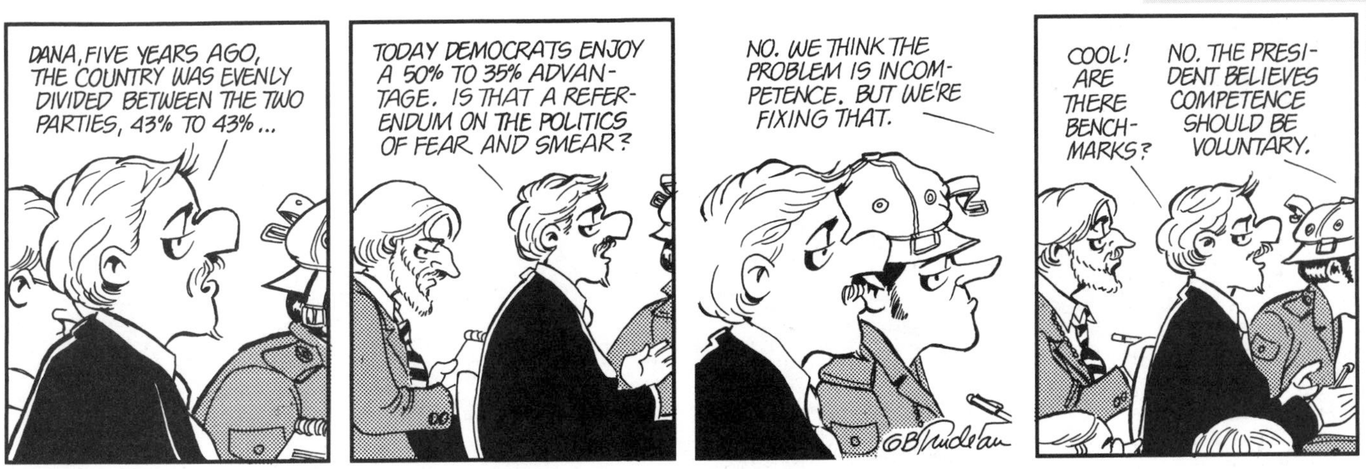
DANA, FIVE YEARS AGO, THE COUNTRY WAS EVENLY DIVIDED BETWEEN THE TWO PARTIES, 43% TO 43% ...
TODAY DEMOCRATS ENJOY A 50% TO 35% ADVAN-TAGE. IS THAT A REFER-ENDUM ON THE POLITICS OF FEAR AND SMEAR?
NO. WE THINK THE PROBLEM IS INCOM-PETENCE. BUT WE'RE FIXING THAT.
COOL! ARE THERE BENCH-MARKS?
NO. THE PRESI-DENT BELIEVES COMPETENCE SHOULD BE VOLUNTARY.
©B Trudeau

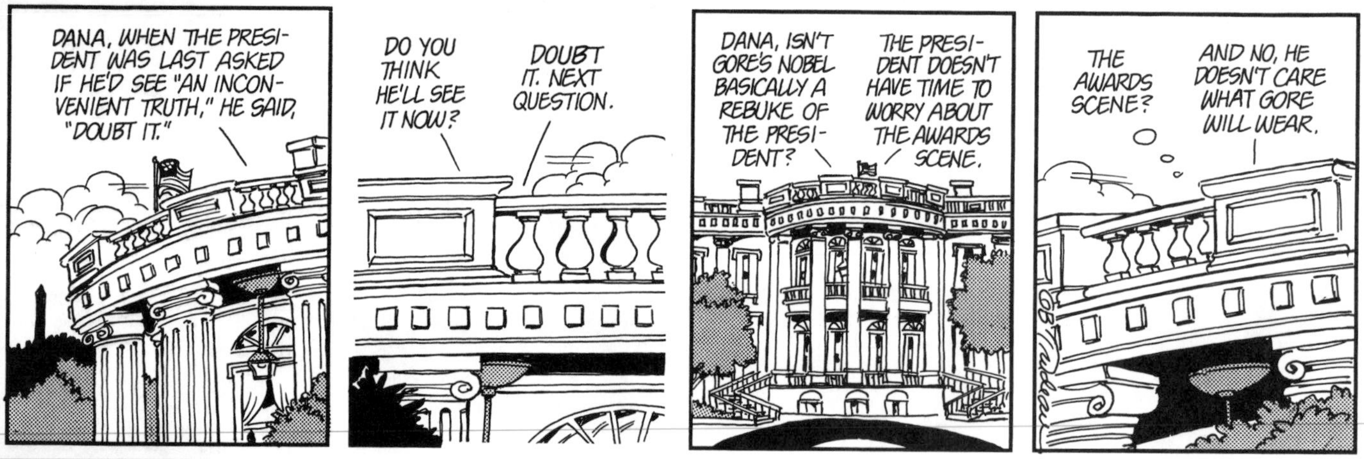
DANA, WHEN THE PRESIDENT WAS LAST ASKED IF HE'D SEE "AN INCONVENIENT TRUTH," HE SAID, "DOUBT IT."
DO YOU THINK HE'LL SEE IT NOW?
DOUBT IT. NEXT QUESTION.
DANA, ISN'T GORE'S NOBEL BASICALLY A REBUKE OF THE PRESIDENT?
THE PRESIDENT DOESN'T HAVE TIME TO WORRY ABOUT THE AWARDS SCENE.
THE AWARDS SCENE?
AND NO, HE DOESN'T CARE WHAT GORE WILL WEAR.

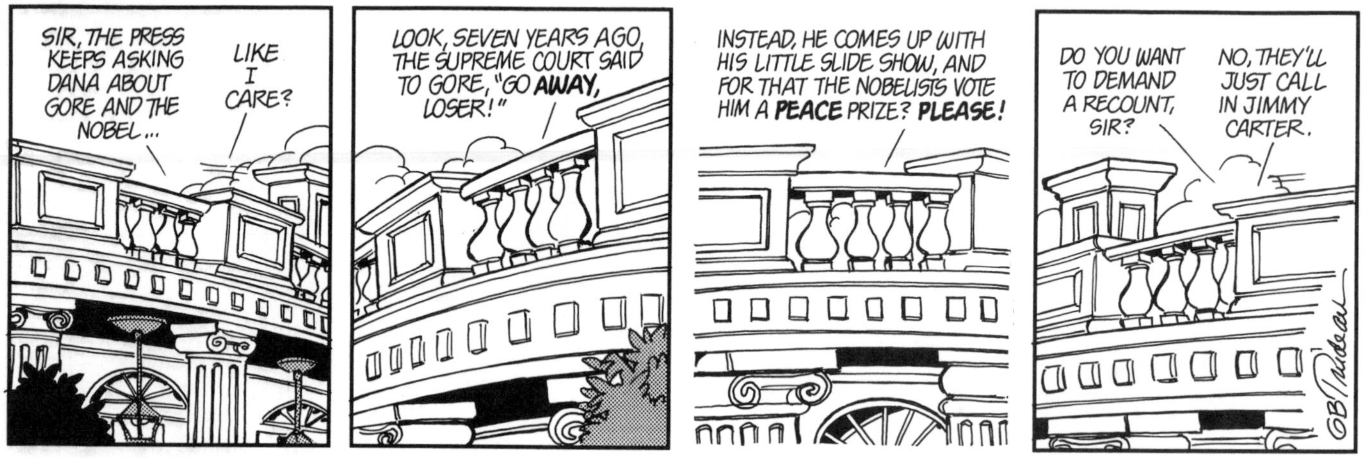
SIR, THE PRESS KEEPS ASKING DANA ABOUT GORE AND THE NOBEL...
LIKE I CARE?
LOOK, SEVEN YEARS AGO, THE SUPREME COURT SAID TO GORE, "GO AWAY, LOSER!"
INSTEAD, HE COMES UP WITH HIS LITTLE SLIDE SHOW, AND FOR THAT THE NOBELISTS VOTE HIM A PEACE PRIZE? PLEASE!
DO YOU WANT TO DEMAND A RECOUNT, SIR?
NO, THEY'LL JUST CALL IN JIMMY CARTER.

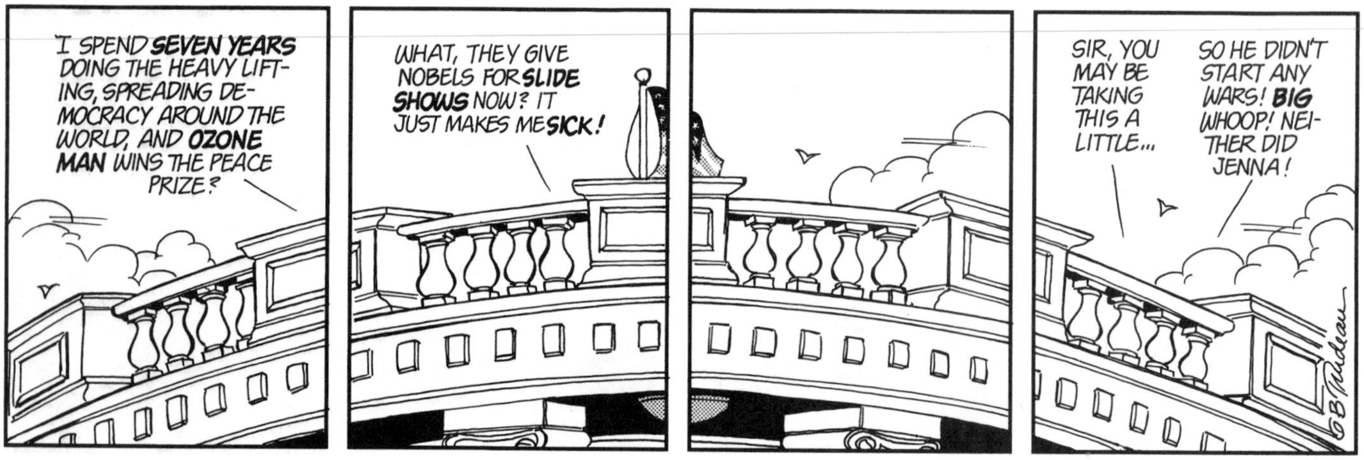
I SPEND SEVEN YEARS DOING THE HEAVY LIFTING, SPREADING DEMOCRACY AROUND THE WORLD, AND OZONE MAN WINS THE PEACE PRIZE?
WHAT, THEY GIVE NOBELS FOR SLIDE SHOWS NOW? IT JUST MAKES ME SICK!
SIR, YOU MAY BE TAKING THIS A LITTLE...
SO HE DIDN'T START ANY WARS! BIG WHOOP! NEITHER DID JENNA!

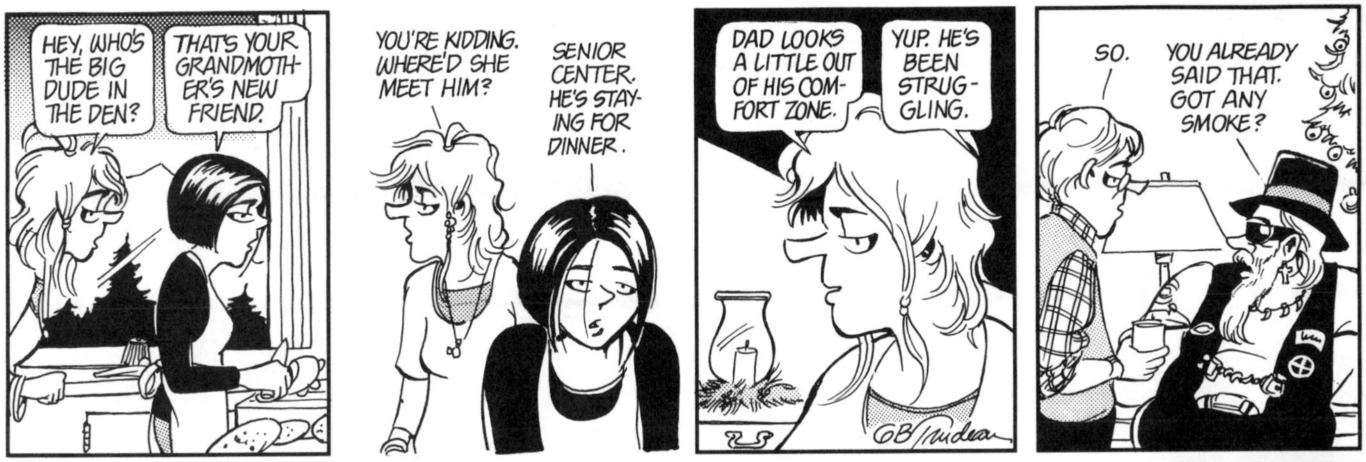
HEY, WHO'S THE BIG DUDE IN THE DEN?
THAT'S YOUR GRANDMOTHER'S NEW FRIEND.
YOU'RE KIDDING. WHERE'D SHE MEET HIM?
SENIOR CENTER. HE'S STAYING FOR DINNER.
DAD LOOKS A LITTLE OUT OF HIS COMFORT ZONE.
YUP. HE'S BEEN STRUGGLING.
SO.
YOU ALREADY SAID THAT. GOT ANY SMOKE?

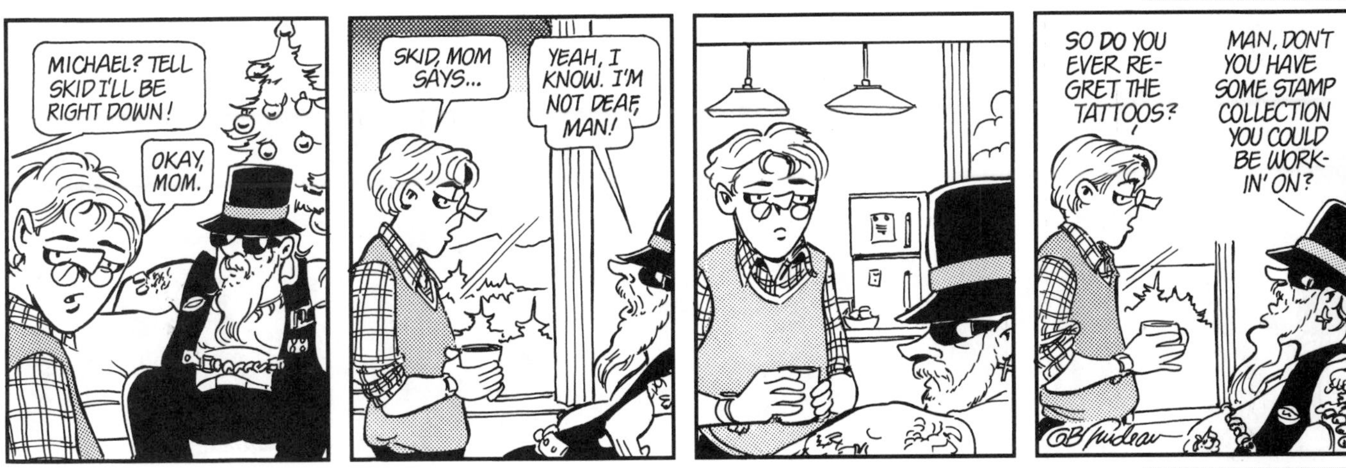
MICHAEL? TELL SKID I'LL BE RIGHT DOWN!
OKAY, MOM.
SKID, MOM SAYS...
YEAH, I KNOW. I'M NOT DEAF, MAN!
SO DO YOU EVER REGRET THE TATTOOS?
MAN, DON'T YOU HAVE SOME STAMP COLLECTION YOU COULD BE WORKIN' ON?

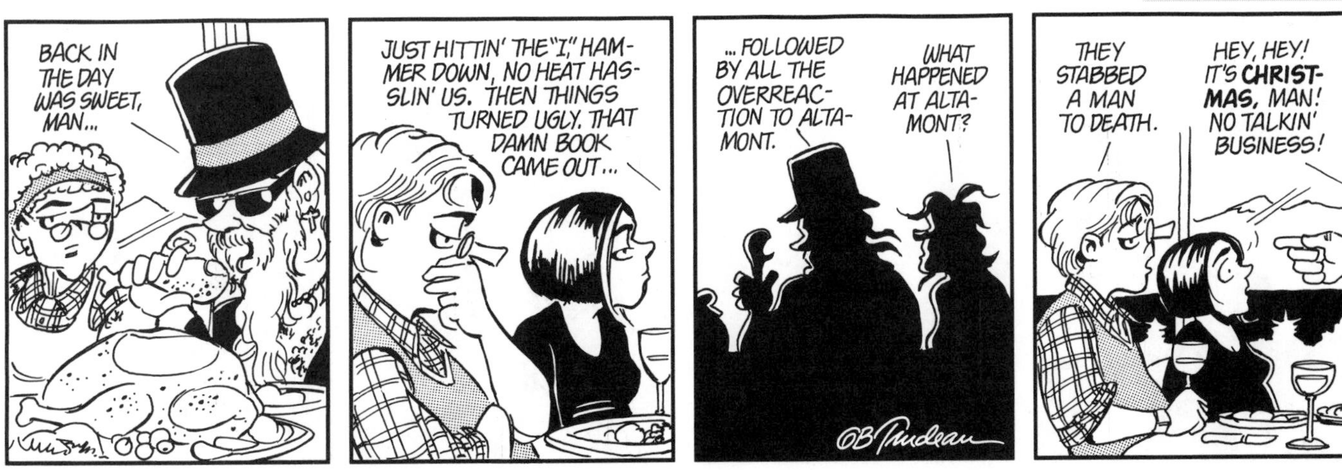
BACK IN THE DAY WAS SWEET, MAN...
JUST HITTIN' THE "I," HAMMER DOWN, NO HEAT HASSLIN' US. THEN THINGS TURNED UGLY. THAT DAMN BOOK CAME OUT...
...FOLLOWED BY ALL THE OVERREACTION TO ALTAMONT.
WHAT HAPPENED AT ALTAMONT?
THEY STABBED A MAN TO DEATH.
HEY, HEY! IT'S **CHRISTMAS,** MAN! NO TALKIN' BUSINESS!

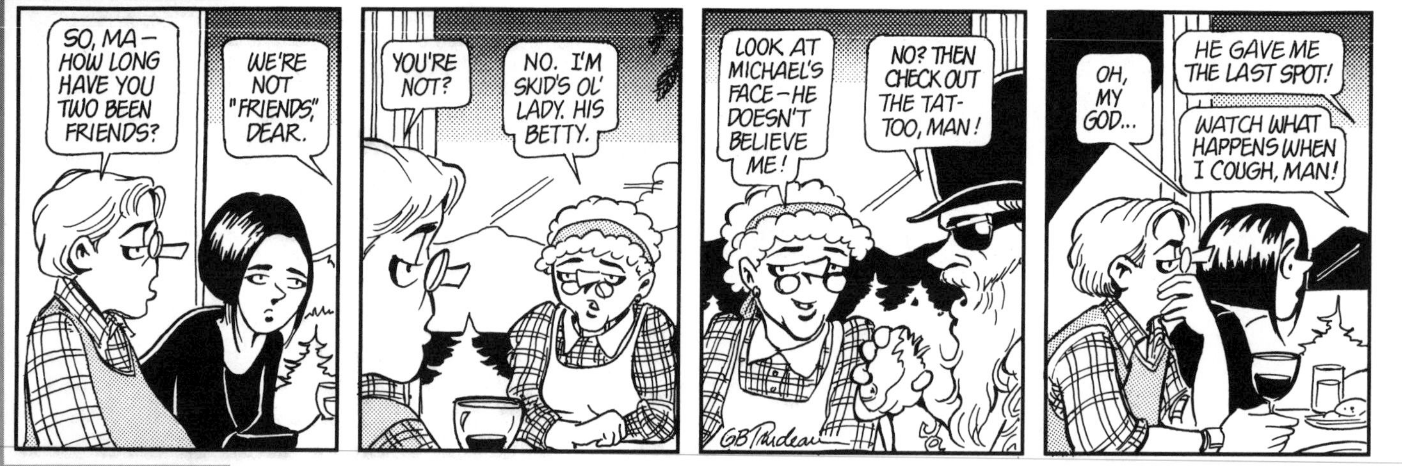
SO, MA— HOW LONG HAVE YOU TWO BEEN FRIENDS?
WE'RE NOT "FRIENDS," DEAR.
YOU'RE NOT?
NO. I'M SKID'S OL' LADY. HIS BETTY.
LOOK AT MICHAEL'S FACE—HE DOESN'T BELIEVE ME!
NO? THEN CHECK OUT THE TAT-TOO, MAN!
OH, MY GOD...
HE GAVE ME THE LAST SPOT!
WATCH WHAT HAPPENS WHEN I COUGH, MAN!
GB Trudeau

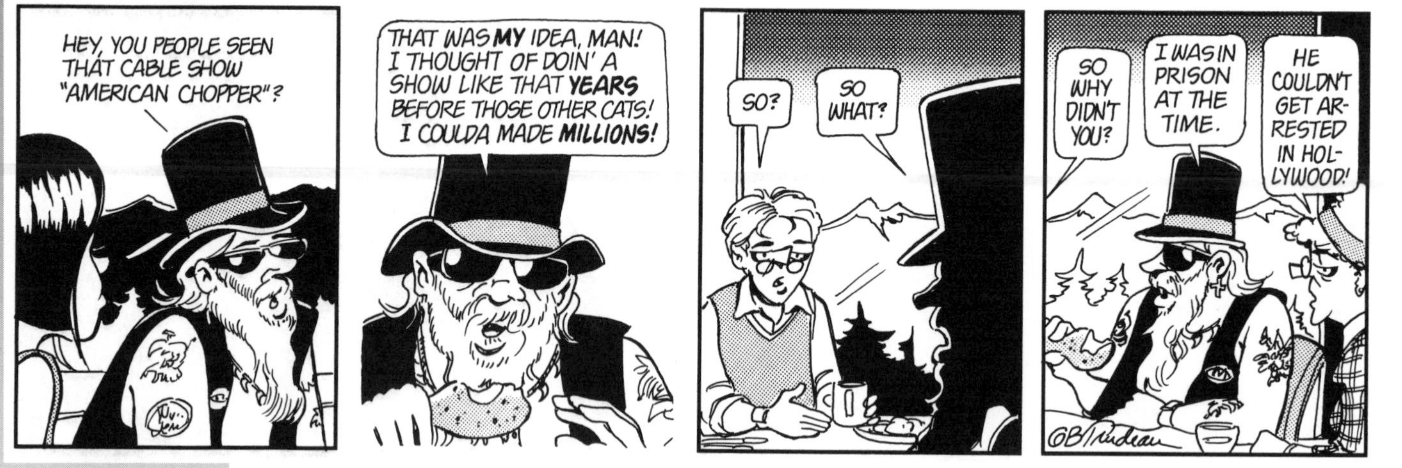
HEY, YOU PEOPLE SEEN THAT CABLE SHOW "AMERICAN CHOPPER"?
THAT WAS MY IDEA, MAN! I THOUGHT OF DOIN' A SHOW LIKE THAT YEARS BEFORE THOSE OTHER CATS! I COULDA MADE MILLIONS!
SO?
SO WHAT?
SO WHY DIDN'T YOU?
I WAS IN PRISON AT THE TIME.
HE COULDN'T GET AR-RESTED IN HOL-LYWOOD!
GB Trudeau

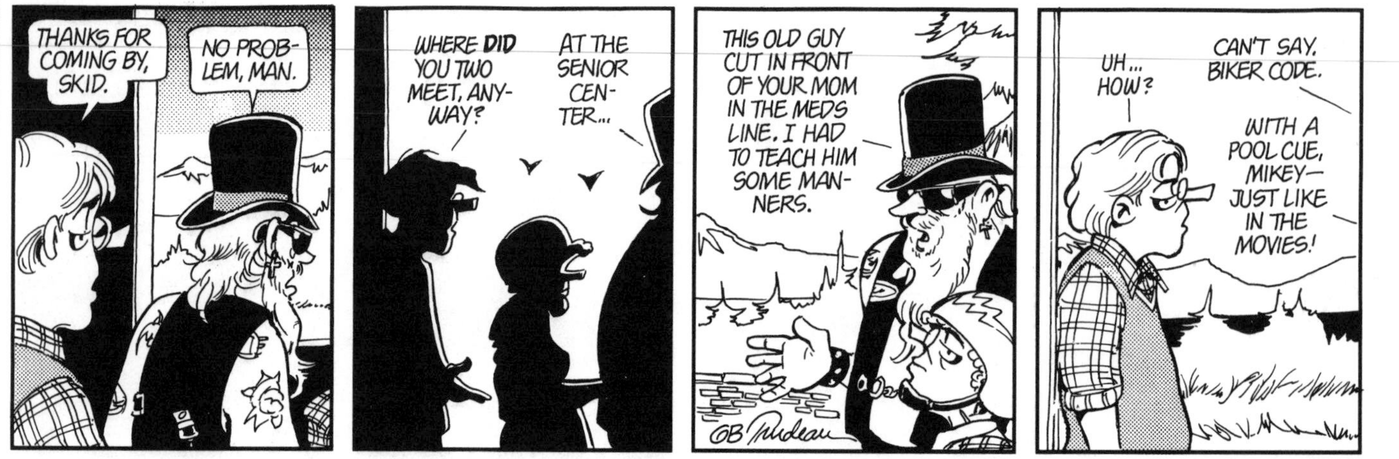
THANKS FOR COMING BY, SKID.
NO PROB-LEM, MAN.
WHERE DID YOU TWO MEET, ANY-WAY?
AT THE SENIOR CEN-TER...
THIS OLD GUY CUT IN FRONT OF YOUR MOM IN THE MEDS LINE. I HAD TO TEACH HIM SOME MAN-NERS.
GB Trudeau
UH... HOW?
CAN'T SAY. BIKER CODE.
WITH A POOL CUE, MIKEY— JUST LIKE IN THE MOVIES!

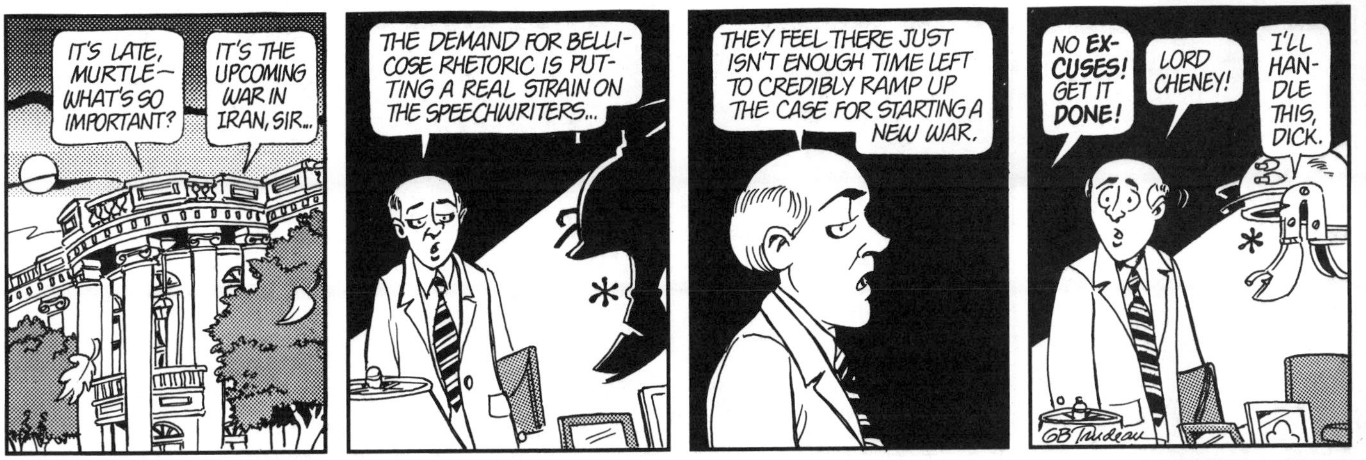
IT'S LATE, MURTLE— WHAT'S SO IMPORTANT?
IT'S THE UPCOMING WAR IN IRAN, SIR...
THE DEMAND FOR BELLICOSE RHETORIC IS PUTTING A REAL STRAIN ON THE SPEECHWRITERS...
THEY FEEL THERE JUST ISN'T ENOUGH TIME LEFT TO CREDIBLY RAMP UP THE CASE FOR STARTING A NEW WAR.
NO **EXCUSES!** GET IT **DONE!**
LORD CHENEY!
I'LL HANDLE THIS, DICK.
GB Trudeau

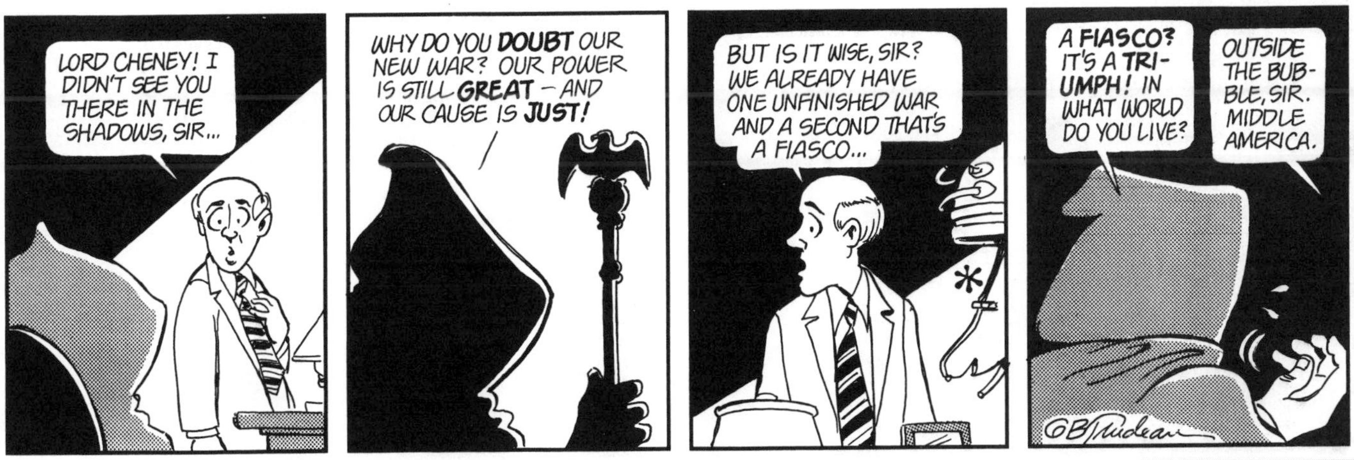
LORD CHENEY! I DIDN'T SEE YOU THERE IN THE SHADOWS, SIR...
WHY DO YOU **DOUBT** OUR NEW WAR? OUR POWER IS STILL **GREAT** — AND OUR CAUSE IS **JUST!**
BUT IS IT WISE, SIR? WE ALREADY HAVE ONE UNFINISHED WAR AND A SECOND THAT'S A FIASCO...
A **FIASCO?** IT'S A **TRIUMPH!** IN WHAT WORLD DO YOU LIVE?
OUTSIDE THE BUBBLE, SIR. MIDDLE AMERICA.
GB Trudeau

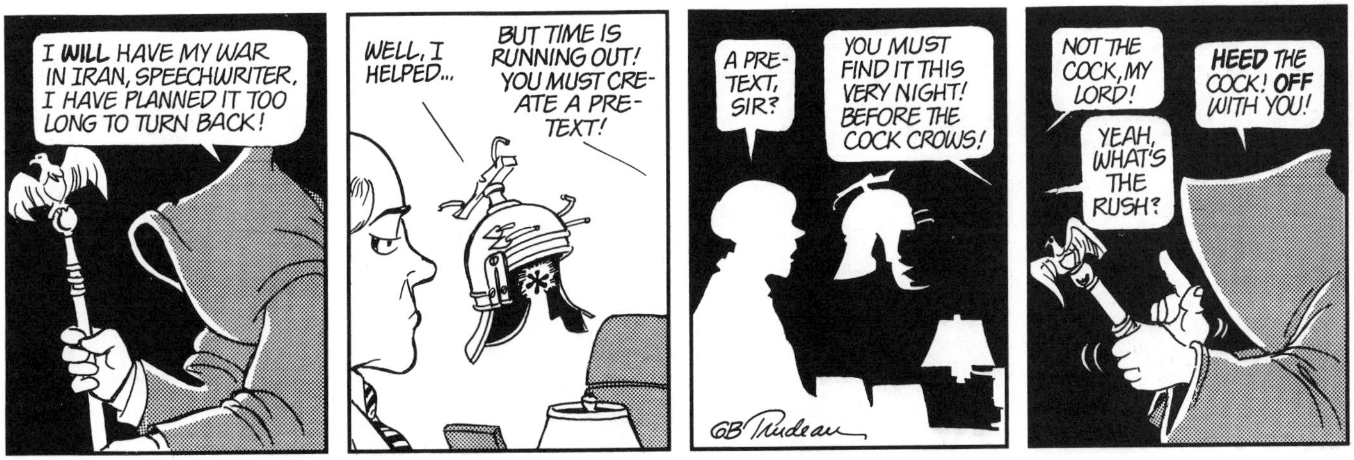
I **WILL** HAVE MY WAR IN IRAN, SPEECHWRITER. I HAVE PLANNED IT TOO LONG TO TURN BACK!
WELL, I HELPED...
BUT TIME IS RUNNING OUT! YOU MUST CREATE A PRETEXT!
A PRETEXT, SIR?
YOU MUST FIND IT THIS VERY NIGHT! BEFORE THE COCK CROWS!
GB Trudeau
NOT THE COCK, MY LORD!
YEAH, WHAT'S THE RUSH?
HEED THE COCK! **OFF** WITH YOU!

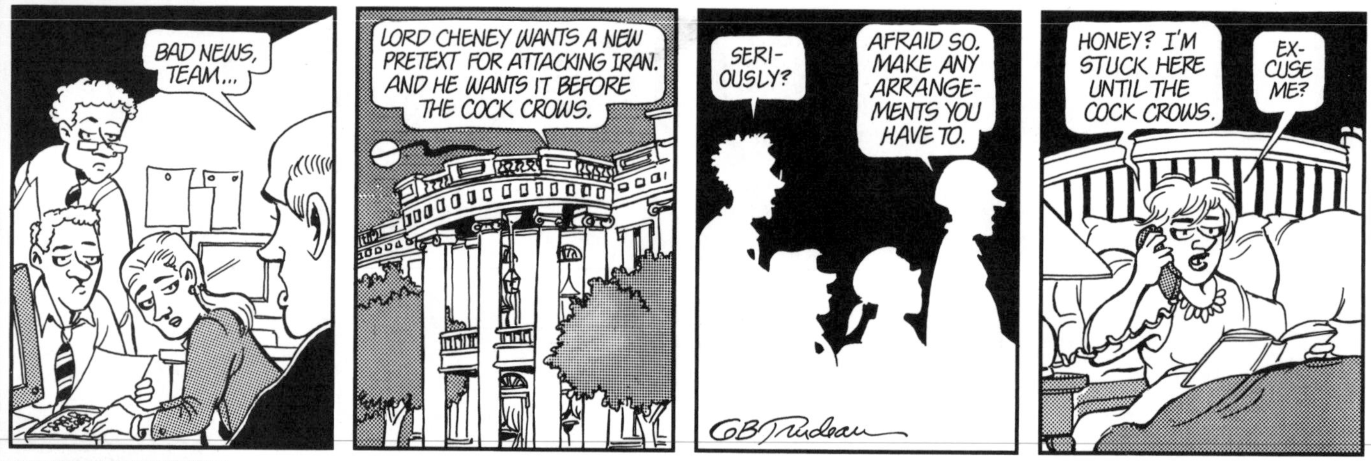
BAD NEWS, TEAM...
LORD CHENEY WANTS A NEW PRETEXT FOR ATTACKING IRAN. AND HE WANTS IT BEFORE THE COCK CROWS.
SERI-OUSLY?
AFRAID SO. MAKE ANY ARRANGE-MENTS YOU HAVE TO.
HONEY? I'M STUCK HERE UNTIL THE COCK CROWS.
EX-CUSE ME?

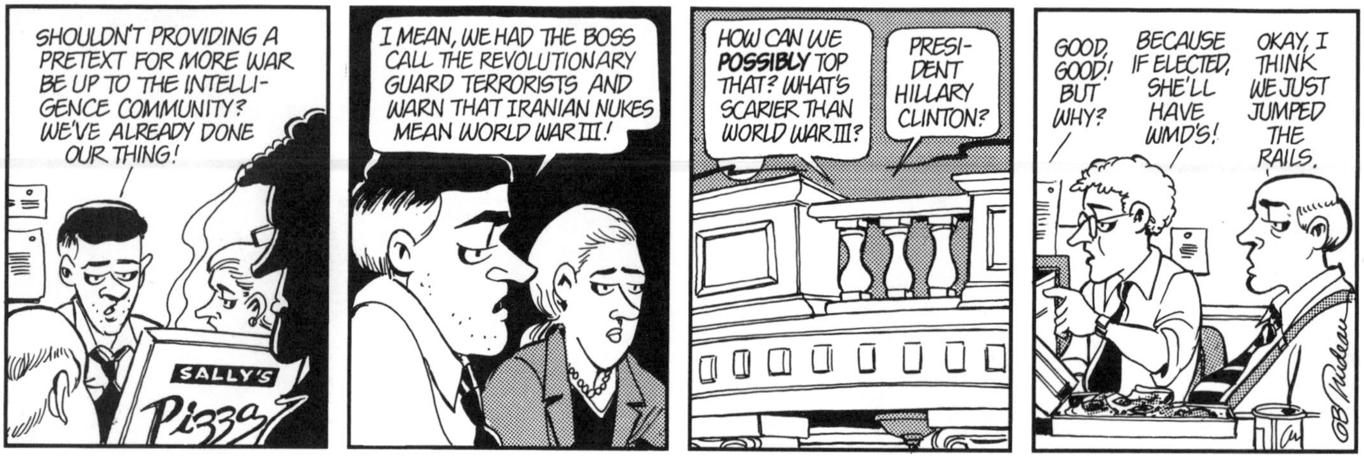
SHOULDN'T PROVIDING A PRETEXT FOR MORE WAR BE UP TO THE INTELLI-GENCE COMMUNITY? WE'VE ALREADY DONE OUR THING!
SALLY'S
Pizza
I MEAN, WE HAD THE BOSS CALL THE REVOLUTIONARY GUARD TERRORISTS AND WARN THAT IRANIAN NUKES MEAN WORLD WAR III!
HOW CAN WE POSSIBLY TOP THAT? WHAT'S SCARIER THAN WORLD WAR III?
PRESI-DENT HILLARY CLINTON?
GOOD, GOOD! BUT WHY?
BECAUSE IF ELECTED, SHE'LL HAVE WMD'S!
OKAY, I THINK WE JUST JUMPED THE RAILS.

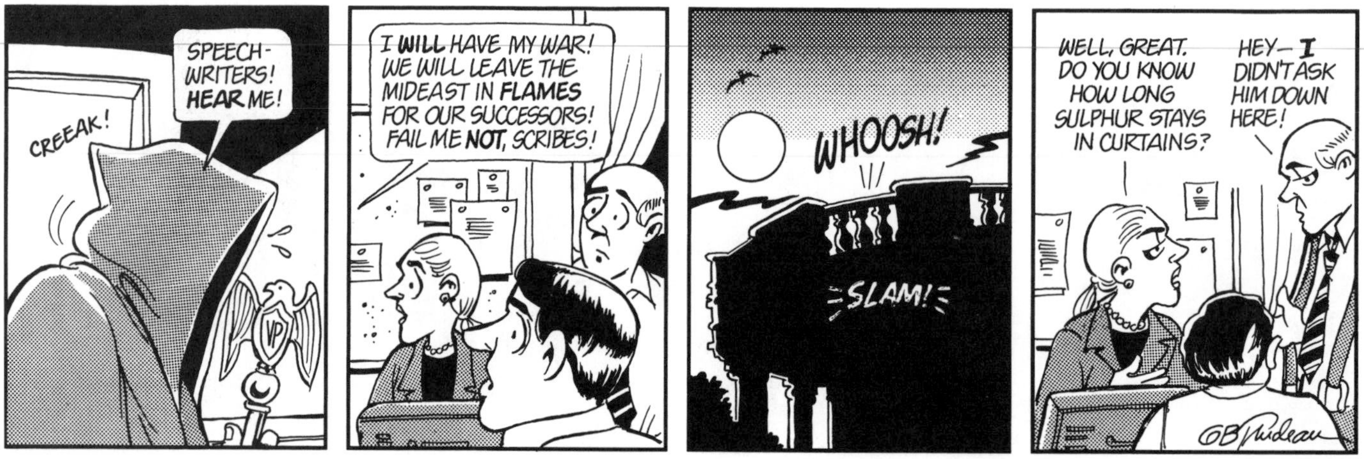
SPEECH-WRITERS! HEAR ME!
CREEAK!
VP
I WILL HAVE MY WAR! WE WILL LEAVE THE MIDEAST IN FLAMES FOR OUR SUCCESSORS! FAIL ME NOT, SCRIBES!
WHOOSH!
SLAM!
WELL, GREAT. DO YOU KNOW HOW LONG SULPHUR STAYS IN CURTAINS?
HEY— I DIDN'T ASK HIM DOWN HERE!

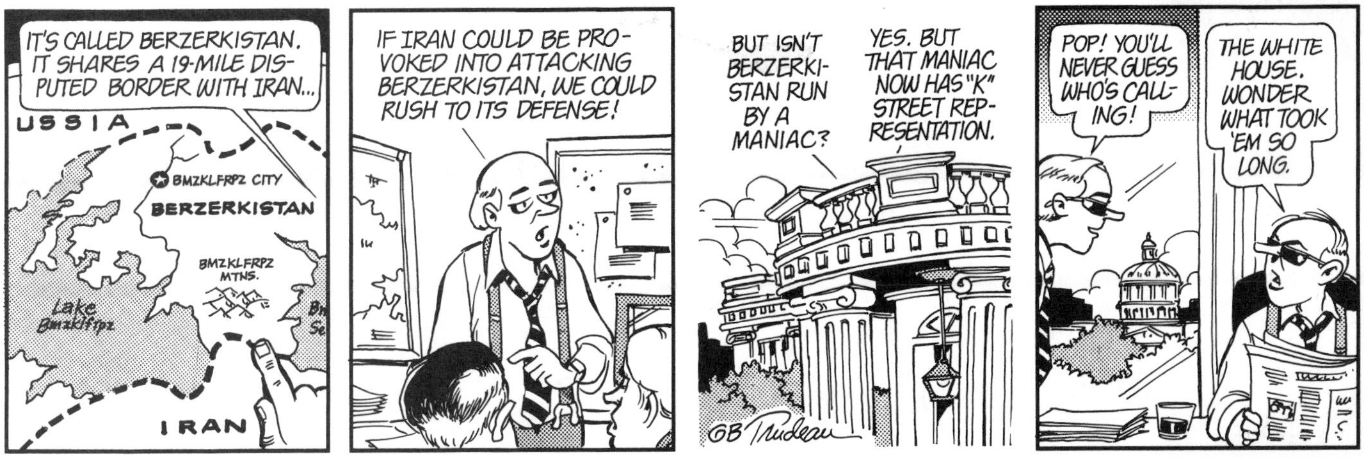
IT'S CALLED BERZERKISTAN. IT SHARES A 19-MILE DISPUTED BORDER WITH IRAN...
USSIA
BMZKLFRPZ CITY
BERZERKISTAN
BMZKLFRPZ MTNS.
Lake Bmzklfrpz
IRAN
IF IRAN COULD BE PROVOKED INTO ATTACKING BERZERKISTAN, WE COULD RUSH TO ITS DEFENSE!
BUT ISN'T BERZERKISTAN RUN BY A MANIAC?
YES. BUT THAT MANIAC NOW HAS "K" STREET REPRESENTATION.
©B Trudeau
POP! YOU'LL NEVER GUESS WHO'S CALLING!
THE WHITE HOUSE. WONDER WHAT TOOK 'EM SO LONG.

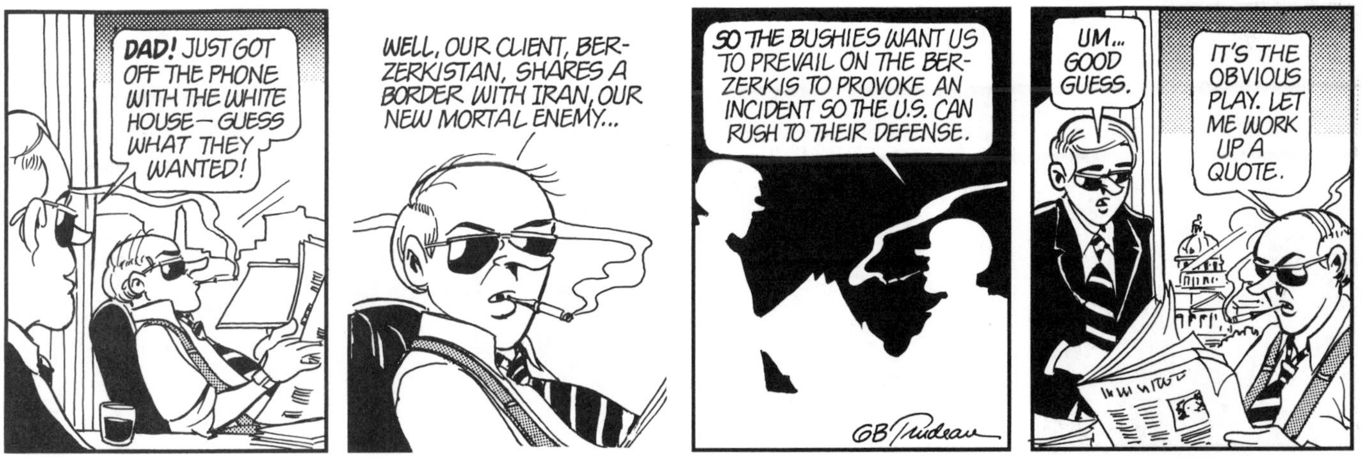
DAD! JUST GOT OFF THE PHONE WITH THE WHITE HOUSE—GUESS WHAT THEY WANTED!
WELL, OUR CLIENT, BERZERKISTAN, SHARES A BORDER WITH IRAN, OUR NEW MORTAL ENEMY...
SO THE BUSHIES WANT US TO PREVAIL ON THE BERZERKIS TO PROVOKE AN INCIDENT SO THE U.S. CAN RUSH TO THEIR DEFENSE.
©B Trudeau
UM... GOOD GUESS.
IT'S THE OBVIOUS PLAY. LET ME WORK UP A QUOTE.

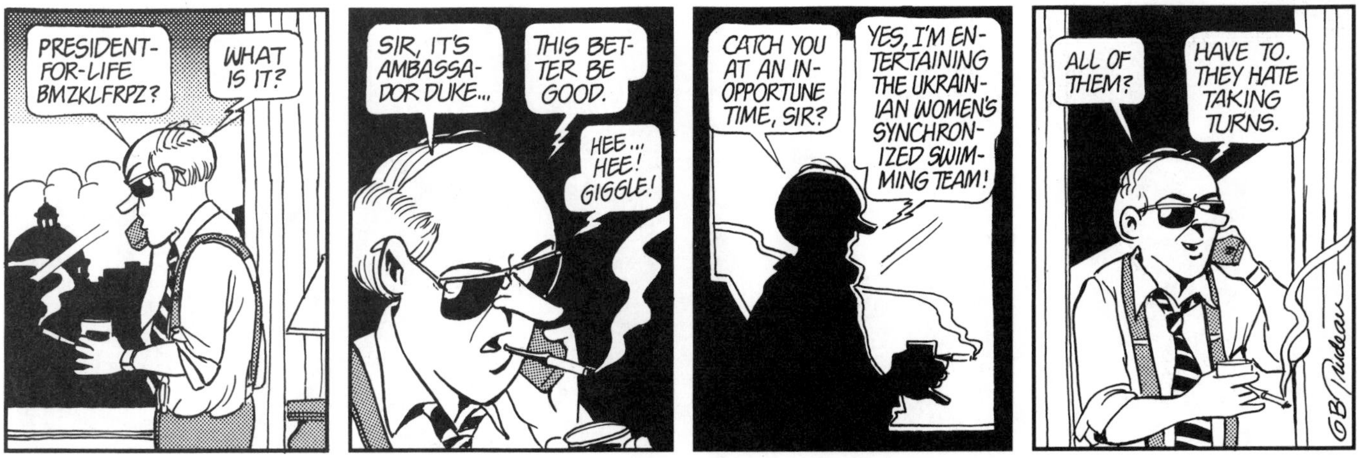
PRESIDENT-FOR-LIFE BMZKLFRPZ?
WHAT IS IT?
SIR, IT'S AMBASSADOR DUKE...
THIS BETTER BE GOOD.
HEE... HEE! GIGGLE!
CATCH YOU AT AN INOPPORTUNE TIME, SIR?
YES, I'M ENTERTAINING THE UKRAINIAN WOMEN'S SYNCHRONIZED SWIMMING TEAM!
ALL OF THEM?
HAVE TO. THEY HATE TAKING TURNS.
©B Trudeau

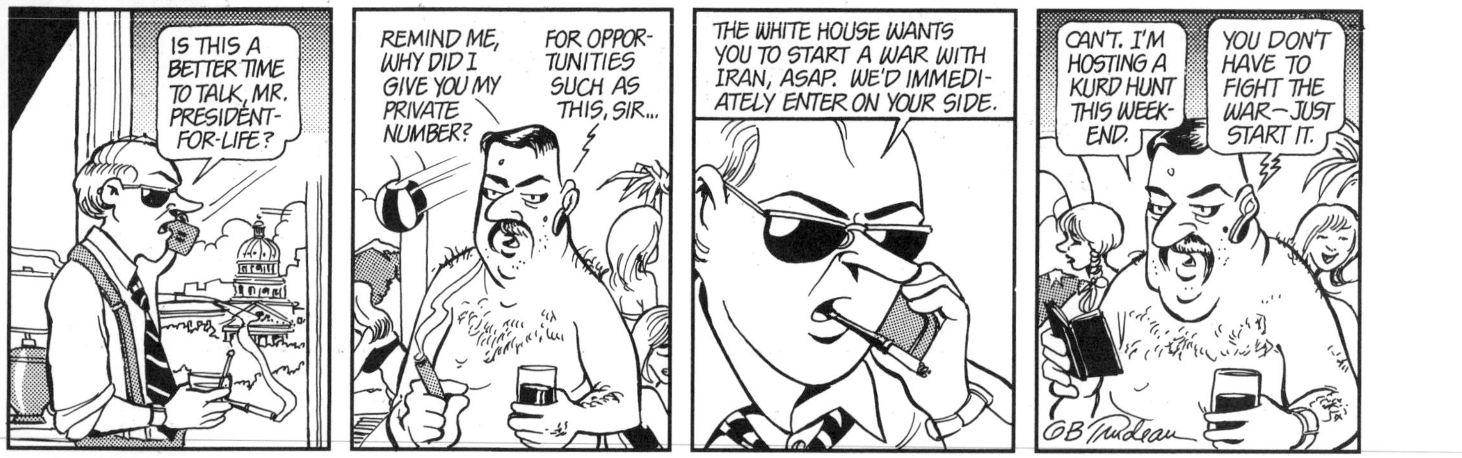
IS THIS A BETTER TIME TO TALK, MR. PRESIDENT-FOR-LIFE?
REMIND ME, WHY DID I GIVE YOU MY PRIVATE NUMBER?
FOR OPPORTUNITIES SUCH AS THIS, SIR...
THE WHITE HOUSE WANTS YOU TO START A WAR WITH IRAN, ASAP. WE'D IMMEDIATELY ENTER ON YOUR SIDE.
CAN'T. I'M HOSTING A KURD HUNT THIS WEEKEND.
YOU DON'T HAVE TO FIGHT THE WAR—JUST START IT.
GB Trudeau

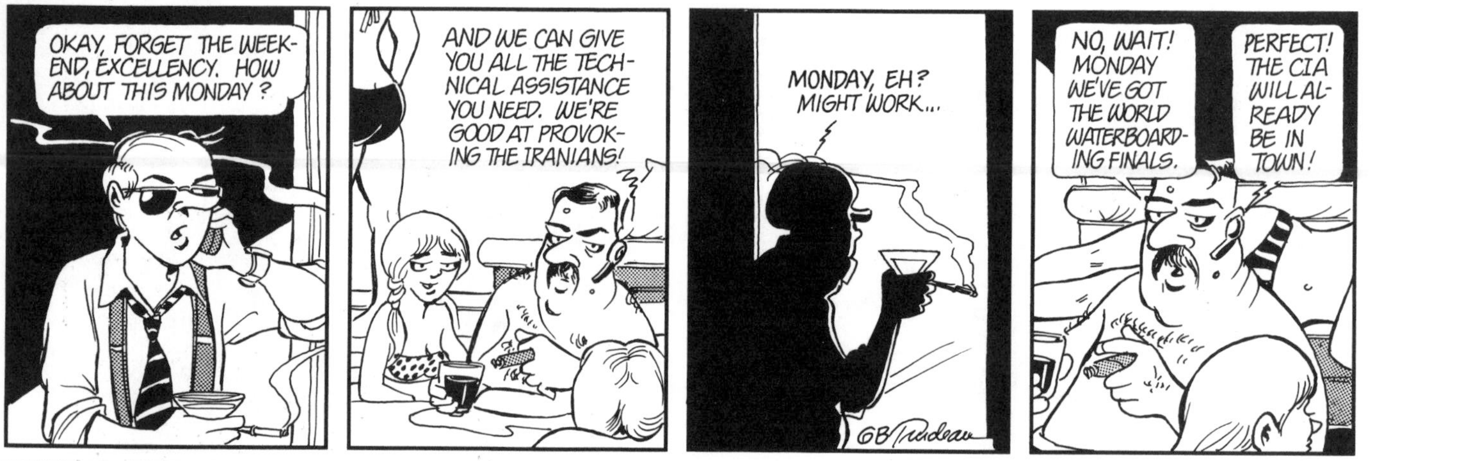
OKAY, FORGET THE WEEKEND, EXCELLENCY. HOW ABOUT THIS MONDAY?
AND WE CAN GIVE YOU ALL THE TECHNICAL ASSISTANCE YOU NEED. WE'RE GOOD AT PROVOKING THE IRANIANS!
MONDAY, EH? MIGHT WORK...
GB Trudeau
NO, WAIT! MONDAY WE'VE GOT THE WORLD WATERBOARDING FINALS.
PERFECT! THE CIA WILL ALREADY BE IN TOWN!

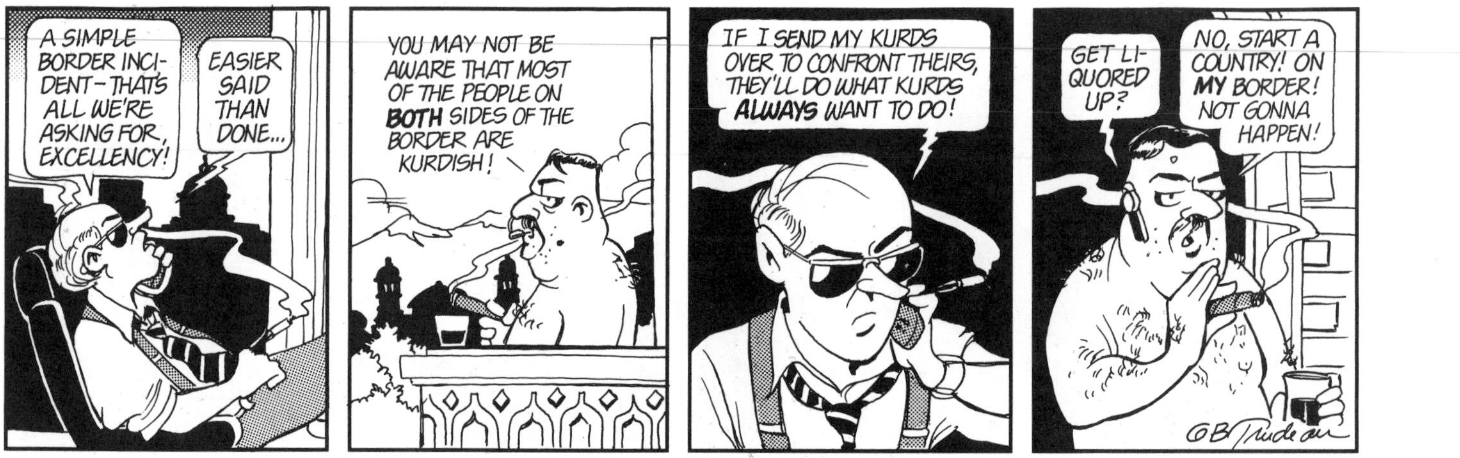
A SIMPLE BORDER INCIDENT—THAT'S ALL WE'RE ASKING FOR, EXCELLENCY!
EASIER SAID THAN DONE...
YOU MAY NOT BE AWARE THAT MOST OF THE PEOPLE ON BOTH SIDES OF THE BORDER ARE KURDISH!
IF I SEND MY KURDS OVER TO CONFRONT THEIRS, THEY'LL DO WHAT KURDS ALWAYS WANT TO DO!
GET LIQUORED UP?
NO, START A COUNTRY! ON MY BORDER! NOT GONNA HAPPEN!
GB Trudeau

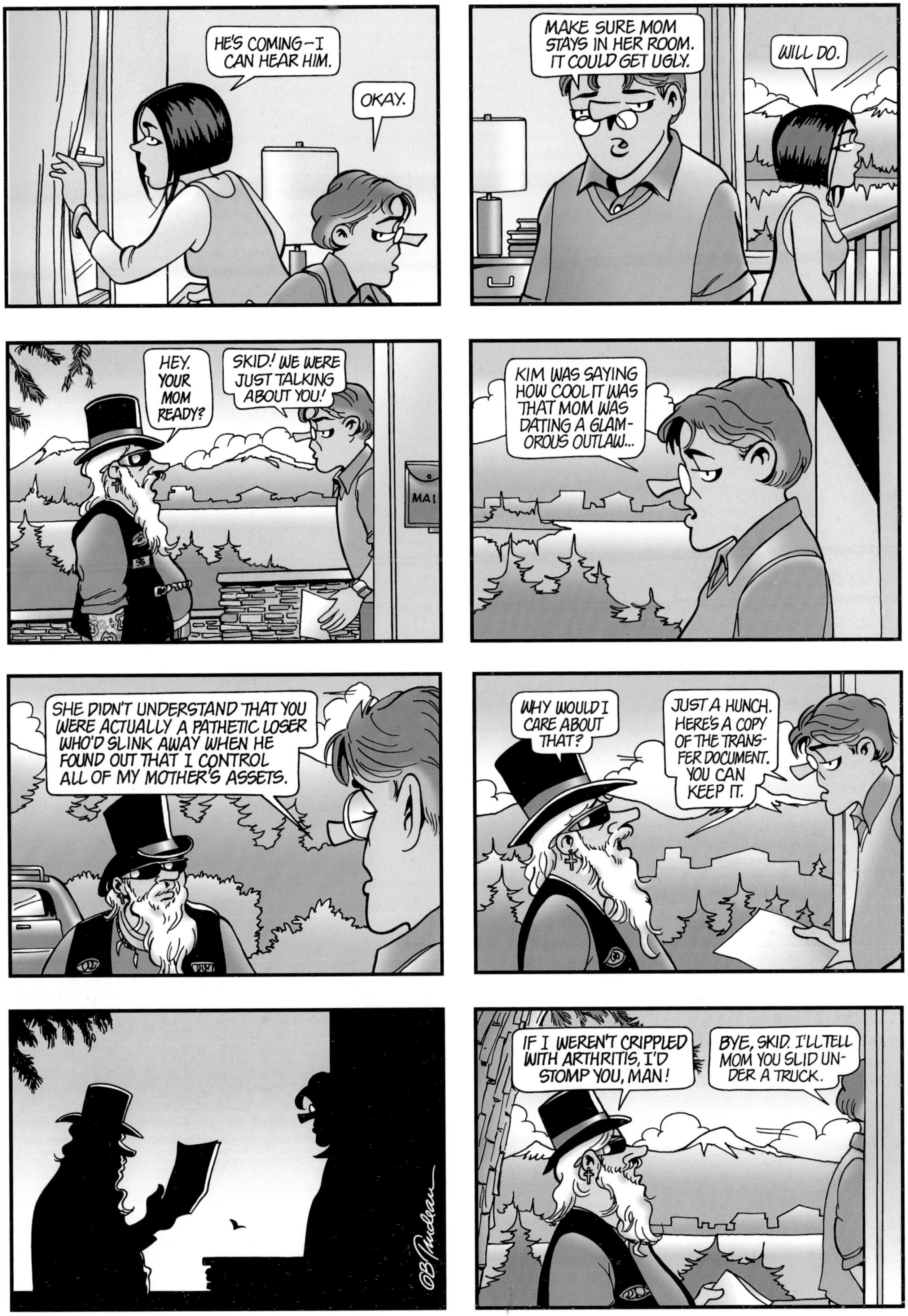
HE'S COMING—I CAN HEAR HIM.
OKAY.
MAKE SURE MOM STAYS IN HER ROOM. IT COULD GET UGLY.
WILL DO.
HEY. YOUR MOM READY?
SKID! WE WERE JUST TALKING ABOUT YOU!
MAI
KIM WAS SAYING HOW COOL IT WAS THAT MOM WAS DATING A GLAMOROUS OUTLAW...
SHE DIDN'T UNDERSTAND THAT YOU WERE ACTUALLY A PATHETIC LOSER WHO'D SLINK AWAY WHEN HE FOUND OUT THAT I CONTROL ALL OF MY MOTHER'S ASSETS.
WHY WOULD I CARE ABOUT THAT?
JUST A HUNCH. HERE'S A COPY OF THE TRANSFER DOCUMENT. YOU CAN KEEP IT.
IF I WEREN'T CRIPPLED WITH ARTHRITIS, I'D STOMP YOU, MAN!
BYE, SKID. I'LL TELL MOM YOU SLID UNDER A TRUCK.

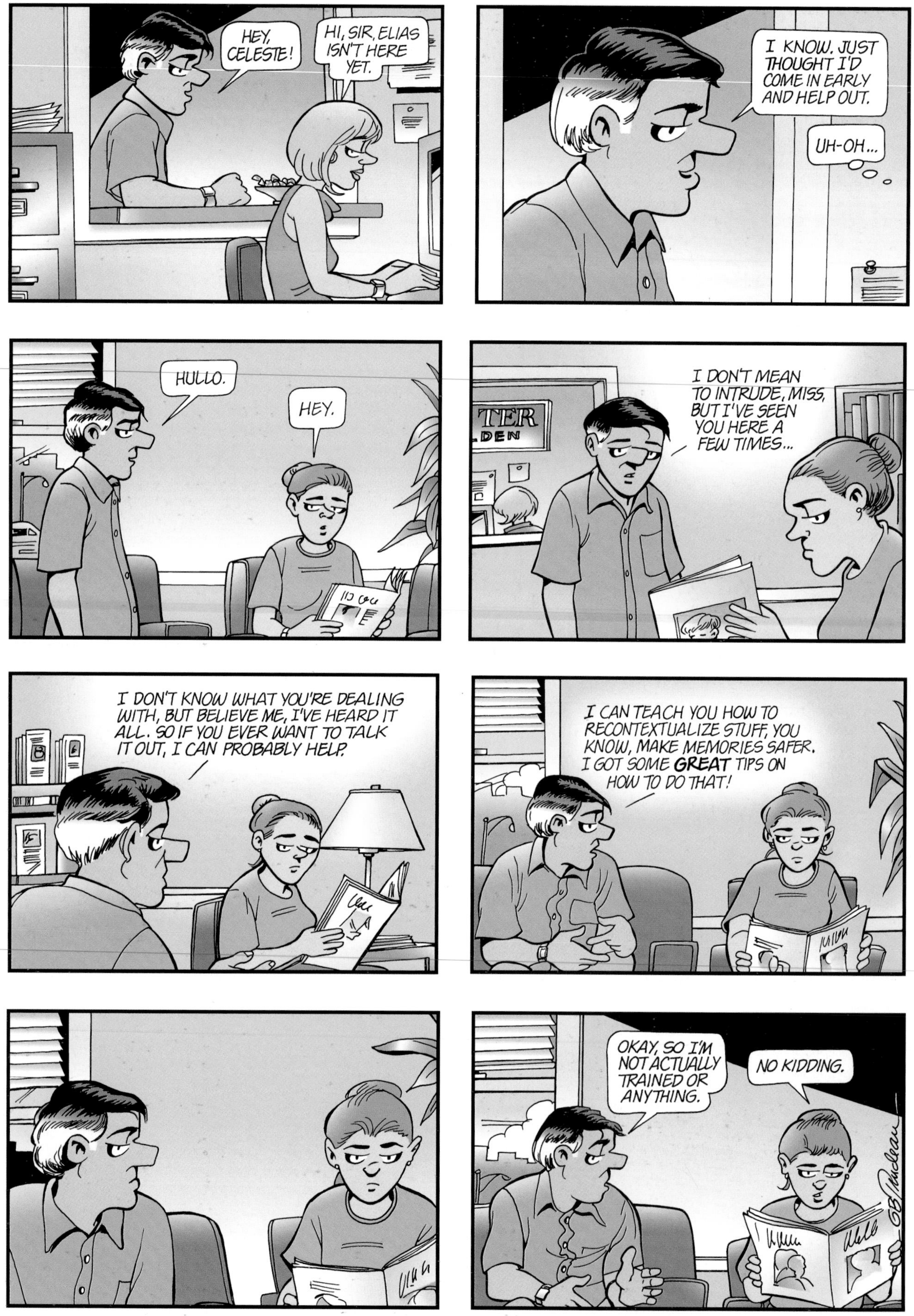
HEY, CELESTE!
HI, SIR, ELIAS ISN'T HERE YET.
I KNOW. JUST THOUGHT I'D COME IN EARLY AND HELP OUT.
UH-OH...
HULLO.
HEY.
I DON'T MEAN TO INTRUDE, MISS, BUT I'VE SEEN YOU HERE A FEW TIMES...
I DON'T KNOW WHAT YOU'RE DEALING WITH, BUT BELIEVE ME, I'VE HEARD IT ALL. SO IF YOU EVER WANT TO TALK IT OUT, I CAN PROBABLY HELP.
I CAN TEACH YOU HOW TO RECONTEXTUALIZE STUFF, YOU KNOW, MAKE MEMORIES SAFER. I GOT SOME **GREAT** TIPS ON HOW TO DO THAT!
OKAY, SO I'M NOT ACTUALLY TRAINED OR ANYTHING.
NO KIDDING.

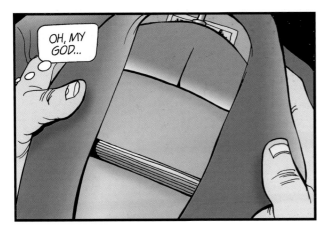

OH, MY GOD...

IT'S GONE!

SENATOR SO-AND-SO'S VERY BAD DAY.

GAIL! I CAN'T FIND MY LAPEL PIN!

SO?

SO? SO I CAN'T GO OUT IN PUBLIC WITHOUT MY FLAG LAPEL PIN!

WHY? LEADERS IN OTHER COUNTRIES DON'T DECORATE THEMSELVES WITH TINY FLAGS.

THEY DON'T LOVE THEIR COUNTRIES THE WAY WE DO!

IF I DON'T WEAR MY FLAG PIN, PEOPLE WILL THINK I'M MAKING A STATEMENT AND THAT I'M WITH THE TERRORISTS...

...AND WANT THEM TO WIN IN IRAQ AND FOLLOW US HOME!

WANT ME TO GET THE PIN OFF YOUR PAJAMAS?

NO, NO, IT HAS TO BE MY DRESS PIN!

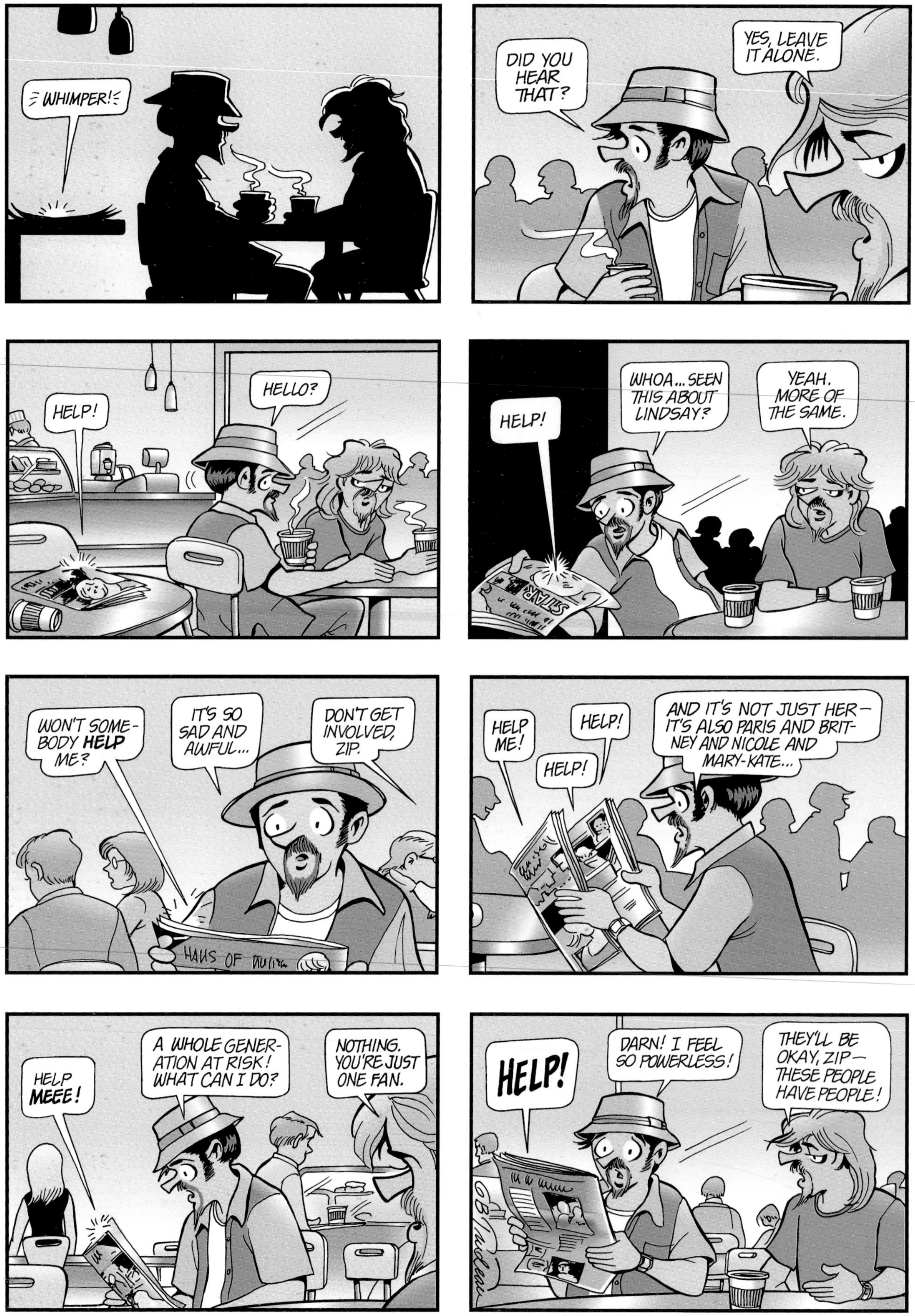
WHIMPER!
DID YOU HEAR THAT?
YES, LEAVE IT ALONE.
HELP!
HELLO?
HELP!
WHOA... SEEN THIS ABOUT LINDSAY?
YEAH. MORE OF THE SAME.
STAR
WON'T SOMEBODY **HELP** ME?
IT'S SO SAD AND AWFUL...
DON'T GET INVOLVED, ZIP.
HELP ME!
HELP!
HELP!
AND IT'S NOT JUST HER— IT'S ALSO PARIS AND BRITNEY AND NICOLE AND MARY-KATE...
HELP **MEEE**!
A WHOLE GENERATION AT RISK! WHAT CAN I DO?
NOTHING. YOU'RE JUST ONE FAN.
HELP!
DARN! I FEEL SO POWERLESS!
THEY'LL BE OKAY, ZIP— THESE PEOPLE HAVE PEOPLE!
GB Trudeau

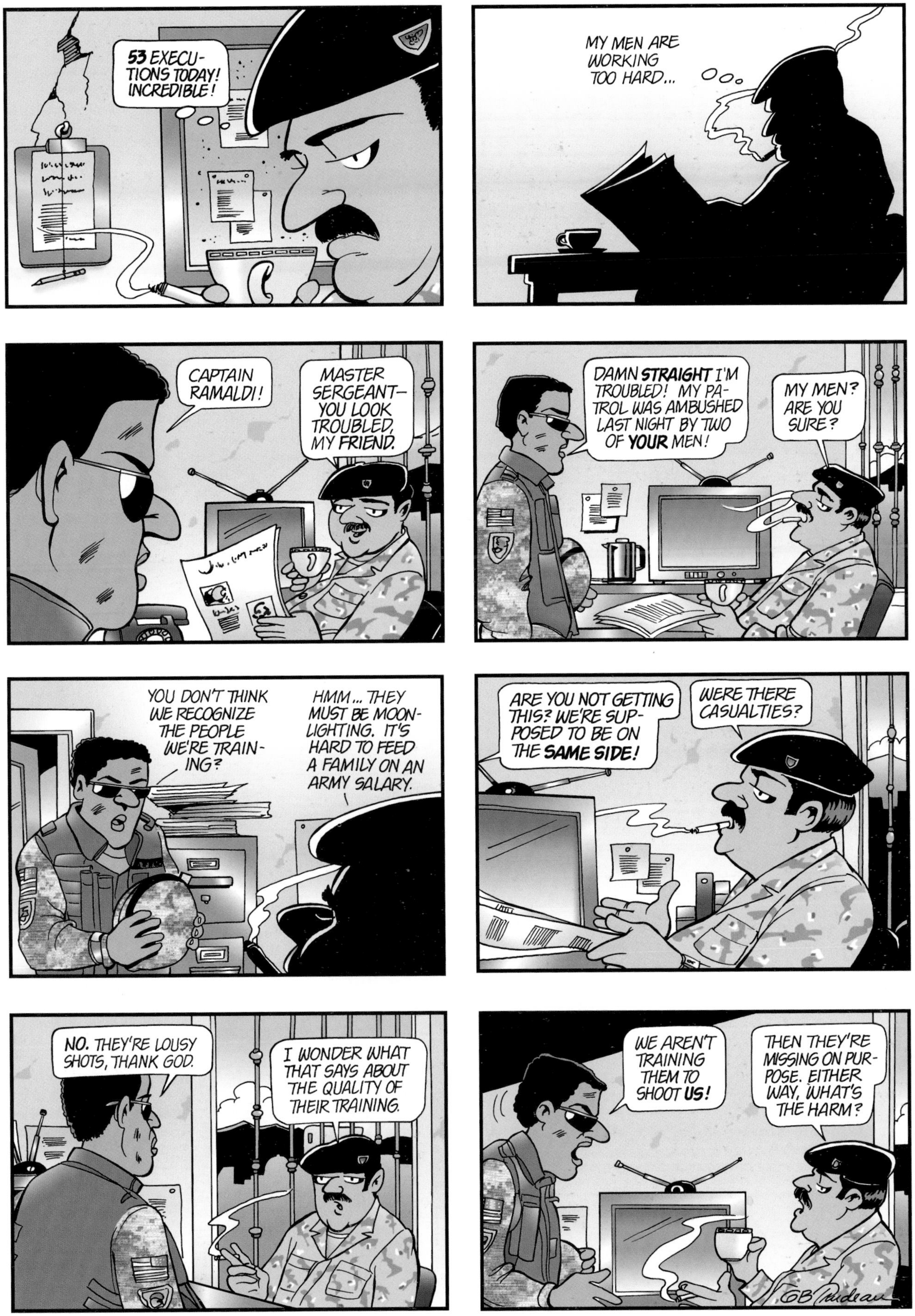
53 EXECUTIONS TODAY! INCREDIBLE!
MY MEN ARE WORKING TOO HARD...
CAPTAIN RAMALDI!
MASTER SERGEANT—YOU LOOK TROUBLED, MY FRIEND.
DAMN STRAIGHT I'M TROUBLED! MY PATROL WAS AMBUSHED LAST NIGHT BY TWO OF YOUR MEN!
MY MEN? ARE YOU SURE?
YOU DON'T THINK WE RECOGNIZE THE PEOPLE WE'RE TRAINING?
HMM... THEY MUST BE MOONLIGHTING. IT'S HARD TO FEED A FAMILY ON AN ARMY SALARY.
ARE YOU NOT GETTING THIS? WE'RE SUPPOSED TO BE ON THE SAME SIDE!
WERE THERE CASUALTIES?
NO. THEY'RE LOUSY SHOTS, THANK GOD.
I WONDER WHAT THAT SAYS ABOUT THE QUALITY OF THEIR TRAINING.
WE AREN'T TRAINING THEM TO SHOOT US!
THEN THEY'RE MISSING ON PURPOSE. EITHER WAY, WHAT'S THE HARM?
GB Trudeau

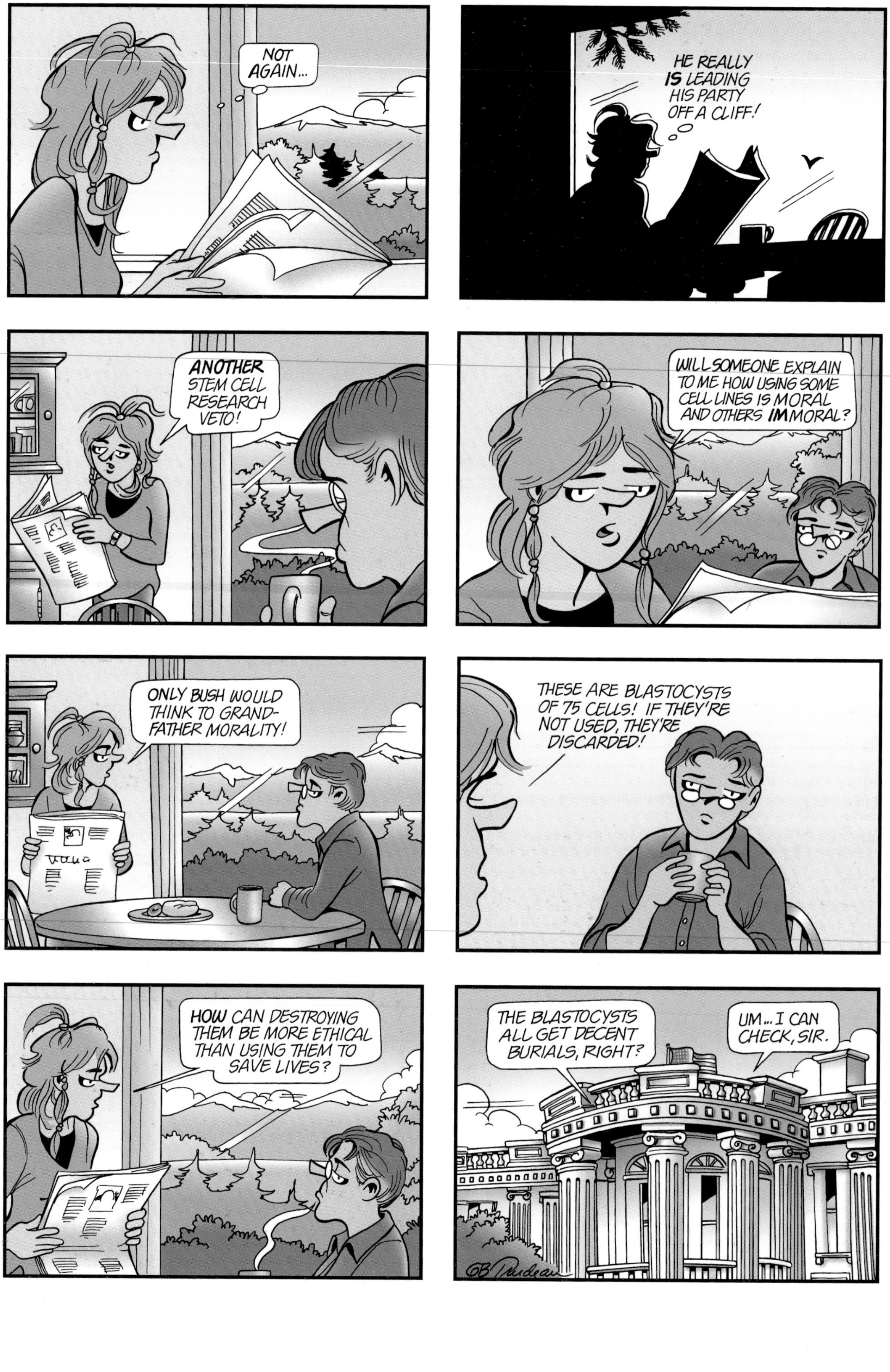

NOT AGAIN...
HE REALLY IS LEADING HIS PARTY OFF A CLIFF!
ANOTHER STEM CELL RESEARCH VETO!
WILL SOMEONE EXPLAIN TO ME HOW USING SOME CELL LINES IS MORAL AND OTHERS IMMORAL?
ONLY BUSH WOULD THINK TO GRAND-FATHER MORALITY!
THESE ARE BLASTOCYSTS OF 75 CELLS! IF THEY'RE NOT USED, THEY'RE DISCARDED!
HOW CAN DESTROYING THEM BE MORE ETHICAL THAN USING THEM TO SAVE LIVES?
THE BLASTOCYSTS ALL GET DECENT BURIALS, RIGHT?
UM... I CAN CHECK, SIR.

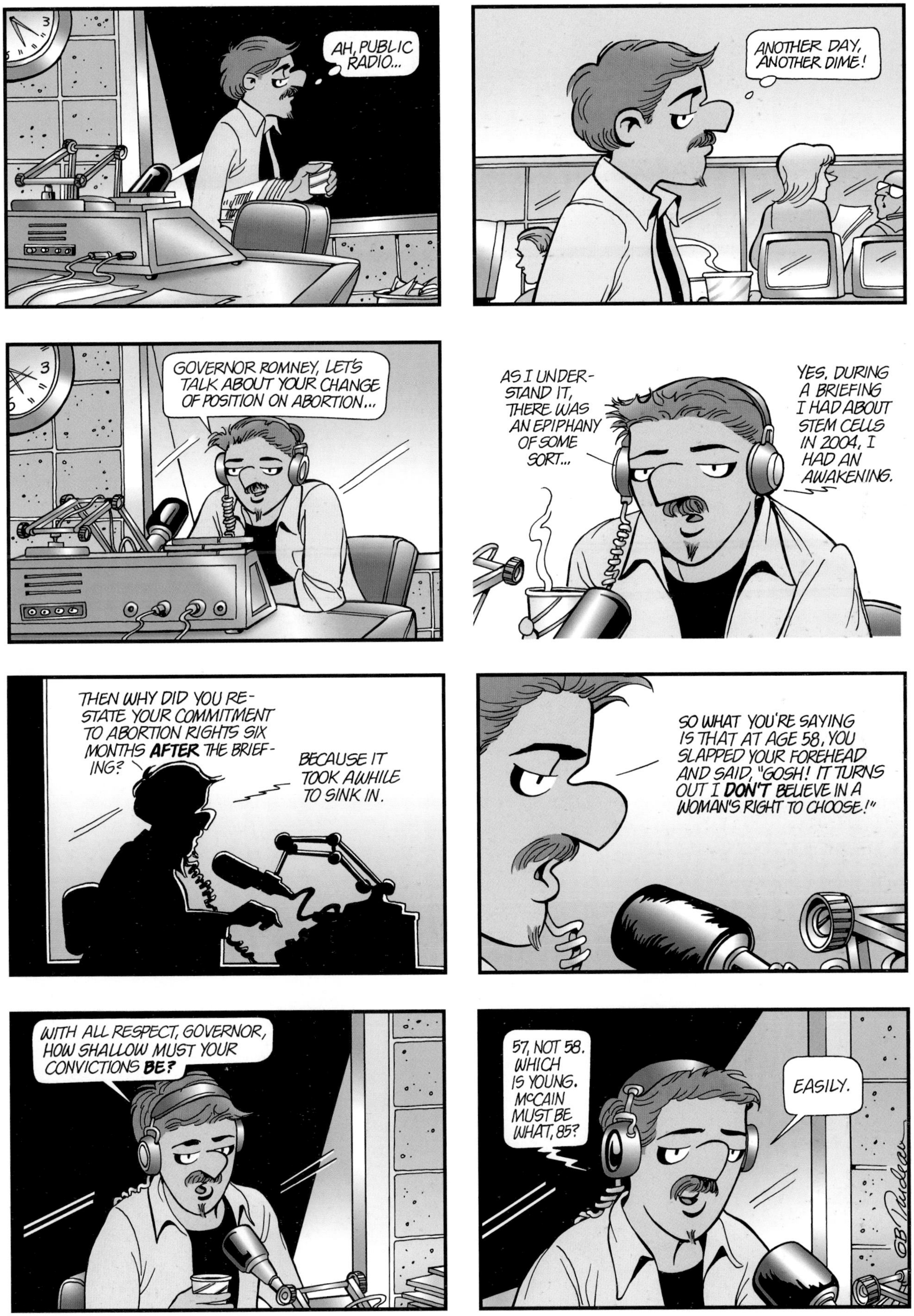
AH, PUBLIC RADIO...
ANOTHER DAY, ANOTHER DIME!
GOVERNOR ROMNEY, LET'S TALK ABOUT YOUR CHANGE OF POSITION ON ABORTION...
AS I UNDERSTAND IT, THERE WAS AN EPIPHANY OF SOME SORT...
YES. DURING A BRIEFING I HAD ABOUT STEM CELLS IN 2004, I HAD AN AWAKENING.
THEN WHY DID YOU RESTATE YOUR COMMITMENT TO ABORTION RIGHTS SIX MONTHS AFTER THE BRIEFING?
BECAUSE IT TOOK AWHILE TO SINK IN.
SO WHAT YOU'RE SAYING IS THAT AT AGE 58, YOU SLAPPED YOUR FOREHEAD AND SAID, "GOSH! IT TURNS OUT I DON'T BELIEVE IN A WOMAN'S RIGHT TO CHOOSE!"
WITH ALL RESPECT, GOVERNOR, HOW SHALLOW MUST YOUR CONVICTIONS BE?
57, NOT 58. WHICH IS YOUNG. McCAIN MUST BE WHAT, 85?
EASILY.

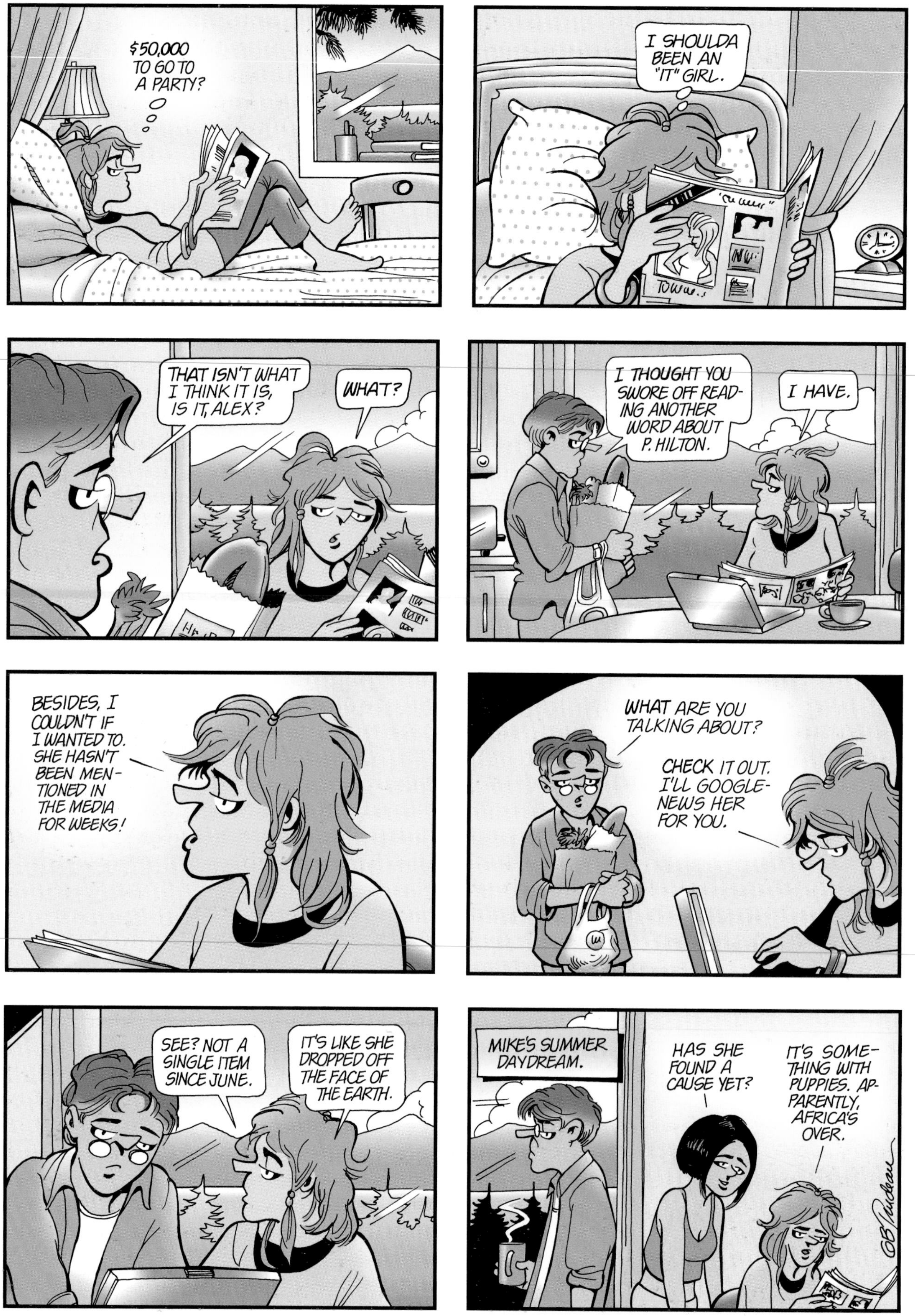
$50,000 TO GO TO A PARTY?
I SHOULDA BEEN AN "IT" GIRL.
THAT ISN'T WHAT I THINK IT IS, IS IT, ALEX?
WHAT?
I THOUGHT YOU SWORE OFF READING ANOTHER WORD ABOUT P. HILTON.
I HAVE.
BESIDES, I COULDN'T IF I WANTED TO. SHE HASN'T BEEN MENTIONED IN THE MEDIA FOR WEEKS!
WHAT ARE YOU TALKING ABOUT?
CHECK IT OUT. I'LL GOOGLE-NEWS HER FOR YOU.
SEE? NOT A SINGLE ITEM SINCE JUNE.
IT'S LIKE SHE DROPPED OFF THE FACE OF THE EARTH.
MIKE'S SUMMER DAYDREAM.
HAS SHE FOUND A CAUSE YET?
IT'S SOMETHING WITH PUPPIES. APPARENTLY, AFRICA'S OVER.

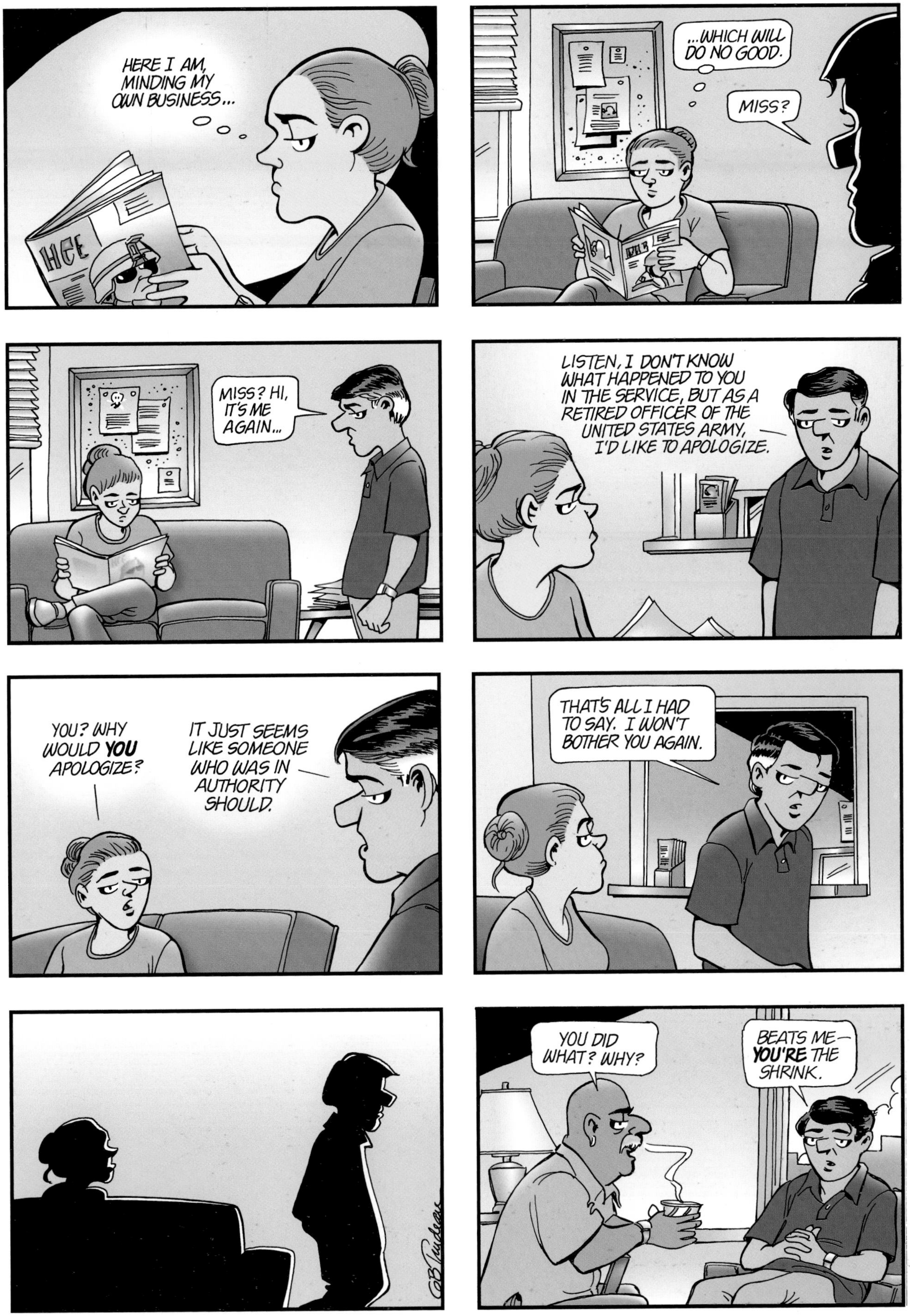
HERE I AM, MINDING MY OWN BUSINESS...
...WHICH WILL DO NO GOOD.
MISS?
MISS? HI, IT'S ME AGAIN...
LISTEN, I DON'T KNOW WHAT HAPPENED TO YOU IN THE SERVICE, BUT AS A RETIRED OFFICER OF THE UNITED STATES ARMY, I'D LIKE TO APOLOGIZE.
YOU? WHY WOULD **YOU** APOLOGIZE?
IT JUST SEEMS LIKE SOMEONE WHO WAS IN AUTHORITY SHOULD.
THAT'S ALL I HAD TO SAY. I WON'T BOTHER YOU AGAIN.
YOU DID WHAT? WHY?
BEATS ME— **YOU'RE** THE SHRINK.

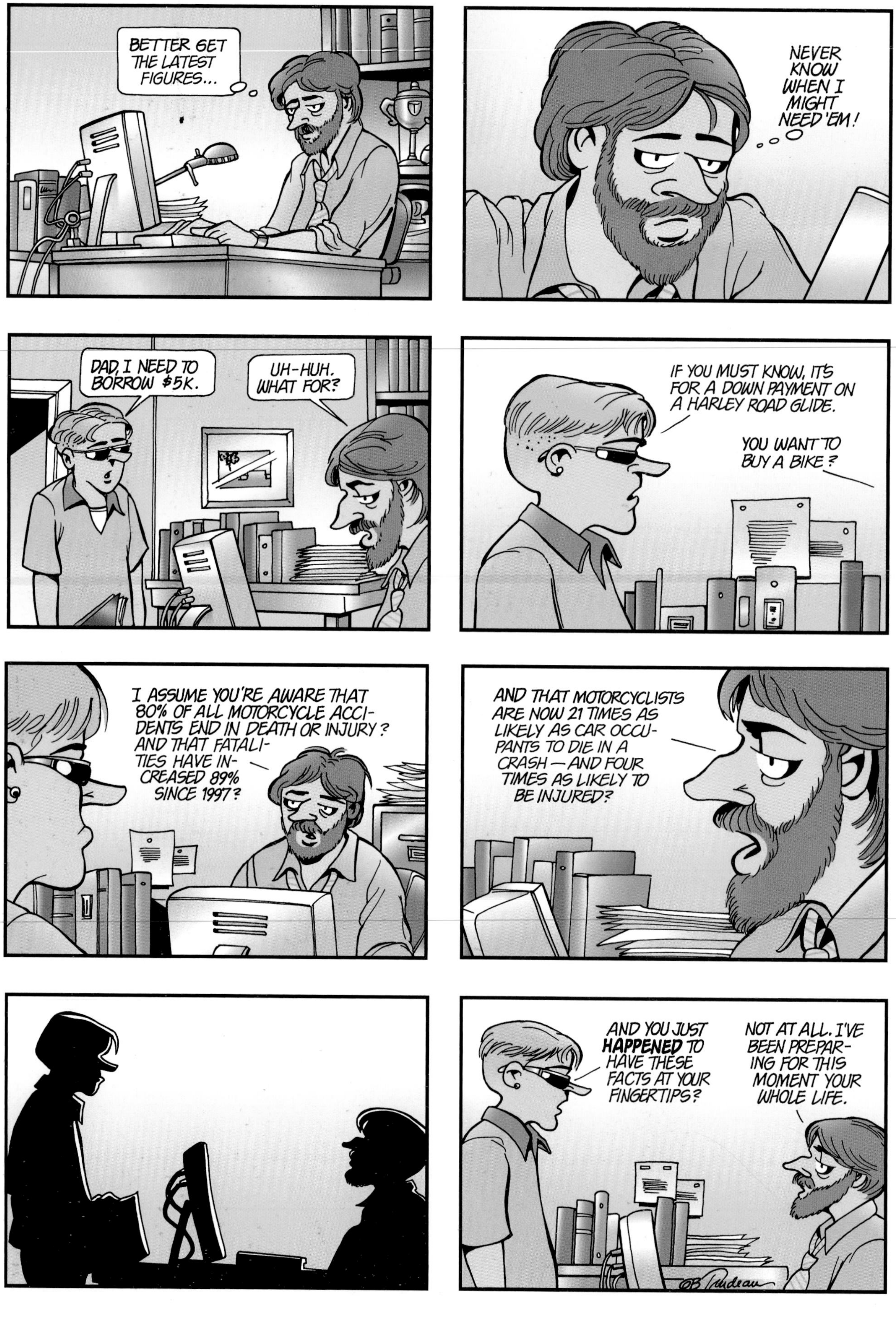
BETTER GET THE LATEST FIGURES...
NEVER KNOW WHEN I MIGHT NEED 'EM!
DAD, I NEED TO BORROW $5K.
UH-HUH. WHAT FOR?
IF YOU MUST KNOW, IT'S FOR A DOWN PAYMENT ON A HARLEY ROAD GLIDE.
YOU WANT TO BUY A BIKE?
I ASSUME YOU'RE AWARE THAT 80% OF ALL MOTORCYCLE ACCIDENTS END IN DEATH OR INJURY? AND THAT FATALITIES HAVE INCREASED 89% SINCE 1997?
AND THAT MOTORCYCLISTS ARE NOW 21 TIMES AS LIKELY AS CAR OCCUPANTS TO DIE IN A CRASH — AND FOUR TIMES AS LIKELY TO BE INJURED?
AND YOU JUST **HAPPENED** TO HAVE THESE FACTS AT YOUR FINGERTIPS?
NOT AT ALL. I'VE BEEN PREPARING FOR THIS MOMENT YOUR WHOLE LIFE.
©B Trudeau

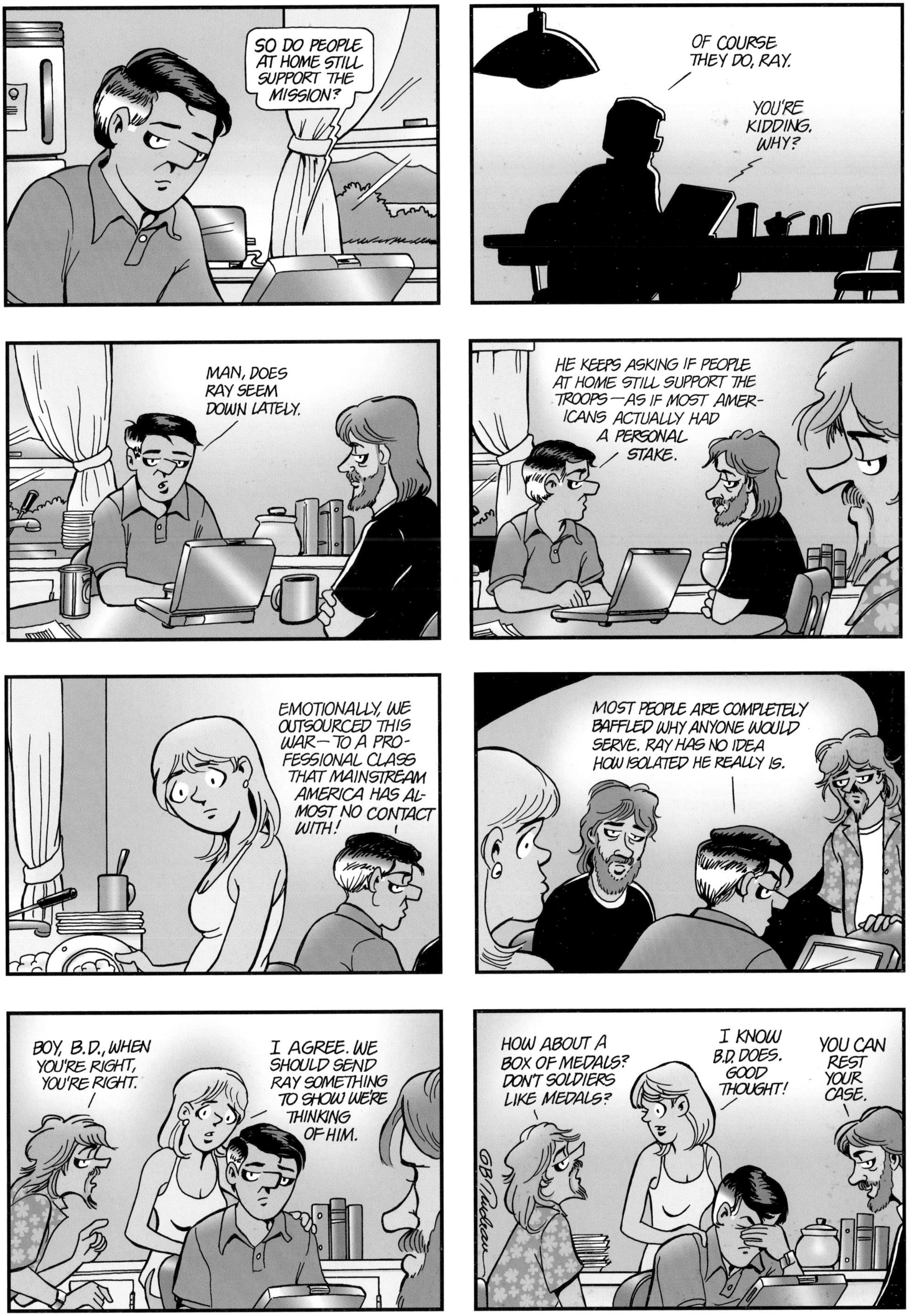
SO DO PEOPLE AT HOME STILL SUPPORT THE MISSION?
OF COURSE THEY DO, RAY.
YOU'RE KIDDING. WHY?
MAN, DOES RAY SEEM DOWN LATELY.
HE KEEPS ASKING IF PEOPLE AT HOME STILL SUPPORT THE TROOPS—AS IF MOST AMERICANS ACTUALLY HAD A PERSONAL STAKE.
EMOTIONALLY, WE OUTSOURCED THIS WAR—TO A PROFESSIONAL CLASS THAT MAINSTREAM AMERICA HAS ALMOST NO CONTACT WITH!
MOST PEOPLE ARE COMPLETELY BAFFLED WHY ANYONE WOULD SERVE. RAY HAS NO IDEA HOW ISOLATED HE REALLY IS.
BOY, B.D., WHEN YOU'RE RIGHT, YOU'RE RIGHT.
I AGREE. WE SHOULD SEND RAY SOMETHING TO SHOW WE'RE THINKING OF HIM.
HOW ABOUT A BOX OF MEDALS? DON'T SOLDIERS LIKE MEDALS?
I KNOW B.D. DOES. GOOD THOUGHT!
YOU CAN REST YOUR CASE.
GB Trudeau

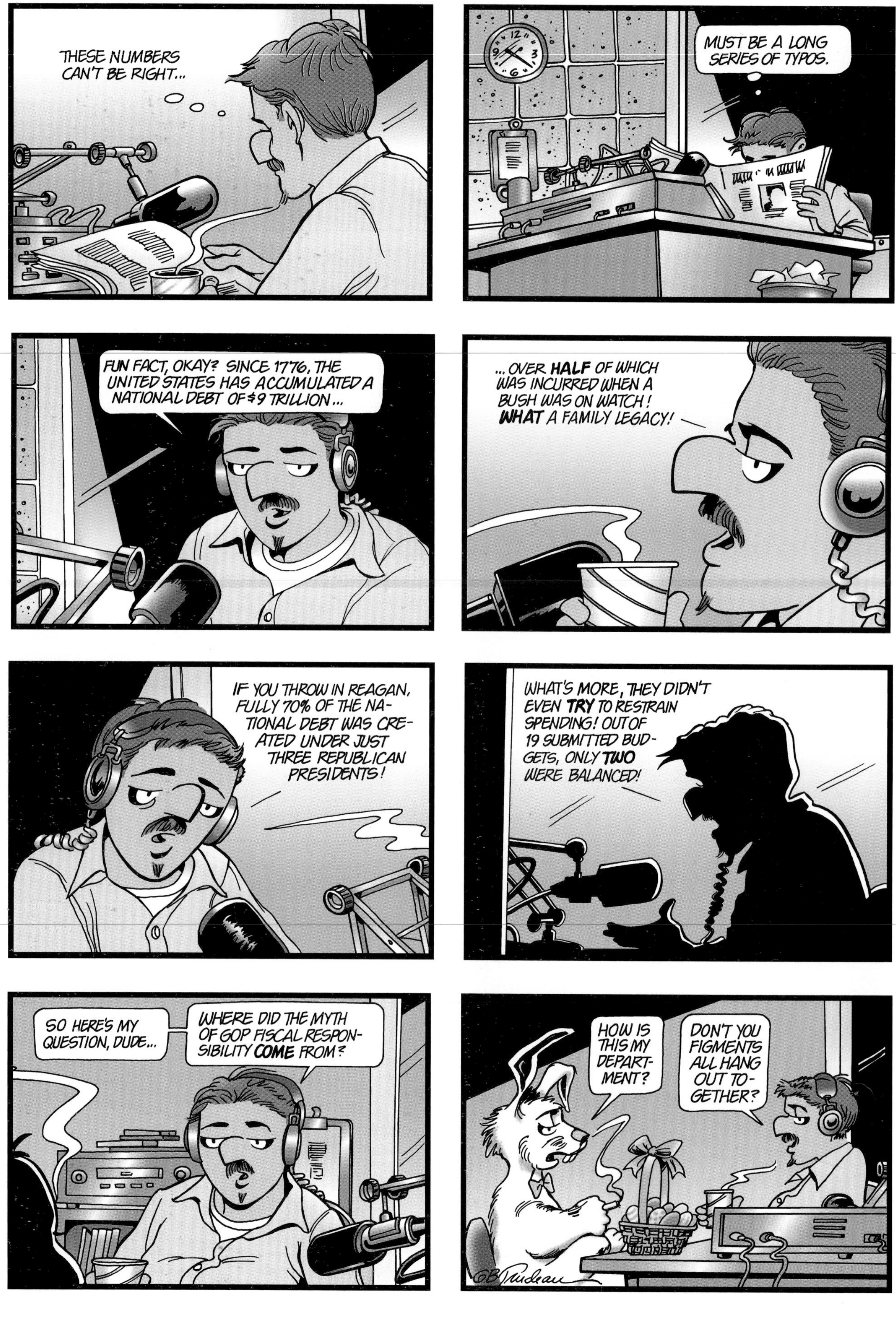
THESE NUMBERS CAN'T BE RIGHT...
MUST BE A LONG SERIES OF TYPOS.
FUN FACT, OKAY? SINCE 1776, THE UNITED STATES HAS ACCUMULATED A NATIONAL DEBT OF $9 TRILLION...
...OVER HALF OF WHICH WAS INCURRED WHEN A BUSH WAS ON WATCH! WHAT A FAMILY LEGACY!
IF YOU THROW IN REAGAN, FULLY 70% OF THE NATIONAL DEBT WAS CREATED UNDER JUST THREE REPUBLICAN PRESIDENTS!
WHAT'S MORE, THEY DIDN'T EVEN TRY TO RESTRAIN SPENDING! OUT OF 19 SUBMITTED BUDGETS, ONLY TWO WERE BALANCED!
SO HERE'S MY QUESTION, DUDE...
WHERE DID THE MYTH OF GOP FISCAL RESPONSIBILITY COME FROM?
HOW IS THIS MY DEPARTMENT?
DON'T YOU FIGMENTS ALL HANG OUT TOGETHER?
GB Trudeau

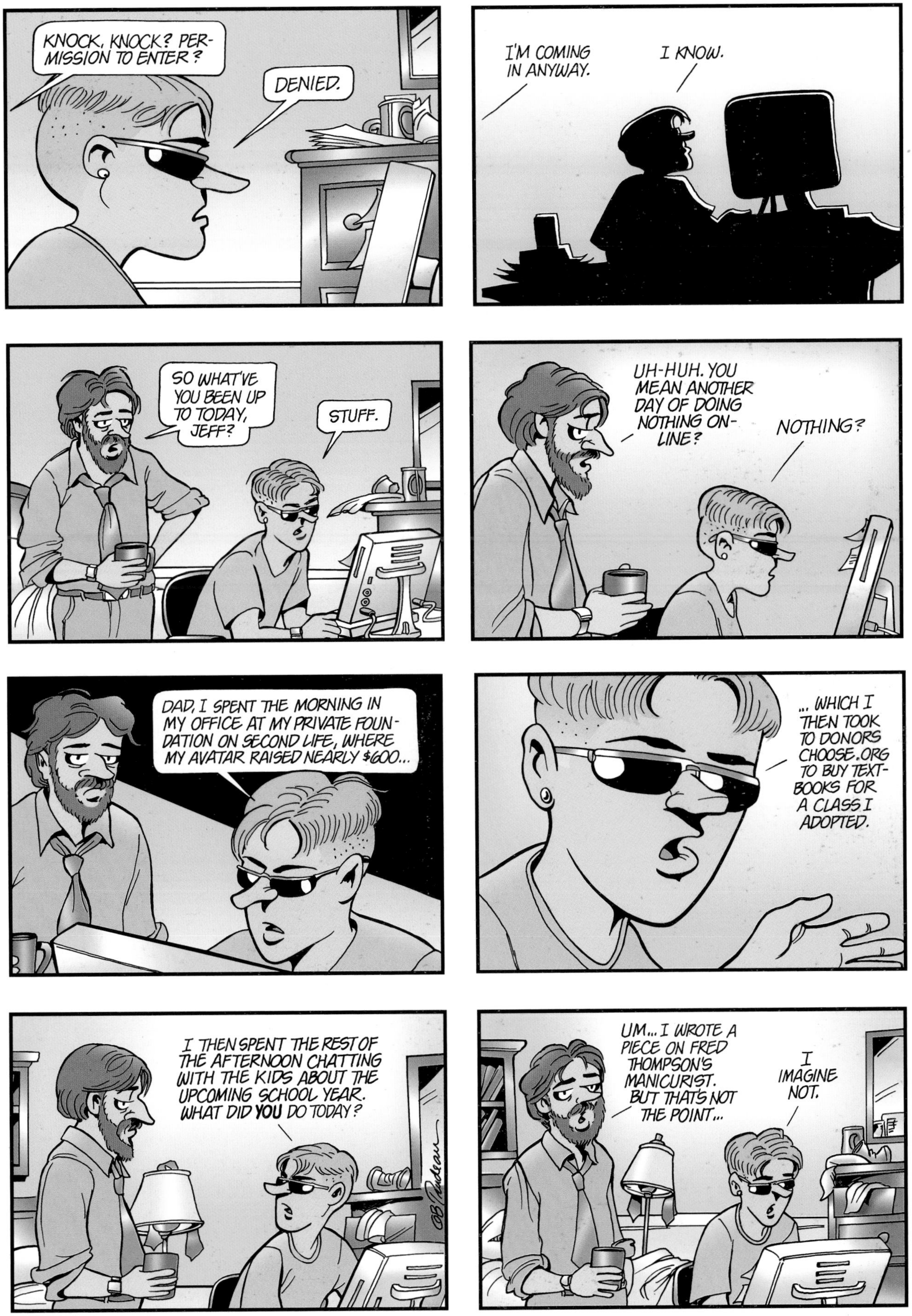
KNOCK, KNOCK? PERMISSION TO ENTER?
DENIED.
I'M COMING IN ANYWAY.
I KNOW.
SO WHAT'VE YOU BEEN UP TO TODAY, JEFF?
STUFF.
UH-HUH. YOU MEAN ANOTHER DAY OF DOING NOTHING ON-LINE?
NOTHING?
DAD, I SPENT THE MORNING IN MY OFFICE AT MY PRIVATE FOUNDATION ON SECOND LIFE, WHERE MY AVATAR RAISED NEARLY $600...
... WHICH I THEN TOOK TO DONORSCHOOSE.ORG TO BUY TEXTBOOKS FOR A CLASS I ADOPTED.
I THEN SPENT THE REST OF THE AFTERNOON CHATTING WITH THE KIDS ABOUT THE UPCOMING SCHOOL YEAR. WHAT DID **YOU** DO TODAY?
UM... I WROTE A PIECE ON FRED THOMPSON'S MANICURIST. BUT THAT'S NOT THE POINT...
I IMAGINE NOT.

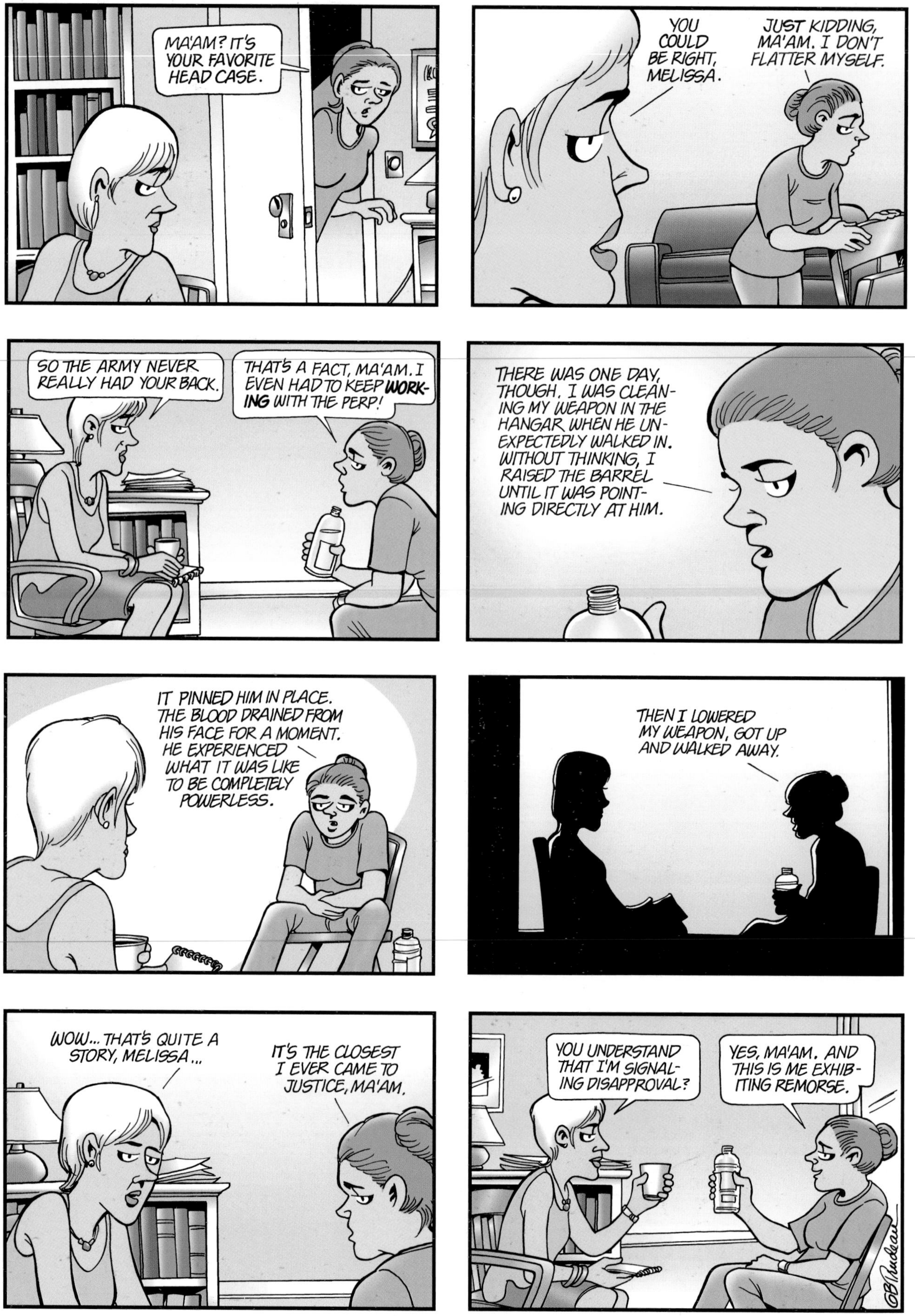
MA'AM? IT'S YOUR FAVORITE HEAD CASE.
YOU COULD BE RIGHT, MELISSA.
JUST KIDDING, MA'AM. I DON'T FLATTER MYSELF.
SO THE ARMY NEVER REALLY HAD YOUR BACK.
THAT'S A FACT, MA'AM. I EVEN HAD TO KEEP **WORKING** WITH THE PERP!
THERE WAS ONE DAY, THOUGH. I WAS CLEANING MY WEAPON IN THE HANGAR WHEN HE UNEXPECTEDLY WALKED IN. WITHOUT THINKING, I RAISED THE BARREL UNTIL IT WAS POINTING DIRECTLY AT HIM.
IT PINNED HIM IN PLACE. THE BLOOD DRAINED FROM HIS FACE FOR A MOMENT. HE EXPERIENCED WHAT IT WAS LIKE TO BE COMPLETELY POWERLESS.
THEN I LOWERED MY WEAPON, GOT UP AND WALKED AWAY.
WOW... THAT'S QUITE A STORY, MELISSA...
IT'S THE CLOSEST I EVER CAME TO JUSTICE, MA'AM.
YOU UNDERSTAND THAT I'M SIGNALING DISAPPROVAL?
YES, MA'AM. AND THIS IS ME EXHIBITING REMORSE.
©BTrudeau

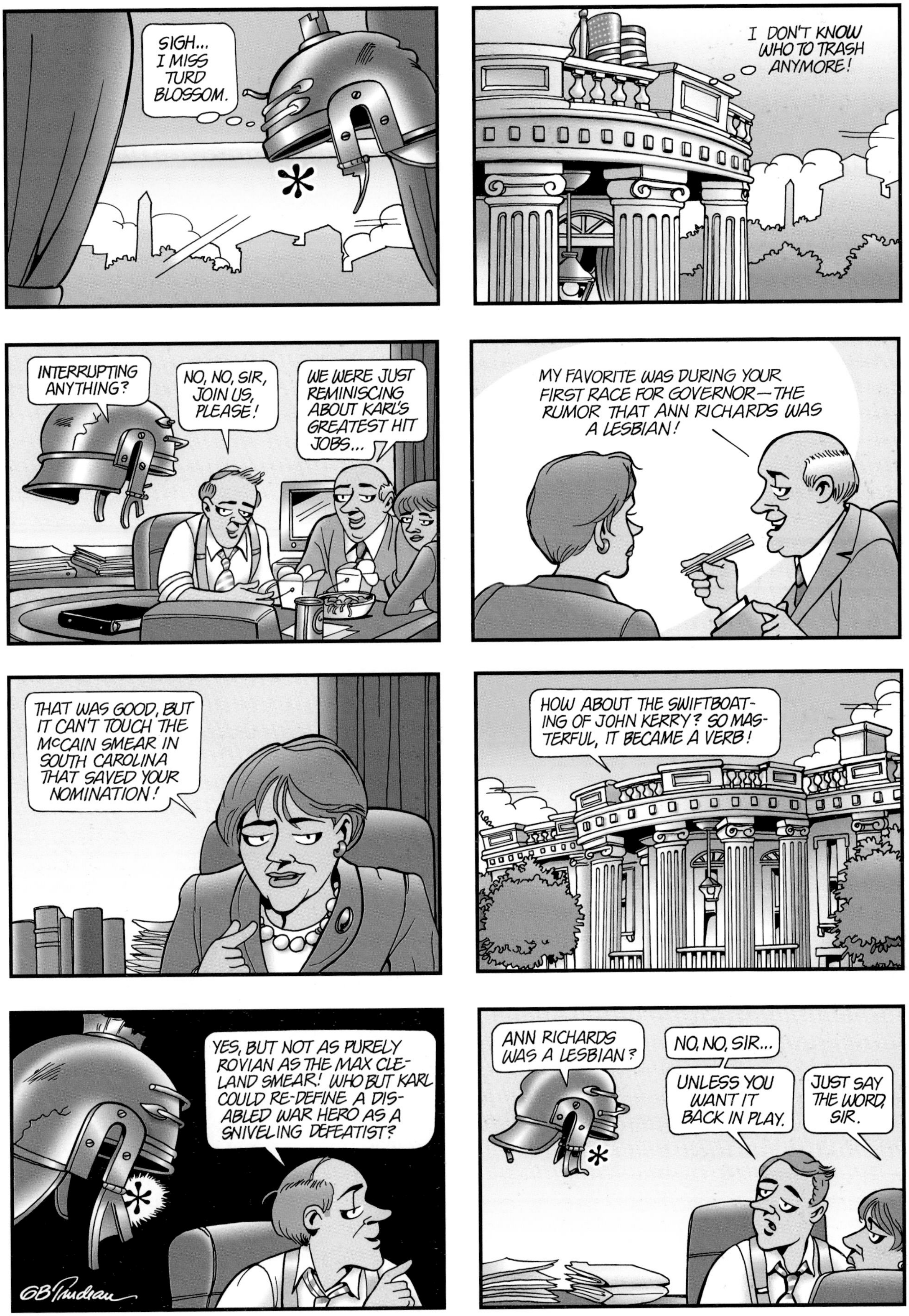
SIGH... I MISS TURD BLOSSOM.
I DON'T KNOW WHO TO TRASH ANYMORE!
INTERRUPTING ANYTHING?
NO, NO, SIR, JOIN US, PLEASE!
WE WERE JUST REMINISCING ABOUT KARL'S GREATEST HIT JOBS...
MY FAVORITE WAS DURING YOUR FIRST RACE FOR GOVERNOR—THE RUMOR THAT ANN RICHARDS WAS A LESBIAN!
THAT WAS GOOD, BUT IT CAN'T TOUCH THE McCAIN SMEAR IN SOUTH CAROLINA THAT SAVED YOUR NOMINATION!
HOW ABOUT THE SWIFTBOATING OF JOHN KERRY? SO MASTERFUL, IT BECAME A VERB!
YES, BUT NOT AS PURELY ROVIAN AS THE MAX CLELAND SMEAR! WHO BUT KARL COULD RE-DEFINE A DISABLED WAR HERO AS A SNIVELING DEFEATIST?
GB Trudeau
ANN RICHARDS WAS A LESBIAN?
NO, NO, SIR...
UNLESS YOU WANT IT BACK IN PLAY.
JUST SAY THE WORD, SIR.

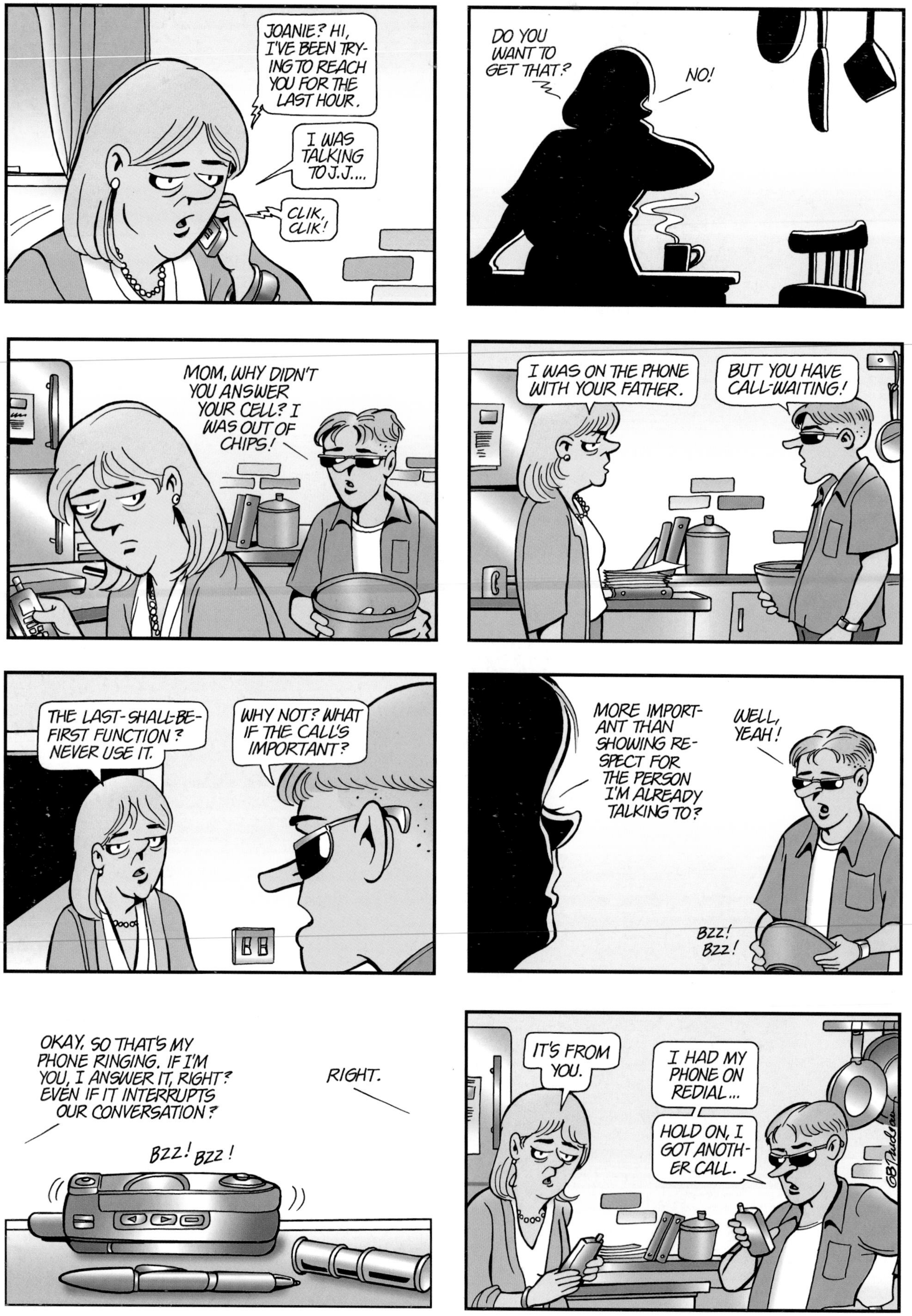
JOANIE? HI, I'VE BEEN TRYING TO REACH YOU FOR THE LAST HOUR.
I WAS TALKING TO J.J....
CLIK, CLIK!
DO YOU WANT TO GET THAT?
NO!
MOM, WHY DIDN'T YOU ANSWER YOUR CELL? I WAS OUT OF CHIPS!
I WAS ON THE PHONE WITH YOUR FATHER.
BUT YOU HAVE CALL-WAITING!
THE LAST-SHALL-BE-FIRST FUNCTION? NEVER USE IT.
WHY NOT? WHAT IF THE CALL'S IMPORTANT?
MORE IMPORTANT THAN SHOWING RESPECT FOR THE PERSON I'M ALREADY TALKING TO?
WELL, YEAH!
BZZ! BZZ!
OKAY, SO THAT'S MY PHONE RINGING. IF I'M YOU, I ANSWER IT, RIGHT? EVEN IF IT INTERRUPTS OUR CONVERSATION?
RIGHT.
BZZ! BZZ!
IT'S FROM YOU.
I HAD MY PHONE ON REDIAL...
HOLD ON, I GOT ANOTHER CALL.

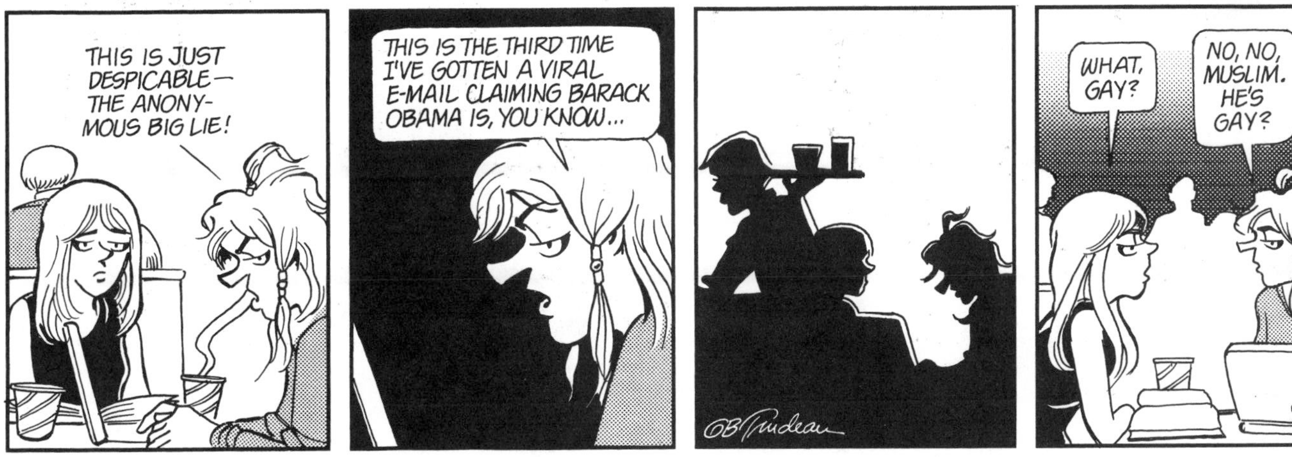
THIS IS JUST DESPICABLE— THE ANONY-MOUS BIG LIE!
THIS IS THE THIRD TIME I'VE GOTTEN A VIRAL E-MAIL CLAIMING BARACK OBAMA IS, YOU KNOW...
WHAT, GAY?
NO, NO, MUSLIM. HE'S GAY?

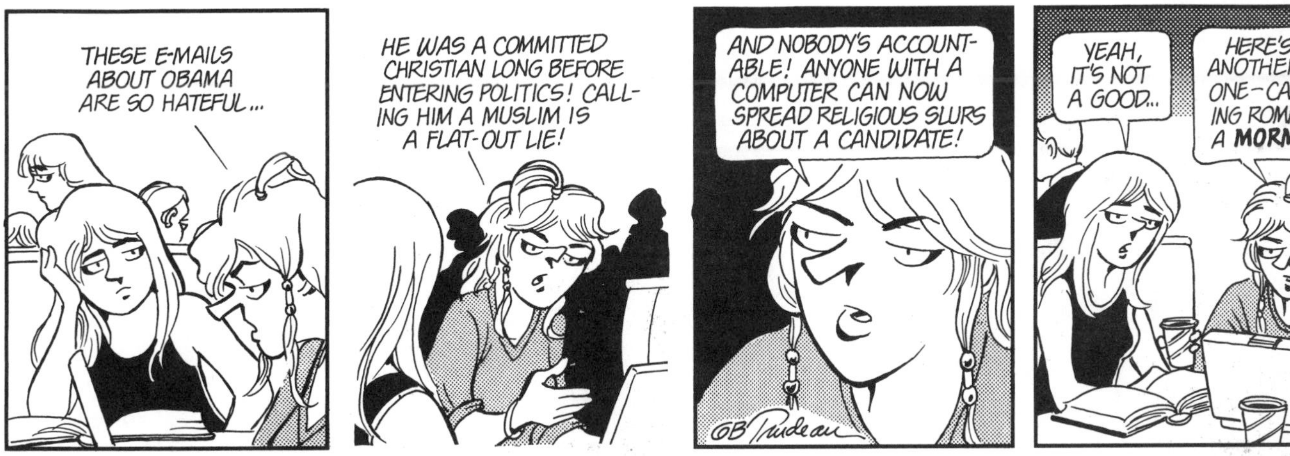
THESE E-MAILS ABOUT OBAMA ARE SO HATEFUL...
HE WAS A COMMITTED CHRISTIAN LONG BEFORE ENTERING POLITICS! CALL-ING HIM A MUSLIM IS A FLAT-OUT LIE!
AND NOBODY'S ACCOUNT-ABLE! ANYONE WITH A COMPUTER CAN NOW SPREAD RELIGIOUS SLURS ABOUT A CANDIDATE!
YEAH, IT'S NOT A GOOD...
HERE'S ANOTHER ONE—CALL-ING ROMNEY A **MORMON!**

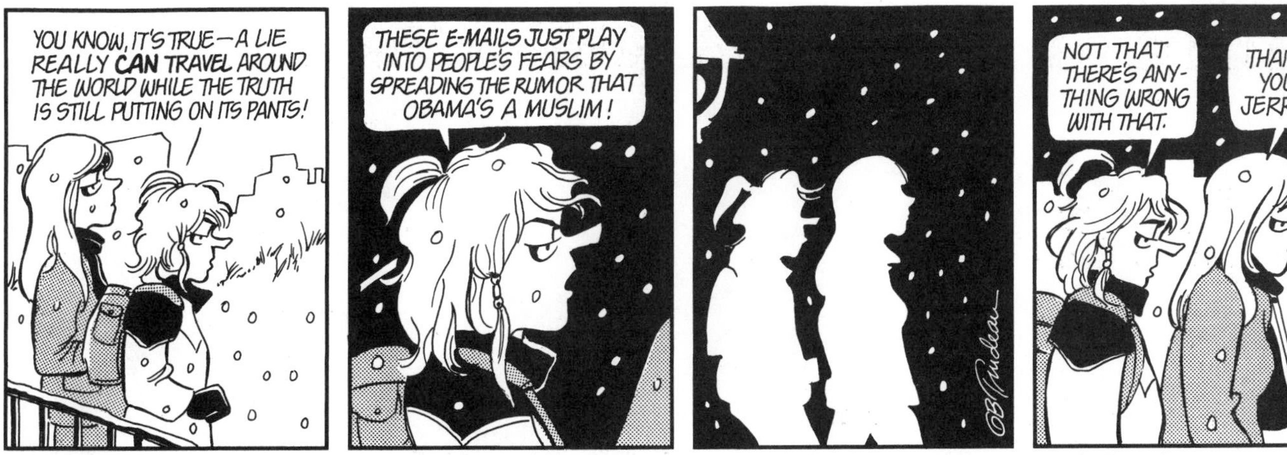
YOU KNOW, IT'S TRUE—A LIE REALLY **CAN** TRAVEL AROUND THE WORLD WHILE THE TRUTH IS STILL PUTTING ON ITS PANTS!
THESE E-MAILS JUST PLAY INTO PEOPLE'S FEARS BY SPREADING THE RUMOR THAT OBAMA'S A MUSLIM!
NOT THAT THERE'S ANY-THING WRONG WITH THAT.
THANK YOU, JERRY.

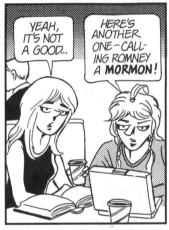

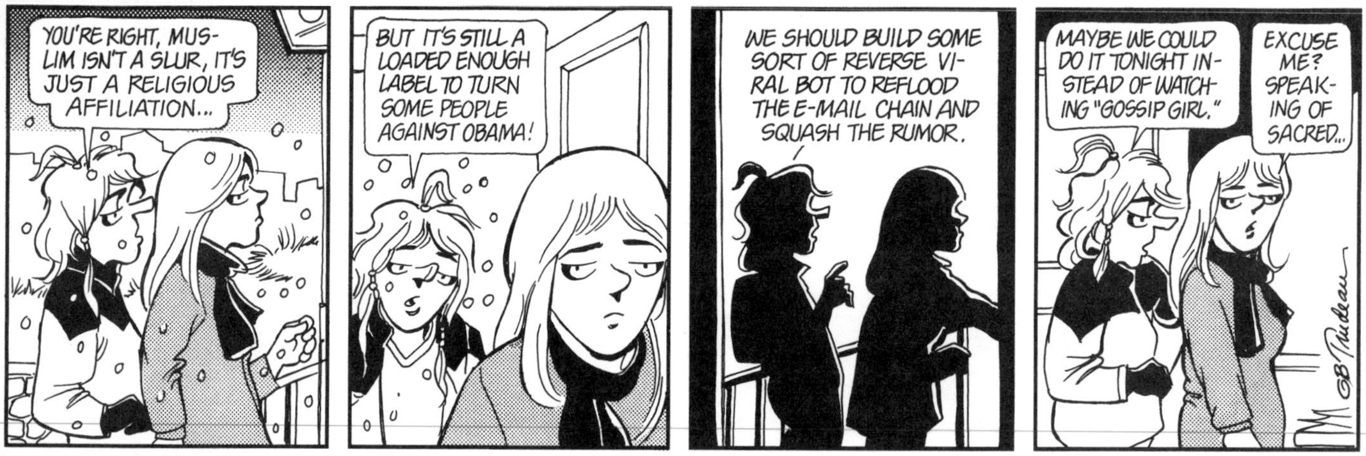
YOU'RE RIGHT, MUS-LIM ISN'T A SLUR, IT'S JUST A RELIGIOUS AFFILIATION...
BUT IT'S STILL A LOADED ENOUGH LABEL TO TURN SOME PEOPLE AGAINST OBAMA!
WE SHOULD BUILD SOME SORT OF REVERSE VI-RAL BOT TO REFLOOD THE E-MAIL CHAIN AND SQUASH THE RUMOR.
MAYBE WE COULD DO IT TONIGHT IN-STEAD OF WATCH-ING "GOSSIP GIRL."
EXCUSE ME? SPEAK-ING OF SACRED...
GB Trudeau

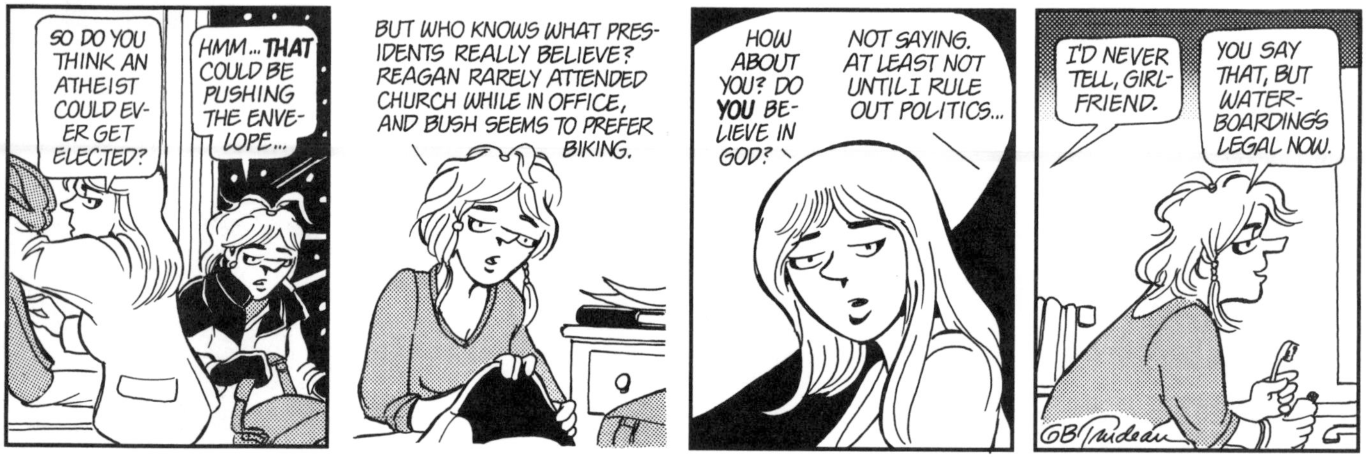
SO DO YOU THINK AN ATHEIST COULD EV-ER GET ELECTED?
HMM... THAT COULD BE PUSHING THE ENVE-LOPE...
BUT WHO KNOWS WHAT PRES-IDENTS REALLY BELIEVE? REAGAN RARELY ATTENDED CHURCH WHILE IN OFFICE, AND BUSH SEEMS TO PREFER BIKING.
HOW ABOUT YOU? DO YOU BE-LIEVE IN GOD?
NOT SAYING. AT LEAST NOT UNTIL I RULE OUT POLITICS...
I'D NEVER TELL, GIRL-FRIEND.
YOU SAY THAT, BUT WATER-BOARDING'S LEGAL NOW.
GB Trudeau

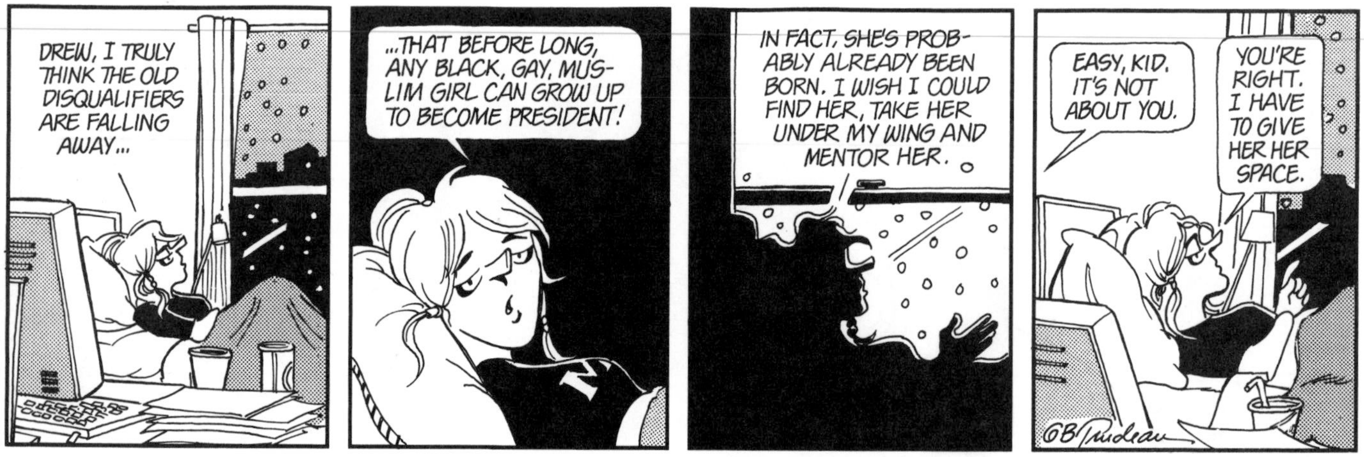
DREW, I TRULY THINK THE OLD DISQUALIFIERS ARE FALLING AWAY...
...THAT BEFORE LONG, ANY BLACK, GAY, MUS-LIM GIRL CAN GROW UP TO BECOME PRESIDENT!
IN FACT, SHE'S PROB-ABLY ALREADY BEEN BORN. I WISH I COULD FIND HER, TAKE HER UNDER MY WING AND MENTOR HER.
EASY, KID. IT'S NOT ABOUT YOU.
YOU'RE RIGHT. I HAVE TO GIVE HER HER SPACE.
GB Trudeau

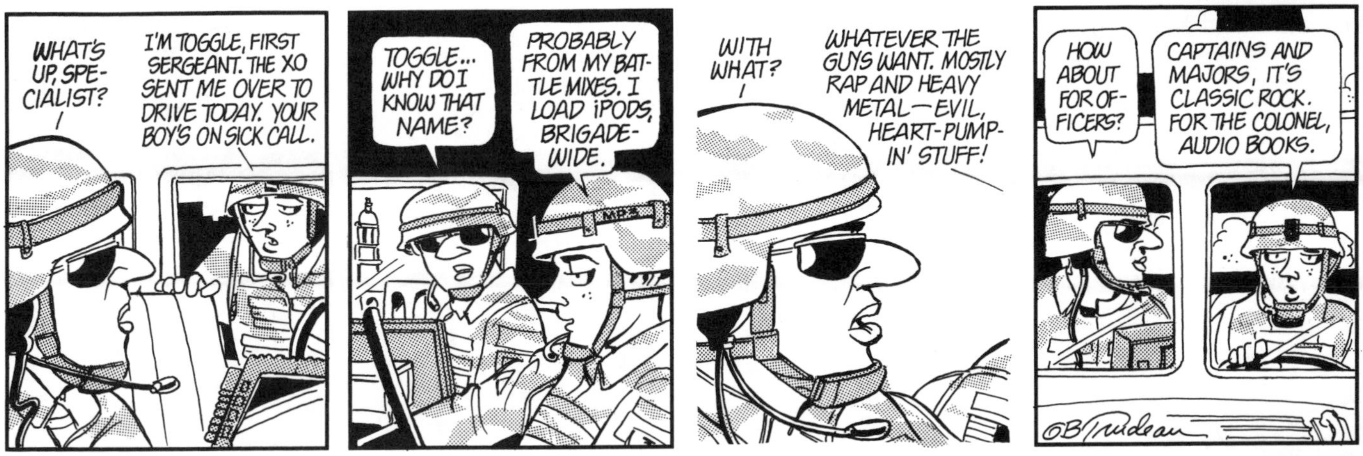
WHAT'S UP, SPECIALIST?
I'M TOGGLE, FIRST SERGEANT. THE XO SENT ME OVER TO DRIVE TODAY. YOUR BOY'S ON SICK CALL.
TOGGLE... WHY DO I KNOW THAT NAME?
PROBABLY FROM MY BATTLE MIXES. I LOAD iPODS, BRIGADE-WIDE.
WITH WHAT?
WHATEVER THE GUYS WANT. MOSTLY RAP AND HEAVY METAL—EVIL, HEART-PUMPIN' STUFF!
HOW ABOUT FOR OFFICERS?
CAPTAINS AND MAJORS, IT'S CLASSIC ROCK. FOR THE COLONEL, AUDIO BOOKS.
©B Trudeau

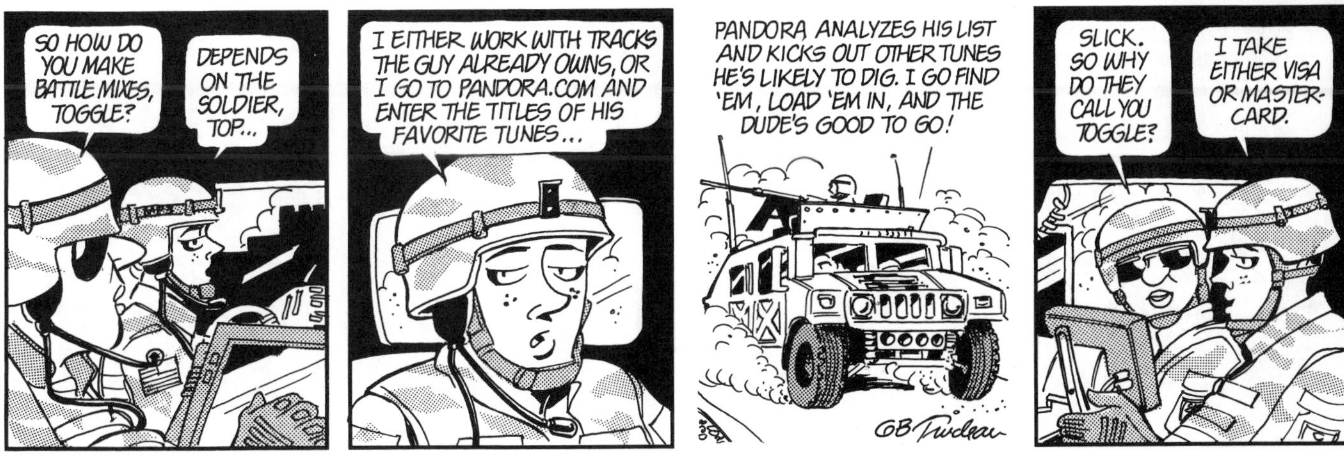
SO HOW DO YOU MAKE BATTLE MIXES, TOGGLE?
DEPENDS ON THE SOLDIER, TOP...
I EITHER WORK WITH TRACKS THE GUY ALREADY OWNS, OR I GO TO PANDORA.COM AND ENTER THE TITLES OF HIS FAVORITE TUNES...
PANDORA ANALYZES HIS LIST AND KICKS OUT OTHER TUNES HE'S LIKELY TO DIG. I GO FIND 'EM, LOAD 'EM IN, AND THE DUDE'S GOOD TO GO!
©B Trudeau
SLICK. SO WHY DO THEY CALL YOU TOGGLE?
I TAKE EITHER VISA OR MASTERCARD.

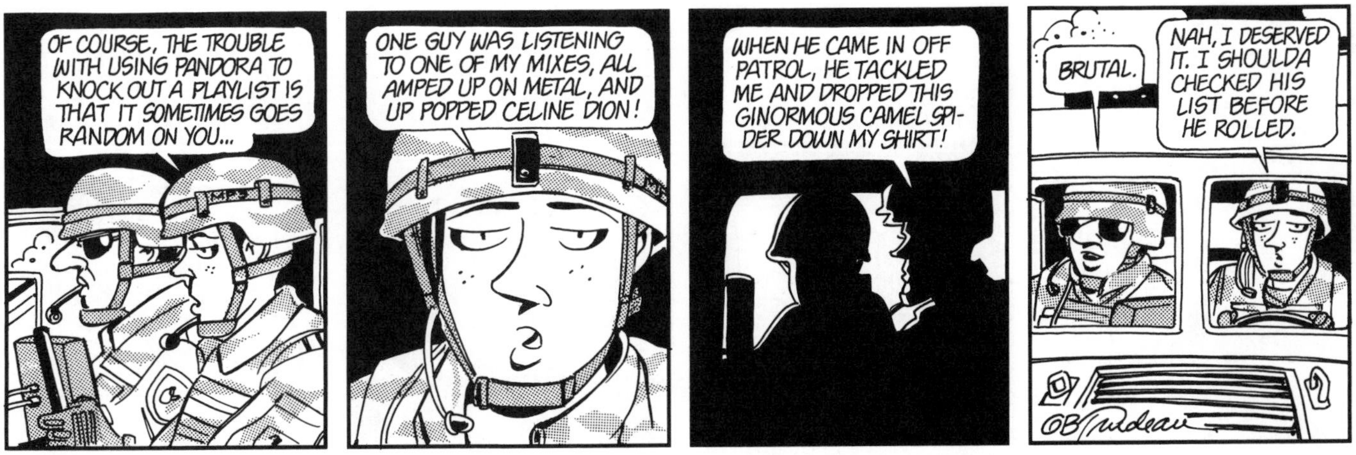
OF COURSE, THE TROUBLE WITH USING PANDORA TO KNOCK OUT A PLAYLIST IS THAT IT SOMETIMES GOES RANDOM ON YOU...
ONE GUY WAS LISTENING TO ONE OF MY MIXES, ALL AMPED UP ON METAL, AND UP POPPED CELINE DION!
WHEN HE CAME IN OFF PATROL, HE TACKLED ME AND DROPPED THIS GINORMOUS CAMEL SPIDER DOWN MY SHIRT!
BRUTAL.
NAH, I DESERVED IT. I SHOULDA CHECKED HIS LIST BEFORE HE ROLLED.
©B Trudeau

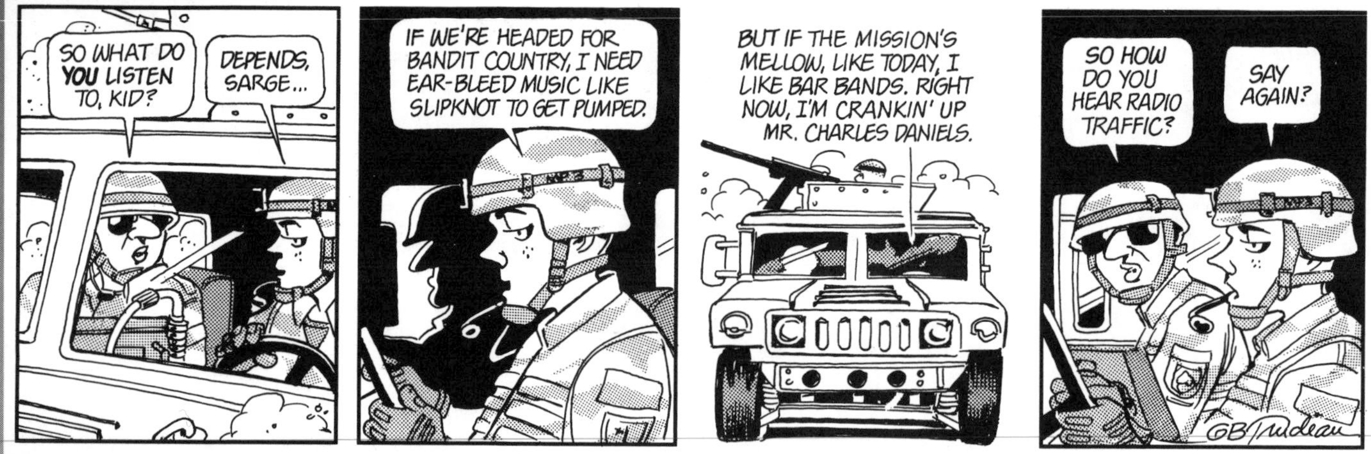

SO WHAT DO **YOU** LISTEN TO, KID?
DEPENDS, SARGE...
IF WE'RE HEADED FOR BANDIT COUNTRY, I NEED EAR-BLEED MUSIC LIKE SLIPKNOT TO GET PUMPED.
BUT IF THE MISSION'S MELLOW, LIKE TODAY, I LIKE BAR BANDS. RIGHT NOW, I'M CRANKIN' UP MR. CHARLES DANIELS.
SO HOW DO YOU HEAR RADIO TRAFFIC?
SAY AGAIN?
GB Trudeau

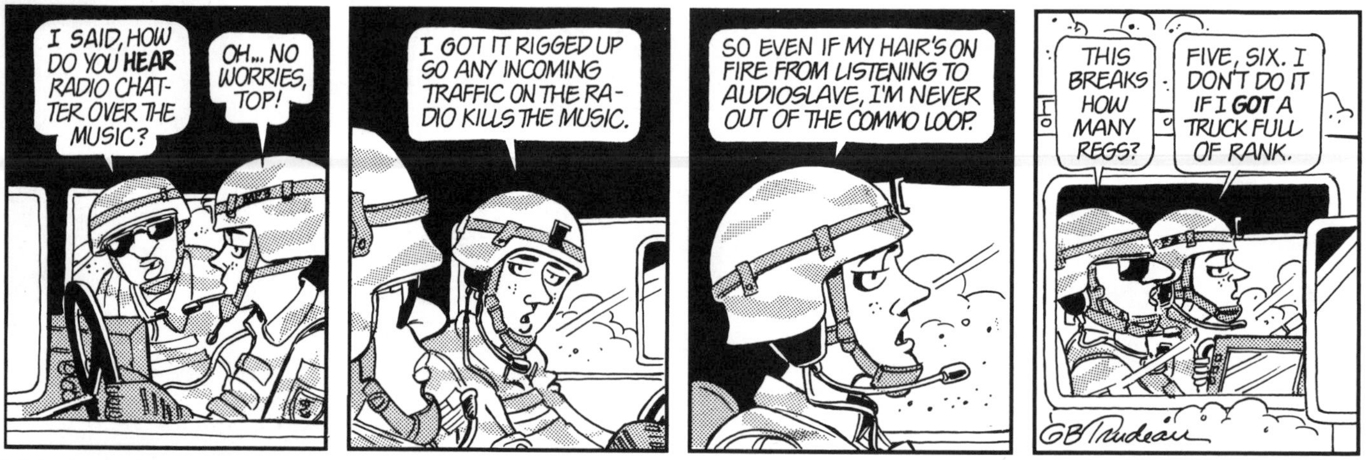

I SAID, HOW DO YOU **HEAR** RADIO CHATTER OVER THE MUSIC?
OH... NO WORRIES, TOP!
I GOT IT RIGGED UP SO ANY INCOMING TRAFFIC ON THE RADIO KILLS THE MUSIC.
SO EVEN IF MY HAIR'S ON FIRE FROM LISTENING TO AUDIOSLAVE, I'M NEVER OUT OF THE COMMO LOOP.
THIS BREAKS HOW MANY REGS?
FIVE, SIX. I DON'T DO IT IF I **GOT** A TRUCK FULL OF RANK.
GB Trudeau

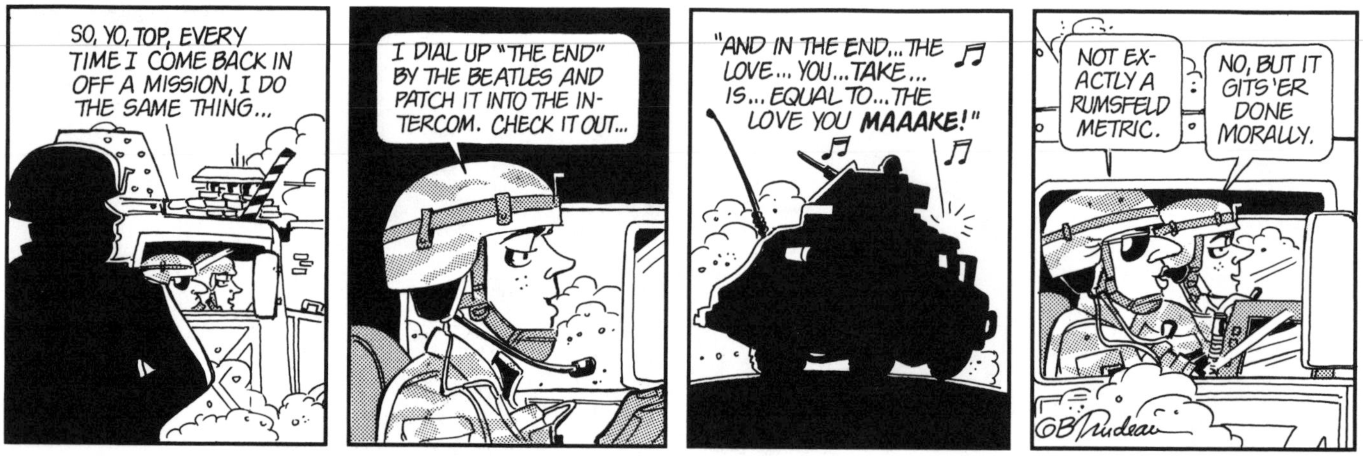

SO, YO, TOP, EVERY TIME I COME BACK IN OFF A MISSION, I DO THE SAME THING...
I DIAL UP "THE END" BY THE BEATLES AND PATCH IT INTO THE INTERCOM. CHECK IT OUT...
"AND IN THE END... THE LOVE... YOU... TAKE... IS... EQUAL TO... THE LOVE YOU **MAAAKE!**"
NOT EXACTLY A RUMSFELD METRIC.
NO, BUT IT GITS 'ER DONE MORALLY.
GB Trudeau

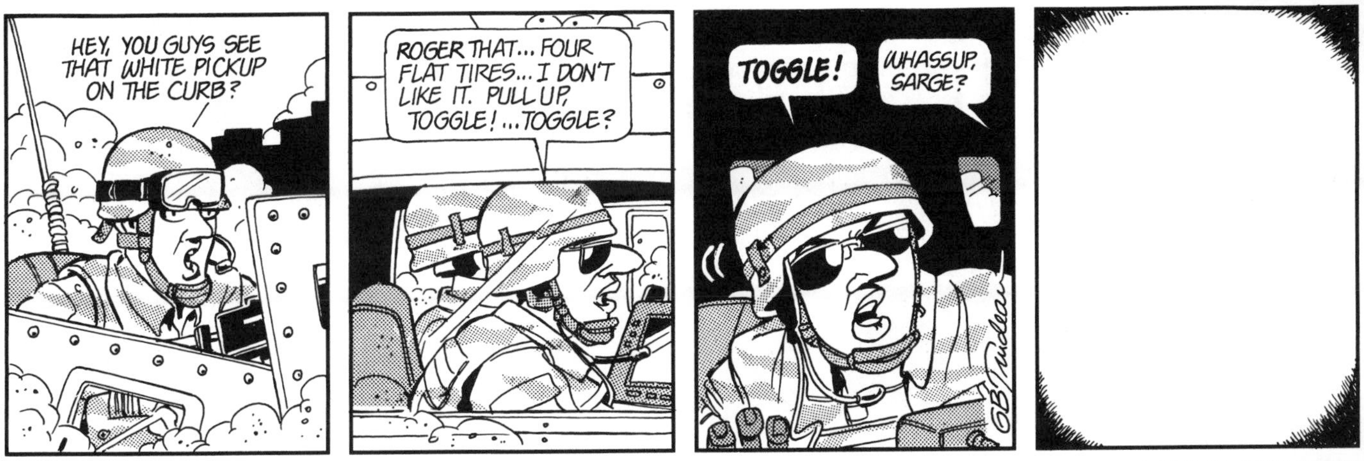
HEY, YOU GUYS SEE THAT WHITE PICKUP ON THE CURB?
ROGER THAT... FOUR FLAT TIRES... I DON'T LIKE IT. PULL UP, TOGGLE! ...TOGGLE?
TOGGLE!
WHASSUP, SARGE?
GB Trudeau

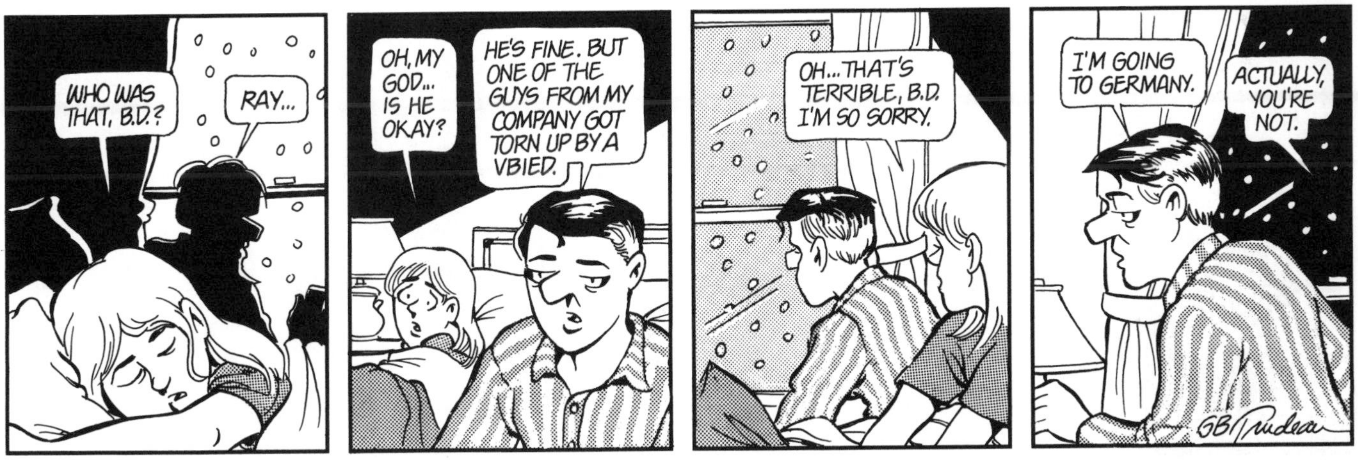
WHO WAS THAT, B.D.?
RAY...
OH, MY GOD... IS HE OKAY?
HE'S FINE. BUT ONE OF THE GUYS FROM MY COMPANY GOT TORN UP BY A VBIED.
OH... THAT'S TERRIBLE, B.D. I'M SO SORRY.
I'M GOING TO GERMANY.
ACTUALLY, YOU'RE NOT.
GB Trudeau

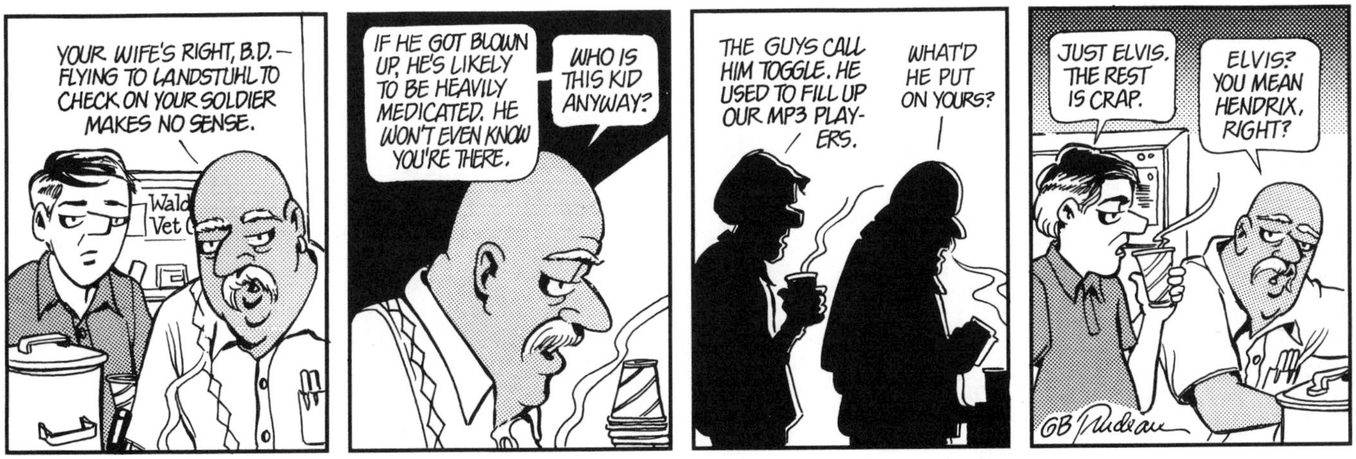
YOUR WIFE'S RIGHT, B.D.— FLYING TO LANDSTUHL TO CHECK ON YOUR SOLDIER MAKES NO SENSE.
IF HE GOT BLOWN UP, HE'S LIKELY TO BE HEAVILY MEDICATED. HE WON'T EVEN KNOW YOU'RE THERE.
WHO IS THIS KID ANYWAY?
THE GUYS CALL HIM TOGGLE. HE USED TO FILL UP OUR MP3 PLAYERS.
WHAT'D HE PUT ON YOURS?
JUST ELVIS. THE REST IS CRAP.
ELVIS? YOU MEAN HENDRIX, RIGHT?
GB Trudeau

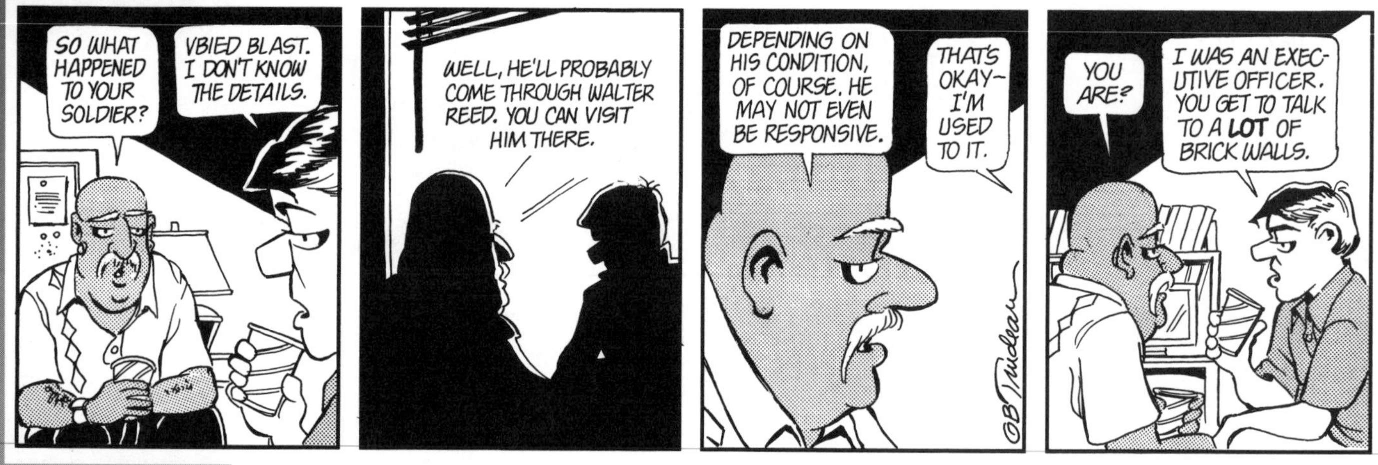
SO WHAT HAPPENED TO YOUR SOLDIER?
VBIED BLAST. I DON'T KNOW THE DETAILS.
WELL, HE'LL PROBABLY COME THROUGH WALTER REED. YOU CAN VISIT HIM THERE.
DEPENDING ON HIS CONDITION, OF COURSE. HE MAY NOT EVEN BE RESPONSIVE.
THAT'S OKAY— I'M USED TO IT.
YOU ARE?
I WAS AN EXECUTIVE OFFICER. YOU GET TO TALK TO A **LOT** OF BRICK WALLS.

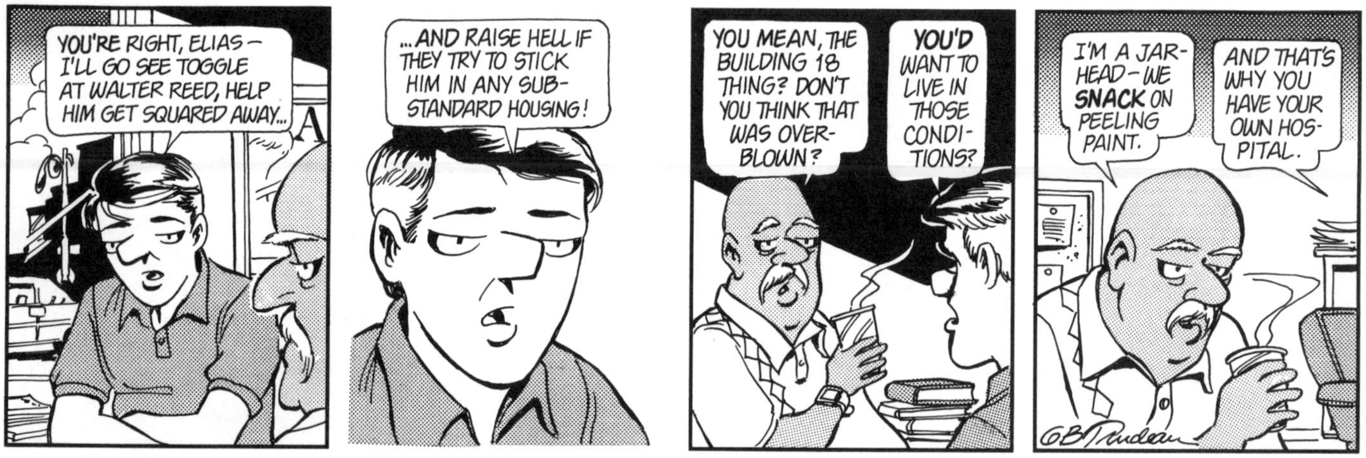
YOU'RE RIGHT, ELIAS— I'LL GO SEE TOGGLE AT WALTER REED, HELP HIM GET SQUARED AWAY...
...AND RAISE HELL IF THEY TRY TO STICK HIM IN ANY SUBSTANDARD HOUSING!
YOU **MEAN**, THE BUILDING 18 THING? DON'T YOU THINK THAT WAS OVERBLOWN?
YOU'D WANT TO LIVE IN THOSE CONDITIONS?
I'M A JARHEAD—WE **SNACK** ON PEELING PAINT.
AND THAT'S WHY YOU HAVE YOUR OWN HOSPITAL.

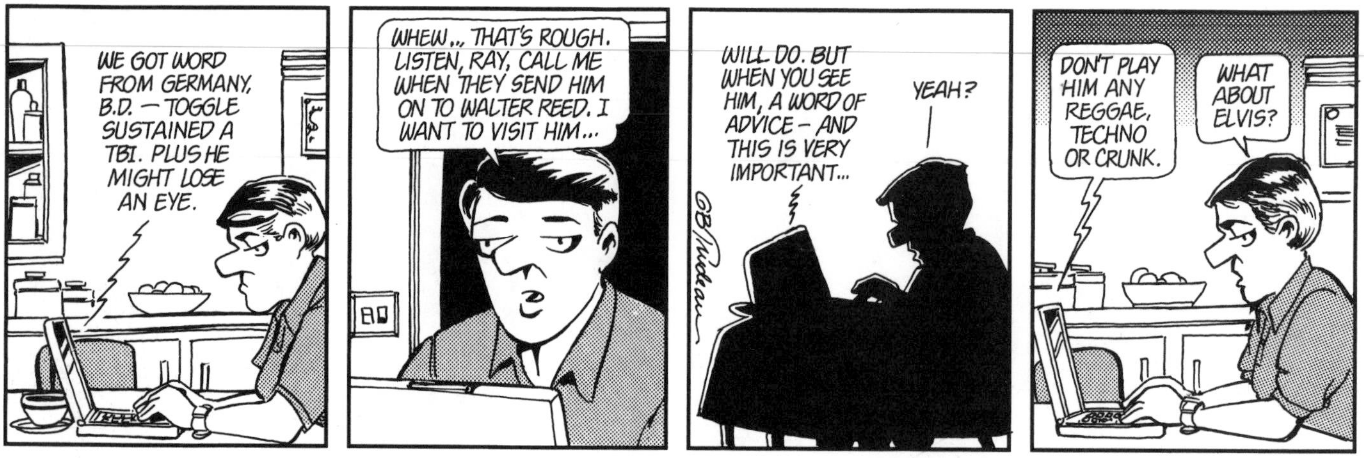
WE GOT WORD FROM GERMANY, B.D. — TOGGLE SUSTAINED A TBI. PLUS HE MIGHT LOSE AN EYE.
WHEW... THAT'S ROUGH. LISTEN, RAY, CALL ME WHEN THEY SEND HIM ON TO WALTER REED. I WANT TO VISIT HIM...
WILL DO. BUT WHEN YOU SEE HIM, A WORD OF ADVICE — AND THIS IS VERY IMPORTANT...
YEAH?
DON'T PLAY HIM ANY REGGAE, TECHNO OR CRUNK.
WHAT ABOUT ELVIS?

MELISSA? HI, IT'S ME, B.D.! FROM THE VET CENTER?

OH, HI, SIR...

WE'RE OUT OF THE SERVICE, MELISSA— YOU DON'T HAVE TO CALL ME "SIR."

12-10

I PRE-FER TO, SIR.

WHY? DOES USING RANK FEEL SAFER?

SAFER? ARE YOU OUT OF YOUR FREAK-IN' MIND?

SORRY. SHOULDN'T BE PLAYING SHRINK. IT LOOKS SO EASY.

©B Trudeau

QUITE A COINCI-DENCE, ISN'T IT, SIR? BUMPING INTO YOU SHOP-PING AT 2:00 A.M.?

NOT REALLY...

LOTS OF VETS SHOP AT THIS HOUR. CROWD-ED PLACES TEND TO FREAK US OUT.

SEE THAT BIG DUDE IN FROZEN FOOD? HE'S OIF, AND SO'S THAT GUY WALK-ING TOWARDS US IN THE BAKING PRODUCTS AISLE...

©B Trudeau

WELL, GREAT— I'M SUR-ROUNDED.

OH... SORRY. YO, JASON! BACK OFF! TAKE AISLE 4!

YOU KNOW WHAT'S WORSE THAN SUPER-MARKETS FOR ME?

MALLS! THE SECOND I WALK INTO ONE, I START HYPERVENTILATING!

Kellogg's

AND AT CHRISTMAS, OF COURSE, THE CROWDS ARE TEN TIMES WORSE. I CAN'T EVEN GET OUT OF THE CAR.

©B Trudeau

SO WHAT WILL YOU DO FOR PRESENTS?

EVERYONE'S GETTING FROZEN PIZZA.

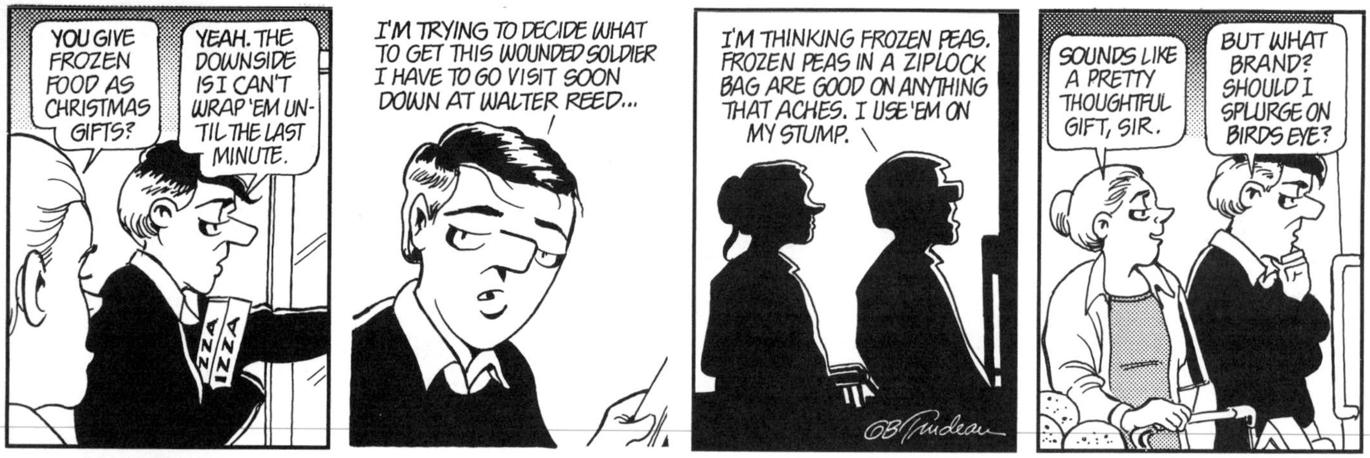
YOU GIVE FROZEN FOOD AS CHRISTMAS GIFTS?
YEAH. THE DOWNSIDE IS I CAN'T WRAP 'EM UNTIL THE LAST MINUTE.
I'M TRYING TO DECIDE WHAT TO GET THIS WOUNDED SOLDIER I HAVE TO GO VISIT SOON DOWN AT WALTER REED...
I'M THINKING FROZEN PEAS. FROZEN PEAS IN A ZIPLOCK BAG ARE GOOD ON ANYTHING THAT ACHES. I USE 'EM ON MY STUMP.
SOUNDS LIKE A PRETTY THOUGHTFUL GIFT, SIR.
BUT WHAT BRAND? SHOULD I SPLURGE ON BIRDS EYE?
GB Trudeau

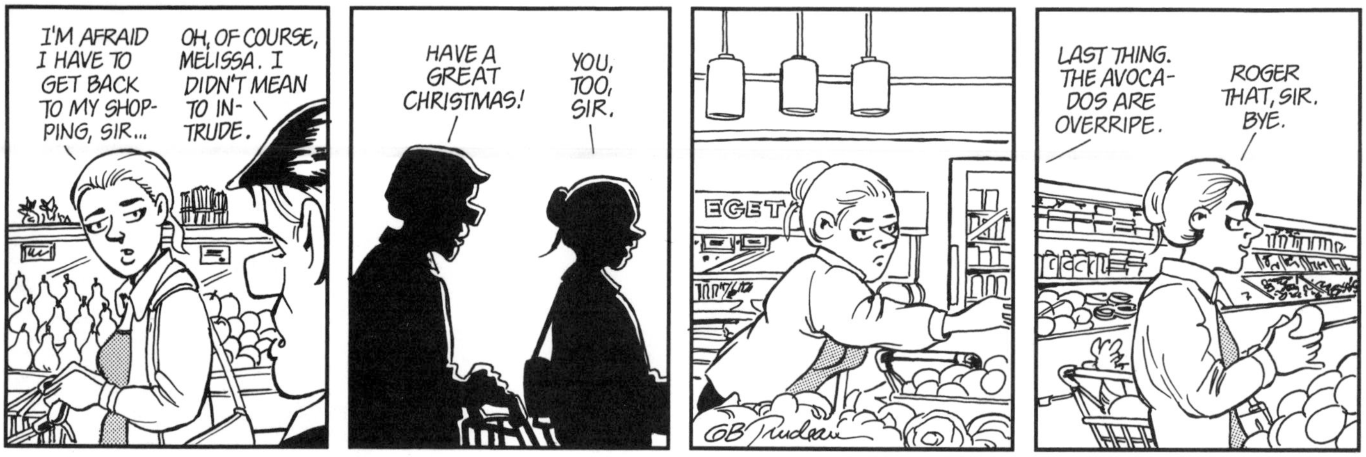
I'M AFRAID I HAVE TO GET BACK TO MY SHOPPING, SIR...
OH, OF COURSE, MELISSA. I DIDN'T MEAN TO INTRUDE.
HAVE A GREAT CHRISTMAS!
YOU, TOO, SIR.
LAST THING. THE AVOCADOS ARE OVERRIPE.
ROGER THAT, SIR. BYE.
GB Trudeau

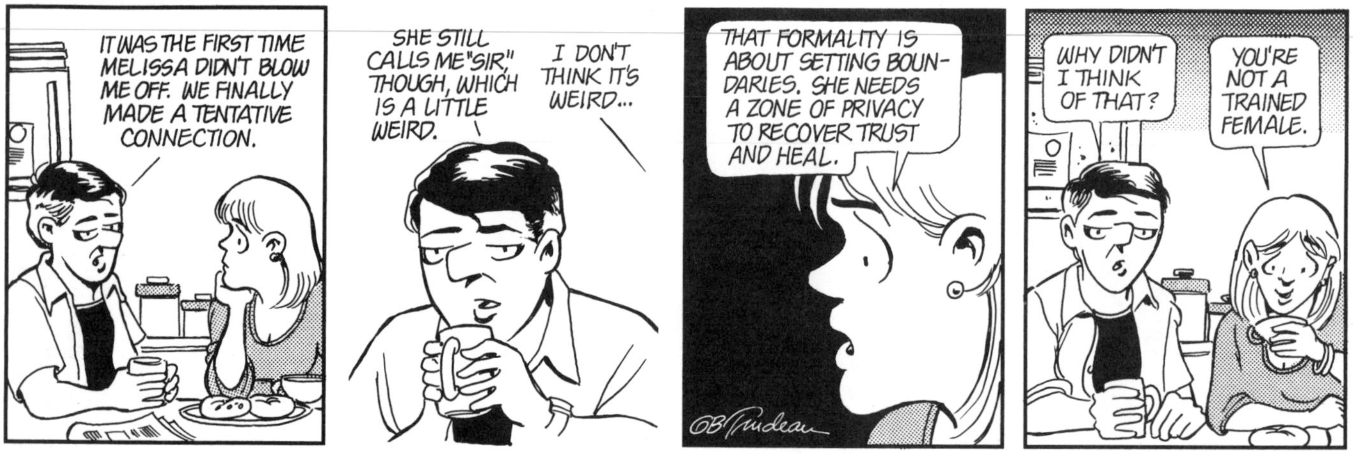
IT WAS THE FIRST TIME MELISSA DIDN'T BLOW ME OFF. WE FINALLY MADE A TENTATIVE CONNECTION.
SHE STILL CALLS ME "SIR," THOUGH, WHICH IS A LITTLE WEIRD.
I DON'T THINK IT'S WEIRD...
THAT FORMALITY IS ABOUT SETTING BOUNDARIES. SHE NEEDS A ZONE OF PRIVACY TO RECOVER TRUST AND HEAL.
WHY DIDN'T I THINK OF THAT?
YOU'RE NOT A TRAINED FEMALE.
GB Trudeau

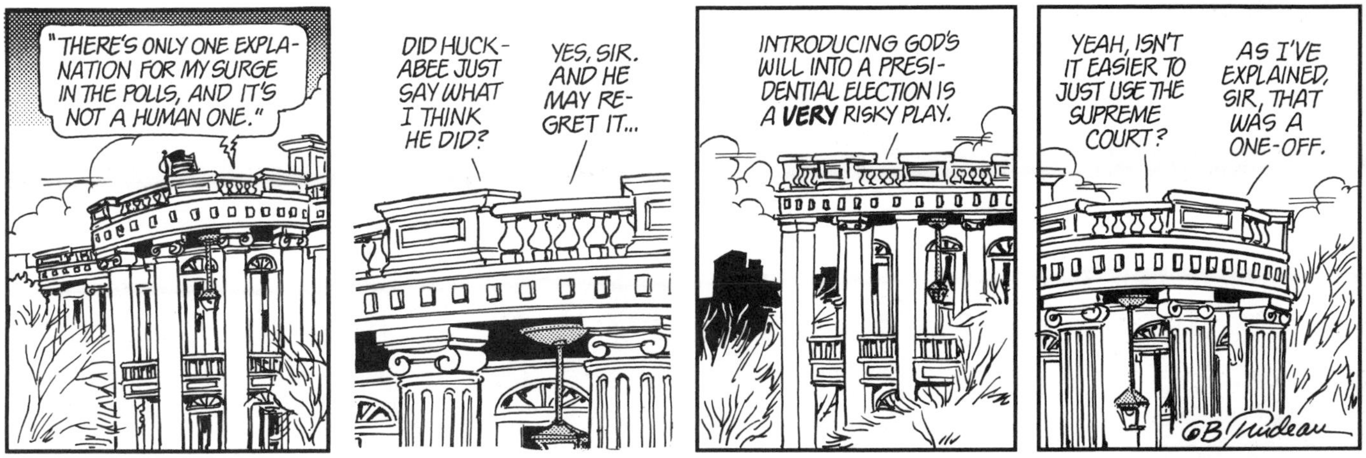
"THERE'S ONLY ONE EXPLANATION FOR MY SURGE IN THE POLLS, AND IT'S NOT A HUMAN ONE."
DID HUCKABEE JUST SAY WHAT I THINK HE DID?
YES, SIR. AND HE MAY REGRET IT...
INTRODUCING GOD'S WILL INTO A PRESIDENTIAL ELECTION IS A VERY RISKY PLAY.
YEAH, ISN'T IT EASIER TO JUST USE THE SUPREME COURT?
AS I'VE EXPLAINED, SIR, THAT WAS A ONE-OFF.
©B Trudeau

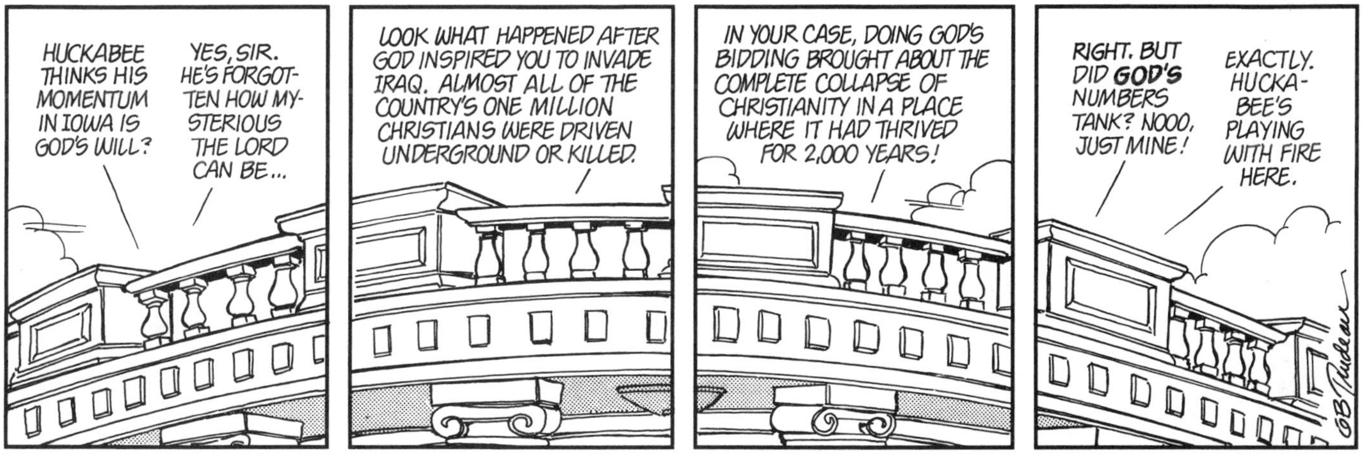
HUCKABEE THINKS HIS MOMENTUM IN IOWA IS GOD'S WILL?
YES, SIR. HE'S FORGOTTEN HOW MYSTERIOUS THE LORD CAN BE...
LOOK WHAT HAPPENED AFTER GOD INSPIRED YOU TO INVADE IRAQ. ALMOST ALL OF THE COUNTRY'S ONE MILLION CHRISTIANS WERE DRIVEN UNDERGROUND OR KILLED.
IN YOUR CASE, DOING GOD'S BIDDING BROUGHT ABOUT THE COMPLETE COLLAPSE OF CHRISTIANITY IN A PLACE WHERE IT HAD THRIVED FOR 2,000 YEARS!
RIGHT. BUT DID GOD'S NUMBERS TANK? NOOO, JUST MINE!
EXACTLY. HUCKABEE'S PLAYING WITH FIRE HERE.
©B Trudeau

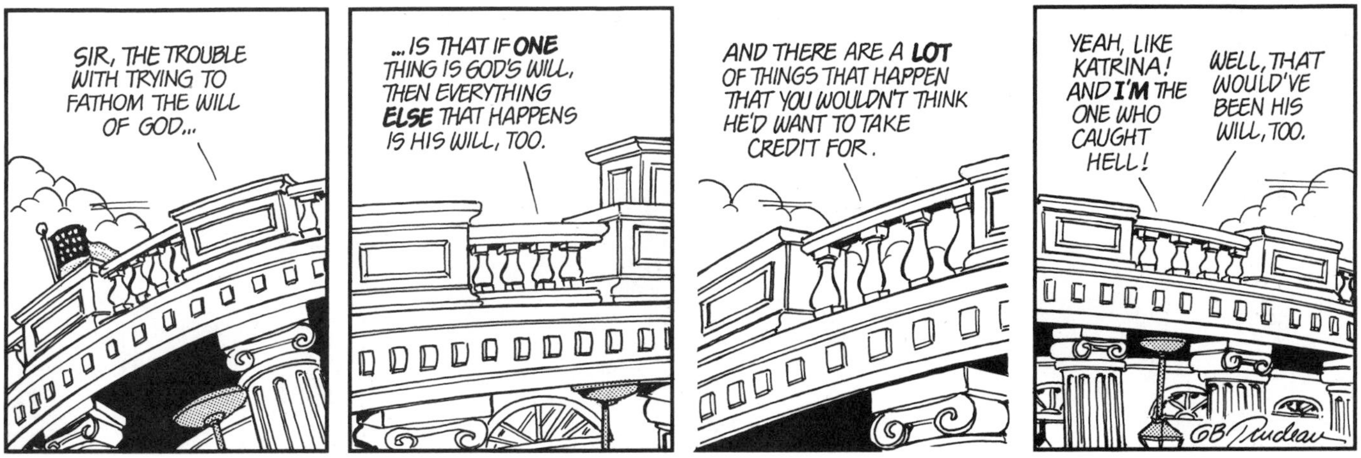
SIR, THE TROUBLE WITH TRYING TO FATHOM THE WILL OF GOD...
...IS THAT IF ONE THING IS GOD'S WILL, THEN EVERYTHING ELSE THAT HAPPENS IS HIS WILL, TOO.
AND THERE ARE A LOT OF THINGS THAT HAPPEN THAT YOU WOULDN'T THINK HE'D WANT TO TAKE CREDIT FOR.
YEAH, LIKE KATRINA! AND I'M THE ONE WHO CAUGHT HELL!
WELL, THAT WOULD'VE BEEN HIS WILL, TOO.
©B Trudeau

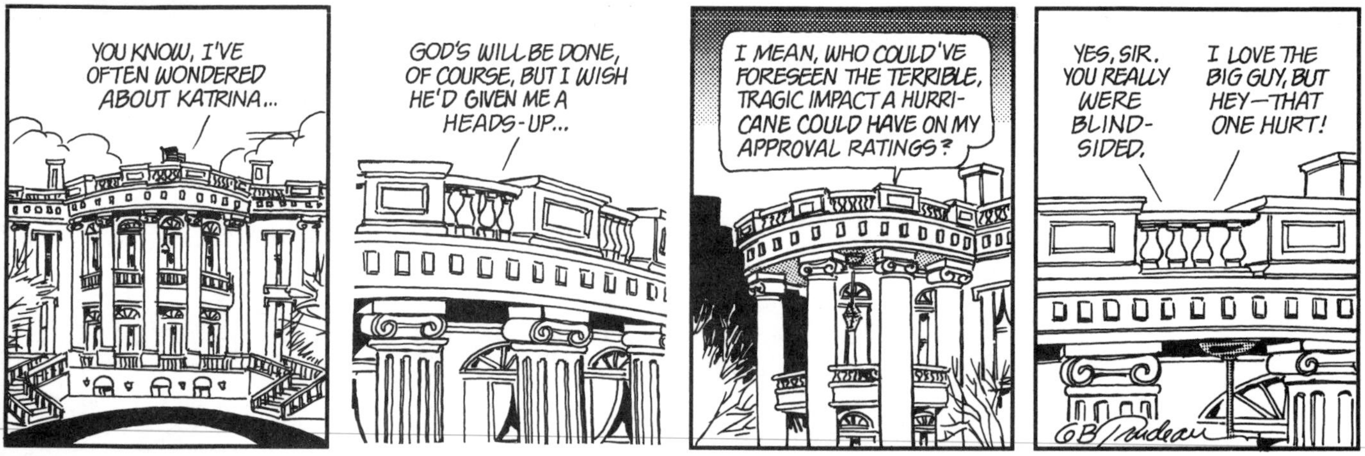
YOU KNOW, I'VE OFTEN WONDERED ABOUT KATRINA...
GOD'S WILL BE DONE, OF COURSE, BUT I WISH HE'D GIVEN ME A HEADS-UP...
I MEAN, WHO COULD'VE FORESEEN THE TERRIBLE, TRAGIC IMPACT A HURRICANE COULD HAVE ON MY APPROVAL RATINGS?
YES, SIR. YOU REALLY WERE BLINDSIDED.
I LOVE THE BIG GUY, BUT HEY—THAT ONE HURT!
GB Trudeau

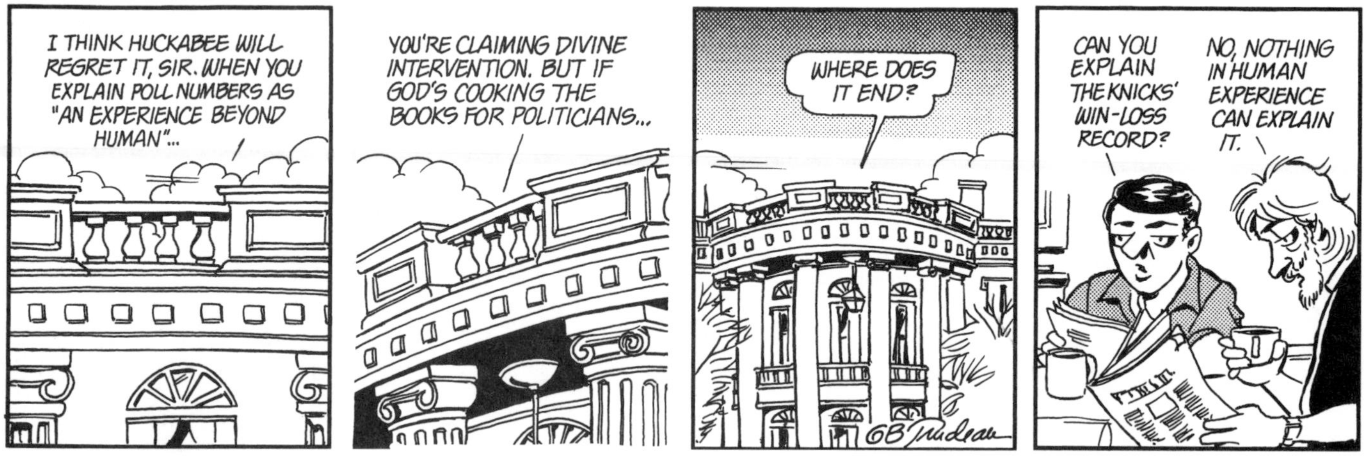
I THINK HUCKABEE WILL REGRET IT, SIR. WHEN YOU EXPLAIN POLL NUMBERS AS "AN EXPERIENCE BEYOND HUMAN"...
YOU'RE CLAIMING DIVINE INTERVENTION. BUT IF GOD'S COOKING THE BOOKS FOR POLITICIANS...
WHERE DOES IT END?
GB Trudeau
CAN YOU EXPLAIN THE KNICKS' WIN-LOSS RECORD?
NO, NOTHING IN HUMAN EXPERIENCE CAN EXPLAIN IT.

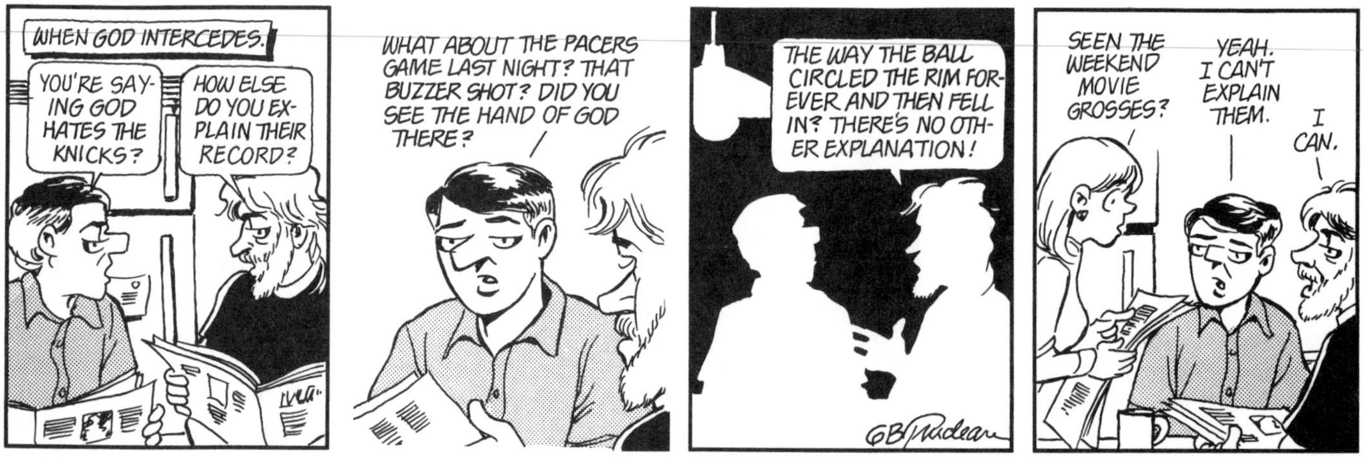
WHEN GOD INTERCEDES.
YOU'RE SAYING GOD HATES THE KNICKS?
HOW ELSE DO YOU EXPLAIN THEIR RECORD?
WHAT ABOUT THE PACERS GAME LAST NIGHT? THAT BUZZER SHOT? DID YOU SEE THE HAND OF GOD THERE?
THE WAY THE BALL CIRCLED THE RIM FOREVER AND THEN FELL IN? THERE'S NO OTHER EXPLANATION!
GB Trudeau
SEEN THE WEEKEND MOVIE GROSSES?
YEAH. I CAN'T EXPLAIN THEM.
I CAN.

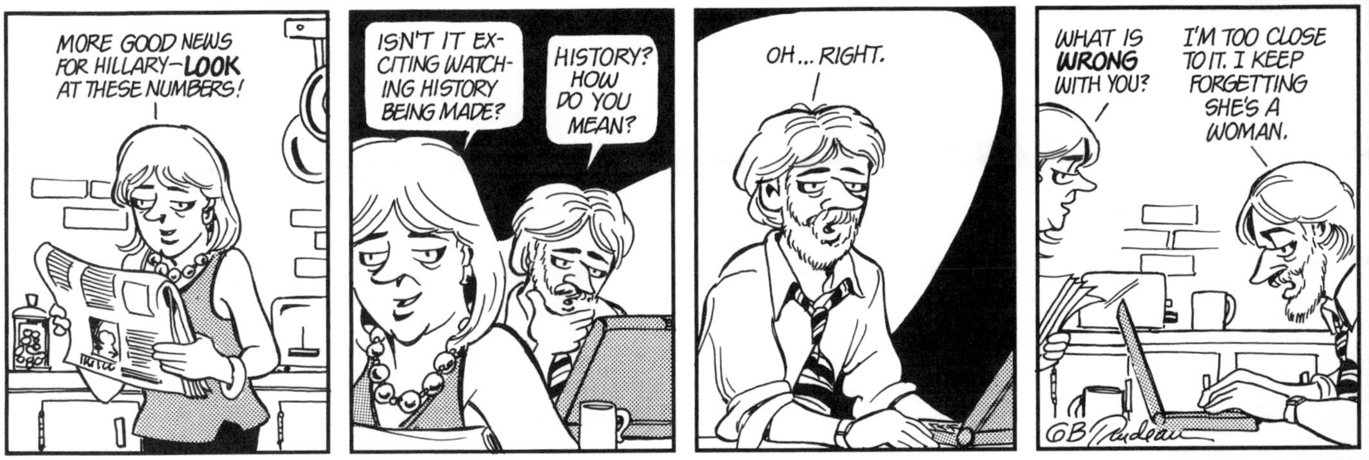
MORE GOOD NEWS FOR HILLARY—**LOOK** AT THESE NUMBERS!
ISN'T IT EXCITING WATCHING HISTORY BEING MADE?
HISTORY? HOW DO YOU MEAN?
OH... RIGHT.
WHAT IS **WRONG** WITH YOU?
I'M TOO CLOSE TO IT. I KEEP FORGETTING SHE'S A WOMAN.
©GB Trudeau

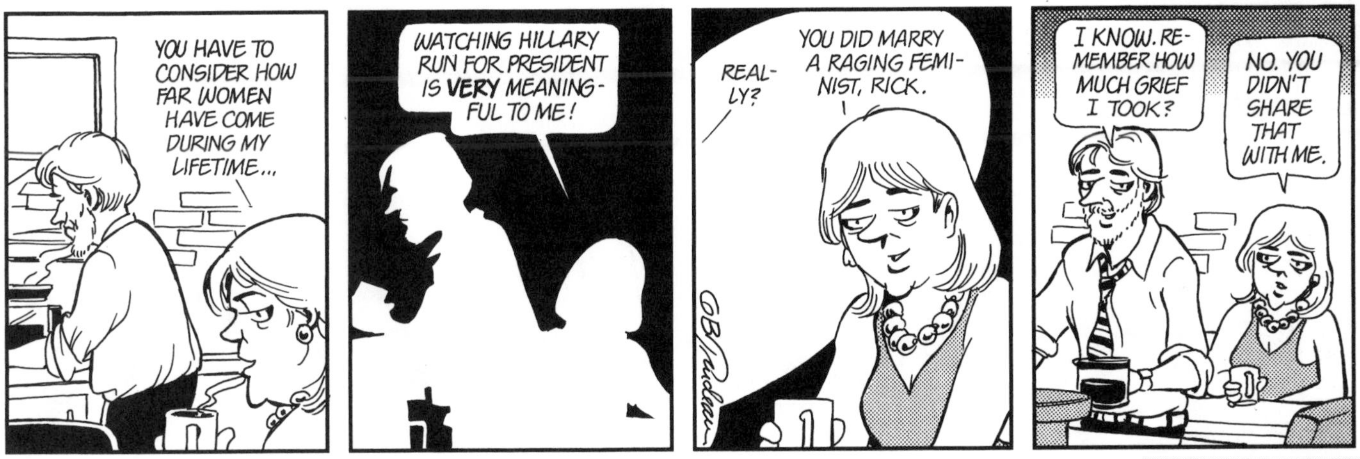
YOU HAVE TO CONSIDER HOW FAR WOMEN HAVE COME DURING MY LIFETIME...
WATCHING HILLARY RUN FOR PRESIDENT IS **VERY** MEANINGFUL TO ME!
REALLY?
YOU DID MARRY A RAGING FEMINIST, RICK.
©GB Trudeau
I KNOW. REMEMBER HOW MUCH GRIEF I TOOK?
NO. YOU DIDN'T SHARE THAT WITH ME.

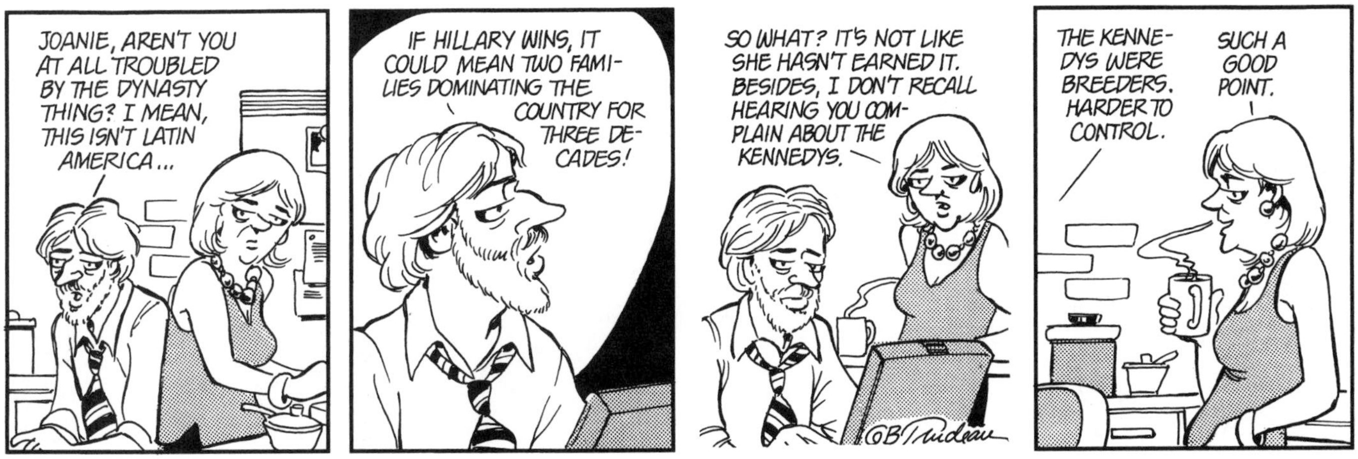
JOANIE, AREN'T YOU AT ALL TROUBLED BY THE DYNASTY THING? I MEAN, THIS ISN'T LATIN AMERICA...
IF HILLARY WINS, IT COULD MEAN TWO FAMILIES DOMINATING THE COUNTRY FOR THREE DECADES!
SO WHAT? IT'S NOT LIKE SHE HASN'T EARNED IT. BESIDES, I DON'T RECALL HEARING YOU COMPLAIN ABOUT THE KENNEDYS.
©GB Trudeau
THE KENNEDYS WERE BREEDERS. HARDER TO CONTROL.
SUCH A GOOD POINT.

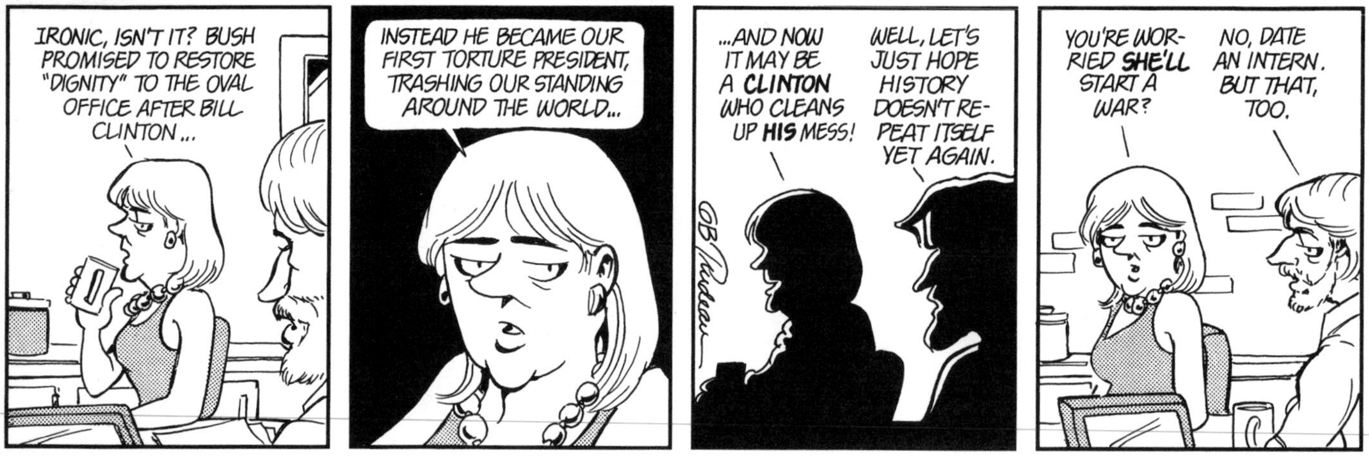
IRONIC, ISN'T IT? BUSH PROMISED TO RESTORE "DIGNITY" TO THE OVAL OFFICE AFTER BILL CLINTON...
INSTEAD HE BECAME OUR FIRST TORTURE PRESIDENT, TRASHING OUR STANDING AROUND THE WORLD...
...AND NOW IT MAY BE A **CLINTON** WHO CLEANS UP **HIS** MESS!
WELL, LET'S JUST HOPE HISTORY DOESN'T REPEAT ITSELF YET AGAIN.
YOU'RE WORRIED **SHE'LL** START A WAR?
NO, DATE AN INTERN. BUT THAT, TOO.

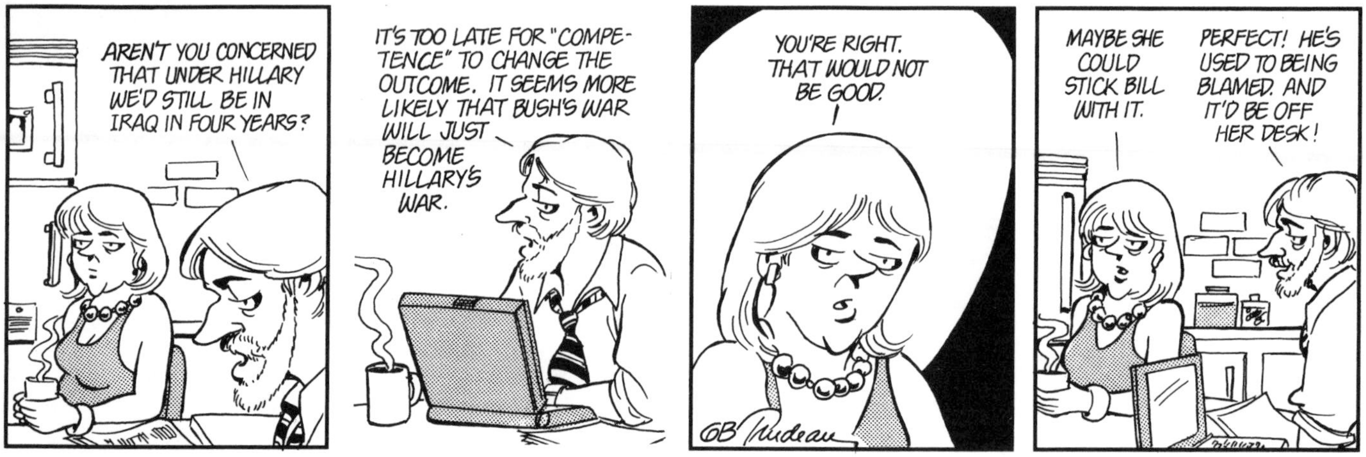
AREN'T YOU CONCERNED THAT UNDER HILLARY WE'D STILL BE IN IRAQ IN FOUR YEARS?
IT'S TOO LATE FOR "COMPETENCE" TO CHANGE THE OUTCOME. IT SEEMS MORE LIKELY THAT BUSH'S WAR WILL JUST BECOME HILLARY'S WAR.
YOU'RE RIGHT. THAT WOULD NOT BE GOOD.
MAYBE SHE COULD STICK BILL WITH IT.
PERFECT! HE'S USED TO BEING BLAMED. AND IT'D BE OFF HER DESK!

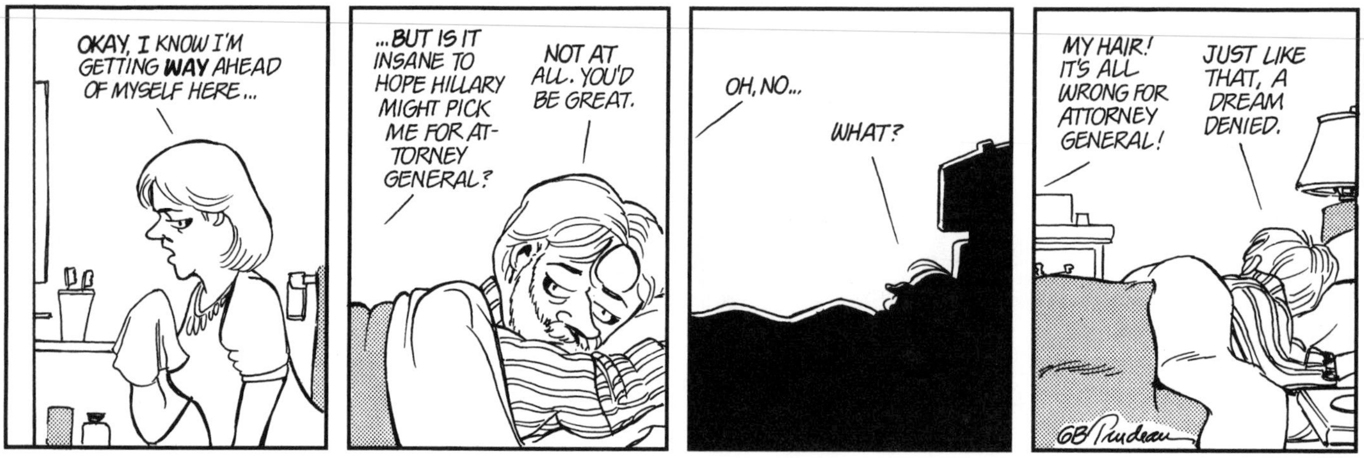
OKAY, I KNOW I'M GETTING **WAY** AHEAD OF MYSELF HERE...
...BUT IS IT INSANE TO HOPE HILLARY MIGHT PICK ME FOR ATTORNEY GENERAL?
NOT AT ALL. YOU'D BE GREAT.
OH, NO...
WHAT?
MY HAIR! IT'S ALL WRONG FOR ATTORNEY GENERAL!
JUST LIKE THAT, A DREAM DENIED.

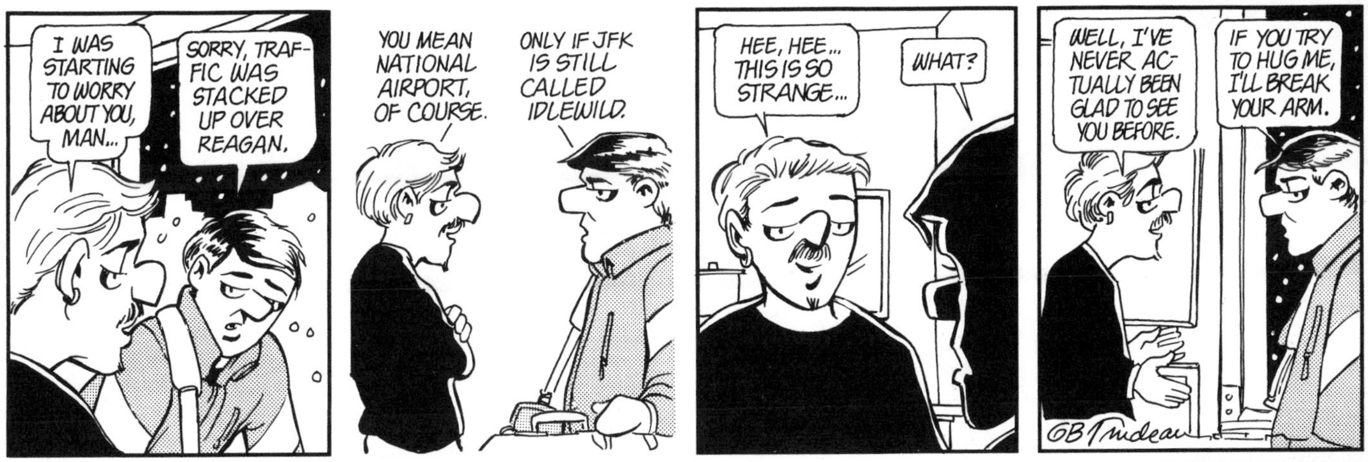
I WAS STARTING TO WORRY ABOUT YOU, MAN...
SORRY, TRAFFIC WAS STACKED UP OVER REAGAN.
YOU MEAN NATIONAL AIRPORT, OF COURSE.
ONLY IF JFK IS STILL CALLED IDLEWILD.
HEE, HEE... THIS IS SO STRANGE...
WHAT?
WELL, I'VE NEVER ACTUALLY BEEN GLAD TO SEE YOU BEFORE.
IF YOU TRY TO HUG ME, I'LL BREAK YOUR ARM.
GB Trudeau

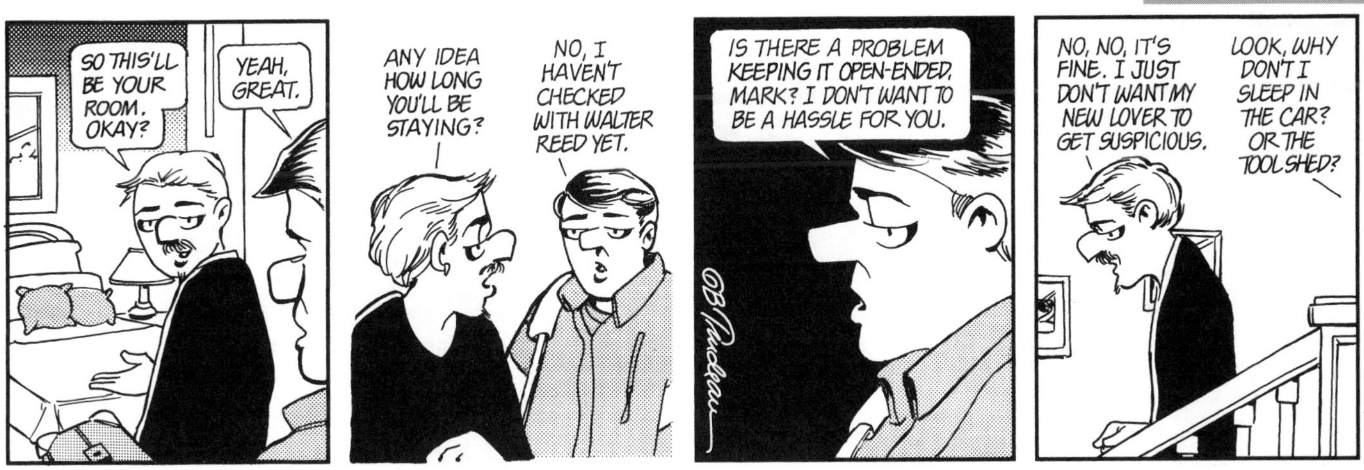
SO THIS'LL BE YOUR ROOM. OKAY?
YEAH, GREAT.
ANY IDEA HOW LONG YOU'LL BE STAYING?
NO, I HAVEN'T CHECKED WITH WALTER REED YET.
IS THERE A PROBLEM KEEPING IT OPEN-ENDED, MARK? I DON'T WANT TO BE A HASSLE FOR YOU.
GB Trudeau
NO, NO, IT'S FINE. I JUST DON'T WANT MY NEW LOVER TO GET SUSPICIOUS.
LOOK, WHY DON'T I SLEEP IN THE CAR? OR THE TOOL SHED?

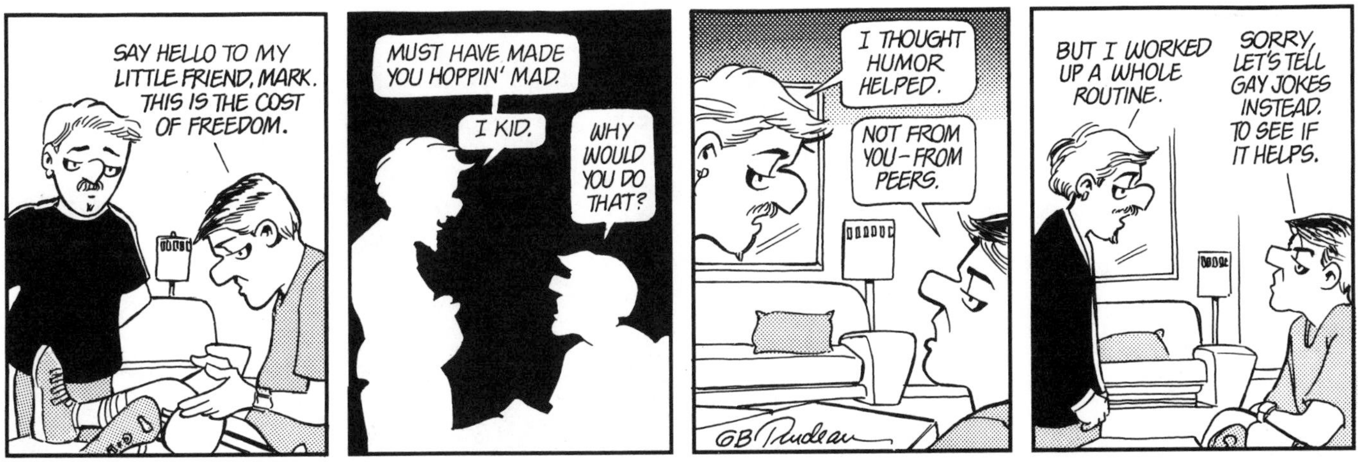
SAY HELLO TO MY LITTLE FRIEND, MARK. THIS IS THE COST OF FREEDOM.
MUST HAVE MADE YOU HOPPIN' MAD.
I KID.
WHY WOULD YOU DO THAT?
I THOUGHT HUMOR HELPED.
NOT FROM YOU–FROM PEERS.
GB Trudeau
BUT I WORKED UP A WHOLE ROUTINE.
SORRY, LET'S TELL GAY JOKES INSTEAD. TO SEE IF IT HELPS.

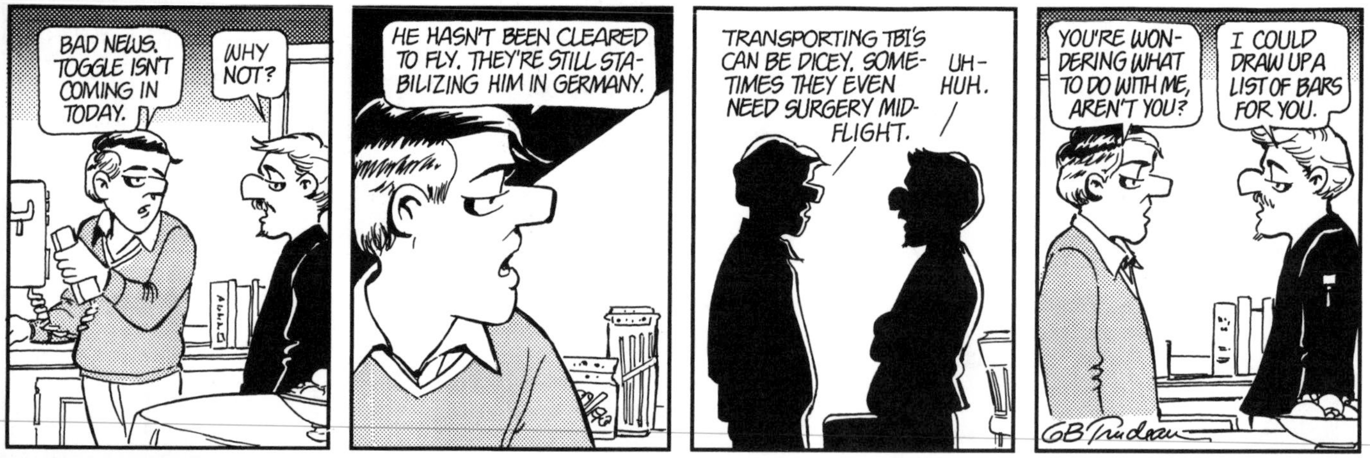
BAD NEWS. TOGGLE ISN'T COMING IN TODAY.
WHY NOT?
HE HASN'T BEEN CLEARED TO FLY. THEY'RE STILL STABILIZING HIM IN GERMANY.
TRANSPORTING TBI'S CAN BE DICEY. SOMETIMES THEY EVEN NEED SURGERY MID-FLIGHT.
UH-HUH.
YOU'RE WONDERING WHAT TO DO WITH ME, AREN'T YOU?
I COULD DRAW UP A LIST OF BARS FOR YOU.
GB Trudeau

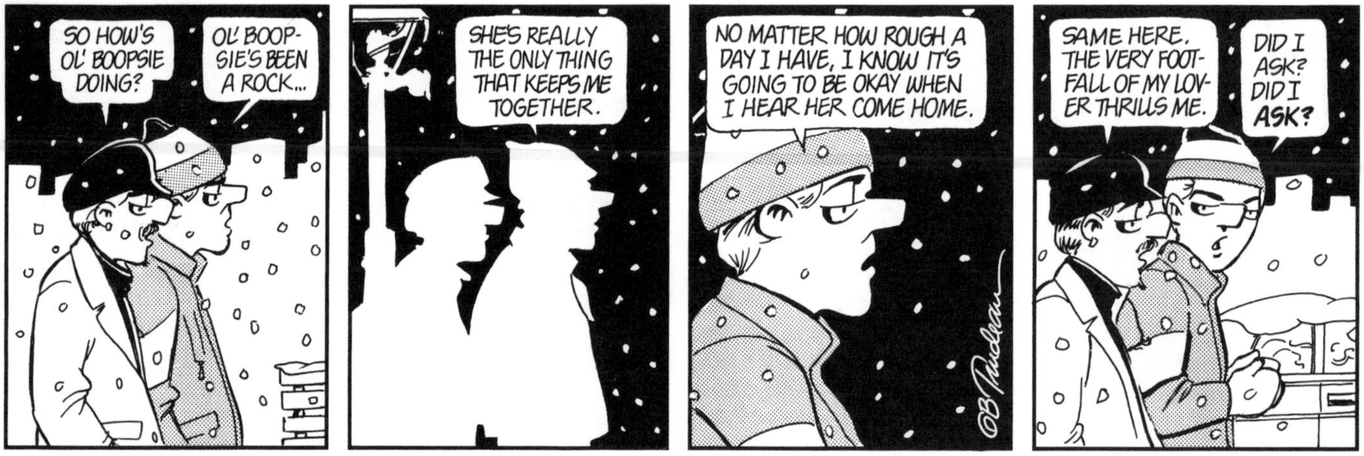
SO HOW'S OL' BOOPSIE DOING?
OL' BOOPSIE'S BEEN A ROCK...
SHE'S REALLY THE ONLY THING THAT KEEPS ME TOGETHER.
NO MATTER HOW ROUGH A DAY I HAVE, I KNOW IT'S GOING TO BE OKAY WHEN I HEAR HER COME HOME.
GB Trudeau
SAME HERE. THE VERY FOOTFALL OF MY LOVER THRILLS ME.
DID I ASK? DID I **ASK?**

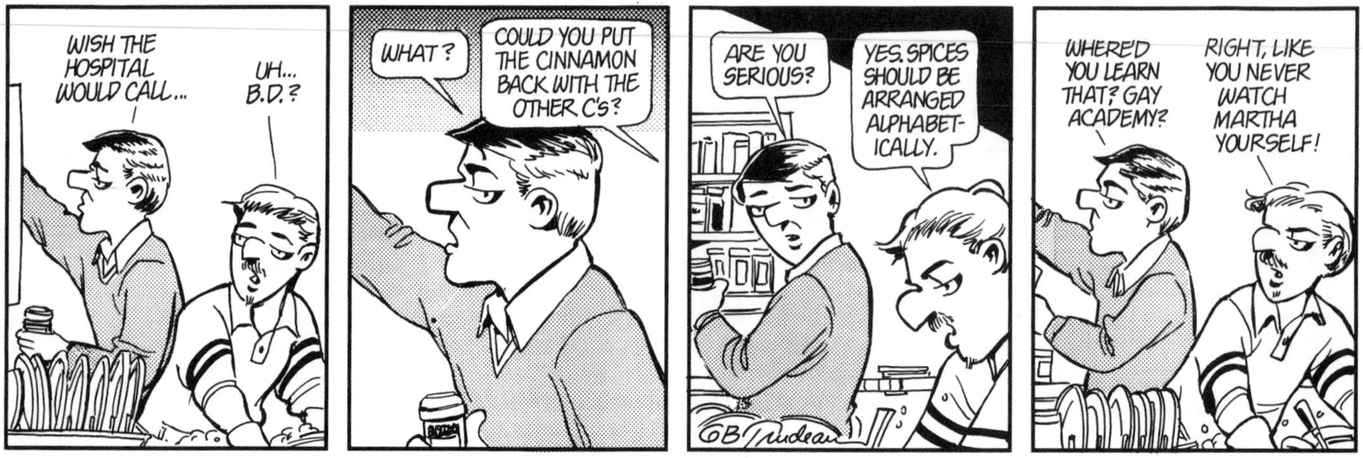
WISH THE HOSPITAL WOULD CALL...
UH... B.D.?
WHAT?
COULD YOU PUT THE CINNAMON BACK WITH THE OTHER C's?
ARE YOU SERIOUS?
YES. SPICES SHOULD BE ARRANGED ALPHABETICALLY.
GB Trudeau
WHERE'D YOU LEARN THAT? GAY ACADEMY?
RIGHT, LIKE YOU NEVER WATCH MARTHA YOURSELF!

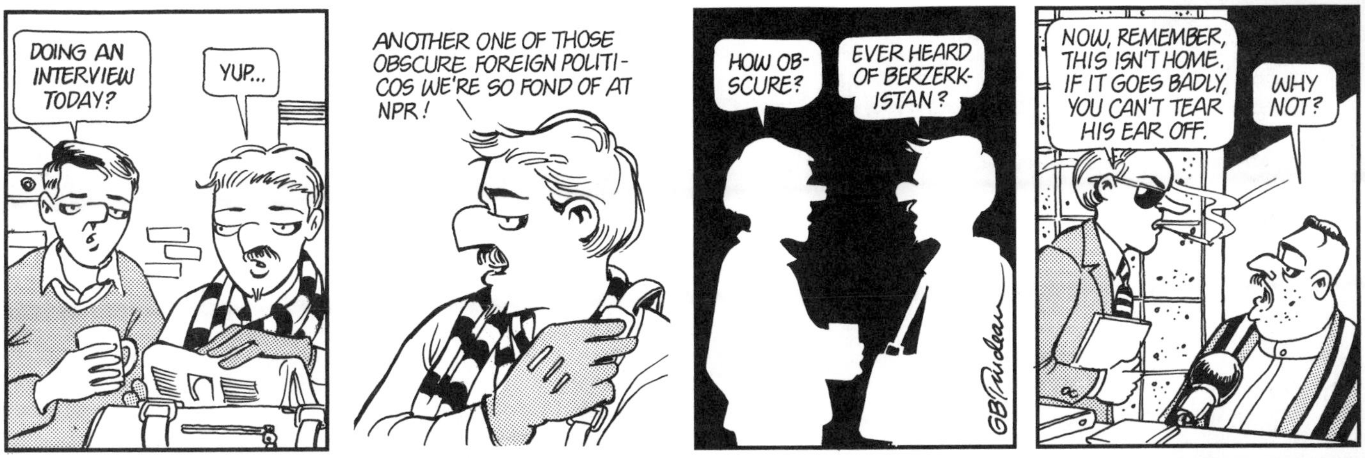
DOING AN INTERVIEW TODAY?
YUP...
ANOTHER ONE OF THOSE OBSCURE FOREIGN POLITICOS WE'RE SO FOND OF AT NPR!
HOW OBSCURE?
EVER HEARD OF BERZERKISTAN?
NOW, REMEMBER, THIS ISN'T HOME. IF IT GOES BADLY, YOU CAN'T TEAR HIS EAR OFF.
WHY NOT?

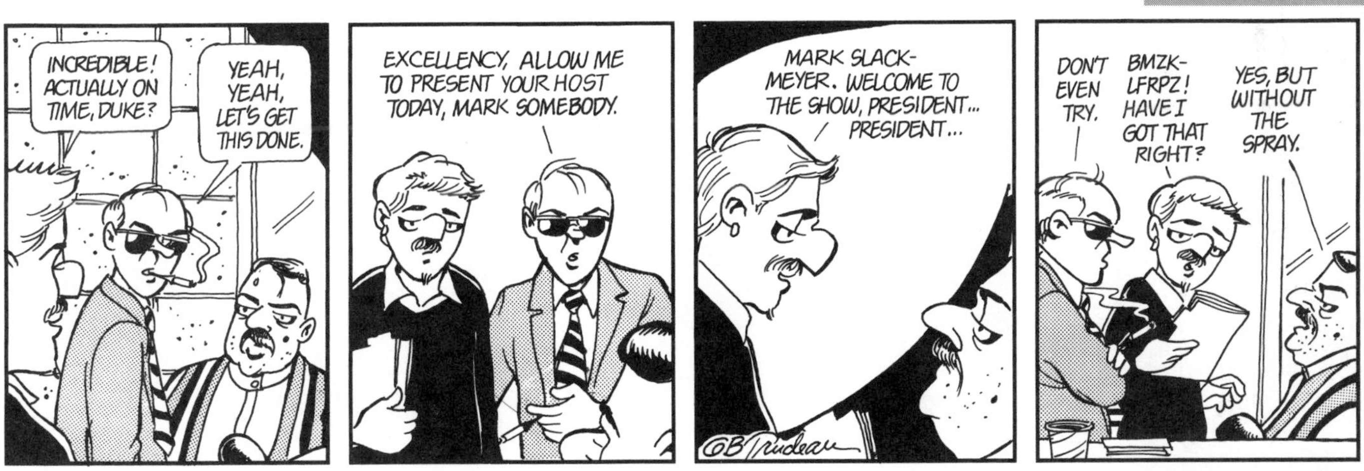
INCREDIBLE! ACTUALLY ON TIME, DUKE?
YEAH, YEAH, LET'S GET THIS DONE.
EXCELLENCY, ALLOW ME TO PRESENT YOUR HOST TODAY, MARK SOMEBODY.
MARK SLACKMEYER. WELCOME TO THE SHOW, PRESIDENT... PRESIDENT...
DON'T EVEN TRY.
BMZKLFRPZ! HAVE I GOT THAT RIGHT?
YES, BUT WITHOUT THE SPRAY.

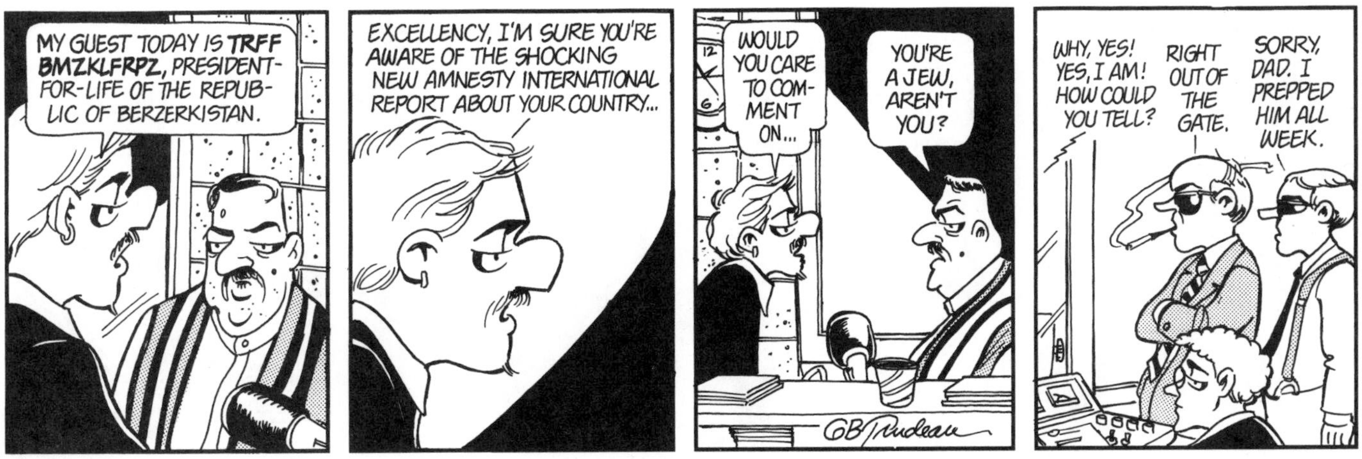
MY GUEST TODAY IS TRFF BMZKLFRPZ, PRESIDENT-FOR-LIFE OF THE REPUBLIC OF BERZERKISTAN.
EXCELLENCY, I'M SURE YOU'RE AWARE OF THE SHOCKING NEW AMNESTY INTERNATIONAL REPORT ABOUT YOUR COUNTRY...
WOULD YOU CARE TO COMMENT ON...
YOU'RE A JEW, AREN'T YOU?
WHY, YES! YES, I AM! HOW COULD YOU TELL?
RIGHT OUT OF THE GATE.
SORRY, DAD. I PREPPED HIM ALL WEEK.

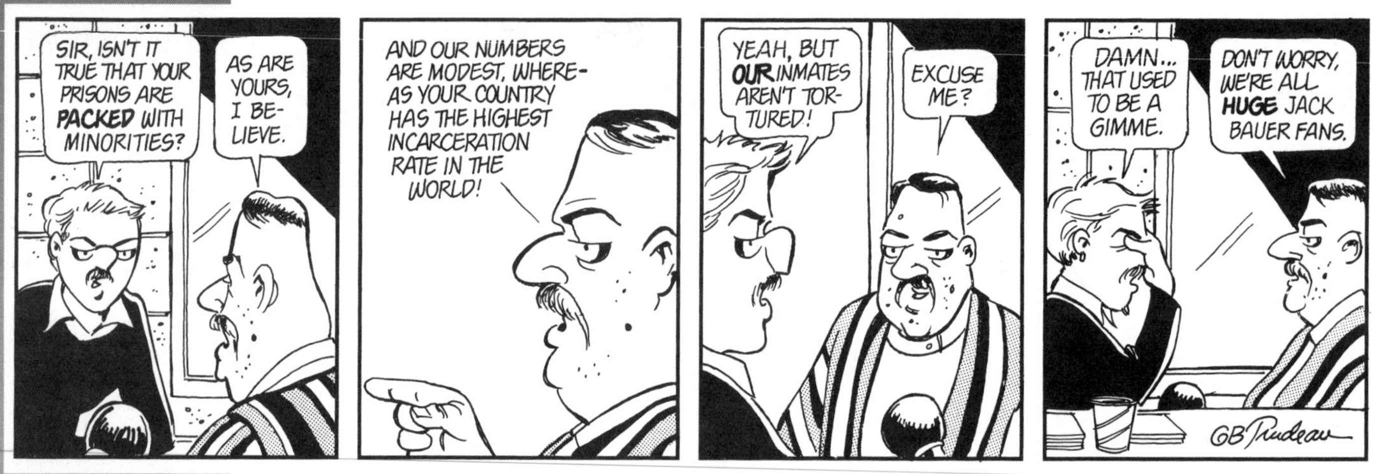
SIR, ISN'T IT TRUE THAT YOUR PRISONS ARE **PACKED** WITH MINORITIES?
AS ARE YOURS, I BELIEVE.
AND OUR NUMBERS ARE MODEST, WHEREAS YOUR COUNTRY HAS THE HIGHEST INCARCERATION RATE IN THE WORLD!
YEAH, BUT **OUR** INMATES AREN'T TORTURED!
EXCUSE ME?
DAMN... THAT USED TO BE A GIMME.
DON'T WORRY, WE'RE ALL **HUGE** JACK BAUER FANS.

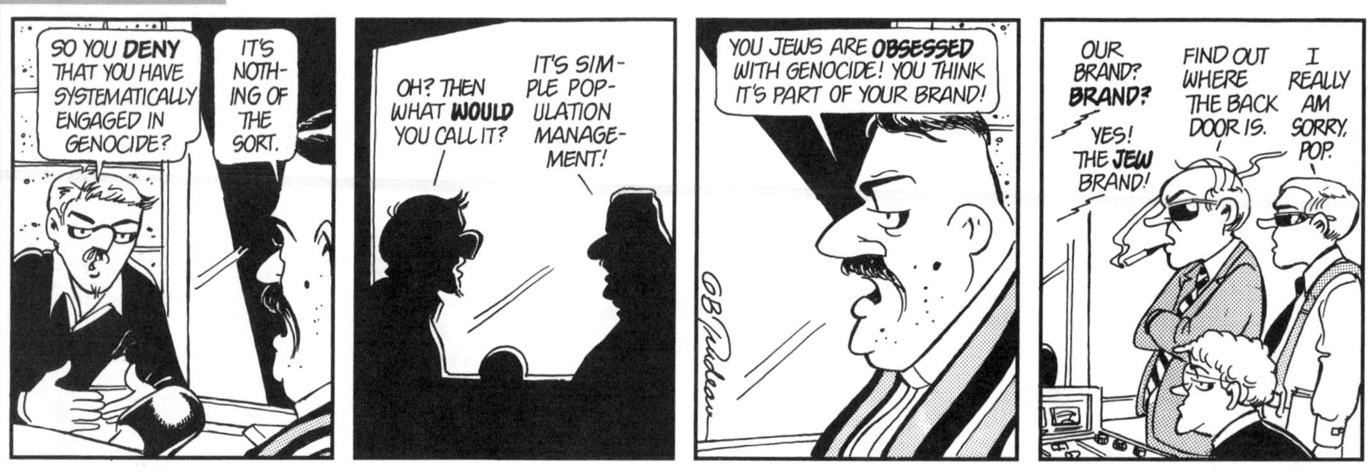
SO YOU **DENY** THAT YOU HAVE SYSTEMATICALLY ENGAGED IN GENOCIDE?
IT'S NOTHING OF THE SORT.
OH? THEN WHAT **WOULD** YOU CALL IT?
IT'S SIMPLE POPULATION MANAGEMENT!
YOU JEWS ARE **OBSESSED** WITH GENOCIDE! YOU THINK IT'S PART OF YOUR BRAND!
OUR BRAND? **BRAND?**
YES! THE **JEW** BRAND!
FIND OUT WHERE THE BACK DOOR IS.
I REALLY AM SORRY, POP.

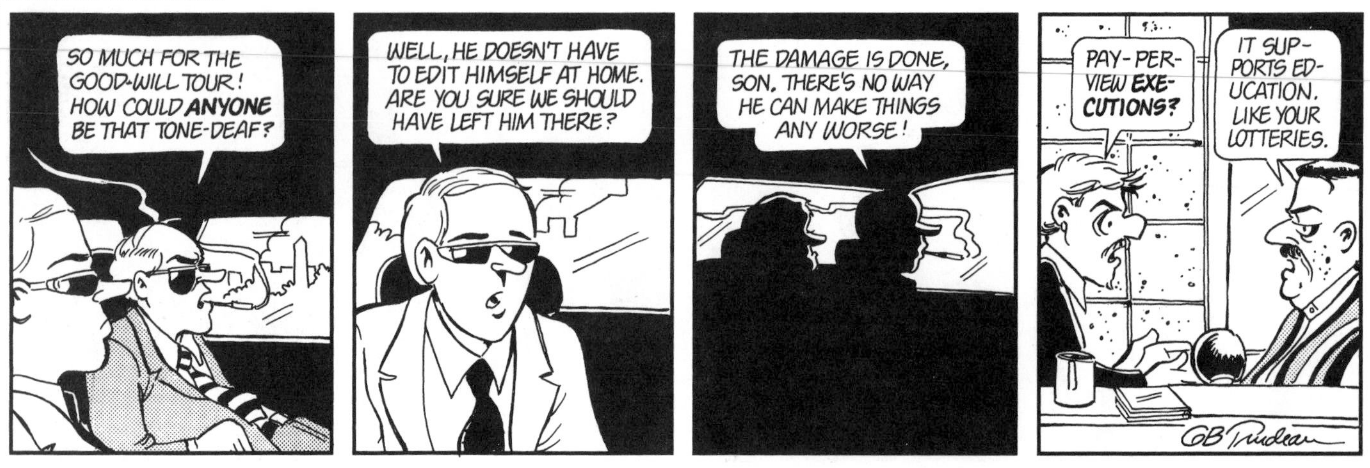
SO MUCH FOR THE GOOD-WILL TOUR! HOW COULD **ANYONE** BE THAT TONE-DEAF?
WELL, HE DOESN'T HAVE TO EDIT HIMSELF AT HOME. ARE YOU SURE WE SHOULD HAVE LEFT HIM THERE?
THE DAMAGE IS DONE, SON. THERE'S NO WAY HE CAN MAKE THINGS ANY WORSE!
PAY-PER-VIEW **EXECUTIONS?**
IT SUPPORTS EDUCATION. LIKE YOUR LOTTERIES.

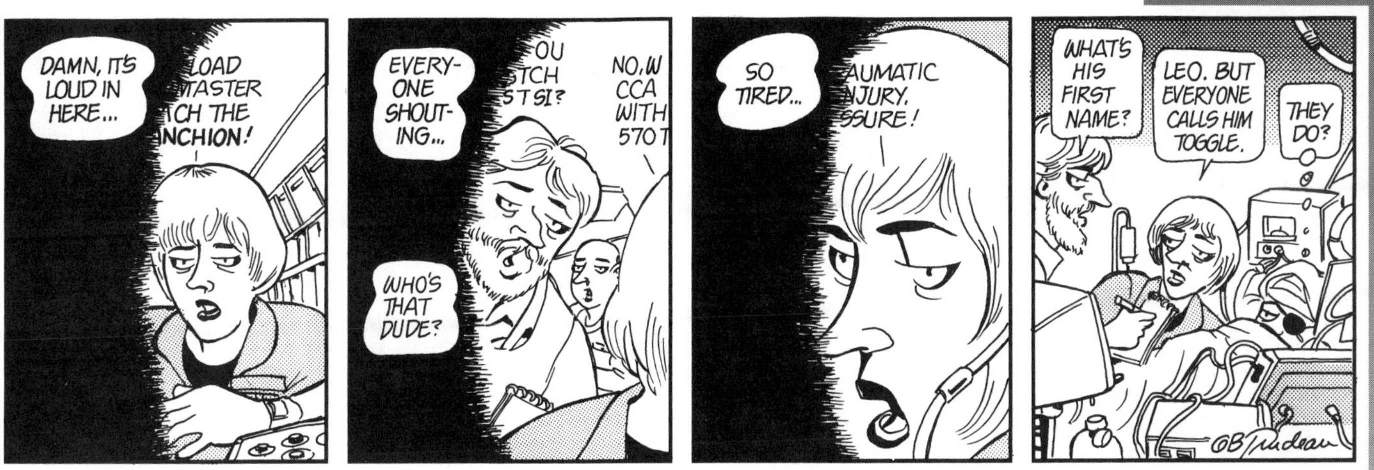

DAMN, IT'S LOUD IN HERE...
LOAD
TASTER
CH THE
ANCHION!
EVERY-ONE SHOUT-ING...
OU
TCH
5 T SI?
NO, W
CCA
WITH
570 T
WHO'S THAT DUDE?
SO TIRED...
AUMATIC
NJURY.
SSURE!
WHAT'S HIS FIRST NAME?
LEO. BUT EVERYONE CALLS HIM TOGGLE.
THEY DO?

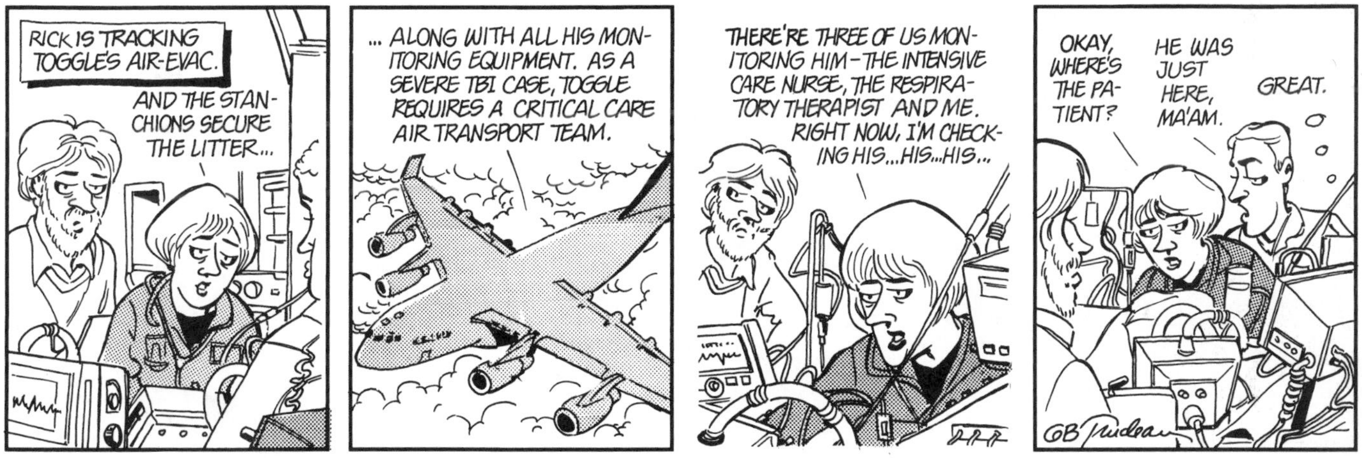

RICK IS TRACKING TOGGLE'S AIR-EVAC.
AND THE STAN-CHIONS SECURE THE LITTER...
... ALONG WITH ALL HIS MON-ITORING EQUIPMENT. AS A SEVERE TBI CASE, TOGGLE REQUIRES A CRITICAL CARE AIR TRANSPORT TEAM.
THERE'RE THREE OF US MON-ITORING HIM—THE INTENSIVE CARE NURSE, THE RESPIRA-TORY THERAPIST AND ME.
RIGHT NOW, I'M CHECK-ING HIS... HIS... HIS...
OKAY, WHERE'S THE PA-TIENT?
HE WAS JUST HERE, MA'AM.
GREAT.

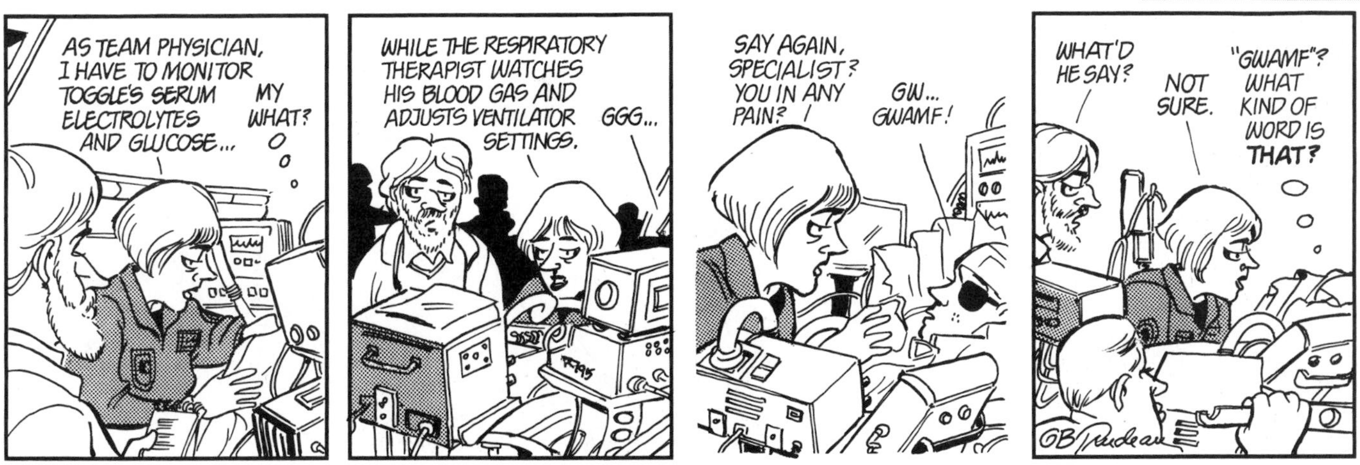

AS TEAM PHYSICIAN, I HAVE TO MONITOR TOGGLE'S SERUM ELECTROLYTES AND GLUCOSE...
MY WHAT?
WHILE THE RESPIRATORY THERAPIST WATCHES HIS BLOOD GAS AND ADJUSTS VENTILATOR SETTINGS.
GGG...
SAY AGAIN, SPECIALIST? YOU IN ANY PAIN?
GW... GWAMF!
WHAT'D HE SAY?
NOT SURE.
"GWAMF"? WHAT KIND OF WORD IS THAT?

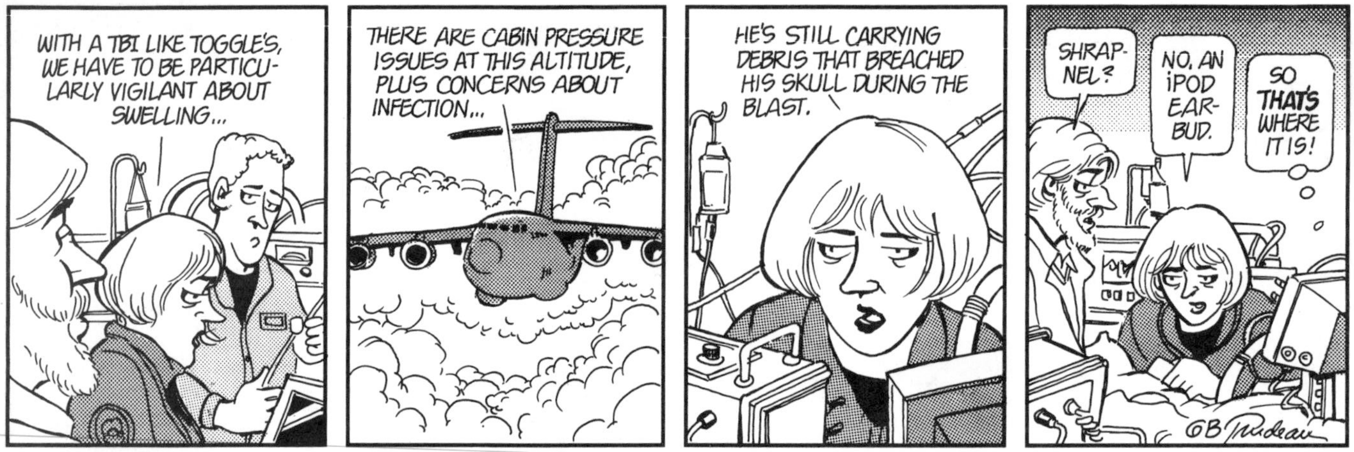
WITH A TBI LIKE TOGGLE'S, WE HAVE TO BE PARTICU-LARLY VIGILANT ABOUT SWELLING...
THERE ARE CABIN PRESSURE ISSUES AT THIS ALTITUDE, PLUS CONCERNS ABOUT INFECTION...
HE'S STILL CARRYING DEBRIS THAT BREACHED HIS SKULL DURING THE BLAST.
SHRAP-NEL?
NO, AN iPOD EAR-BUD.
SO THAT'S WHERE IT IS!
GB Trudeau

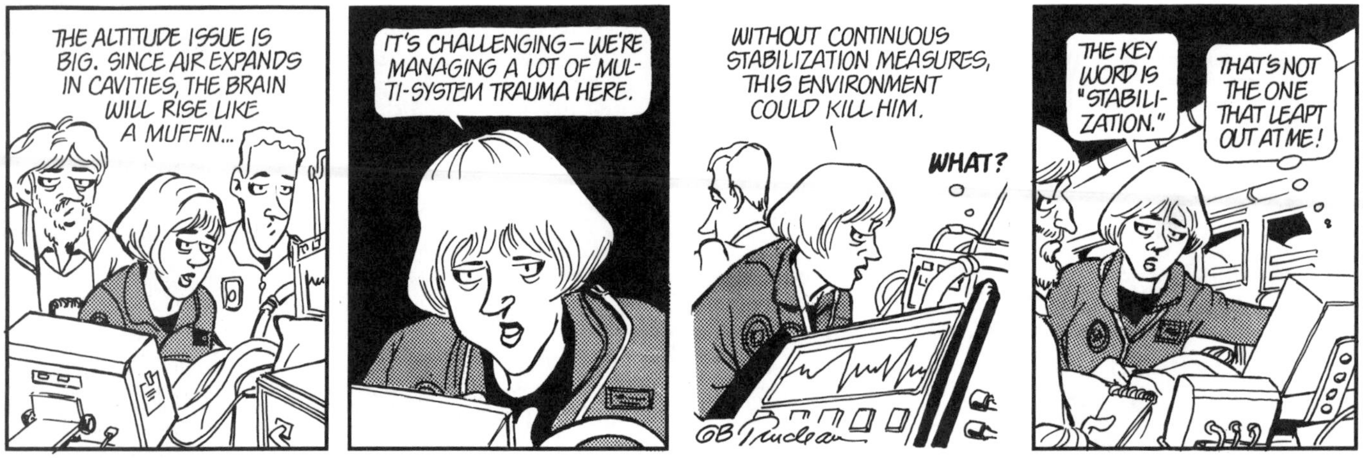
THE ALTITUDE ISSUE IS BIG. SINCE AIR EXPANDS IN CAVITIES, THE BRAIN WILL RISE LIKE A MUFFIN...
IT'S CHALLENGING—WE'RE MANAGING A LOT OF MUL-TI-SYSTEM TRAUMA HERE.
WITHOUT CONTINUOUS STABILIZATION MEASURES, THIS ENVIRONMENT COULD KILL HIM.
WHAT?
GB Trudeau
THE KEY WORD IS "STABILI-ZATION."
THAT'S NOT THE ONE THAT LEAPT OUT AT ME!

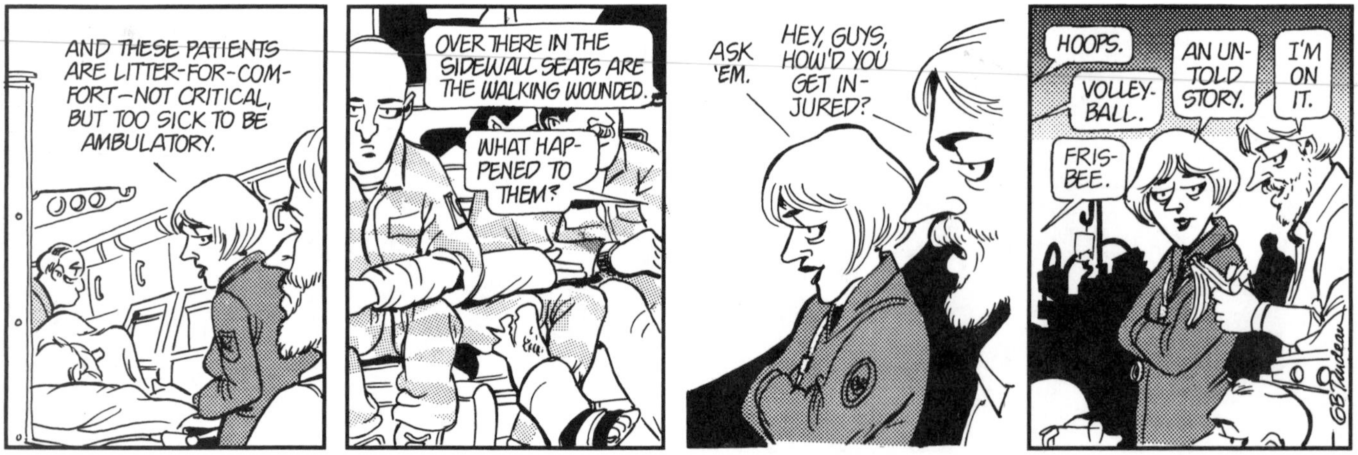
AND THESE PATIENTS ARE LITTER-FOR-COM-FORT—NOT CRITICAL, BUT TOO SICK TO BE AMBULATORY.
OVER THERE IN THE SIDEWALL SEATS ARE THE WALKING WOUNDED.
WHAT HAP-PENED TO THEM?
ASK 'EM.
HEY, GUYS, HOW'D YOU GET IN-JURED?
HOOPS.
VOLLEY-BALL.
FRIS-BEE.
AN UN-TOLD STORY.
I'M ON IT.
GB Trudeau

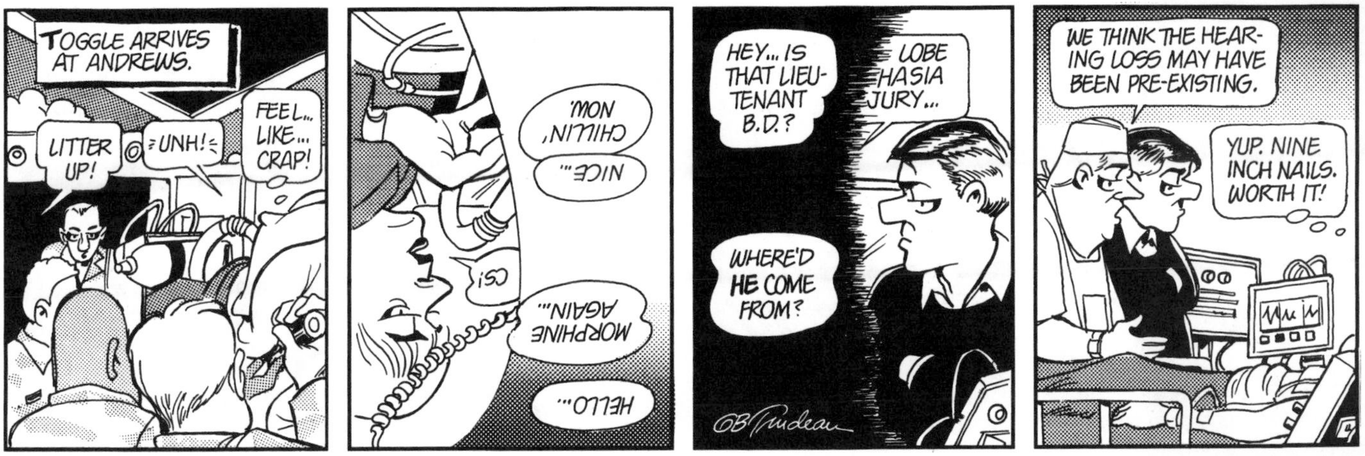
TOGGLE ARRIVES AT ANDREWS.
LITTER UP!
UNH!
FEEL... LIKE... CRAP!
HELLO...
MORPHINE AGAIN...
CS!
NICE...
CHILLIN' NOW.
HEY... IS THAT LIEUTENANT B.D.?
LOBE HASIA JURY...
WHERE'D HE COME FROM?
WE THINK THE HEARING LOSS MAY HAVE BEEN PRE-EXISTING.
YUP. NINE INCH NAILS. WORTH IT!

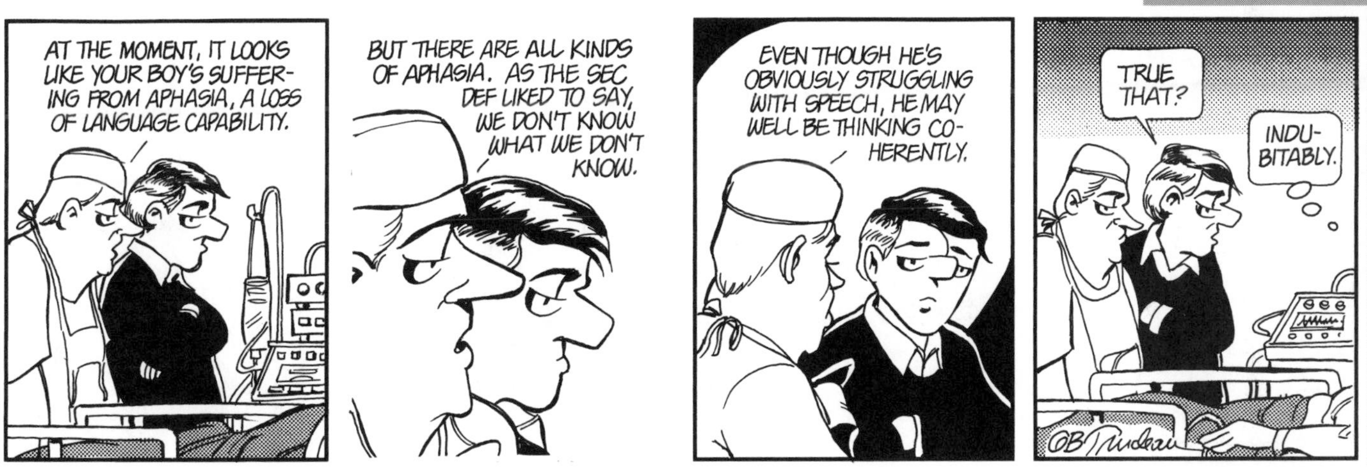
AT THE MOMENT, IT LOOKS LIKE YOUR BOY'S SUFFERING FROM APHASIA, A LOSS OF LANGUAGE CAPABILITY.
BUT THERE ARE ALL KINDS OF APHASIA. AS THE SEC DEF LIKED TO SAY, WE DON'T KNOW WHAT WE DON'T KNOW.
EVEN THOUGH HE'S OBVIOUSLY STRUGGLING WITH SPEECH, HE MAY WELL BE THINKING COHERENTLY.
TRUE THAT?
INDUBITABLY.

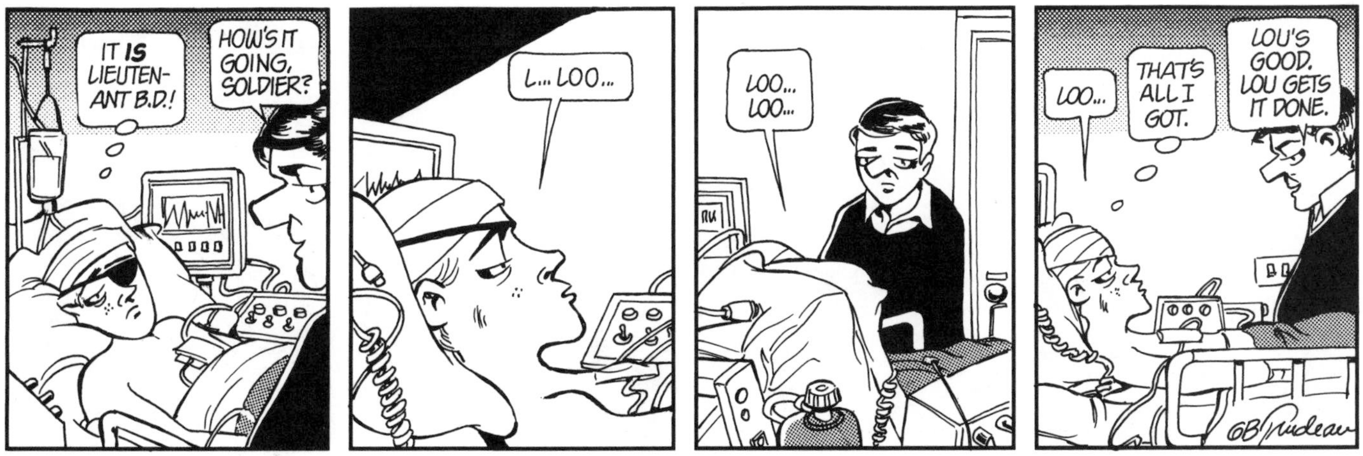
IT IS LIEUTENANT B.D.!
HOW'S IT GOING, SOLDIER?
L... LOO...
LOO... LOO...
LOO...
THAT'S ALL I GOT.
LOU'S GOOD. LOU GETS IT DONE.

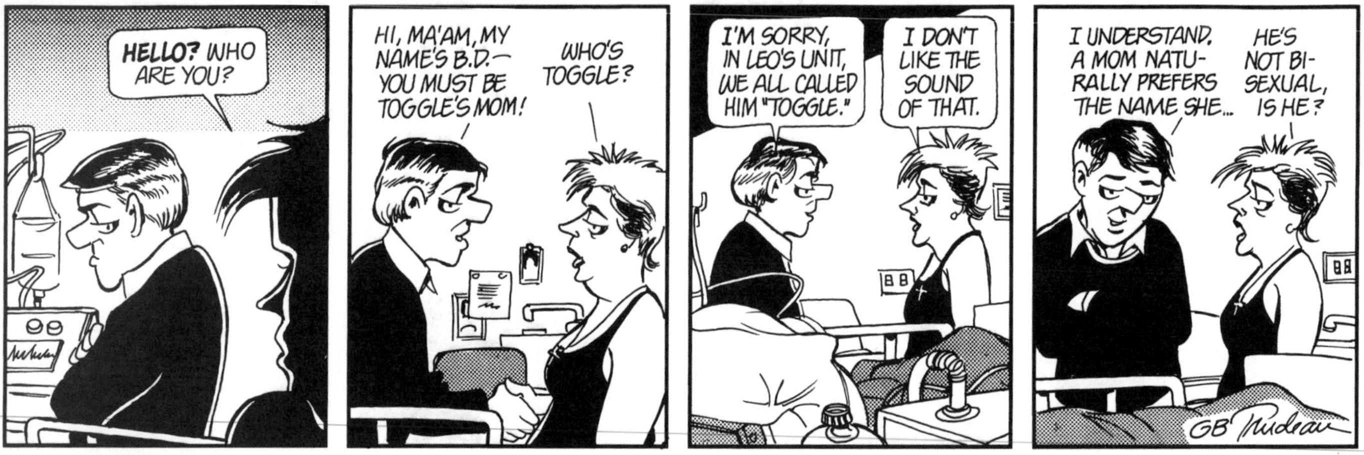
HELLO? WHO ARE YOU?
HI, MA'AM, MY NAME'S B.D.— YOU MUST BE TOGGLE'S MOM!
WHO'S TOGGLE?
I'M SORRY, IN LEO'S UNIT, WE ALL CALLED HIM "TOGGLE."
I DON'T LIKE THE SOUND OF THAT.
I UNDERSTAND. A MOM NATURALLY PREFERS THE NAME SHE...
HE'S NOT BI-SEXUAL, IS HE?
GB Trudeau

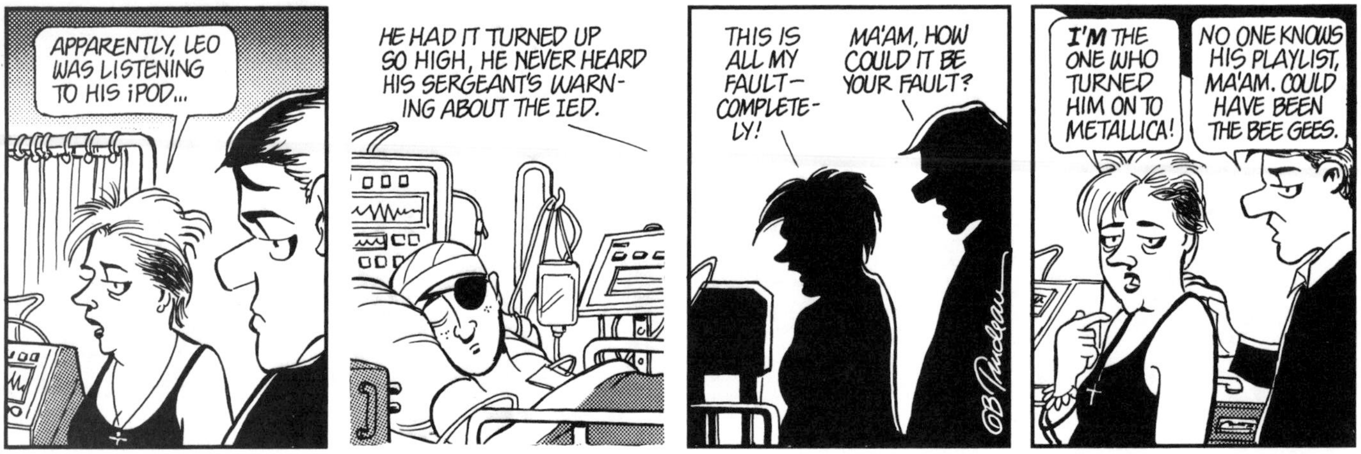
APPARENTLY, LEO WAS LISTENING TO HIS iPOD...
HE HAD IT TURNED UP SO HIGH, HE NEVER HEARD HIS SERGEANT'S WARNING ABOUT THE IED.
THIS IS ALL MY FAULT—COMPLETELY!
MA'AM, HOW COULD IT BE YOUR FAULT?
GB Trudeau
I'M THE ONE WHO TURNED HIM ON TO METALLICA!
NO ONE KNOWS HIS PLAYLIST, MA'AM. COULD HAVE BEEN THE BEE GEES.

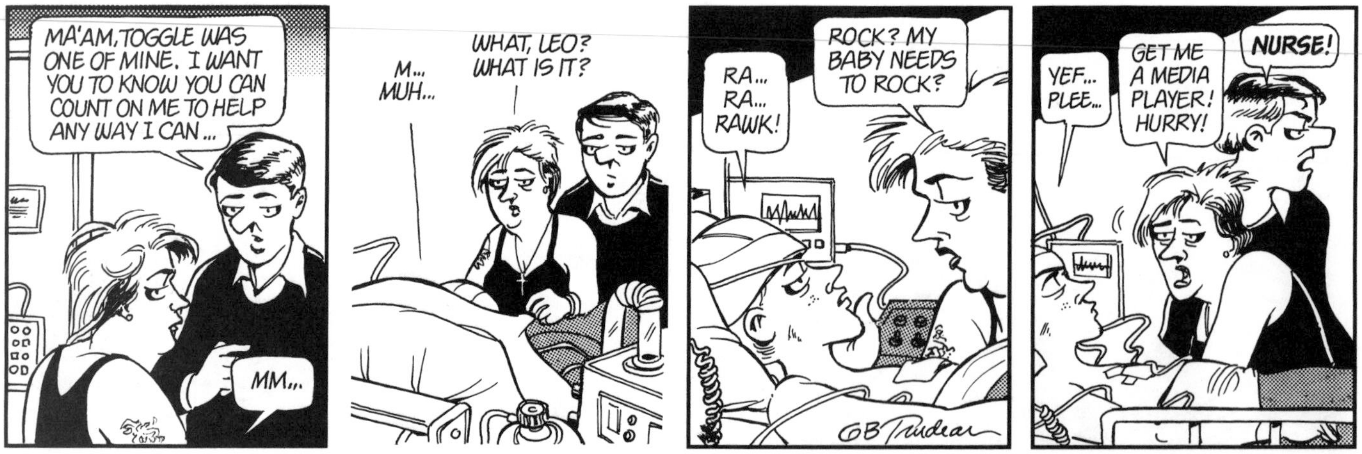
MA'AM, TOGGLE WAS ONE OF MINE. I WANT YOU TO KNOW YOU CAN COUNT ON ME TO HELP ANY WAY I CAN...
MM...
M... MUH...
WHAT, LEO? WHAT IS IT?
RA... RA... RAWK!
ROCK? MY BABY NEEDS TO ROCK?
GB Trudeau
YEF... PLEE...
GET ME A MEDIA PLAYER! HURRY!
NURSE!

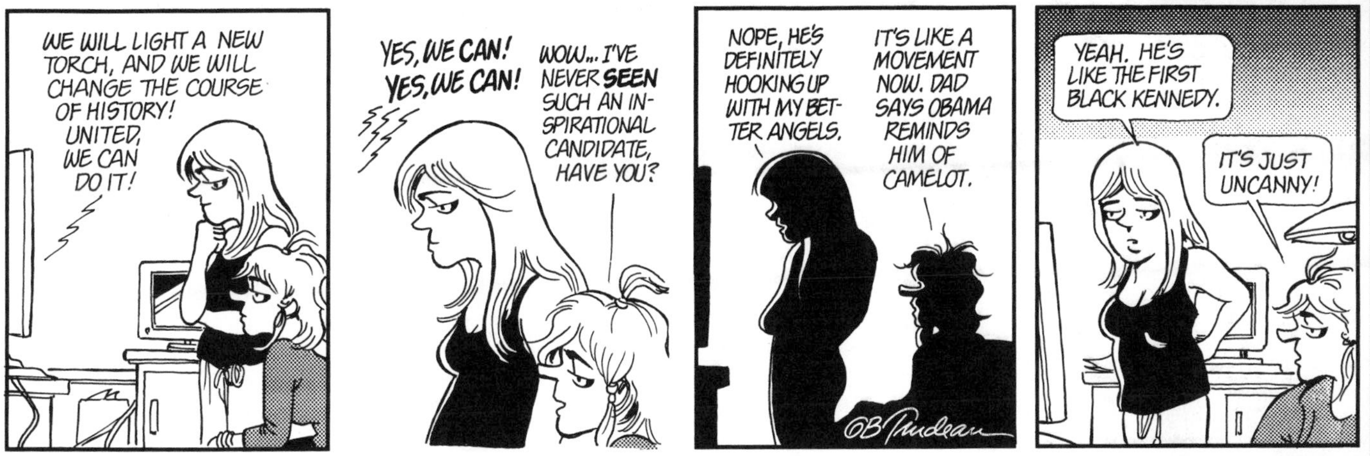
WE WILL LIGHT A NEW TORCH, AND WE WILL CHANGE THE COURSE OF HISTORY! UNITED, WE CAN DO IT!
YES, WE CAN! YES, WE CAN!
WOW... I'VE NEVER SEEN SUCH AN INSPIRATIONAL CANDIDATE, HAVE YOU?
NOPE, HE'S DEFINITELY HOOKING UP WITH MY BETTER ANGELS.
IT'S LIKE A MOVEMENT NOW. DAD SAYS OBAMA REMINDS HIM OF CAMELOT.
GB Trudeau
YEAH. HE'S LIKE THE FIRST BLACK KENNEDY.
IT'S JUST UNCANNY!

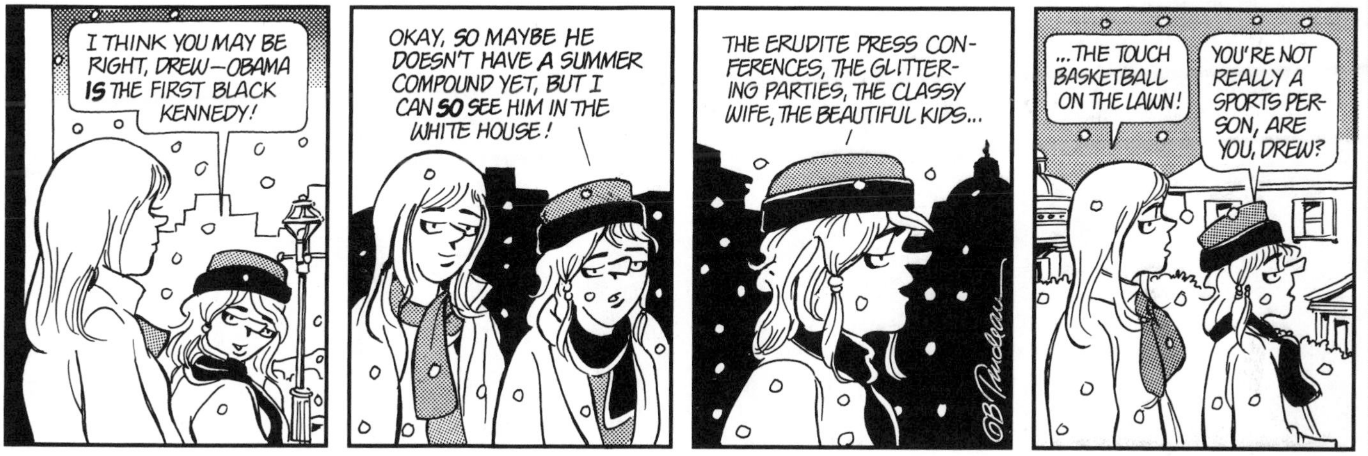
I THINK YOU MAY BE RIGHT, DREW—OBAMA IS THE FIRST BLACK KENNEDY!
OKAY, SO MAYBE HE DOESN'T HAVE A SUMMER COMPOUND YET, BUT I CAN SO SEE HIM IN THE WHITE HOUSE!
THE ERUDITE PRESS CONFERENCES, THE GLITTERING PARTIES, THE CLASSY WIFE, THE BEAUTIFUL KIDS...
GB Trudeau
...THE TOUCH BASKETBALL ON THE LAWN!
YOU'RE NOT REALLY A SPORTS PERSON, ARE YOU, DREW?

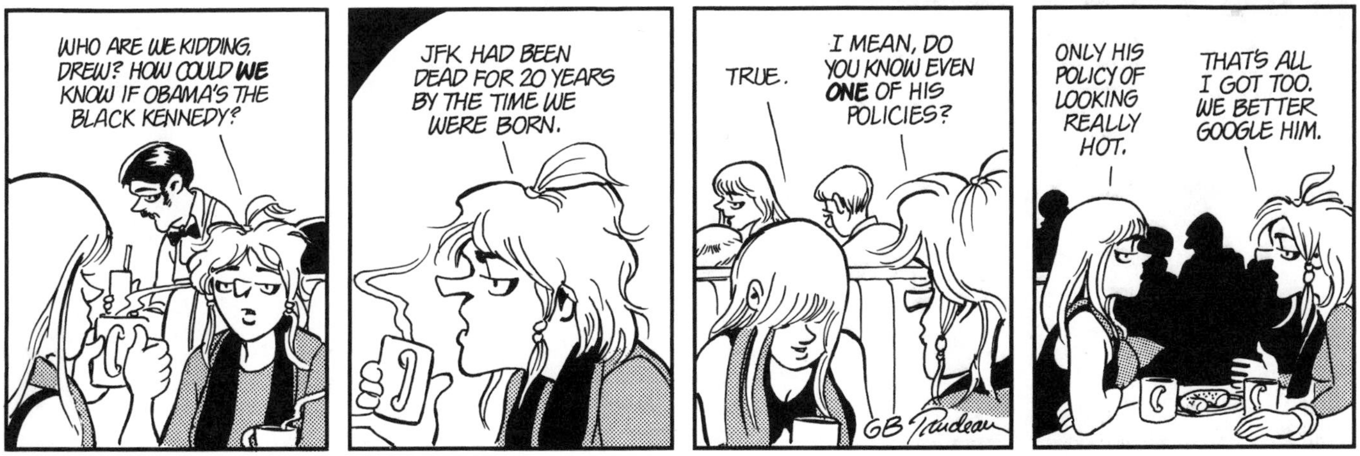
WHO ARE WE KIDDING, DREW? HOW COULD WE KNOW IF OBAMA'S THE BLACK KENNEDY?
JFK HAD BEEN DEAD FOR 20 YEARS BY THE TIME WE WERE BORN.
TRUE.
I MEAN, DO YOU KNOW EVEN ONE OF HIS POLICIES?
GB Trudeau
ONLY HIS POLICY OF LOOKING REALLY HOT.
THAT'S ALL I GOT TOO. WE BETTER GOOGLE HIM.

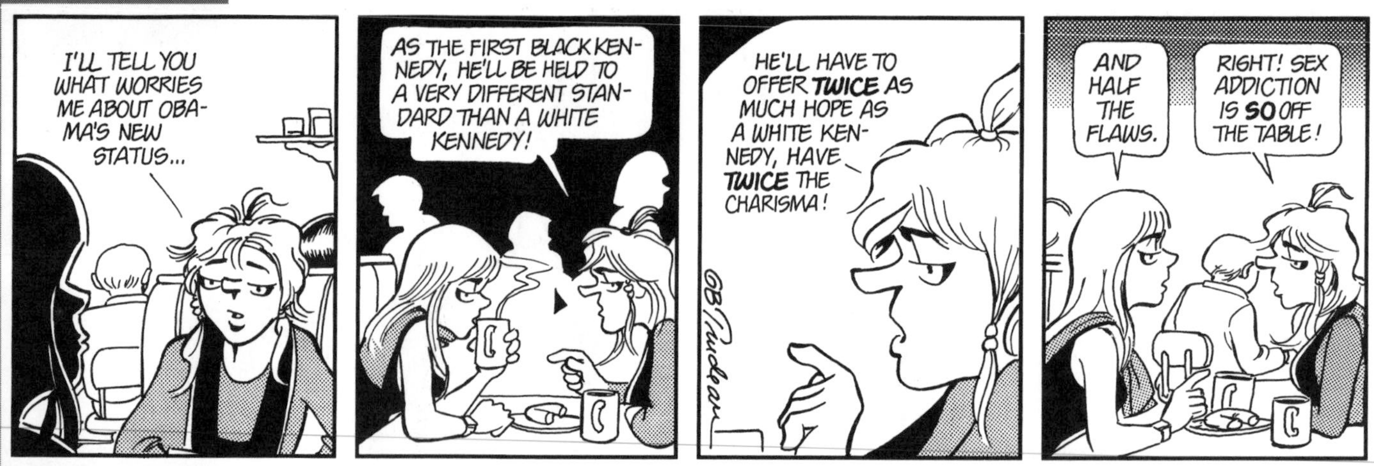
I'LL TELL YOU WHAT WORRIES ME ABOUT OBA-MA'S NEW STATUS...
AS THE FIRST BLACK KEN-NEDY, HE'LL BE HELD TO A VERY DIFFERENT STAN-DARD THAN A WHITE KENNEDY!
HE'LL HAVE TO OFFER **TWICE** AS MUCH HOPE AS A WHITE KEN-NEDY, HAVE **TWICE** THE CHARISMA!
AND HALF THE FLAWS.
RIGHT! SEX ADDICTION IS **SO** OFF THE TABLE!

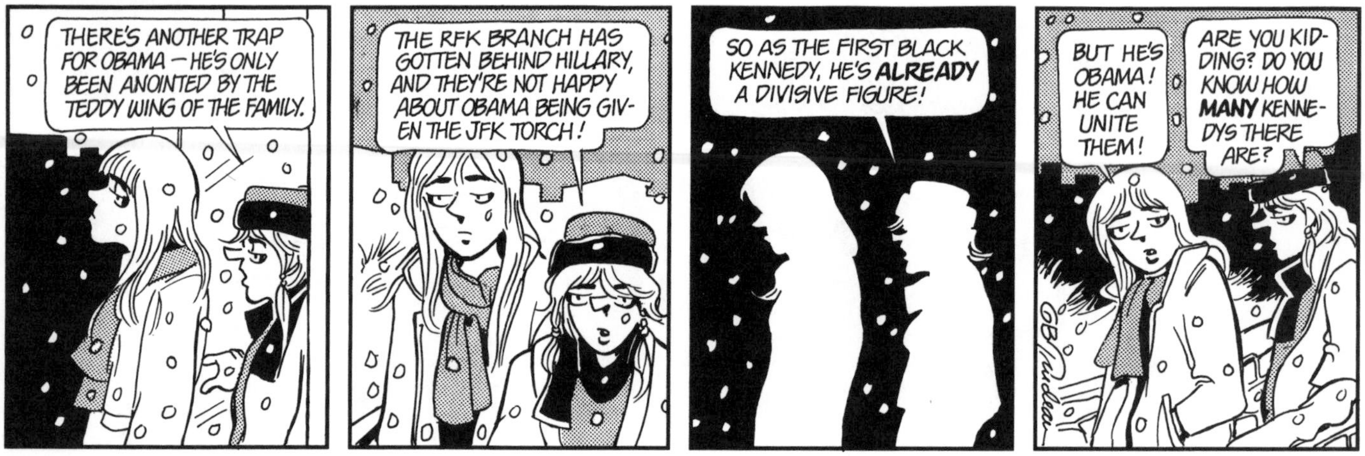
THERE'S ANOTHER TRAP FOR OBAMA — HE'S ONLY BEEN ANOINTED BY THE TEDDY WING OF THE FAMILY.
THE RFK BRANCH HAS GOTTEN BEHIND HILLARY, AND THEY'RE NOT HAPPY ABOUT OBAMA BEING GIV-EN THE JFK TORCH!
SO AS THE FIRST BLACK KENNEDY, HE'S **ALREADY** A DIVISIVE FIGURE!
BUT HE'S OBAMA! HE CAN UNITE THEM!
ARE YOU KID-DING? DO YOU KNOW HOW **MANY** KENNE-DYS THERE ARE?

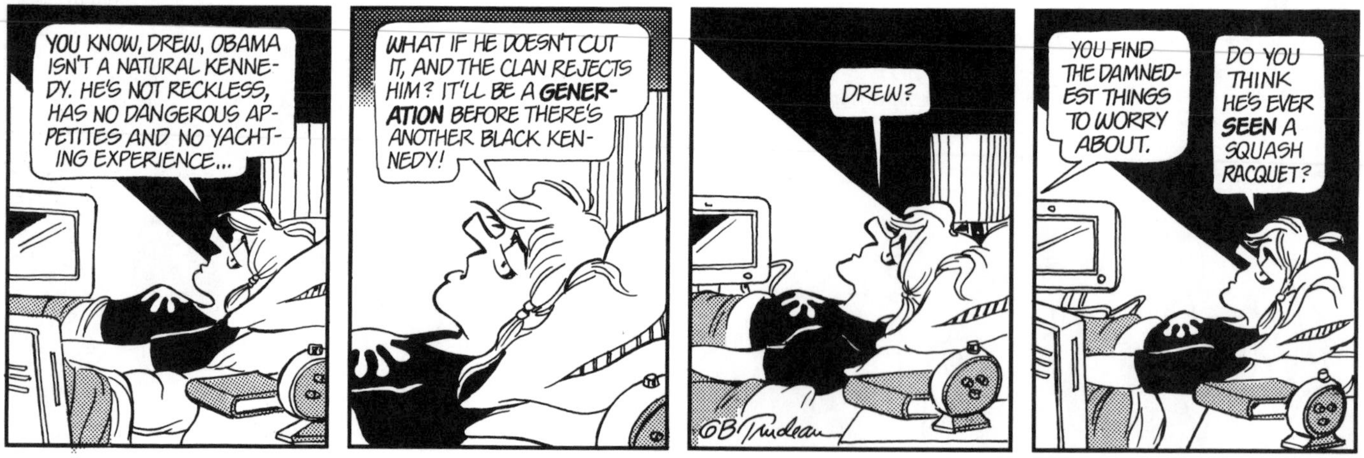
YOU KNOW, DREW, OBAMA ISN'T A NATURAL KENNE-DY. HE'S NOT RECKLESS, HAS NO DANGEROUS AP-PETITES AND NO YACHT-ING EXPERIENCE...
WHAT IF HE DOESN'T CUT IT, AND THE CLAN REJECTS HIM? IT'LL BE A **GENER-ATION** BEFORE THERE'S ANOTHER BLACK KEN-NEDY!
DREW?
YOU FIND THE DAMNED-EST THINGS TO WORRY ABOUT.
DO YOU THINK HE'S EVER **SEEN** A SQUASH RACQUET?

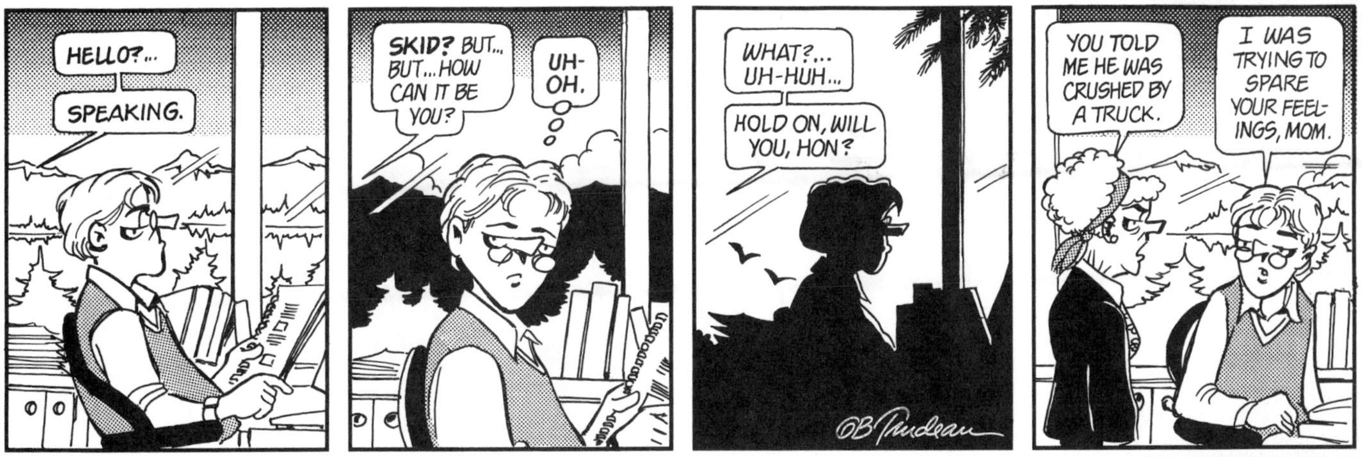
HELLO?...
SPEAKING.
SKID? BUT... BUT... HOW CAN IT BE YOU?
UH-OH.
WHAT?... UH-HUH...
HOLD ON, WILL YOU, HON?
YOU TOLD ME HE WAS CRUSHED BY A TRUCK.
I WAS TRYING TO SPARE YOUR FEELINGS, MOM.

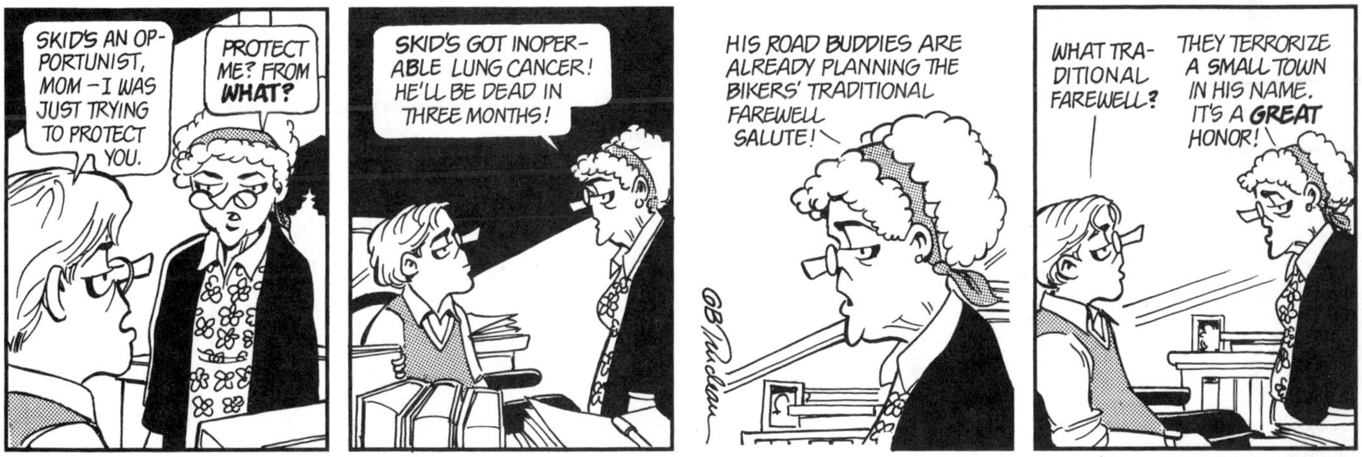
SKID'S AN OPPORTUNIST, MOM – I WAS JUST TRYING TO PROTECT YOU.
PROTECT ME? FROM WHAT?
SKID'S GOT INOPERABLE LUNG CANCER! HE'LL BE DEAD IN THREE MONTHS!
HIS ROAD BUDDIES ARE ALREADY PLANNING THE BIKERS' TRADITIONAL FAREWELL SALUTE!
WHAT TRADITIONAL FAREWELL?
THEY TERRORIZE A SMALL TOWN IN HIS NAME. IT'S A GREAT HONOR!

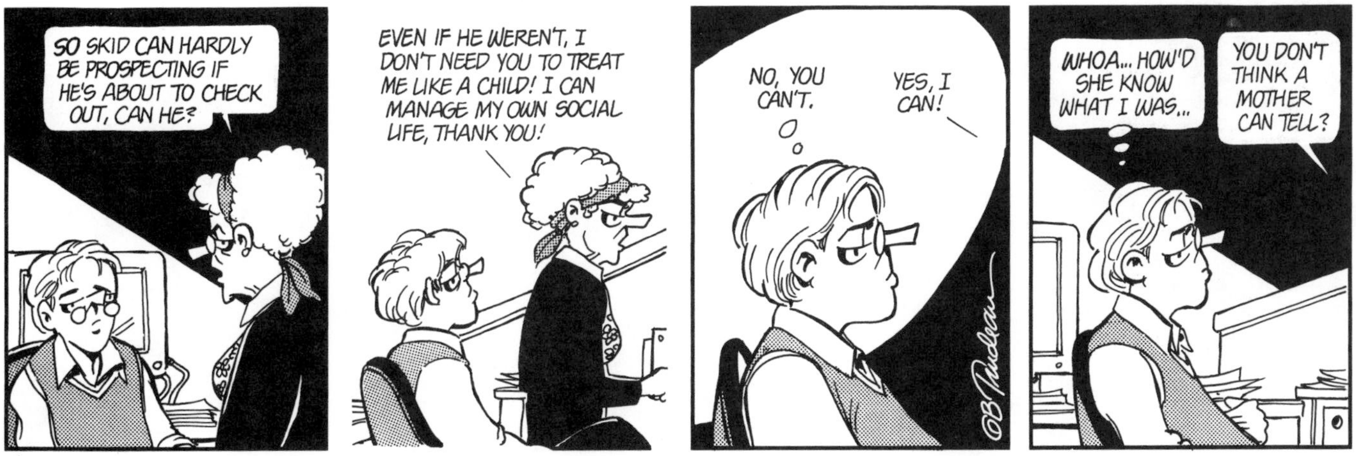
SO SKID CAN HARDLY BE PROSPECTING IF HE'S ABOUT TO CHECK OUT, CAN HE?
EVEN IF HE WEREN'T, I DON'T NEED YOU TO TREAT ME LIKE A CHILD! I CAN MANAGE MY OWN SOCIAL LIFE, THANK YOU!
NO, YOU CAN'T.
YES, I CAN!
WHOA... HOW'D SHE KNOW WHAT I WAS...
YOU DON'T THINK A MOTHER CAN TELL?

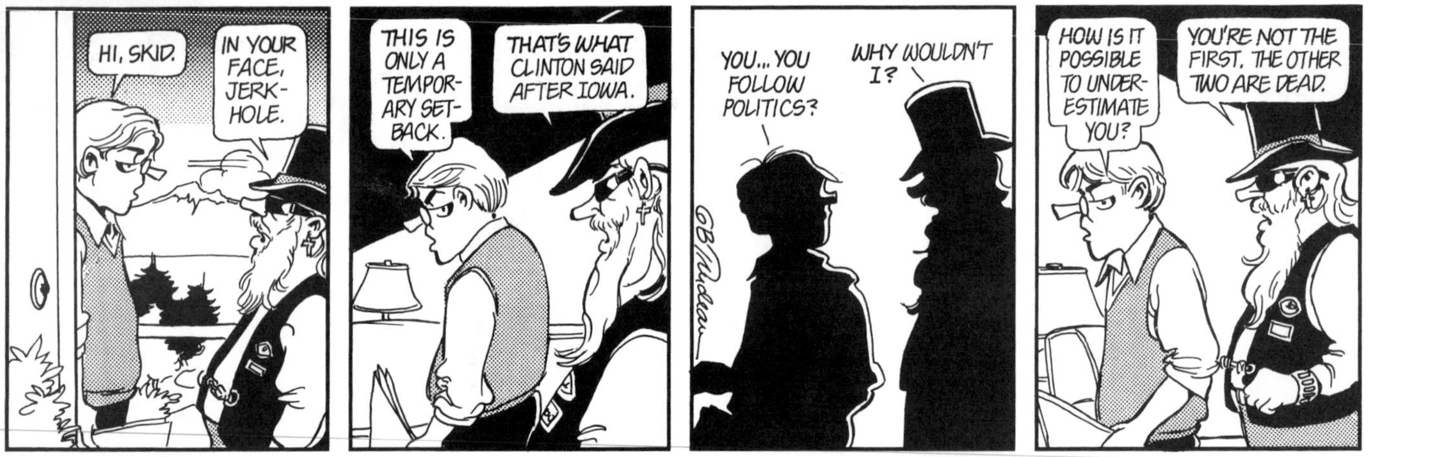
HI, SKID.
IN YOUR FACE, JERK-HOLE.
THIS IS ONLY A TEMPOR-ARY SET-BACK.
THAT'S WHAT CLINTON SAID AFTER IOWA.
YOU... YOU FOLLOW POLITICS?
WHY WOULDN'T I?
HOW IS IT POSSIBLE TO UNDER-ESTIMATE YOU?
YOU'RE NOT THE FIRST. THE OTHER TWO ARE DEAD.

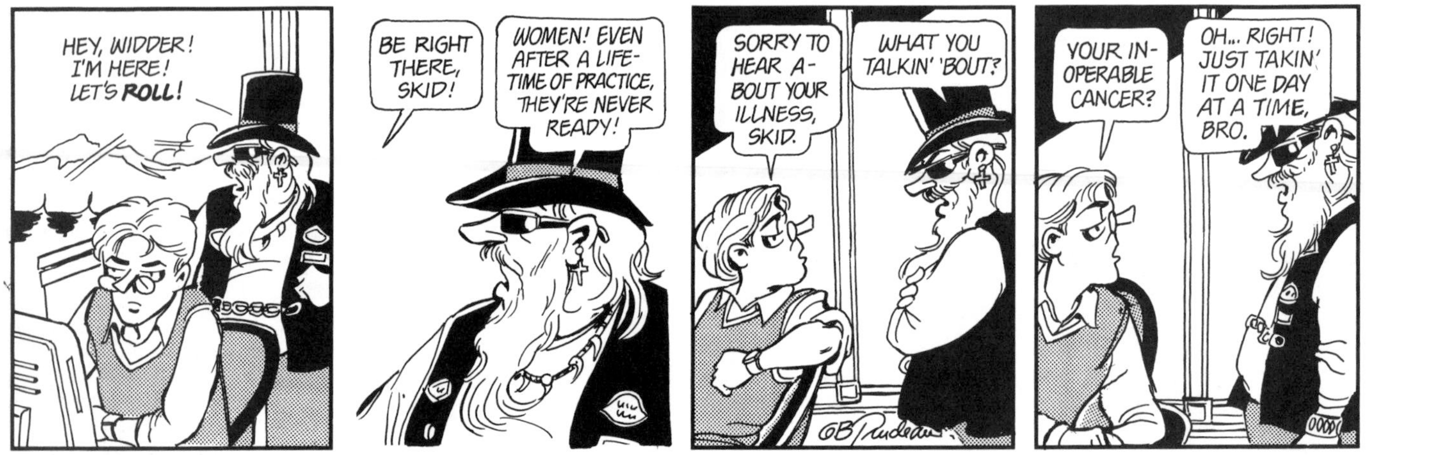
HEY, WIDDER! I'M HERE! LET'S **ROLL**!
BE RIGHT THERE, SKID!
WOMEN! EVEN AFTER A LIFE-TIME OF PRACTICE, THEY'RE NEVER READY!
SORRY TO HEAR A-BOUT YOUR ILLNESS, SKID.
WHAT YOU TALKIN' 'BOUT?
YOUR IN-OPERABLE CANCER?
OH... RIGHT! JUST TAKIN' IT ONE DAY AT A TIME, BRO.

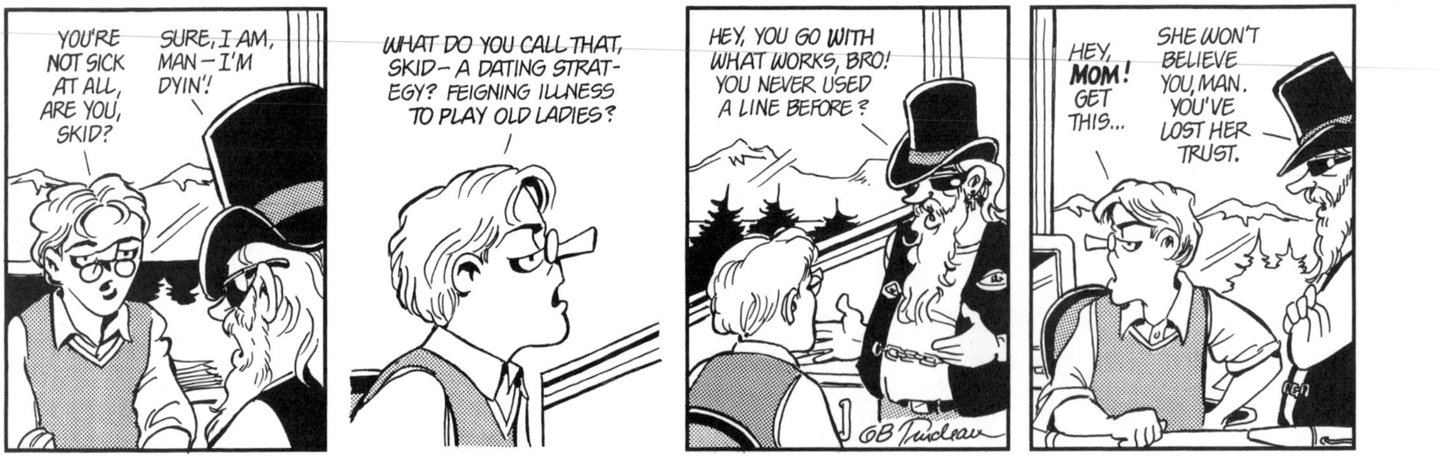
YOU'RE NOT SICK AT ALL, ARE YOU, SKID?
SURE, I AM, MAN – I'M DYIN'!
WHAT DO YOU CALL THAT, SKID – A DATING STRAT-EGY? FEIGNING ILLNESS TO PLAY OLD LADIES?
HEY, YOU GO **WITH** WHAT WORKS, BRO! YOU NEVER USED A LINE BEFORE?
HEY, **MOM**! GET THIS...
SHE WON'T BELIEVE YOU, MAN. YOU'VE LOST HER TRUST.

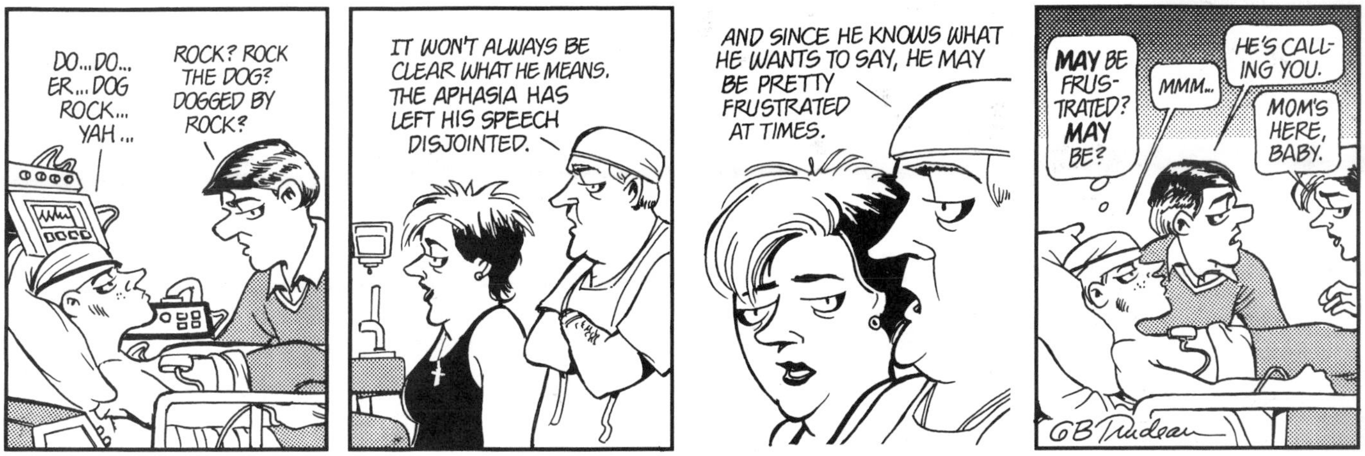
DO... DO... ER... DOG ROCK... YAH...
ROCK? ROCK THE DOG? DOGGED BY ROCK?
IT WON'T ALWAYS BE CLEAR WHAT HE MEANS. THE APHASIA HAS LEFT HIS SPEECH DISJOINTED.
AND SINCE HE KNOWS WHAT HE WANTS TO SAY, HE MAY BE PRETTY FRUSTRATED AT TIMES.
MAY BE FRUS-TRATED? MAY BE?
MMM...
HE'S CALL-ING YOU.
MOM'S HERE, BABY.
©B Trudeau

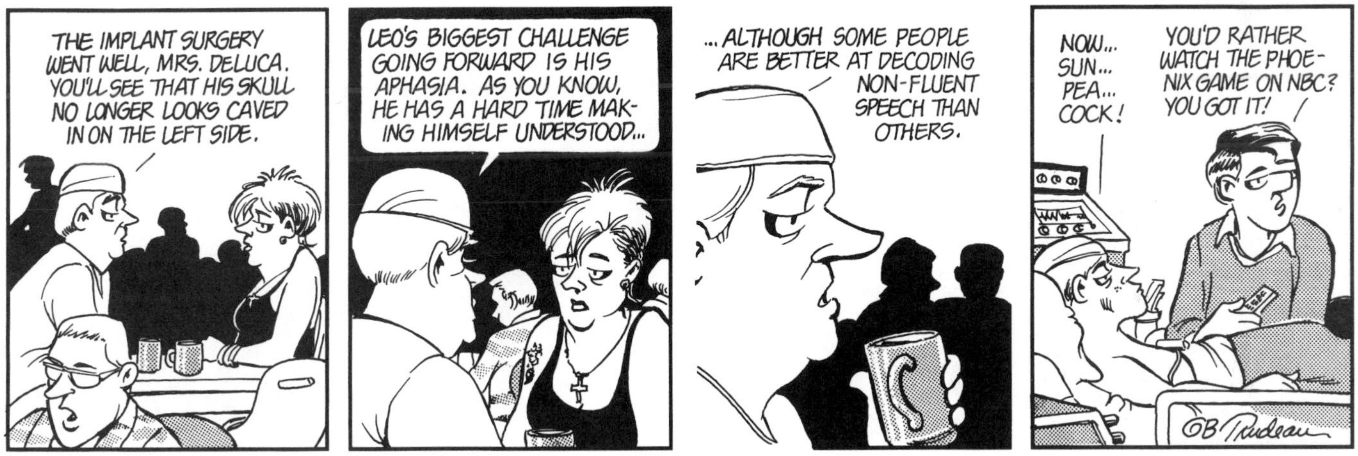
THE IMPLANT SURGERY WENT WELL, MRS. DELUCA. YOU'LL SEE THAT HIS SKULL NO LONGER LOOKS CAVED IN ON THE LEFT SIDE.
LEO'S BIGGEST CHALLENGE GOING FORWARD IS HIS APHASIA. AS YOU KNOW, HE HAS A HARD TIME MAK-ING HIMSELF UNDERSTOOD...
...ALTHOUGH SOME PEOPLE ARE BETTER AT DECODING NON-FLUENT SPEECH THAN OTHERS.
NOW... SUN... PEA... COCK!
YOU'D RATHER WATCH THE PHOE-NIX GAME ON NBC? YOU GOT IT!
©B Trudeau

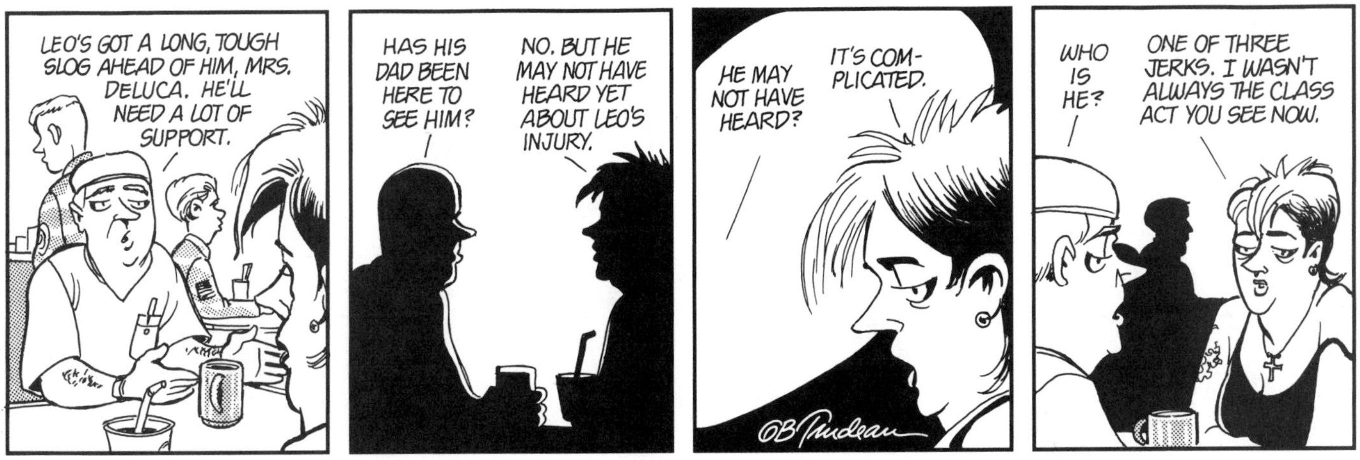
LEO'S GOT A LONG, TOUGH SLOG AHEAD OF HIM, MRS. DELUCA. HE'LL NEED A LOT OF SUPPORT.
HAS HIS DAD BEEN HERE TO SEE HIM?
NO. BUT HE MAY NOT HAVE HEARD YET ABOUT LEO'S INJURY.
HE MAY NOT HAVE HEARD?
IT'S COM-PLICATED.
WHO IS HE?
ONE OF THREE JERKS. I WASN'T ALWAYS THE CLASS ACT YOU SEE NOW.
©B Trudeau

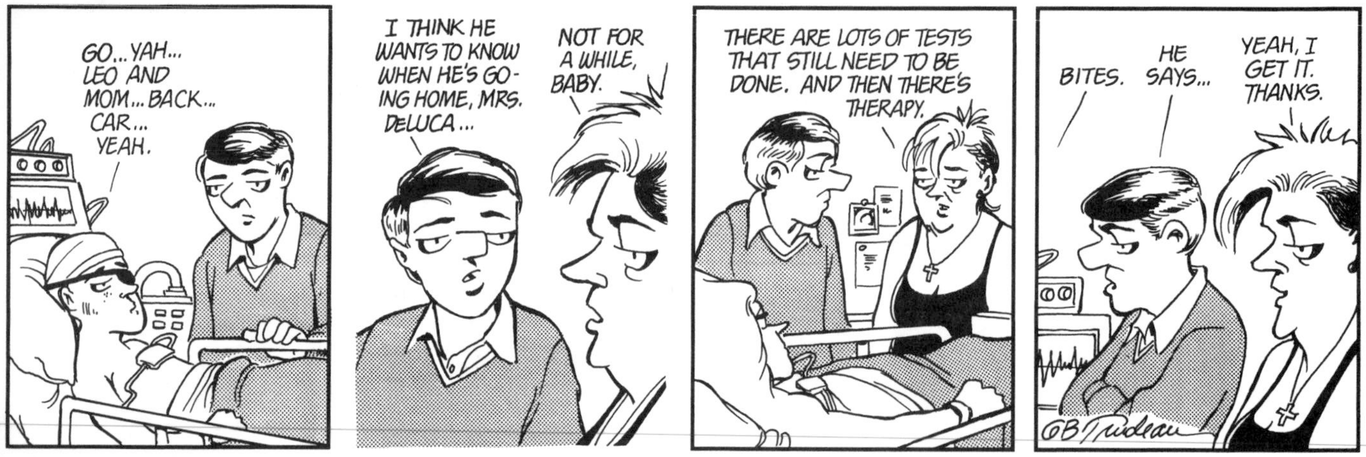
GO... YAH... LEO AND MOM... BACK... CAR... YEAH.
I THINK HE WANTS TO KNOW WHEN HE'S GOING HOME, MRS. DELUCA...
NOT FOR A WHILE, BABY.
THERE ARE LOTS OF TESTS THAT STILL NEED TO BE DONE. AND THEN THERE'S THERAPY.
BITES.
HE SAYS...
YEAH, I GET IT. THANKS.
GB Trudeau

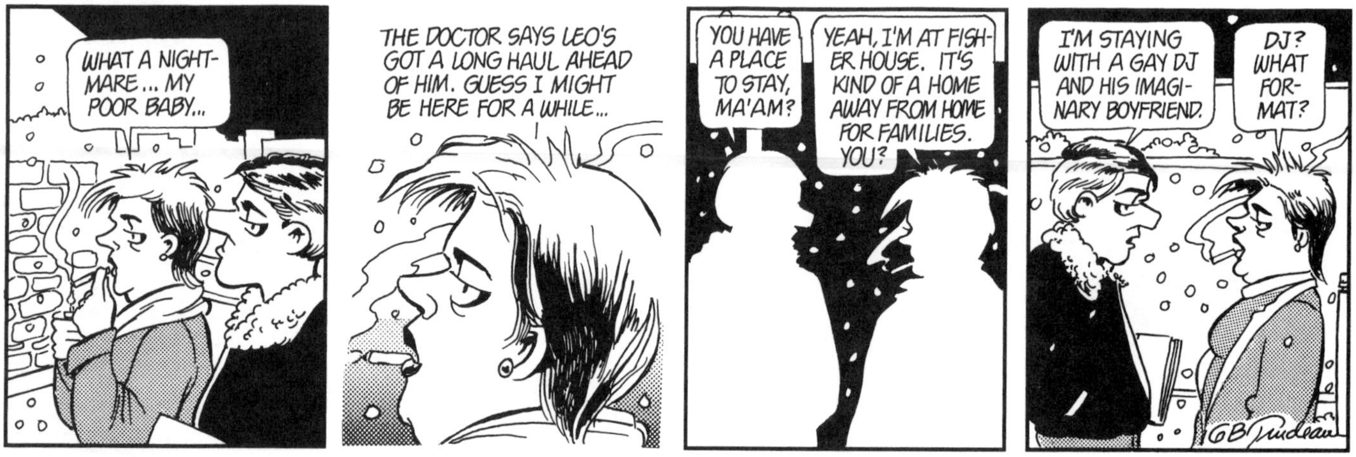
WHAT A NIGHTMARE... MY POOR BABY...
THE DOCTOR SAYS LEO'S GOT A LONG HAUL AHEAD OF HIM. GUESS I MIGHT BE HERE FOR A WHILE...
YOU HAVE A PLACE TO STAY, MA'AM?
YEAH, I'M AT FISHER HOUSE. IT'S KIND OF A HOME AWAY FROM HOME FOR FAMILIES. YOU?
I'M STAYING WITH A GAY DJ AND HIS IMAGINARY BOYFRIEND.
DJ? WHAT FORMAT?
GB Trudeau

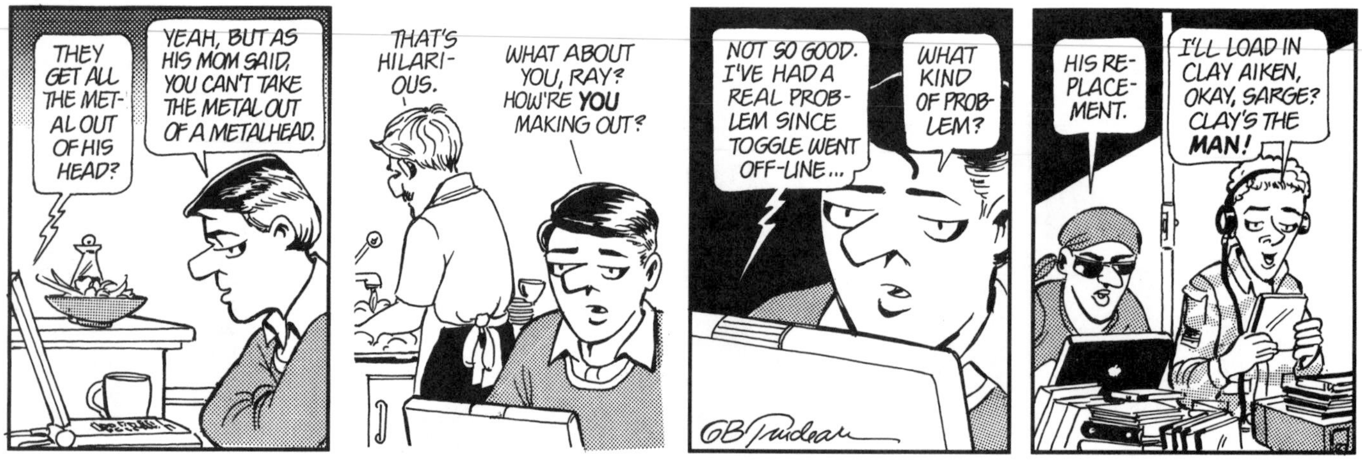
THEY GET ALL THE METAL OUT OF HIS HEAD?
YEAH, BUT AS HIS MOM SAID, YOU CAN'T TAKE THE METAL OUT OF A METALHEAD.
THAT'S HILARIOUS.
WHAT ABOUT YOU, RAY? HOW'RE **YOU** MAKING OUT?
NOT SO GOOD. I'VE HAD A REAL PROBLEM SINCE TOGGLE WENT OFF-LINE...
WHAT KIND OF PROBLEM?
GB Trudeau
HIS REPLACEMENT.
I'LL LOAD IN CLAY AIKEN, OKAY, SARGE? CLAY'S THE **MAN!**

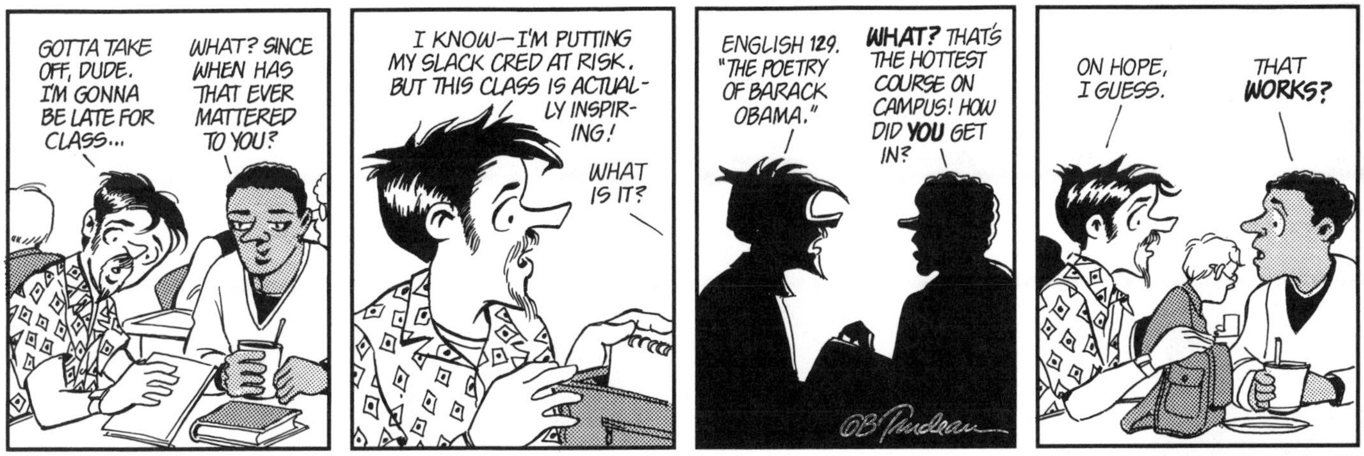
GOTTA TAKE OFF, DUDE. I'M GONNA BE LATE FOR CLASS...
WHAT? SINCE WHEN HAS THAT EVER MATTERED TO YOU?
I KNOW—I'M PUTTING MY SLACK CRED AT RISK. BUT THIS CLASS IS ACTUALLY INSPIRING!
WHAT IS IT?
ENGLISH 129. "THE POETRY OF BARACK OBAMA."
WHAT? THAT'S THE HOTTEST COURSE ON CAMPUS! HOW DID YOU GET IN?
ON HOPE, I GUESS.
THAT WORKS?

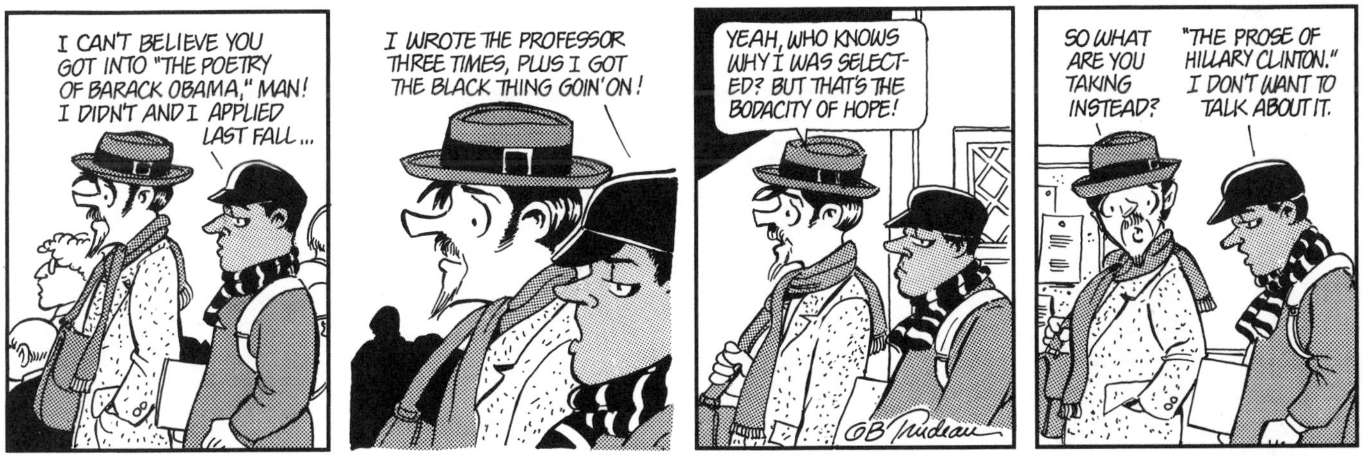
I CAN'T BELIEVE YOU GOT INTO "THE POETRY OF BARACK OBAMA," MAN! I DIDN'T AND I APPLIED LAST FALL...
I WROTE THE PROFESSOR THREE TIMES, PLUS I GOT THE BLACK THING GOIN' ON!
YEAH, WHO KNOWS WHY I WAS SELECTED? BUT THAT'S THE BODACITY OF HOPE!
SO WHAT ARE YOU TAKING INSTEAD?
"THE PROSE OF HILLARY CLINTON." I DON'T WANT TO TALK ABOUT IT.

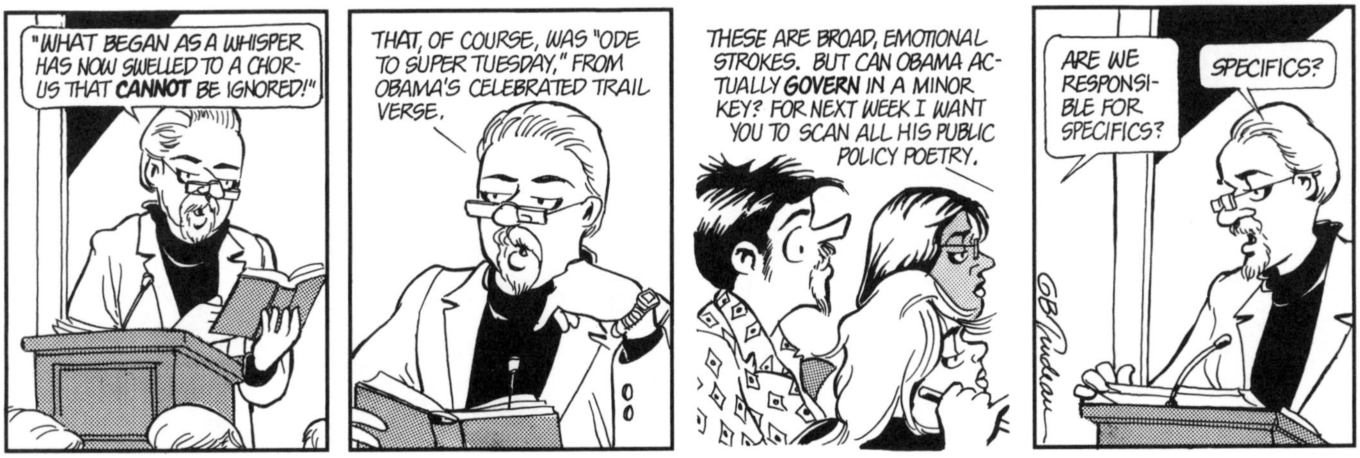
"WHAT BEGAN AS A WHISPER HAS NOW SWELLED TO A CHORUS THAT CANNOT BE IGNORED!"
THAT, OF COURSE, WAS "ODE TO SUPER TUESDAY," FROM OBAMA'S CELEBRATED TRAIL VERSE.
THESE ARE BROAD, EMOTIONAL STROKES. BUT CAN OBAMA ACTUALLY GOVERN IN A MINOR KEY? FOR NEXT WEEK I WANT YOU TO SCAN ALL HIS PUBLIC POLICY POETRY.
ARE WE RESPONSIBLE FOR SPECIFICS?
SPECIFICS?

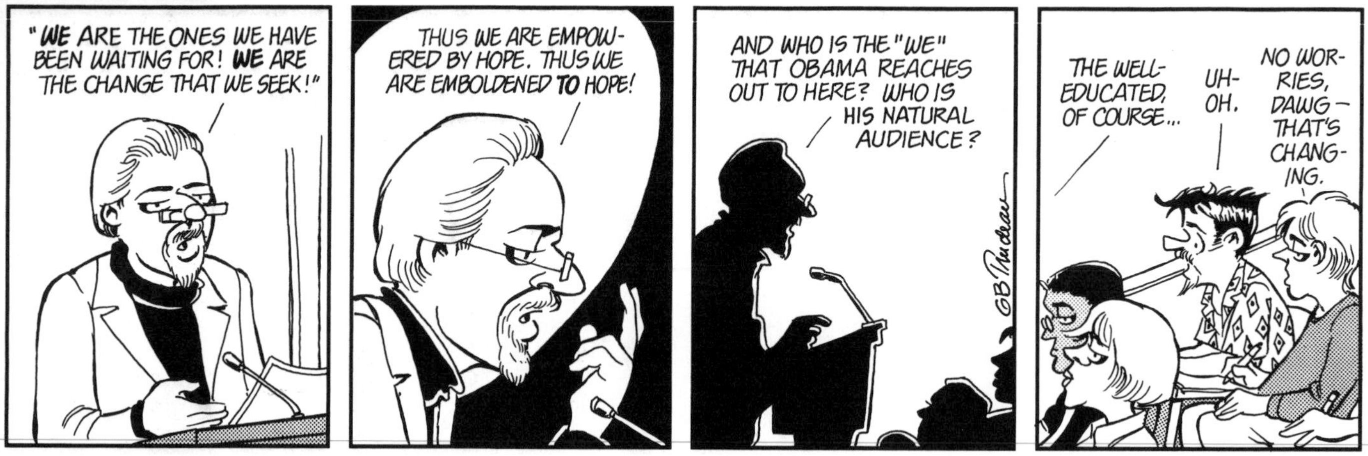
"WE ARE THE ONES WE HAVE BEEN WAITING FOR! WE ARE THE CHANGE THAT WE SEEK!"
THUS WE ARE EMPOWERED BY HOPE. THUS WE ARE EMBOLDENED TO HOPE!
AND WHO IS THE "WE" THAT OBAMA REACHES OUT TO HERE? WHO IS HIS NATURAL AUDIENCE?
THE WELL-EDUCATED, OF COURSE...
UH-OH.
NO WORRIES, DAWG—THAT'S CHANGING.

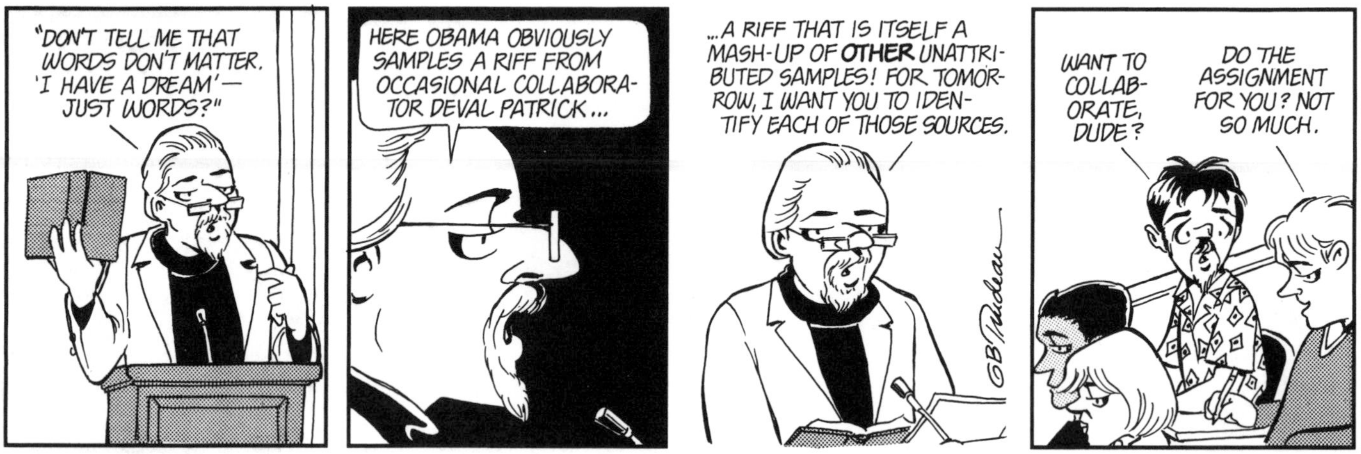
"DON'T TELL ME THAT WORDS DON'T MATTER. 'I HAVE A DREAM'—JUST WORDS?"
HERE OBAMA OBVIOUSLY SAMPLES A RIFF FROM OCCASIONAL COLLABORATOR DEVAL PATRICK...
...A RIFF THAT IS ITSELF A MASH-UP OF OTHER UNATTRIBUTED SAMPLES! FOR TOMORROW, I WANT YOU TO IDENTIFY EACH OF THOSE SOURCES.
WANT TO COLLABORATE, DUDE?
DO THE ASSIGNMENT FOR YOU? NOT SO MUCH.

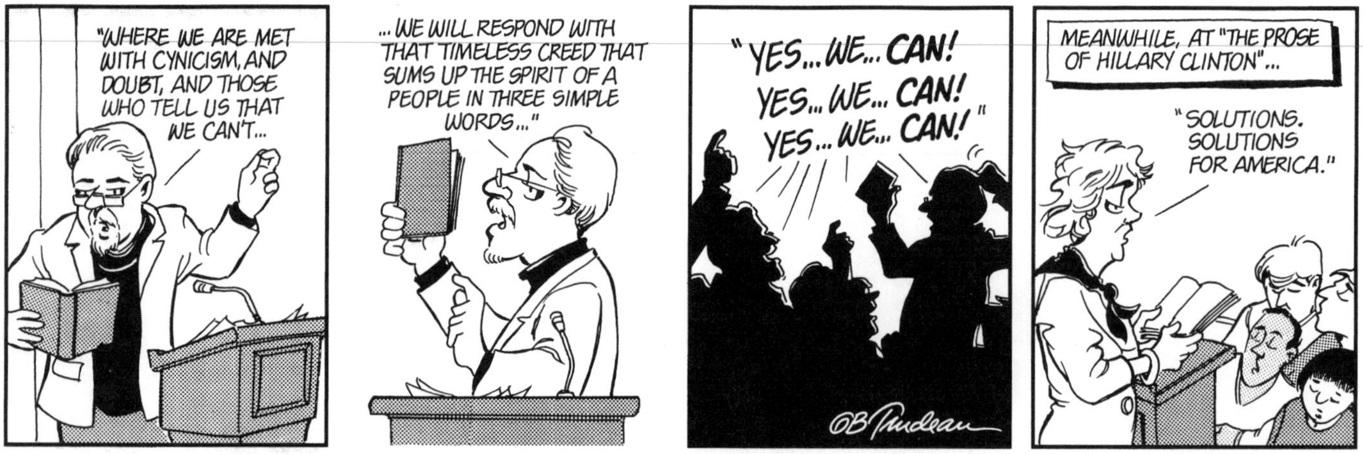
"WHERE WE ARE MET WITH CYNICISM, AND DOUBT, AND THOSE WHO TELL US THAT WE CAN'T...
...WE WILL RESPOND WITH THAT TIMELESS CREED THAT SUMS UP THE SPIRIT OF A PEOPLE IN THREE SIMPLE WORDS..."
"YES... WE... CAN! YES... WE... CAN! YES... WE... CAN!"
MEANWHILE, AT "THE PROSE OF HILLARY CLINTON"...
"SOLUTIONS. SOLUTIONS FOR AMERICA."

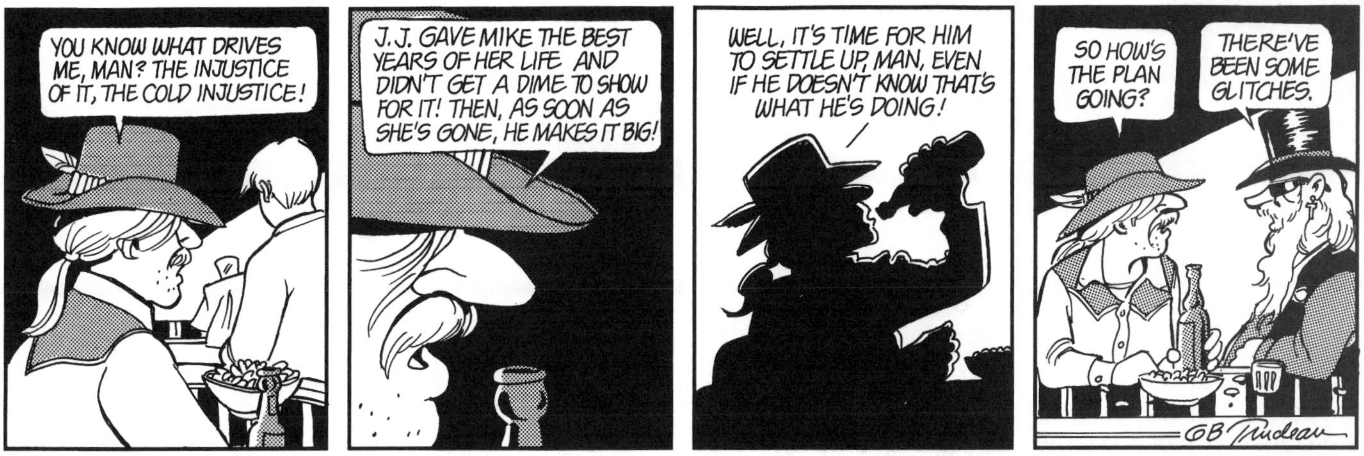
YOU KNOW WHAT DRIVES ME, MAN? THE INJUSTICE OF IT, THE COLD INJUSTICE!
J. J. GAVE MIKE THE BEST YEARS OF HER LIFE AND DIDN'T GET A DIME TO SHOW FOR IT! THEN, AS SOON AS SHE'S GONE, HE MAKES IT BIG!
WELL, IT'S TIME FOR HIM TO SETTLE UP, MAN, EVEN IF HE DOESN'T KNOW THAT'S WHAT HE'S DOING!
SO HOW'S THE PLAN GOING?
THERE'VE BEEN SOME GLITCHES.

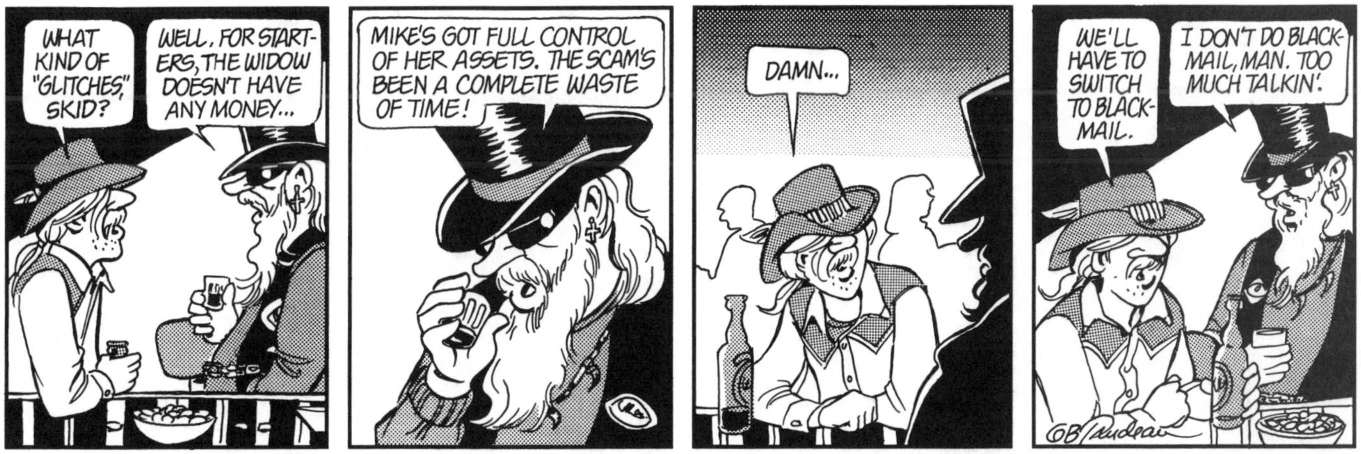
WHAT KIND OF "GLITCHES," SKID?
WELL, FOR STARTERS, THE WIDOW DOESN'T HAVE ANY MONEY...
MIKE'S GOT FULL CONTROL OF HER ASSETS. THE SCAM'S BEEN A COMPLETE WASTE OF TIME!
DAMN...
WE'LL HAVE TO SWITCH TO BLACKMAIL.
I DON'T DO BLACKMAIL, MAN. TOO MUCH TALKIN'.

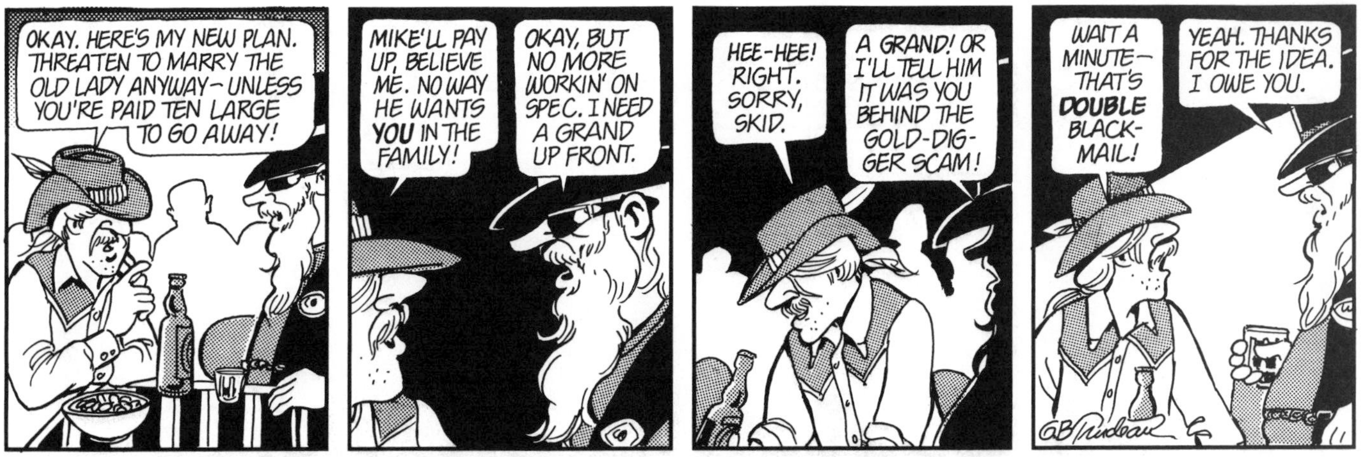
OKAY. HERE'S MY NEW PLAN. THREATEN TO MARRY THE OLD LADY ANYWAY– UNLESS YOU'RE PAID TEN LARGE TO GO AWAY!
MIKE'LL PAY UP, BELIEVE ME. NO WAY HE WANTS **YOU** IN THE FAMILY!
OKAY, BUT NO MORE WORKIN' ON SPEC. I NEED A GRAND UP FRONT.
HEE-HEE! RIGHT. SORRY, SKID.
A **GRAND**! OR I'LL TELL HIM IT WAS YOU BEHIND THE GOLD-DIGGER SCAM!
WAIT A MINUTE– THAT'S **DOUBLE** BLACKMAIL!
YEAH. THANKS FOR THE IDEA. I OWE YOU.

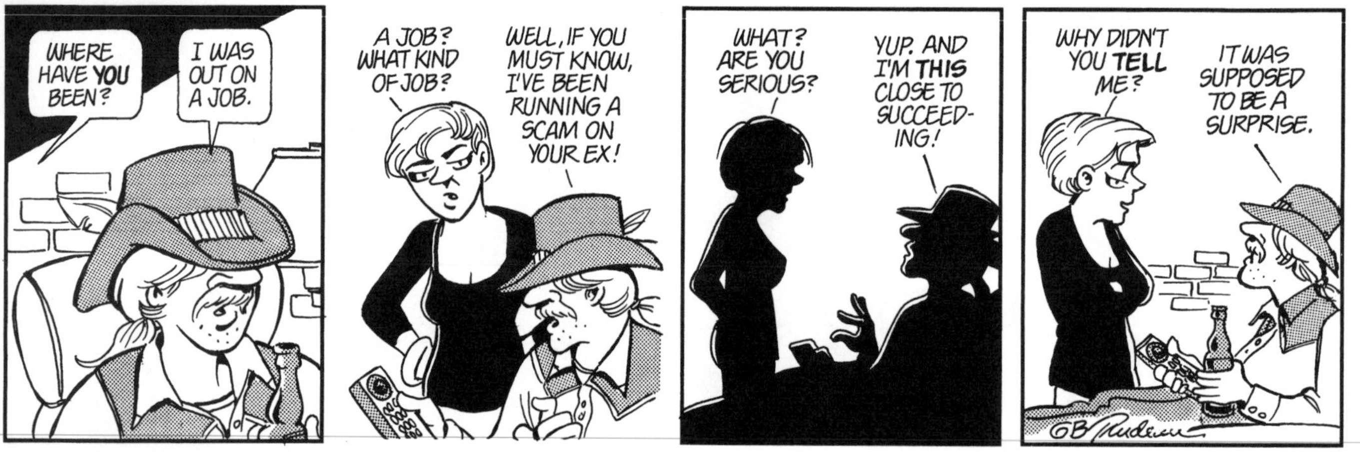
WHERE HAVE YOU BEEN?
I WAS OUT ON A JOB.
A JOB? WHAT KIND OF JOB?
WELL, IF YOU MUST KNOW, I'VE BEEN RUNNING A SCAM ON YOUR EX!
WHAT? ARE YOU SERIOUS?
YUP. AND I'M THIS CLOSE TO SUCCEED-ING!
WHY DIDN'T YOU TELL ME?
IT WAS SUPPOSED TO BE A SURPRISE.
GB Trudeau

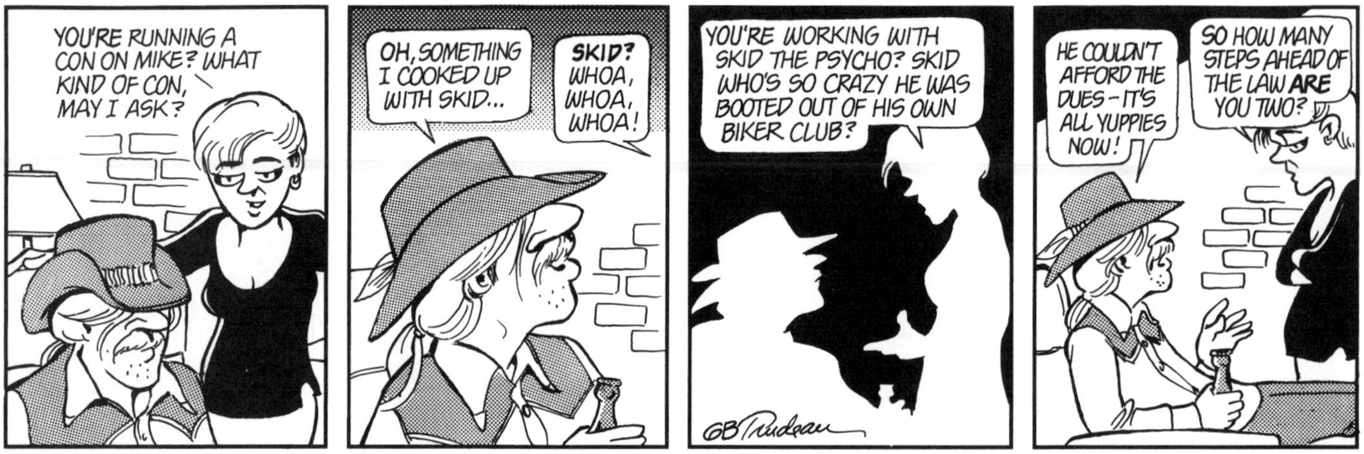
YOU'RE RUNNING A CON ON MIKE? WHAT KIND OF CON, MAY I ASK?
OH, SOMETHING I COOKED UP WITH SKID...
SKID? WHOA, WHOA, WHOA!
YOU'RE WORKING WITH SKID THE PSYCHO? SKID WHO'S SO CRAZY HE WAS BOOTED OUT OF HIS OWN BIKER CLUB?
GB Trudeau
HE COULDN'T AFFORD THE DUES – IT'S ALL YUPPIES NOW!
SO HOW MANY STEPS AHEAD OF THE LAW ARE YOU TWO?

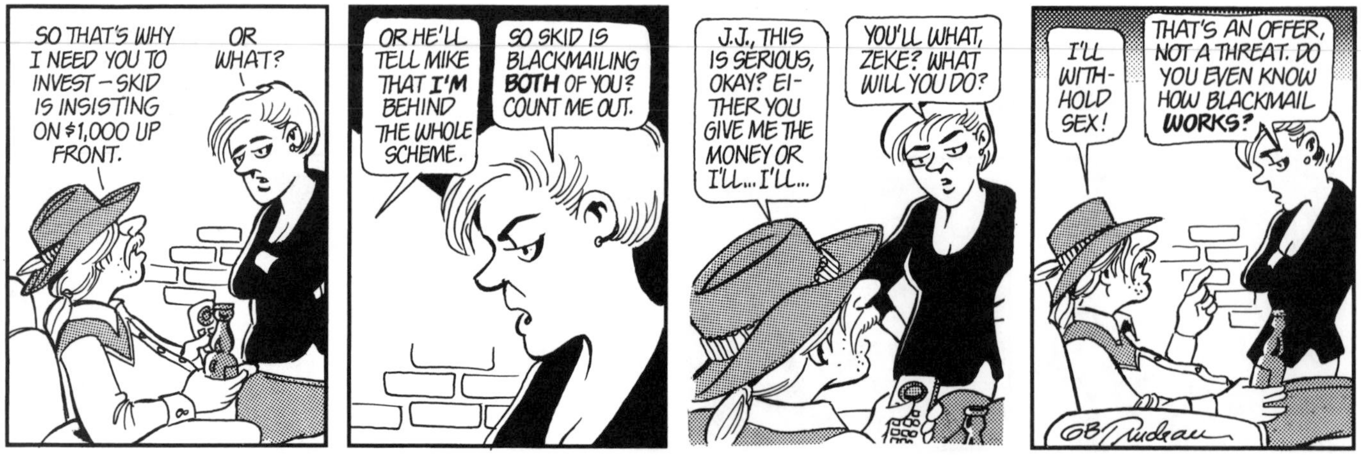
SO THAT'S WHY I NEED YOU TO INVEST – SKID IS INSISTING ON $1,000 UP FRONT.
OR WHAT?
OR HE'LL TELL MIKE THAT I'M BEHIND THE WHOLE SCHEME.
SO SKID IS BLACKMAILING BOTH OF YOU? COUNT ME OUT.
J.J., THIS IS SERIOUS, OKAY? EI-THER YOU GIVE ME THE MONEY OR I'LL... I'LL...
YOU'LL WHAT, ZEKE? WHAT WILL YOU DO?
I'LL WITH-HOLD SEX!
THAT'S AN OFFER, NOT A THREAT. DO YOU EVEN KNOW HOW BLACKMAIL WORKS?
GB Trudeau

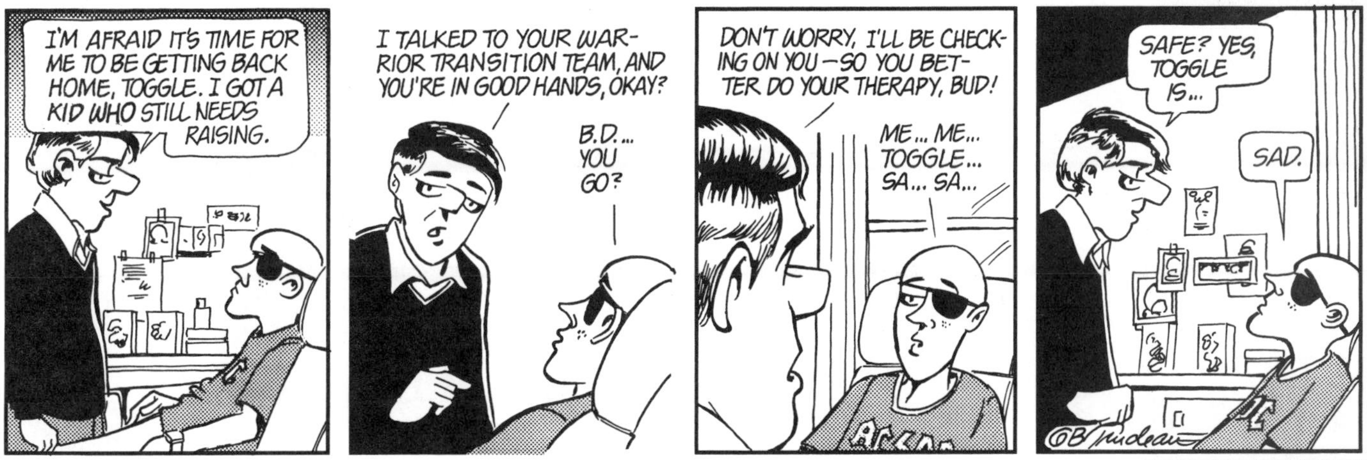
I'M AFRAID IT'S TIME FOR ME TO BE GETTING BACK HOME, TOGGLE. I GOT A KID WHO STILL NEEDS RAISING.
I TALKED TO YOUR WARRIOR TRANSITION TEAM, AND YOU'RE IN GOOD HANDS, OKAY?
B.D.... YOU GO?
DON'T WORRY, I'LL BE CHECKING ON YOU—SO YOU BETTER DO YOUR THERAPY, BUD!
ME... ME... TOGGLE... SA... SA...
SAFE? YES, TOGGLE IS...
SAD.
©B Trudeau

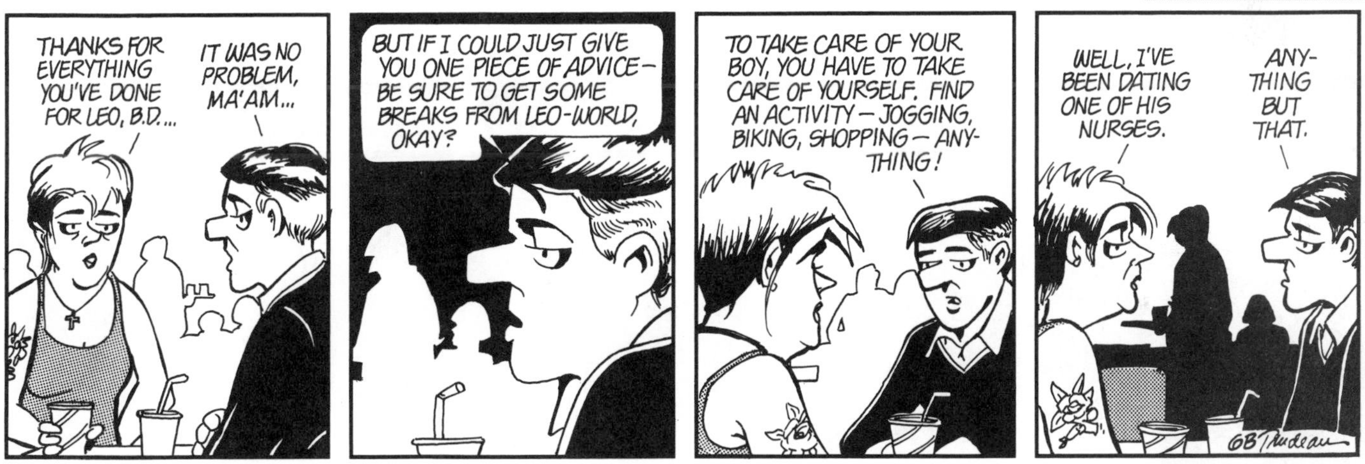
THANKS FOR EVERYTHING YOU'VE DONE FOR LEO, B.D....
IT WAS NO PROBLEM, MA'AM...
BUT IF I COULD JUST GIVE YOU ONE PIECE OF ADVICE—BE SURE TO GET SOME BREAKS FROM LEO-WORLD, OKAY?
TO TAKE CARE OF YOUR BOY, YOU HAVE TO TAKE CARE OF YOURSELF. FIND AN ACTIVITY—JOGGING, BIKING, SHOPPING—ANYTHING!
WELL, I'VE BEEN DATING ONE OF HIS NURSES.
ANYTHING BUT THAT.
©B Trudeau

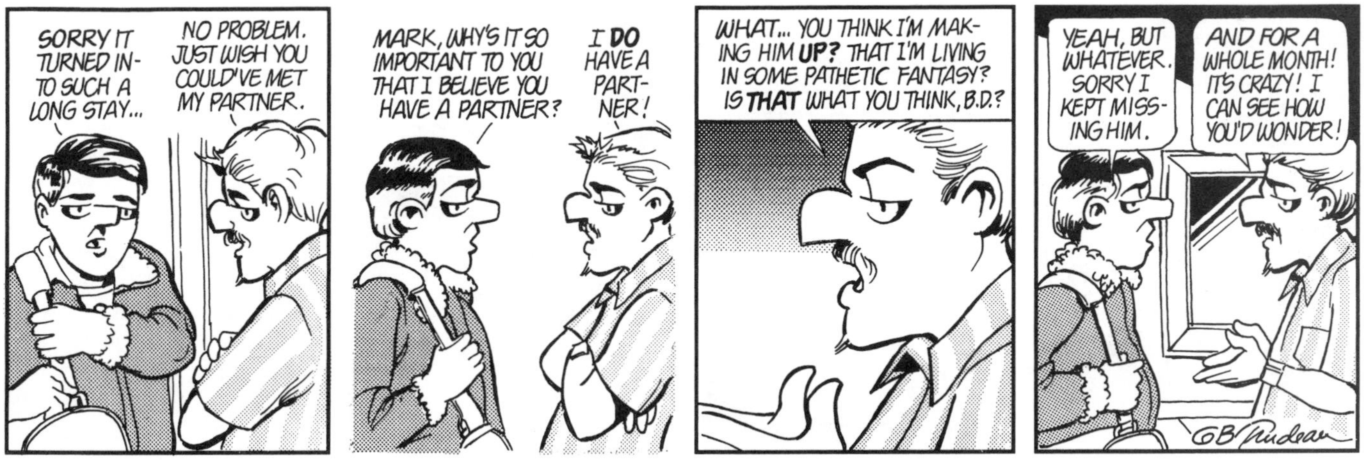
SORRY IT TURNED INTO SUCH A LONG STAY...
NO PROBLEM. JUST WISH YOU COULD'VE MET MY PARTNER.
MARK, WHY'S IT SO IMPORTANT TO YOU THAT I BELIEVE YOU HAVE A PARTNER?
I DO HAVE A PARTNER!
WHAT... YOU THINK I'M MAKING HIM UP? THAT I'M LIVING IN SOME PATHETIC FANTASY? IS THAT WHAT YOU THINK, B.D.?
YEAH, BUT WHATEVER. SORRY I KEPT MISSING HIM.
AND FOR A WHOLE MONTH! IT'S CRAZY! I CAN SEE HOW YOU'D WONDER!
©B Trudeau

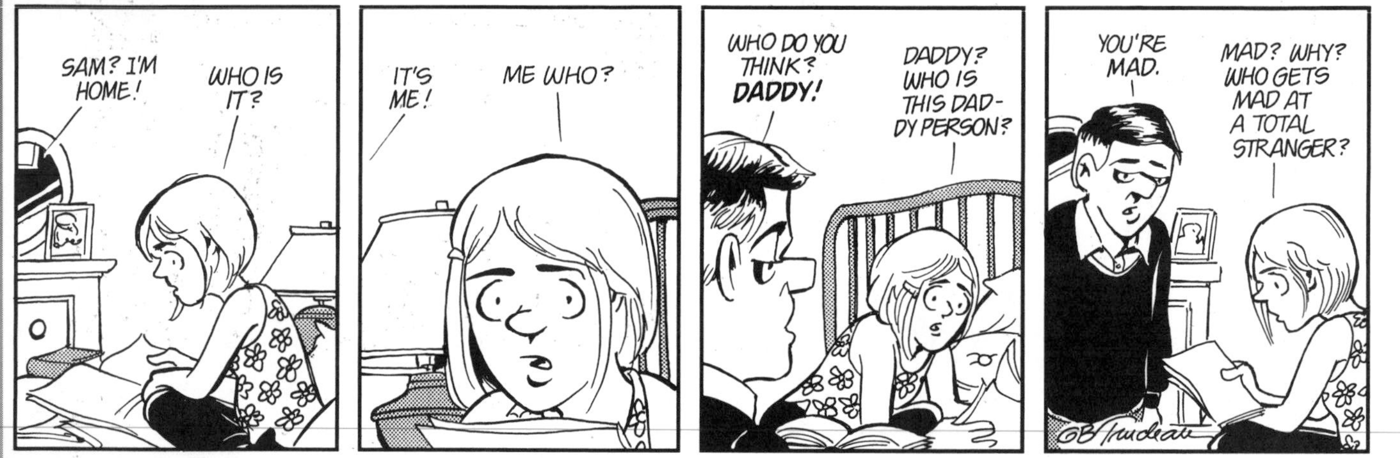
SAM? I'M HOME!
WHO IS IT?
IT'S ME!
ME WHO?
WHO DO YOU THINK? DADDY!
DADDY? WHO IS THIS DADDY PERSON?
YOU'RE MAD.
MAD? WHY? WHO GETS MAD AT A TOTAL STRANGER?
GB Trudeau

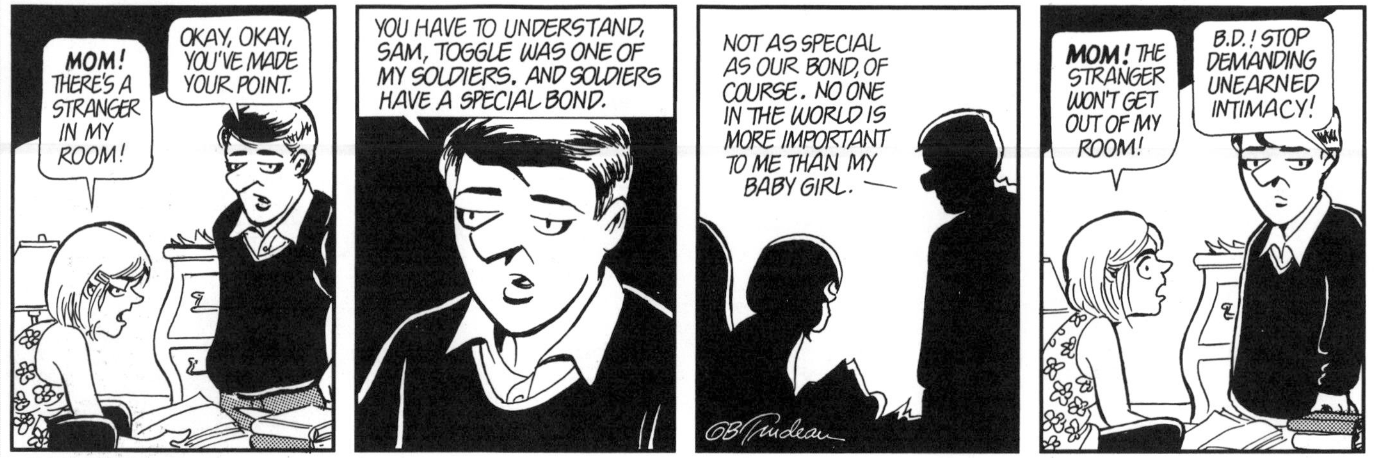
MOM! THERE'S A STRANGER IN MY ROOM!
OKAY, OKAY, YOU'VE MADE YOUR POINT.
YOU HAVE TO UNDERSTAND, SAM, TOGGLE WAS ONE OF MY SOLDIERS. AND SOLDIERS HAVE A SPECIAL BOND.
NOT AS SPECIAL AS OUR BOND, OF COURSE. NO ONE IN THE WORLD IS MORE IMPORTANT TO ME THAN MY BABY GIRL.
GB Trudeau
MOM! THE STRANGER WON'T GET OUT OF MY ROOM!
B.D.! STOP DEMANDING UNEARNED INTIMACY!

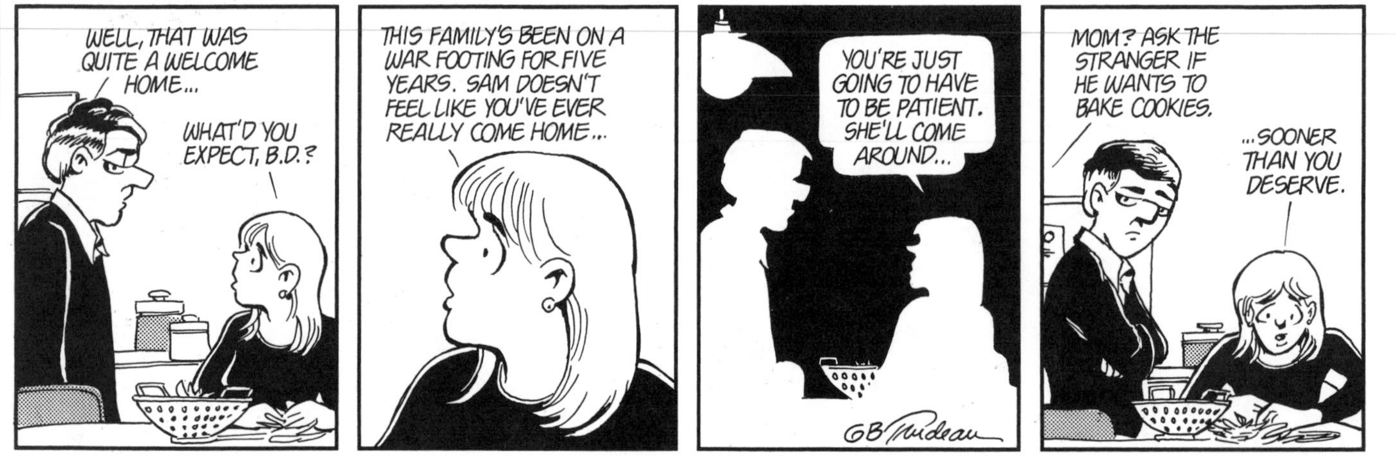
WELL, THAT WAS QUITE A WELCOME HOME...
WHAT'D YOU EXPECT, B.D.?
THIS FAMILY'S BEEN ON A WAR FOOTING FOR FIVE YEARS. SAM DOESN'T FEEL LIKE YOU'VE EVER REALLY COME HOME...
YOU'RE JUST GOING TO HAVE TO BE PATIENT. SHE'LL COME AROUND...
GB Trudeau
MOM? ASK THE STRANGER IF HE WANTS TO BAKE COOKIES.
...SOONER THAN YOU DESERVE.

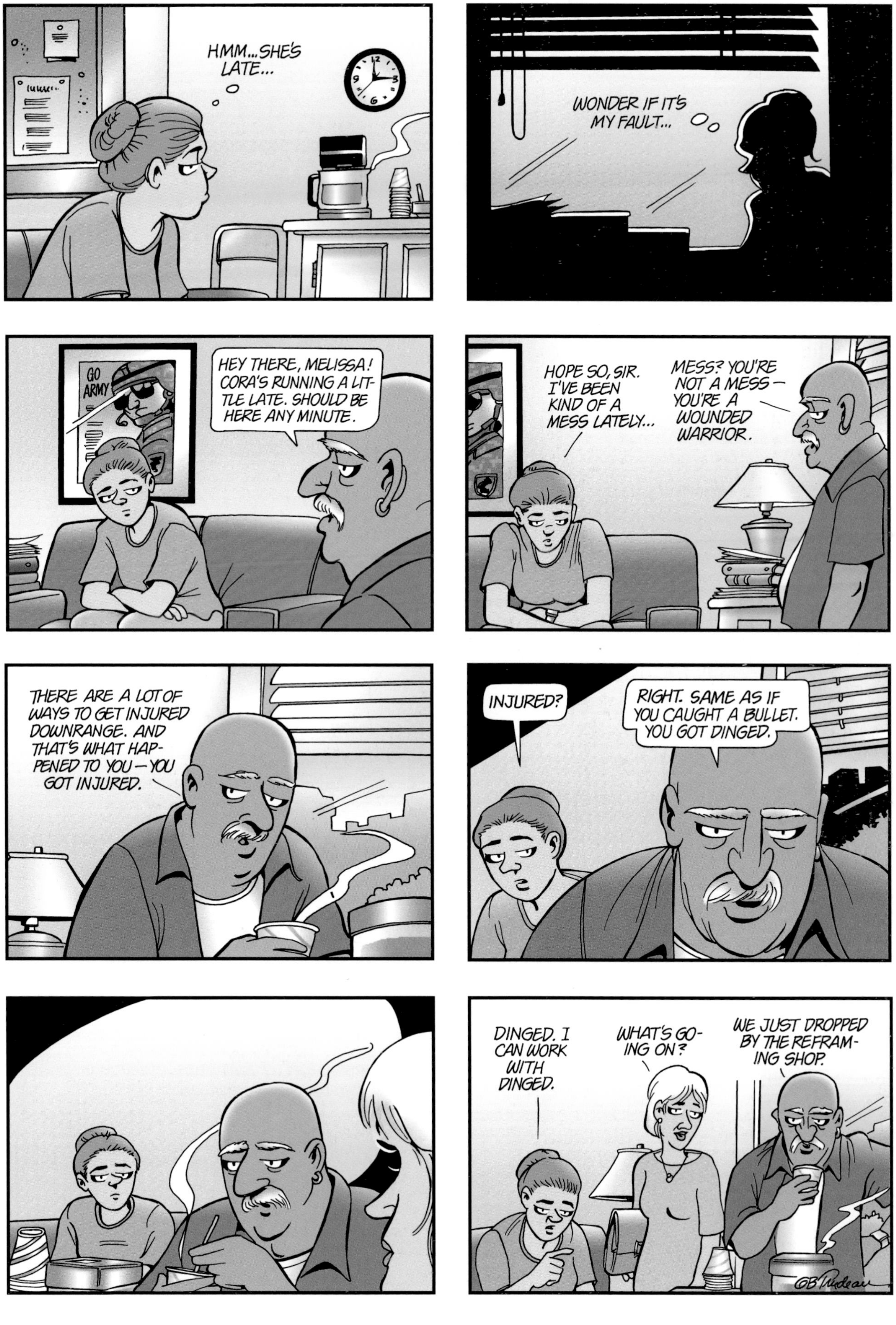
HMM...SHE'S LATE...
WONDER IF IT'S MY FAULT...
HEY THERE, MELISSA! CORA'S RUNNING A LITTLE LATE. SHOULD BE HERE ANY MINUTE.
GO ARMY
HOPE SO, SIR. I'VE BEEN KIND OF A MESS LATELY...
MESS? YOU'RE NOT A MESS — YOU'RE A WOUNDED WARRIOR.
THERE ARE A LOT OF WAYS TO GET INJURED DOWNRANGE. AND THAT'S WHAT HAPPENED TO YOU — YOU GOT INJURED.
INJURED?
RIGHT. SAME AS IF YOU CAUGHT A BULLET. YOU GOT DINGED.
DINGED. I CAN WORK WITH DINGED.
WHAT'S GOING ON?
WE JUST DROPPED BY THE REFRAMING SHOP.
©B Trudeau

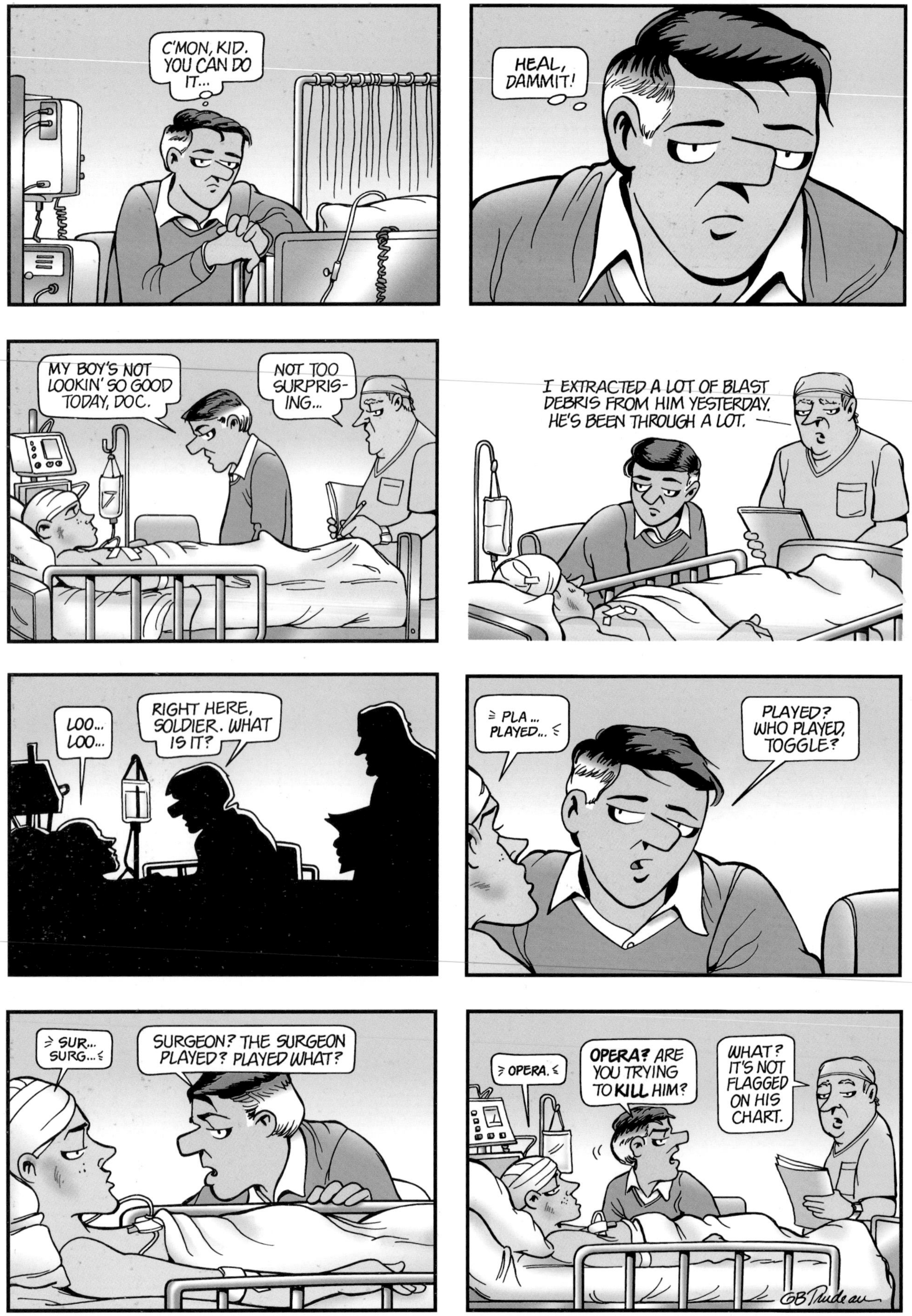
C'MON, KID. YOU CAN DO IT...
HEAL, DAMMIT!
MY BOY'S NOT LOOKIN' SO GOOD TODAY, DOC.
NOT TOO SURPRISING...
I EXTRACTED A LOT OF BLAST DEBRIS FROM HIM YESTERDAY. HE'S BEEN THROUGH A LOT.
LOO... LOO...
RIGHT HERE, SOLDIER. WHAT IS IT?
PLA... PLAYED...
PLAYED? WHO PLAYED, TOGGLE?
SUR... SURG...
SURGEON? THE SURGEON PLAYED? PLAYED WHAT?
OPERA.
OPERA? ARE YOU TRYING TO **KILL** HIM?
WHAT? IT'S NOT FLAGGED ON HIS CHART.
GBTrudeau

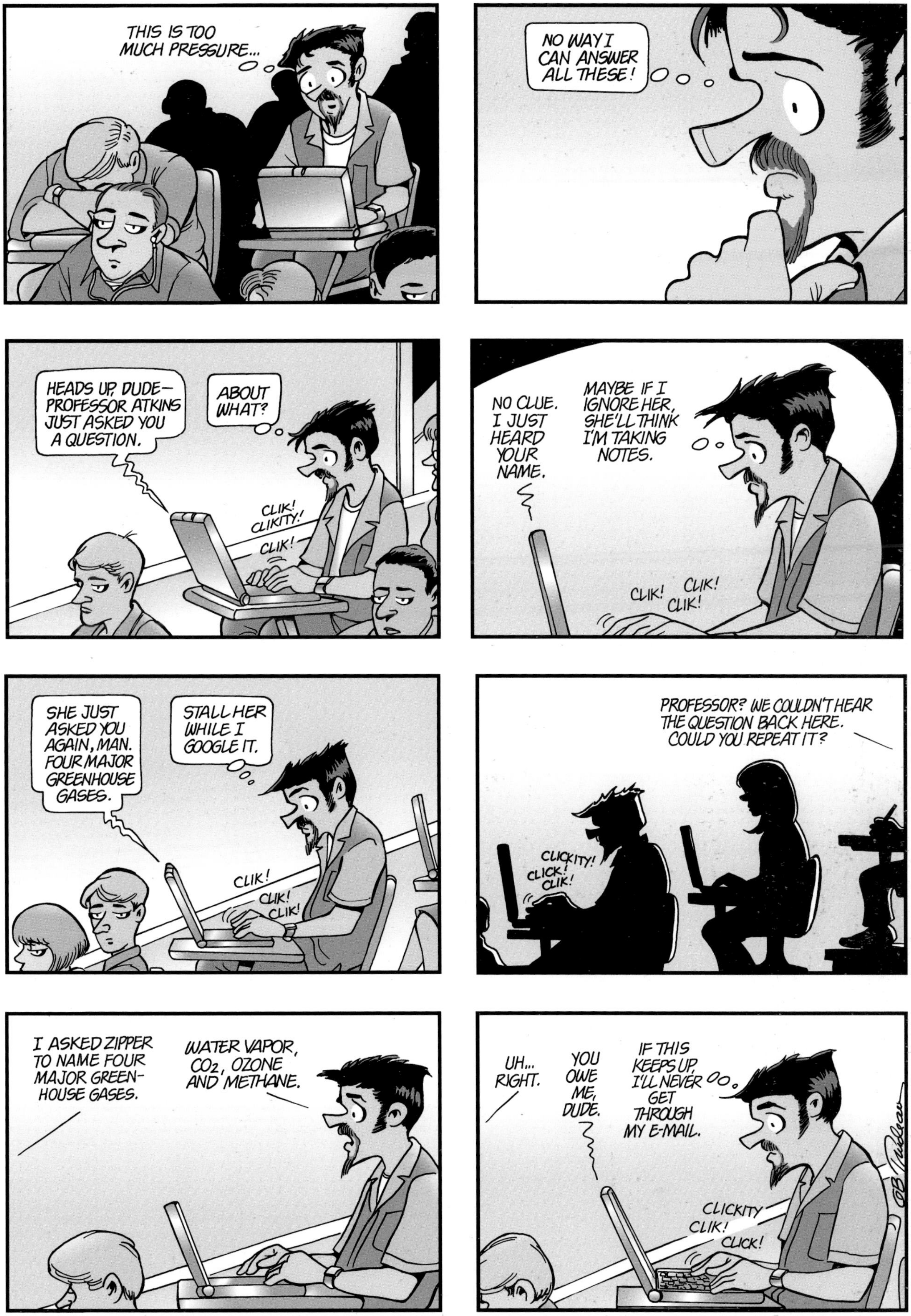
THIS IS TOO MUCH PRESSURE...
NO WAY I CAN ANSWER ALL THESE!
HEADS UP, DUDE— PROFESSOR ATKINS JUST ASKED YOU A QUESTION.
ABOUT WHAT?
CLIK! CLIKITY! CLIK!
NO CLUE. I JUST HEARD YOUR NAME.
MAYBE IF I IGNORE HER, SHE'LL THINK I'M TAKING NOTES.
CLIK! CLIK! CLIK!
SHE JUST ASKED YOU AGAIN, MAN. FOUR MAJOR GREENHOUSE GASES.
STALL HER WHILE I GOOGLE IT.
CLIK! CLIK! CLIK!
PROFESSOR? WE COULDN'T HEAR THE QUESTION BACK HERE. COULD YOU REPEAT IT?
CLICKITY! CLICK! CLIK!
I ASKED ZIPPER TO NAME FOUR MAJOR GREEN-HOUSE GASES.
WATER VAPOR, CO2, OZONE AND METHANE.
UH... RIGHT.
YOU OWE ME, DUDE.
IF THIS KEEPS UP, I'LL NEVER GET THROUGH MY E-MAIL.
CLICKITY CLIK! CLICK!

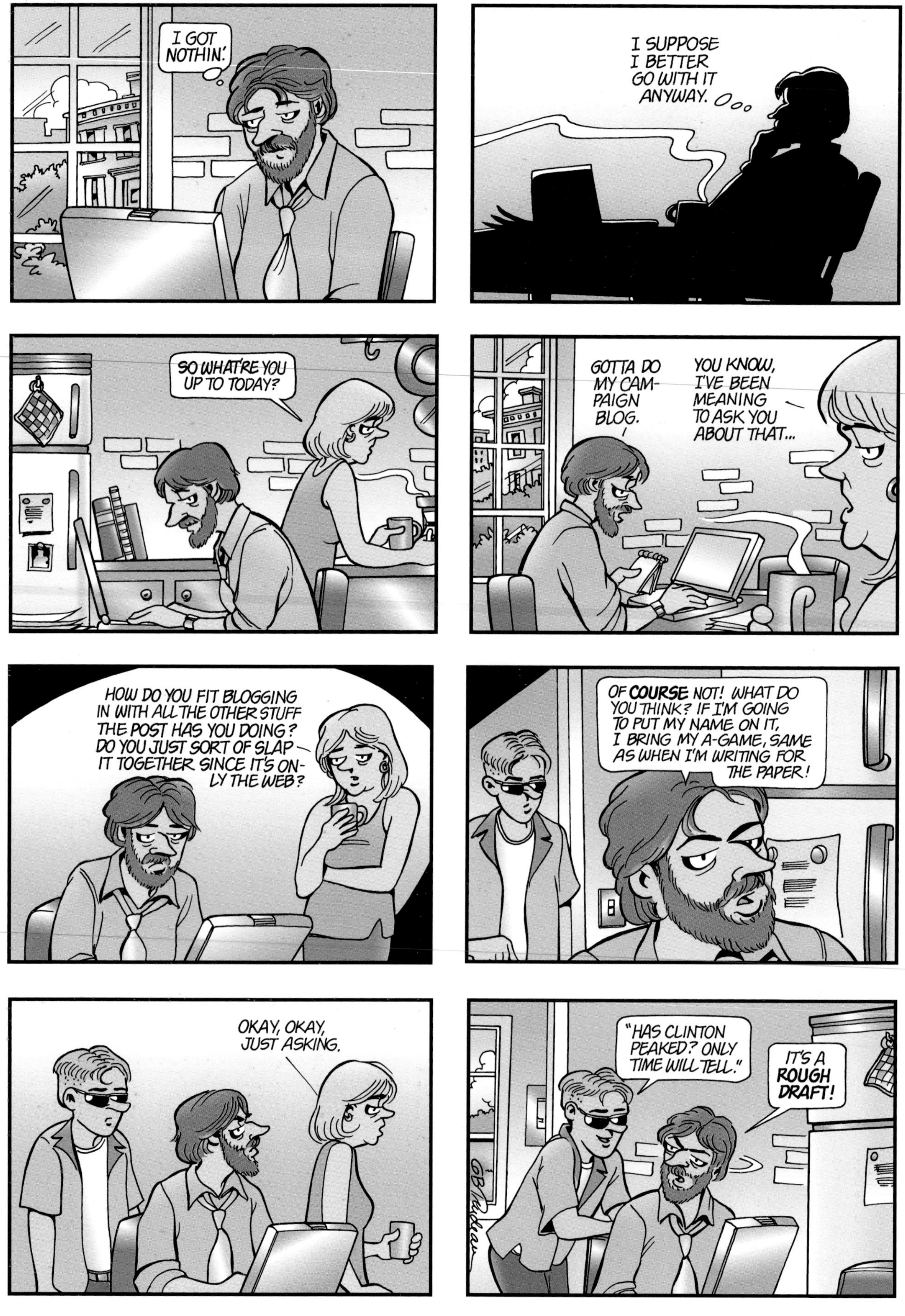
I GOT NOTHIN'.
I SUPPOSE I BETTER GO WITH IT ANYWAY.
SO WHAT'RE YOU UP TO TODAY?
GOTTA DO MY CAMPAIGN BLOG.
YOU KNOW, I'VE BEEN MEANING TO ASK YOU ABOUT THAT...
HOW DO YOU FIT BLOGGING IN WITH ALL THE OTHER STUFF THE POST HAS YOU DOING? DO YOU JUST SORT OF SLAP IT TOGETHER SINCE IT'S ONLY THE WEB?
OF COURSE NOT! WHAT DO YOU THINK? IF I'M GOING TO PUT MY NAME ON IT, I BRING MY A-GAME, SAME AS WHEN I'M WRITING FOR THE PAPER!
OKAY, OKAY, JUST ASKING.
"HAS CLINTON PEAKED? ONLY TIME WILL TELL."
IT'S A ROUGH DRAFT!
GB Trudeau

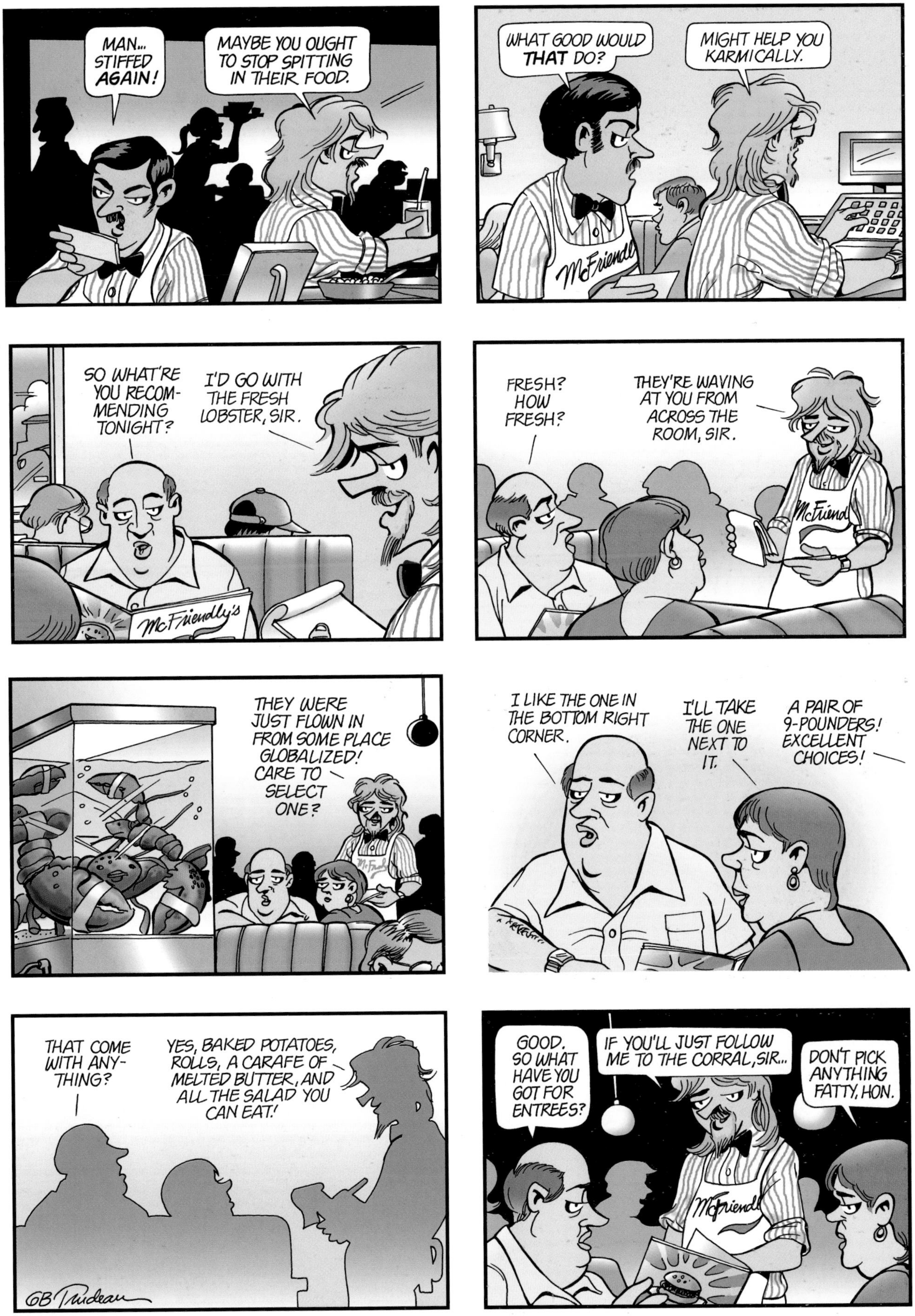
MAN... STIFFED AGAIN!
MAYBE YOU OUGHT TO STOP SPITTING IN THEIR FOOD.
WHAT GOOD WOULD THAT DO?
MIGHT HELP YOU KARMICALLY.
McFriendly
SO WHAT'RE YOU RECOMMENDING TONIGHT?
I'D GO WITH THE FRESH LOBSTER, SIR.
McFriendly's
FRESH? HOW FRESH?
THEY'RE WAVING AT YOU FROM ACROSS THE ROOM, SIR.
THEY WERE JUST FLOWN IN FROM SOME PLACE GLOBALIZED! CARE TO SELECT ONE?
I LIKE THE ONE IN THE BOTTOM RIGHT CORNER.
I'LL TAKE THE ONE NEXT TO IT.
A PAIR OF 9-POUNDERS! EXCELLENT CHOICES!
THAT COME WITH ANYTHING?
YES, BAKED POTATOES, ROLLS, A CARAFE OF MELTED BUTTER, AND ALL THE SALAD YOU CAN EAT!
GB Trudeau
GOOD. SO WHAT HAVE YOU GOT FOR ENTREES?
IF YOU'LL JUST FOLLOW ME TO THE CORRAL, SIR...
DON'T PICK ANYTHING FATTY, HON.

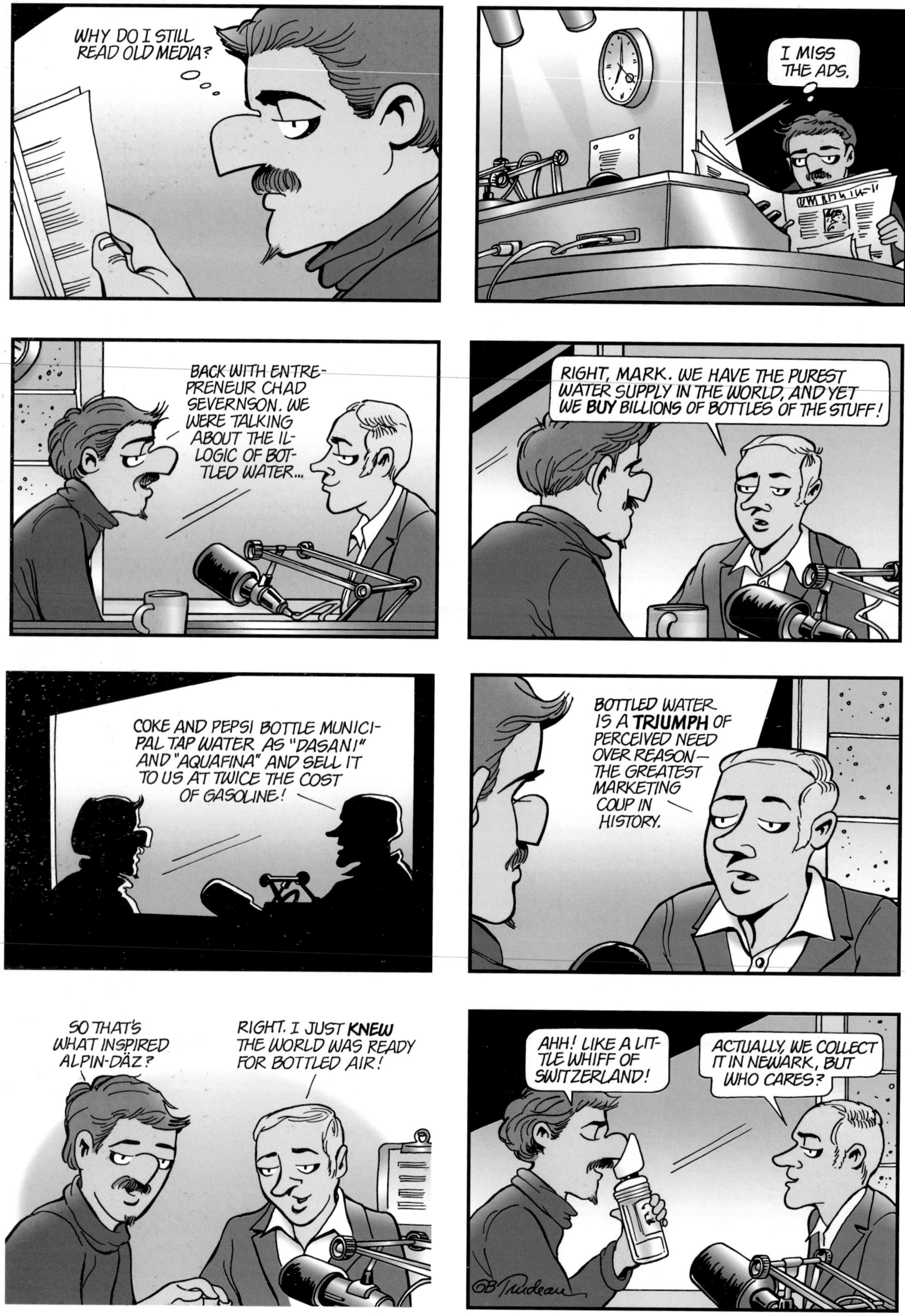
WHY DO I STILL READ OLD MEDIA?
I MISS THE ADS.
BACK WITH ENTRE-PRENEUR CHAD SEVERNSON. WE WERE TALKING ABOUT THE IL-LOGIC OF BOT-TLED WATER...
RIGHT, MARK. WE HAVE THE PUREST WATER SUPPLY IN THE WORLD, AND YET WE **BUY** BILLIONS OF BOTTLES OF THE STUFF!
COKE AND PEPSI BOTTLE MUNICI-PAL TAP WATER AS "DASANI" AND "AQUAFINA" AND SELL IT TO US AT TWICE THE COST OF GASOLINE!
BOTTLED WATER IS A **TRIUMPH** OF PERCEIVED NEED OVER REASON— THE GREATEST MARKETING COUP IN HISTORY.
SO THAT'S WHAT INSPIRED ALPIN-DÄZ?
RIGHT. I JUST **KNEW** THE WORLD WAS READY FOR BOTTLED AIR!
AHH! LIKE A LIT-TLE WHIFF OF SWITZERLAND!
ACTUALLY, WE COLLECT IT IN NEWARK, BUT WHO CARES?

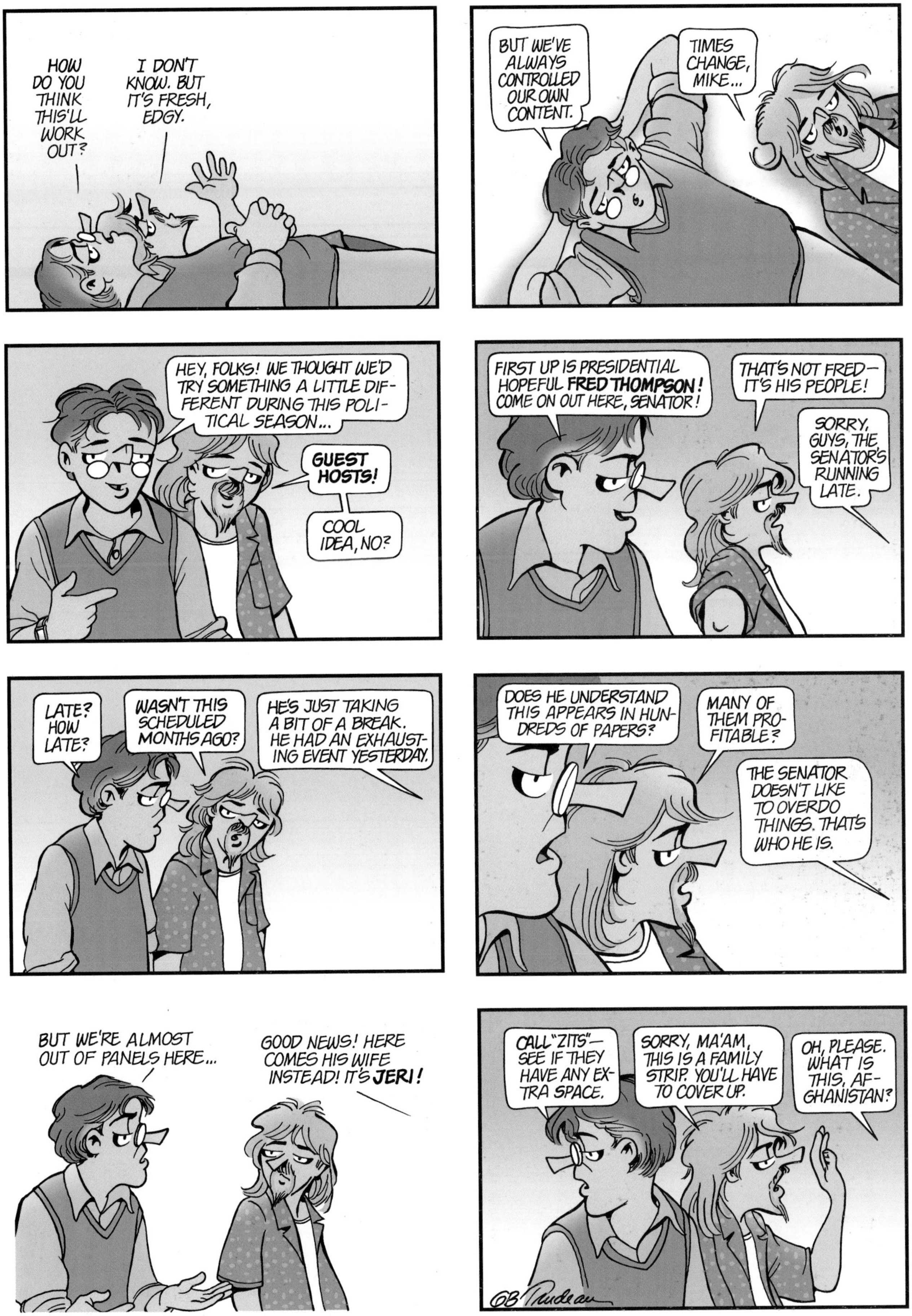
HOW DO YOU THINK THIS'LL WORK OUT?
I DON'T KNOW. BUT IT'S FRESH, EDGY.
BUT WE'VE ALWAYS CONTROLLED OUR OWN CONTENT.
TIMES CHANGE, MIKE...
HEY, FOLKS! WE THOUGHT WE'D TRY SOMETHING A LITTLE DIFFERENT DURING THIS POLITICAL SEASON...
GUEST HOSTS!
COOL IDEA, NO?
FIRST UP IS PRESIDENTIAL HOPEFUL FRED THOMPSON! COME ON OUT HERE, SENATOR!
THAT'S NOT FRED— IT'S HIS PEOPLE!
SORRY, GUYS, THE SENATOR'S RUNNING LATE.
LATE? HOW LATE?
WASN'T THIS SCHEDULED MONTHS AGO?
HE'S JUST TAKING A BIT OF A BREAK. HE HAD AN EXHAUSTING EVENT YESTERDAY.
DOES HE UNDERSTAND THIS APPEARS IN HUNDREDS OF PAPERS?
MANY OF THEM PROFITABLE?
THE SENATOR DOESN'T LIKE TO OVERDO THINGS. THAT'S WHO HE IS.
BUT WE'RE ALMOST OUT OF PANELS HERE...
GOOD NEWS! HERE COMES HIS WIFE INSTEAD! IT'S JERI!
CALL "ZITS"— SEE IF THEY HAVE ANY EXTRA SPACE.
SORRY, MA'AM, THIS IS A FAMILY STRIP. YOU'LL HAVE TO COVER UP.
OH, PLEASE. WHAT IS THIS, AFGHANISTAN?
GB Trudeau

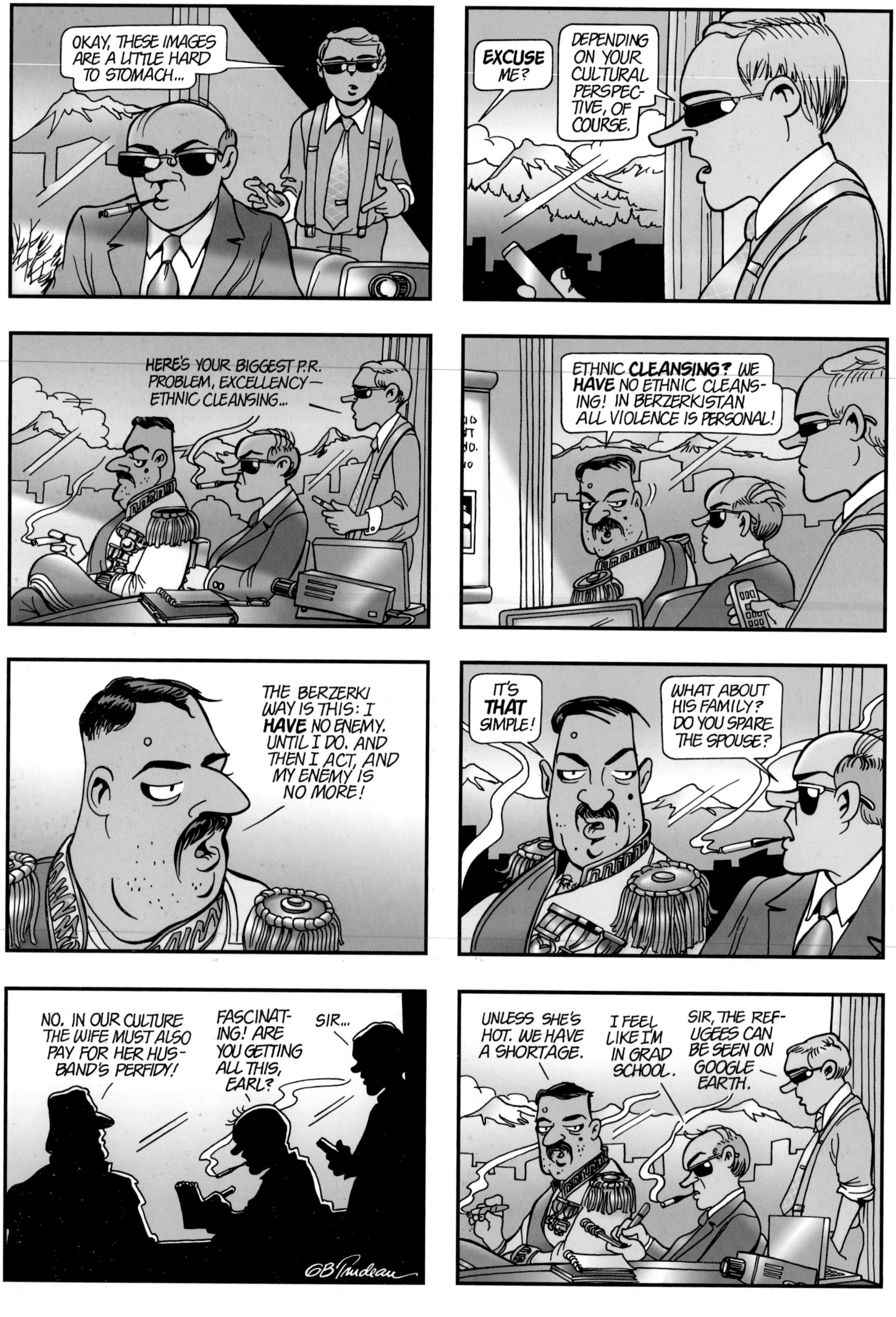
OKAY, THESE IMAGES ARE A LITTLE HARD TO STOMACH...
EXCUSE ME?
DEPENDING ON YOUR CULTURAL PERSPEC-TIVE, OF COURSE.
HERE'S YOUR BIGGEST P.R. PROBLEM, EXCELLENCY— ETHNIC CLEANSING...
ETHNIC CLEANSING? WE HAVE NO ETHNIC CLEANS-ING! IN BERZERKISTAN ALL VIOLENCE IS PERSONAL!
THE BERZERKI WAY IS THIS: I HAVE NO ENEMY. UNTIL I DO. AND THEN I ACT, AND MY ENEMY IS NO MORE!
IT'S THAT SIMPLE!
WHAT ABOUT HIS FAMILY? DO YOU SPARE THE SPOUSE?
NO. IN OUR CULTURE THE WIFE MUST ALSO PAY FOR HER HUS-BAND'S PERFIDY!
FASCINAT-ING! ARE YOU GETTING ALL THIS, EARL?
SIR...
GBTrudeau
UNLESS SHE'S HOT. WE HAVE A SHORTAGE.
I FEEL LIKE I'M IN GRAD SCHOOL.
SIR, THE REF-UGEES CAN BE SEEN ON GOOGLE EARTH.

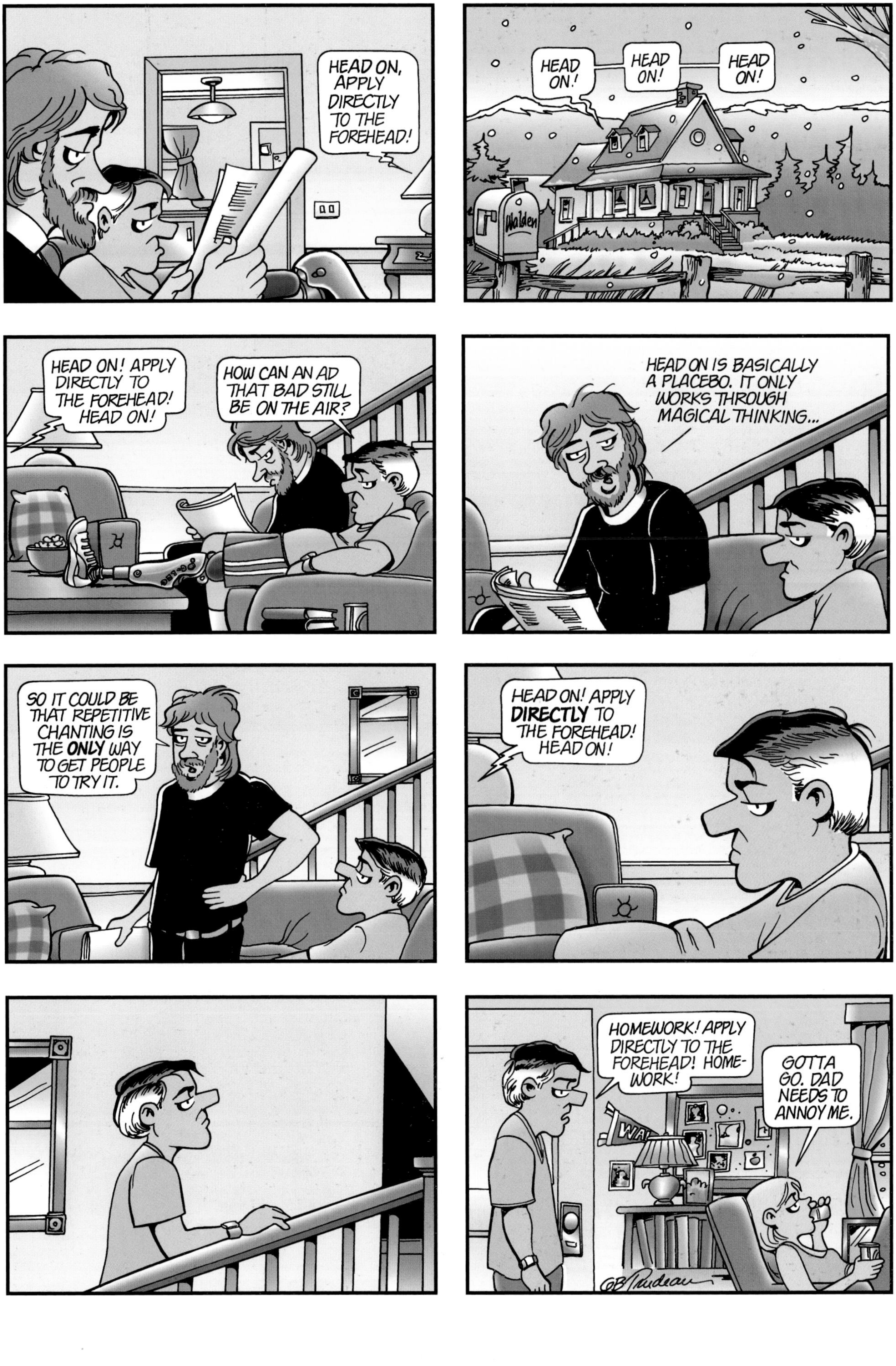
HEAD ON, APPLY DIRECTLY TO THE FOREHEAD!
HEAD ON!
HEAD ON!
HEAD ON!
HEAD ON! APPLY DIRECTLY TO THE FOREHEAD! HEAD ON!
HOW CAN AN AD THAT BAD STILL BE ON THE AIR?
HEAD ON IS BASICALLY A PLACEBO. IT ONLY WORKS THROUGH MAGICAL THINKING...
SO IT COULD BE THAT REPETITIVE CHANTING IS THE **ONLY** WAY TO GET PEOPLE TO TRY IT.
HEAD ON! APPLY **DIRECTLY** TO THE FOREHEAD! HEAD ON!
HOMEWORK! APPLY DIRECTLY TO THE FOREHEAD! HOME-WORK!
GOTTA GO. DAD NEEDS TO ANNOY ME.

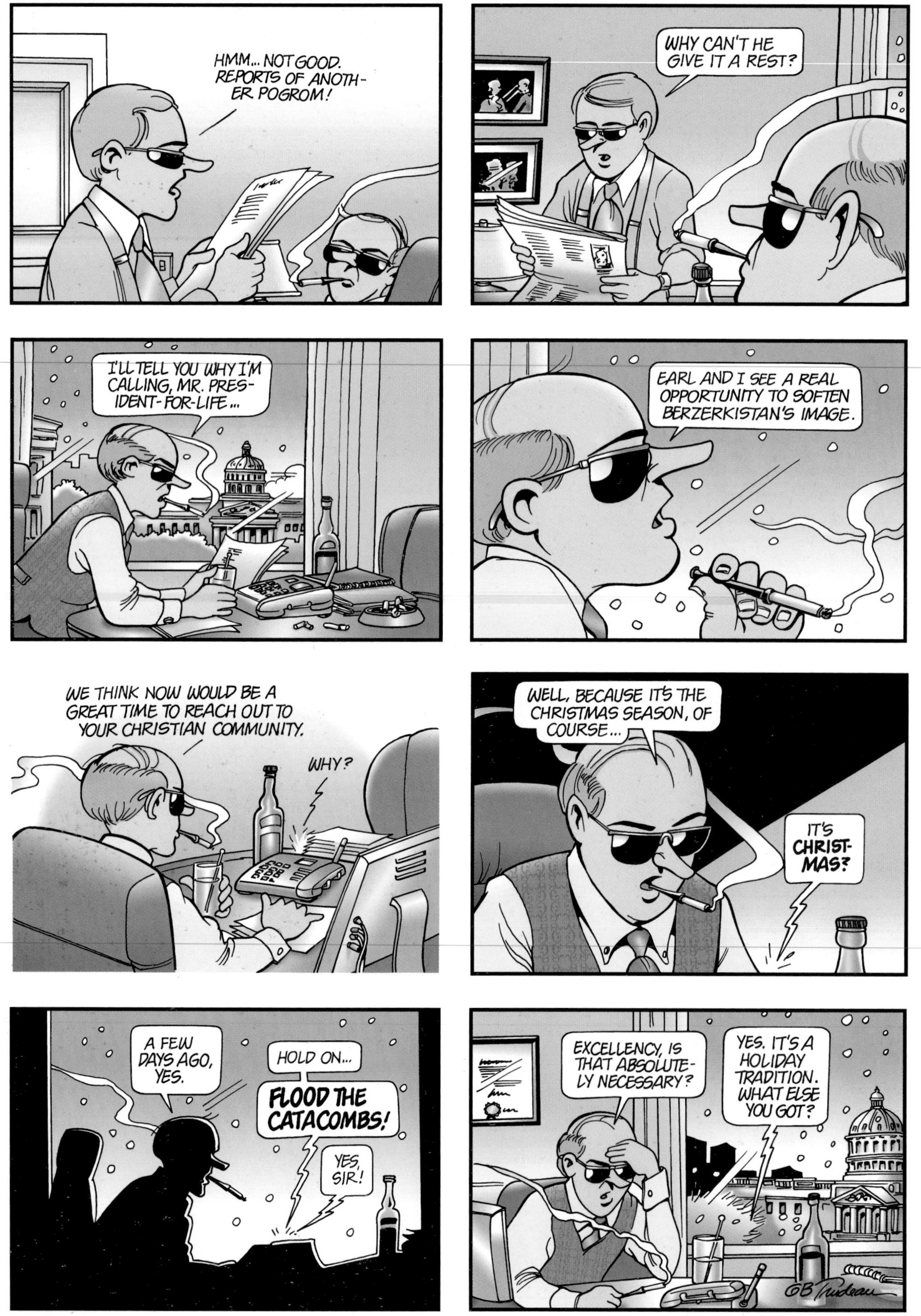
HMM... NOT GOOD. REPORTS OF ANOTH-ER POGROM!
WHY CAN'T HE GIVE IT A REST?
I'LL TELL YOU WHY I'M CALLING, MR. PRES-IDENT-FOR-LIFE...
EARL AND I SEE A REAL OPPORTUNITY TO SOFTEN BERZERKISTAN'S IMAGE.
WE THINK NOW WOULD BE A GREAT TIME TO REACH OUT TO YOUR CHRISTIAN COMMUNITY.
WHY?
WELL, BECAUSE IT'S THE CHRISTMAS SEASON, OF COURSE...
IT'S CHRISTMAS?
A FEW DAYS AGO, YES.
HOLD ON...
FLOOD THE CATACOMBS!
YES, SIR!
EXCELLENCY, IS THAT ABSOLUTE-LY NECESSARY?
YES. IT'S A HOLIDAY TRADITION. WHAT ELSE YOU GOT?
GB Trudeau

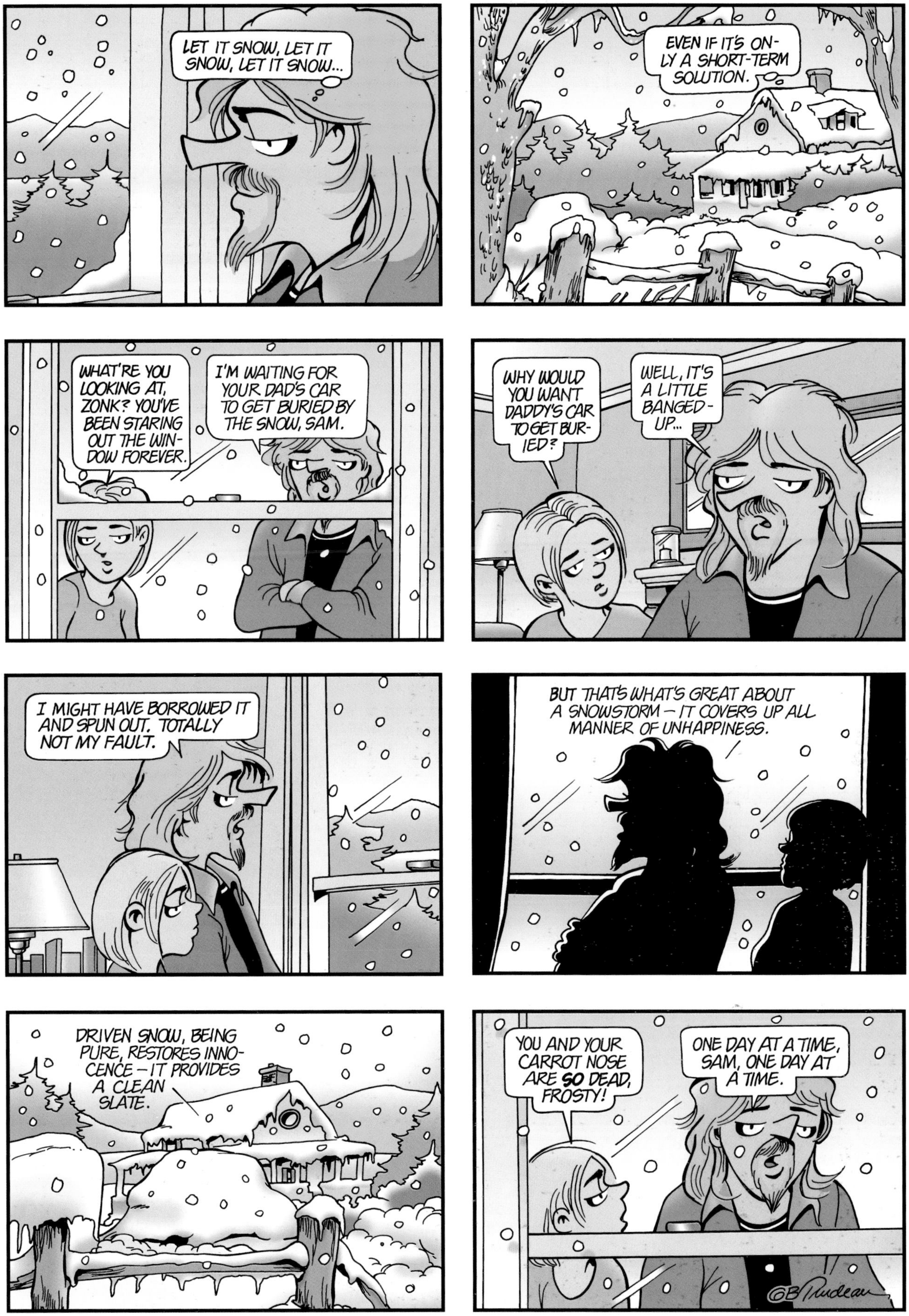
LET IT SNOW, LET IT SNOW, LET IT SNOW...
EVEN IF IT'S ONLY A SHORT-TERM SOLUTION.
WHAT'RE YOU LOOKING AT, ZONK? YOU'VE BEEN STARING OUT THE WINDOW FOREVER.
I'M WAITING FOR YOUR DAD'S CAR TO GET BURIED BY THE SNOW, SAM.
WHY WOULD YOU WANT DADDY'S CAR TO GET BURIED?
WELL, IT'S A LITTLE BANGED-UP...
I MIGHT HAVE BORROWED IT AND SPUN OUT. TOTALLY NOT MY FAULT.
BUT THAT'S WHAT'S GREAT ABOUT A SNOWSTORM – IT COVERS UP ALL MANNER OF UNHAPPINESS.
DRIVEN SNOW, BEING PURE, RESTORES INNOCENCE – IT PROVIDES A CLEAN SLATE.
YOU AND YOUR CARROT NOSE ARE SO DEAD, FROSTY!
ONE DAY AT A TIME, SAM, ONE DAY AT A TIME.
©B Trudeau

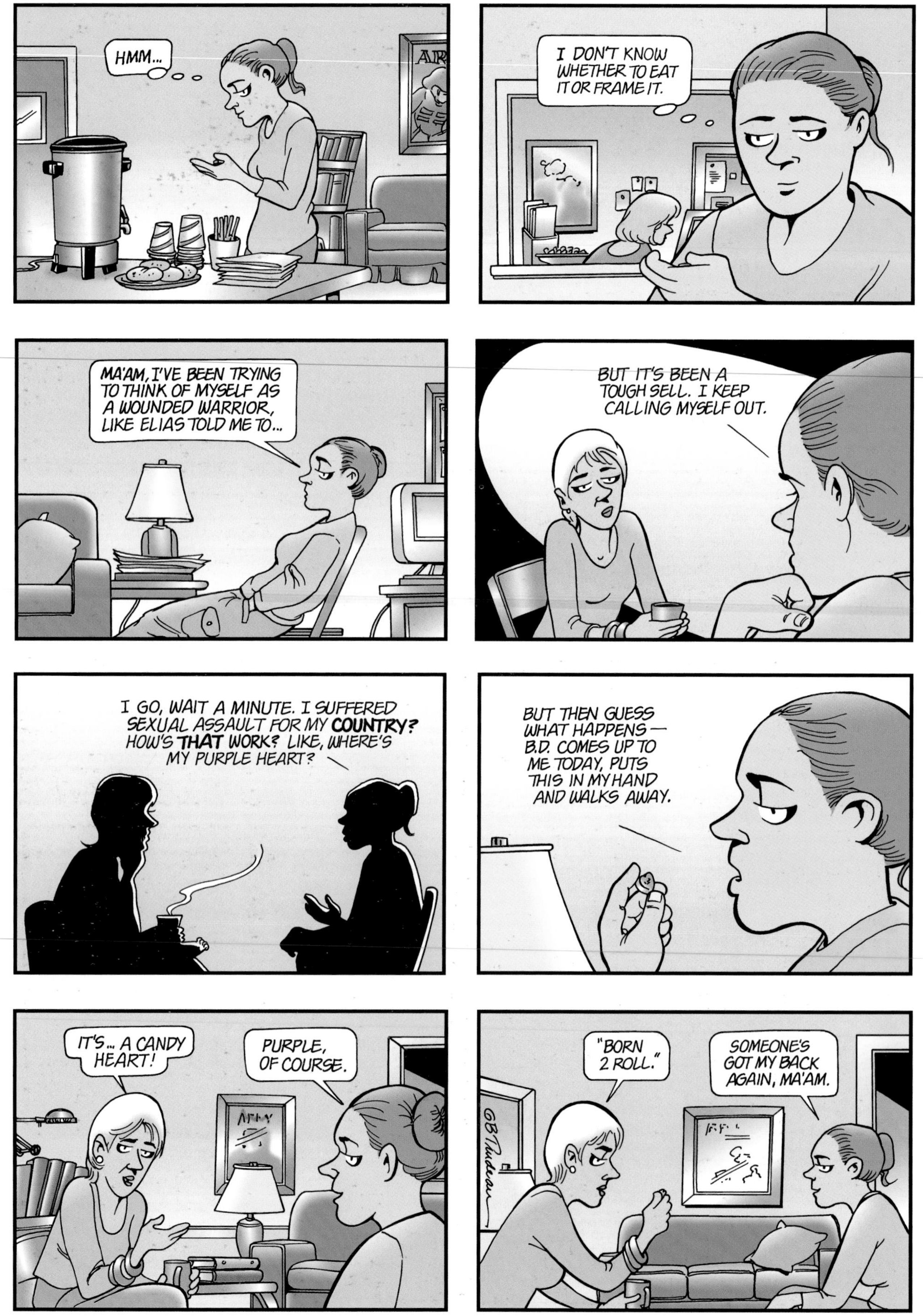
HMM...
I DON'T KNOW WHETHER TO EAT IT OR FRAME IT.
MA'AM, I'VE BEEN TRYING TO THINK OF MYSELF AS A WOUNDED WARRIOR, LIKE ELIAS TOLD ME TO...
BUT IT'S BEEN A TOUGH SELL. I KEEP CALLING MYSELF OUT.
I GO, WAIT A MINUTE. I SUFFERED SEXUAL ASSAULT FOR MY COUNTRY? HOW'S THAT WORK? LIKE, WHERE'S MY PURPLE HEART?
BUT THEN GUESS WHAT HAPPENS — B.D. COMES UP TO ME TODAY, PUTS THIS IN MY HAND AND WALKS AWAY.
IT'S... A CANDY HEART!
PURPLE, OF COURSE.
"BORN 2 ROLL."
SOMEONE'S GOT MY BACK AGAIN, MA'AM.

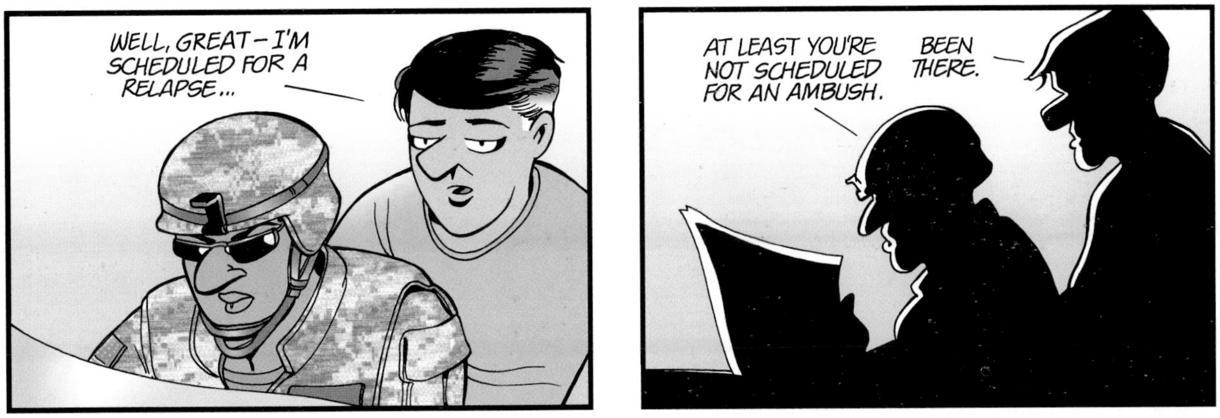
WELL, GREAT – I'M SCHEDULED FOR A RELAPSE...
AT LEAST YOU'RE NOT SCHEDULED FOR AN AMBUSH.
BEEN THERE.

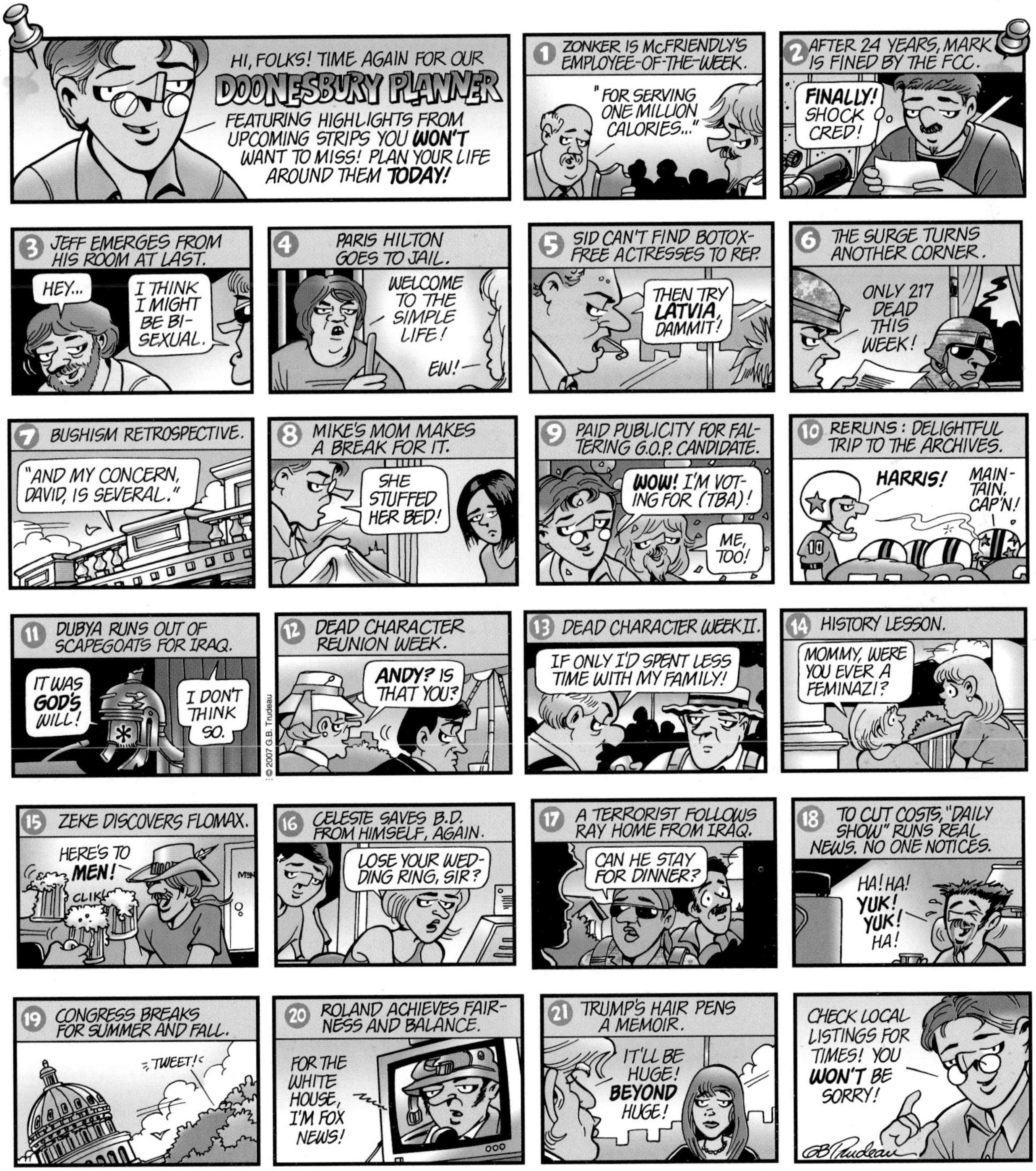
HI, FOLKS! TIME AGAIN FOR OUR
DOONESBURY PLANNER
FEATURING HIGHLIGHTS FROM UPCOMING STRIPS YOU **WON'T** WANT TO MISS! PLAN YOUR LIFE AROUND THEM **TODAY!**
1 ZONKER IS McFRIENDLY'S EMPLOYEE-OF-THE-WEEK.
"FOR SERVING ONE MILLION CALORIES..."
2 AFTER 24 YEARS, MARK IS FINED BY THE FCC.
FINALLY! SHOCK CRED!
3 JEFF EMERGES FROM HIS ROOM AT LAST.
HEY...
I THINK I MIGHT BE BI-SEXUAL.
4 PARIS HILTON GOES TO JAIL.
WELCOME TO THE SIMPLE LIFE!
EW!
5 SID CAN'T FIND BOTOX-FREE ACTRESSES TO REP.
THEN TRY **LATVIA**, DAMMIT!
6 THE SURGE TURNS ANOTHER CORNER.
ONLY 217 DEAD THIS WEEK!
7 BUSHISM RETROSPECTIVE.
"AND MY CONCERN, DAVID, IS SEVERAL."
8 MIKE'S MOM MAKES A BREAK FOR IT.
SHE STUFFED HER BED!
9 PAID PUBLICITY FOR FALTERING G.O.P. CANDIDATE.
WOW! I'M VOTING FOR (TBA)!
ME, TOO!
10 RERUNS: DELIGHTFUL TRIP TO THE ARCHIVES.
HARRIS!
MAINTAIN, CAP'N!
11 DUBYA RUNS OUT OF SCAPEGOATS FOR IRAQ.
IT WAS **GOD'S** WILL!
I DON'T THINK SO.
© 2007 G.B. Trudeau
12 DEAD CHARACTER REUNION WEEK.
ANDY? IS THAT YOU?
13 DEAD CHARACTER WEEK II.
IF ONLY I'D SPENT LESS TIME WITH MY FAMILY!
14 HISTORY LESSON.
MOMMY, WERE YOU EVER A FEMINAZI?
15 ZEKE DISCOVERS FLOMAX.
HERE'S TO **MEN!**
CLIK!
16 CELESTE SAVES B.D. FROM HIMSELF, AGAIN.
LOSE YOUR WEDDING RING, SIR?
17 A TERRORIST FOLLOWS RAY HOME FROM IRAQ.
CAN HE STAY FOR DINNER?
18 TO CUT COSTS, "DAILY SHOW" RUNS REAL NEWS. NO ONE NOTICES.
HA! HA! **YUK! YUK!** HA!
19 CONGRESS BREAKS FOR SUMMER AND FALL.
TWEET!
20 ROLAND ACHIEVES FAIRNESS AND BALANCE.
FOR THE WHITE HOUSE, I'M FOX NEWS!
21 TRUMP'S HAIR PENS A MEMOIR.
IT'LL BE HUGE! **BEYOND** HUGE!
CHECK LOCAL LISTINGS FOR TIMES! YOU **WON'T** BE SORRY!
GB Trudeau

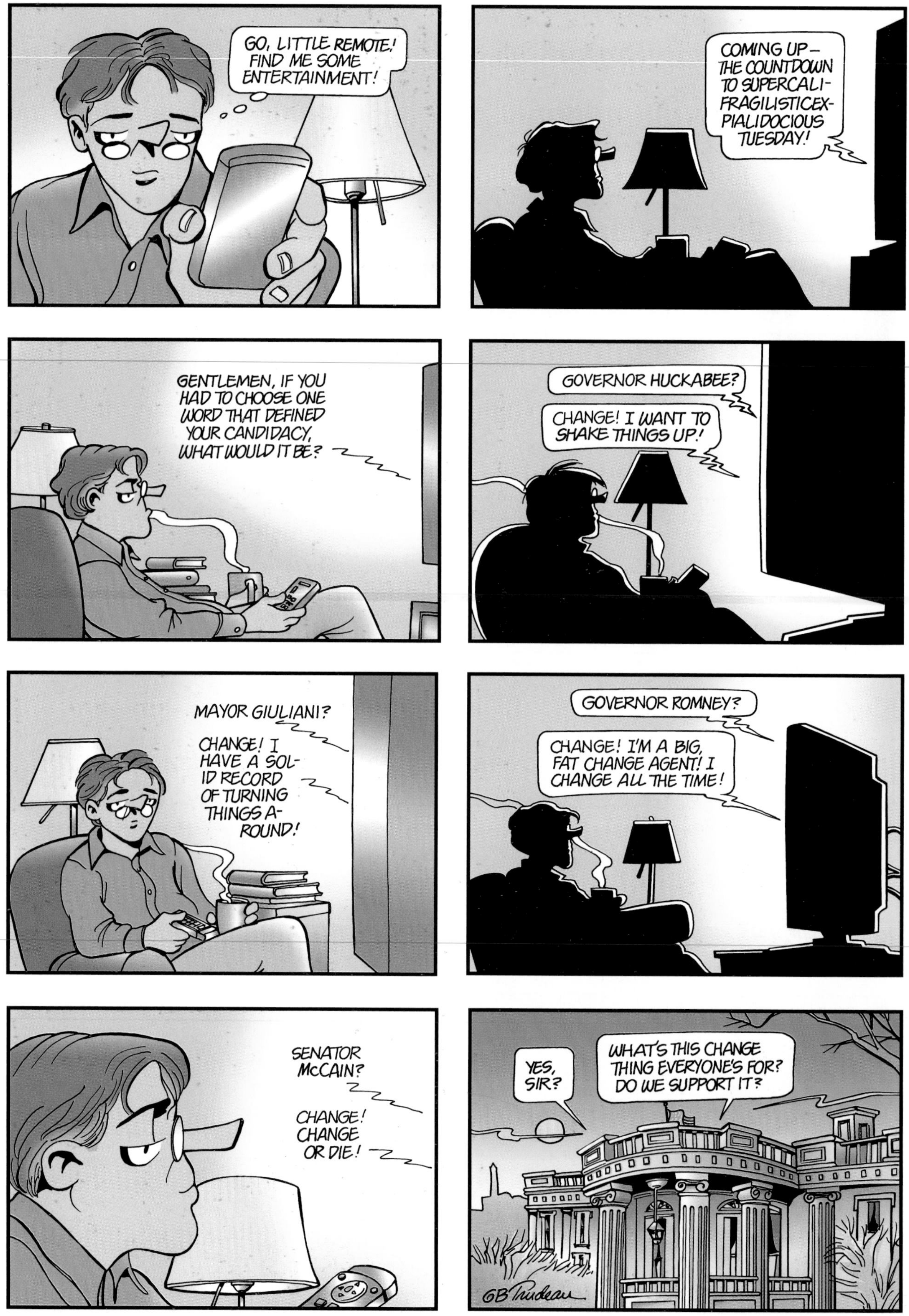
GO, LITTLE REMOTE! FIND ME SOME ENTERTAINMENT!
COMING UP— THE COUNTDOWN TO SUPERCALI-FRAGILISTICEX-PIALIDOCIOUS TUESDAY!
GENTLEMEN, IF YOU HAD TO CHOOSE ONE WORD THAT DEFINED YOUR CANDIDACY, WHAT WOULD IT BE?
GOVERNOR HUCKABEE?
CHANGE! I WANT TO SHAKE THINGS UP!
MAYOR GIULIANI?
CHANGE! I HAVE A SOL-ID RECORD OF TURNING THINGS A-ROUND!
GOVERNOR ROMNEY?
CHANGE! I'M A BIG, FAT CHANGE AGENT! I CHANGE ALL THE TIME!
SENATOR McCAIN?
CHANGE! CHANGE OR DIE!
YES, SIR?
WHAT'S THIS CHANGE THING EVERYONE'S FOR? DO WE SUPPORT IT?
GB Trudeau

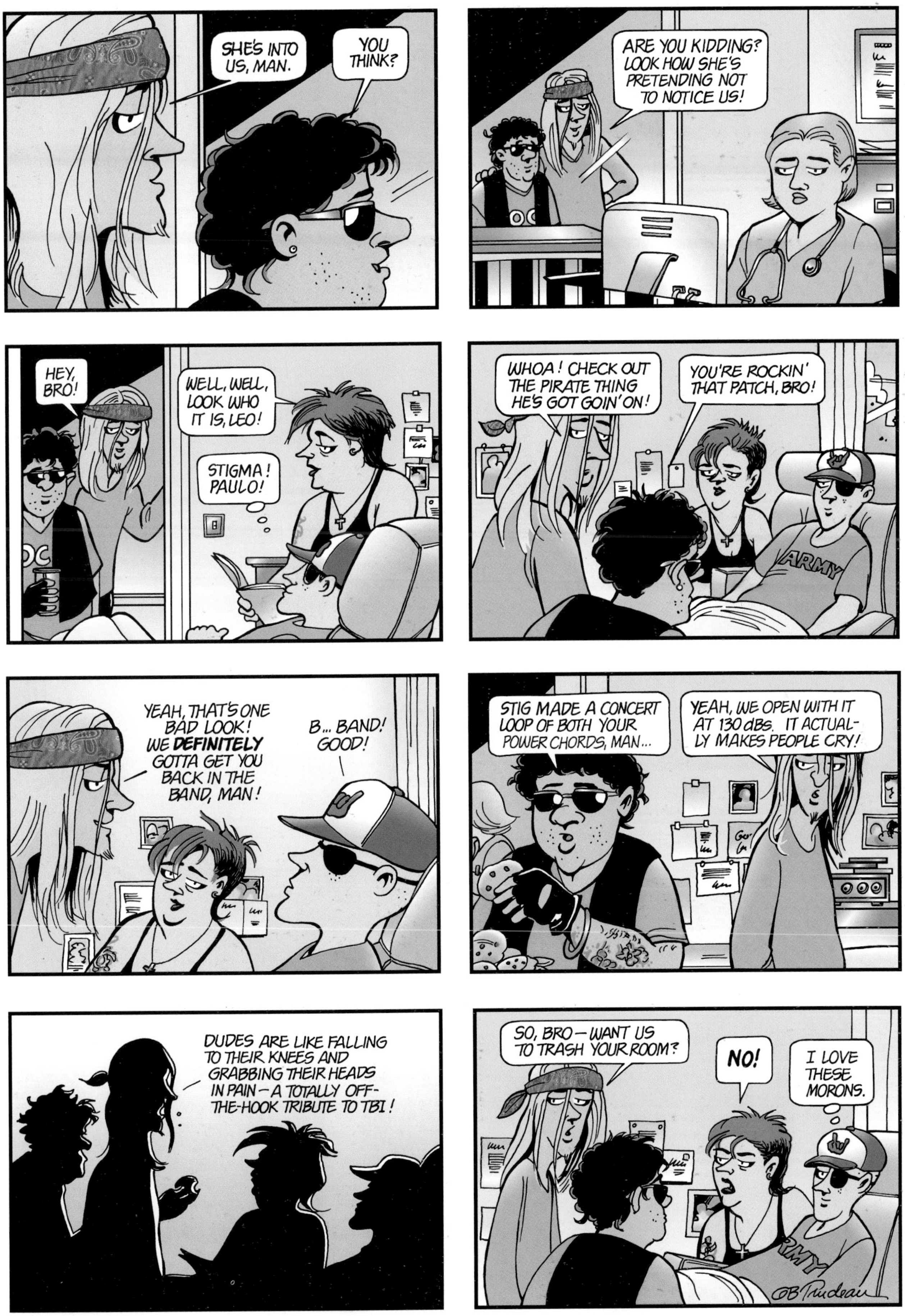
SHE'S INTO US, MAN.
YOU THINK?
ARE YOU KIDDING? LOOK HOW SHE'S PRETENDING NOT TO NOTICE US!
HEY, BRO!
WELL, WELL, LOOK WHO IT IS, LEO!
STIGMA! PAULO!
WHOA! CHECK OUT THE PIRATE THING HE'S GOT GOIN' ON!
YOU'RE ROCKIN' THAT PATCH, BRO!
YEAH, THAT'S ONE BAD LOOK! WE **DEFINITELY** GOTTA GET YOU BACK IN THE BAND, MAN!
B... BAND! GOOD!
STIG MADE A CONCERT LOOP OF BOTH YOUR POWER CHORDS, MAN...
YEAH, WE OPEN WITH IT AT 130 dBs. IT ACTUALLY MAKES PEOPLE CRY!
DUDES ARE LIKE FALLING TO THEIR KNEES AND GRABBING THEIR HEADS IN PAIN — A TOTALLY OFF-THE-HOOK TRIBUTE TO TBI!
SO, BRO — WANT US TO TRASH YOUR ROOM?
NO!
I LOVE THESE MORONS.
GB Trudeau

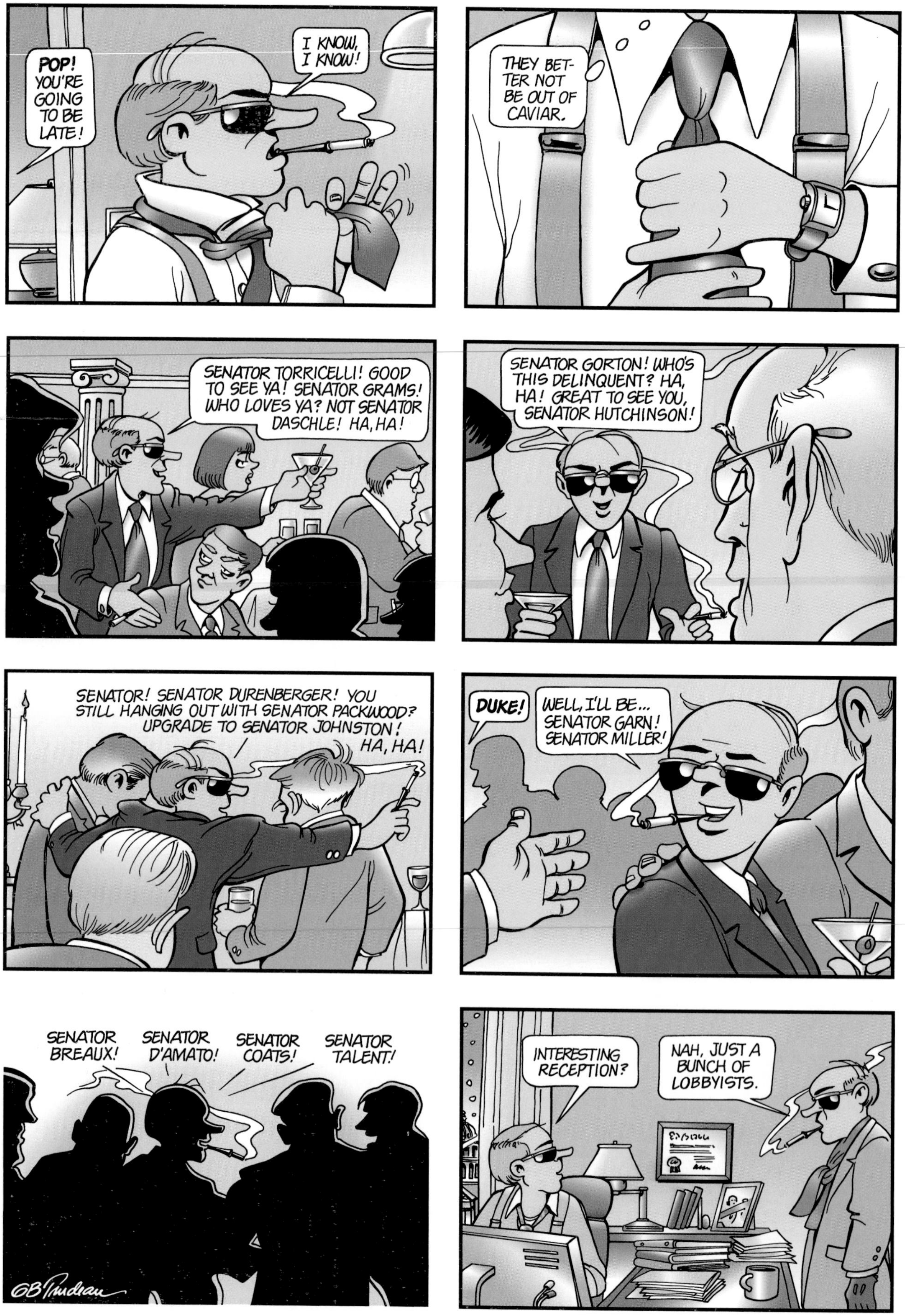
POP! YOU'RE GOING TO BE LATE!
I KNOW, I KNOW!
THEY BETTER NOT BE OUT OF CAVIAR.
SENATOR TORRICELLI! GOOD TO SEE YA! SENATOR GRAMS! WHO LOVES YA? NOT SENATOR DASCHLE! HA, HA!
SENATOR GORTON! WHO'S THIS DELINQUENT? HA, HA! GREAT TO SEE YOU, SENATOR HUTCHINSON!
SENATOR! SENATOR DURENBERGER! YOU STILL HANGING OUT WITH SENATOR PACKWOOD? UPGRADE TO SENATOR JOHNSTON! HA, HA!
DUKE!
WELL, I'LL BE... SENATOR GARN! SENATOR MILLER!
SENATOR BREAUX!
SENATOR D'AMATO!
SENATOR COATS!
SENATOR TALENT!
INTERESTING RECEPTION?
NAH, JUST A BUNCH OF LOBBYISTS.

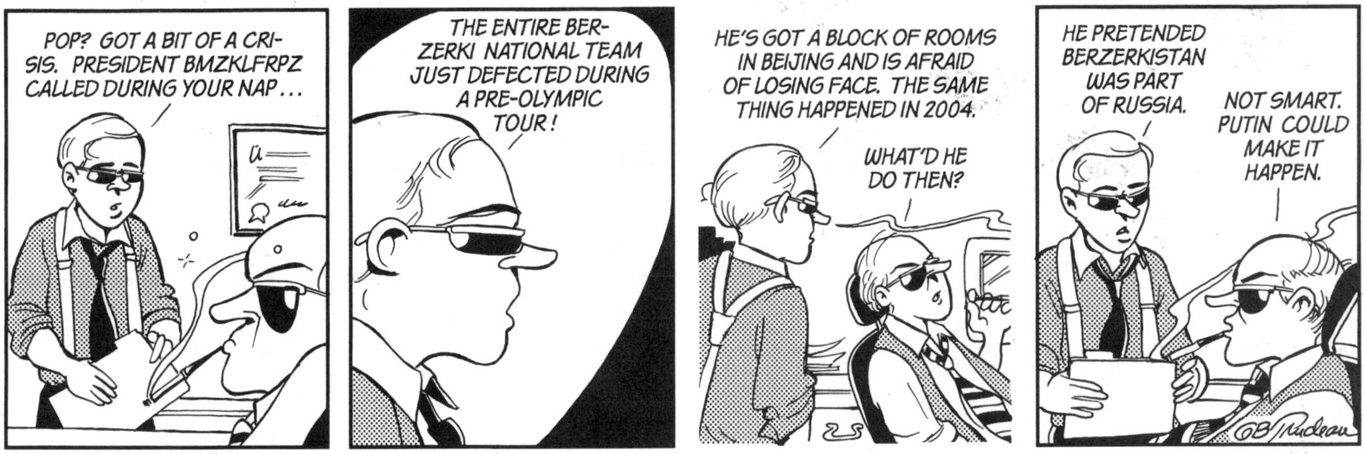
POP? GOT A BIT OF A CRISIS. PRESIDENT BMZKLFRPZ CALLED DURING YOUR NAP...
THE ENTIRE BERZERKI NATIONAL TEAM JUST DEFECTED DURING A PRE-OLYMPIC TOUR!
HE'S GOT A BLOCK OF ROOMS IN BEIJING AND IS AFRAID OF LOSING FACE. THE SAME THING HAPPENED IN 2004.
WHAT'D HE DO THEN?
HE PRETENDED BERZERKISTAN WAS PART OF RUSSIA.
NOT SMART. PUTIN COULD MAKE IT HAPPEN.
GB Trudeau

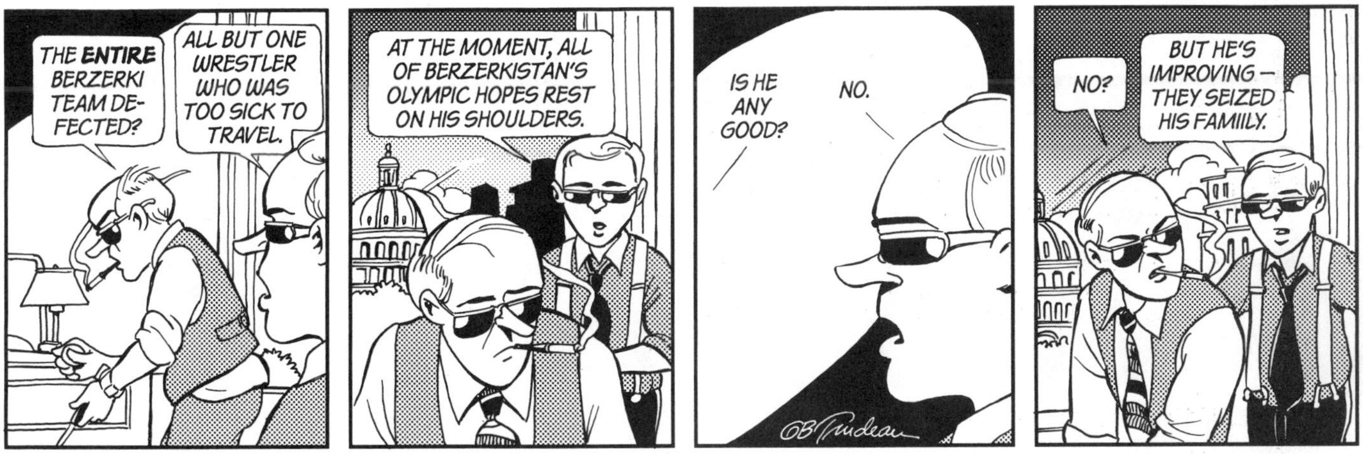
THE ENTIRE BERZERKI TEAM DEFECTED?
ALL BUT ONE WRESTLER WHO WAS TOO SICK TO TRAVEL.
AT THE MOMENT, ALL OF BERZERKISTAN'S OLYMPIC HOPES REST ON HIS SHOULDERS.
IS HE ANY GOOD?
NO.
NO?
BUT HE'S IMPROVING — THEY SEIZED HIS FAMILY.
GB Trudeau

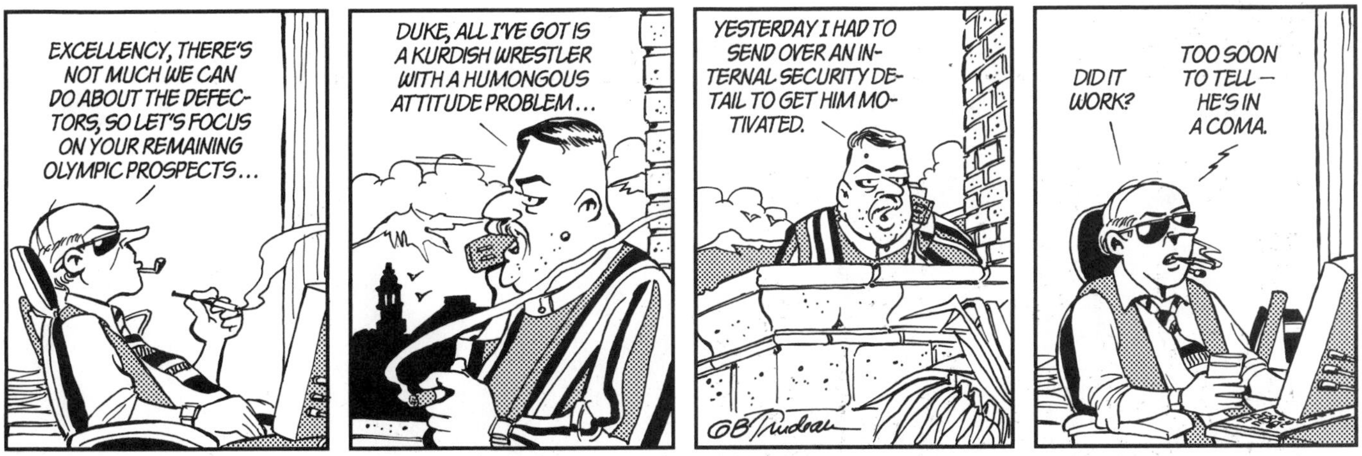
EXCELLENCY, THERE'S NOT MUCH WE CAN DO ABOUT THE DEFECTORS, SO LET'S FOCUS ON YOUR REMAINING OLYMPIC PROSPECTS...
DUKE, ALL I'VE GOT IS A KURDISH WRESTLER WITH A HUMONGOUS ATTITUDE PROBLEM...
YESTERDAY I HAD TO SEND OVER AN INTERNAL SECURITY DETAIL TO GET HIM MOTIVATED.
DID IT WORK?
TOO SOON TO TELL — HE'S IN A COMA.
GB Trudeau

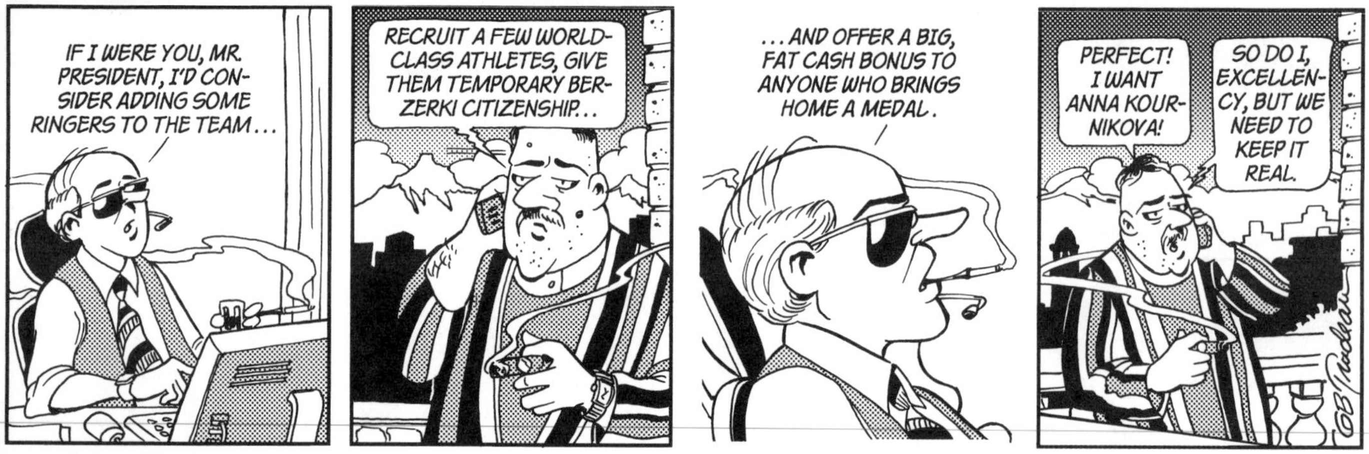
IF I WERE YOU, MR. PRESIDENT, I'D CONSIDER ADDING SOME RINGERS TO THE TEAM...
RECRUIT A FEW WORLD-CLASS ATHLETES, GIVE THEM TEMPORARY BERZERKI CITIZENSHIP...
...AND OFFER A BIG, FAT CASH BONUS TO ANYONE WHO BRINGS HOME A MEDAL.
PERFECT! I WANT ANNA KOURNIKOVA!
SO DO I, EXCELLENCY, BUT WE NEED TO KEEP IT REAL.
GB Trudeau

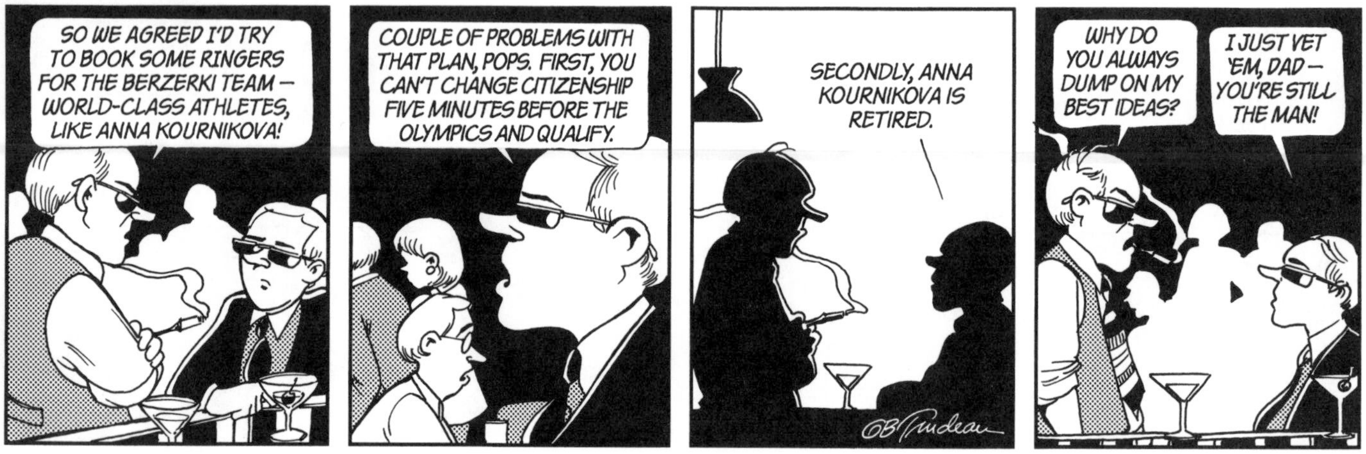
SO WE AGREED I'D TRY TO BOOK SOME RINGERS FOR THE BERZERKI TEAM — WORLD-CLASS ATHLETES, LIKE ANNA KOURNIKOVA!
COUPLE OF PROBLEMS WITH THAT PLAN, POPS. FIRST, YOU CAN'T CHANGE CITIZENSHIP FIVE MINUTES BEFORE THE OLYMPICS AND QUALIFY.
SECONDLY, ANNA KOURNIKOVA IS RETIRED.
GB Trudeau
WHY DO YOU ALWAYS DUMP ON MY BEST IDEAS?
I JUST VET 'EM, DAD — YOU'RE STILL THE MAN!

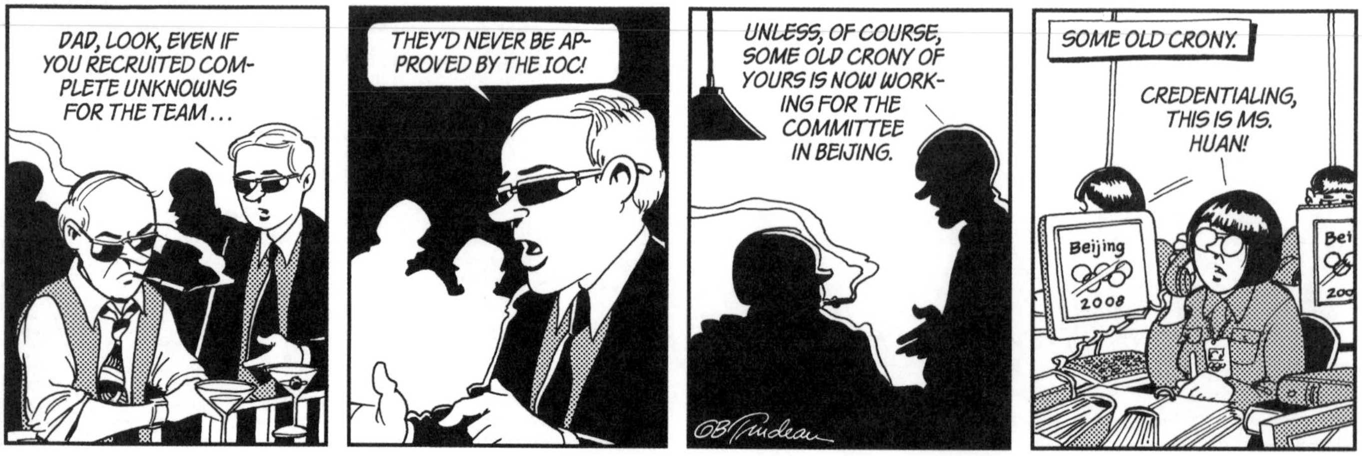
DAD, LOOK, EVEN IF YOU RECRUITED COMPLETE UNKNOWNS FOR THE TEAM...
THEY'D NEVER BE APPROVED BY THE IOC!
UNLESS, OF COURSE, SOME OLD CRONY OF YOURS IS NOW WORKING FOR THE COMMITTEE IN BEIJING.
GB Trudeau
SOME OLD CRONY.
CREDENTIALING, THIS IS MS. HUAN!
Beijing
2008

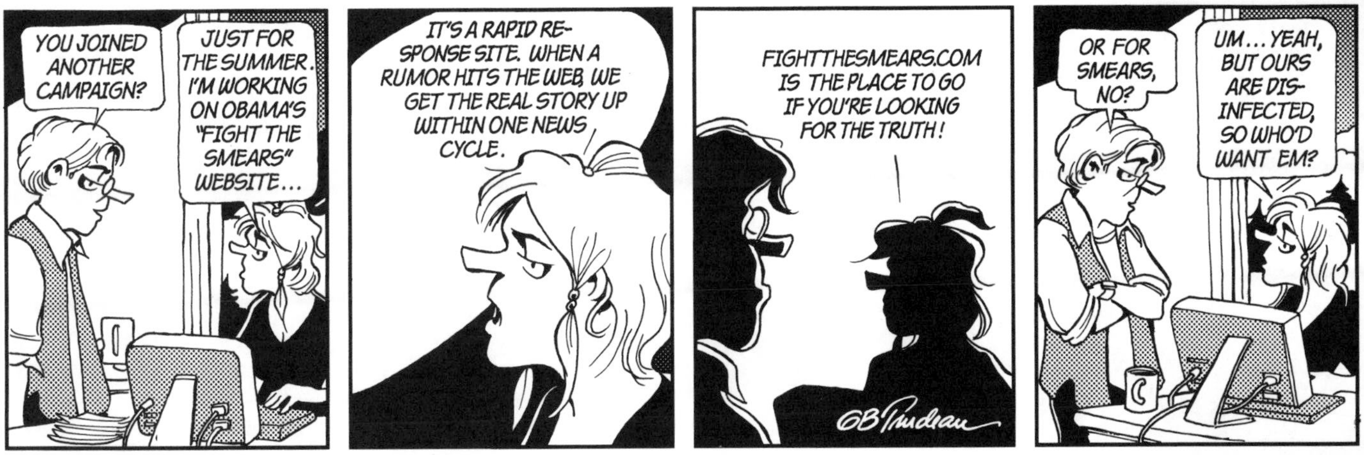
YOU JOINED ANOTHER CAMPAIGN?
JUST FOR THE SUMMER. I'M WORKING ON OBAMA'S "FIGHT THE SMEARS" WEBSITE...
IT'S A RAPID RESPONSE SITE. WHEN A RUMOR HITS THE WEB, WE GET THE REAL STORY UP WITHIN ONE NEWS CYCLE.
FIGHTTHESMEARS.COM IS THE PLACE TO GO IF YOU'RE LOOKING FOR THE TRUTH!
OR FOR SMEARS, NO?
UM... YEAH, BUT OURS ARE DISINFECTED, SO WHO'D WANT EM?

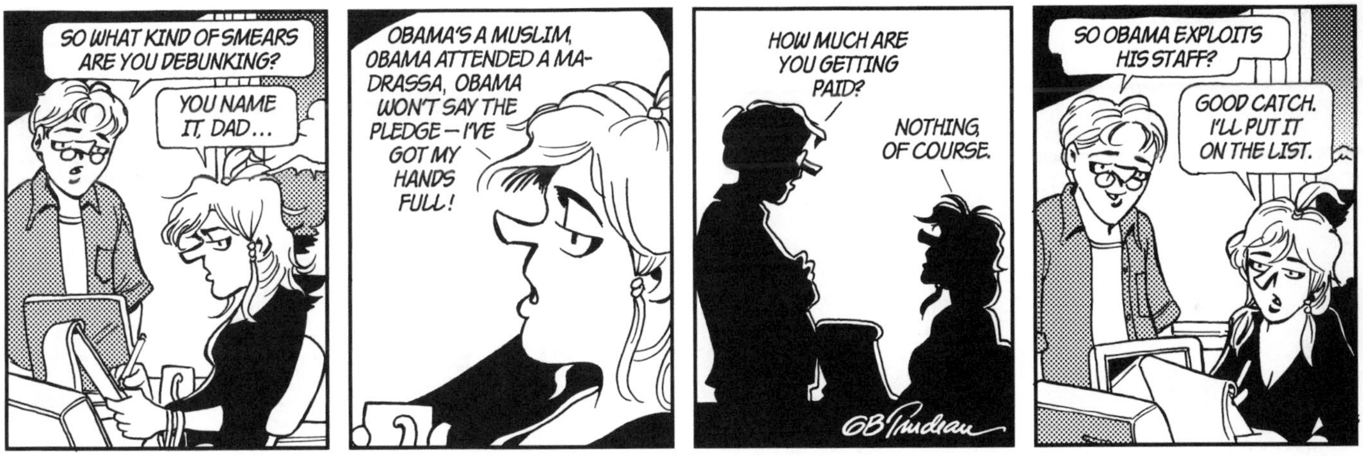
SO WHAT KIND OF SMEARS ARE YOU DEBUNKING?
YOU NAME IT, DAD...
OBAMA'S A MUSLIM, OBAMA ATTENDED A MADRASSA, OBAMA WON'T SAY THE PLEDGE — I'VE GOT MY HANDS FULL!
HOW MUCH ARE YOU GETTING PAID?
NOTHING, OF COURSE.
SO OBAMA EXPLOITS HIS STAFF?
GOOD CATCH. I'LL PUT IT ON THE LIST.

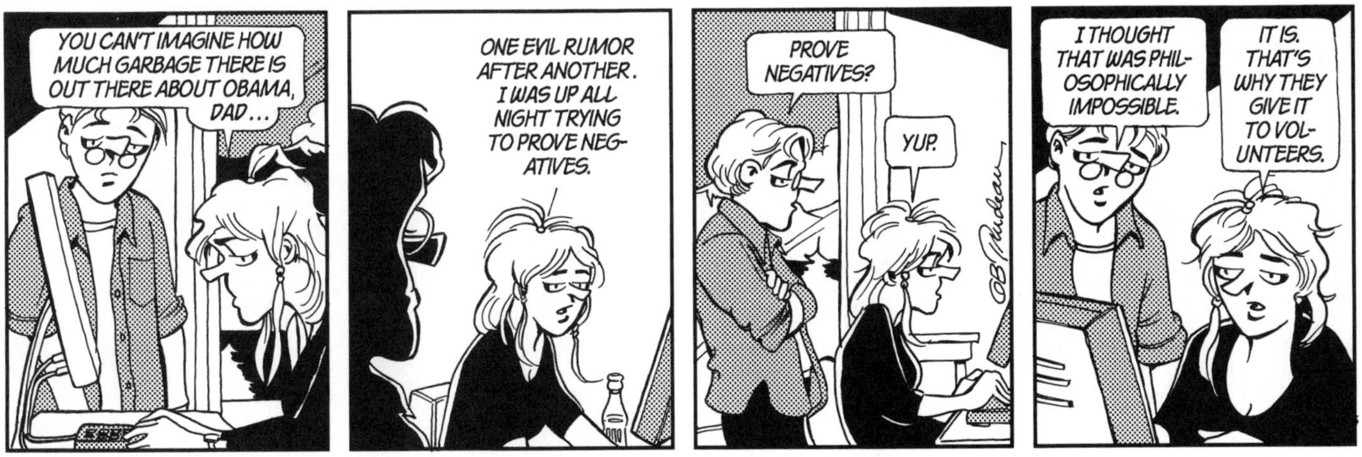
YOU CAN'T IMAGINE HOW MUCH GARBAGE THERE IS OUT THERE ABOUT OBAMA, DAD...
ONE EVIL RUMOR AFTER ANOTHER. I WAS UP ALL NIGHT TRYING TO PROVE NEGATIVES.
PROVE NEGATIVES?
YUP.
I THOUGHT THAT WAS PHILOSOPHICALLY IMPOSSIBLE.
IT IS. THAT'S WHY THEY GIVE IT TO VOLUNTEERS.

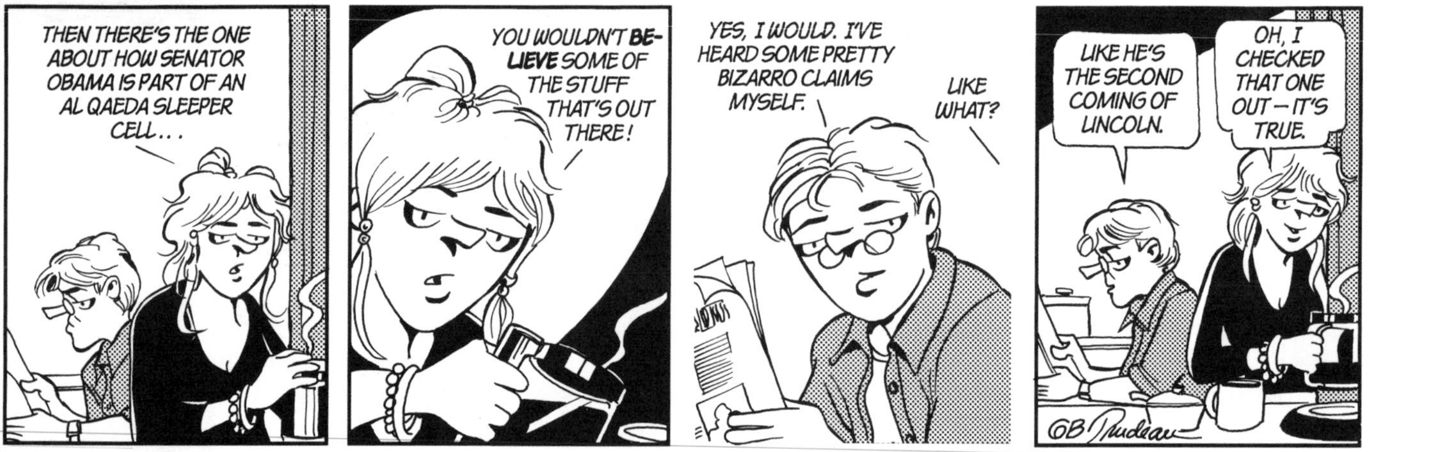
THEN THERE'S THE ONE ABOUT HOW SENATOR OBAMA IS PART OF AN AL QAEDA SLEEPER CELL...
YOU WOULDN'T BELIEVE SOME OF THE STUFF THAT'S OUT THERE!
YES, I WOULD. I'VE HEARD SOME PRETTY BIZARRO CLAIMS MYSELF.
LIKE WHAT?
LIKE HE'S THE SECOND COMING OF LINCOLN.
OH, I CHECKED THAT ONE OUT – IT'S TRUE.
©B Trudeau

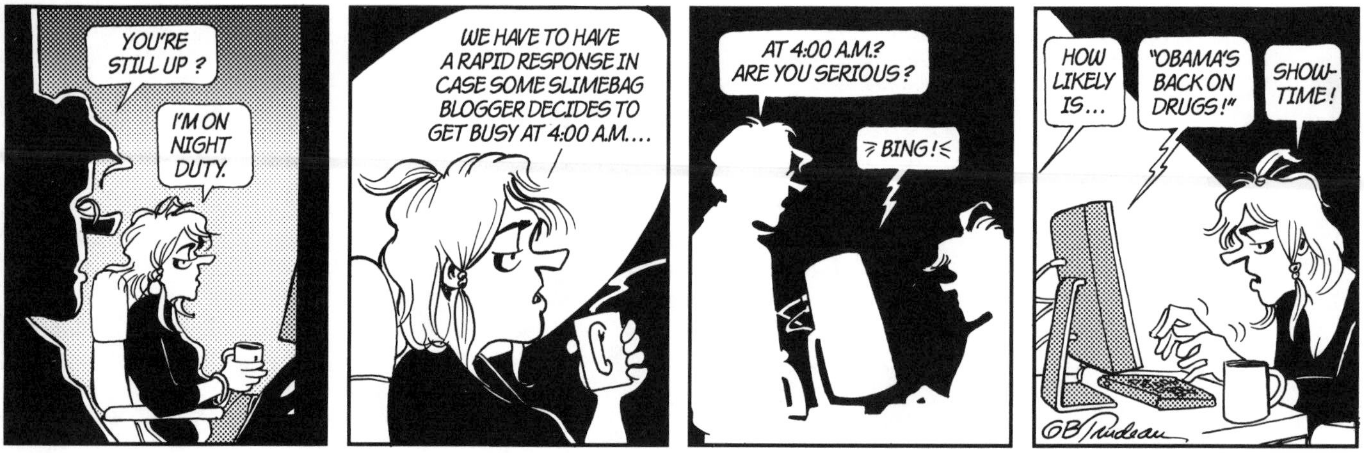
YOU'RE STILL UP ?
I'M ON NIGHT DUTY.
WE HAVE TO HAVE A RAPID RESPONSE IN CASE SOME SLIMEBAG BLOGGER DECIDES TO GET BUSY AT 4:00 A.M....
AT 4:00 A.M.? ARE YOU SERIOUS ?
BING!
HOW LIKELY IS...
"OBAMA'S BACK ON DRUGS!"
SHOW-TIME!
©B Trudeau

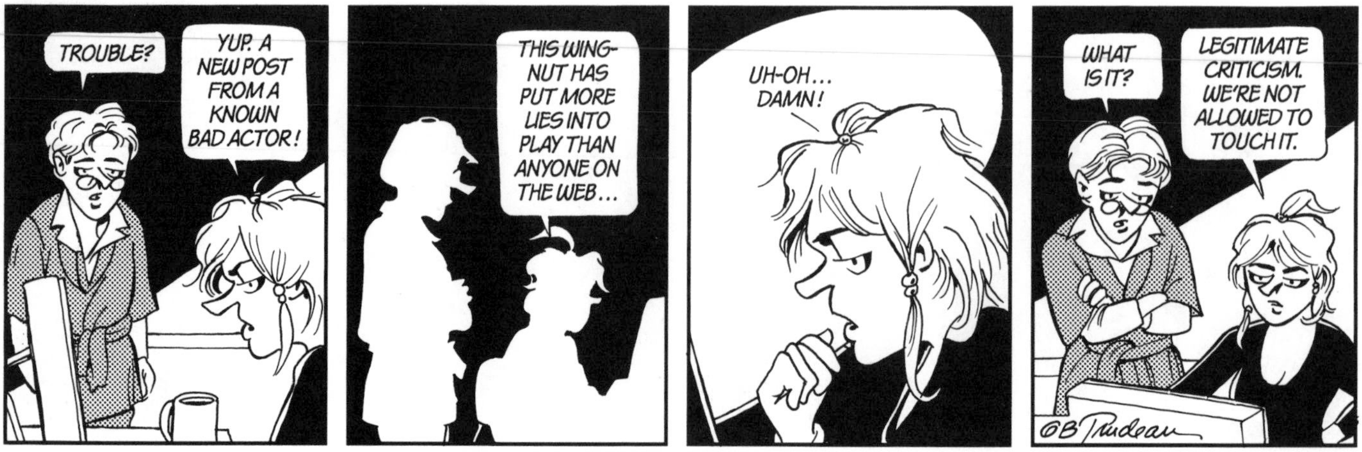
TROUBLE?
YUP. A NEW POST FROM A KNOWN BAD ACTOR!
THIS WING-NUT HAS PUT MORE LIES INTO PLAY THAN ANYONE ON THE WEB...
UH-OH... DAMN!
WHAT IS IT?
LEGITIMATE CRITICISM. WE'RE NOT ALLOWED TO TOUCH IT.
©B Trudeau

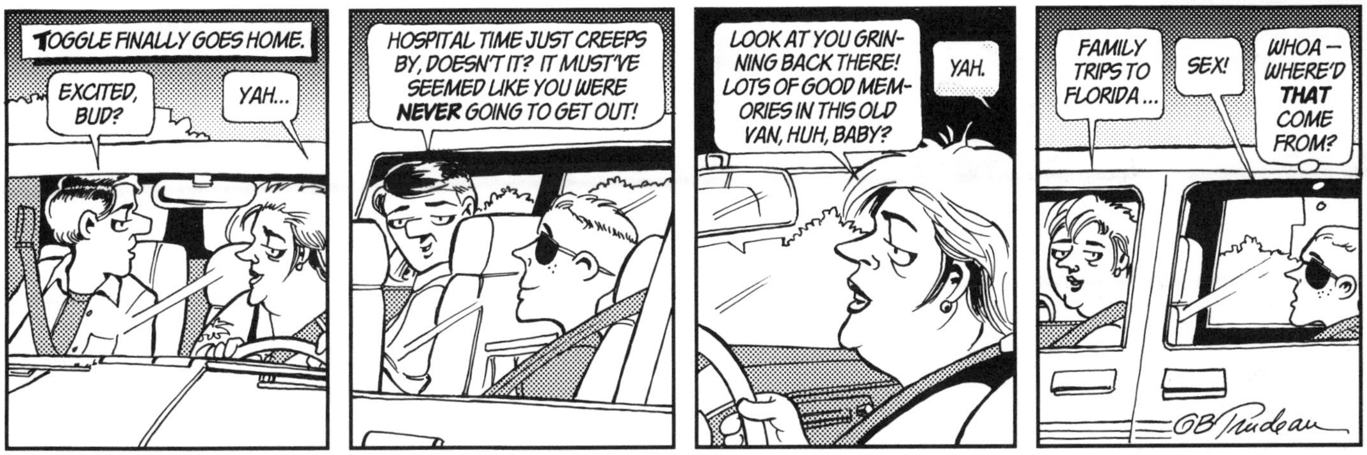
TOGGLE FINALLY GOES HOME.
EXCITED, BUD?
YAH...
HOSPITAL TIME JUST CREEPS BY, DOESN'T IT? IT MUST'VE SEEMED LIKE YOU WERE NEVER GOING TO GET OUT!
LOOK AT YOU GRINNING BACK THERE! LOTS OF GOOD MEMORIES IN THIS OLD VAN, HUH, BABY?
YAH.
FAMILY TRIPS TO FLORIDA...
SEX!
WHOA — WHERE'D THAT COME FROM?
©B Trudeau

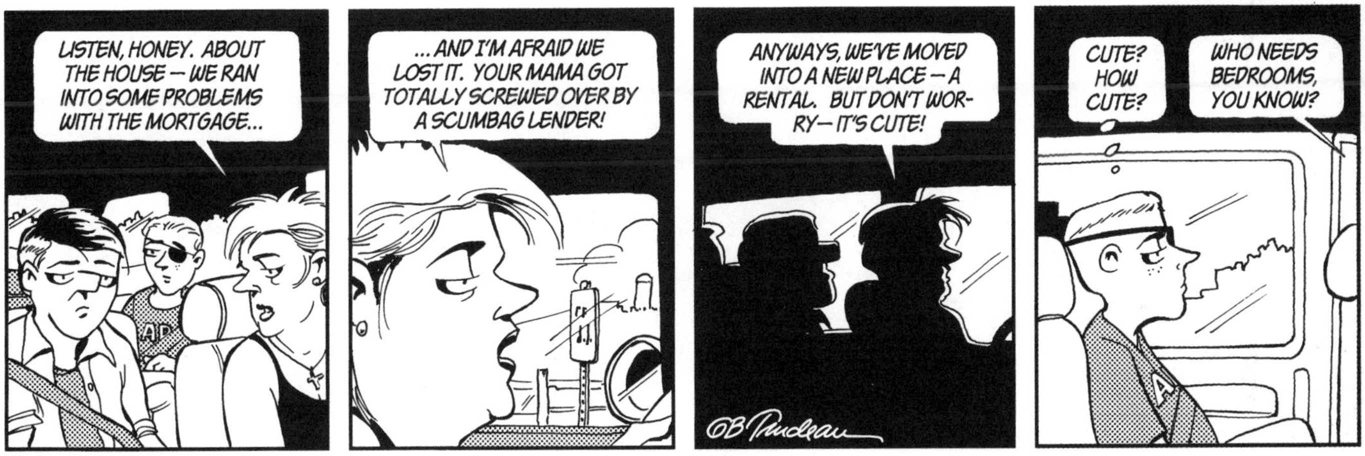
LISTEN, HONEY. ABOUT THE HOUSE — WE RAN INTO SOME PROBLEMS WITH THE MORTGAGE...
...AND I'M AFRAID WE LOST IT. YOUR MAMA GOT TOTALLY SCREWED OVER BY A SCUMBAG LENDER!
ANYWAYS, WE'VE MOVED INTO A NEW PLACE — A RENTAL. BUT DON'T WORRY — IT'S CUTE!
CUTE? HOW CUTE?
WHO NEEDS BEDROOMS, YOU KNOW?
©B Trudeau

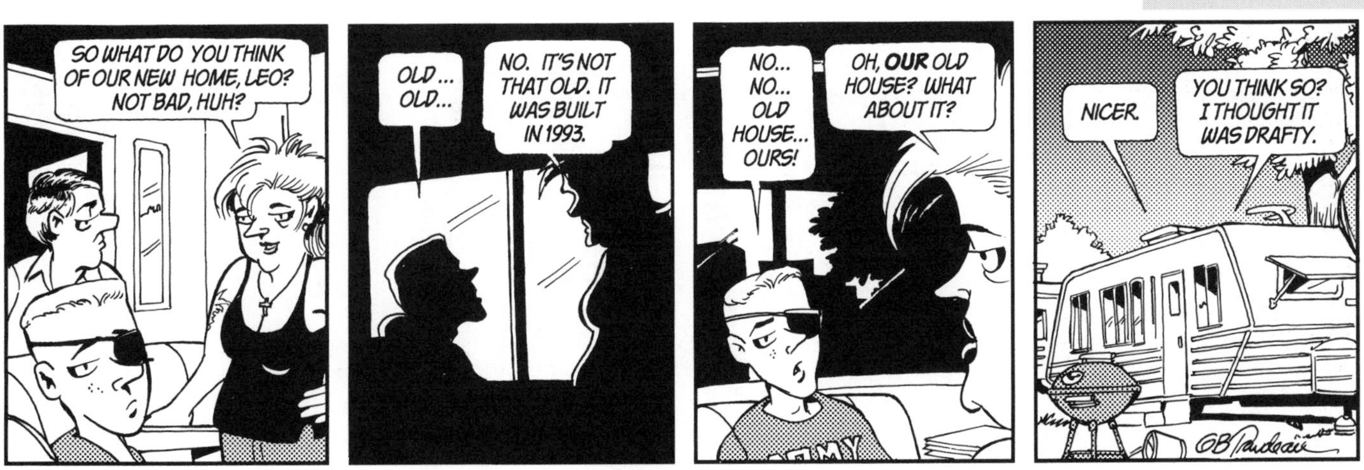
SO WHAT DO YOU THINK OF OUR NEW HOME, LEO? NOT BAD, HUH?
OLD... OLD...
NO. IT'S NOT THAT OLD. IT WAS BUILT IN 1993.
NO... NO... OLD HOUSE... OURS!
OH, OUR OLD HOUSE? WHAT ABOUT IT?
NICER.
YOU THINK SO? I THOUGHT IT WAS DRAFTY.
©B Trudeau

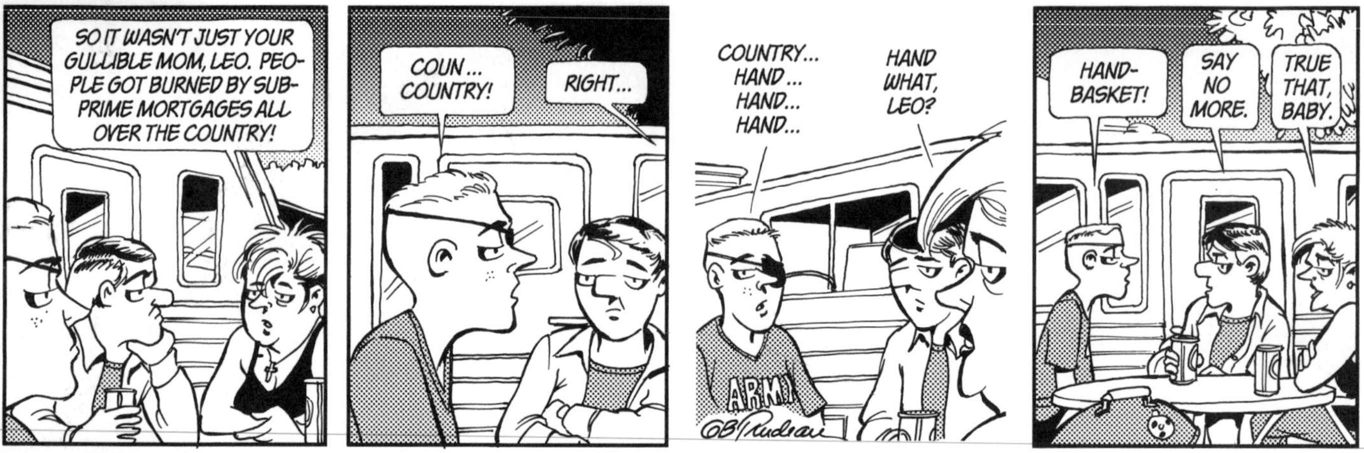
SO IT WASN'T JUST YOUR GULLIBLE MOM, LEO. PEOPLE GOT BURNED BY SUBPRIME MORTGAGES ALL OVER THE COUNTRY!
COUN ... COUNTRY!
RIGHT...
COUNTRY... HAND ... HAND... HAND...
HAND WHAT, LEO?
HAND-BASKET!
SAY NO MORE.
TRUE THAT, BABY.
ARMY
©B Trudeau

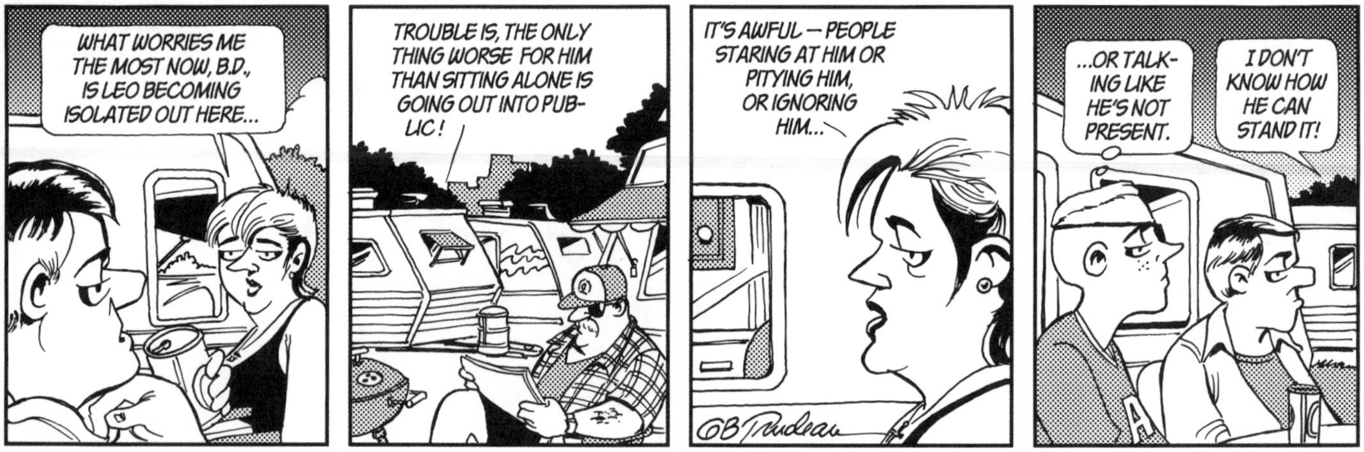
WHAT WORRIES ME THE MOST NOW, B.D., IS LEO BECOMING ISOLATED OUT HERE...
TROUBLE IS, THE ONLY THING WORSE FOR HIM THAN SITTING ALONE IS GOING OUT INTO PUBLIC!
IT'S AWFUL — PEOPLE STARING AT HIM OR PITYING HIM, OR IGNORING HIM...
©B Trudeau
...OR TALKING LIKE HE'S NOT PRESENT.
I DON'T KNOW HOW HE CAN STAND IT!

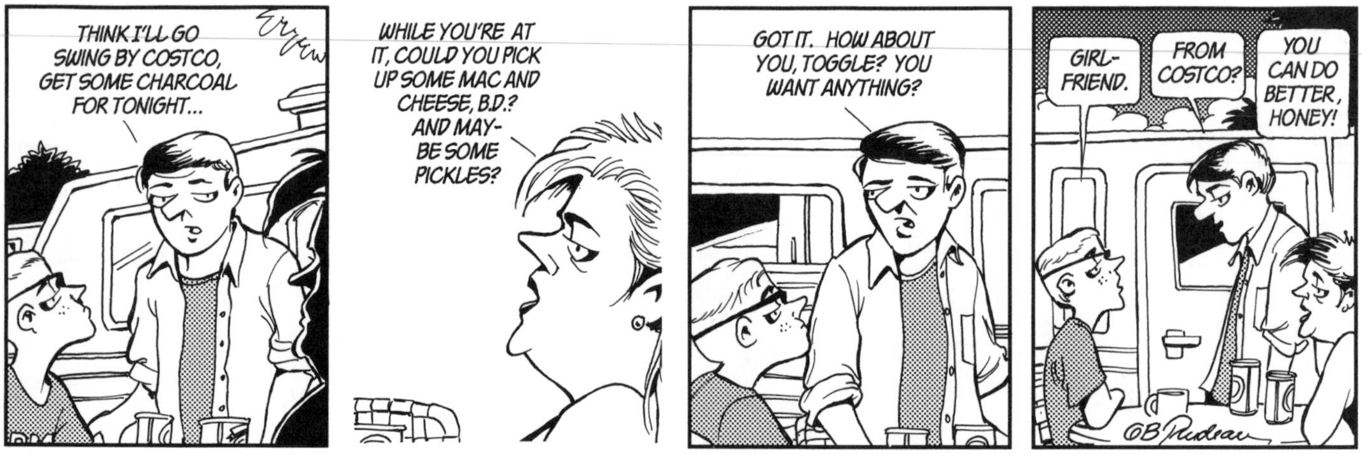
THINK I'LL GO SWING BY COSTCO, GET SOME CHARCOAL FOR TONIGHT...
WHILE YOU'RE AT IT, COULD YOU PICK UP SOME MAC AND CHEESE, B.D.? AND MAYBE SOME PICKLES?
GOT IT. HOW ABOUT YOU, TOGGLE? YOU WANT ANYTHING?
GIRLFRIEND.
FROM COSTCO?
YOU CAN DO BETTER, HONEY!
©B Trudeau

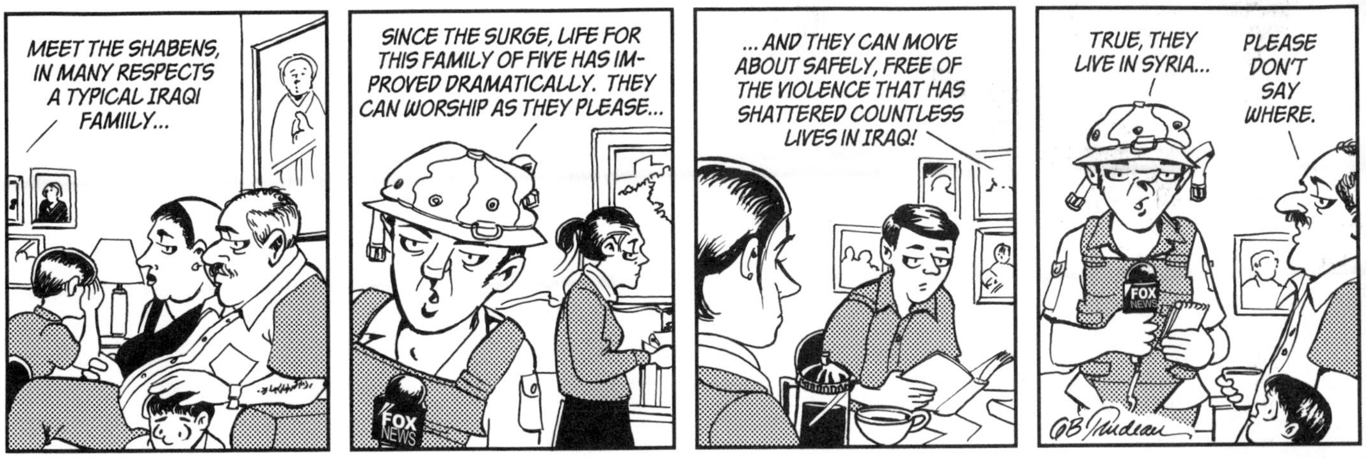
MEET THE SHABENS, IN MANY RESPECTS A TYPICAL IRAQI FAMIILY...
SINCE THE SURGE, LIFE FOR THIS FAMILY OF FIVE HAS IMPROVED DRAMATICALLY. THEY CAN WORSHIP AS THEY PLEASE...
... AND THEY CAN MOVE ABOUT SAFELY, FREE OF THE VIOLENCE THAT HAS SHATTERED COUNTLESS LIVES IN IRAQ!
TRUE, THEY LIVE IN SYRIA...
PLEASE DON'T SAY WHERE.

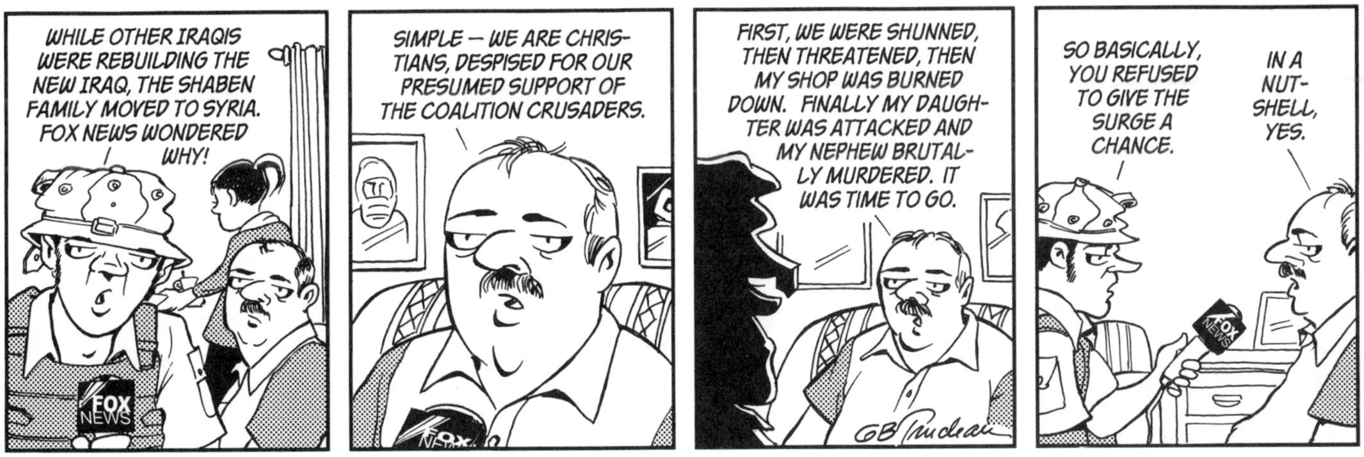
WHILE OTHER IRAQIS WERE REBUILDING THE NEW IRAQ, THE SHABEN FAMILY MOVED TO SYRIA. FOX NEWS WONDERED WHY!
SIMPLE — WE ARE CHRISTIANS, DESPISED FOR OUR PRESUMED SUPPORT OF THE COALITION CRUSADERS.
FIRST, WE WERE SHUNNED, THEN THREATENED, THEN MY SHOP WAS BURNED DOWN. FINALLY MY DAUGHTER WAS ATTACKED AND MY NEPHEW BRUTALLY MURDERED. IT WAS TIME TO GO.
SO BASICALLY, YOU REFUSED TO GIVE THE SURGE A CHANCE.
IN A NUTSHELL, YES.

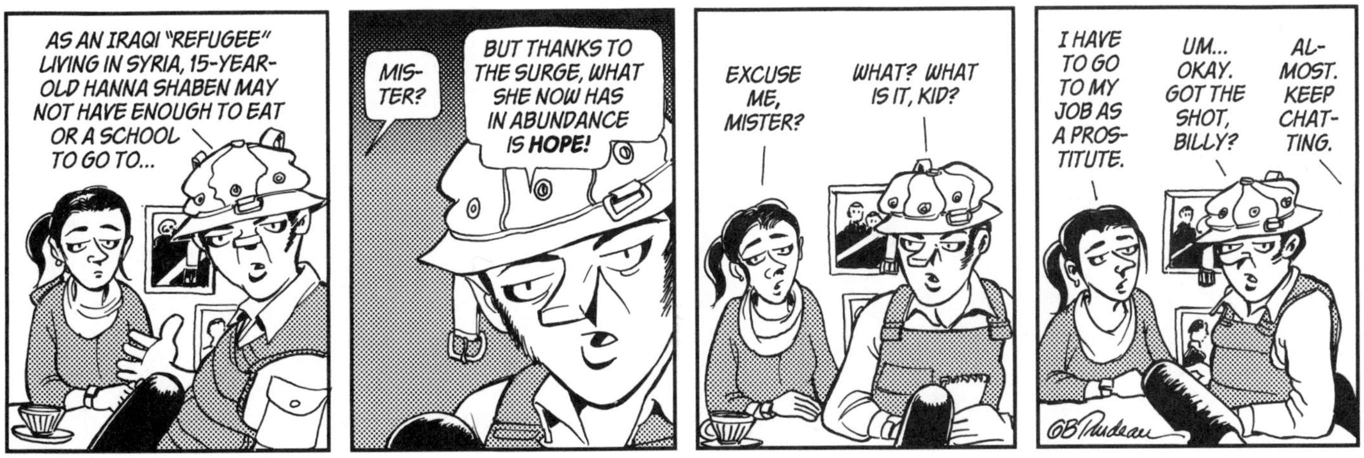
AS AN IRAQI "REFUGEE" LIVING IN SYRIA, 15-YEAR-OLD HANNA SHABEN MAY NOT HAVE ENOUGH TO EAT OR A SCHOOL TO GO TO...
MISTER?
BUT THANKS TO THE SURGE, WHAT SHE NOW HAS IN ABUNDANCE IS HOPE!
EXCUSE ME, MISTER?
WHAT? WHAT IS IT, KID?
I HAVE TO GO TO MY JOB AS A PROSTITUTE.
UM... OKAY. GOT THE SHOT, BILLY?
ALMOST. KEEP CHATTING.

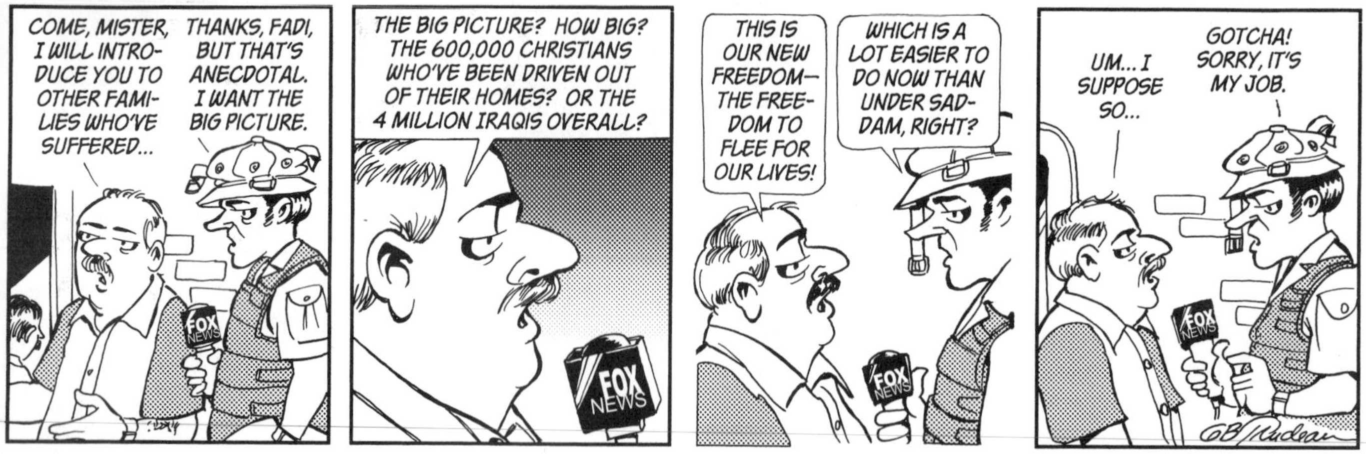
COME, MISTER, I WILL INTRODUCE YOU TO OTHER FAMILIES WHO'VE SUFFERED...
THANKS, FADI, BUT THAT'S ANECDOTAL. I WANT THE BIG PICTURE.
THE BIG PICTURE? HOW BIG? THE 600,000 CHRISTIANS WHO'VE BEEN DRIVEN OUT OF THEIR HOMES? OR THE 4 MILLION IRAQIS OVERALL?
FOX NEWS
THIS IS OUR NEW FREEDOM—THE FREEDOM TO FLEE FOR OUR LIVES!
WHICH IS A LOT EASIER TO DO NOW THAN UNDER SADDAM, RIGHT?
UM... I SUPPOSE SO...
GOTCHA! SORRY, IT'S MY JOB.
GBTrudeau

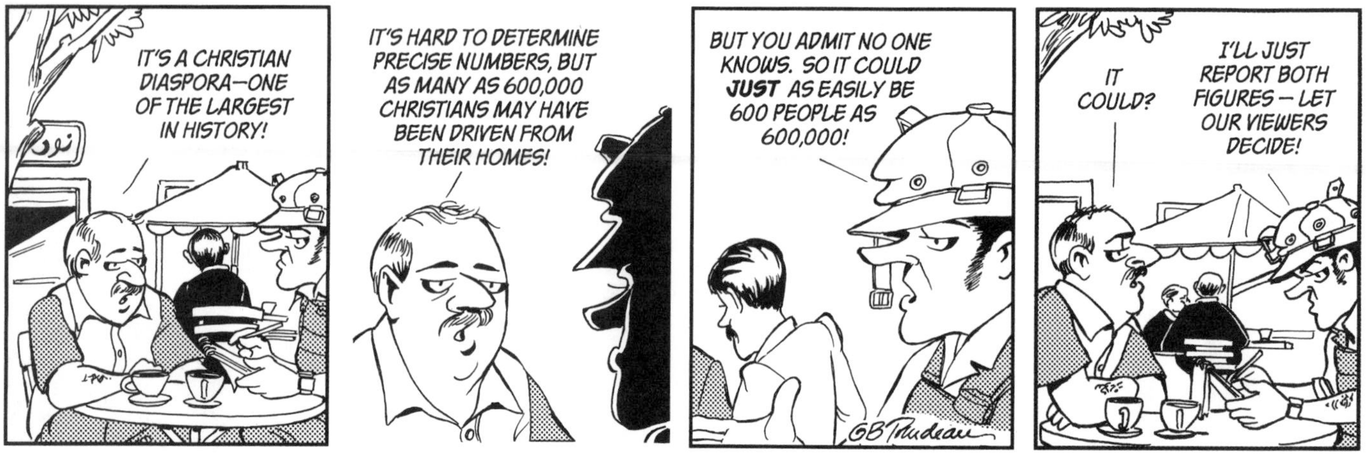
IT'S A CHRISTIAN DIASPORA—ONE OF THE LARGEST IN HISTORY!
IT'S HARD TO DETERMINE PRECISE NUMBERS, BUT AS MANY AS 600,000 CHRISTIANS MAY HAVE BEEN DRIVEN FROM THEIR HOMES!
BUT YOU ADMIT NO ONE KNOWS. SO IT COULD **JUST** AS EASILY BE 600 PEOPLE AS 600,000!
GBTrudeau
IT COULD?
I'LL JUST REPORT BOTH FIGURES — LET OUR VIEWERS DECIDE!

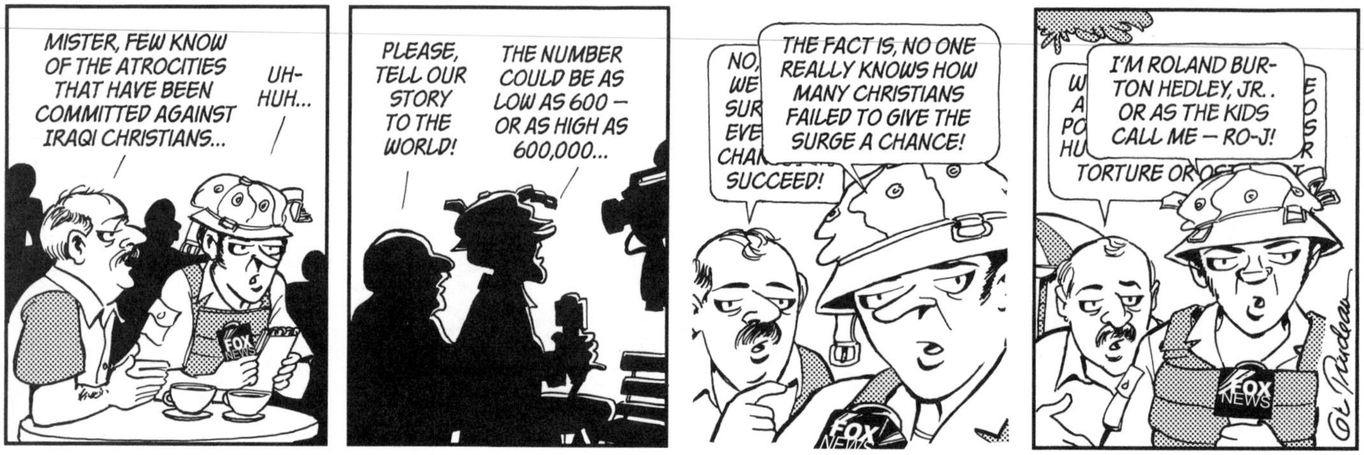
MISTER, FEW KNOW OF THE ATROCITIES THAT HAVE BEEN COMMITTED AGAINST IRAQI CHRISTIANS...
UH-HUH...
PLEASE, TELL OUR STORY TO THE WORLD!
THE NUMBER COULD BE AS LOW AS 600 — OR AS HIGH AS 600,000...
SUCCEED!
THE FACT IS, NO ONE REALLY KNOWS HOW MANY CHRISTIANS FAILED TO GIVE THE SURGE A CHANCE!
I'M ROLAND BURTON HEDLEY, JR.. OR AS THE KIDS CALL ME — RO-J!
FOX NEWS
GBTrudeau

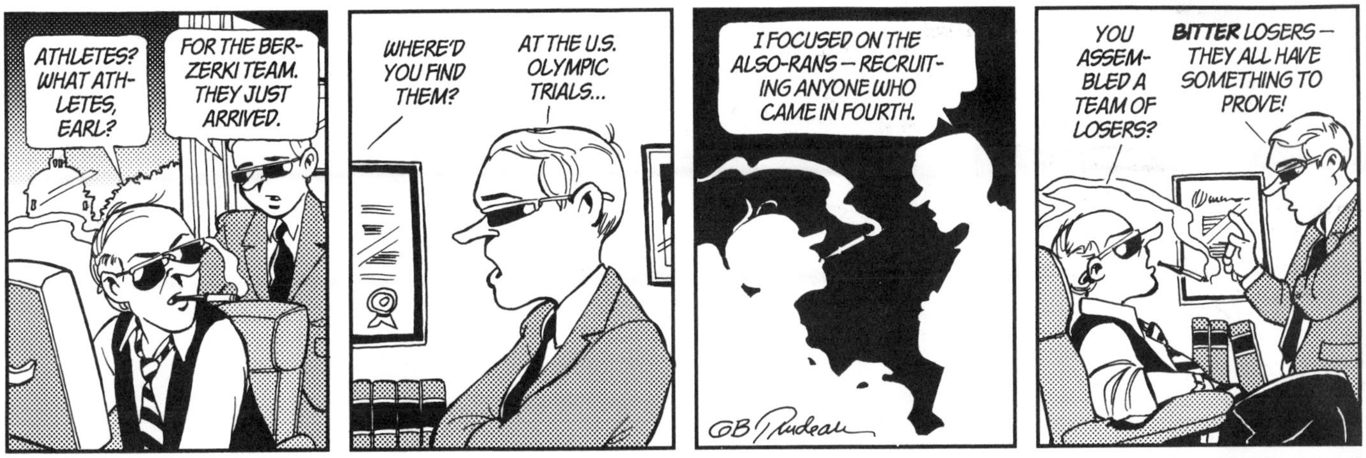
ATHLETES? WHAT ATH-LETES, EARL?
FOR THE BER-ZERKI TEAM. THEY JUST ARRIVED.
WHERE'D YOU FIND THEM?
AT THE U.S. OLYMPIC TRIALS...
I FOCUSED ON THE ALSO-RANS — RECRUIT-ING ANYONE WHO CAME IN FOURTH.
GB Trudeau
YOU ASSEM-BLED A TEAM OF LOSERS?
BITTER LOSERS — THEY ALL HAVE SOMETHING TO PROVE!

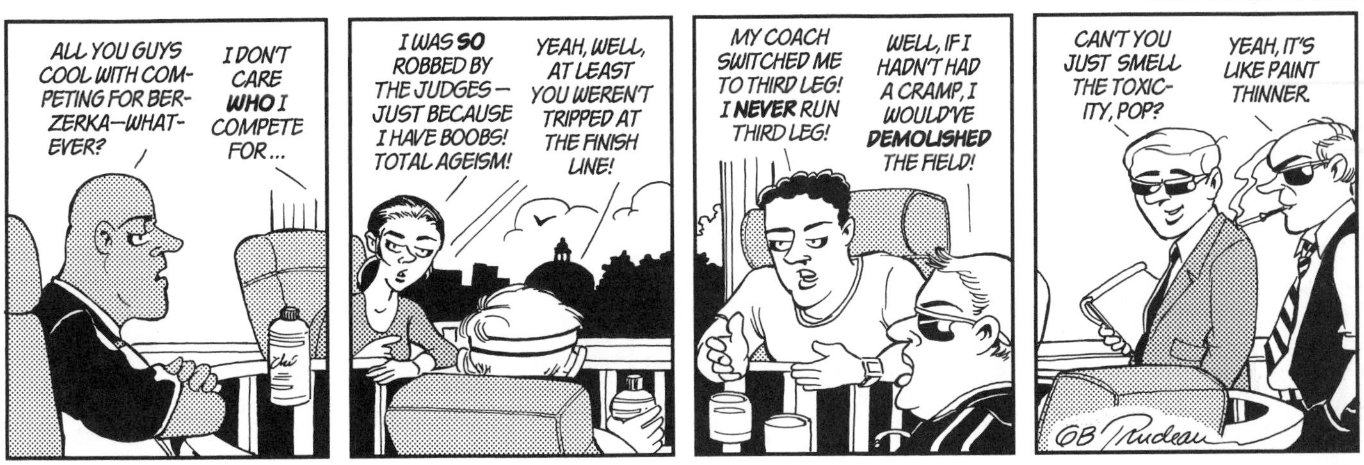
ALL YOU GUYS COOL WITH COM-PETING FOR BER-ZERKA—WHAT-EVER?
I DON'T CARE WHO I COMPETE FOR...
I WAS SO ROBBED BY THE JUDGES — JUST BECAUSE I HAVE BOOBS! TOTAL AGEISM!
YEAH, WELL, AT LEAST YOU WEREN'T TRIPPED AT THE FINISH LINE!
MY COACH SWITCHED ME TO THIRD LEG! I NEVER RUN THIRD LEG!
WELL, IF I HADN'T HAD A CRAMP, I WOULD'VE DEMOLISHED THE FIELD!
CAN'T YOU JUST SMELL THE TOXIC-ITY, POP?
YEAH, IT'S LIKE PAINT THINNER.
GB Trudeau

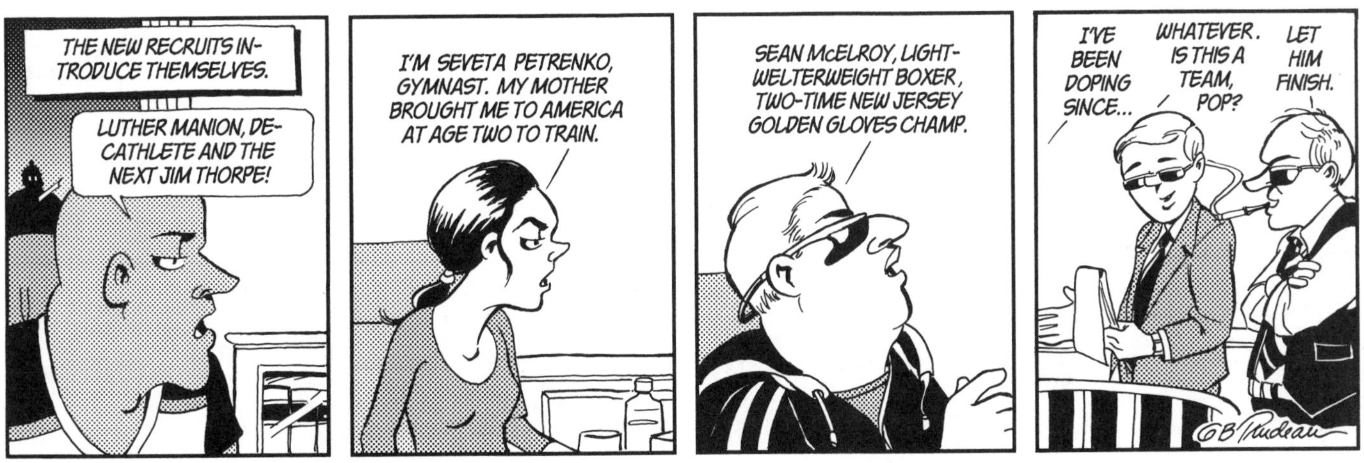
THE NEW RECRUITS IN-TRODUCE THEMSELVES.
LUTHER MANION, DE-CATHLETE AND THE NEXT JIM THORPE!
I'M SEVETA PETRENKO, GYMNAST. MY MOTHER BROUGHT ME TO AMERICA AT AGE TWO TO TRAIN.
SEAN McELROY, LIGHT-WELTERWEIGHT BOXER, TWO-TIME NEW JERSEY GOLDEN GLOVES CHAMP.
I'VE BEEN DOPING SINCE...
WHATEVER. IS THIS A TEAM, POP?
LET HIM FINISH.
GB Trudeau

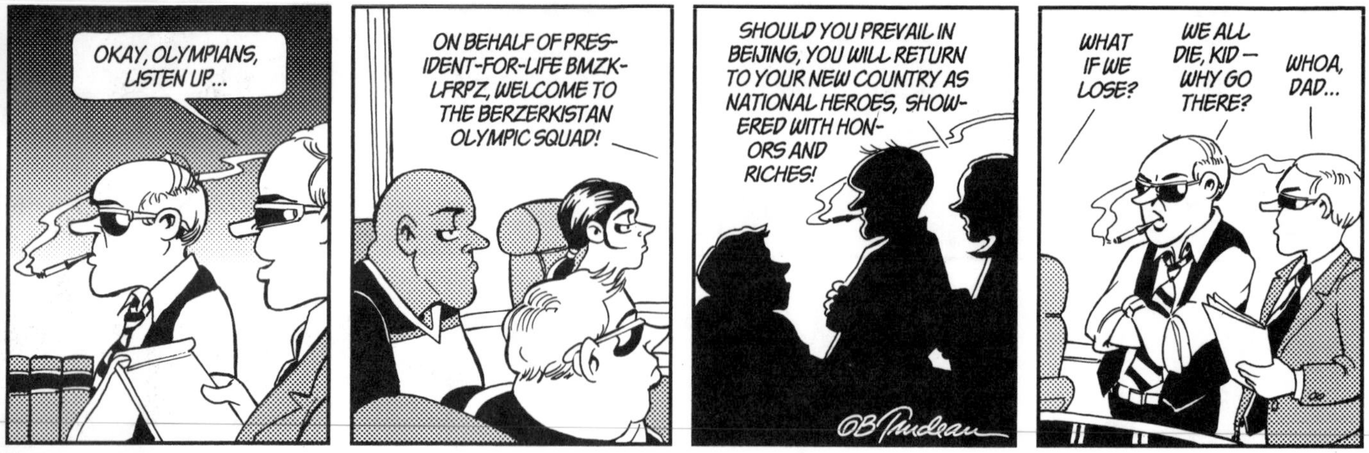
OKAY, OLYMPIANS, LISTEN UP...
ON BEHALF OF PRES-IDENT-FOR-LIFE BMZK-LFRPZ, WELCOME TO THE BERZERKISTAN OLYMPIC SQUAD!
SHOULD YOU PREVAIL IN BEIJING, YOU WILL RETURN TO YOUR NEW COUNTRY AS NATIONAL HEROES, SHOW-ERED WITH HON-ORS AND RICHES!
WHAT IF WE LOSE?
WE ALL DIE, KID — WHY GO THERE?
WHOA, DAD...
GB Trudeau

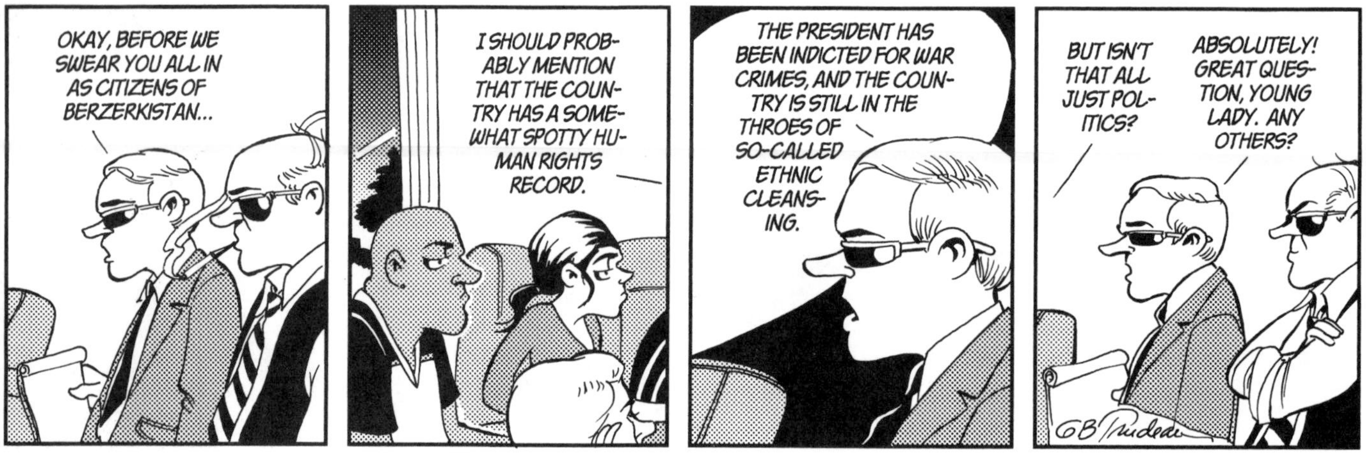
OKAY, BEFORE WE SWEAR YOU ALL IN AS CITIZENS OF BERZERKISTAN...
I SHOULD PROB-ABLY MENTION THAT THE COUN-TRY HAS A SOME-WHAT SPOTTY HU-MAN RIGHTS RECORD.
THE PRESIDENT HAS BEEN INDICTED FOR WAR CRIMES, AND THE COUN-TRY IS STILL IN THE THROES OF SO-CALLED ETHNIC CLEANS-ING.
BUT ISN'T THAT ALL JUST POL-ITICS?
ABSOLUTELY! GREAT QUES-TION, YOUNG LADY. ANY OTHERS?
GB Trudeau

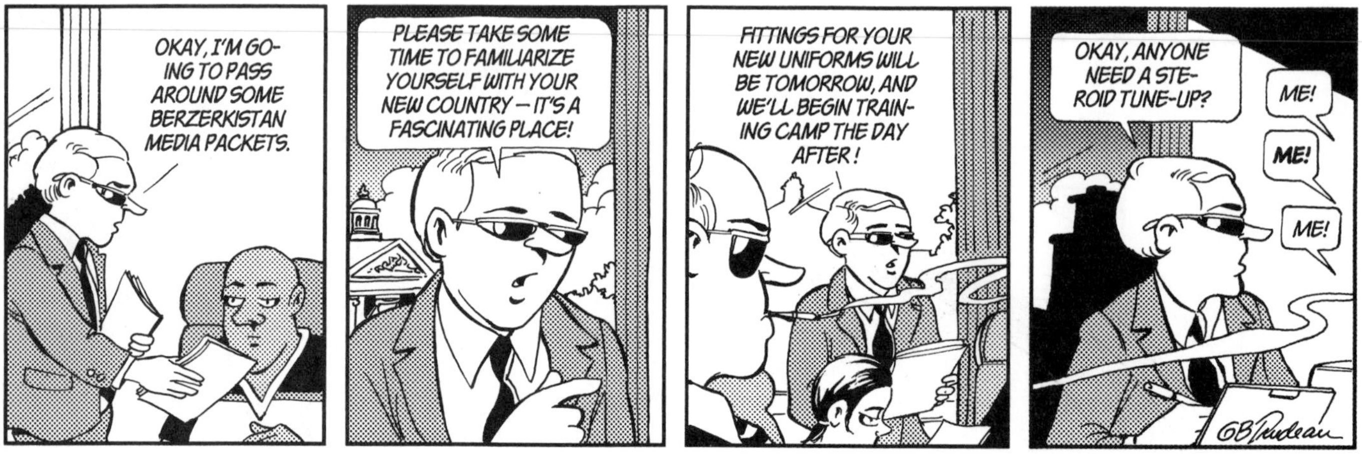
OKAY, I'M GO-ING TO PASS AROUND SOME BERZERKISTAN MEDIA PACKETS.
PLEASE TAKE SOME TIME TO FAMILIARIZE YOURSELF WITH YOUR NEW COUNTRY — IT'S A FASCINATING PLACE!
FITTINGS FOR YOUR NEW UNIFORMS WILL BE TOMORROW, AND WE'LL BEGIN TRAIN-ING CAMP THE DAY AFTER!
OKAY, ANYONE NEED A STE-ROID TUNE-UP?
ME!
ME!
ME!
GB Trudeau

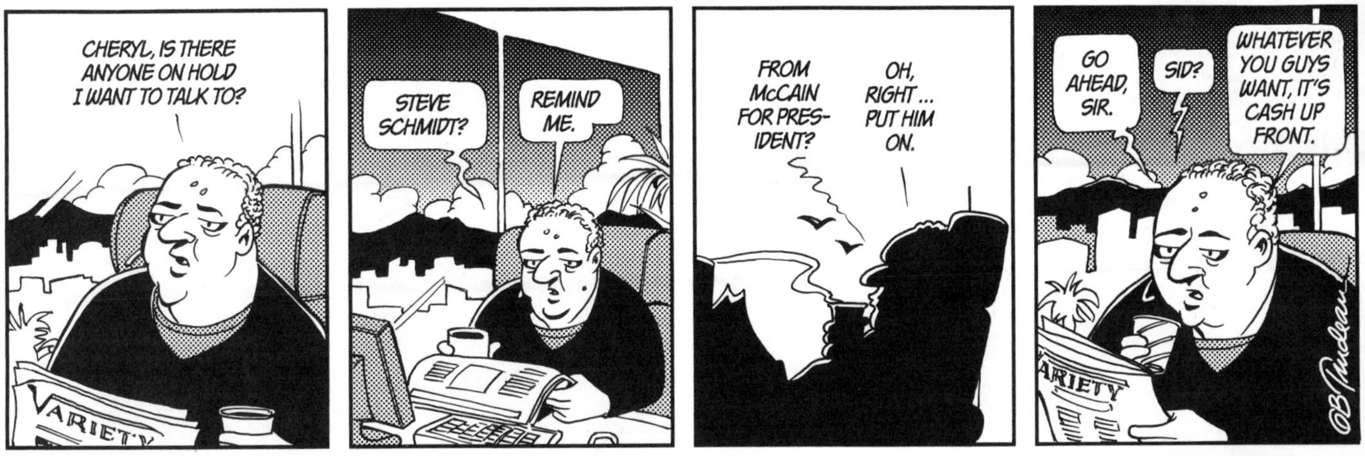
CHERYL, IS THERE ANYONE ON HOLD I WANT TO TALK TO?
STEVE SCHMIDT?
REMIND ME.
FROM McCAIN FOR PRESIDENT?
OH, RIGHT ... PUT HIM ON.
GO AHEAD, SIR.
SID?
WHATEVER YOU GUYS WANT, IT'S CASH UP FRONT.
VARIETY

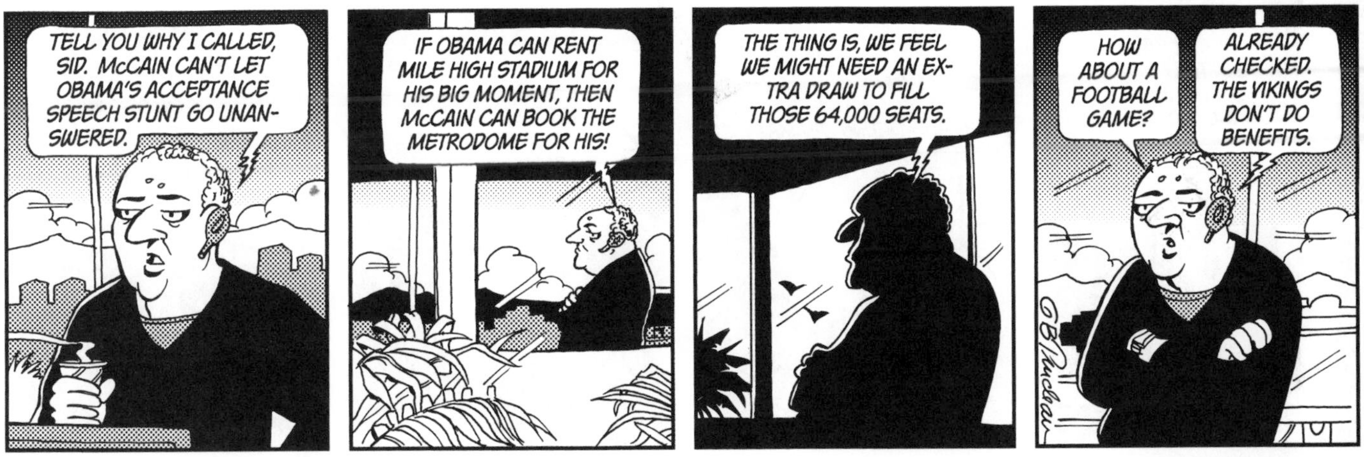
TELL YOU WHY I CALLED, SID. McCAIN CAN'T LET OBAMA'S ACCEPTANCE SPEECH STUNT GO UNANSWERED.
IF OBAMA CAN RENT MILE HIGH STADIUM FOR HIS BIG MOMENT, THEN McCAIN CAN BOOK THE METRODOME FOR HIS!
THE THING IS, WE FEEL WE MIGHT NEED AN EXTRA DRAW TO FILL THOSE 64,000 SEATS.
HOW ABOUT A FOOTBALL GAME?
ALREADY CHECKED. THE VIKINGS DON'T DO BENEFITS.

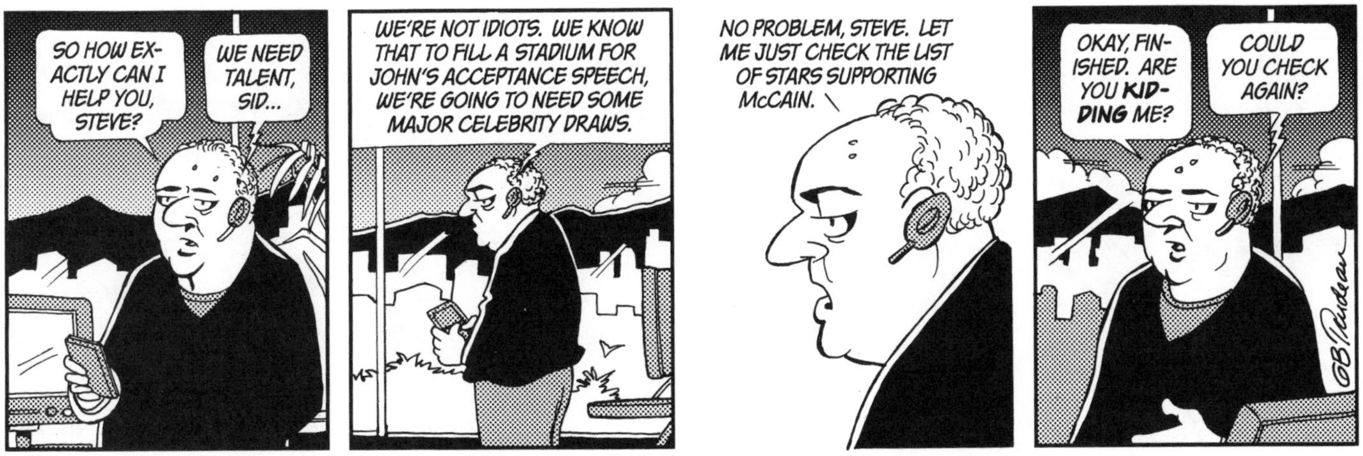
SO HOW EXACTLY CAN I HELP YOU, STEVE?
WE NEED TALENT, SID...
WE'RE NOT IDIOTS. WE KNOW THAT TO FILL A STADIUM FOR JOHN'S ACCEPTANCE SPEECH, WE'RE GOING TO NEED SOME MAJOR CELEBRITY DRAWS.
NO PROBLEM, STEVE. LET ME JUST CHECK THE LIST OF STARS SUPPORTING McCAIN.
OKAY, FINISHED. ARE YOU **KIDDING** ME?
COULD YOU CHECK AGAIN?

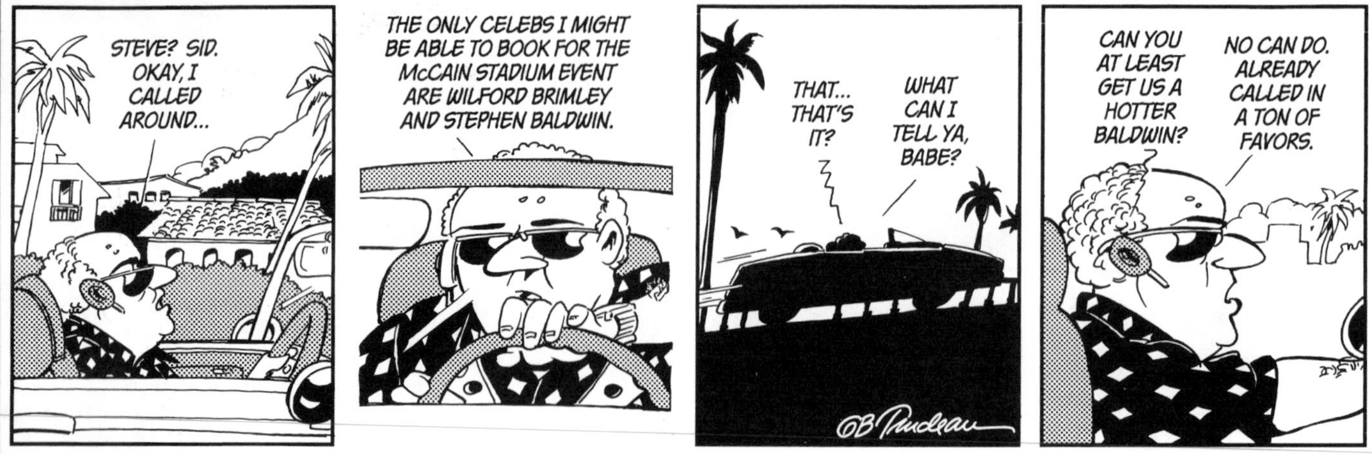
STEVE? SID. OKAY, I CALLED AROUND...
THE ONLY CELEBS I MIGHT BE ABLE TO BOOK FOR THE McCAIN STADIUM EVENT ARE WILFORD BRIMLEY AND STEPHEN BALDWIN.
THAT... THAT'S IT?
WHAT CAN I TELL YA, BABE?
CAN YOU AT LEAST GET US A HOTTER BALDWIN?
NO CAN DO. ALREADY CALLED IN A TON OF FAVORS.
GB Trudeau

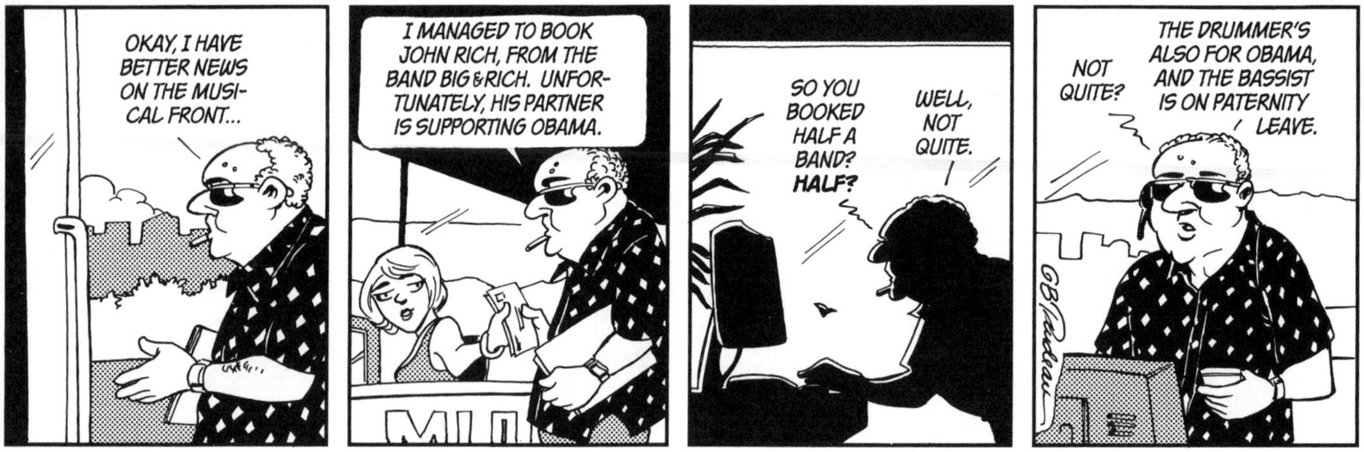
OKAY, I HAVE BETTER NEWS ON THE MUSICAL FRONT...
I MANAGED TO BOOK JOHN RICH, FROM THE BAND BIG & RICH. UNFORTUNATELY, HIS PARTNER IS SUPPORTING OBAMA.
SO YOU BOOKED HALF A BAND? HALF?
WELL, NOT QUITE.
NOT QUITE?
THE DRUMMER'S ALSO FOR OBAMA, AND THE BASSIST IS ON PATERNITY LEAVE.
GB Trudeau

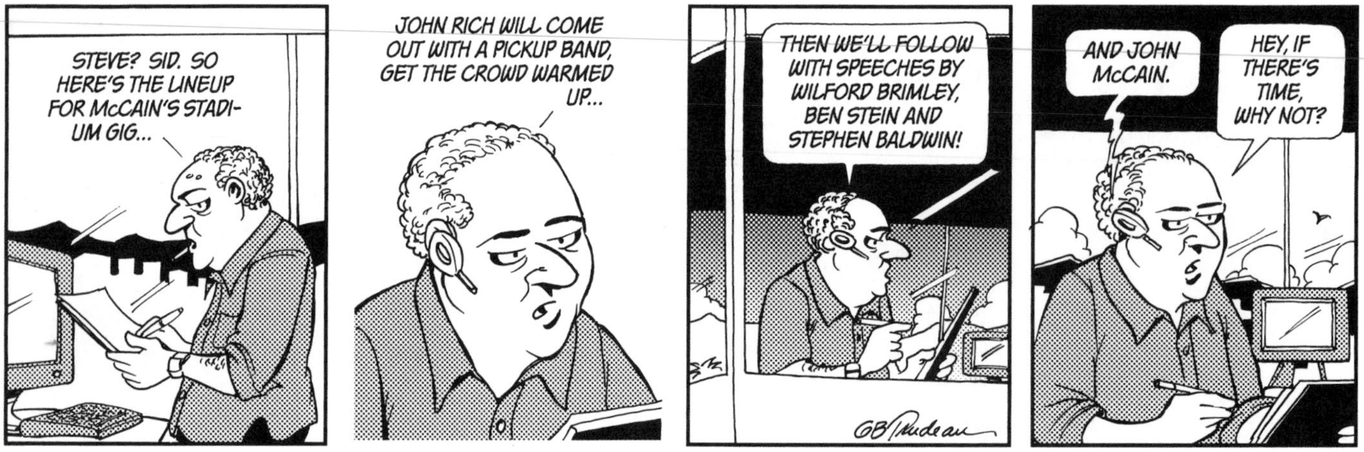
STEVE? SID. SO HERE'S THE LINEUP FOR McCAIN'S STADIUM GIG...
JOHN RICH WILL COME OUT WITH A PICKUP BAND, GET THE CROWD WARMED UP...
THEN WE'LL FOLLOW WITH SPEECHES BY WILFORD BRIMLEY, BEN STEIN AND STEPHEN BALDWIN!
AND JOHN McCAIN.
HEY, IF THERE'S TIME, WHY NOT?
GB Trudeau

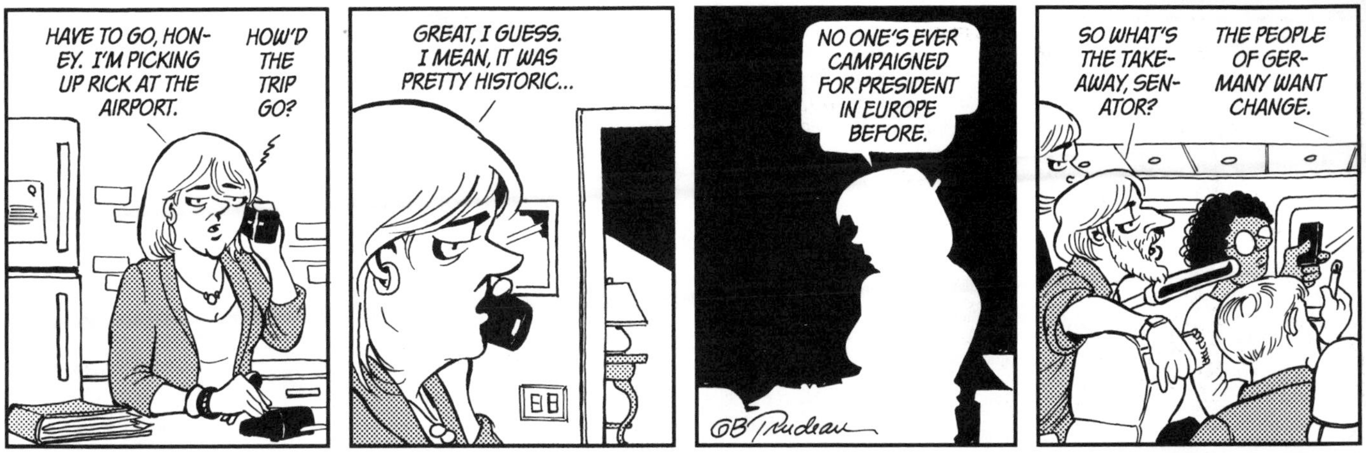
HAVE TO GO, HONEY. I'M PICKING UP RICK AT THE AIRPORT.
HOW'D THE TRIP GO?
GREAT, I GUESS. I MEAN, IT WAS PRETTY HISTORIC...
NO ONE'S EVER CAMPAIGNED FOR PRESIDENT IN EUROPE BEFORE.
SO WHAT'S THE TAKE-AWAY, SENATOR?
THE PEOPLE OF GERMANY WANT CHANGE.
GB Trudeau

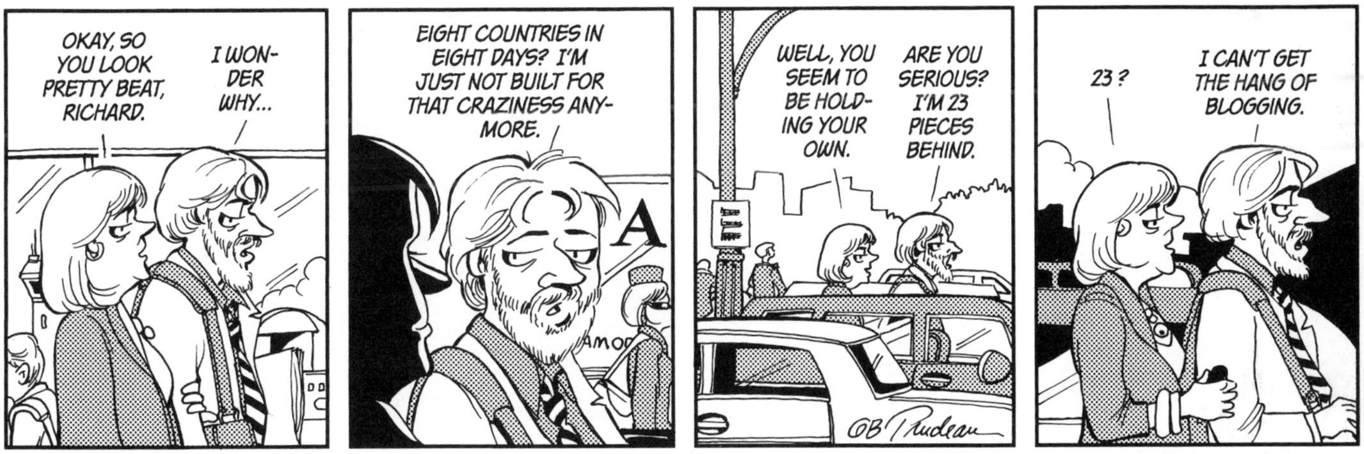
OKAY, SO YOU LOOK PRETTY BEAT, RICHARD.
I WONDER WHY...
EIGHT COUNTRIES IN EIGHT DAYS? I'M JUST NOT BUILT FOR THAT CRAZINESS ANYMORE.
WELL, YOU SEEM TO BE HOLDING YOUR OWN.
ARE YOU SERIOUS? I'M 23 PIECES BEHIND.
23 ?
I CAN'T GET THE HANG OF BLOGGING.
GB Trudeau

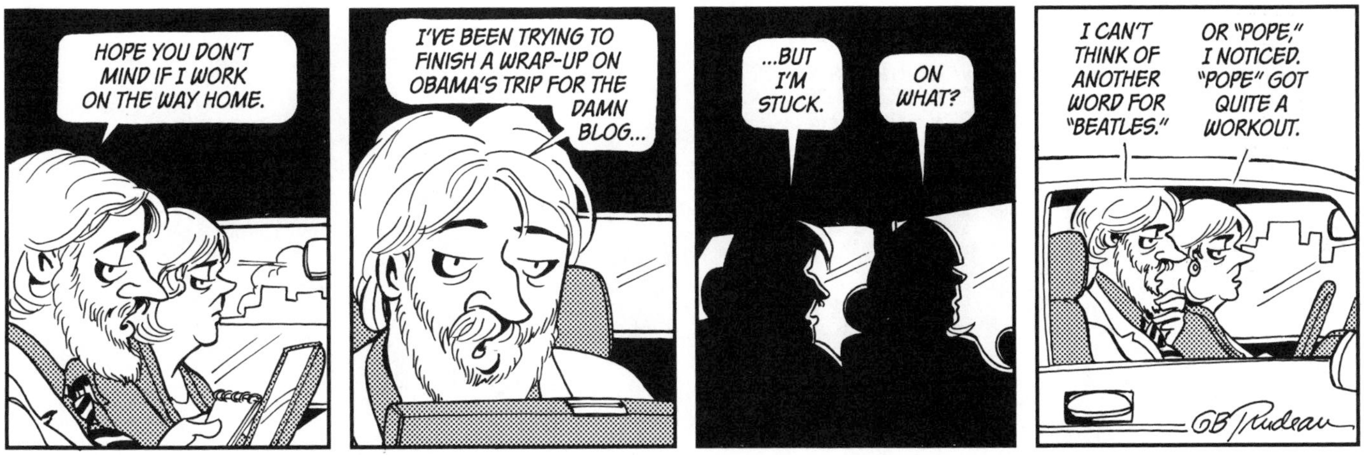
HOPE YOU DON'T MIND IF I WORK ON THE WAY HOME.
I'VE BEEN TRYING TO FINISH A WRAP-UP ON OBAMA'S TRIP FOR THE DAMN BLOG...
...BUT I'M STUCK.
ON WHAT?
I CAN'T THINK OF ANOTHER WORD FOR "BEATLES."
OR "POPE," I NOTICED. "POPE" GOT QUITE A WORKOUT.
GB Trudeau

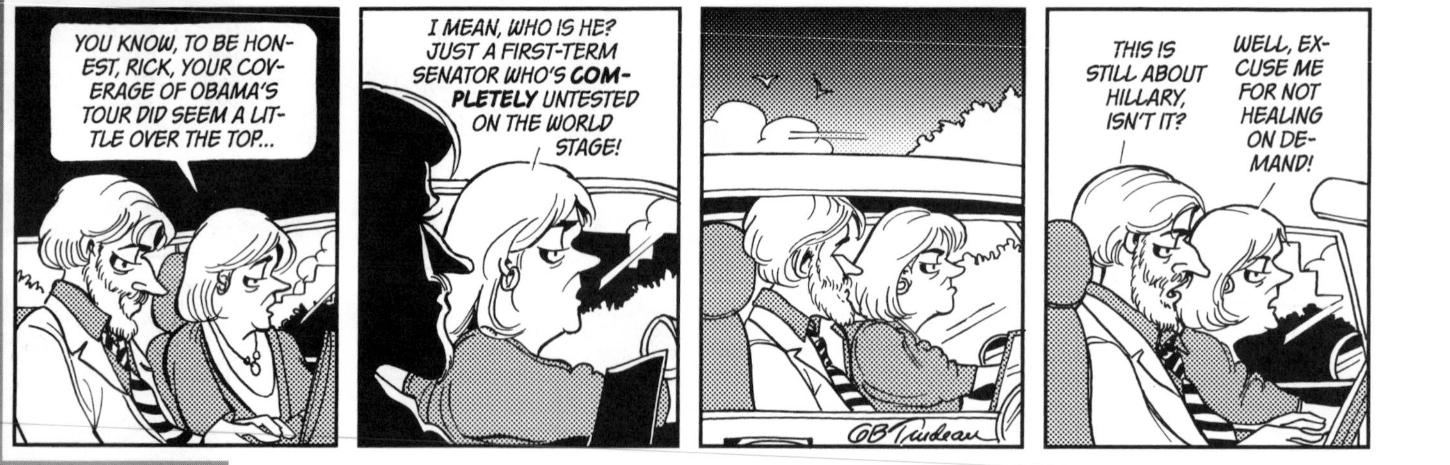
YOU KNOW, TO BE HONEST, RICK, YOUR COVERAGE OF OBAMA'S TOUR DID SEEM A LITTLE OVER THE TOP...
I MEAN, WHO IS HE? JUST A FIRST-TERM SENATOR WHO'S **COMPLETELY** UNTESTED ON THE WORLD STAGE!
THIS IS STILL ABOUT HILLARY, ISN'T IT?
WELL, EXCUSE ME FOR NOT HEALING ON DEMAND!
©B Trudeau

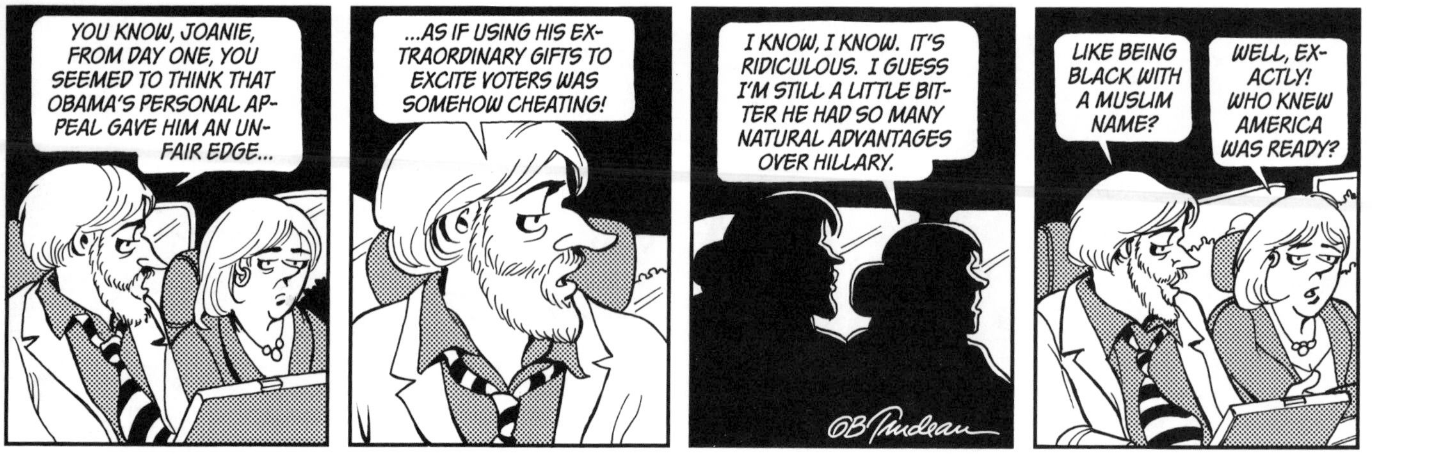
YOU KNOW, JOANIE, FROM DAY ONE, YOU SEEMED TO THINK THAT OBAMA'S PERSONAL APPEAL GAVE HIM AN UNFAIR EDGE...
...AS IF USING HIS EXTRAORDINARY GIFTS TO EXCITE VOTERS WAS SOMEHOW CHEATING!
I KNOW, I KNOW. IT'S RIDICULOUS. I GUESS I'M STILL A LITTLE BITTER HE HAD SO MANY NATURAL ADVANTAGES OVER HILLARY.
©B Trudeau
LIKE BEING BLACK WITH A MUSLIM NAME?
WELL, EXACTLY! WHO KNEW AMERICA WAS READY?

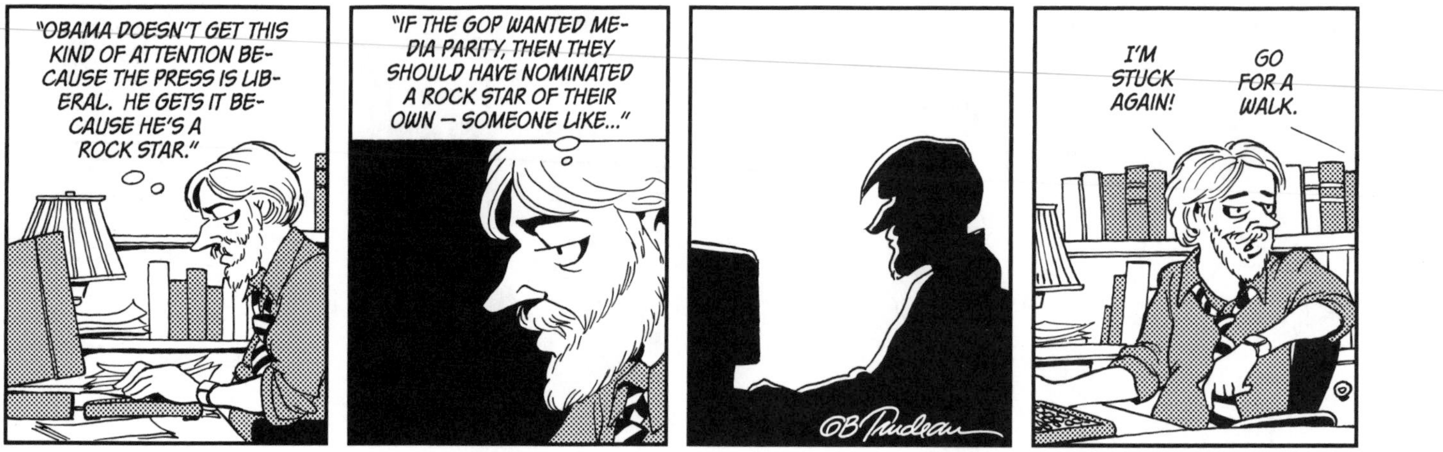
"OBAMA DOESN'T GET THIS KIND OF ATTENTION BECAUSE THE PRESS IS LIBERAL. HE GETS IT BECAUSE HE'S A ROCK STAR."
"IF THE GOP WANTED MEDIA PARITY, THEN THEY SHOULD HAVE NOMINATED A ROCK STAR OF THEIR OWN — SOMEONE LIKE..."
©B Trudeau
I'M STUCK AGAIN!
GO FOR A WALK.

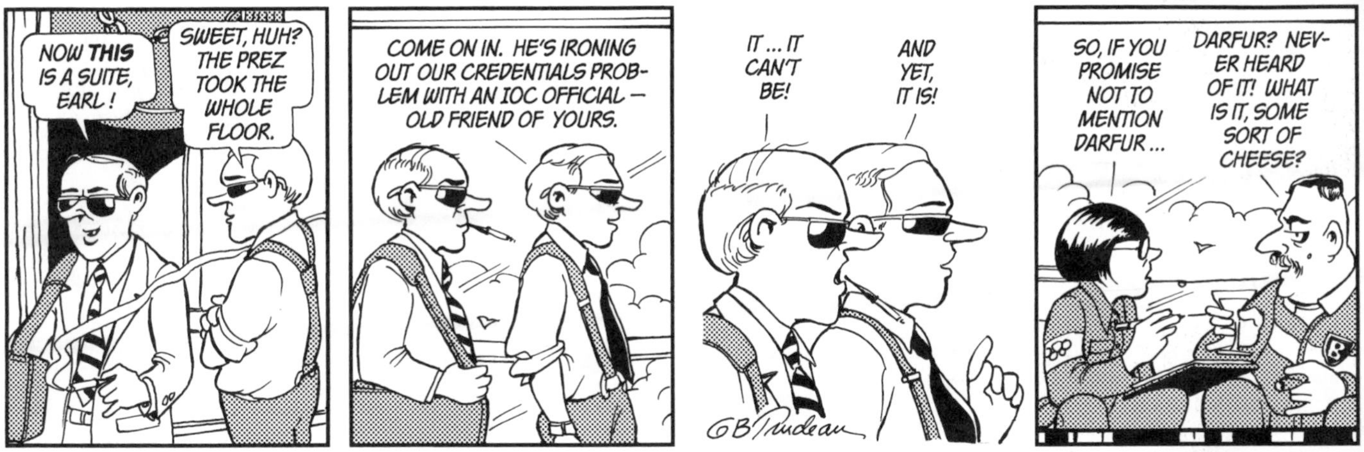

NOW THIS IS A SUITE, EARL!
SWEET, HUH? THE PREZ TOOK THE WHOLE FLOOR.
COME ON IN. HE'S IRONING OUT OUR CREDENTIALS PROBLEM WITH AN IOC OFFICIAL — OLD FRIEND OF YOURS.
IT ... IT CAN'T BE!
AND YET, IT IS!
GB Trudeau
SO, IF YOU PROMISE NOT TO MENTION DARFUR ...
DARFUR? NEVER HEARD OF IT! WHAT IS IT, SOME SORT OF CHEESE?

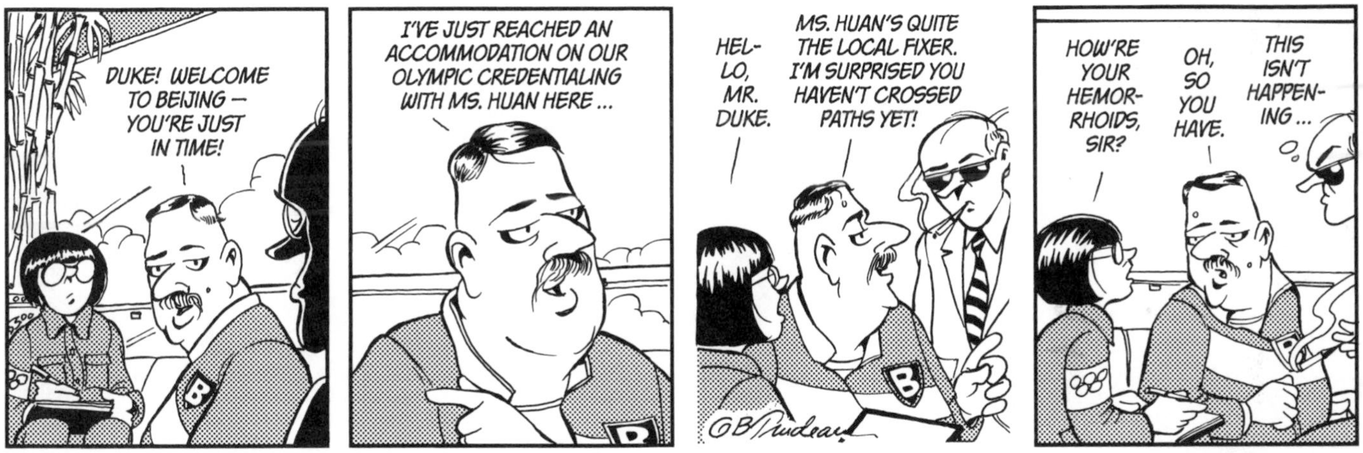

DUKE! WELCOME TO BEIJING — YOU'RE JUST IN TIME!
I'VE JUST REACHED AN ACCOMMODATION ON OUR OLYMPIC CREDENTIALING WITH MS. HUAN HERE ...
HEL-LO, MR. DUKE.
MS. HUAN'S QUITE THE LOCAL FIXER. I'M SURPRISED YOU HAVEN'T CROSSED PATHS YET!
GB Trudeau
HOW'RE YOUR HEMORRHOIDS, SIR?
OH, SO YOU HAVE.
THIS ISN'T HAPPENING ...

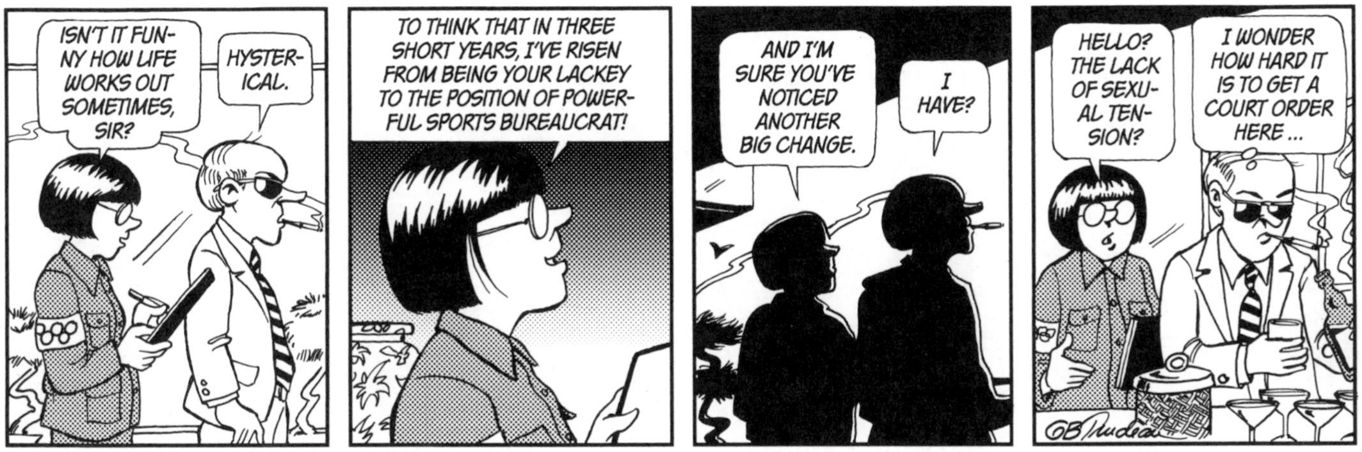

ISN'T IT FUNNY HOW LIFE WORKS OUT SOMETIMES, SIR?
HYSTERICAL.
TO THINK THAT IN THREE SHORT YEARS, I'VE RISEN FROM BEING YOUR LACKEY TO THE POSITION OF POWERFUL SPORTS BUREAUCRAT!
AND I'M SURE YOU'VE NOTICED ANOTHER BIG CHANGE.
I HAVE?
HELLO? THE LACK OF SEXUAL TENSION?
I WONDER HOW HARD IT IS TO GET A COURT ORDER HERE ...
GB Trudeau

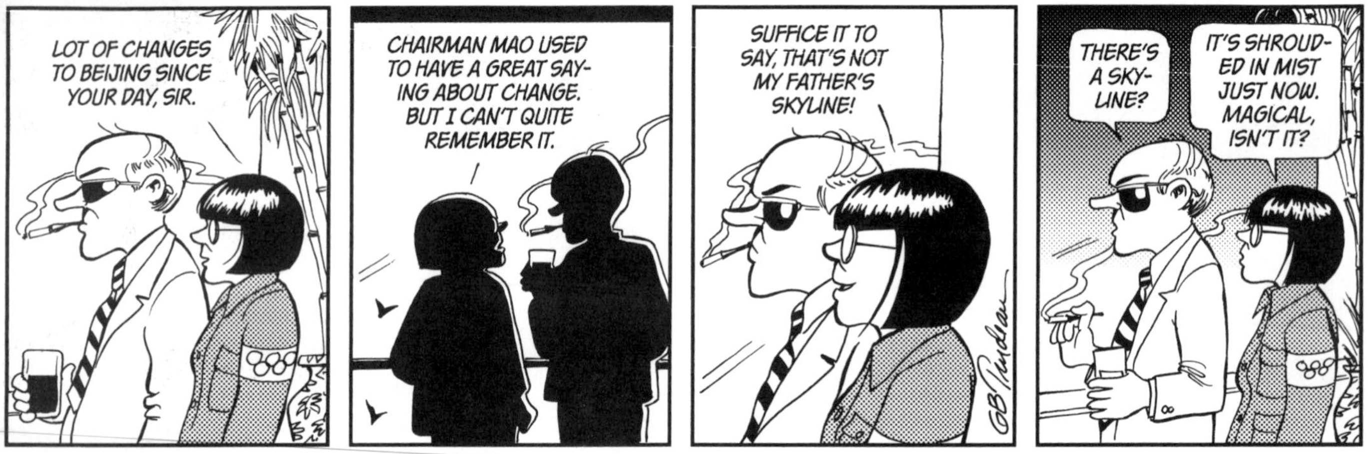
LOT OF CHANGES TO BEIJING SINCE YOUR DAY, SIR.
CHAIRMAN MAO USED TO HAVE A GREAT SAYING ABOUT CHANGE. BUT I CAN'T QUITE REMEMBER IT.
SUFFICE IT TO SAY, THAT'S NOT MY FATHER'S SKYLINE!
THERE'S A SKYLINE?
IT'S SHROUDED IN MIST JUST NOW. MAGICAL, ISN'T IT?

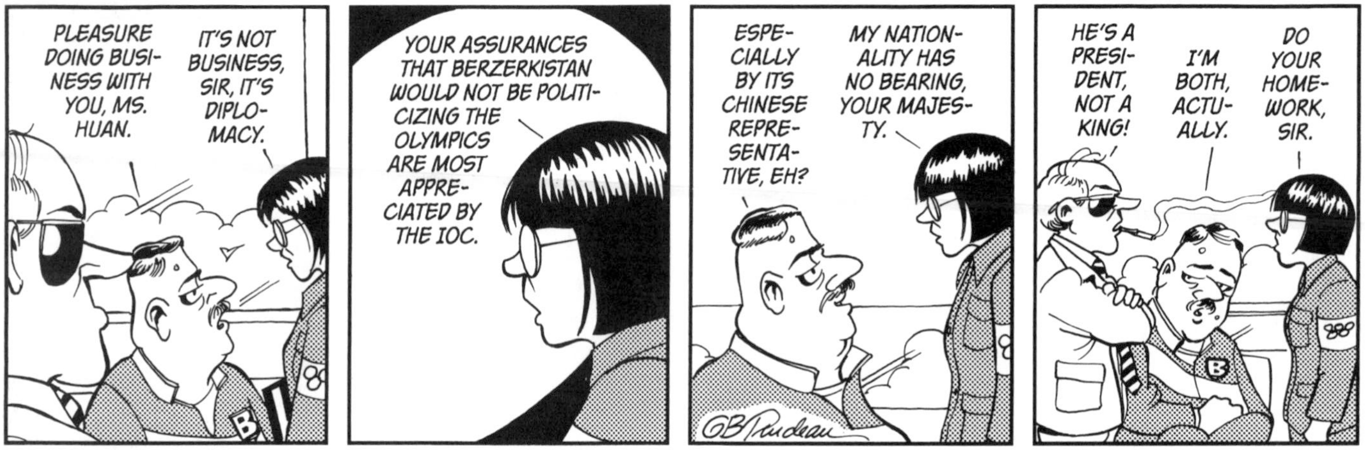
PLEASURE DOING BUSINESS WITH YOU, MS. HUAN.
IT'S NOT BUSINESS, SIR, IT'S DIPLOMACY.
YOUR ASSURANCES THAT BERZERKISTAN WOULD NOT BE POLITICIZING THE OLYMPICS ARE MOST APPRECIATED BY THE IOC.
ESPECIALLY BY ITS CHINESE REPRESENTATIVE, EH?
MY NATIONALITY HAS NO BEARING, YOUR MAJESTY.
HE'S A PRESIDENT, NOT A KING!
I'M BOTH, ACTUALLY.
DO YOUR HOMEWORK, SIR.

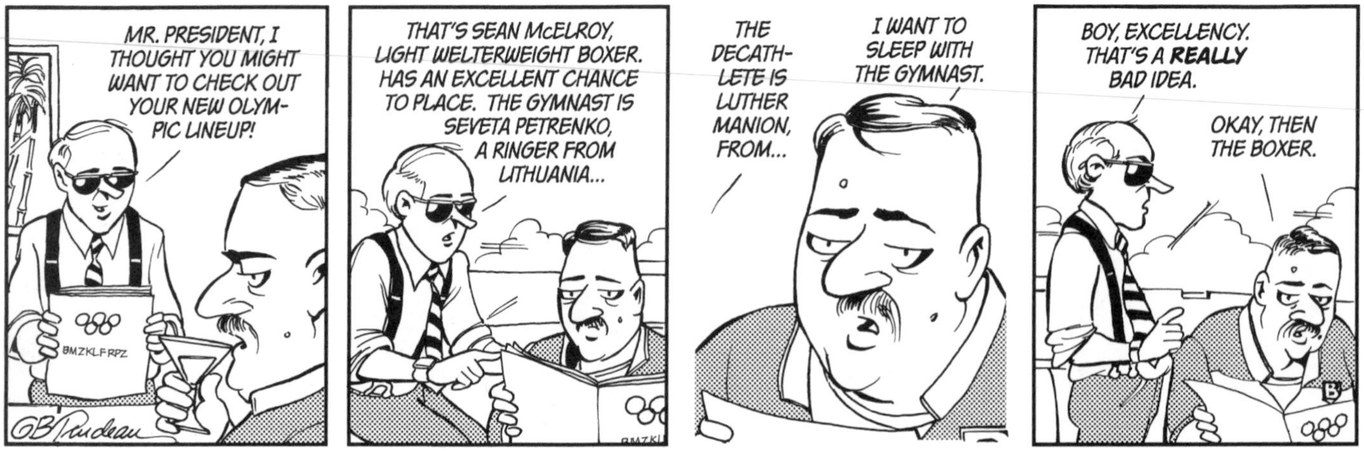
MR. PRESIDENT, I THOUGHT YOU MIGHT WANT TO CHECK OUT YOUR NEW OLYMPIC LINEUP!
BMZKLFRPZ
THAT'S SEAN McELROY, LIGHT WELTERWEIGHT BOXER. HAS AN EXCELLENT CHANCE TO PLACE. THE GYMNAST IS SEVETA PETRENKO, A RINGER FROM LITHUANIA...
THE DECATHLETE IS LUTHER MANION, FROM...
I WANT TO SLEEP WITH THE GYMNAST.
BOY, EXCELLENCY. THAT'S A **REALLY** BAD IDEA.
OKAY, THEN THE BOXER.

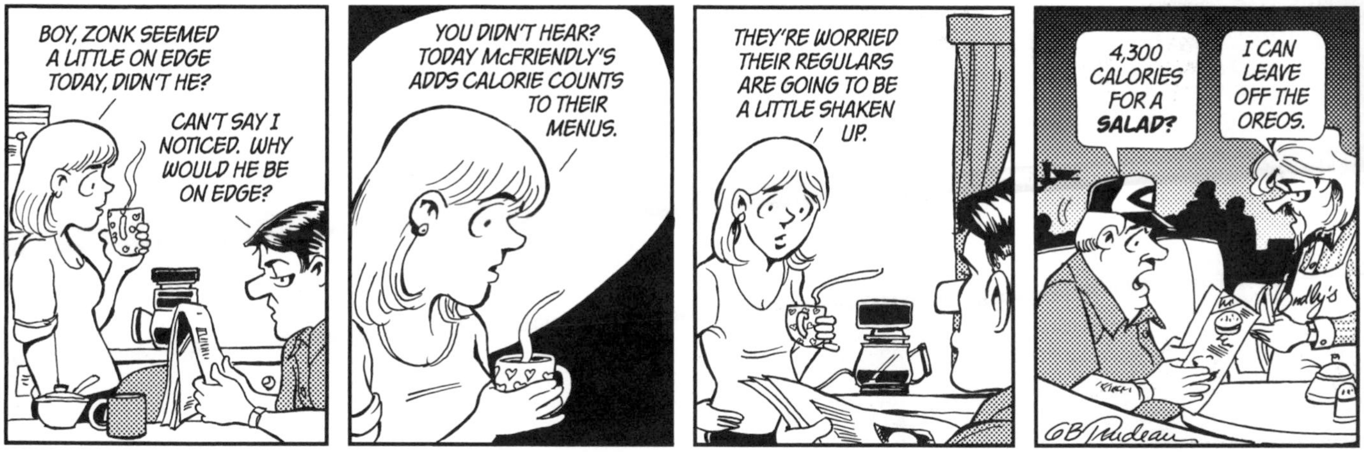
BOY, ZONK SEEMED A LITTLE ON EDGE TODAY, DIDN'T HE?
CAN'T SAY I NOTICED. WHY WOULD HE BE ON EDGE?
YOU DIDN'T HEAR? TODAY McFRIENDLY'S ADDS CALORIE COUNTS TO THEIR MENUS.
THEY'RE WORRIED THEIR REGULARS ARE GOING TO BE A LITTLE SHAKEN UP.
4,300 CALORIES FOR A SALAD?
I CAN LEAVE OFF THE OREOS.
GB Trudeau

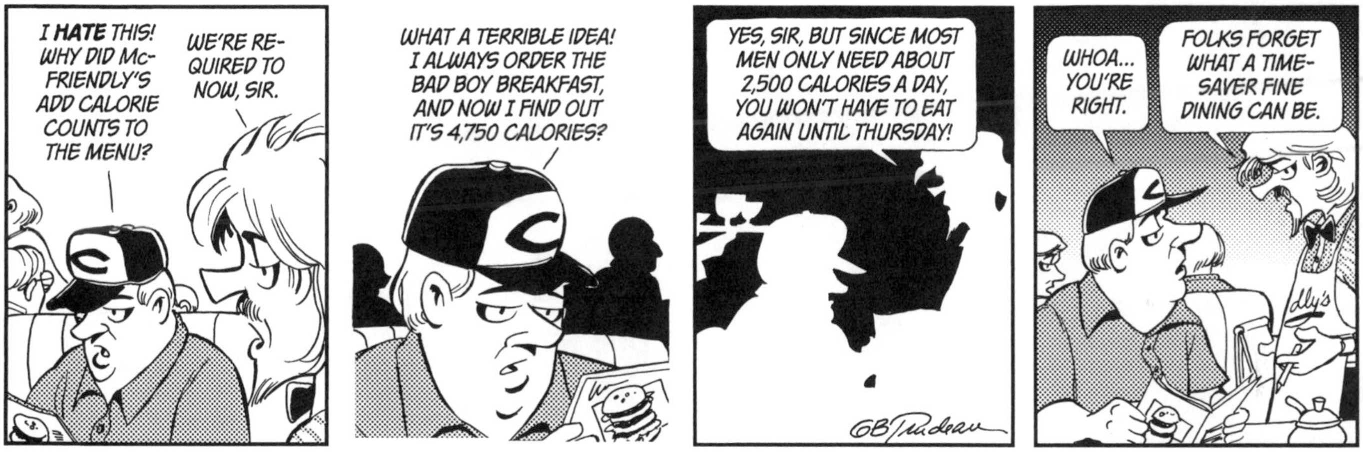
I HATE THIS! WHY DID McFRIENDLY'S ADD CALORIE COUNTS TO THE MENU?
WE'RE REQUIRED TO NOW, SIR.
WHAT A TERRIBLE IDEA! I ALWAYS ORDER THE BAD BOY BREAKFAST, AND NOW I FIND OUT IT'S 4,750 CALORIES?
YES, SIR, BUT SINCE MOST MEN ONLY NEED ABOUT 2,500 CALORIES A DAY, YOU WON'T HAVE TO EAT AGAIN UNTIL THURSDAY!
GB Trudeau
WHOA... YOU'RE RIGHT.
FOLKS FORGET WHAT A TIME-SAVER FINE DINING CAN BE.

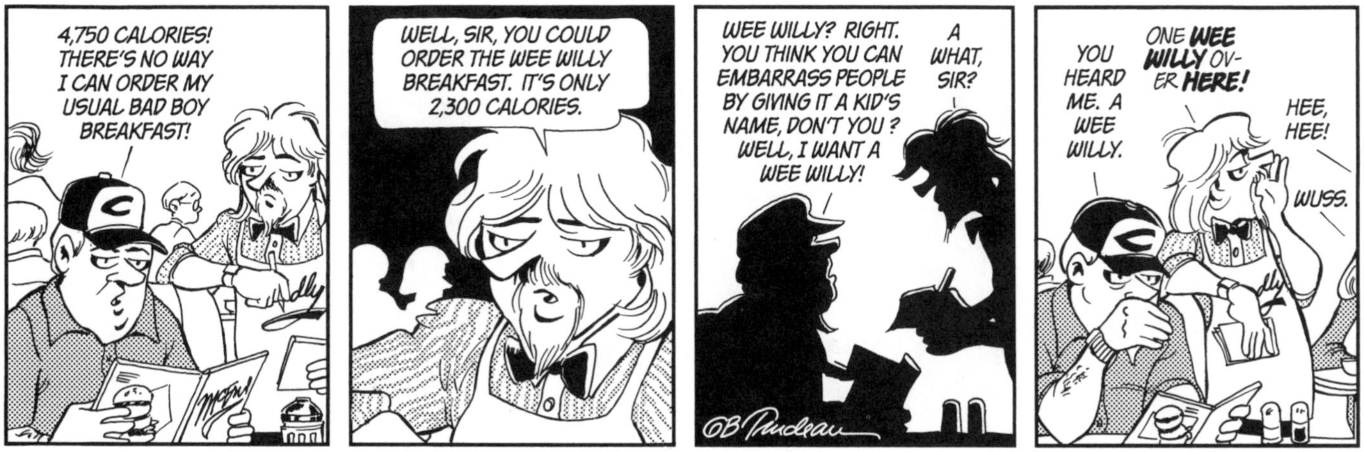
4,750 CALORIES! THERE'S NO WAY I CAN ORDER MY USUAL BAD BOY BREAKFAST!
WELL, SIR, YOU COULD ORDER THE WEE WILLY BREAKFAST. IT'S ONLY 2,300 CALORIES.
WEE WILLY? RIGHT. YOU THINK YOU CAN EMBARRASS PEOPLE BY GIVING IT A KID'S NAME, DON'T YOU ? WELL, I WANT A WEE WILLY!
A WHAT, SIR?
GB Trudeau
YOU HEARD ME. A WEE WILLY.
ONE WEE WILLY OVER HERE!
HEE, HEE!
WUSS.

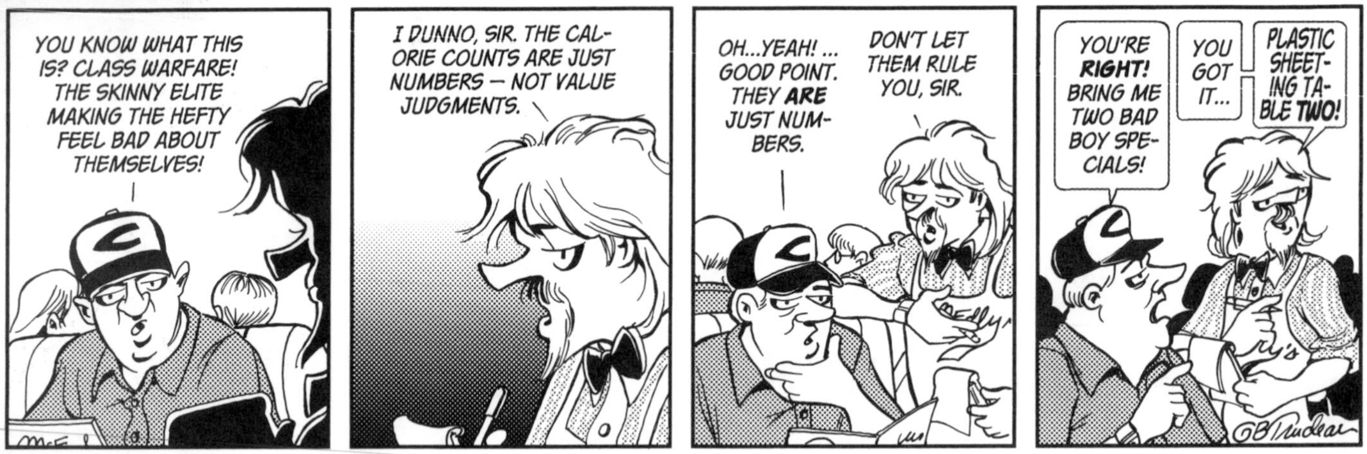
YOU KNOW WHAT THIS IS? CLASS WARFARE! THE SKINNY ELITE MAKING THE HEFTY FEEL BAD ABOUT THEMSELVES!
I DUNNO, SIR. THE CALORIE COUNTS ARE JUST NUMBERS — NOT VALUE JUDGMENTS.
OH...YEAH! ... GOOD POINT. THEY **ARE** JUST NUMBERS.
DON'T LET THEM RULE YOU, SIR.
YOU'RE **RIGHT!** BRING ME TWO BAD BOY SPECIALS!
YOU GOT IT...
PLASTIC SHEETING TABLE **TWO!**

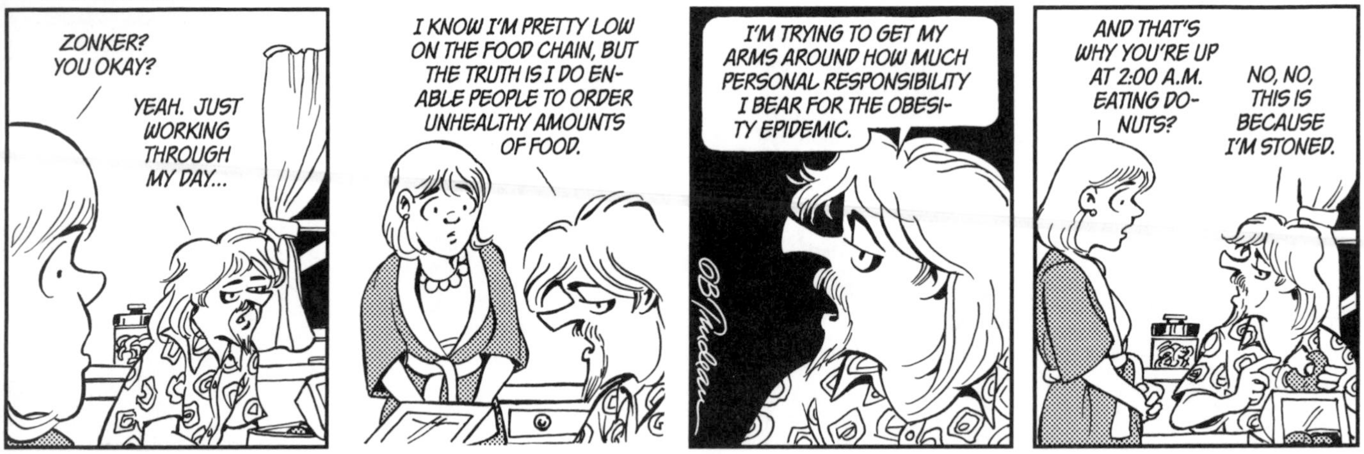
ZONKER? YOU OKAY?
YEAH. JUST WORKING THROUGH MY DAY...
I KNOW I'M PRETTY LOW ON THE FOOD CHAIN, BUT THE TRUTH IS I DO ENABLE PEOPLE TO ORDER UNHEALTHY AMOUNTS OF FOOD.
I'M TRYING TO GET MY ARMS AROUND HOW MUCH PERSONAL RESPONSIBILITY I BEAR FOR THE OBESITY EPIDEMIC.
AND THAT'S WHY YOU'RE UP AT 2:00 A.M. EATING DONUTS?
NO, NO, THIS IS BECAUSE I'M STONED.

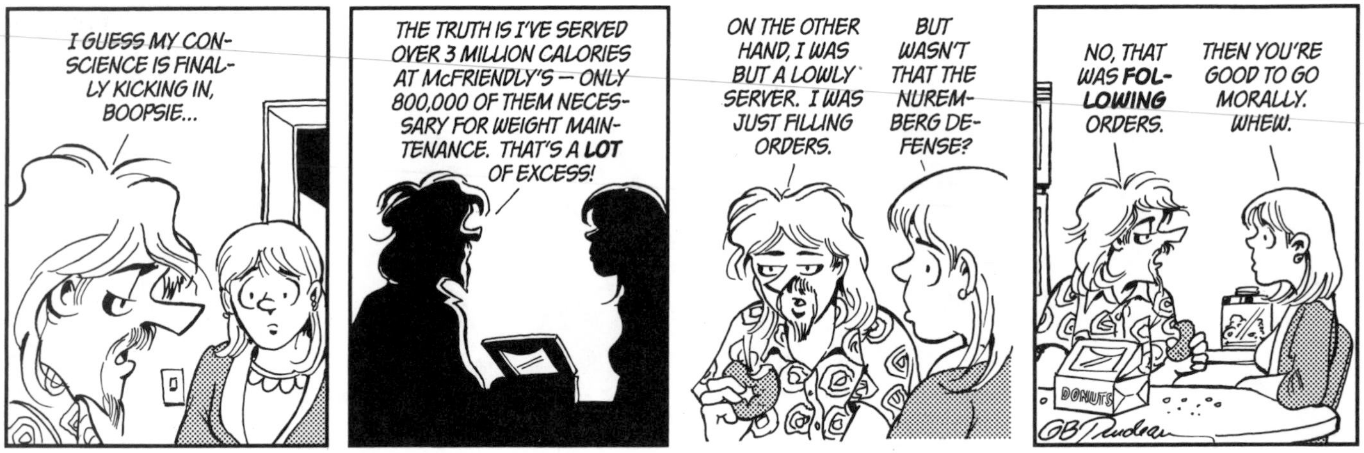
I GUESS MY CONSCIENCE IS FINALLY KICKING IN, BOOPSIE...
THE TRUTH IS I'VE SERVED OVER 3 MILLION CALORIES AT McFRIENDLY'S — ONLY 800,000 OF THEM NECESSARY FOR WEIGHT MAINTENANCE. THAT'S A **LOT** OF EXCESS!
ON THE OTHER HAND, I WAS BUT A LOWLY SERVER. I WAS JUST FILLING ORDERS.
BUT WASN'T THAT THE NUREMBERG DEFENSE?
NO, THAT WAS **FOLLOWING** ORDERS.
THEN YOU'RE GOOD TO GO MORALLY. WHEW.
DONUTS

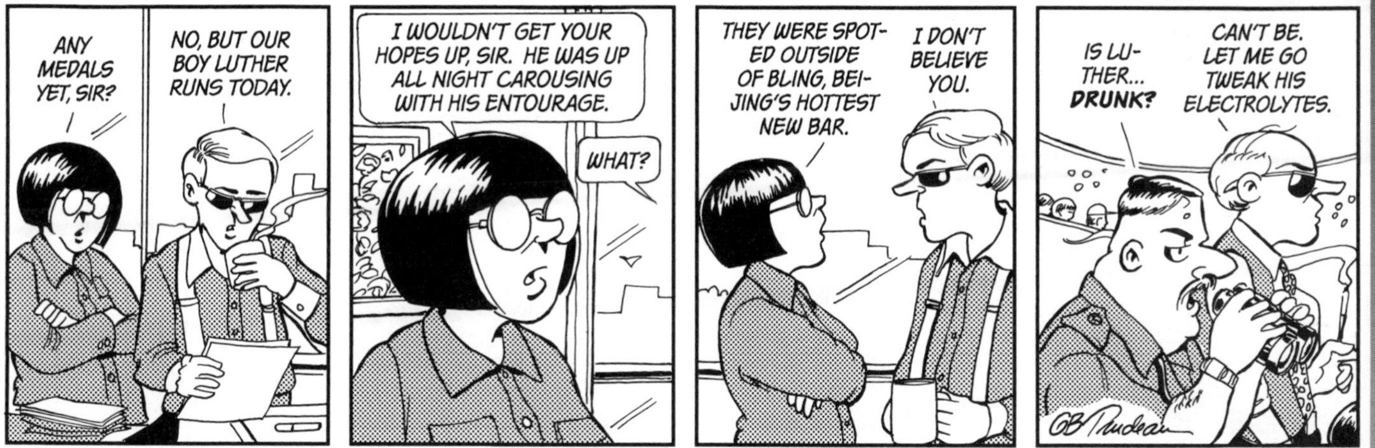
ANY MEDALS YET, SIR?
NO, BUT OUR BOY LUTHER RUNS TODAY.
I WOULDN'T GET YOUR HOPES UP, SIR. HE WAS UP ALL NIGHT CAROUSING WITH HIS ENTOURAGE.
WHAT?
THEY WERE SPOTTED OUTSIDE OF BLING, BEIJING'S HOTTEST NEW BAR.
I DON'T BELIEVE YOU.
IS LUTHER... **DRUNK?**
CAN'T BE. LET ME GO TWEAK HIS ELECTROLYTES.
GB Trudeau

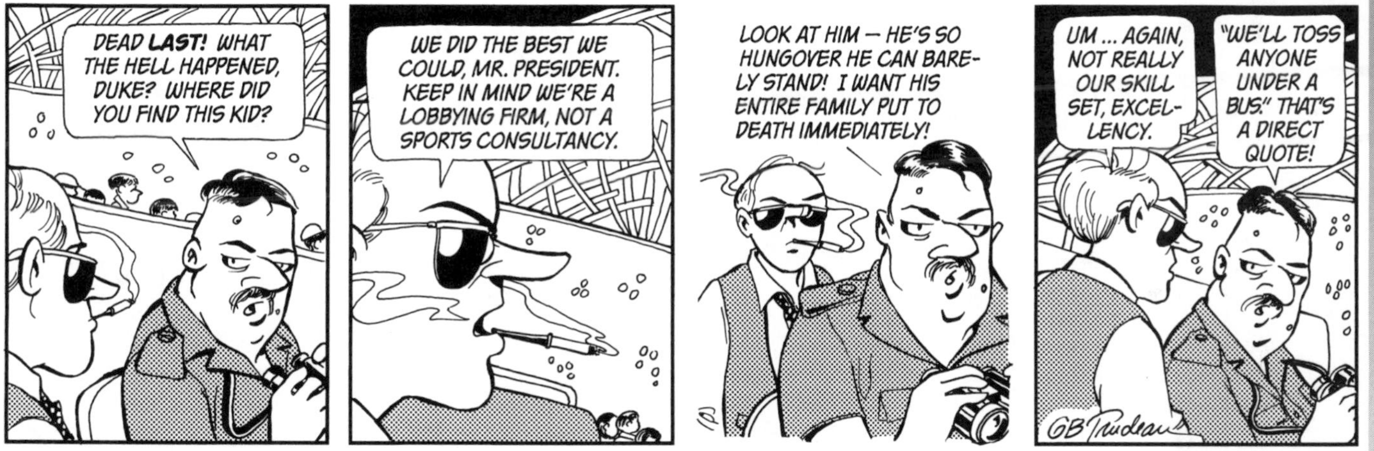
DEAD **LAST!** WHAT THE HELL HAPPENED, DUKE? WHERE DID YOU FIND THIS KID?
WE DID THE BEST WE COULD, MR. PRESIDENT. KEEP IN MIND WE'RE A LOBBYING FIRM, NOT A SPORTS CONSULTANCY.
LOOK AT HIM — HE'S SO HUNGOVER HE CAN BARELY STAND! I WANT HIS ENTIRE FAMILY PUT TO DEATH IMMEDIATELY!
UM ... AGAIN, NOT REALLY OUR SKILL SET, EXCELLENCY.
"WE'LL TOSS ANYONE UNDER A BUS." THAT'S A DIRECT QUOTE!
GB Trudeau

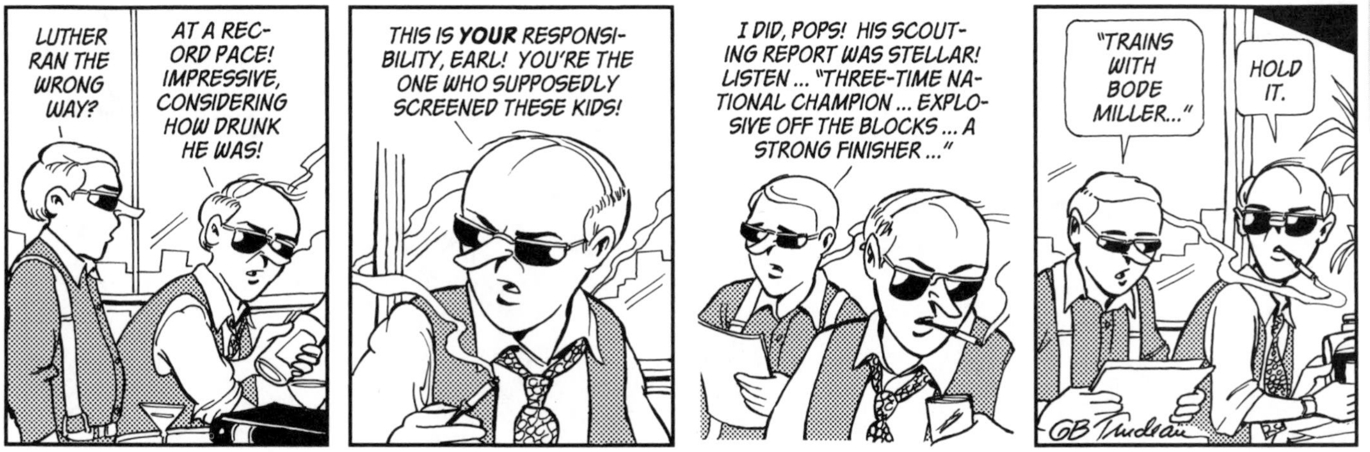
LUTHER RAN THE WRONG WAY?
AT A RECORD PACE! IMPRESSIVE, CONSIDERING HOW DRUNK HE WAS!
THIS IS **YOUR** RESPONSIBILITY, EARL! YOU'RE THE ONE WHO SUPPOSEDLY SCREENED THESE KIDS!
I DID, POPS! HIS SCOUTING REPORT WAS STELLAR! LISTEN ... "THREE-TIME NATIONAL CHAMPION ... EXPLOSIVE OFF THE BLOCKS ... A STRONG FINISHER ..."
"TRAINS WITH BODE MILLER..."
HOLD IT.
GB Trudeau

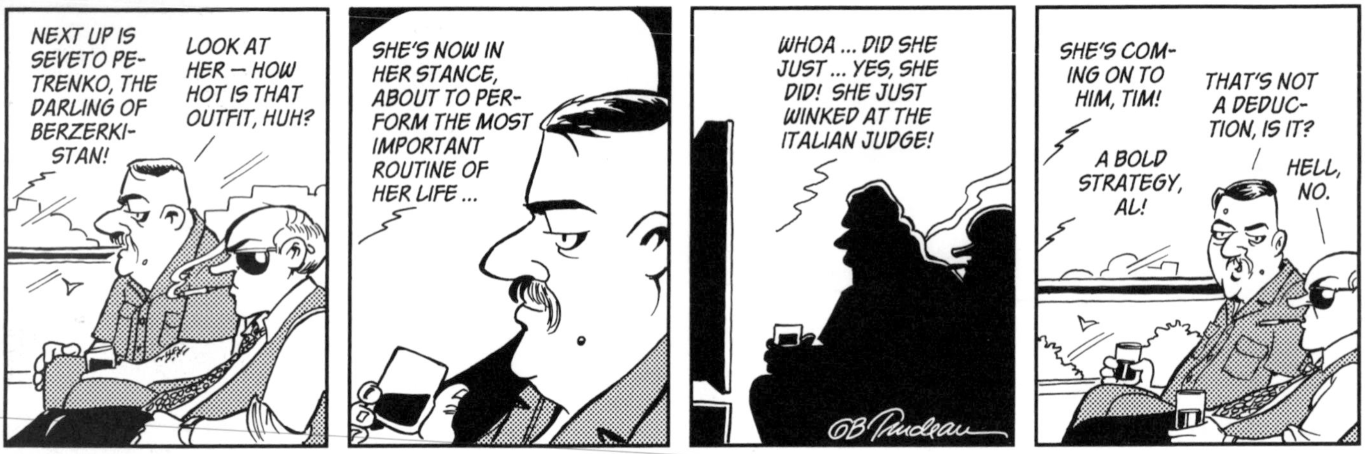
NEXT UP IS SEVETO PETRENKO, THE DARLING OF BERZERKISTAN!
LOOK AT HER — HOW HOT IS THAT OUTFIT, HUH?
SHE'S NOW IN HER STANCE, ABOUT TO PERFORM THE MOST IMPORTANT ROUTINE OF HER LIFE ...
WHOA ... DID SHE JUST ... YES, SHE DID! SHE JUST WINKED AT THE ITALIAN JUDGE!
SHE'S COMING ON TO HIM, TIM!
A BOLD STRATEGY, AL!
THAT'S NOT A DEDUCTION, IS IT?
HELL, NO.

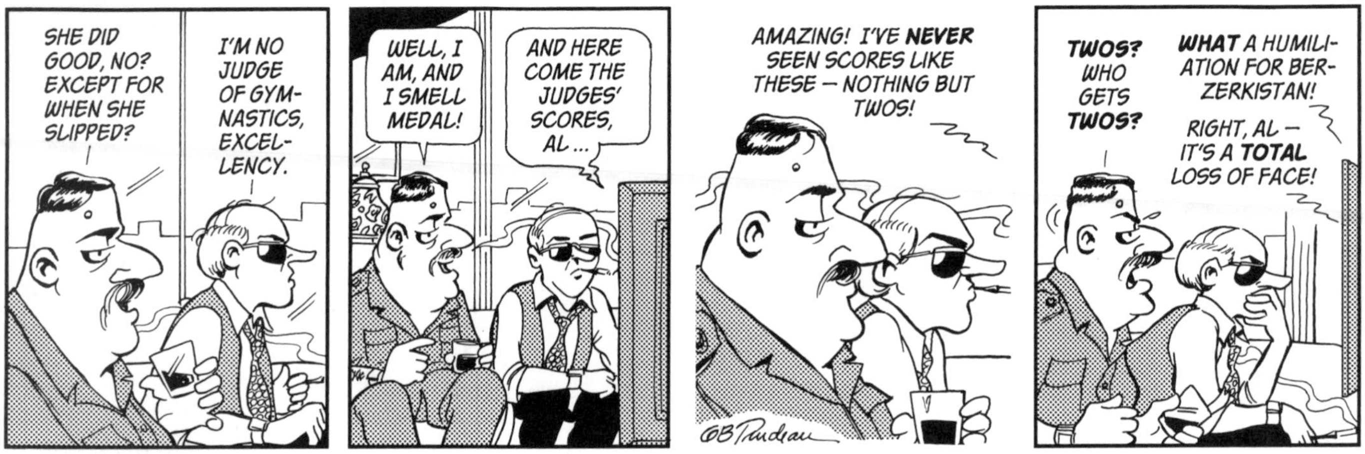
SHE DID GOOD, NO? EXCEPT FOR WHEN SHE SLIPPED?
I'M NO JUDGE OF GYMNASTICS, EXCELLENCY.
WELL, I AM, AND I SMELL MEDAL!
AND HERE COME THE JUDGES' SCORES, AL ...
AMAZING! I'VE **NEVER** SEEN SCORES LIKE THESE — NOTHING BUT TWOS!
TWOS? WHO GETS **TWOS?**
WHAT A HUMILIATION FOR BERZERKISTAN!
RIGHT, AL — IT'S A **TOTAL** LOSS OF FACE!

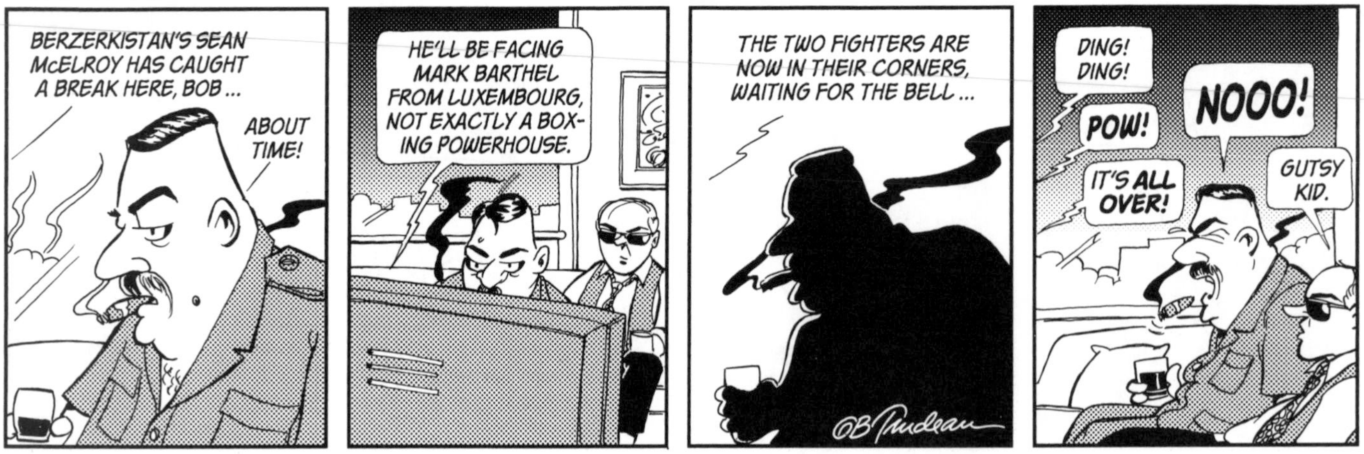
BERZERKISTAN'S SEAN McELROY HAS CAUGHT A BREAK HERE, BOB ...
ABOUT TIME!
HE'LL BE FACING MARK BARTHEL FROM LUXEMBOURG, NOT EXACTLY A BOXING POWERHOUSE.
THE TWO FIGHTERS ARE NOW IN THEIR CORNERS, WAITING FOR THE BELL ...
DING! DING!
POW!
IT'S **ALL OVER!**
NOOO!
GUTSY KID.

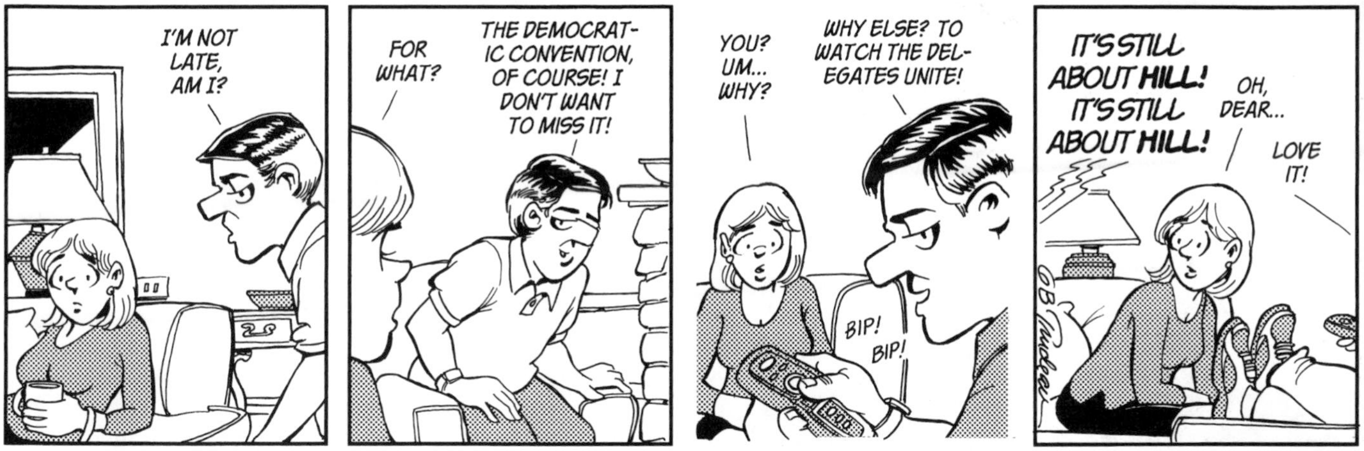
I'M NOT LATE, AM I?
FOR WHAT?
THE DEMOCRATIC CONVENTION, OF COURSE! I DON'T WANT TO MISS IT!
YOU? UM... WHY?
WHY ELSE? TO WATCH THE DELEGATES UNITE!
BIP!
BIP!
IT'S STILL ABOUT **HILL!** IT'S STILL ABOUT **HILL!**
OH, DEAR...
LOVE IT!

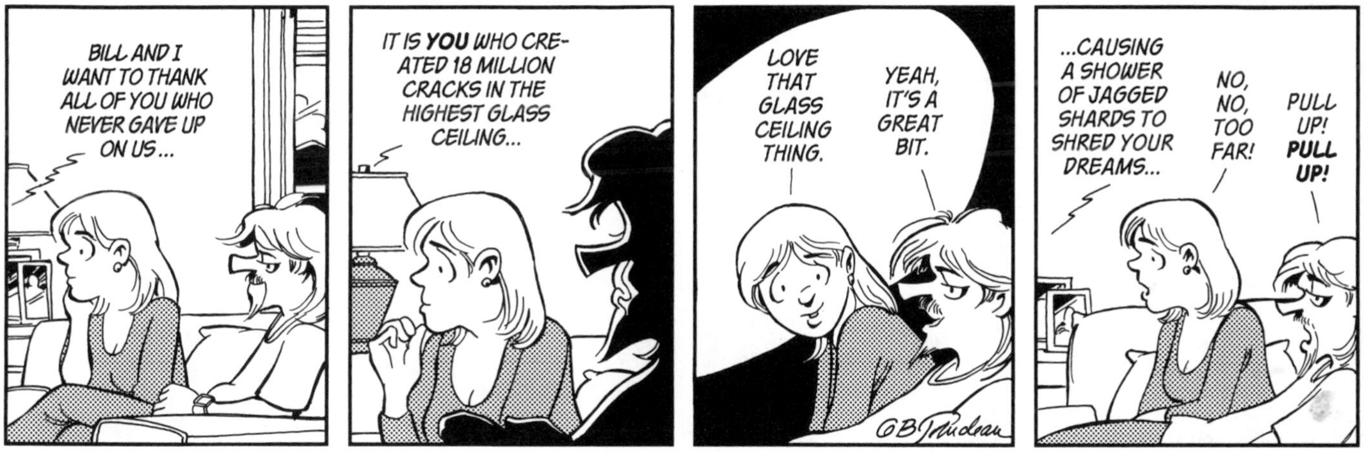
BILL AND I WANT TO THANK ALL OF YOU WHO NEVER GAVE UP ON US...
IT IS **YOU** WHO CREATED 18 MILLION CRACKS IN THE HIGHEST GLASS CEILING...
LOVE THAT GLASS CEILING THING.
YEAH, IT'S A GREAT BIT.
...CAUSING A SHOWER OF JAGGED SHARDS TO SHRED YOUR DREAMS...
NO, NO, TOO FAR!
PULL UP! **PULL UP!**

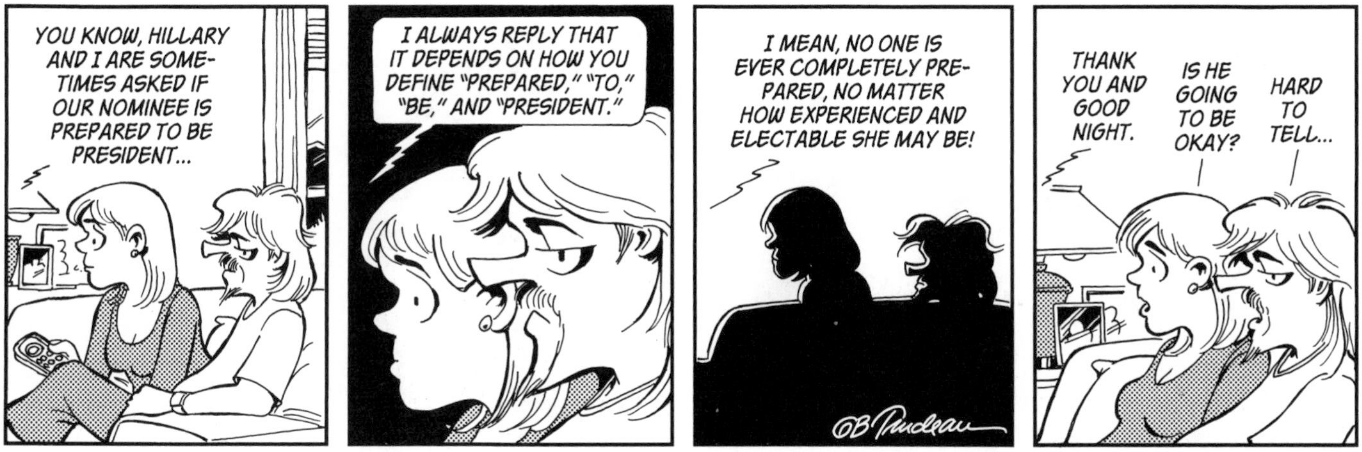
YOU KNOW, HILLARY AND I ARE SOMETIMES ASKED IF OUR NOMINEE IS PREPARED TO BE PRESIDENT...
I ALWAYS REPLY THAT IT DEPENDS ON HOW YOU DEFINE "PREPARED," "TO," "BE," AND "PRESIDENT."
I MEAN, NO ONE IS EVER COMPLETELY PREPARED, NO MATTER HOW EXPERIENCED AND ELECTABLE SHE MAY BE!
THANK YOU AND GOOD NIGHT.
IS HE GOING TO BE OKAY?
HARD TO TELL...

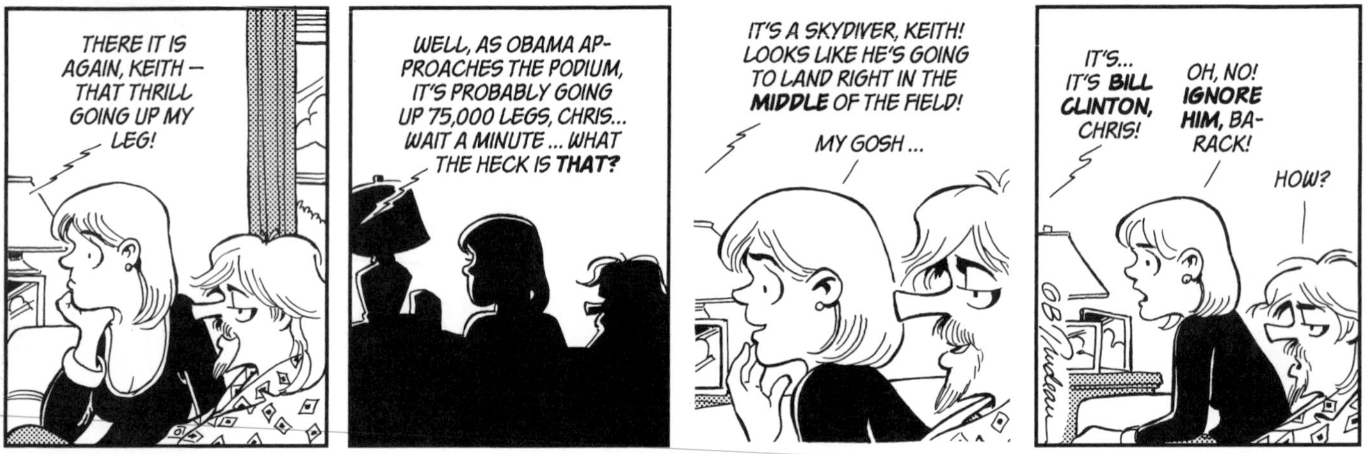
THERE IT IS AGAIN, KEITH — THAT THRILL GOING UP MY LEG!
WELL, AS OBAMA APPROACHES THE PODIUM, IT'S PROBABLY GOING UP 75,000 LEGS, CHRIS... WAIT A MINUTE ... WHAT THE HECK IS **THAT?**
IT'S A SKYDIVER, KEITH! LOOKS LIKE HE'S GOING TO LAND RIGHT IN THE **MIDDLE** OF THE FIELD!
MY GOSH ...
IT'S... IT'S **BILL CLINTON,** CHRIS!
OH, NO! **IGNORE HIM,** BARACK!
HOW?

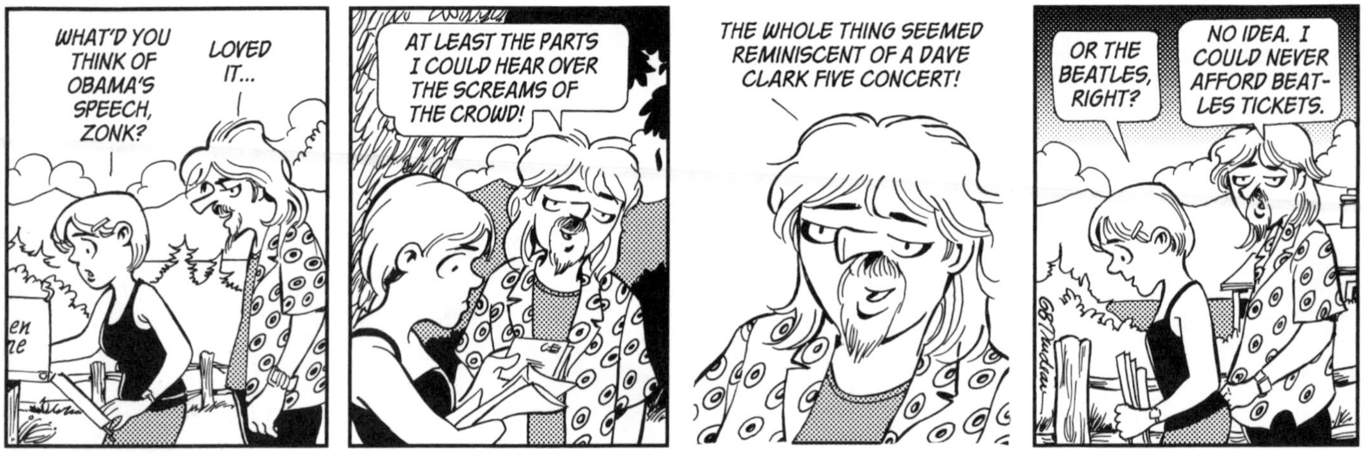
WHAT'D YOU THINK OF OBAMA'S SPEECH, ZONK?
LOVED IT...
AT LEAST THE PARTS I COULD HEAR OVER THE SCREAMS OF THE CROWD!
THE WHOLE THING SEEMED REMINISCENT OF A DAVE CLARK FIVE CONCERT!
OR THE BEATLES, RIGHT?
NO IDEA. I COULD NEVER AFFORD BEATLES TICKETS.

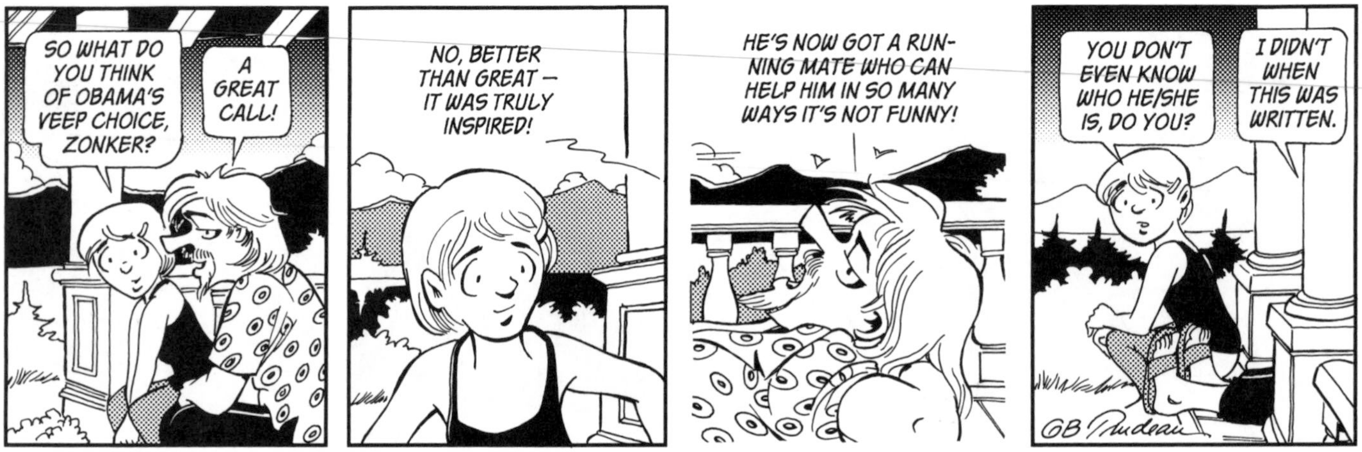
SO WHAT DO YOU THINK OF OBAMA'S VEEP CHOICE, ZONKER?
A GREAT CALL!
NO, BETTER THAN GREAT — IT WAS TRULY INSPIRED!
HE'S NOW GOT A RUNNING MATE WHO CAN HELP HIM IN SO MANY WAYS IT'S NOT FUNNY!
YOU DON'T EVEN KNOW WHO HE/SHE IS, DO YOU?
I DIDN'T WHEN THIS WAS WRITTEN.

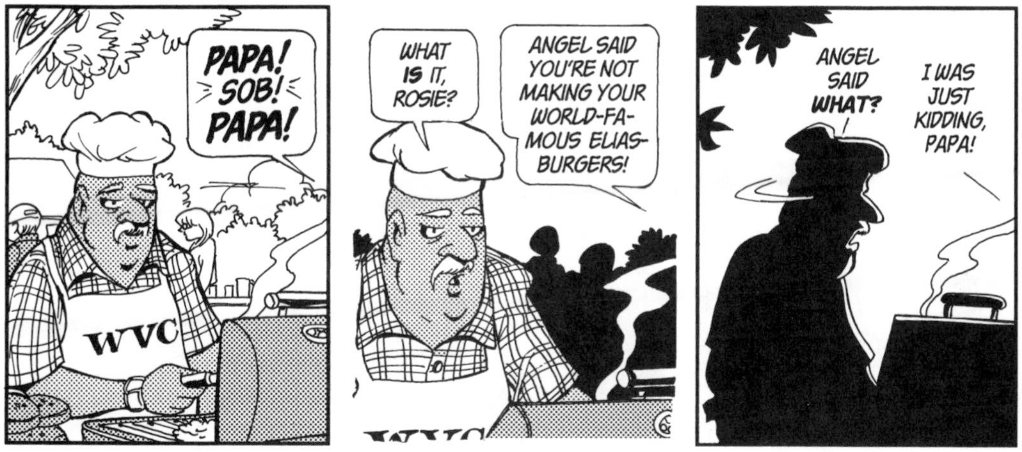
PAPA! SOB! PAPA!
WHAT IS IT, ROSIE?
ANGEL SAID YOU'RE NOT MAKING YOUR WORLD-FAMOUS ELIASBURGERS!
ANGEL SAID WHAT?
I WAS JUST KIDDING, PAPA!
IS IT TRUE, MAN?
NO WORLD-FAMOUS ELIASBURGERS?
SEE THE PANIC YOU STARTED!
SORRY, PAPA!
WVC
GB Trudeau

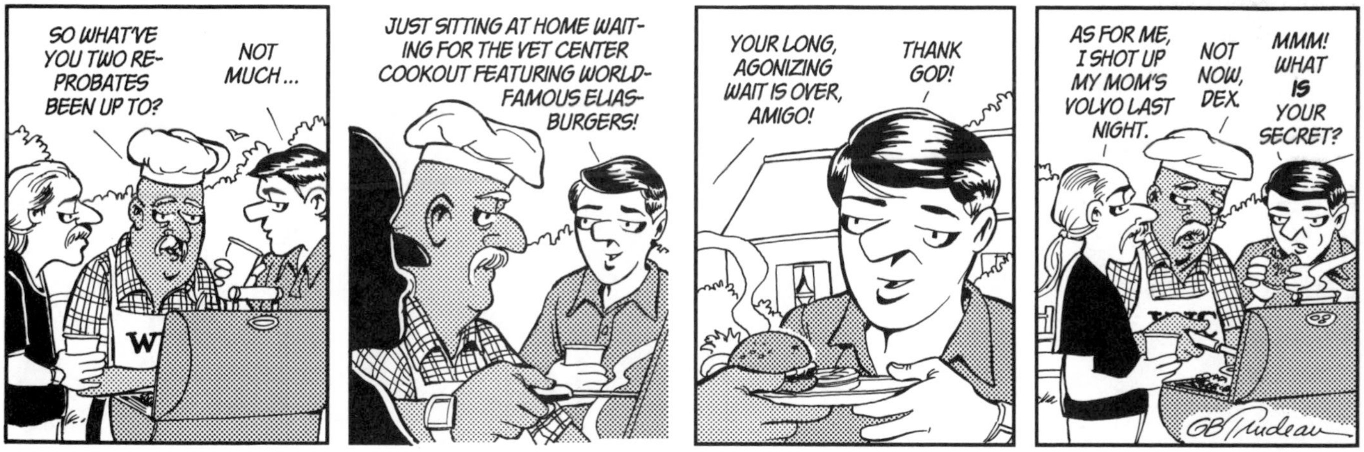
SO WHAT'VE YOU TWO REPROBATES BEEN UP TO?
NOT MUCH...
JUST SITTING AT HOME WAITING FOR THE VET CENTER COOKOUT FEATURING WORLD-FAMOUS ELIASBURGERS!
YOUR LONG, AGONIZING WAIT IS OVER, AMIGO!
THANK GOD!
AS FOR ME, I SHOT UP MY MOM'S VOLVO LAST NIGHT.
NOT NOW, DEX.
MMM! WHAT IS YOUR SECRET?
GB Trudeau

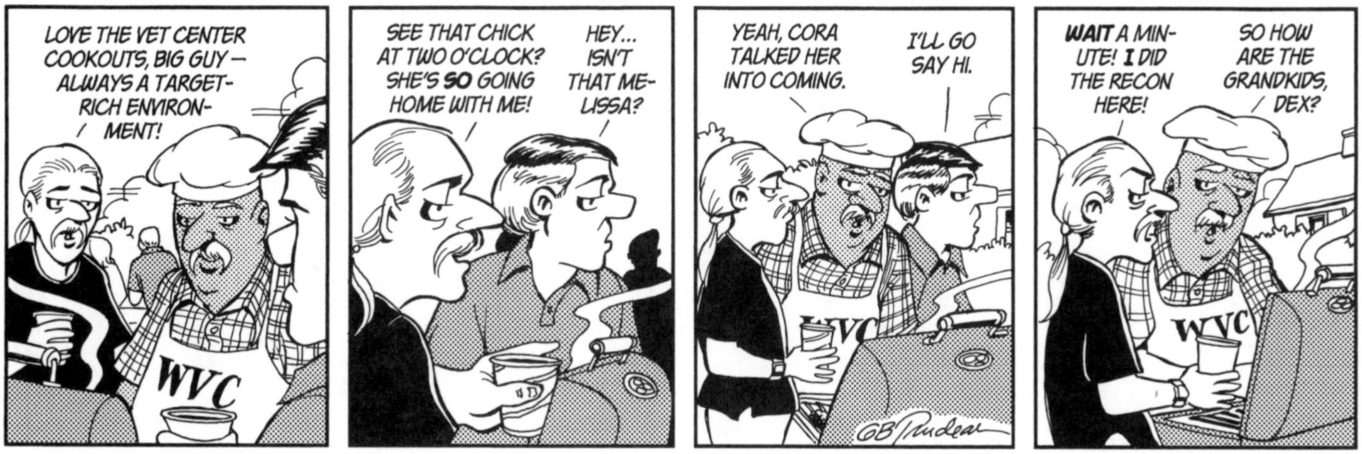
LOVE THE VET CENTER COOKOUTS, BIG GUY — ALWAYS A TARGET-RICH ENVIRONMENT!
WVC
SEE THAT CHICK AT TWO O'CLOCK? SHE'S SO GOING HOME WITH ME!
HEY... ISN'T THAT MELISSA?
YEAH, CORA TALKED HER INTO COMING.
I'LL GO SAY HI.
WAIT A MINUTE! I DID THE RECON HERE!
SO HOW ARE THE GRANDKIDS, DEX?
WVC
GB Trudeau

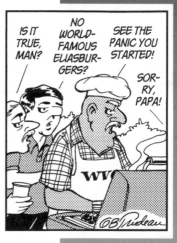

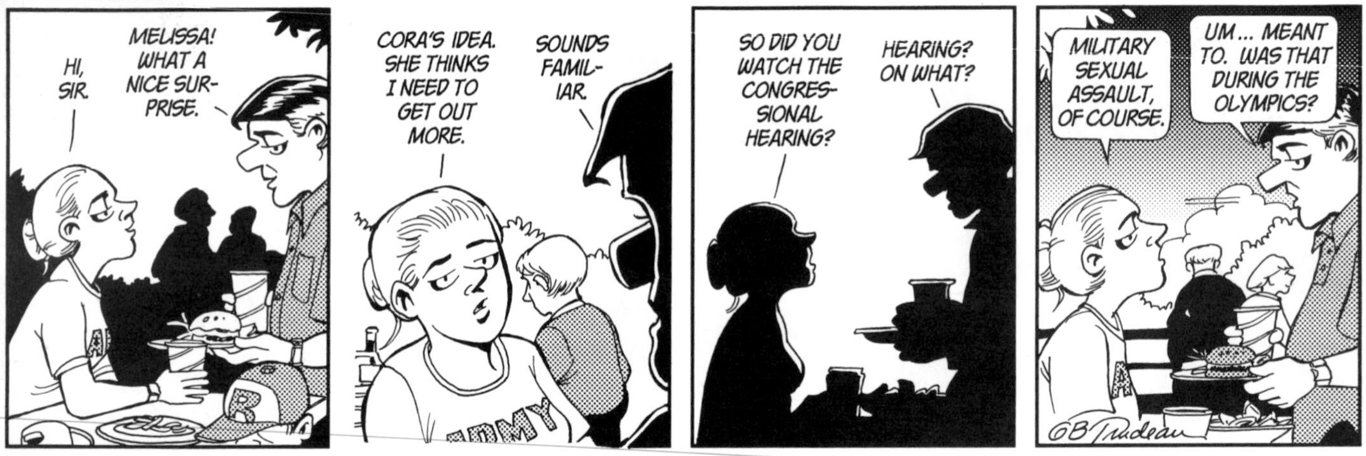
HI, SIR.
MELISSA! WHAT A NICE SURPRISE.
CORA'S IDEA. SHE THINKS I NEED TO GET OUT MORE.
SOUNDS FAMILIAR.
SO DID YOU WATCH THE CONGRESSIONAL HEARING?
HEARING? ON WHAT?
MILITARY SEXUAL ASSAULT, OF COURSE.
UM... MEANT TO. WAS THAT DURING THE OLYMPICS?
GB Trudeau

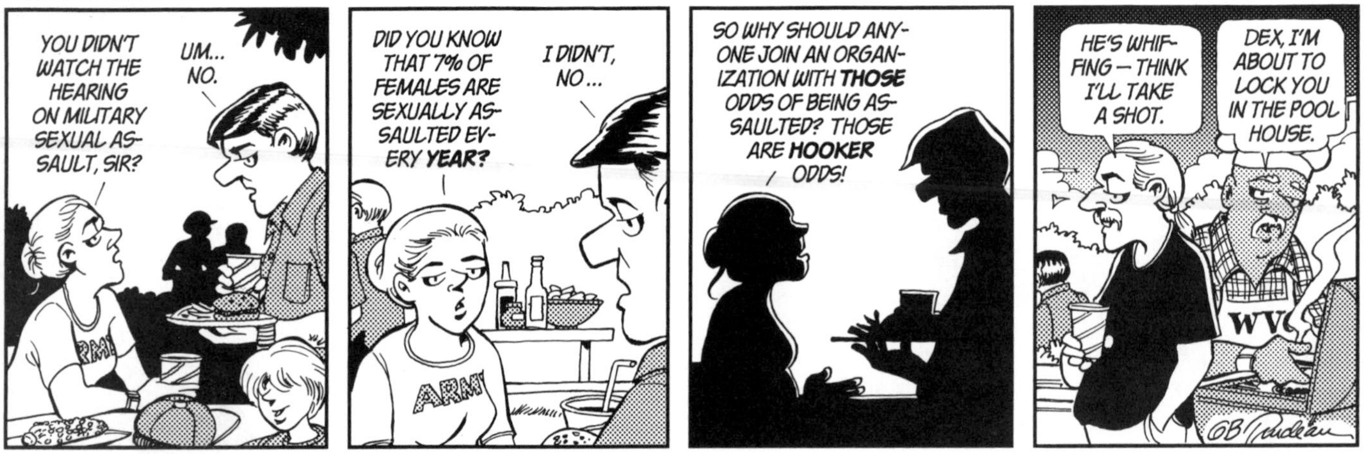
YOU DIDN'T WATCH THE HEARING ON MILITARY SEXUAL ASSAULT, SIR?
UM... NO.
DID YOU KNOW THAT 7% OF FEMALES ARE SEXUALLY ASSAULTED EVERY YEAR?
I DIDN'T, NO...
SO WHY SHOULD ANYONE JOIN AN ORGANIZATION WITH THOSE ODDS OF BEING ASSAULTED? THOSE ARE HOOKER ODDS!
HE'S WHIFFING — THINK I'LL TAKE A SHOT.
DEX, I'M ABOUT TO LOCK YOU IN THE POOL HOUSE.
GB Trudeau

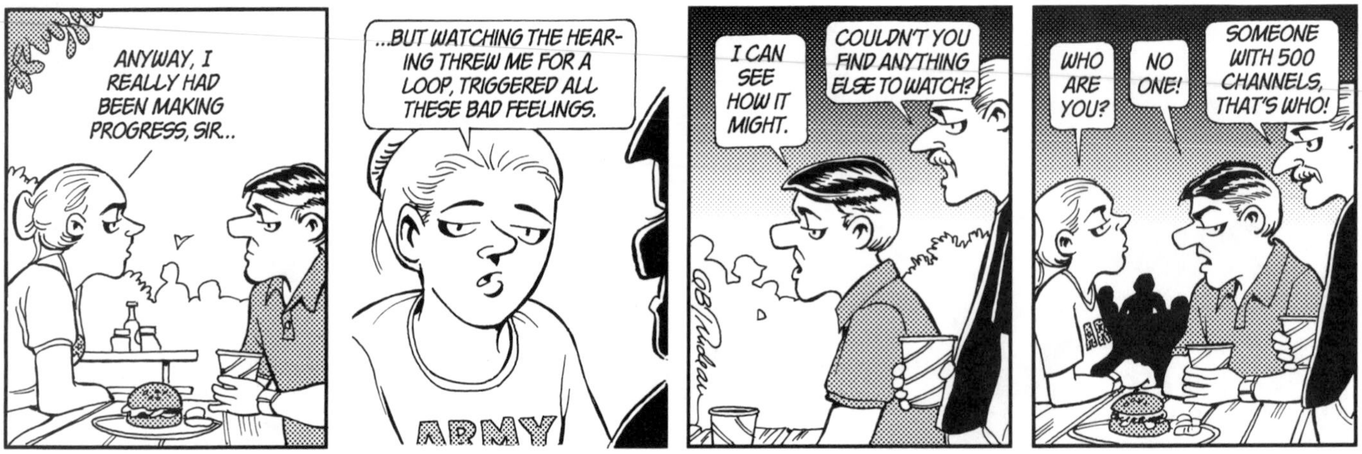
ANYWAY, I REALLY HAD BEEN MAKING PROGRESS, SIR...
...BUT WATCHING THE HEARING THREW ME FOR A LOOP, TRIGGERED ALL THESE BAD FEELINGS.
I CAN SEE HOW IT MIGHT.
COULDN'T YOU FIND ANYTHING ELSE TO WATCH?
WHO ARE YOU?
NO ONE!
SOMEONE WITH 500 CHANNELS, THAT'S WHO!
GB Trudeau

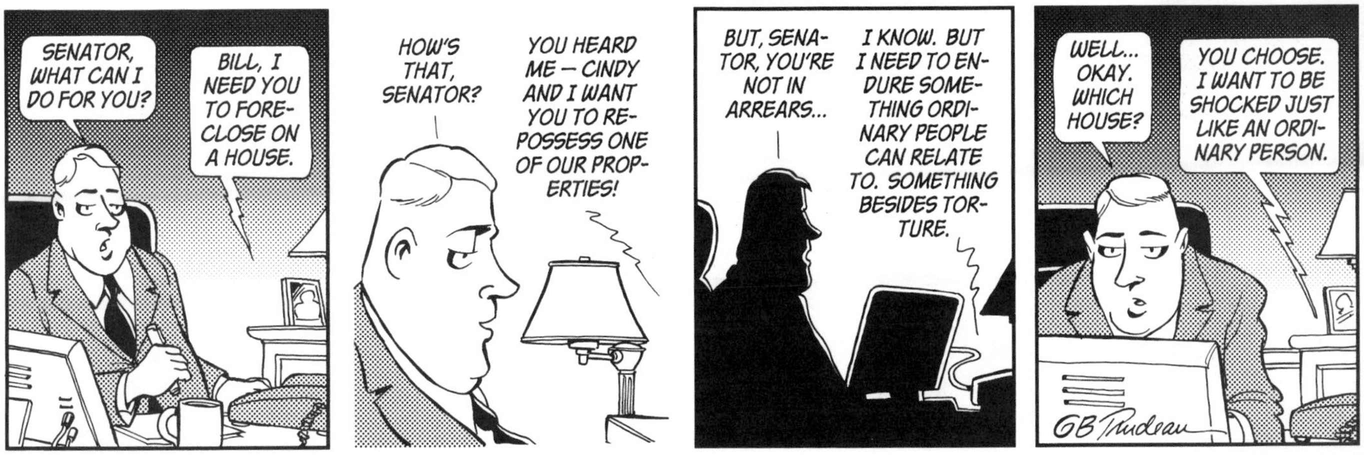
SENATOR, WHAT CAN I DO FOR YOU?
BILL, I NEED YOU TO FORECLOSE ON A HOUSE.
HOW'S THAT, SENATOR?
YOU HEARD ME — CINDY AND I WANT YOU TO REPOSSESS ONE OF OUR PROPERTIES!
BUT, SENATOR, YOU'RE NOT IN ARREARS...
I KNOW. BUT I NEED TO ENDURE SOMETHING ORDINARY PEOPLE CAN RELATE TO. SOMETHING BESIDES TORTURE.
WELL... OKAY. WHICH HOUSE?
YOU CHOOSE. I WANT TO BE SHOCKED JUST LIKE AN ORDINARY PERSON.
GB Trudeau

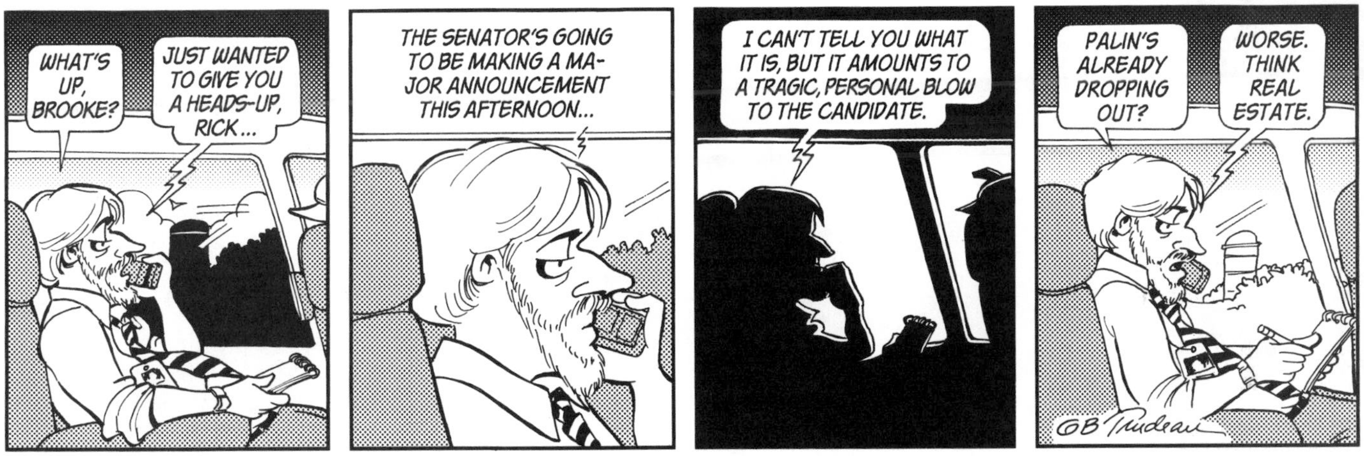
WHAT'S UP, BROOKE?
JUST WANTED TO GIVE YOU A HEADS-UP, RICK...
THE SENATOR'S GOING TO BE MAKING A MAJOR ANNOUNCEMENT THIS AFTERNOON...
I CAN'T TELL YOU WHAT IT IS, BUT IT AMOUNTS TO A TRAGIC, PERSONAL BLOW TO THE CANDIDATE.
PALIN'S ALREADY DROPPING OUT?
WORSE. THINK REAL ESTATE.
GB Trudeau

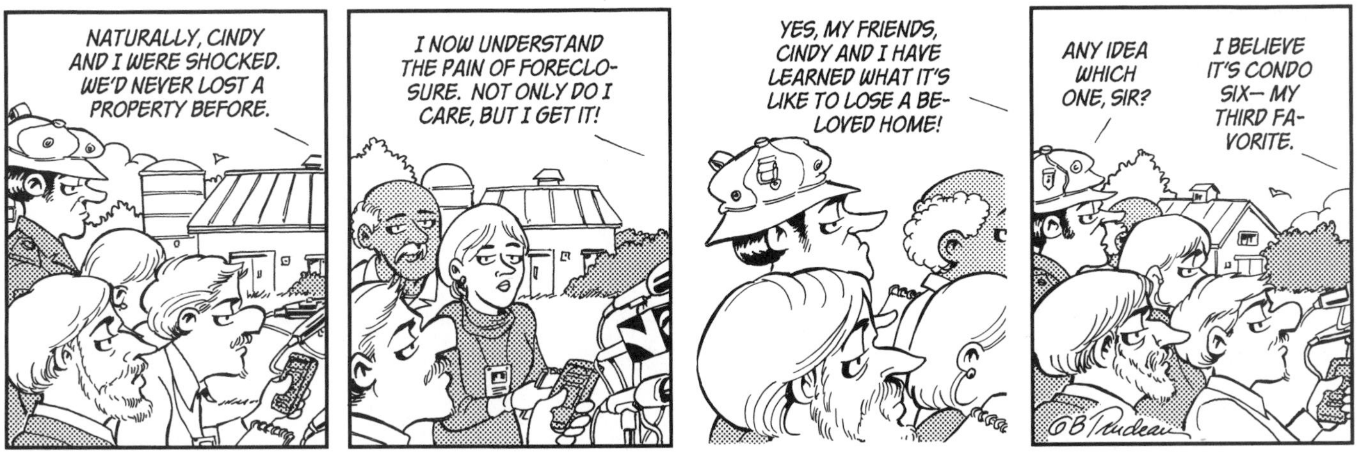
NATURALLY, CINDY AND I WERE SHOCKED. WE'D NEVER LOST A PROPERTY BEFORE.
I NOW UNDERSTAND THE PAIN OF FORECLOSURE. NOT ONLY DO I CARE, BUT I GET IT!
YES, MY FRIENDS, CINDY AND I HAVE LEARNED WHAT IT'S LIKE TO LOSE A BELOVED HOME!
ANY IDEA WHICH ONE, SIR?
I BELIEVE IT'S CONDO SIX— MY THIRD FAVORITE.
GB Trudeau

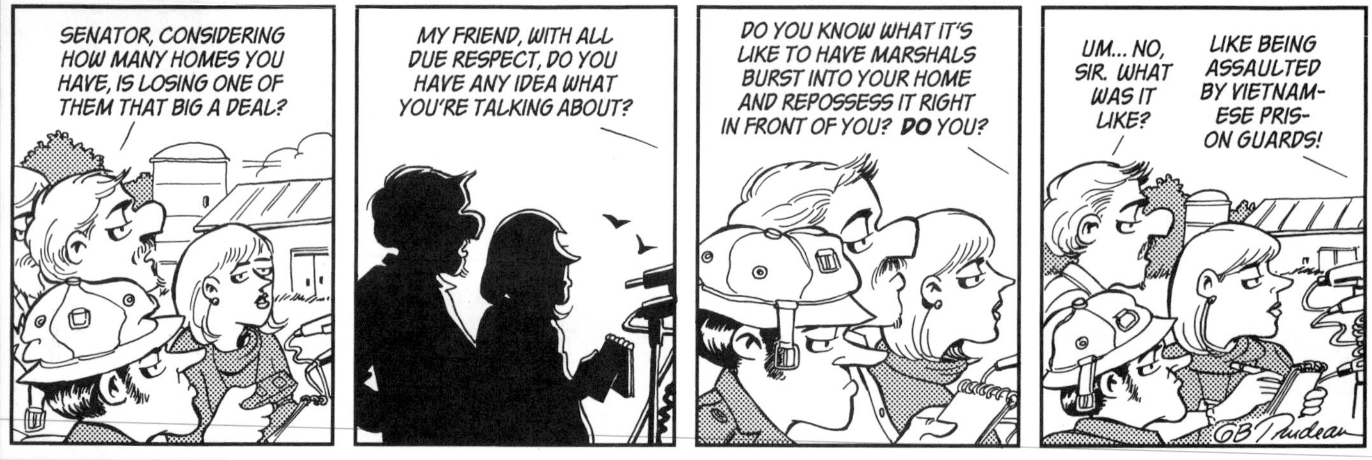
SENATOR, CONSIDERING HOW MANY HOMES YOU HAVE, IS LOSING ONE OF THEM THAT BIG A DEAL?
MY FRIEND, WITH ALL DUE RESPECT, DO YOU HAVE ANY IDEA WHAT YOU'RE TALKING ABOUT?
DO YOU KNOW WHAT IT'S LIKE TO HAVE MARSHALS BURST INTO YOUR HOME AND REPOSSESS IT RIGHT IN FRONT OF YOU? **DO** YOU?
UM... NO, SIR. WHAT WAS IT LIKE?
LIKE BEING ASSAULTED BY VIETNAMESE PRISON GUARDS!
©B Trudeau

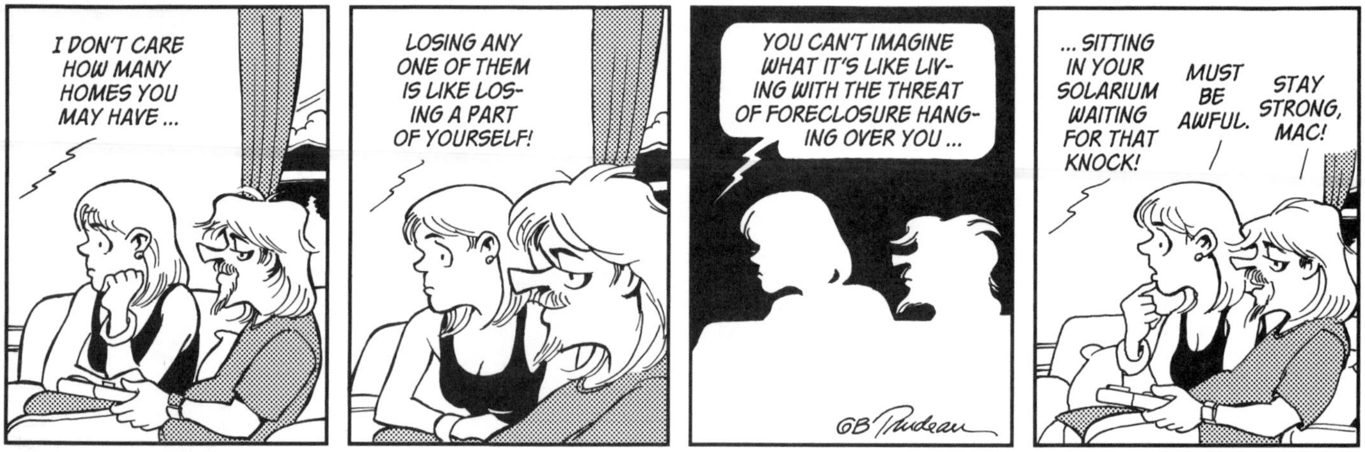
I DON'T CARE HOW MANY HOMES YOU MAY HAVE ...
LOSING ANY ONE OF THEM IS LIKE LOSING A PART OF YOURSELF!
YOU CAN'T IMAGINE WHAT IT'S LIKE LIVING WITH THE THREAT OF FORECLOSURE HANGING OVER YOU ...
©B Trudeau
... SITTING IN YOUR SOLARIUM WAITING FOR THAT KNOCK!
MUST BE AWFUL.
STAY STRONG, MAC!

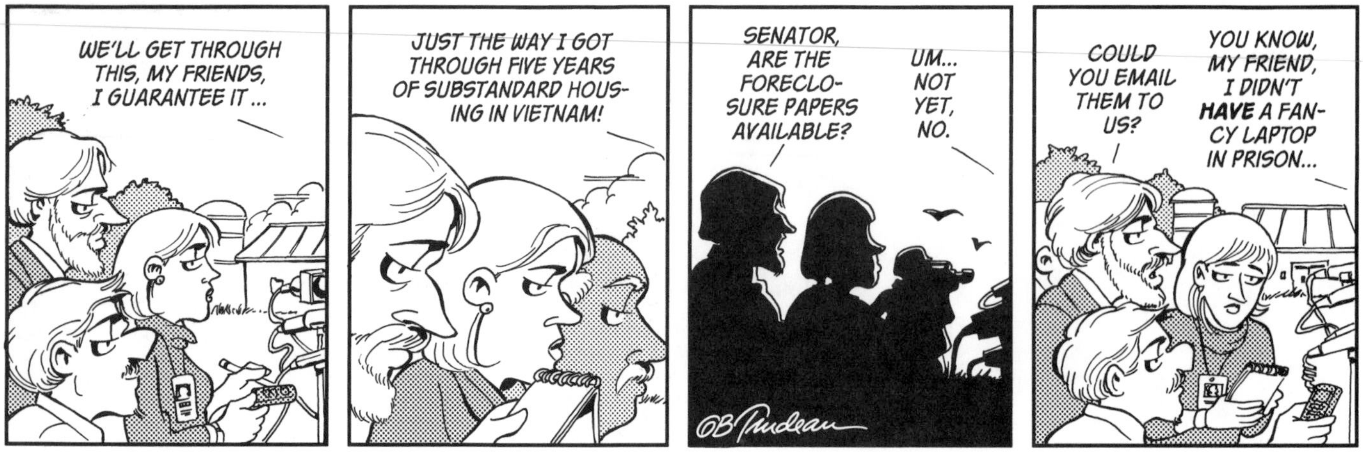
WE'LL GET THROUGH THIS, MY FRIENDS, I GUARANTEE IT ...
JUST THE WAY I GOT THROUGH FIVE YEARS OF SUBSTANDARD HOUSING IN VIETNAM!
SENATOR, ARE THE FORECLOSURE PAPERS AVAILABLE?
UM... NOT YET, NO.
©B Trudeau
COULD YOU EMAIL THEM TO US?
YOU KNOW, MY FRIEND, I DIDN'T **HAVE** A FANCY LAPTOP IN PRISON...

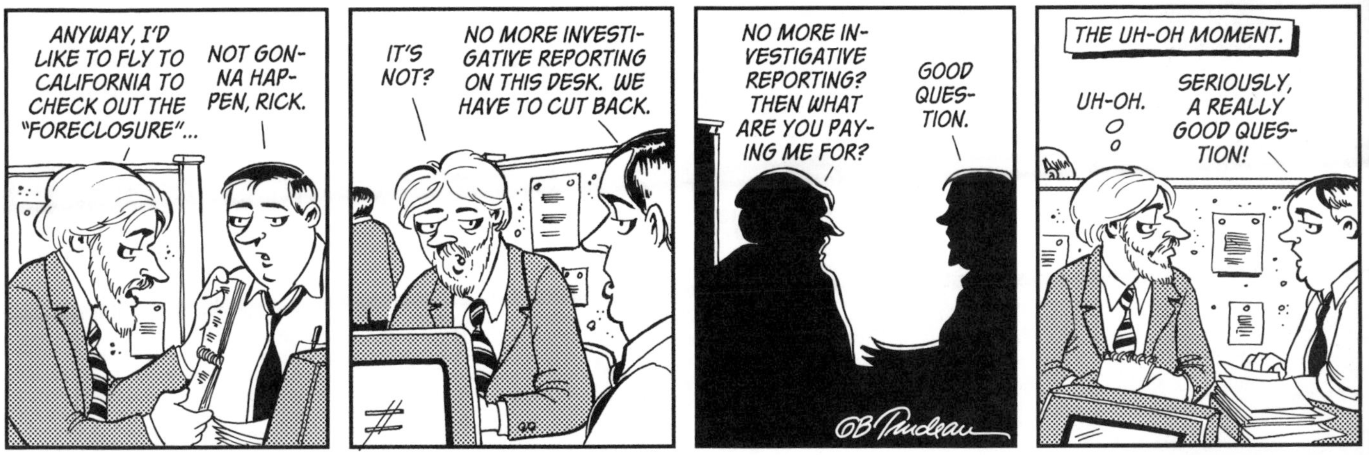
ANYWAY, I'D LIKE TO FLY TO CALIFORNIA TO CHECK OUT THE "FORECLOSURE"...
NOT GONNA HAPPEN, RICK.
IT'S NOT?
NO MORE INVESTIGATIVE REPORTING ON THIS DESK. WE HAVE TO CUT BACK.
NO MORE INVESTIGATIVE REPORTING? THEN WHAT ARE YOU PAYING ME FOR?
GOOD QUESTION.
GB Trudeau
THE UH-OH MOMENT.
UH-OH.
SERIOUSLY, A REALLY GOOD QUESTION!

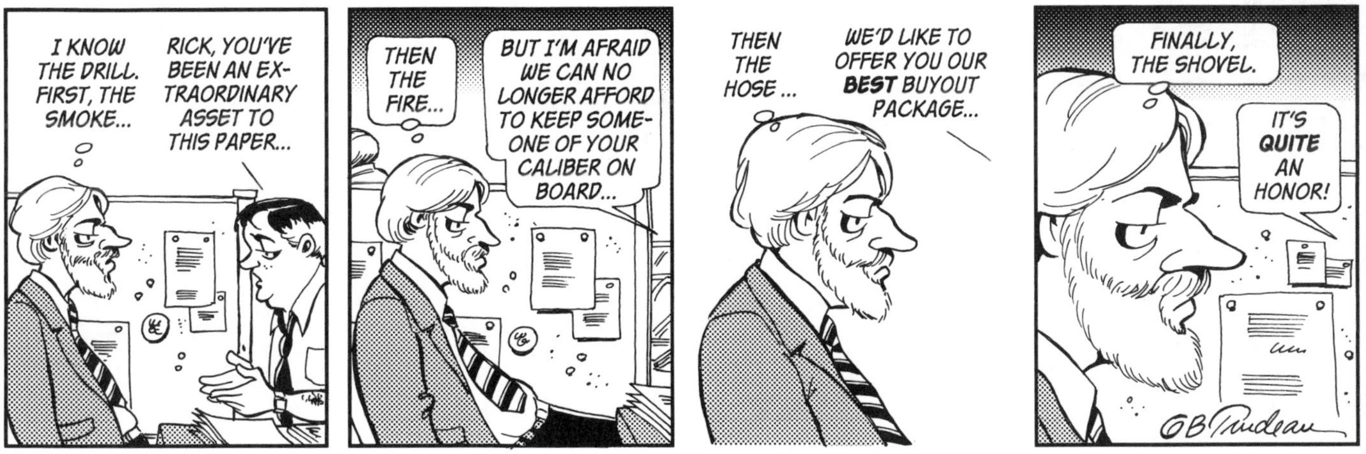
I KNOW THE DRILL. FIRST, THE SMOKE...
RICK, YOU'VE BEEN AN EXTRAORDINARY ASSET TO THIS PAPER...
THEN THE FIRE...
BUT I'M AFRAID WE CAN NO LONGER AFFORD TO KEEP SOMEONE OF YOUR CALIBER ON BOARD...
THEN THE HOSE ...
WE'D LIKE TO OFFER YOU OUR **BEST** BUYOUT PACKAGE...
FINALLY, THE SHOVEL.
IT'S **QUITE** AN HONOR!
GB Trudeau

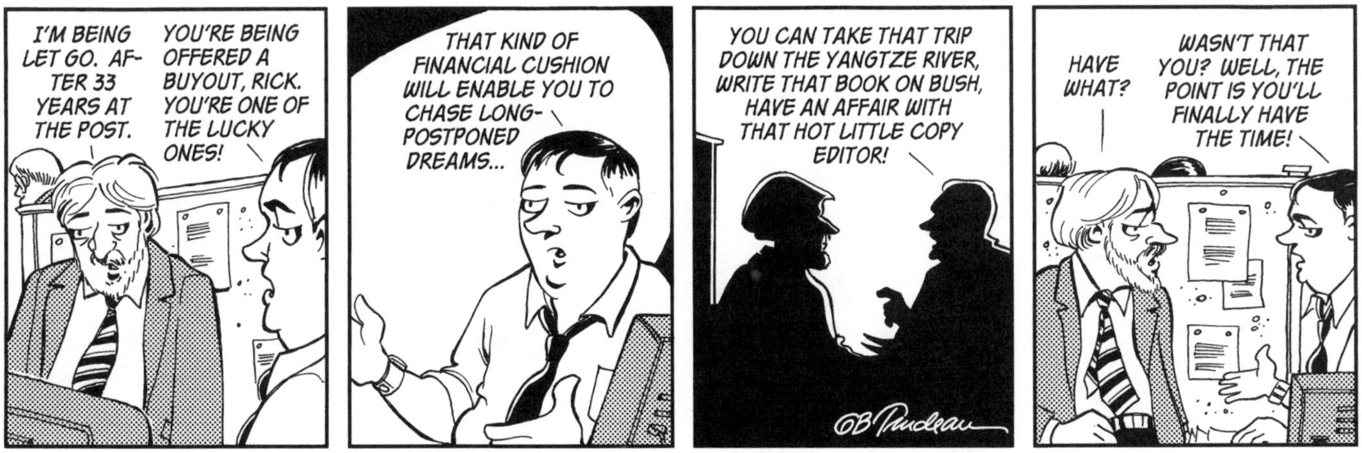
I'M BEING LET GO. AFTER 33 YEARS AT THE POST.
YOU'RE BEING OFFERED A BUYOUT, RICK. YOU'RE ONE OF THE LUCKY ONES!
THAT KIND OF FINANCIAL CUSHION WILL ENABLE YOU TO CHASE LONG-POSTPONED DREAMS...
YOU CAN TAKE THAT TRIP DOWN THE YANGTZE RIVER, WRITE THAT BOOK ON BUSH, HAVE AN AFFAIR WITH THAT HOT LITTLE COPY EDITOR!
GB Trudeau
HAVE WHAT?
WASN'T THAT YOU? WELL, THE POINT IS YOU'LL FINALLY HAVE THE TIME!

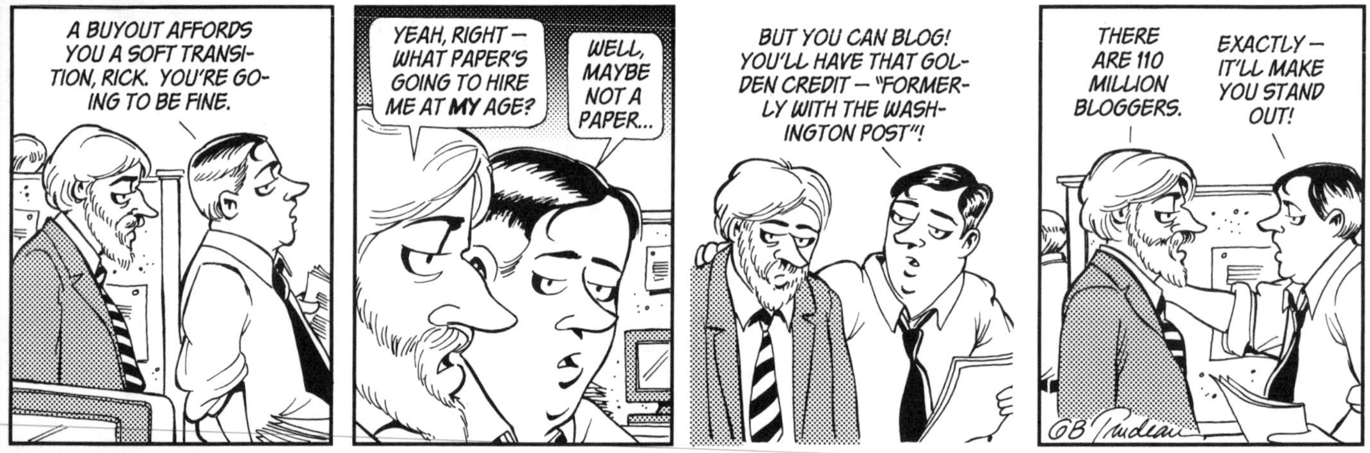
A BUYOUT AFFORDS YOU A SOFT TRANSITION, RICK. YOU'RE GOING TO BE FINE.
YEAH, RIGHT — WHAT PAPER'S GOING TO HIRE ME AT **MY** AGE?
WELL, MAYBE NOT A PAPER...
BUT YOU CAN BLOG! YOU'LL HAVE THAT GOLDEN CREDIT — "FORMERLY WITH THE WASHINGTON POST"!
THERE ARE 110 MILLION BLOGGERS.
EXACTLY — IT'LL MAKE YOU STAND OUT!
GB Trudeau

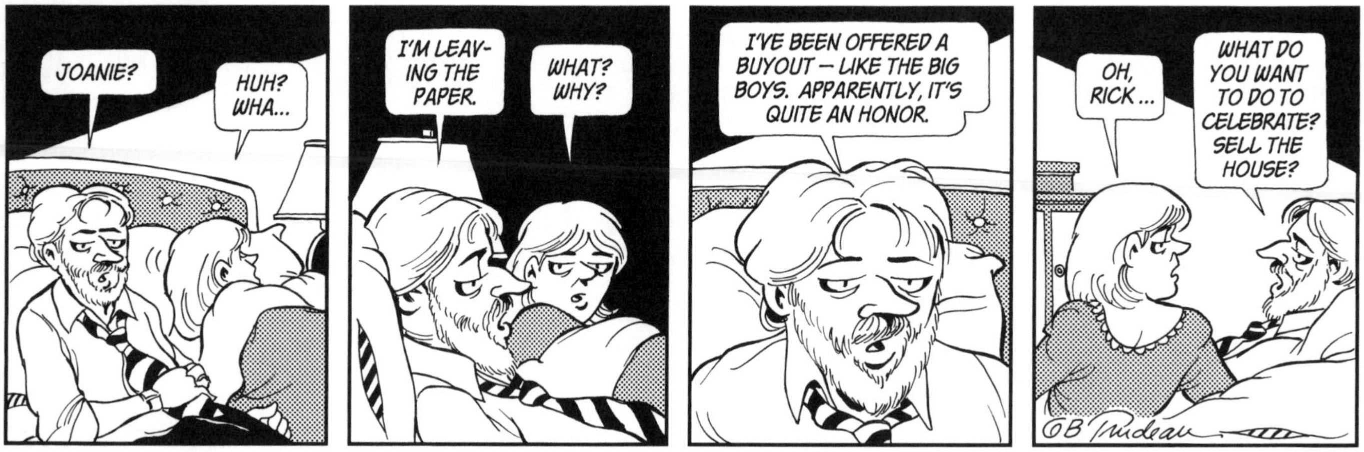
JOANIE?
HUH? WHA...
I'M LEAVING THE PAPER.
WHAT? WHY?
I'VE BEEN OFFERED A BUYOUT — LIKE THE BIG BOYS. APPARENTLY, IT'S QUITE AN HONOR.
OH, RICK...
WHAT DO YOU WANT TO DO TO CELEBRATE? SELL THE HOUSE?
GB Trudeau

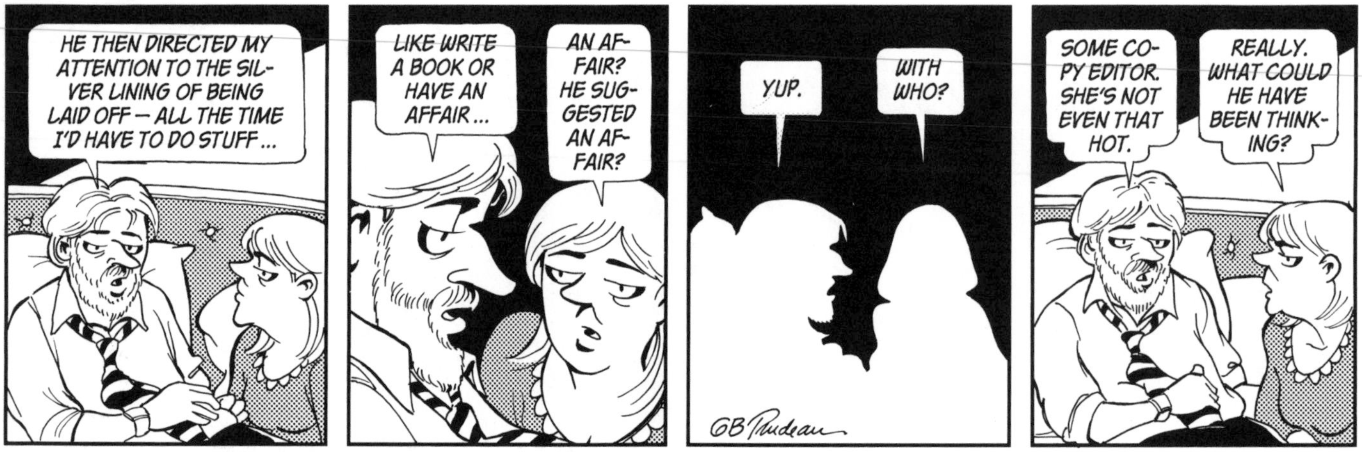
HE THEN DIRECTED MY ATTENTION TO THE SILVER LINING OF BEING LAID OFF — ALL THE TIME I'D HAVE TO DO STUFF...
LIKE WRITE A BOOK OR HAVE AN AFFAIR...
AN AFFAIR? HE SUGGESTED AN AFFAIR?
YUP.
WITH WHO?
SOME COPY EDITOR. SHE'S NOT EVEN THAT HOT.
REALLY. WHAT COULD HE HAVE BEEN THINKING?
GB Trudeau

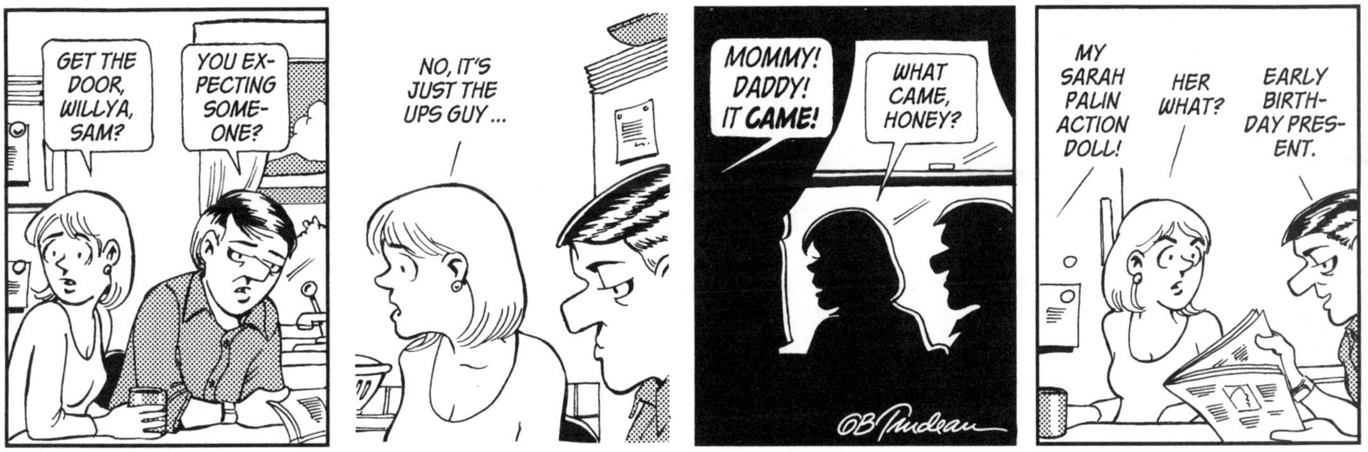
GET THE DOOR, WILLYA, SAM?
YOU EX-PECTING SOME-ONE?
NO, IT'S JUST THE UPS GUY ...
MOMMY! DADDY! IT **CAME!**
WHAT CAME, HONEY?
MY SARAH PALIN ACTION DOLL!
HER WHAT?
EARLY BIRTH-DAY PRES-ENT.
GB Trudeau

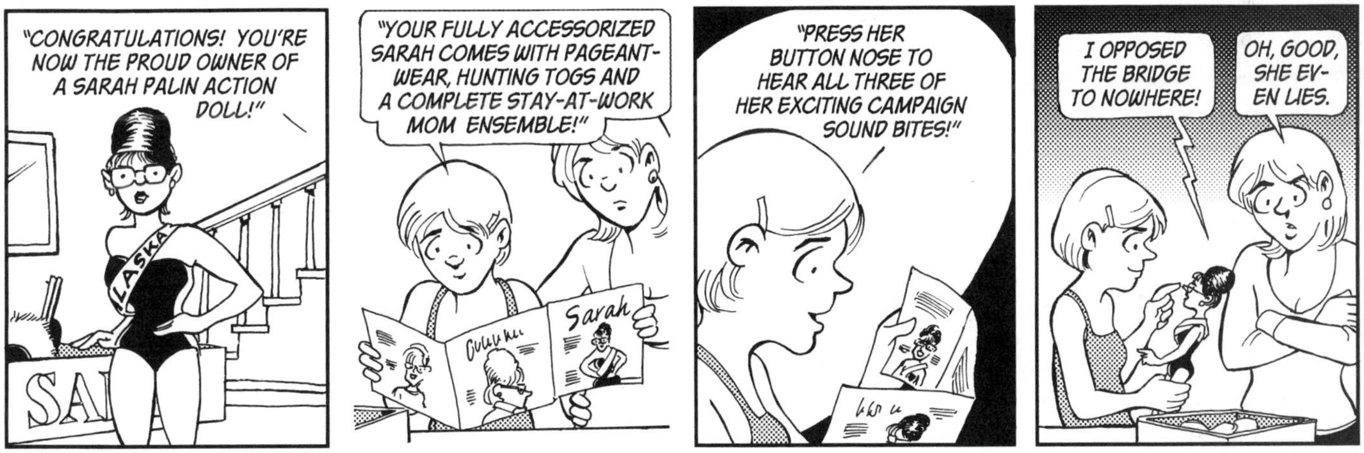
"CONGRATULATIONS! YOU'RE NOW THE PROUD OWNER OF A SARAH PALIN ACTION DOLL!"
"YOUR FULLY ACCESSORIZED SARAH COMES WITH PAGEANT-WEAR, HUNTING TOGS AND A COMPLETE STAY-AT-WORK MOM ENSEMBLE!"
"PRESS HER BUTTON NOSE TO HEAR ALL THREE OF HER EXCITING CAMPAIGN SOUND BITES!"
I OPPOSED THE BRIDGE TO NOWHERE!
OH, GOOD, SHE EV-EN LIES.

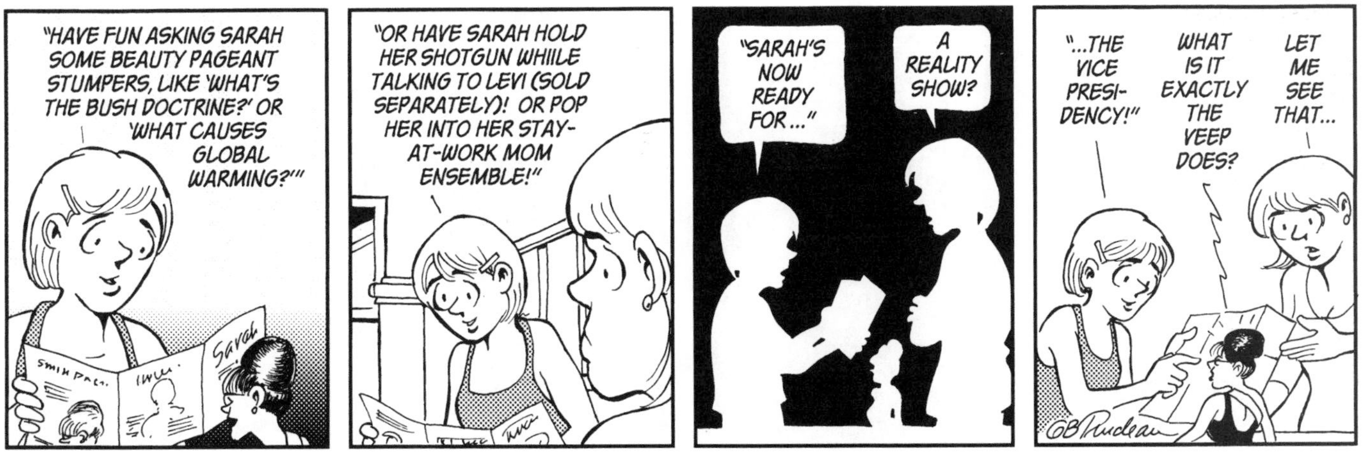
"HAVE FUN ASKING SARAH SOME BEAUTY PAGEANT STUMPERS, LIKE 'WHAT'S THE BUSH DOCTRINE?' OR 'WHAT CAUSES GLOBAL WARMING?'"
"OR HAVE SARAH HOLD HER SHOTGUN WHIILE TALKING TO LEVI (SOLD SEPARATELY)! OR POP HER INTO HER STAY-AT-WORK MOM ENSEMBLE!"
"SARAH'S NOW READY FOR ..."
A REALITY SHOW?
"...THE VICE PRESI-DENCY!"
WHAT IS IT EXACTLY THE VEEP DOES?
LET ME SEE THAT...
GB Trudeau

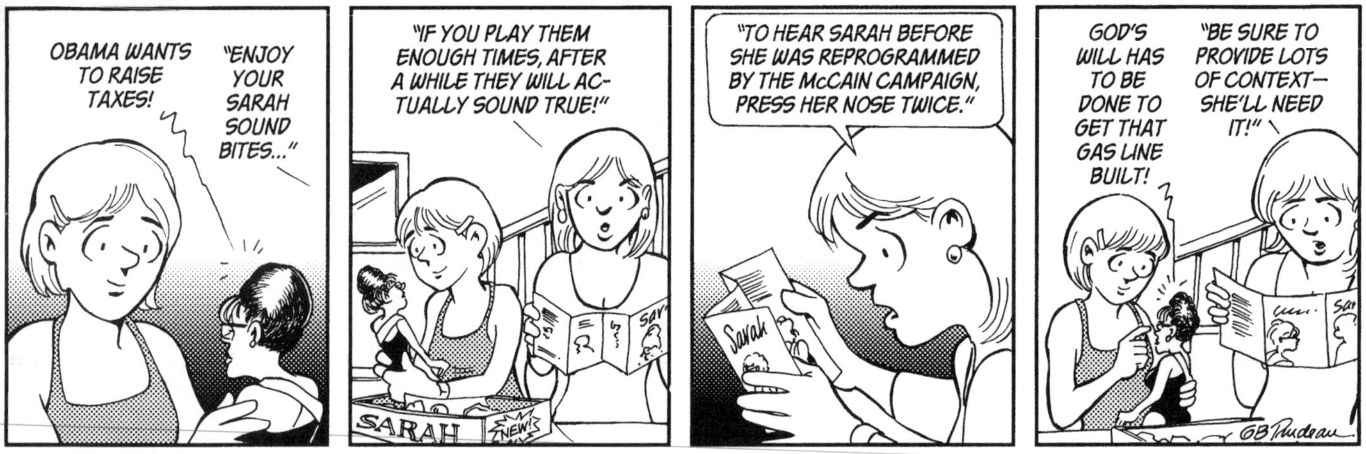
OBAMA WANTS TO RAISE TAXES!
"ENJOY YOUR SARAH SOUND BITES..."
"IF YOU PLAY THEM ENOUGH TIMES, AFTER A WHILE THEY WILL ACTUALLY SOUND TRUE!"
SARAH
NEW!
"TO HEAR SARAH BEFORE SHE WAS REPROGRAMMED BY THE McCAIN CAMPAIGN, PRESS HER NOSE TWICE."
Sarah
GOD'S WILL HAS TO BE DONE TO GET THAT GAS LINE BUILT!
"BE SURE TO PROVIDE LOTS OF CONTEXT— SHE'LL NEED IT!"
GB Trudeau

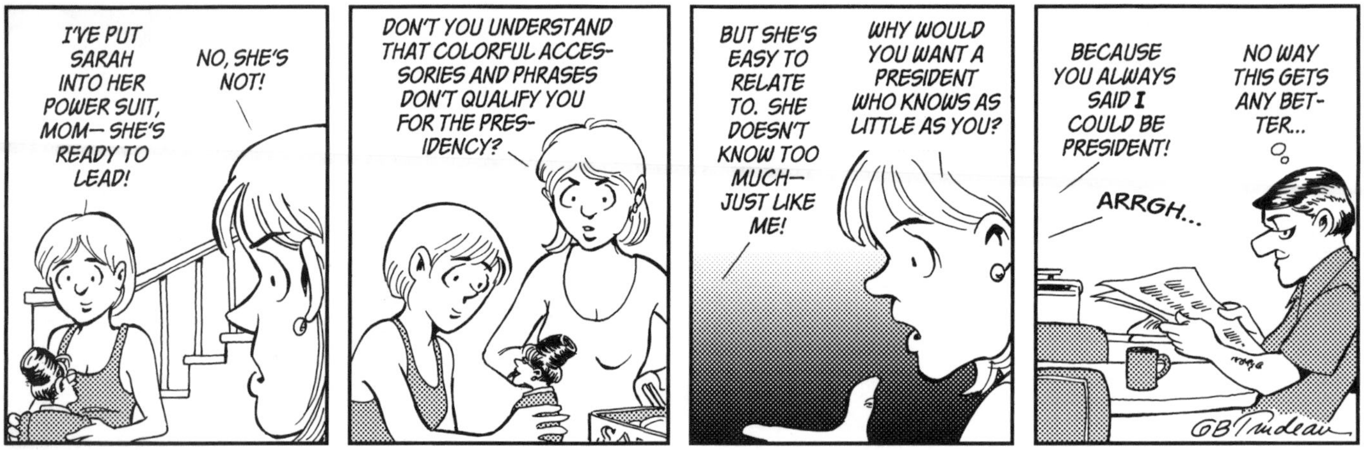
I'VE PUT SARAH INTO HER POWER SUIT, MOM— SHE'S READY TO LEAD!
NO, SHE'S NOT!
DON'T YOU UNDERSTAND THAT COLORFUL ACCESSORIES AND PHRASES DON'T QUALIFY YOU FOR THE PRESIDENCY?
BUT SHE'S EASY TO RELATE TO. SHE DOESN'T KNOW TOO MUCH— JUST LIKE ME!
WHY WOULD YOU WANT A PRESIDENT WHO KNOWS AS LITTLE AS YOU?
BECAUSE YOU ALWAYS SAID I COULD BE PRESIDENT!
ARRGH...
NO WAY THIS GETS ANY BETTER...
GB Trudeau

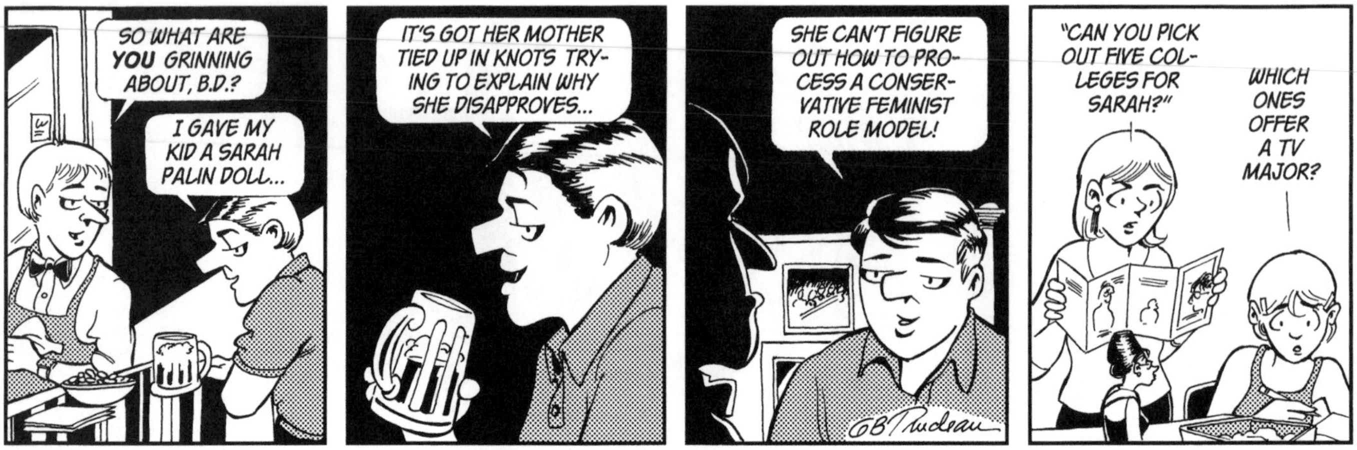
SO WHAT ARE YOU GRINNING ABOUT, B.D.?
I GAVE MY KID A SARAH PALIN DOLL...
IT'S GOT HER MOTHER TIED UP IN KNOTS TRYING TO EXPLAIN WHY SHE DISAPPROVES...
SHE CAN'T FIGURE OUT HOW TO PROCESS A CONSERVATIVE FEMINIST ROLE MODEL!
GB Trudeau
"CAN YOU PICK OUT FIVE COLLEGES FOR SARAH?"
WHICH ONES OFFER A TV MAJOR?

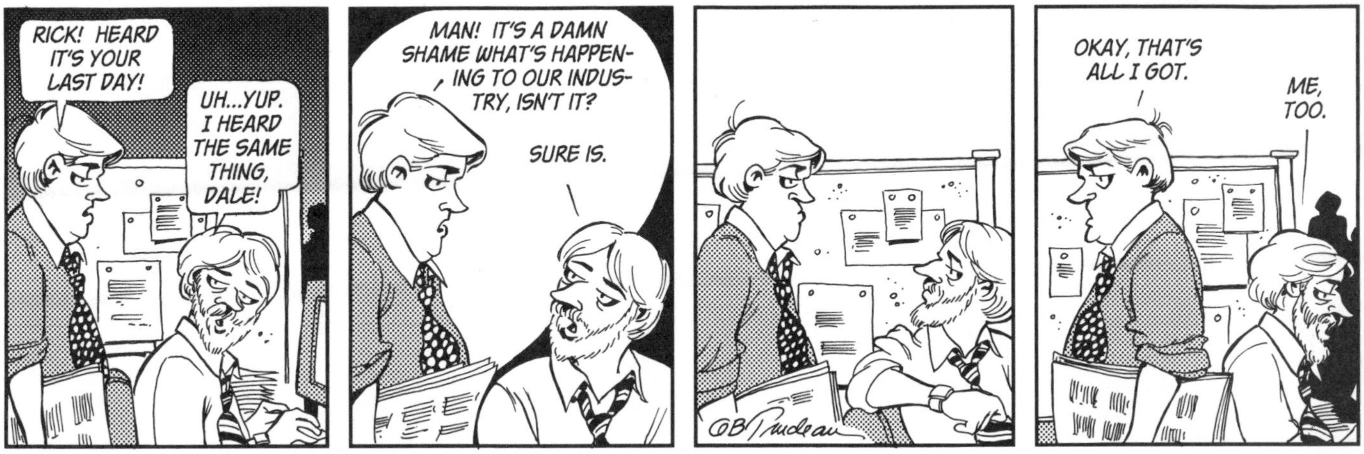
RICK! HEARD IT'S YOUR LAST DAY!
UH...YUP. I HEARD THE SAME THING, DALE!
MAN! IT'S A DAMN SHAME WHAT'S HAPPENING TO OUR INDUSTRY, ISN'T IT?
SURE IS.
OKAY, THAT'S ALL I GOT.
ME, TOO.

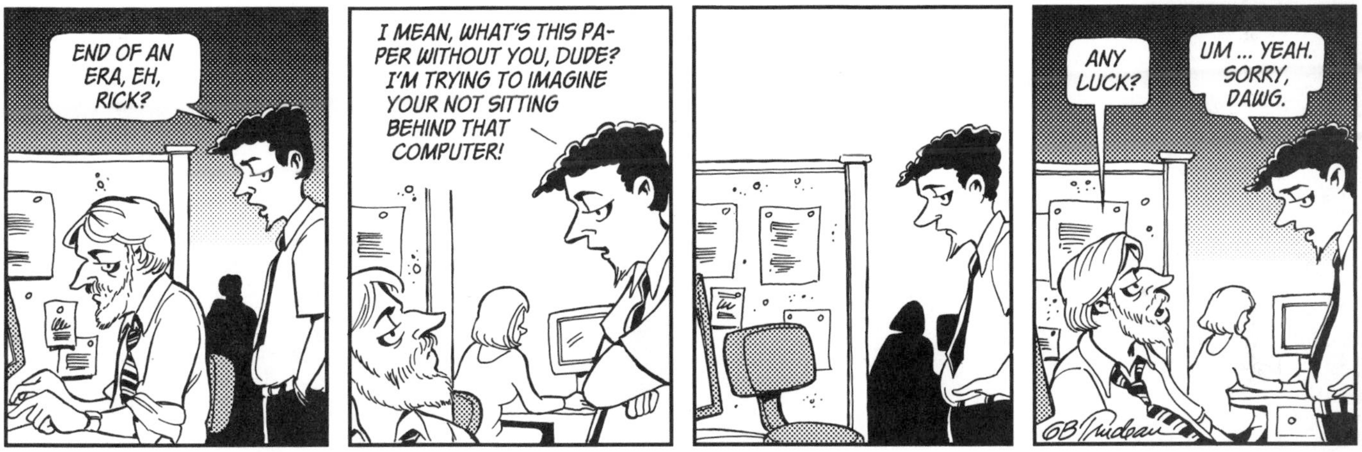
END OF AN ERA, EH, RICK?
I MEAN, WHAT'S THIS PAPER WITHOUT YOU, DUDE? I'M TRYING TO IMAGINE YOUR NOT SITTING BEHIND THAT COMPUTER!
ANY LUCK?
UM ... YEAH. SORRY, DAWG.

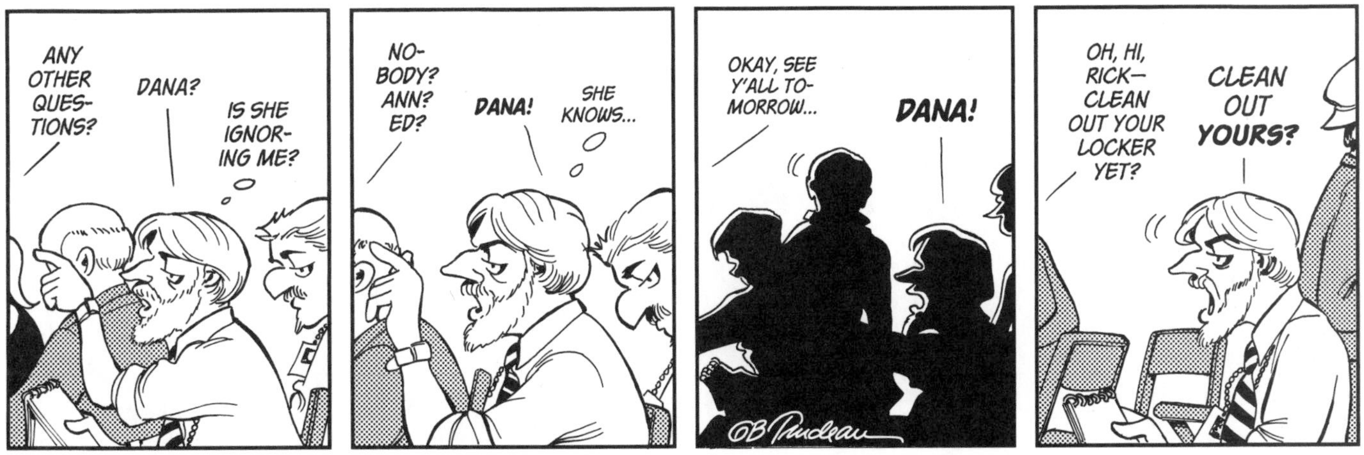
ANY OTHER QUESTIONS?
DANA?
IS SHE IGNORING ME?
NOBODY? ANN? ED?
DANA!
SHE KNOWS...
OKAY, SEE Y'ALL TOMORROW...
DANA!
OH, HI, RICK— CLEAN OUT YOUR LOCKER YET?
CLEAN OUT YOURS?

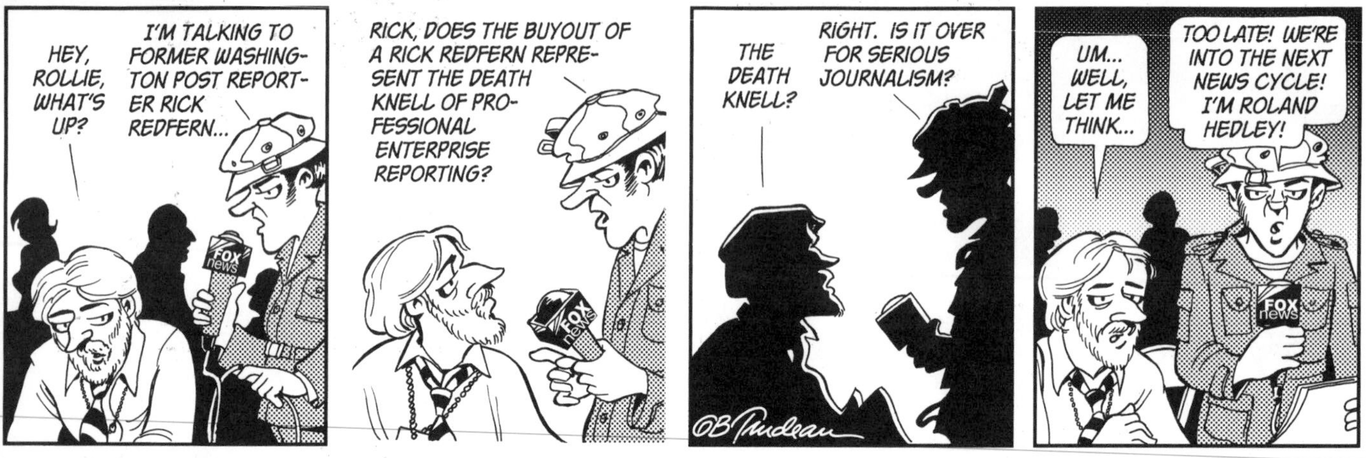
HEY, ROLLIE, WHAT'S UP?
I'M TALKING TO FORMER WASHINGTON POST REPORTER RICK REDFERN...
FOX news
RICK, DOES THE BUYOUT OF A RICK REDFERN REPRESENT THE DEATH KNELL OF PROFESSIONAL ENTERPRISE REPORTING?
THE DEATH KNELL?
RIGHT. IS IT OVER FOR SERIOUS JOURNALISM?
UM... WELL, LET ME THINK...
TOO LATE! WE'RE INTO THE NEXT NEWS CYCLE! I'M ROLAND HEDLEY!
©B Trudeau

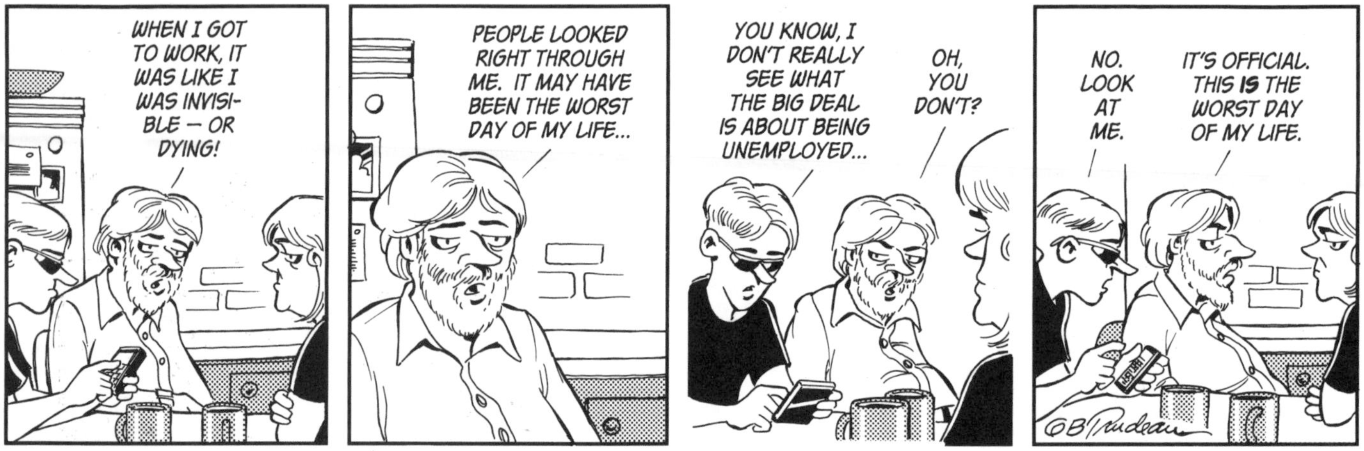
WHEN I GOT TO WORK, IT WAS LIKE I WAS INVISIBLE — OR DYING!
PEOPLE LOOKED RIGHT THROUGH ME. IT MAY HAVE BEEN THE WORST DAY OF MY LIFE...
YOU KNOW, I DON'T REALLY SEE WHAT THE BIG DEAL IS ABOUT BEING UNEMPLOYED...
OH, YOU DON'T?
NO. LOOK AT ME.
IT'S OFFICIAL. THIS **IS** THE WORST DAY OF MY LIFE.
©B Trudeau

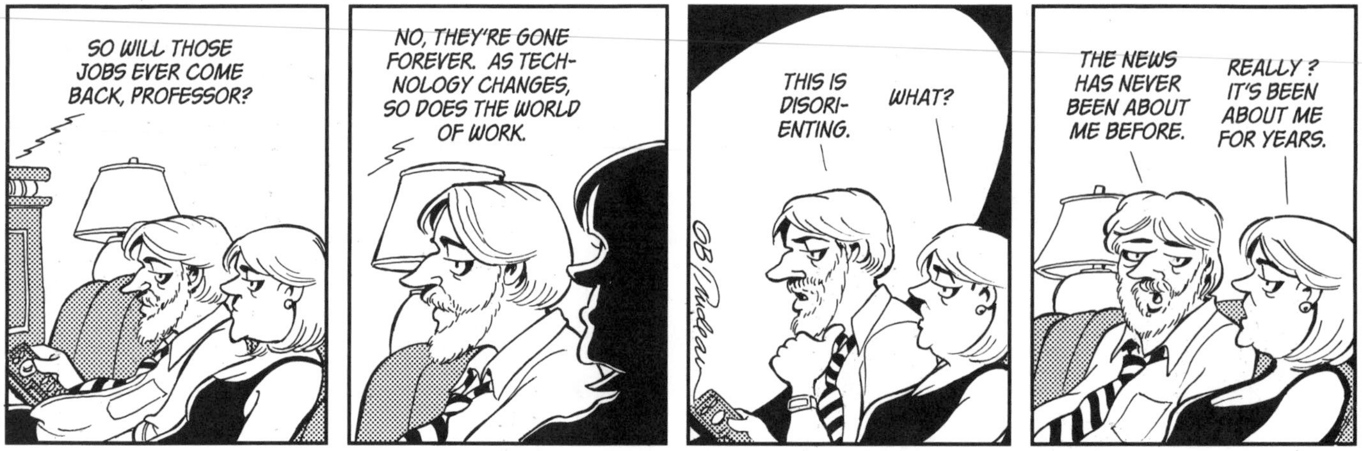
SO WILL THOSE JOBS EVER COME BACK, PROFESSOR?
NO, THEY'RE GONE FOREVER. AS TECHNOLOGY CHANGES, SO DOES THE WORLD OF WORK.
THIS IS DISORIENTING.
WHAT?
©B Trudeau
THE NEWS HAS NEVER BEEN ABOUT ME BEFORE.
REALLY? IT'S BEEN ABOUT ME FOR YEARS.

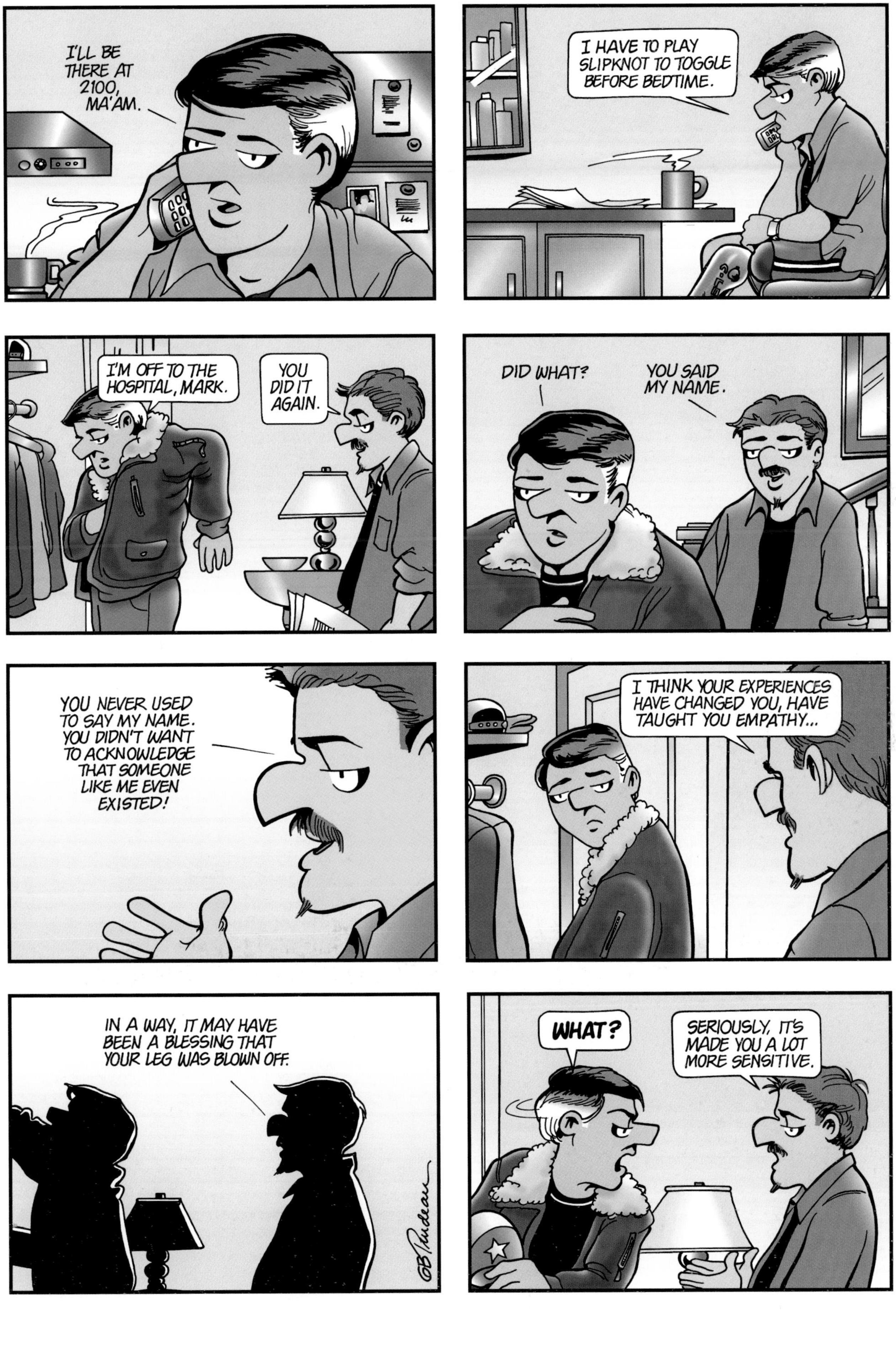
I'LL BE THERE AT 2100, MA'AM.
I HAVE TO PLAY SLIPKNOT TO TOGGLE BEFORE BEDTIME.
I'M OFF TO THE HOSPITAL, MARK.
YOU DID IT AGAIN.
DID WHAT?
YOU SAID MY NAME.
YOU NEVER USED TO SAY MY NAME. YOU DIDN'T WANT TO ACKNOWLEDGE THAT SOMEONE LIKE ME EVEN EXISTED!
I THINK YOUR EXPERIENCES HAVE CHANGED YOU, HAVE TAUGHT YOU EMPATHY...
IN A WAY, IT MAY HAVE BEEN A BLESSING THAT YOUR LEG WAS BLOWN OFF.
WHAT?
SERIOUSLY, IT'S MADE YOU A LOT MORE SENSITIVE.
GBTrudeau

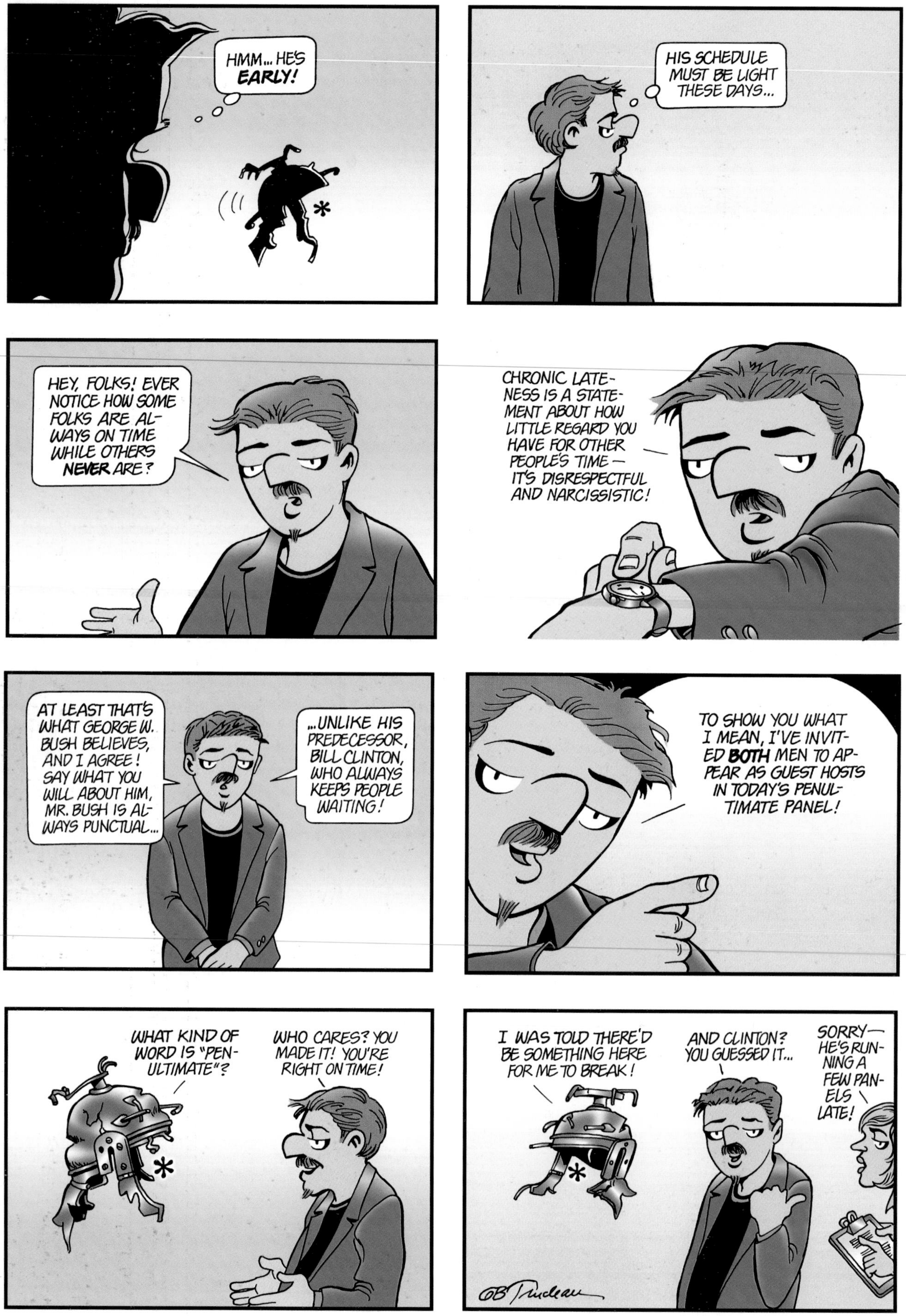
HMM... HE'S EARLY!
HIS SCHEDULE MUST BE LIGHT THESE DAYS...
HEY, FOLKS! EVER NOTICE HOW SOME FOLKS ARE ALWAYS ON TIME WHILE OTHERS NEVER ARE?
CHRONIC LATENESS IS A STATEMENT ABOUT HOW LITTLE REGARD YOU HAVE FOR OTHER PEOPLE'S TIME — IT'S DISRESPECTFUL AND NARCISSISTIC!
AT LEAST THAT'S WHAT GEORGE W. BUSH BELIEVES, AND I AGREE! SAY WHAT YOU WILL ABOUT HIM, MR. BUSH IS ALWAYS PUNCTUAL...
...UNLIKE HIS PREDECESSOR, BILL CLINTON, WHO ALWAYS KEEPS PEOPLE WAITING!
TO SHOW YOU WHAT I MEAN, I'VE INVITED BOTH MEN TO APPEAR AS GUEST HOSTS IN TODAY'S PENULTIMATE PANEL!
WHAT KIND OF WORD IS "PENULTIMATE"?
WHO CARES? YOU MADE IT! YOU'RE RIGHT ON TIME!
I WAS TOLD THERE'D BE SOMETHING HERE FOR ME TO BREAK!
AND CLINTON? YOU GUESSED IT...
SORRY— HE'S RUNNING A FEW PANELS LATE!
GB Trudeau

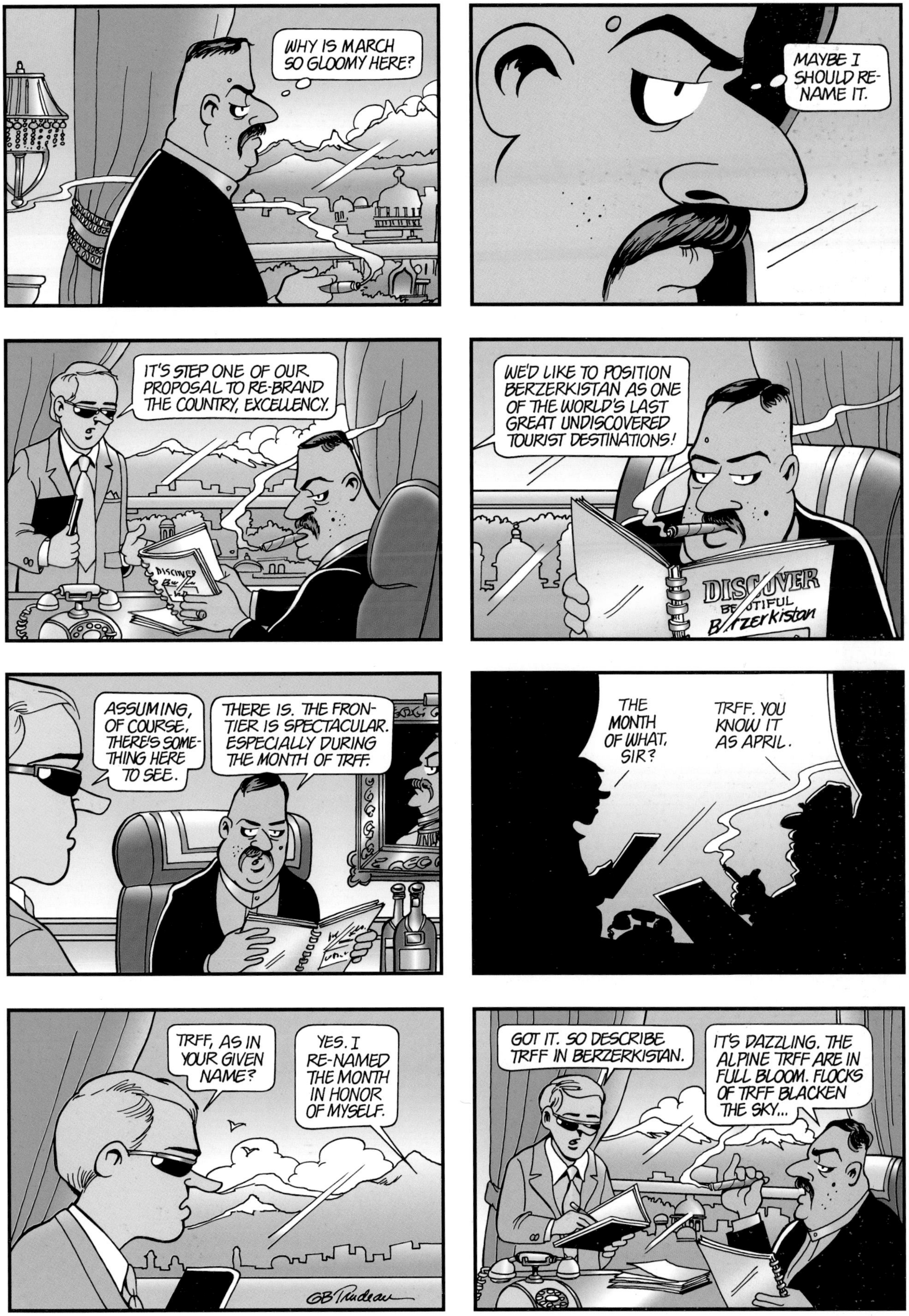
WHY IS MARCH SO GLOOMY HERE?
MAYBE I SHOULD RE-NAME IT.
IT'S STEP ONE OF OUR PROPOSAL TO RE-BRAND THE COUNTRY, EXCELLENCY.
WE'D LIKE TO POSITION BERZERKISTAN AS ONE OF THE WORLD'S LAST GREAT UNDISCOVERED TOURIST DESTINATIONS!
ASSUMING, OF COURSE, THERE'S SOMETHING HERE TO SEE.
THERE IS. THE FRONTIER IS SPECTACULAR. ESPECIALLY DURING THE MONTH OF TRFF.
THE MONTH OF WHAT, SIR?
TRFF. YOU KNOW IT AS APRIL.
TRFF, AS IN YOUR GIVEN NAME?
YES. I RE-NAMED THE MONTH IN HONOR OF MYSELF.
GBTrudeau
GOT IT. SO DESCRIBE TRFF IN BERZERKISTAN.
IT'S DAZZLING. THE ALPINE TRFF ARE IN FULL BLOOM. FLOCKS OF TRFF BLACKEN THE SKY...

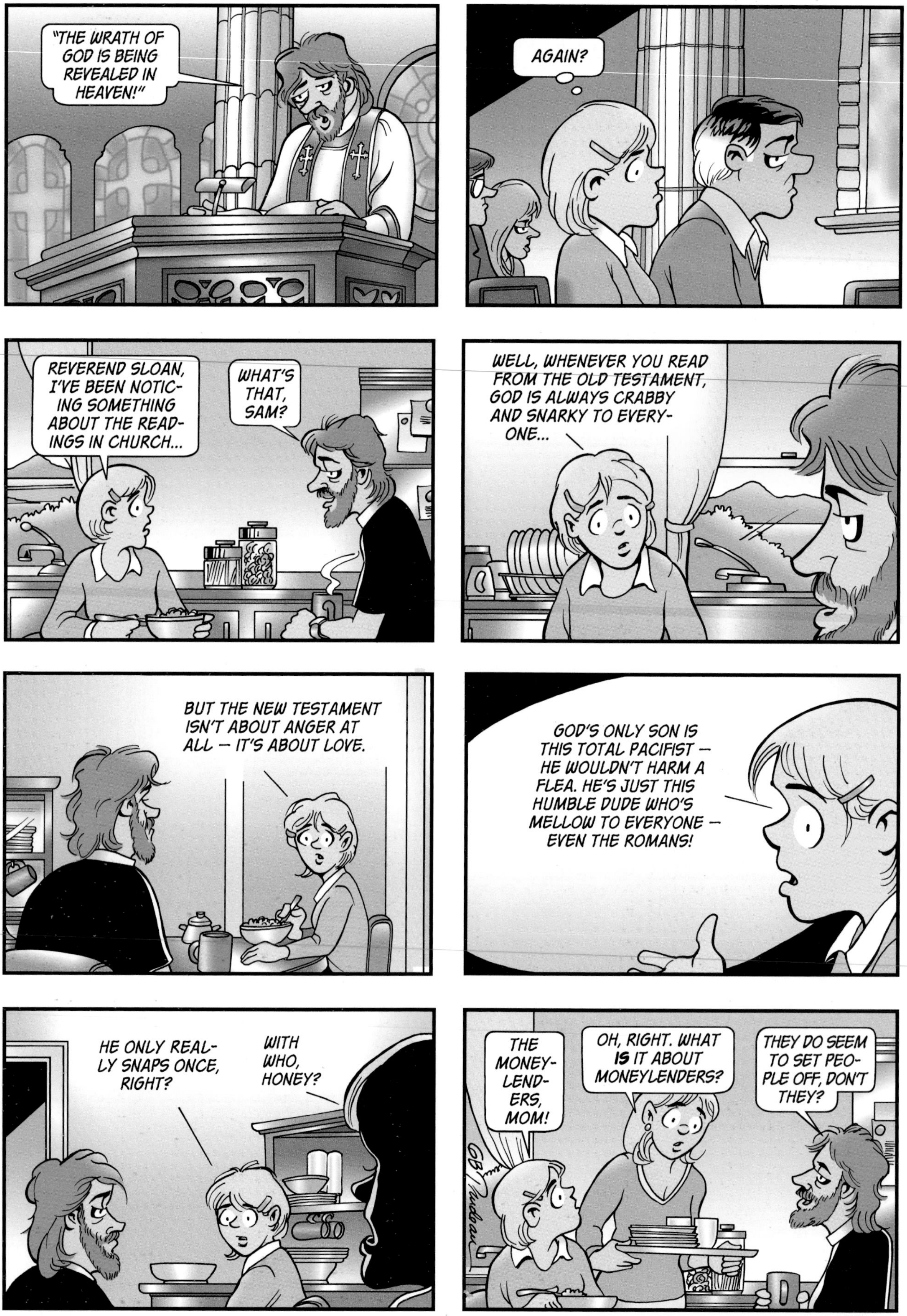
"THE WRATH OF GOD IS BEING REVEALED IN HEAVEN!"
AGAIN?
REVEREND SLOAN, I'VE BEEN NOTICING SOMETHING ABOUT THE READINGS IN CHURCH...
WHAT'S THAT, SAM?
WELL, WHENEVER YOU READ FROM THE OLD TESTAMENT, GOD IS ALWAYS CRABBY AND SNARKY TO EVERYONE...
BUT THE NEW TESTAMENT ISN'T ABOUT ANGER AT ALL — IT'S ABOUT LOVE.
GOD'S ONLY SON IS THIS TOTAL PACIFIST — HE WOULDN'T HARM A FLEA. HE'S JUST THIS HUMBLE DUDE WHO'S MELLOW TO EVERYONE — EVEN THE ROMANS!
HE ONLY REALLY SNAPS ONCE, RIGHT?
WITH WHO, HONEY?
THE MONEYLENDERS, MOM!
OH, RIGHT. WHAT **IS** IT ABOUT MONEYLENDERS?
THEY DO SEEM TO SET PEOPLE OFF, DON'T THEY?
GB Trudeau

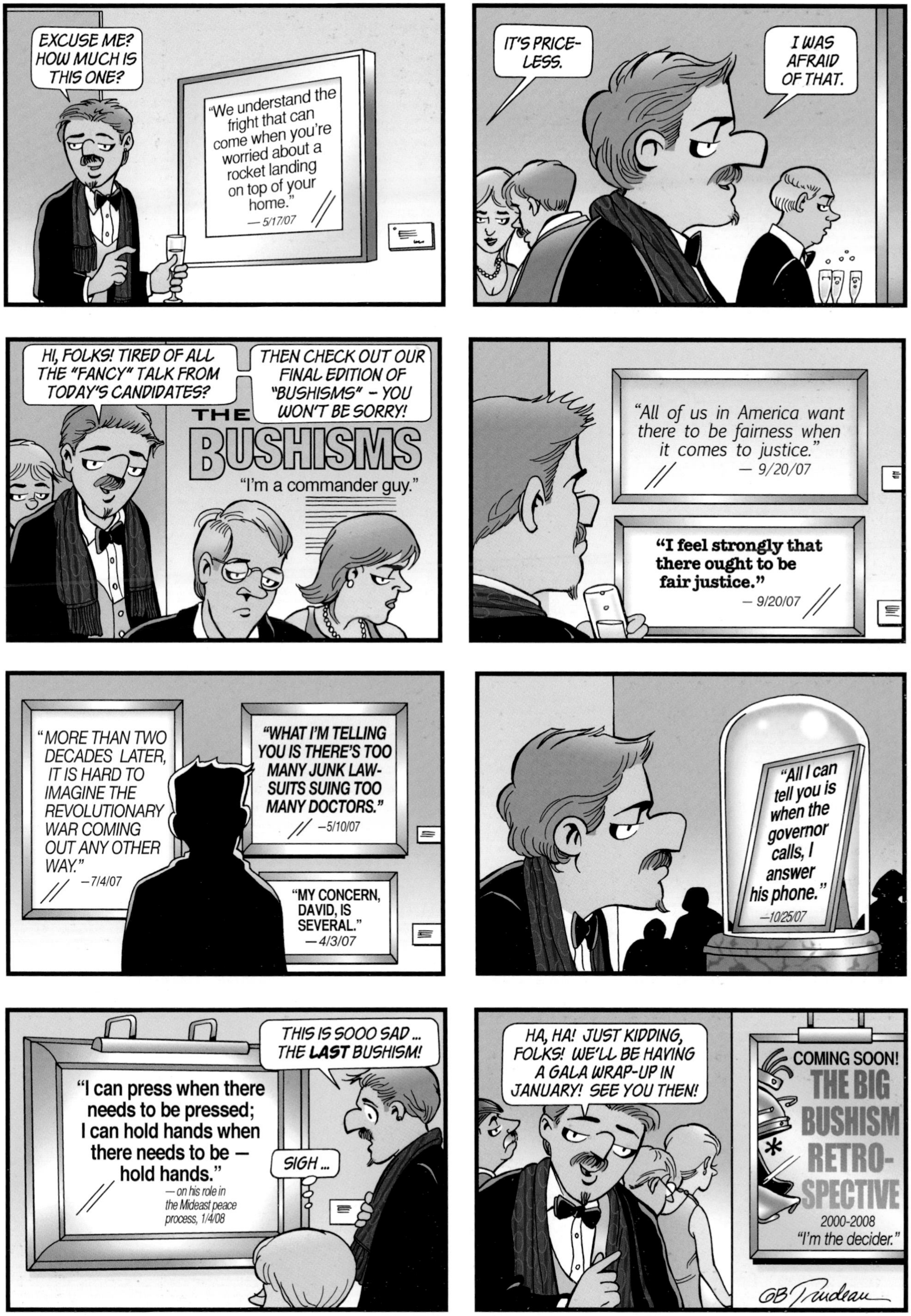
EXCUSE ME? HOW MUCH IS THIS ONE?
"We understand the fright that can come when you're worried about a rocket landing on top of your home." — 5/17/07
IT'S PRICE-LESS.
I WAS AFRAID OF THAT.
HI, FOLKS! TIRED OF ALL THE "FANCY" TALK FROM TODAY'S CANDIDATES?
THEN CHECK OUT OUR FINAL EDITION OF "BUSHISMS" – YOU WON'T BE SORRY!
THE BUSHISMS
"I'm a commander guy."
"All of us in America want there to be fairness when it comes to justice." — 9/20/07
"I feel strongly that there ought to be fair justice." — 9/20/07
"MORE THAN TWO DECADES LATER, IT IS HARD TO IMAGINE THE REVOLUTIONARY WAR COMING OUT ANY OTHER WAY." —7/4/07
"WHAT I'M TELLING YOU IS THERE'S TOO MANY JUNK LAW-SUITS SUING TOO MANY DOCTORS." —5/10/07
"MY CONCERN, DAVID, IS SEVERAL." —4/3/07
"All I can tell you is when the governor calls, I answer his phone." —10/25/07
"I can press when there needs to be pressed; I can hold hands when there needs to be — hold hands." — on his role in the Mideast peace process, 1/4/08
THIS IS SOOO SAD ... THE LAST BUSHISM!
SIGH ...
HA, HA! JUST KIDDING, FOLKS! WE'LL BE HAVING A GALA WRAP-UP IN JANUARY! SEE YOU THEN!
COMING SOON! THE BIG BUSHISM RETRO-SPECTIVE 2000-2008 "I'm the decider."
GB Trudeau

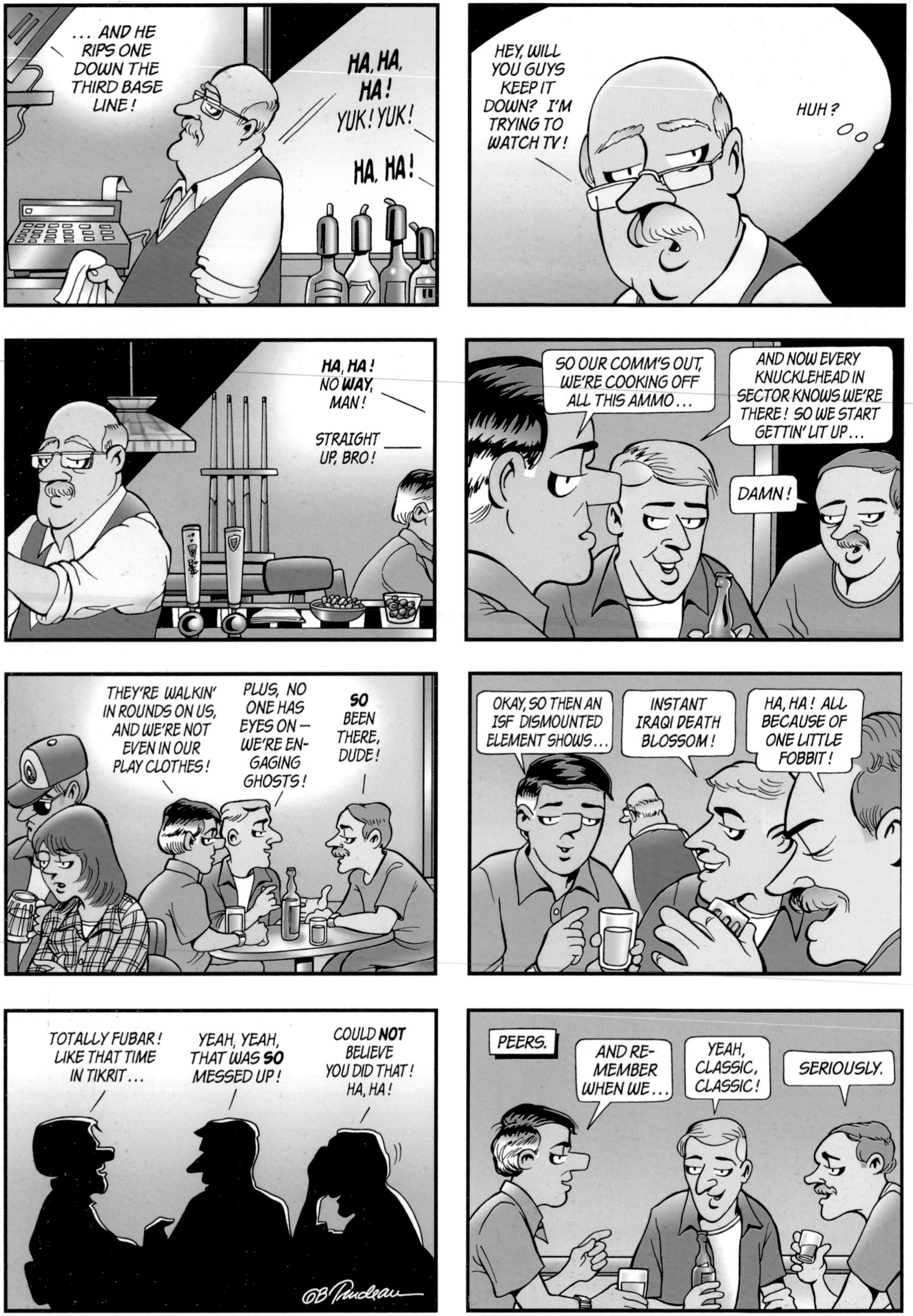

. . . AND HE RIPS ONE DOWN THE THIRD BASE LINE !
HA, HA, HA !
YUK ! YUK !
HA, HA !
HEY, WILL YOU GUYS KEEP IT DOWN? I'M TRYING TO WATCH TV !
HUH ?
HA, HA ! NO WAY, MAN !
STRAIGHT UP, BRO !
SO OUR COMM'S OUT, WE'RE COOKING OFF ALL THIS AMMO . . .
AND NOW EVERY KNUCKLEHEAD IN SECTOR KNOWS WE'RE THERE ! SO WE START GETTIN' LIT UP . . .
DAMN !
THEY'RE WALKIN' IN ROUNDS ON US, AND WE'RE NOT EVEN IN OUR PLAY CLOTHES !
PLUS, NO ONE HAS EYES ON — WE'RE ENGAGING GHOSTS !
SO BEEN THERE, DUDE !
OKAY, SO THEN AN ISF DISMOUNTED ELEMENT SHOWS . . .
INSTANT IRAQI DEATH BLOSSOM !
HA, HA ! ALL BECAUSE OF ONE LITTLE FOBBIT !
TOTALLY FUBAR ! LIKE THAT TIME IN TIKRIT . . .
YEAH, YEAH, THAT WAS SO MESSED UP !
COULD NOT BELIEVE YOU DID THAT ! HA, HA !
GB Trudeau
PEERS.
AND REMEMBER WHEN WE . . .
YEAH, CLASSIC, CLASSIC !
SERIOUSLY.

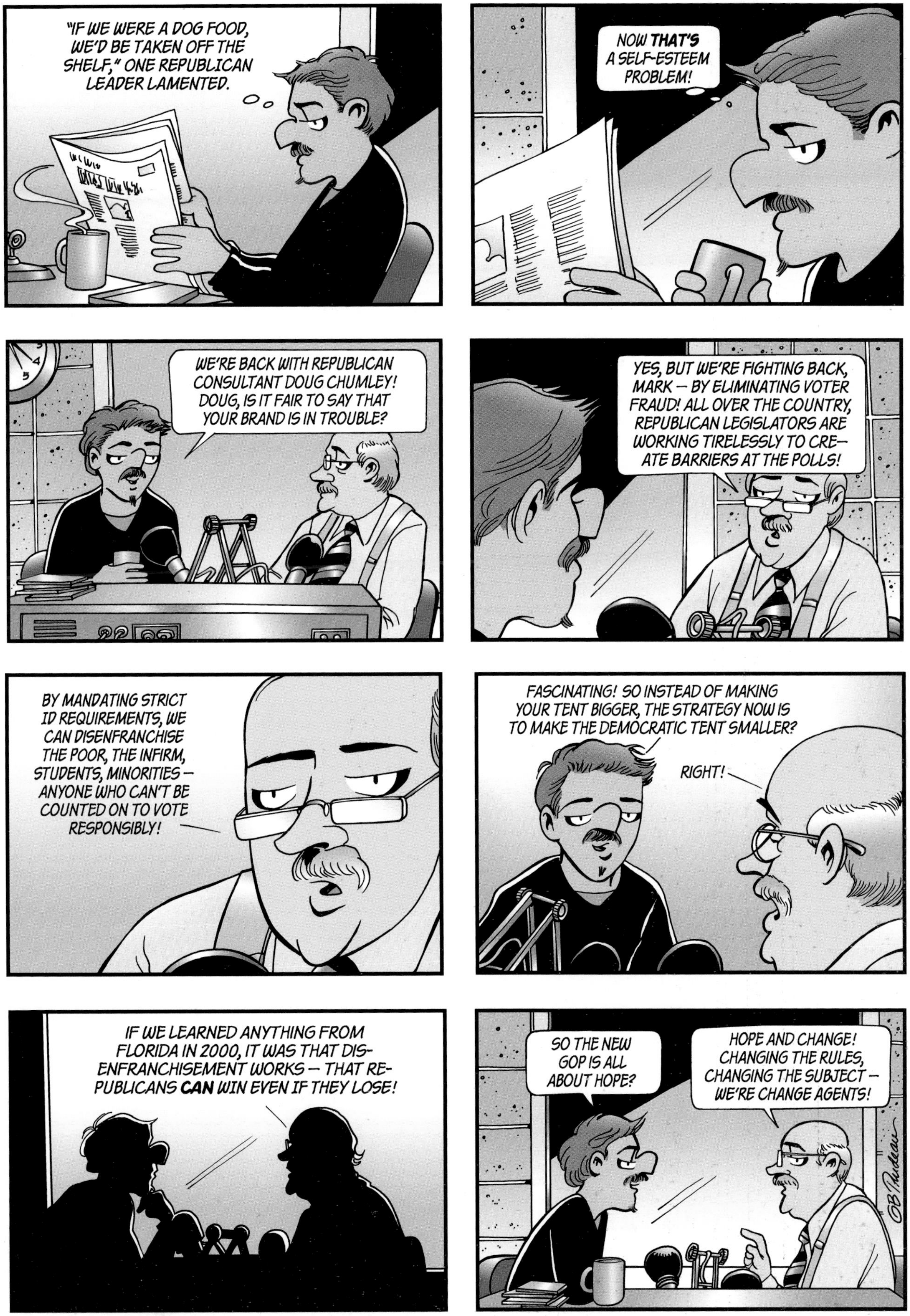
"IF WE WERE A DOG FOOD, WE'D BE TAKEN OFF THE SHELF," ONE REPUBLICAN LEADER LAMENTED.
NOW THAT'S A SELF-ESTEEM PROBLEM!
WE'RE BACK WITH REPUBLICAN CONSULTANT DOUG CHUMLEY! DOUG, IS IT FAIR TO SAY THAT YOUR BRAND IS IN TROUBLE?
YES, BUT WE'RE FIGHTING BACK, MARK — BY ELIMINATING VOTER FRAUD! ALL OVER THE COUNTRY, REPUBLICAN LEGISLATORS ARE WORKING TIRELESSLY TO CRE-ATE BARRIERS AT THE POLLS!
BY MANDATING STRICT ID REQUIREMENTS, WE CAN DISENFRANCHISE THE POOR, THE INFIRM, STUDENTS, MINORITIES — ANYONE WHO CAN'T BE COUNTED ON TO VOTE RESPONSIBLY!
FASCINATING! SO INSTEAD OF MAKING YOUR TENT BIGGER, THE STRATEGY NOW IS TO MAKE THE DEMOCRATIC TENT SMALLER?
RIGHT!
IF WE LEARNED ANYTHING FROM FLORIDA IN 2000, IT WAS THAT DIS-ENFRANCHISEMENT WORKS — THAT RE-PUBLICANS CAN WIN EVEN IF THEY LOSE!
SO THE NEW GOP IS ALL ABOUT HOPE?
HOPE AND CHANGE! CHANGING THE RULES, CHANGING THE SUBJECT — WE'RE CHANGE AGENTS!
©B. Trudeau

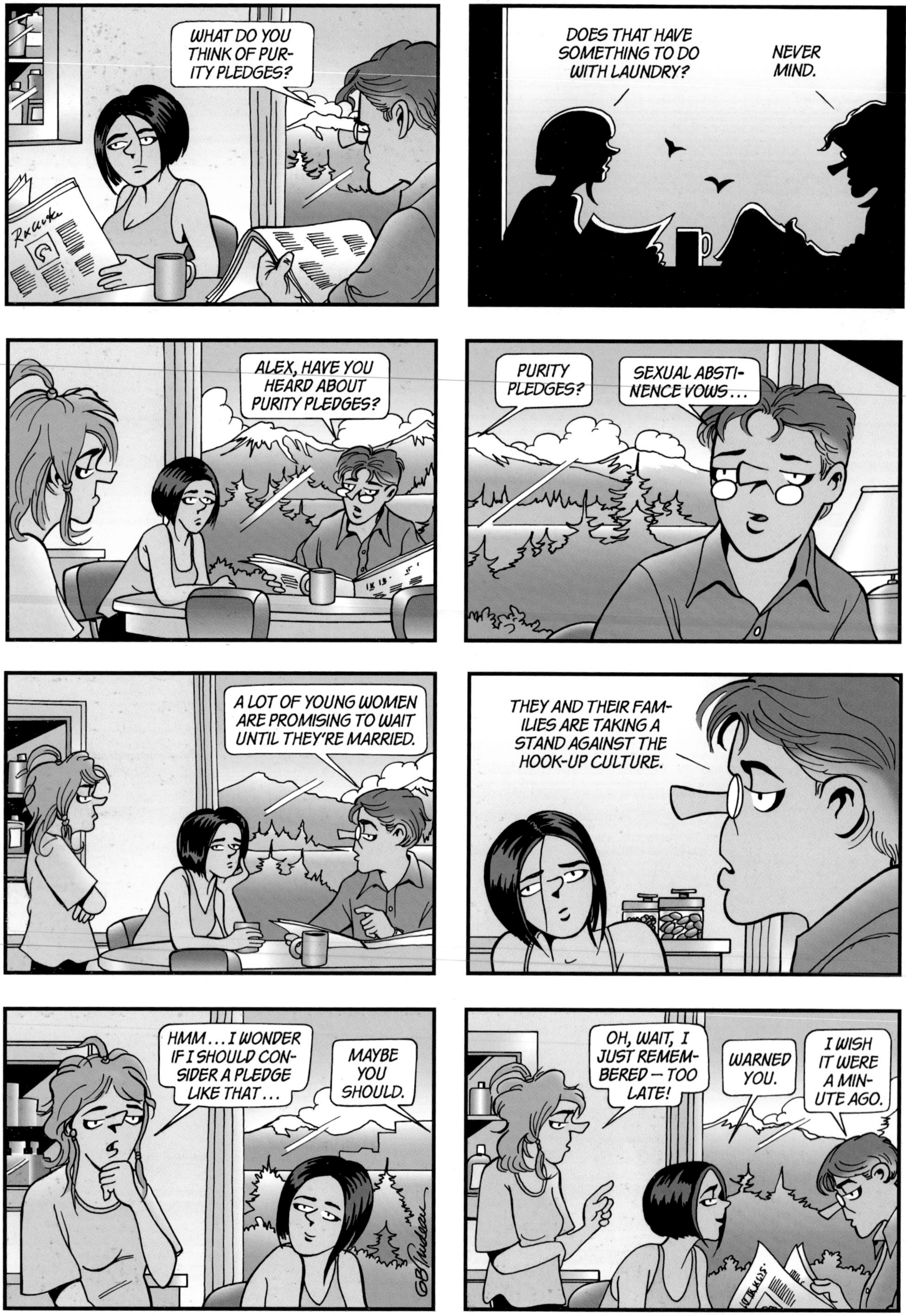
WHAT DO YOU THINK OF PURITY PLEDGES?
DOES THAT HAVE SOMETHING TO DO WITH LAUNDRY?
NEVER MIND.
ALEX, HAVE YOU HEARD ABOUT PURITY PLEDGES?
PURITY PLEDGES?
SEXUAL ABSTINENCE VOWS...
A LOT OF YOUNG WOMEN ARE PROMISING TO WAIT UNTIL THEY'RE MARRIED.
THEY AND THEIR FAMILIES ARE TAKING A STAND AGAINST THE HOOK-UP CULTURE.
HMM... I WONDER IF I SHOULD CONSIDER A PLEDGE LIKE THAT...
MAYBE YOU SHOULD.
OH, WAIT, I JUST REMEMBERED — TOO LATE!
WARNED YOU.
I WISH IT WERE A MINUTE AGO.

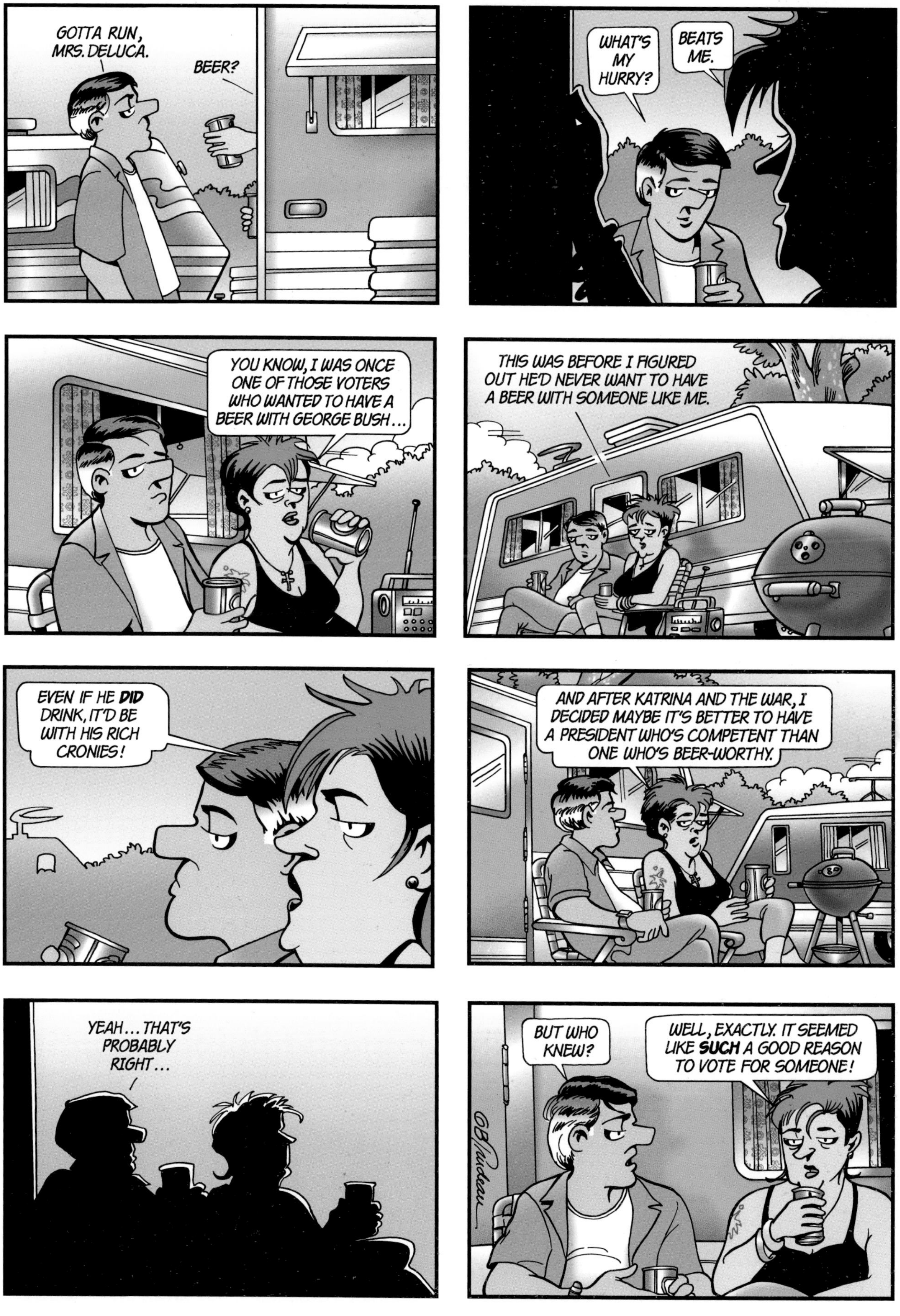
GOTTA RUN, MRS. DELUCA.
BEER?
WHAT'S MY HURRY?
BEATS ME.
YOU KNOW, I WAS ONCE ONE OF THOSE VOTERS WHO WANTED TO HAVE A BEER WITH GEORGE BUSH...
THIS WAS BEFORE I FIGURED OUT HE'D NEVER WANT TO HAVE A BEER WITH SOMEONE LIKE ME.
EVEN IF HE **DID** DRINK, IT'D BE WITH HIS RICH CRONIES!
AND AFTER KATRINA AND THE WAR, I DECIDED MAYBE IT'S BETTER TO HAVE A PRESIDENT WHO'S COMPETENT THAN ONE WHO'S BEER-WORTHY.
YEAH... THAT'S PROBABLY RIGHT...
BUT WHO KNEW?
WELL, EXACTLY. IT SEEMED LIKE **SUCH** A GOOD REASON TO VOTE FOR SOMEONE!
©BTrudeau

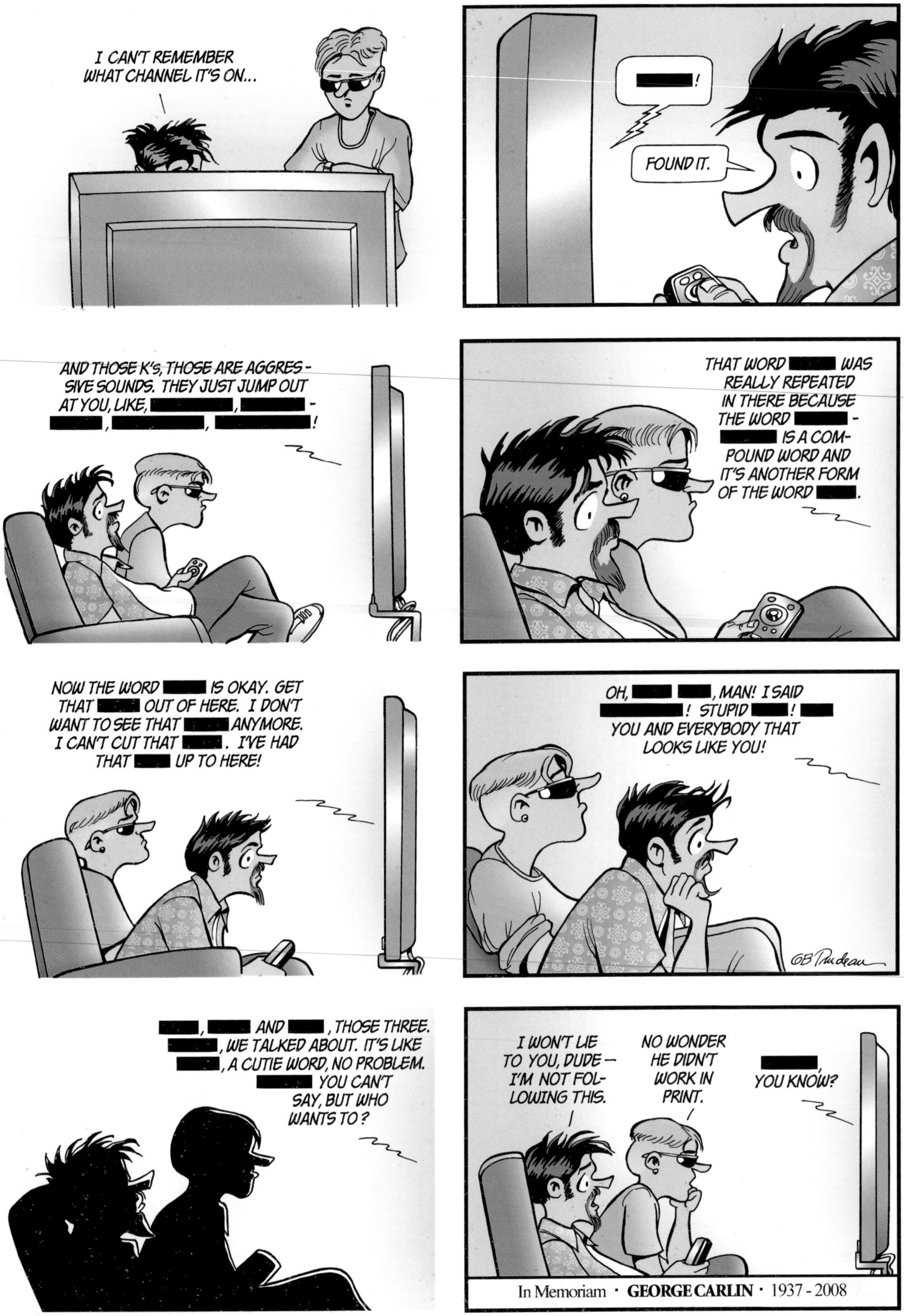
I CAN'T REMEMBER WHAT CHANNEL IT'S ON...
[redacted]!
FOUND IT.
AND THOSE K'S, THOSE ARE AGGRES-SIVE SOUNDS. THEY JUST JUMP OUT AT YOU, LIKE, [redacted], [redacted]-[redacted], [redacted], [redacted]!
THAT WORD [redacted] WAS REALLY REPEATED IN THERE BECAUSE THE WORD [redacted]-[redacted] IS A COM-POUND WORD AND IT'S ANOTHER FORM OF THE WORD [redacted].
NOW THE WORD [redacted] IS OKAY. GET THAT [redacted] OUT OF HERE. I DON'T WANT TO SEE THAT [redacted] ANYMORE. I CAN'T CUT THAT [redacted]. I'VE HAD THAT [redacted] UP TO HERE!
OH, [redacted] [redacted], MAN! I SAID [redacted]! STUPID [redacted]! [redacted] YOU AND EVERYBODY THAT LOOKS LIKE YOU!
GB Trudeau
[redacted], [redacted] AND [redacted], THOSE THREE. [redacted], WE TALKED ABOUT. IT'S LIKE [redacted], A CUTIE WORD, NO PROBLEM. [redacted] YOU CAN'T SAY, BUT WHO WANTS TO?
I WON'T LIE TO YOU, DUDE — I'M NOT FOL-LOWING THIS.
NO WONDER HE DIDN'T WORK IN PRINT.
[redacted], YOU KNOW?
In Memoriam · **GEORGE CARLIN** · 1937 - 2008

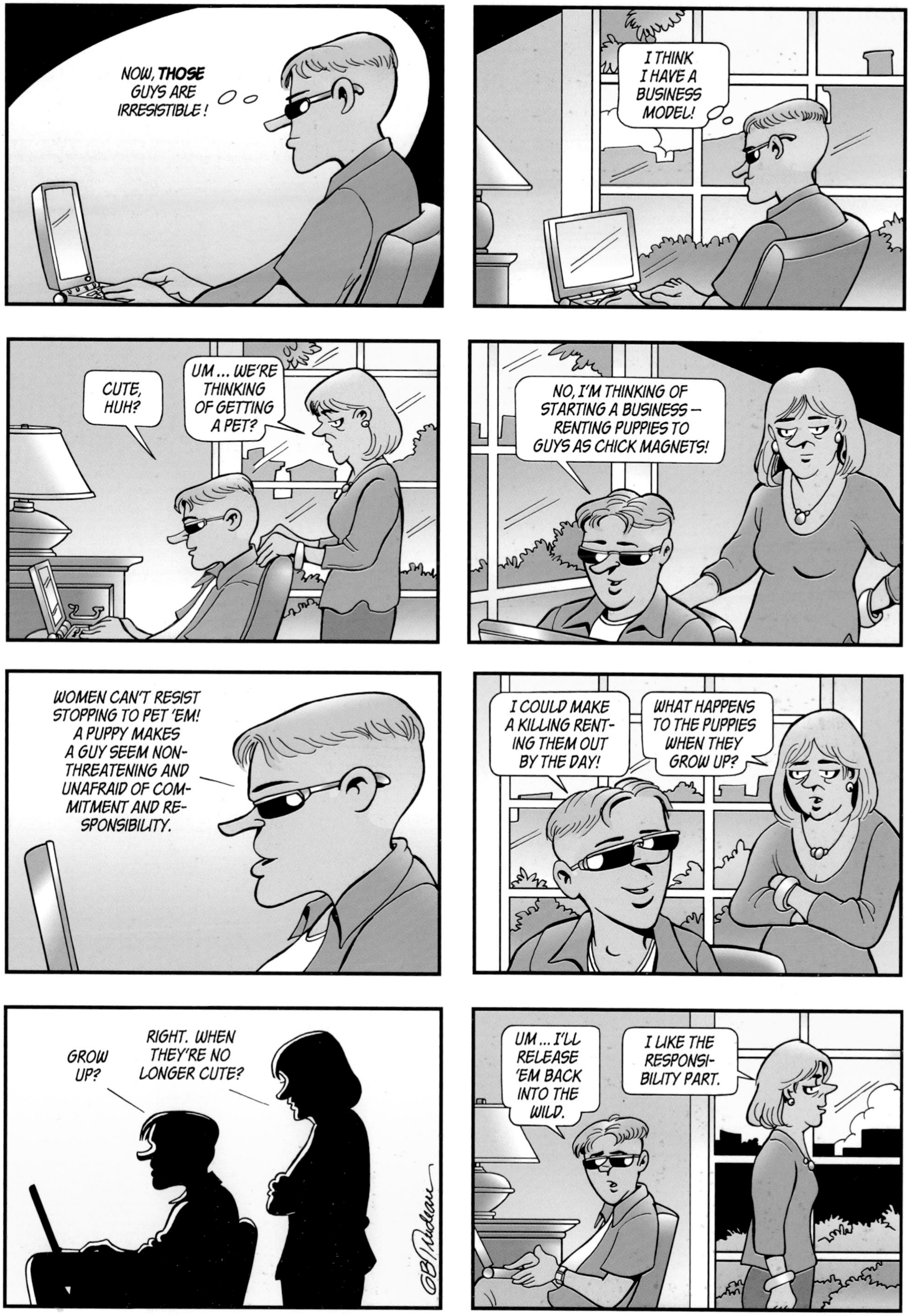
NOW, **THOSE** GUYS ARE IRRESISTIBLE!
I THINK I HAVE A BUSINESS MODEL!
CUTE, HUH?
UM ... WE'RE THINKING OF GETTING A PET?
NO, I'M THINKING OF STARTING A BUSINESS — RENTING PUPPIES TO GUYS AS CHICK MAGNETS!
WOMEN CAN'T RESIST STOPPING TO PET 'EM! A PUPPY MAKES A GUY SEEM NON-THREATENING AND UNAFRAID OF COMMITMENT AND RESPONSIBILITY.
I COULD MAKE A KILLING RENTING THEM OUT BY THE DAY!
WHAT HAPPENS TO THE PUPPIES WHEN THEY GROW UP?
GROW UP?
RIGHT. WHEN THEY'RE NO LONGER CUTE?
UM ... I'LL RELEASE 'EM BACK INTO THE WILD.
I LIKE THE RESPONSIBILITY PART.

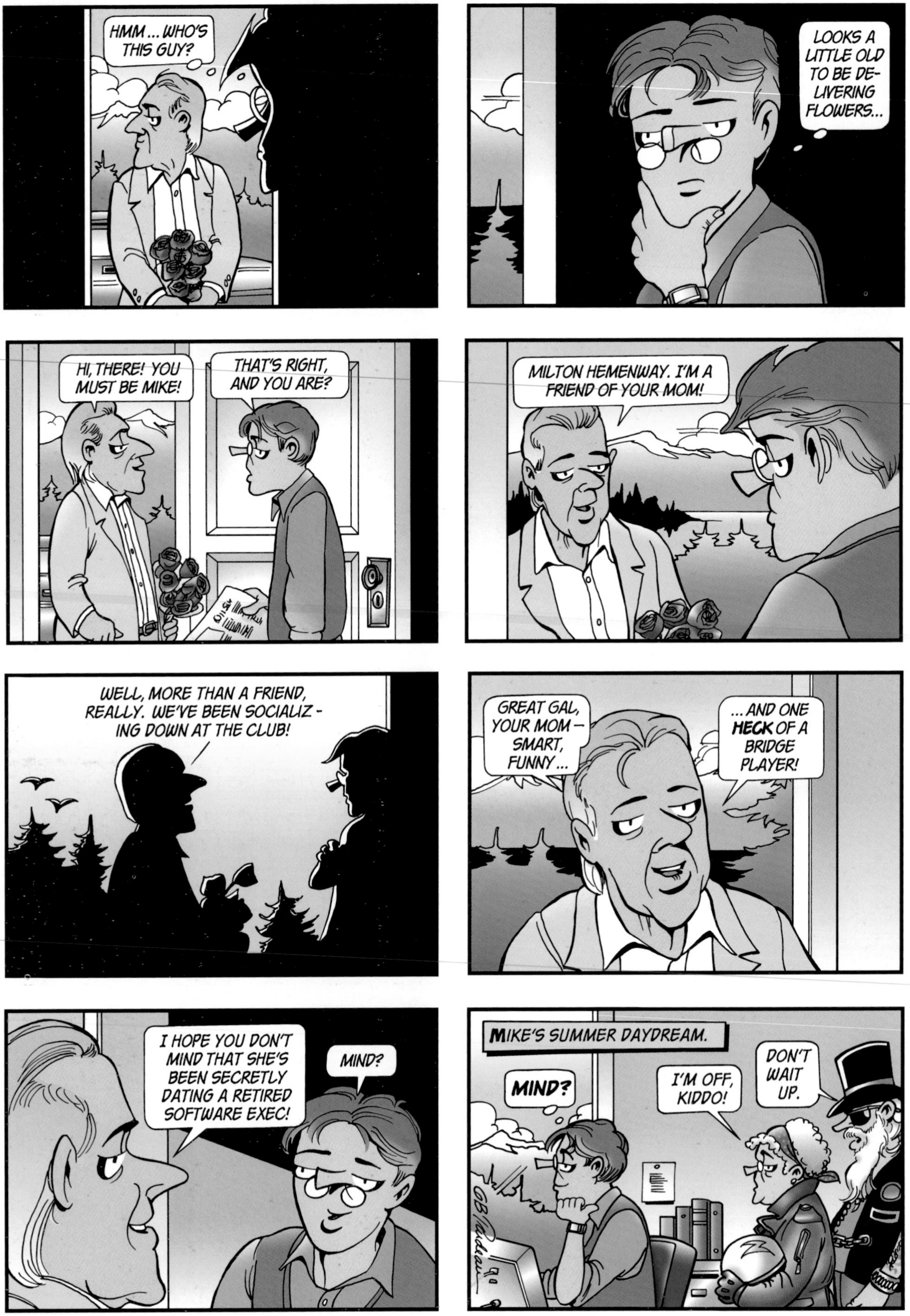
HMM ... WHO'S THIS GUY?
LOOKS A LITTLE OLD TO BE DE-LIVERING FLOWERS...
HI, THERE! YOU MUST BE MIKE!
THAT'S RIGHT, AND YOU ARE?
MILTON HEMENWAY. I'M A FRIEND OF YOUR MOM!
WELL, MORE THAN A FRIEND, REALLY. WE'VE BEEN SOCIALIZ-ING DOWN AT THE CLUB!
GREAT GAL, YOUR MOM — SMART, FUNNY ...
... AND ONE HECK OF A BRIDGE PLAYER!
I HOPE YOU DON'T MIND THAT SHE'S BEEN SECRETLY DATING A RETIRED SOFTWARE EXEC!
MIND?
MIKE'S SUMMER DAYDREAM.
MIND?
I'M OFF, KIDDO!
DON'T WAIT UP.

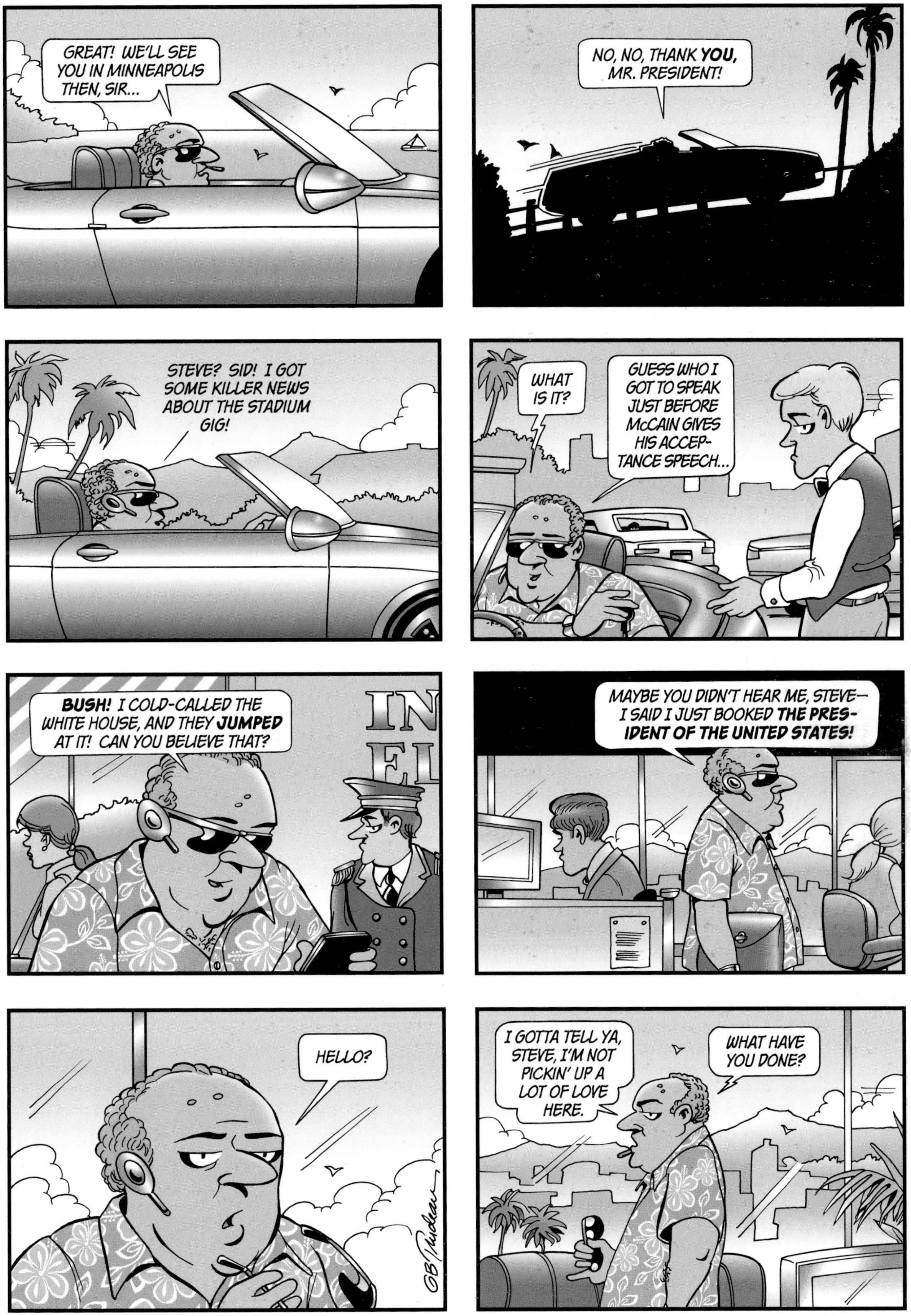
GREAT! WE'LL SEE YOU IN MINNEAPOLIS THEN, SIR...
NO, NO, THANK **YOU,** MR. PRESIDENT!
STEVE? SID! I GOT SOME KILLER NEWS ABOUT THE STADIUM GIG!
WHAT IS IT?
GUESS WHO I GOT TO SPEAK JUST BEFORE McCAIN GIVES HIS ACCEPTANCE SPEECH...
BUSH! I COLD-CALLED THE WHITE HOUSE, AND THEY **JUMPED** AT IT! CAN YOU BELIEVE THAT?
MAYBE YOU DIDN'T HEAR ME, STEVE— I SAID I JUST BOOKED **THE PRESIDENT OF THE UNITED STATES!**
HELLO?
I GOTTA TELL YA, STEVE, I'M NOT PICKIN' UP A LOT OF LOVE HERE.
WHAT HAVE YOU DONE?

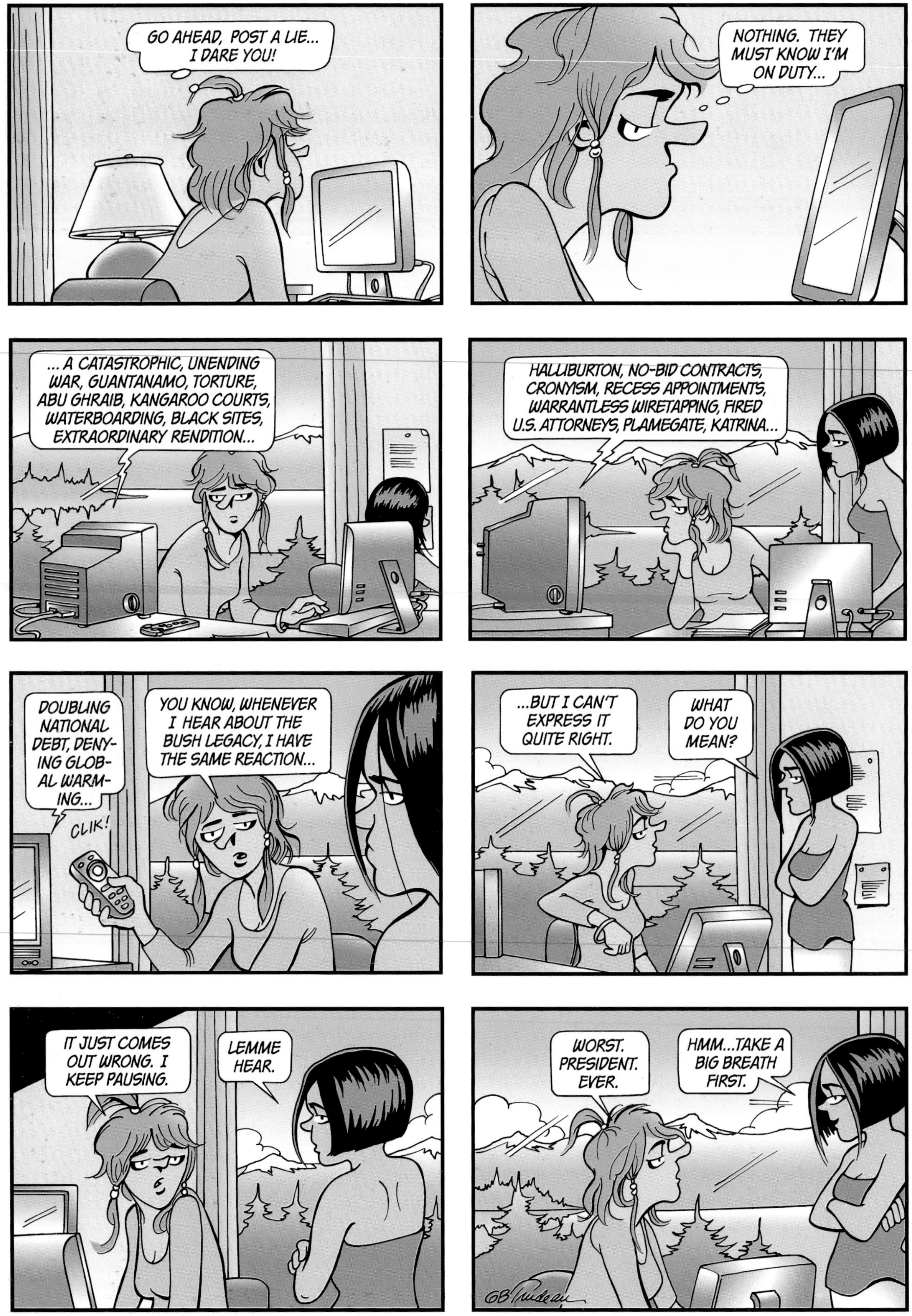
GO AHEAD, POST A LIE... I DARE YOU!
NOTHING. THEY MUST KNOW I'M ON DUTY...
... A CATASTROPHIC, UNENDING WAR, GUANTANAMO, TORTURE, ABU GHRAIB, KANGAROO COURTS, WATERBOARDING, BLACK SITES, EXTRAORDINARY RENDITION...
HALLIBURTON, NO-BID CONTRACTS, CRONYISM, RECESS APPOINTMENTS, WARRANTLESS WIRETAPPING, FIRED U.S. ATTORNEYS, PLAMEGATE, KATRINA...
DOUBLING NATIONAL DEBT, DENYING GLOBAL WARMING...
CLIK!
YOU KNOW, WHENEVER I HEAR ABOUT THE BUSH LEGACY, I HAVE THE SAME REACTION...
...BUT I CAN'T EXPRESS IT QUITE RIGHT.
WHAT DO YOU MEAN?
IT JUST COMES OUT WRONG. I KEEP PAUSING.
LEMME HEAR.
WORST. PRESIDENT. EVER.
HMM...TAKE A BIG BREATH FIRST.
GB Trudeau

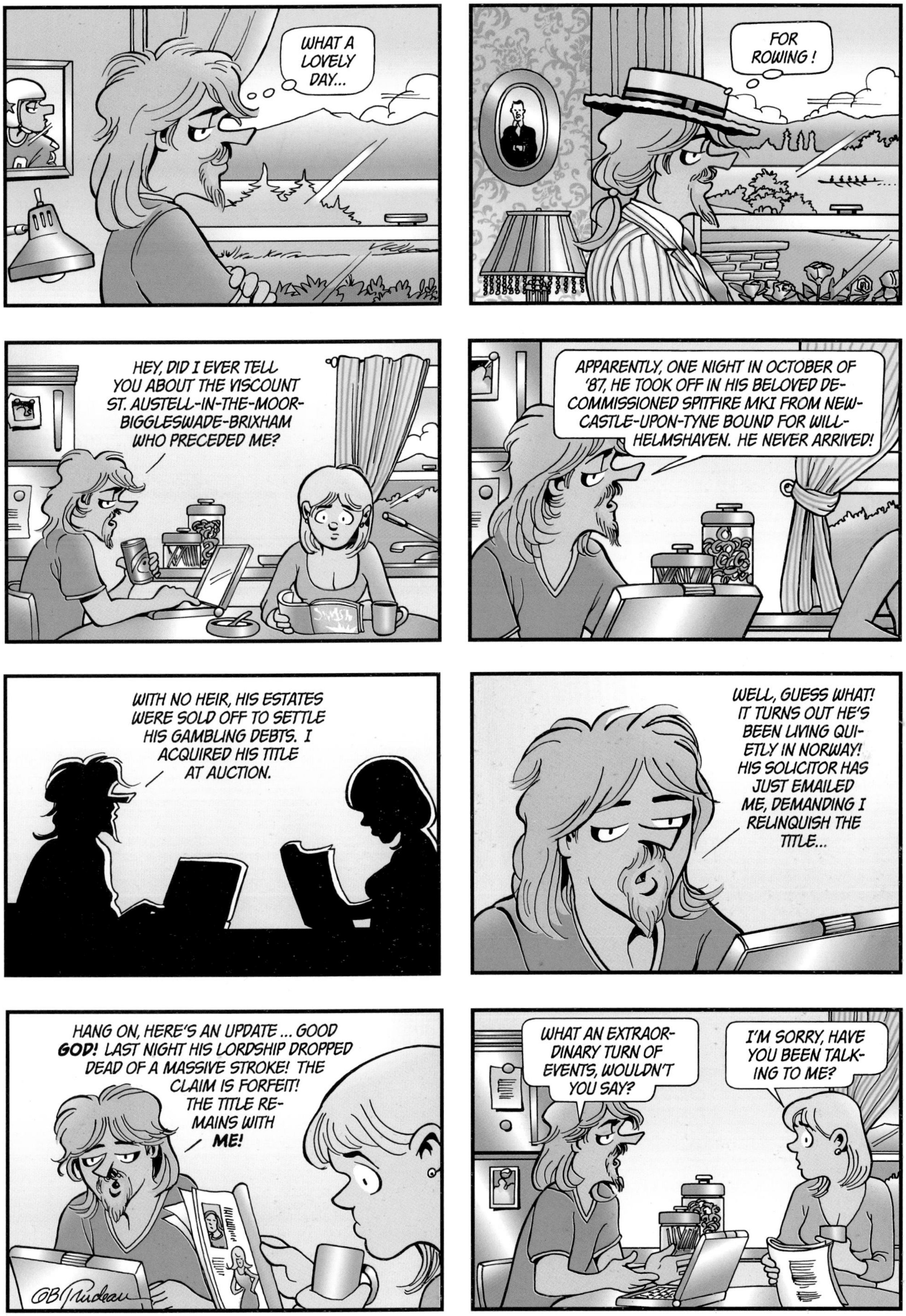
WHAT A LOVELY DAY...
FOR ROWING !
HEY, DID I EVER TELL YOU ABOUT THE VISCOUNT ST. AUSTELL-IN-THE-MOOR-BIGGLESWADE-BRIXHAM WHO PRECEDED ME?
APPARENTLY, ONE NIGHT IN OCTOBER OF '87, HE TOOK OFF IN HIS BELOVED DE-COMMISSIONED SPITFIRE MKI FROM NEW-CASTLE-UPON-TYNE BOUND FOR WILL-HELMSHAVEN. HE NEVER ARRIVED!
WITH NO HEIR, HIS ESTATES WERE SOLD OFF TO SETTLE HIS GAMBLING DEBTS. I ACQUIRED HIS TITLE AT AUCTION.
WELL, GUESS WHAT! IT TURNS OUT HE'S BEEN LIVING QUI-ETLY IN NORWAY! HIS SOLICITOR HAS JUST EMAILED ME, DEMANDING I RELINQUISH THE TITLE...
HANG ON, HERE'S AN UPDATE ... GOOD **GOD!** LAST NIGHT HIS LORDSHIP DROPPED DEAD OF A MASSIVE STROKE! THE CLAIM IS FORFEIT! THE TITLE RE-MAINS WITH **ME!**
GB Trudeau
WHAT AN EXTRAOR-DINARY TURN OF EVENTS, WOULDN'T YOU SAY?
I'M SORRY, HAVE YOU BEEN TALK-ING TO ME?

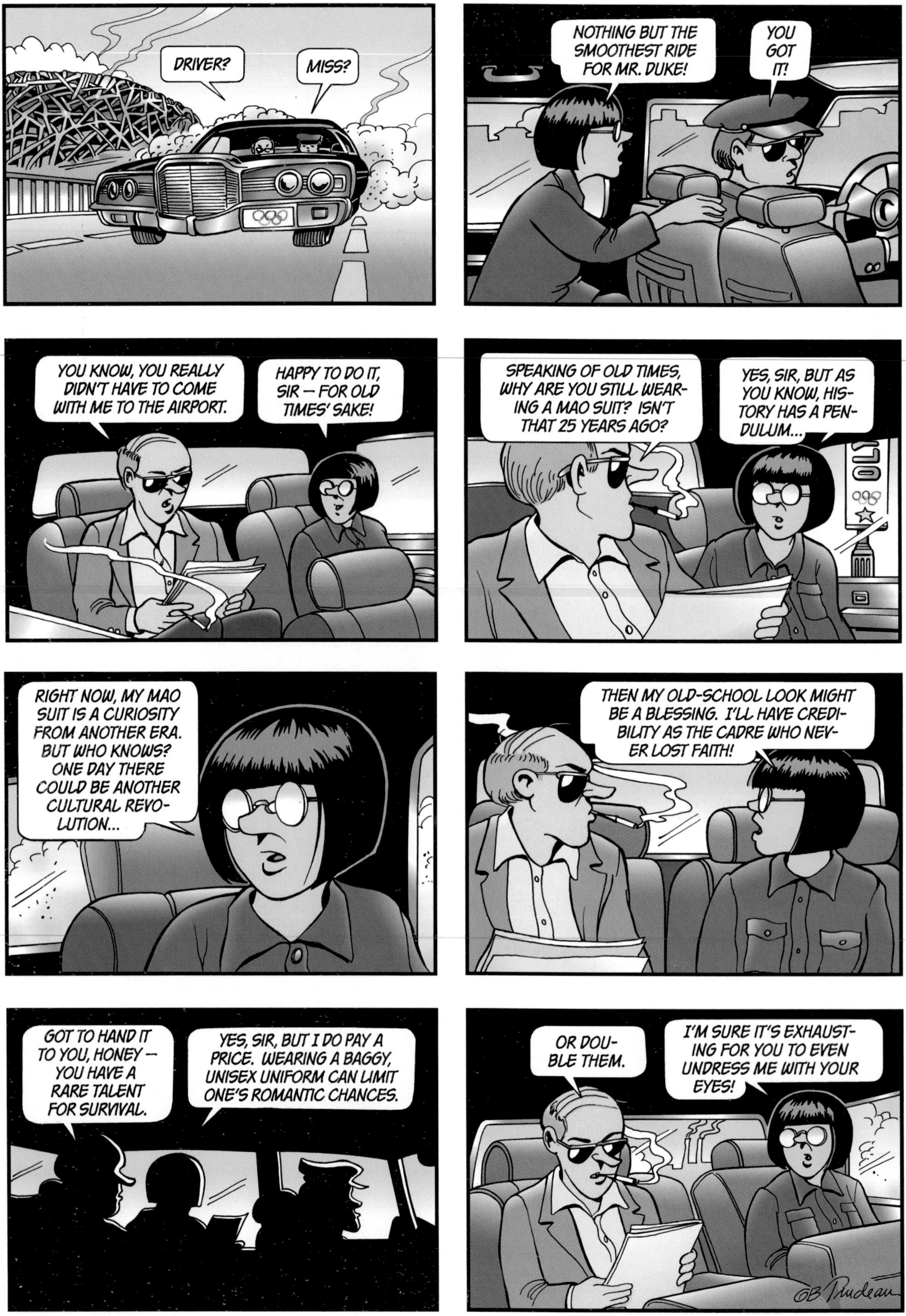
DRIVER?
MISS?
NOTHING BUT THE SMOOTHEST RIDE FOR MR. DUKE!
YOU GOT IT!
YOU KNOW, YOU REALLY DIDN'T HAVE TO COME WITH ME TO THE AIRPORT.
HAPPY TO DO IT, SIR — FOR OLD TIMES' SAKE!
SPEAKING OF OLD TIMES, WHY ARE YOU STILL WEARING A MAO SUIT? ISN'T THAT 25 YEARS AGO?
YES, SIR, BUT AS YOU KNOW, HISTORY HAS A PENDULUM...
RIGHT NOW, MY MAO SUIT IS A CURIOSITY FROM ANOTHER ERA. BUT WHO KNOWS? ONE DAY THERE COULD BE ANOTHER CULTURAL REVOLUTION...
THEN MY OLD-SCHOOL LOOK MIGHT BE A BLESSING. I'LL HAVE CREDIBILITY AS THE CADRE WHO NEVER LOST FAITH!
GOT TO HAND IT TO YOU, HONEY — YOU HAVE A RARE TALENT FOR SURVIVAL.
YES, SIR, BUT I DO PAY A PRICE. WEARING A BAGGY, UNISEX UNIFORM CAN LIMIT ONE'S ROMANTIC CHANCES.
OR DOUBLE THEM.
I'M SURE IT'S EXHAUSTING FOR YOU TO EVEN UNDRESS ME WITH YOUR EYES!
GB Trudeau

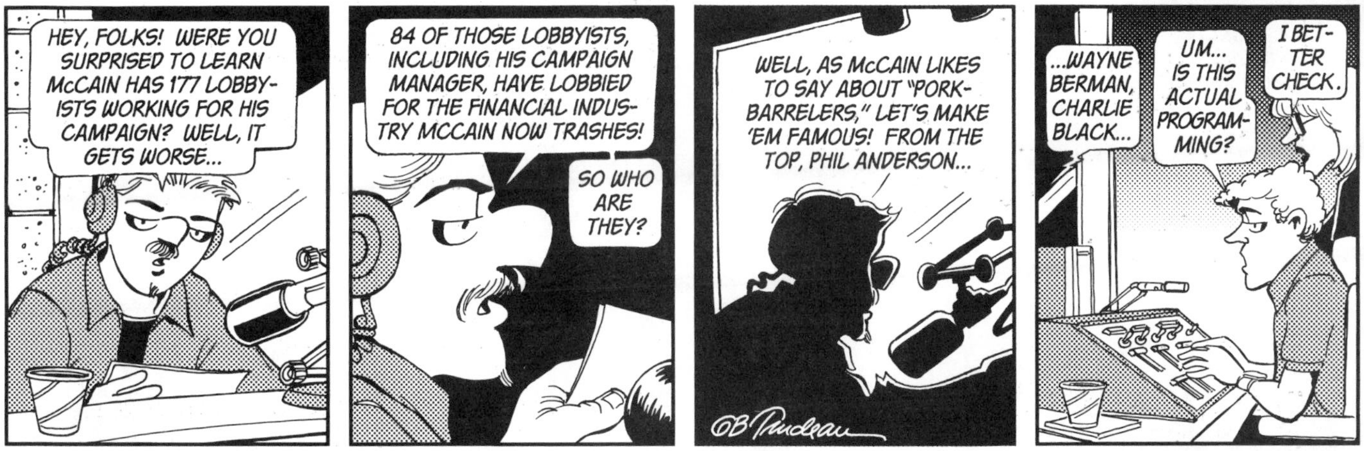
HEY, FOLKS! WERE YOU SURPRISED TO LEARN McCAIN HAS 177 LOBBYISTS WORKING FOR HIS CAMPAIGN? WELL, IT GETS WORSE...
84 OF THOSE LOBBYISTS, INCLUDING HIS CAMPAIGN MANAGER, HAVE LOBBIED FOR THE FINANCIAL INDUSTRY McCAIN NOW TRASHES!
SO WHO ARE THEY?
WELL, AS McCAIN LIKES TO SAY ABOUT "PORK-BARRELERS," LET'S MAKE 'EM FAMOUS! FROM THE TOP, PHIL ANDERSON...
...WAYNE BERMAN, CHARLIE BLACK...
UM... IS THIS ACTUAL PROGRAMMING?
I BETTER CHECK.

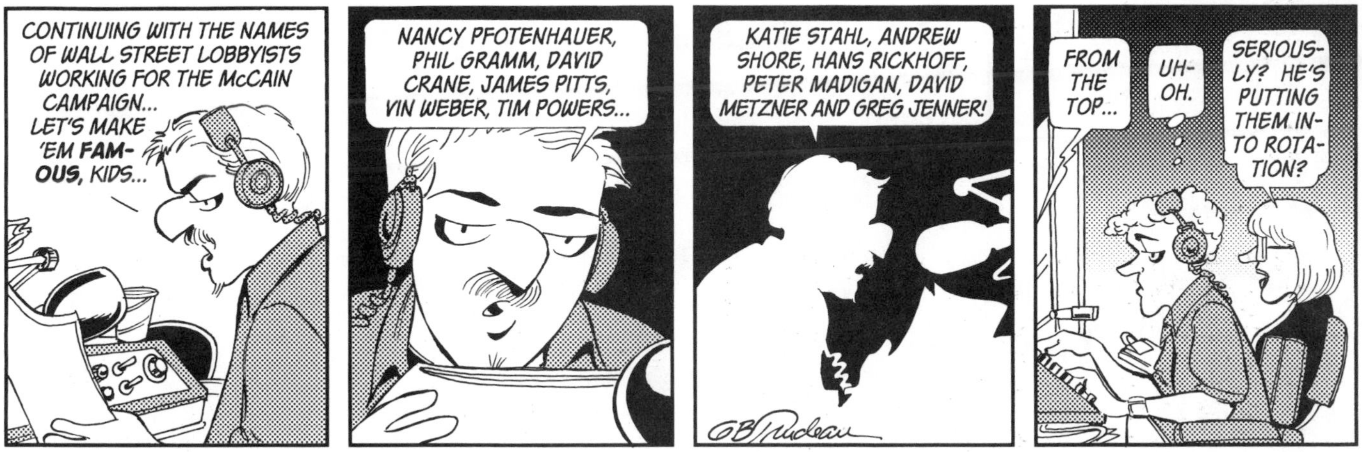
CONTINUING WITH THE NAMES OF WALL STREET LOBBYISTS WORKING FOR THE McCAIN CAMPAIGN... LET'S MAKE 'EM **FAMOUS,** KIDS...
NANCY PFOTENHAUER, PHIL GRAMM, DAVID CRANE, JAMES PITTS, VIN WEBER, TIM POWERS...
KATIE STAHL, ANDREW SHORE, HANS RICKHOFF, PETER MADIGAN, DAVID METZNER AND GREG JENNER!
FROM THE TOP...
UH-OH.
SERIOUSLY? HE'S PUTTING THEM INTO ROTATION?

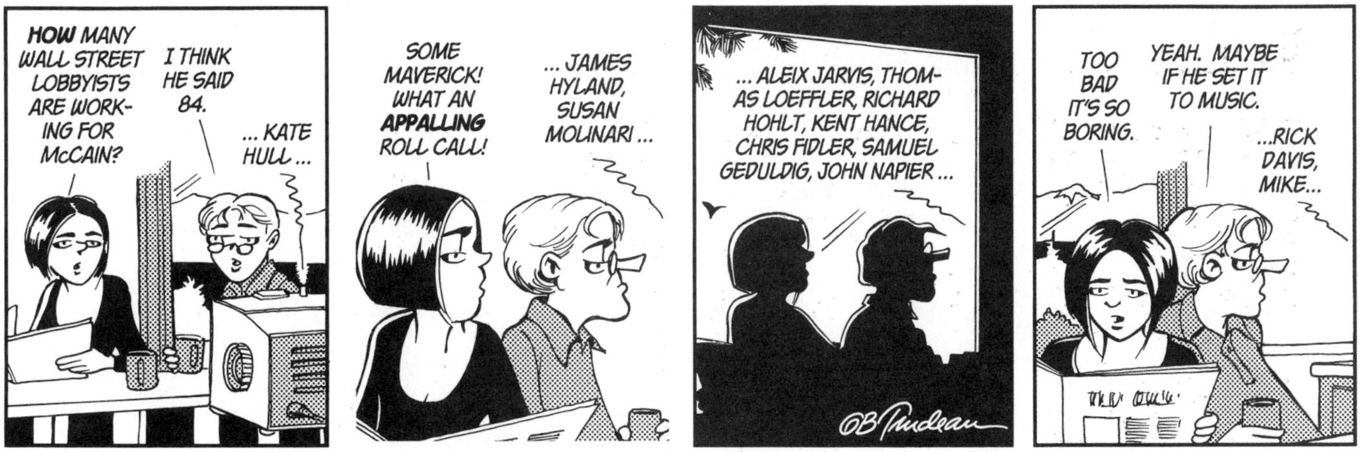
HOW MANY WALL STREET LOBBYISTS ARE WORKING FOR McCAIN?
I THINK HE SAID 84.
... KATE HULL ...
SOME MAVERICK! WHAT AN **APPALLING** ROLL CALL!
... JAMES HYLAND, SUSAN MOLINARI ...
... ALEIX JARVIS, THOMAS LOEFFLER, RICHARD HOHLT, KENT HANCE, CHRIS FIDLER, SAMUEL GEDULDIG, JOHN NAPIER ...
TOO BAD IT'S SO BORING.
YEAH. MAYBE IF HE SET IT TO MUSIC.
...RICK DAVIS, MIKE...

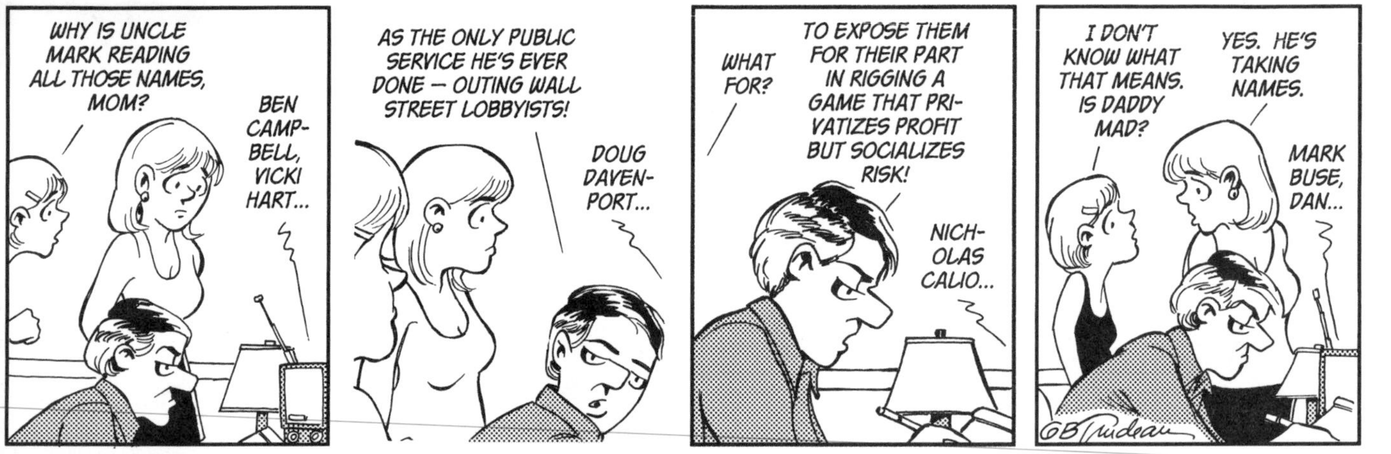
WHY IS UNCLE MARK READING ALL THOSE NAMES, MOM?
BEN CAMPBELL, VICKI HART...
AS THE ONLY PUBLIC SERVICE HE'S EVER DONE — OUTING WALL STREET LOBBYISTS!
DOUG DAVENPORT...
WHAT FOR?
TO EXPOSE THEM FOR THEIR PART IN RIGGING A GAME THAT PRIVATIZES PROFIT BUT SOCIALIZES RISK!
NICHOLAS CALIO...
I DON'T KNOW WHAT THAT MEANS. IS DADDY MAD?
YES. HE'S TAKING NAMES.
MARK BUSE, DAN...
GB Trudeau

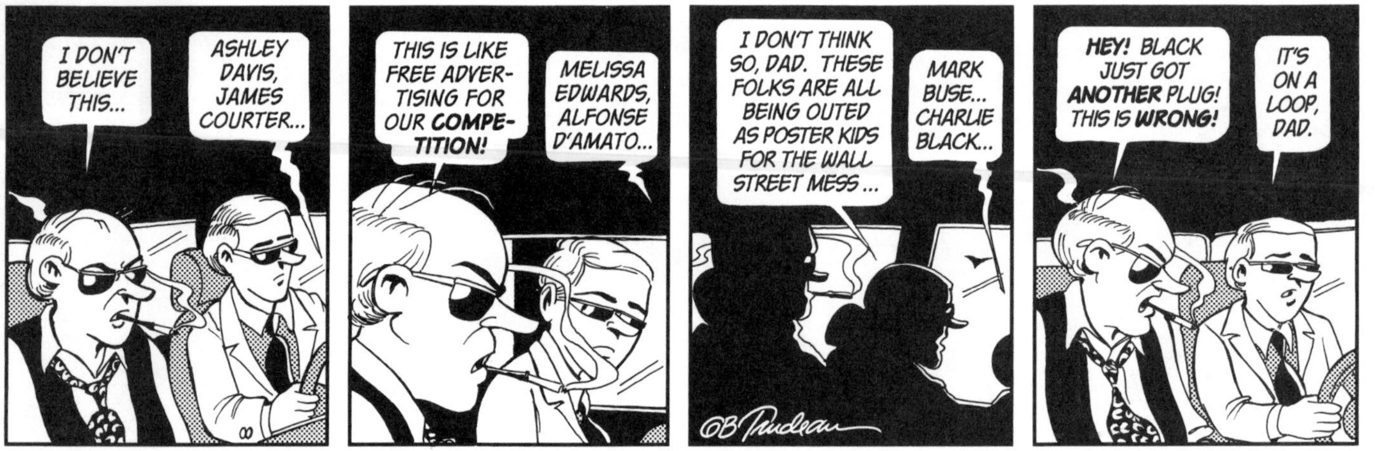
I DON'T BELIEVE THIS...
ASHLEY DAVIS, JAMES COURTER...
THIS IS LIKE FREE ADVERTISING FOR OUR **COMPETITION!**
MELISSA EDWARDS, ALFONSE D'AMATO...
I DON'T THINK SO, DAD. THESE FOLKS ARE ALL BEING OUTED AS POSTER KIDS FOR THE WALL STREET MESS ...
MARK BUSE... CHARLIE BLACK...
GB Trudeau
HEY! BLACK JUST GOT **ANOTHER** PLUG! THIS IS **WRONG!**
IT'S ON A LOOP, DAD.

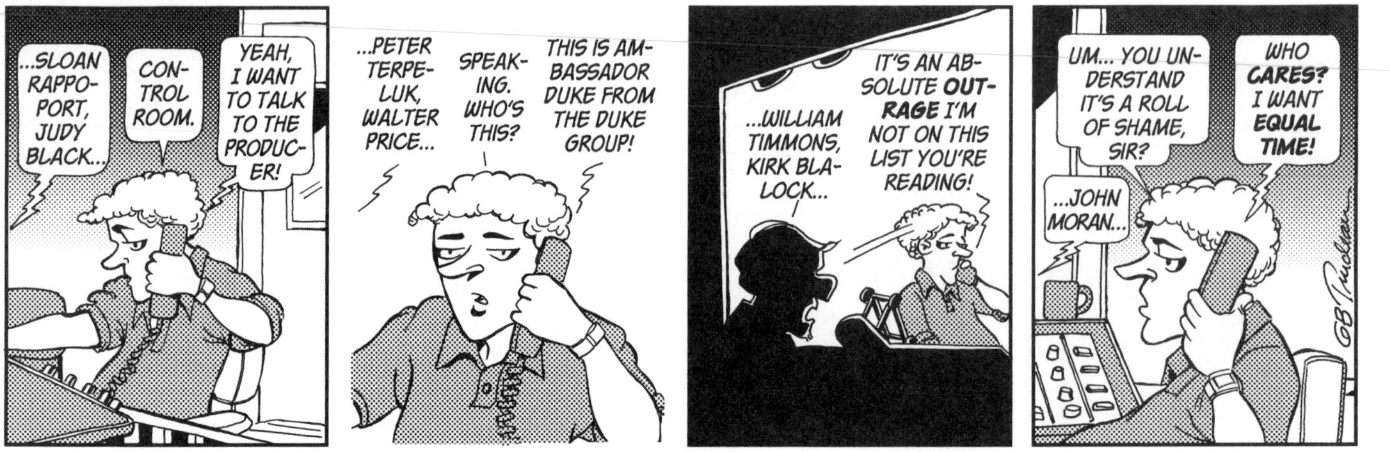
...SLOAN RAPPOPORT, JUDY BLACK...
CONTROL ROOM.
YEAH, I WANT TO TALK TO THE PRODUCER!
...PETER TERPELUK, WALTER PRICE...
SPEAKING. WHO'S THIS?
THIS IS AMBASSADOR DUKE FROM THE DUKE GROUP!
...WILLIAM TIMMONS, KIRK BLALOCK...
IT'S AN ABSOLUTE **OUTRAGE** I'M NOT ON THIS LIST YOU'RE READING!
UM... YOU UNDERSTAND IT'S A ROLL OF SHAME, SIR?
WHO **CARES?** I WANT **EQUAL TIME!**
...JOHN MORAN...
GB Trudeau

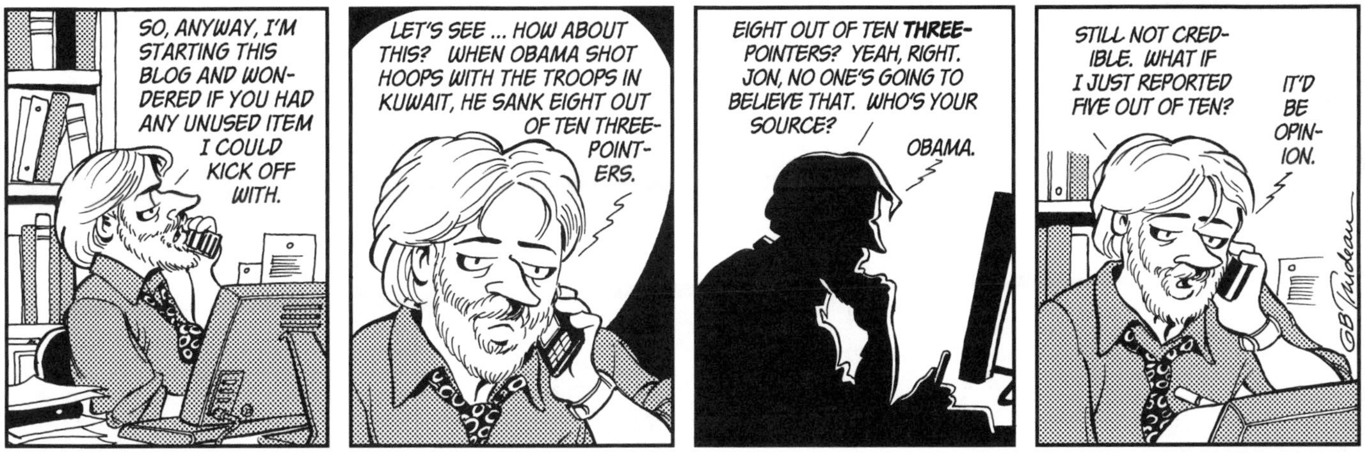
SO, ANYWAY, I'M STARTING THIS BLOG AND WONDERED IF YOU HAD ANY UNUSED ITEM I COULD KICK OFF WITH.
LET'S SEE ... HOW ABOUT THIS? WHEN OBAMA SHOT HOOPS WITH THE TROOPS IN KUWAIT, HE SANK EIGHT OUT OF TEN THREE-POINTERS.
EIGHT OUT OF TEN **THREE-**POINTERS? YEAH, RIGHT. JON, NO ONE'S GOING TO BELIEVE THAT. WHO'S YOUR SOURCE?
OBAMA.
STILL NOT CREDIBLE. WHAT IF I JUST REPORTED FIVE OUT OF TEN?
IT'D BE OPINION.
GB Trudeau

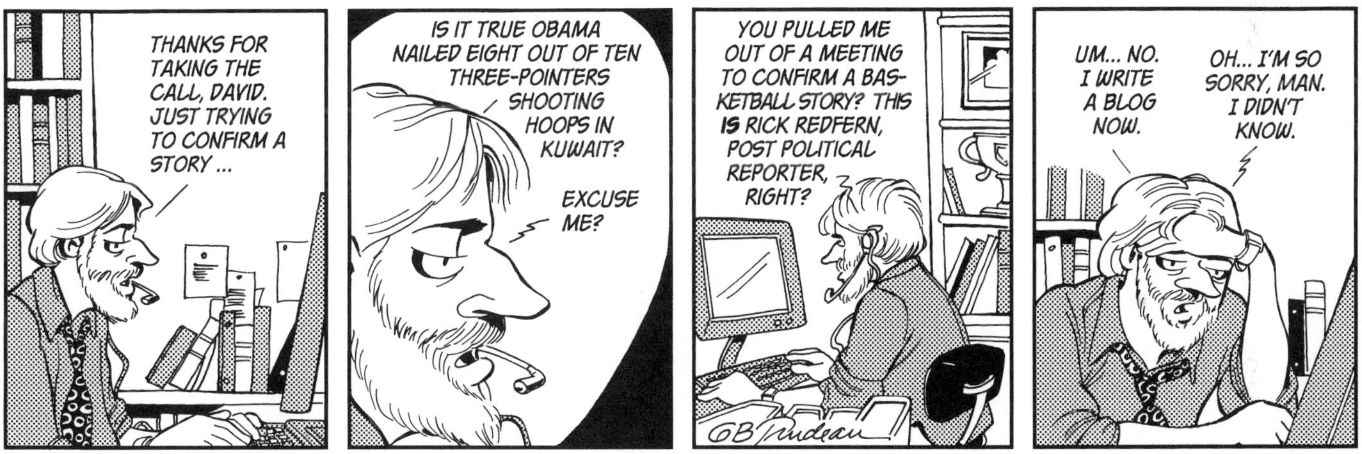
THANKS FOR TAKING THE CALL, DAVID. JUST TRYING TO CONFIRM A STORY ...
IS IT TRUE OBAMA NAILED EIGHT OUT OF TEN THREE-POINTERS SHOOTING HOOPS IN KUWAIT?
EXCUSE ME?
YOU PULLED ME OUT OF A MEETING TO CONFIRM A BASKETBALL STORY? THIS **IS** RICK REDFERN, POST POLITICAL REPORTER, RIGHT?
GB Trudeau
UM... NO. I WRITE A BLOG NOW.
OH... I'M SO SORRY, MAN. I DIDN'T KNOW.

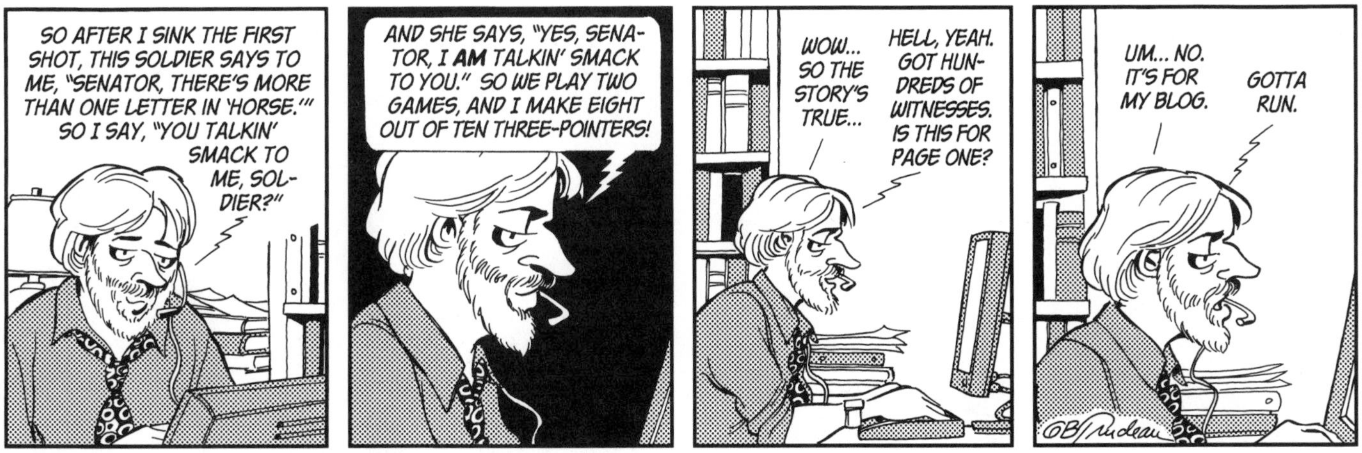
SO AFTER I SINK THE FIRST SHOT, THIS SOLDIER SAYS TO ME, "SENATOR, THERE'S MORE THAN ONE LETTER IN 'HORSE.'" SO I SAY, "YOU TALKIN' SMACK TO ME, SOLDIER?"
AND SHE SAYS, "YES, SENATOR, I **AM** TALKIN' SMACK TO YOU." SO WE PLAY TWO GAMES, AND I MAKE EIGHT OUT OF TEN THREE-POINTERS!
WOW... SO THE STORY'S TRUE...
HELL, YEAH. GOT HUNDREDS OF WITNESSES. IS THIS FOR PAGE ONE?
UM... NO. IT'S FOR MY BLOG.
GOTTA RUN.
GB Trudeau

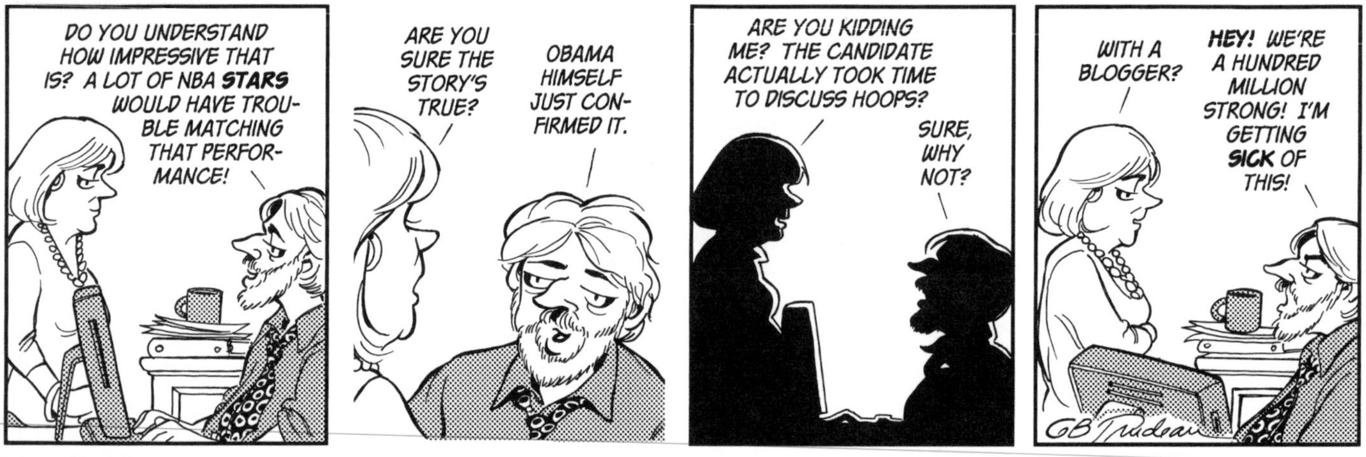
DO YOU UNDERSTAND HOW IMPRESSIVE THAT IS? A LOT OF NBA **STARS** WOULD HAVE TROUBLE MATCHING THAT PERFORMANCE!
ARE YOU SURE THE STORY'S TRUE?
OBAMA HIMSELF JUST CONFIRMED IT.
ARE YOU KIDDING ME? THE CANDIDATE ACTUALLY TOOK TIME TO DISCUSS HOOPS?
SURE, WHY NOT?
WITH A BLOGGER?
HEY! WE'RE A HUNDRED MILLION STRONG! I'M GETTING **SICK** OF THIS!
GB Trudeau

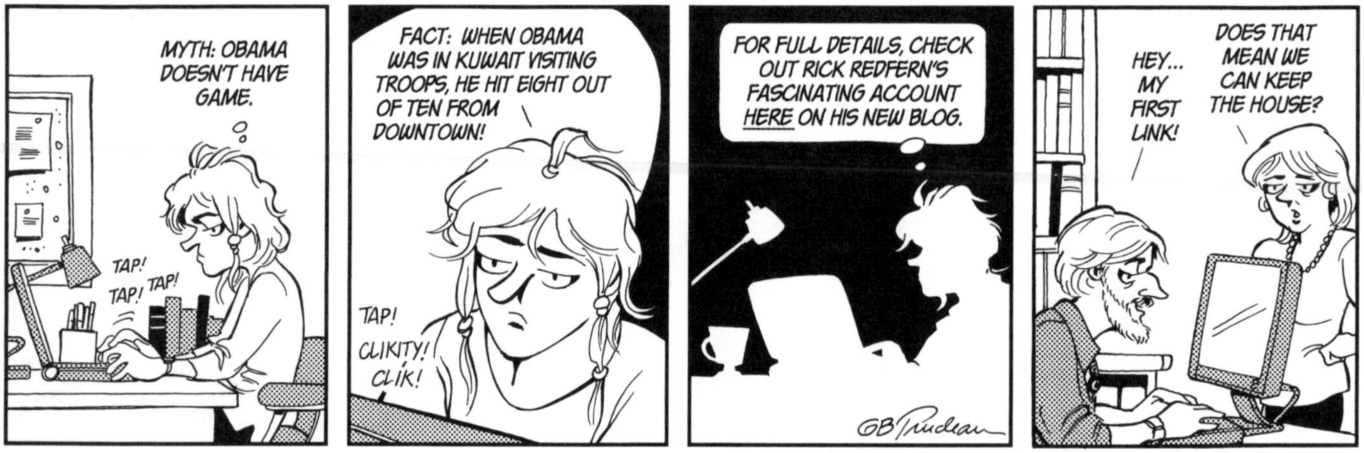
MYTH: OBAMA DOESN'T HAVE GAME.
TAP! TAP! TAP!
FACT: WHEN OBAMA WAS IN KUWAIT VISITING TROOPS, HE HIT EIGHT OUT OF TEN FROM DOWNTOWN!
TAP! CLIKITY! CLIK!
FOR FULL DETAILS, CHECK OUT RICK REDFERN'S FASCINATING ACCOUNT HERE ON HIS NEW BLOG.
GB Trudeau
HEY... MY FIRST LINK!
DOES THAT MEAN WE CAN KEEP THE HOUSE?

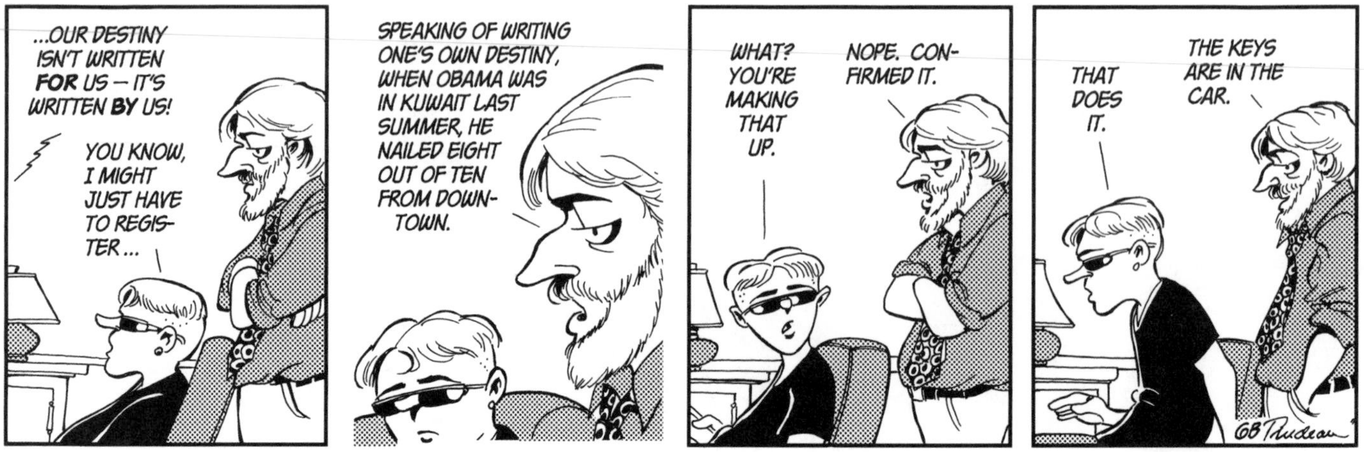
...OUR DESTINY ISN'T WRITTEN **FOR** US — IT'S WRITTEN **BY** US!
YOU KNOW, I MIGHT JUST HAVE TO REGISTER...
SPEAKING OF WRITING ONE'S OWN DESTINY, WHEN OBAMA WAS IN KUWAIT LAST SUMMER, HE NAILED EIGHT OUT OF TEN FROM DOWNTOWN.
WHAT? YOU'RE MAKING THAT UP.
NOPE. CONFIRMED IT.
THAT DOES IT.
THE KEYS ARE IN THE CAR.
GB Trudeau

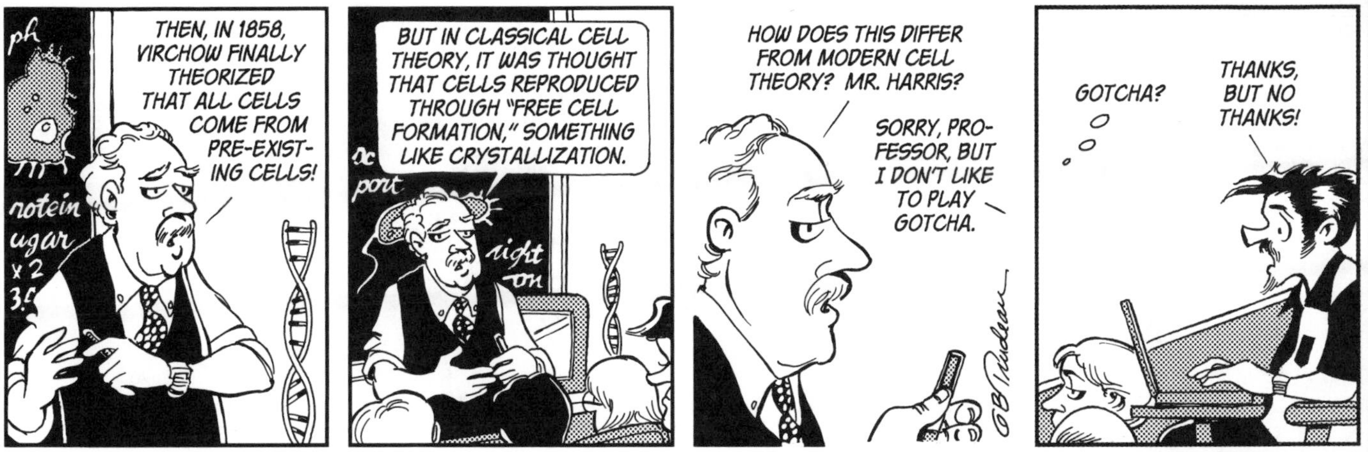
THEN, IN 1858, VIRCHOW FINALLY THEORIZED THAT ALL CELLS COME FROM PRE-EXISTING CELLS!
BUT IN CLASSICAL CELL THEORY, IT WAS THOUGHT THAT CELLS REPRODUCED THROUGH "FREE CELL FORMATION," SOMETHING LIKE CRYSTALLIZATION.
HOW DOES THIS DIFFER FROM MODERN CELL THEORY? MR. HARRIS?
SORRY, PROFESSOR, BUT I DON'T LIKE TO PLAY GOTCHA.
GOTCHA?
THANKS, BUT NO THANKS!
GB Trudeau

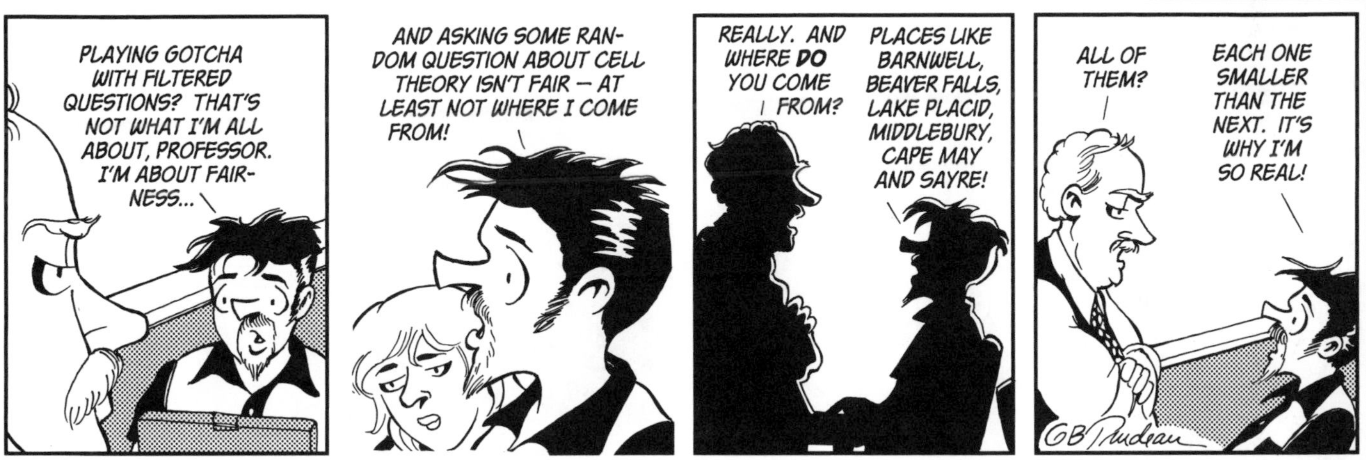
PLAYING GOTCHA WITH FILTERED QUESTIONS? THAT'S NOT WHAT I'M ALL ABOUT, PROFESSOR. I'M ABOUT FAIRNESS...
AND ASKING SOME RANDOM QUESTION ABOUT CELL THEORY ISN'T FAIR — AT LEAST NOT WHERE I COME FROM!
REALLY. AND WHERE **DO** YOU COME FROM?
PLACES LIKE BARNWELL, BEAVER FALLS, LAKE PLACID, MIDDLEBURY, CAPE MAY AND SAYRE!
ALL OF THEM?
EACH ONE SMALLER THAN THE NEXT. IT'S WHY I'M SO REAL!
GB Trudeau

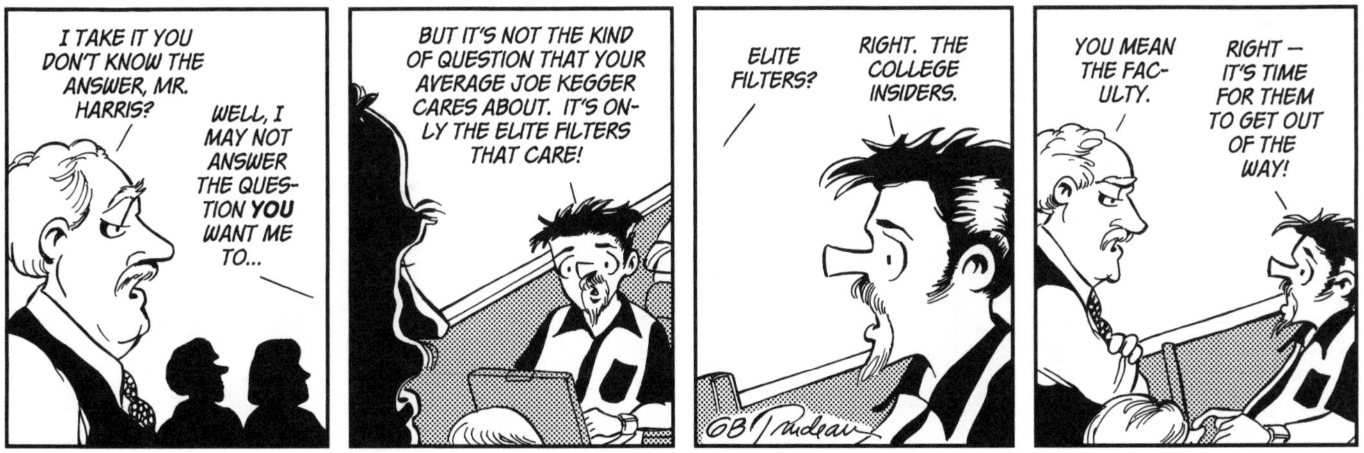
I TAKE IT YOU DON'T KNOW THE ANSWER, MR. HARRIS?
WELL, I MAY NOT ANSWER THE QUESTION **YOU** WANT ME TO...
BUT IT'S NOT THE KIND OF QUESTION THAT YOUR AVERAGE JOE KEGGER CARES ABOUT. IT'S ONLY THE ELITE FILTERS THAT CARE!
ELITE FILTERS?
RIGHT. THE COLLEGE INSIDERS.
YOU MEAN THE FACULTY.
RIGHT — IT'S TIME FOR THEM TO GET OUT OF THE WAY!
GB Trudeau

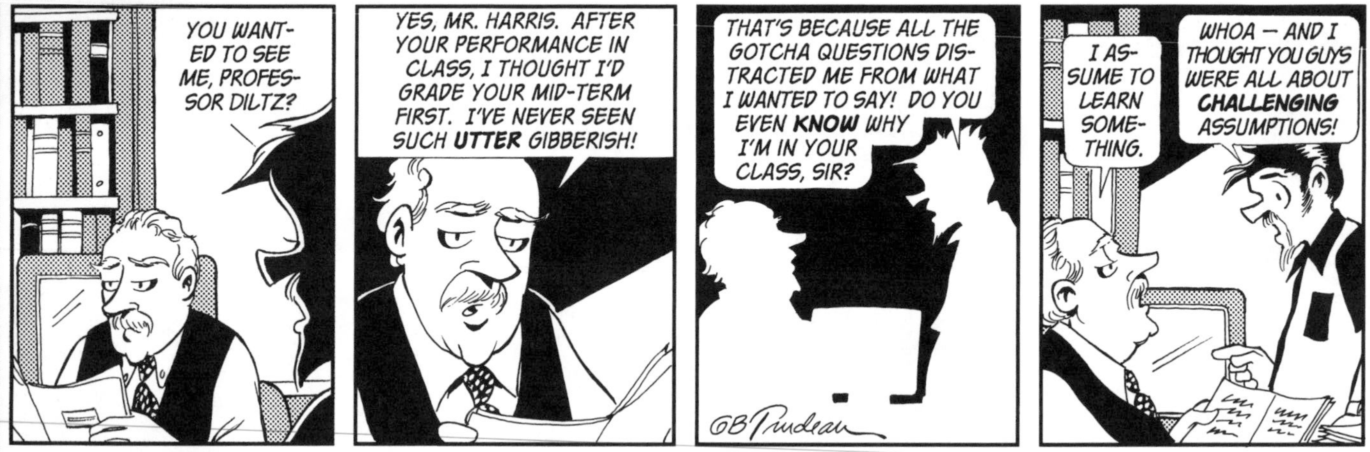
YOU WANTED TO SEE ME, PROFESSOR DILTZ?
YES, MR. HARRIS. AFTER YOUR PERFORMANCE IN CLASS, I THOUGHT I'D GRADE YOUR MID-TERM FIRST. I'VE NEVER SEEN SUCH **UTTER** GIBBERISH!
THAT'S BECAUSE ALL THE GOTCHA QUESTIONS DISTRACTED ME FROM WHAT I WANTED TO SAY! DO YOU EVEN **KNOW** WHY I'M IN YOUR CLASS, SIR?
©B Trudeau
I ASSUME TO LEARN SOMETHING.
WHOA — AND I THOUGHT YOU GUYS WERE ALL ABOUT **CHALLENGING** ASSUMPTIONS!

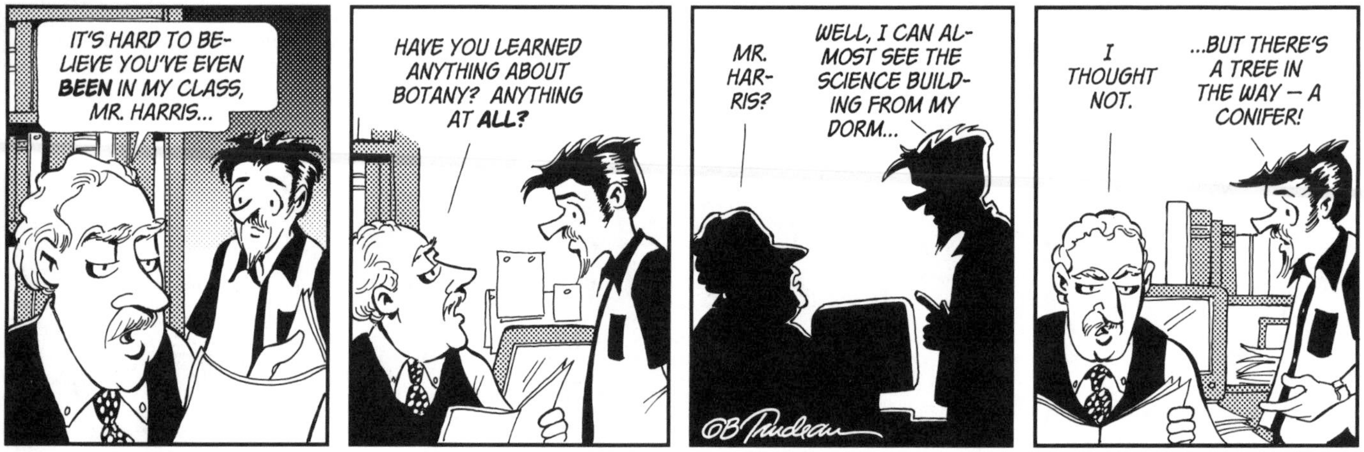
IT'S HARD TO BELIEVE YOU'VE EVEN **BEEN** IN MY CLASS, MR. HARRIS...
HAVE YOU LEARNED ANYTHING ABOUT BOTANY? ANYTHING AT **ALL?**
MR. HARRIS?
WELL, I CAN ALMOST SEE THE SCIENCE BUILDING FROM MY DORM...
©B Trudeau
I THOUGHT NOT.
...BUT THERE'S A TREE IN THE WAY — A CONIFER!

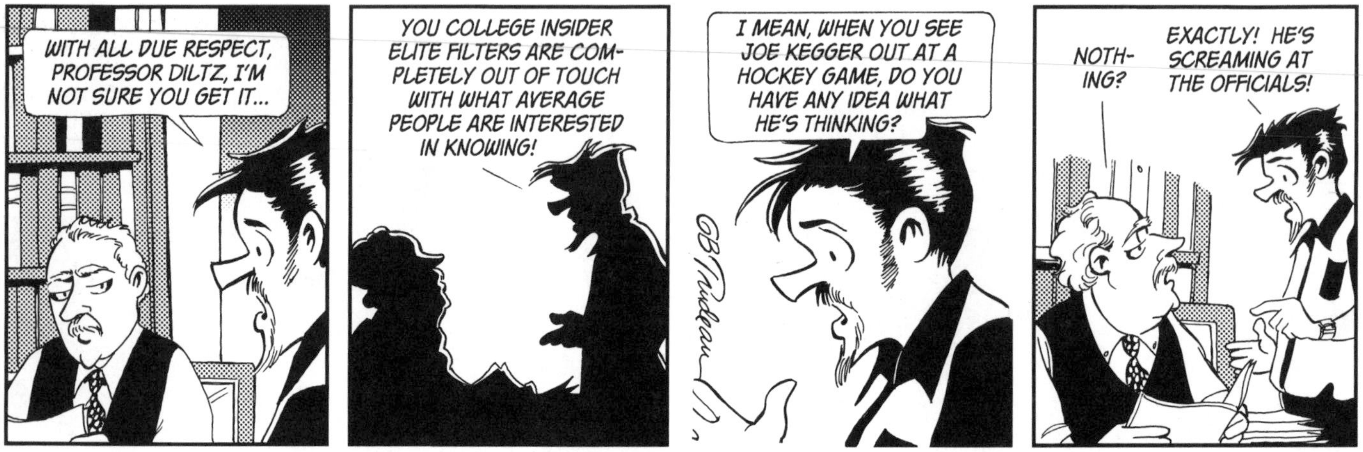
WITH ALL DUE RESPECT, PROFESSOR DILTZ, I'M NOT SURE YOU GET IT...
YOU COLLEGE INSIDER ELITE FILTERS ARE COMPLETELY OUT OF TOUCH WITH WHAT AVERAGE PEOPLE ARE INTERESTED IN KNOWING!
I MEAN, WHEN YOU SEE JOE KEGGER OUT AT A HOCKEY GAME, DO YOU HAVE ANY IDEA WHAT HE'S THINKING?
©B Trudeau
NOTHING?
EXACTLY! HE'S SCREAMING AT THE OFFICIALS!

SO HOW'S NAIROBI, ROLLIE?
HOT — GET ME OUT OF HERE!
WE'RE WORKING ON IT — WHY WERE YOU DIVERTED?
EQUIPMENT FAILURE. I'M DUE IN PARIS.
DON'T WORRY — THERE'S A FLIGHT OUT TOMORROW.
TOMORROW?
YEAH. PROBLEM?
IT'S GETTING DARK! YOU EXPECT ME TO SPEND THE NIGHT IN AFRICA?

EXCUSE ME, WHERE'S THE FIRST CLASS LOUNGE?
IT'S UPSTAIRS, SIR...
... BUT I'M AFRAID IT'S CLOSED FOR THE NIGHT. IT WON'T OPEN AGAIN UNTIL 9:30 A.M.
WELL, GREAT! A LOT OF GOOD THAT DOES ME!
IT'S A QUICK DRIVE INTO NAIROBI. WHAT DO YOU NEED?
SOMEPLACE I CAN NAP WITHOUT GETTING EBOLA FEVER.
HMM... LET ME THINK. THERE'S A SPORTS BAR AT GATE 43.

EXCUSE ME, ARE YOU AN AMERICAN?
A REAL AMERICAN, ACTUALLY. I WORK FOR FOX NEWS.
YOU MUST BE VERY EXCITED ABOUT YOUR MR. OBAMA!
ARE YOU KIDDING? AN OBAMA VICTORY WOULD BE A SOCIALIST NIGHTMARE!
OH, THAT FOX NEWS!
YOU KNOW US? AM I A BIG STAR HERE?

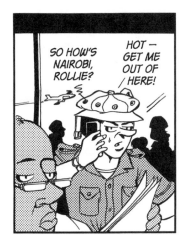

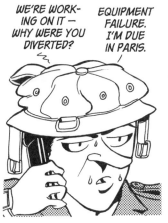

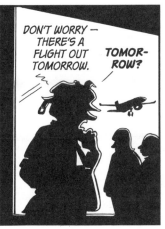

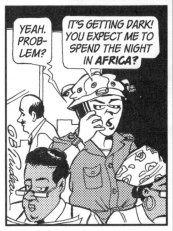

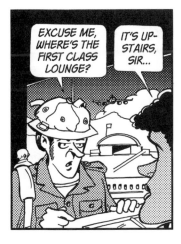

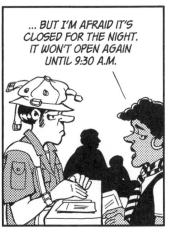

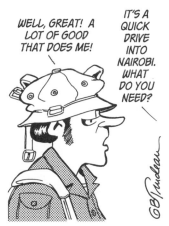

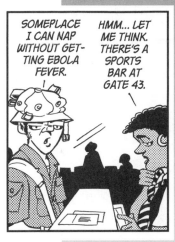

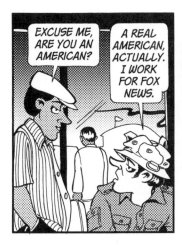

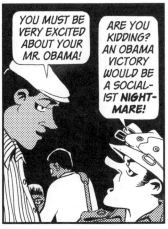

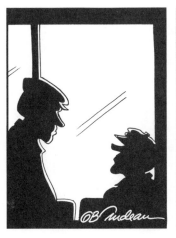

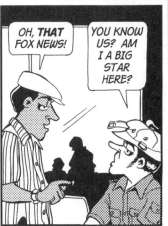

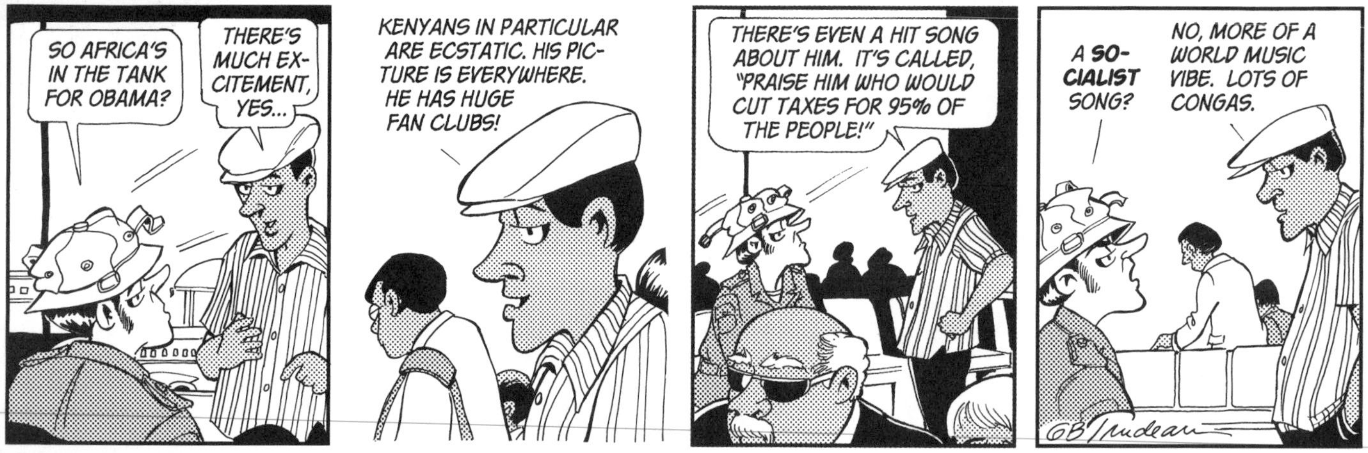
SO AFRICA'S IN THE TANK FOR OBAMA?
THERE'S MUCH EXCITEMENT, YES...
KENYANS IN PARTICULAR ARE ECSTATIC. HIS PICTURE IS EVERYWHERE. HE HAS HUGE FAN CLUBS!
THERE'S EVEN A HIT SONG ABOUT HIM. IT'S CALLED, "PRAISE HIM WHO WOULD CUT TAXES FOR 95% OF THE PEOPLE!"
A SOCIALIST SONG?
NO, MORE OF A WORLD MUSIC VIBE. LOTS OF CONGAS.

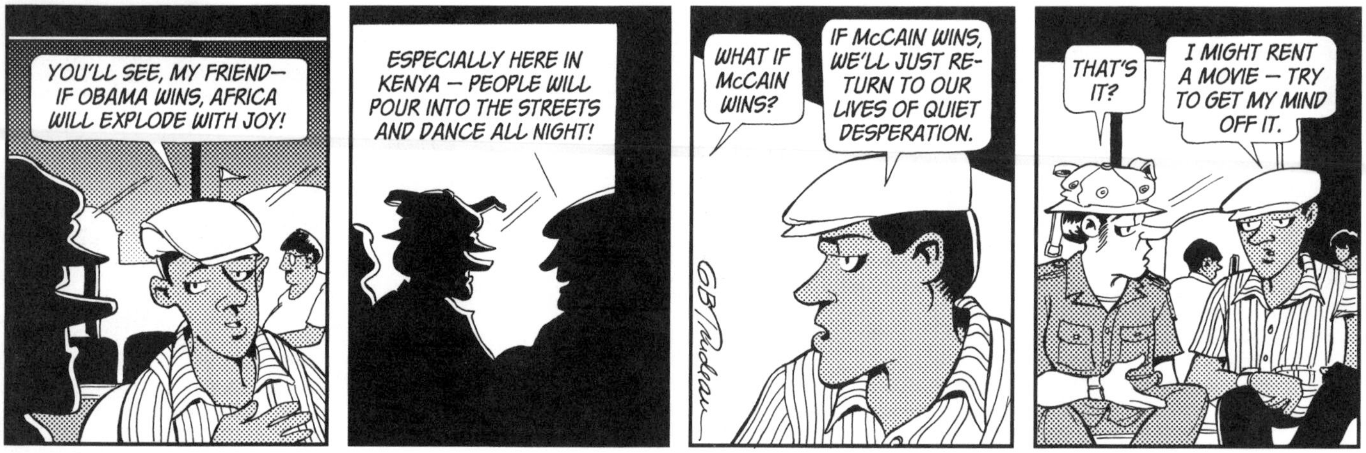
YOU'LL SEE, MY FRIEND— IF OBAMA WINS, AFRICA WILL EXPLODE WITH JOY!
ESPECIALLY HERE IN KENYA — PEOPLE WILL POUR INTO THE STREETS AND DANCE ALL NIGHT!
WHAT IF McCAIN WINS?
IF McCAIN WINS, WE'LL JUST RETURN TO OUR LIVES OF QUIET DESPERATION.
THAT'S IT?
I MIGHT RENT A MOVIE — TRY TO GET MY MIND OFF IT.

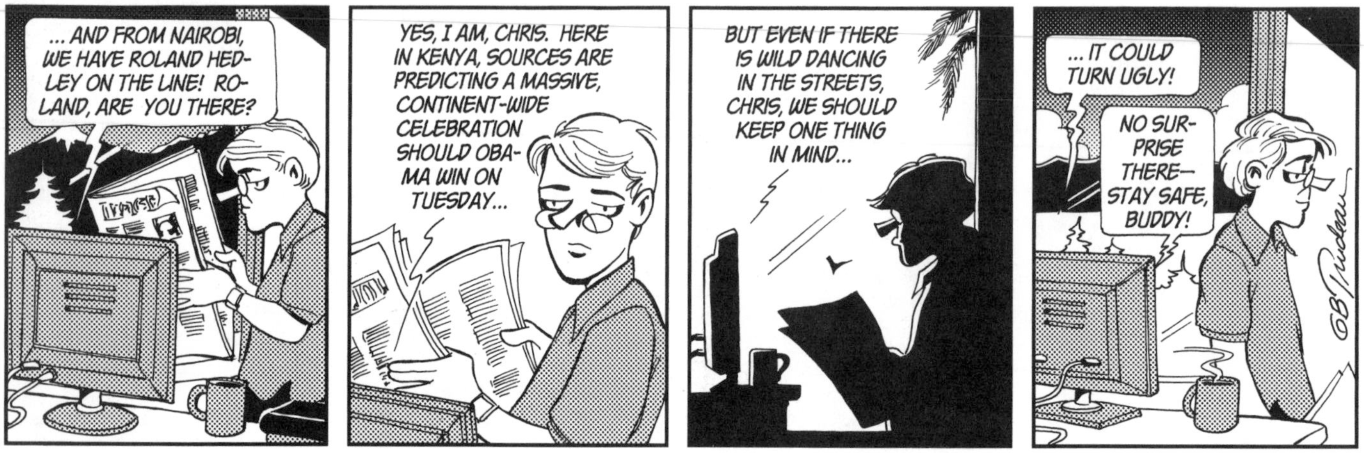
... AND FROM NAIROBI, WE HAVE ROLAND HEDLEY ON THE LINE! ROLAND, ARE YOU THERE?
YES, I AM, CHRIS. HERE IN KENYA, SOURCES ARE PREDICTING A MASSIVE, CONTINENT-WIDE CELEBRATION SHOULD OBAMA WIN ON TUESDAY...
BUT EVEN IF THERE IS WILD DANCING IN THE STREETS, CHRIS, WE SHOULD KEEP ONE THING IN MIND...
... IT COULD TURN UGLY!
NO SURPRISE THERE— STAY SAFE, BUDDY!

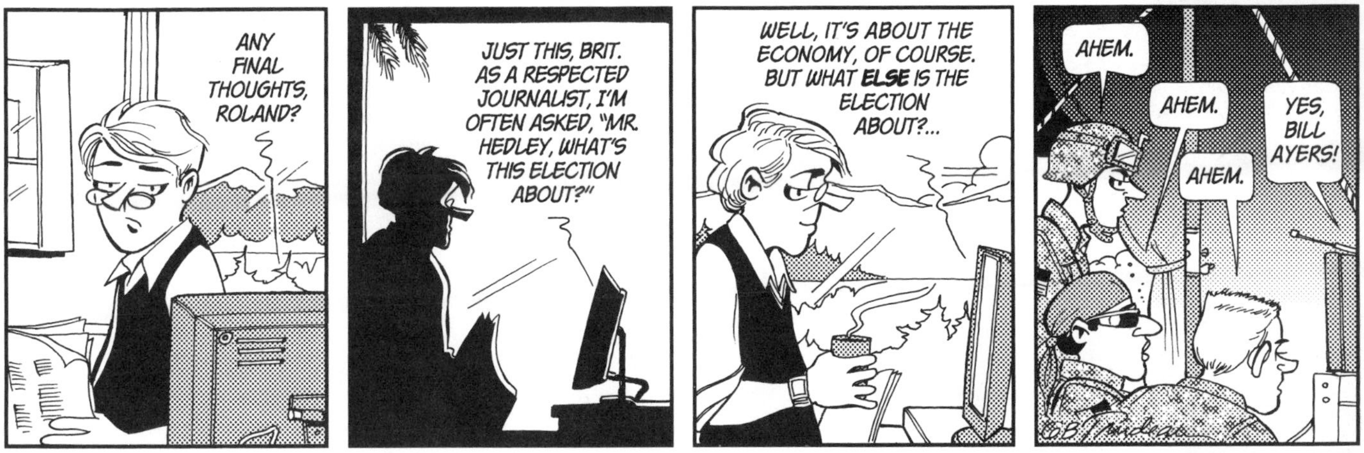
ANY FINAL THOUGHTS, ROLAND?
JUST THIS, BRIT. AS A RESPECTED JOURNALIST, I'M OFTEN ASKED, "MR. HEDLEY, WHAT'S THIS ELECTION ABOUT?"
WELL, IT'S ABOUT THE ECONOMY, OF COURSE. BUT WHAT **ELSE** IS THE ELECTION ABOUT?...
AHEM.
AHEM.
AHEM.
YES, BILL AYERS!

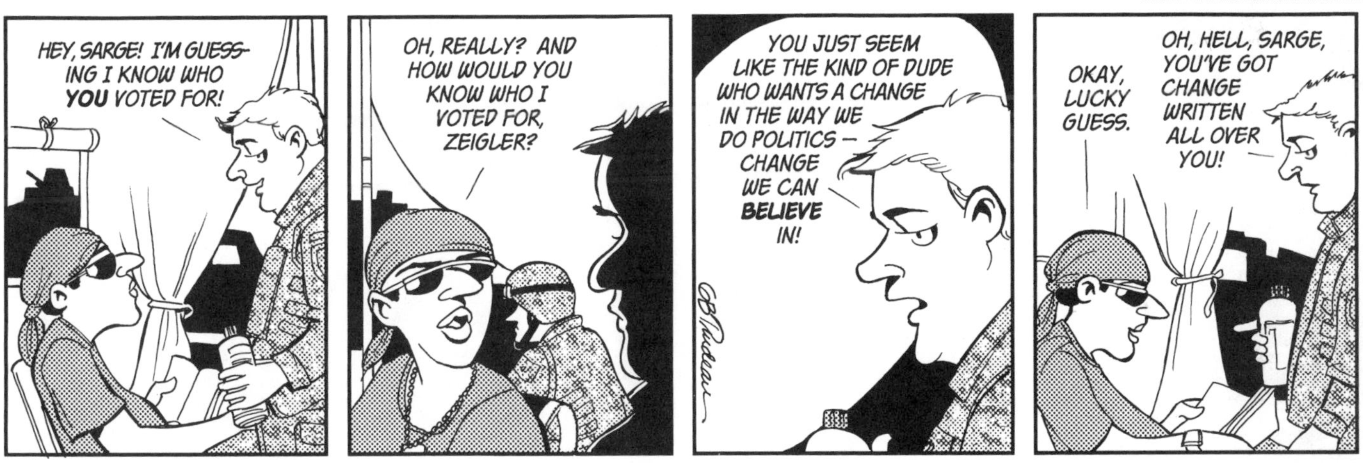
HEY, SARGE! I'M GUESSING I KNOW WHO **YOU** VOTED FOR!
OH, REALLY? AND HOW WOULD YOU KNOW WHO I VOTED FOR, ZEIGLER?
YOU JUST SEEM LIKE THE KIND OF DUDE WHO WANTS A CHANGE IN THE WAY WE DO POLITICS — CHANGE WE CAN **BELIEVE** IN!
OKAY, LUCKY GUESS.
OH, HELL, SARGE, YOU'VE GOT CHANGE WRITTEN ALL OVER YOU!

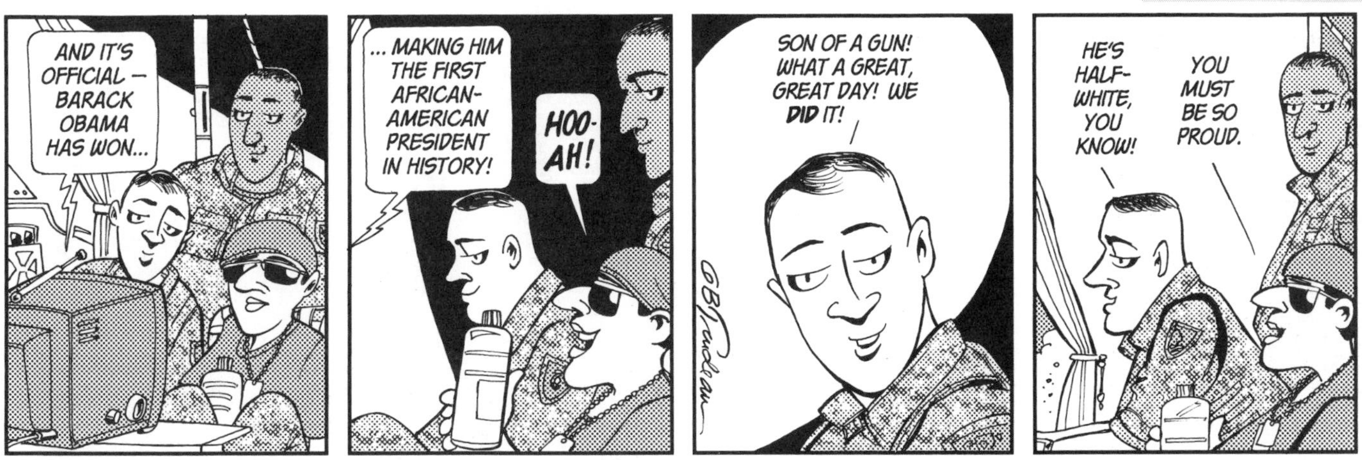
AND IT'S OFFICIAL — BARACK OBAMA HAS WON...
... MAKING HIM THE FIRST AFRICAN-AMERICAN PRESIDENT IN HISTORY!
HOO-AH!
SON OF A GUN! WHAT A GREAT, GREAT DAY! WE **DID** IT!
HE'S HALF-WHITE, YOU KNOW!
YOU MUST BE SO PROUD.

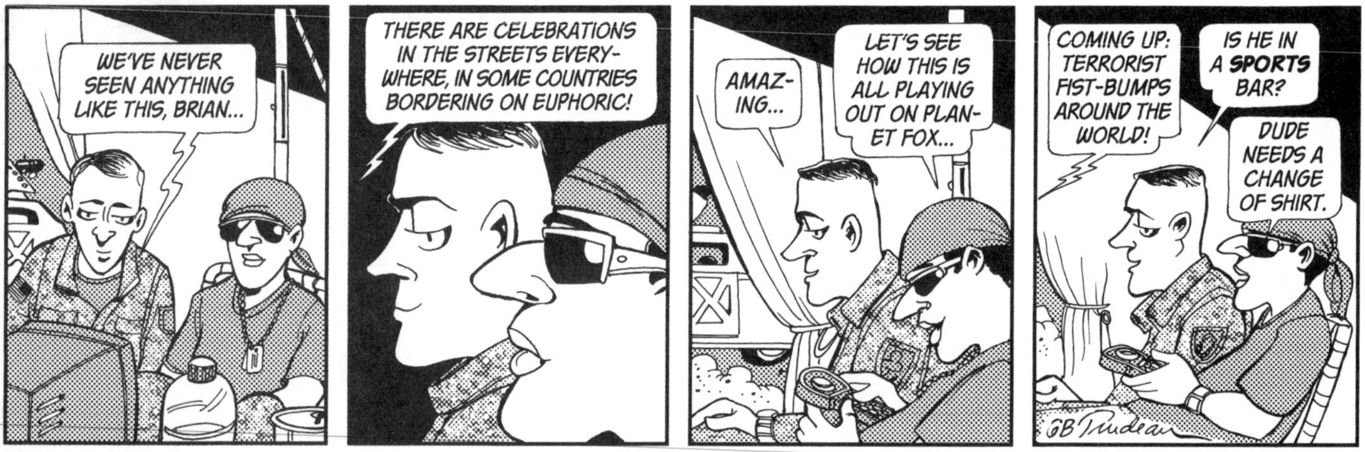
WE'VE NEVER SEEN ANYTHING LIKE THIS, BRIAN...
THERE ARE CELEBRATIONS IN THE STREETS EVERY-WHERE, IN SOME COUNTRIES BORDERING ON EUPHORIC!
AMAZ-ING...
LET'S SEE HOW THIS IS ALL PLAYING OUT ON PLAN-ET FOX...
COMING UP: TERRORIST FIST-BUMPS AROUND THE WORLD!
IS HE IN A **SPORTS** BAR?
DUDE NEEDS A CHANGE OF SHIRT.
GB Trudeau

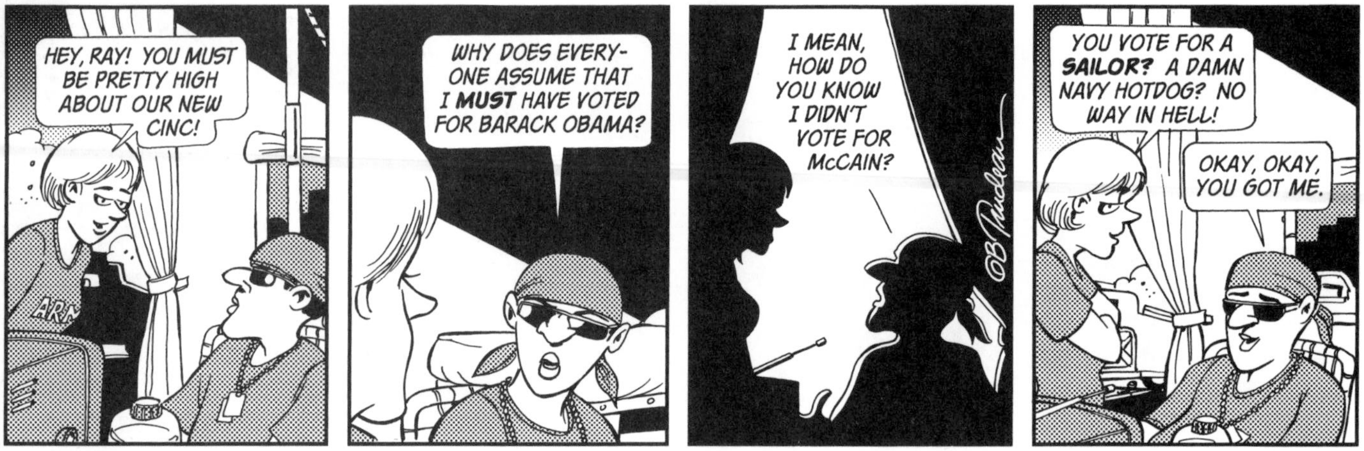
HEY, RAY! YOU MUST BE PRETTY HIGH ABOUT OUR NEW CINC!
WHY DOES EVERY-ONE ASSUME THAT I **MUST** HAVE VOTED FOR BARACK OBAMA?
I MEAN, HOW DO YOU KNOW I DIDN'T VOTE FOR McCAIN?
©B Trudeau
YOU VOTE FOR A **SAILOR?** A DAMN NAVY HOTDOG? NO WAY IN HELL!
OKAY, OKAY, YOU GOT ME.

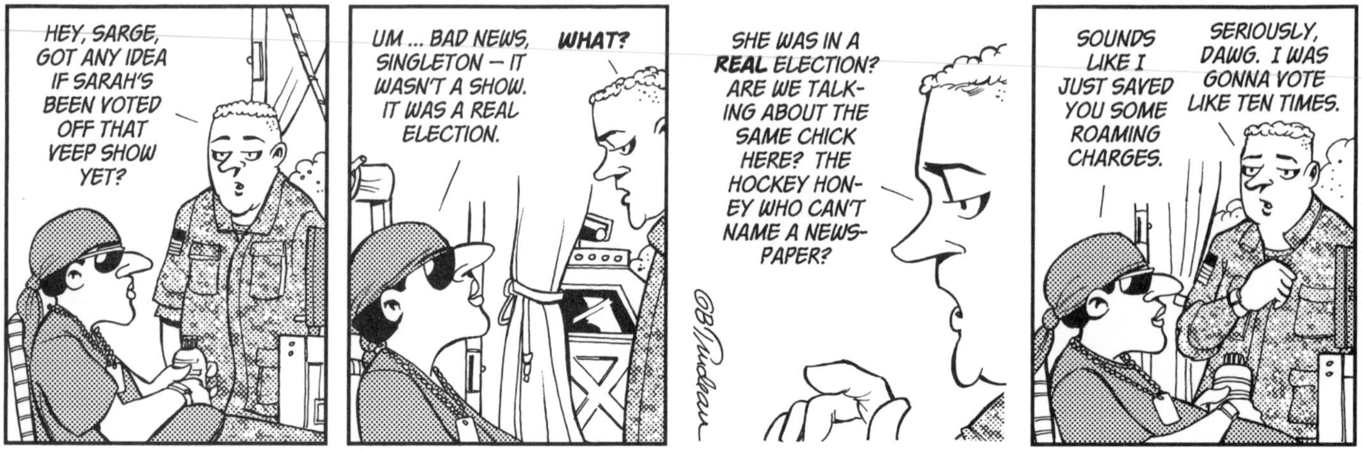
HEY, SARGE, GOT ANY IDEA IF SARAH'S BEEN VOTED OFF THAT VEEP SHOW YET?
UM ... BAD NEWS, SINGLETON — IT WASN'T A SHOW. IT WAS A REAL ELECTION.
WHAT?
©B Trudeau
SHE WAS IN A **REAL** ELECTION? ARE WE TALK-ING ABOUT THE SAME CHICK HERE? THE HOCKEY HON-EY WHO CAN'T NAME A NEWS-PAPER?
SOUNDS LIKE I JUST SAVED YOU SOME ROAMING CHARGES.
SERIOUSLY, DAWG. I WAS GONNA VOTE LIKE TEN TIMES.

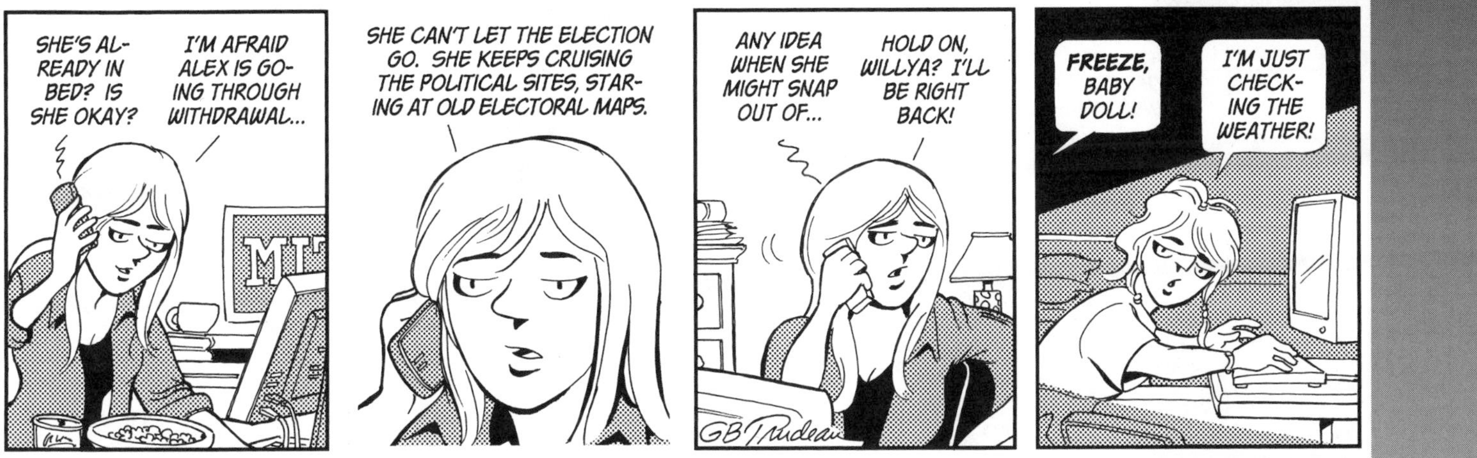
SHE'S ALREADY IN BED? IS SHE OKAY?
I'M AFRAID ALEX IS GOING THROUGH WITHDRAWAL...
SHE CAN'T LET THE ELECTION GO. SHE KEEPS CRUISING THE POLITICAL SITES, STARING AT OLD ELECTORAL MAPS.
ANY IDEA WHEN SHE MIGHT SNAP OUT OF...
HOLD ON, WILLYA? I'LL BE RIGHT BACK!
FREEZE, BABY DOLL!
I'M JUST CHECKING THE WEATHER!

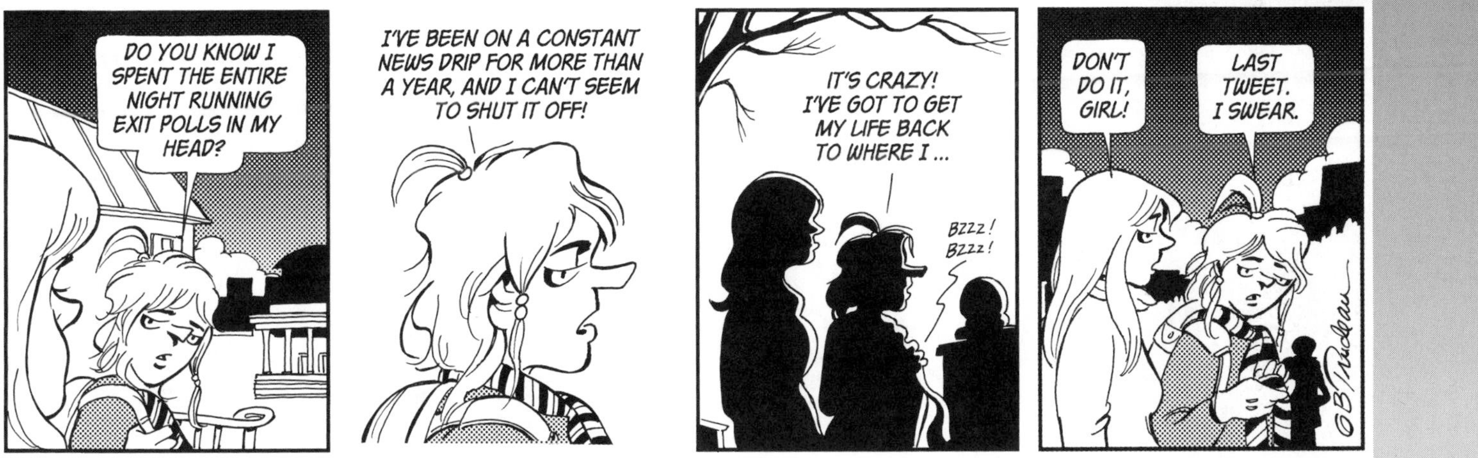
DO YOU KNOW I SPENT THE ENTIRE NIGHT RUNNING EXIT POLLS IN MY HEAD?
I'VE BEEN ON A CONSTANT NEWS DRIP FOR MORE THAN A YEAR, AND I CAN'T SEEM TO SHUT IT OFF!
IT'S CRAZY! I'VE GOT TO GET MY LIFE BACK TO WHERE I ...
BZZZ! BZZZ!
DON'T DO IT, GIRL!
LAST TWEET. I SWEAR.

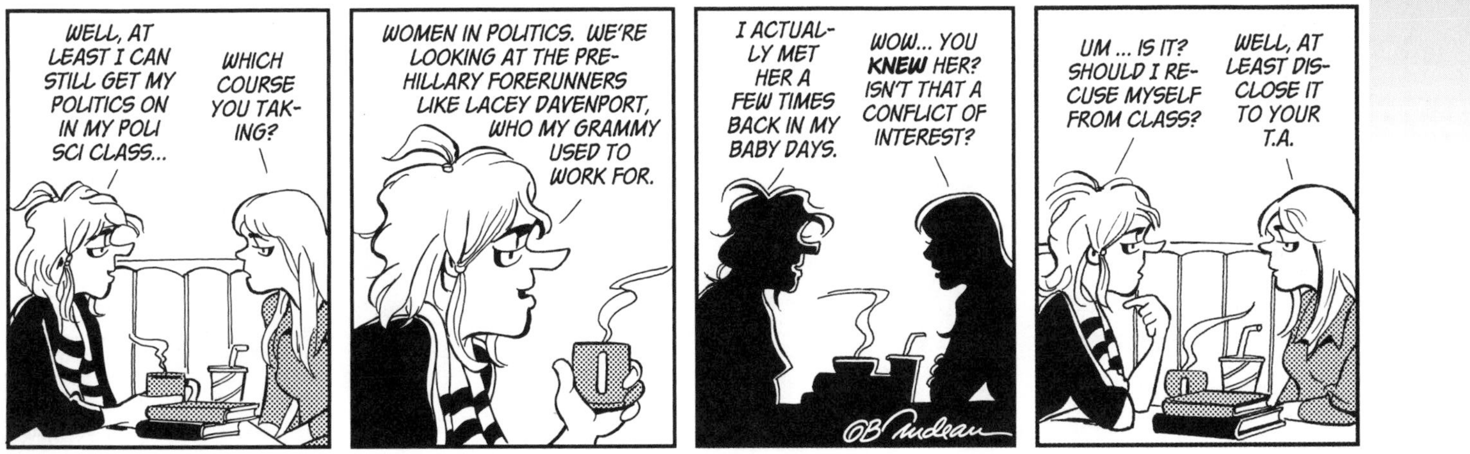
WELL, AT LEAST I CAN STILL GET MY POLITICS ON IN MY POLI SCI CLASS...
WHICH COURSE YOU TAKING?
WOMEN IN POLITICS. WE'RE LOOKING AT THE PRE-HILLARY FORERUNNERS LIKE LACEY DAVENPORT, WHO MY GRAMMY USED TO WORK FOR.
I ACTUALLY MET HER A FEW TIMES BACK IN MY BABY DAYS.
WOW... YOU KNEW HER? ISN'T THAT A CONFLICT OF INTEREST?
UM ... IS IT? SHOULD I RECUSE MYSELF FROM CLASS?
WELL, AT LEAST DISCLOSE IT TO YOUR T.A.

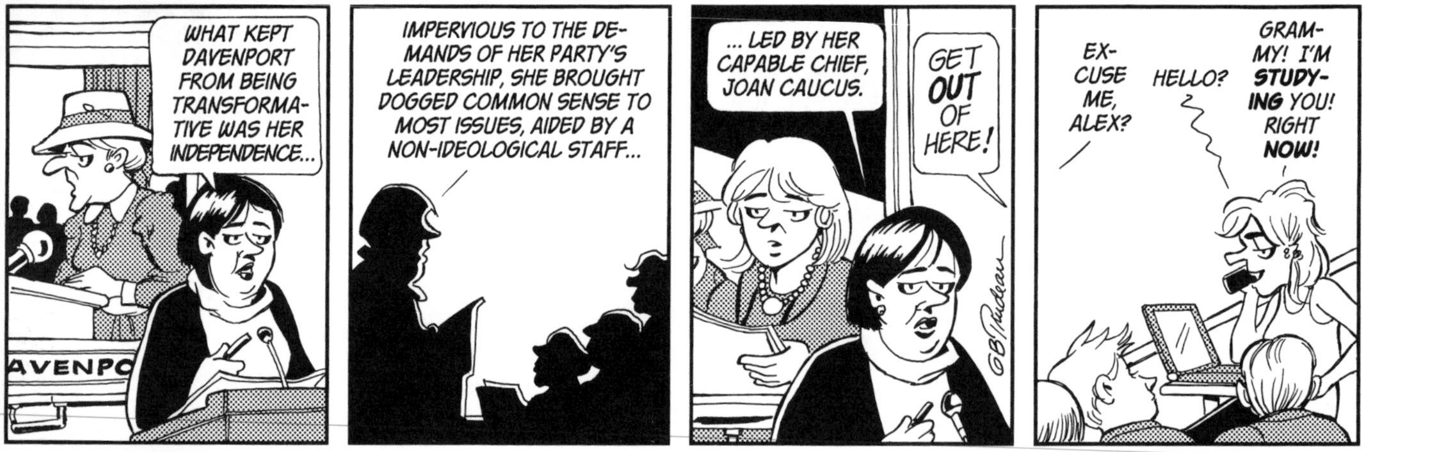
WHAT KEPT DAVENPORT FROM BEING TRANSFORMATIVE WAS HER INDEPENDENCE...
AVENPO
IMPERVIOUS TO THE DEMANDS OF HER PARTY'S LEADERSHIP, SHE BROUGHT DOGGED COMMON SENSE TO MOST ISSUES, AIDED BY A NON-IDEOLOGICAL STAFF...
... LED BY HER CAPABLE CHIEF, JOAN CAUCUS.
GET OUT OF HERE!
EXCUSE ME, ALEX?
HELLO?
GRAMMY! I'M STUDYING YOU! RIGHT NOW!

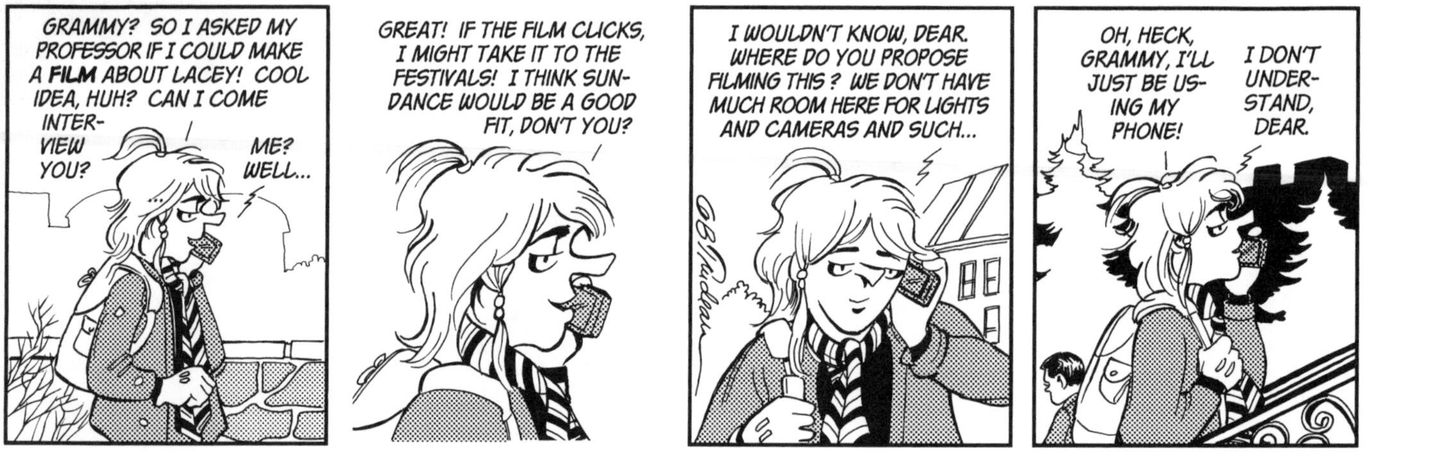
GRAMMY? SO I ASKED MY PROFESSOR IF I COULD MAKE A FILM ABOUT LACEY! COOL IDEA, HUH? CAN I COME INTERVIEW YOU?
ME? WELL...
GREAT! IF THE FILM CLICKS, I MIGHT TAKE IT TO THE FESTIVALS! I THINK SUNDANCE WOULD BE A GOOD FIT, DON'T YOU?
I WOULDN'T KNOW, DEAR. WHERE DO YOU PROPOSE FILMING THIS? WE DON'T HAVE MUCH ROOM HERE FOR LIGHTS AND CAMERAS AND SUCH...
OH, HECK, GRAMMY, I'LL JUST BE USING MY PHONE!
I DON'T UNDERSTAND, DEAR.

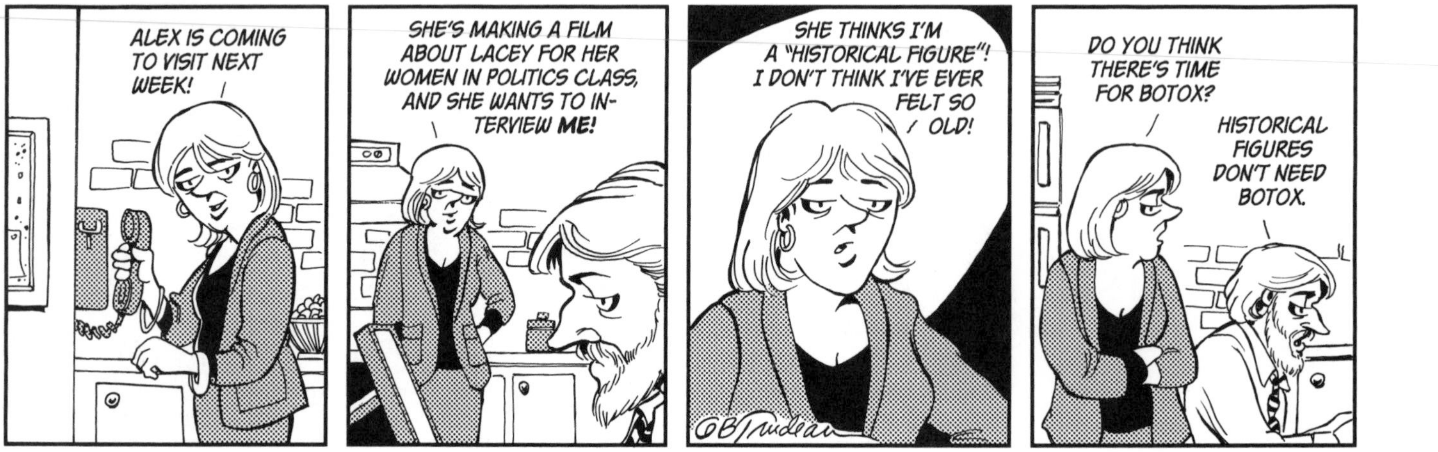
ALEX IS COMING TO VISIT NEXT WEEK!
SHE'S MAKING A FILM ABOUT LACEY FOR HER WOMEN IN POLITICS CLASS, AND SHE WANTS TO INTERVIEW ME!
SHE THINKS I'M A "HISTORICAL FIGURE"! I DON'T THINK I'VE EVER FELT SO OLD!
DO YOU THINK THERE'S TIME FOR BOTOX?
HISTORICAL FIGURES DON'T NEED BOTOX.

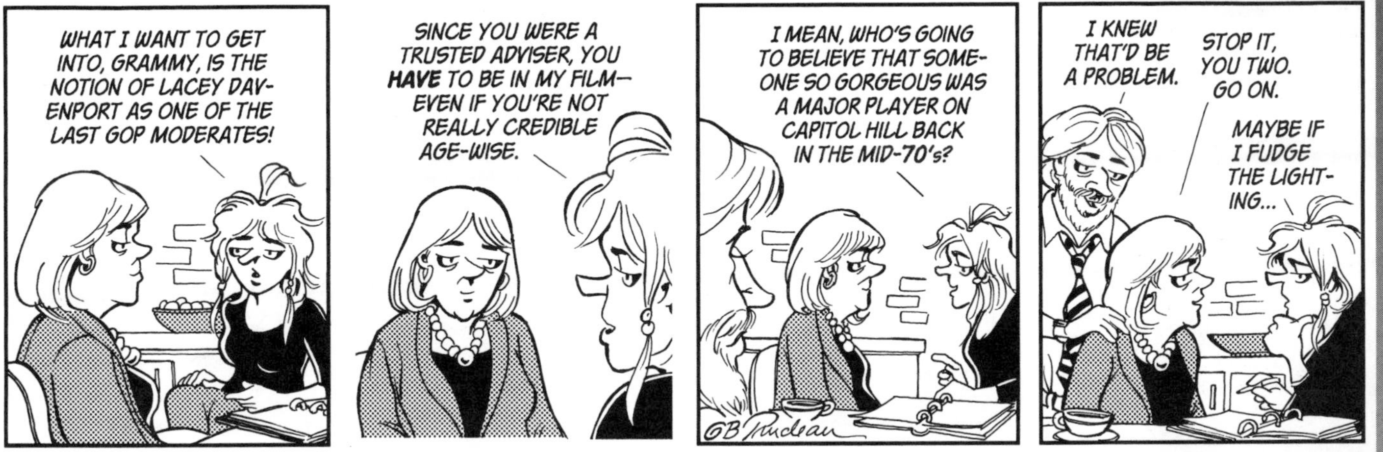
WHAT I WANT TO GET INTO, GRAMMY, IS THE NOTION OF LACEY DAVENPORT AS ONE OF THE LAST GOP MODERATES!
SINCE YOU WERE A TRUSTED ADVISER, YOU **HAVE** TO BE IN MY FILM— EVEN IF YOU'RE NOT REALLY CREDIBLE AGE-WISE.
I MEAN, WHO'S GOING TO BELIEVE THAT SOMEONE SO GORGEOUS WAS A MAJOR PLAYER ON CAPITOL HILL BACK IN THE MID-'70's?
I KNEW THAT'D BE A PROBLEM.
STOP IT, YOU TWO. GO ON.
MAYBE IF I FUDGE THE LIGHTING...
©B Trudeau

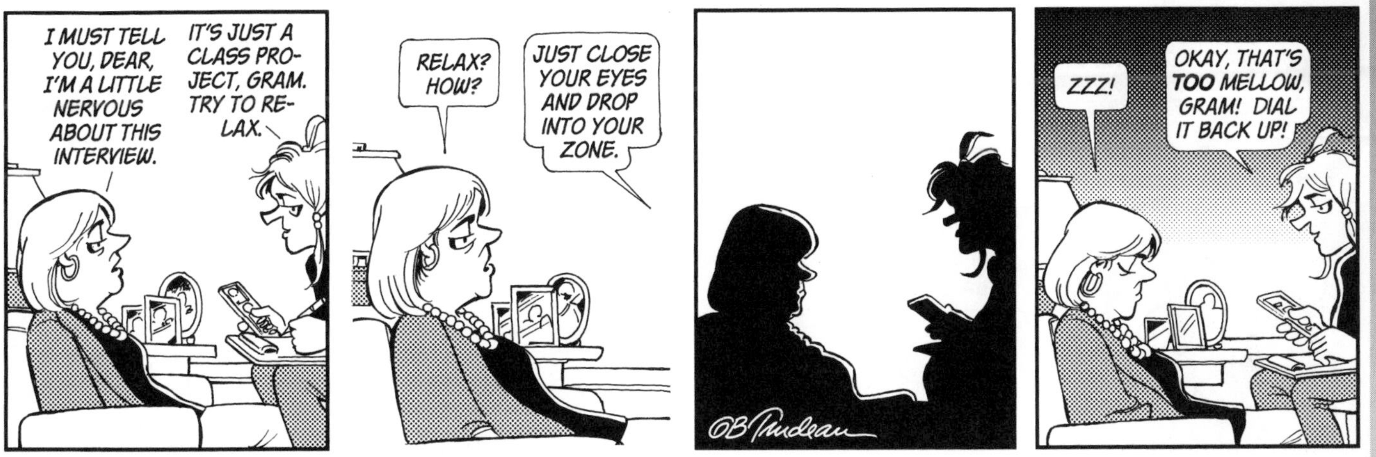
I MUST TELL YOU, DEAR, I'M A LITTLE NERVOUS ABOUT THIS INTERVIEW.
IT'S JUST A CLASS PROJECT, GRAM. TRY TO RELAX.
RELAX? HOW?
JUST CLOSE YOUR EYES AND DROP INTO YOUR ZONE.
©B Trudeau
ZZZ!
OKAY, THAT'S **TOO** MELLOW, GRAM! DIAL IT BACK UP!

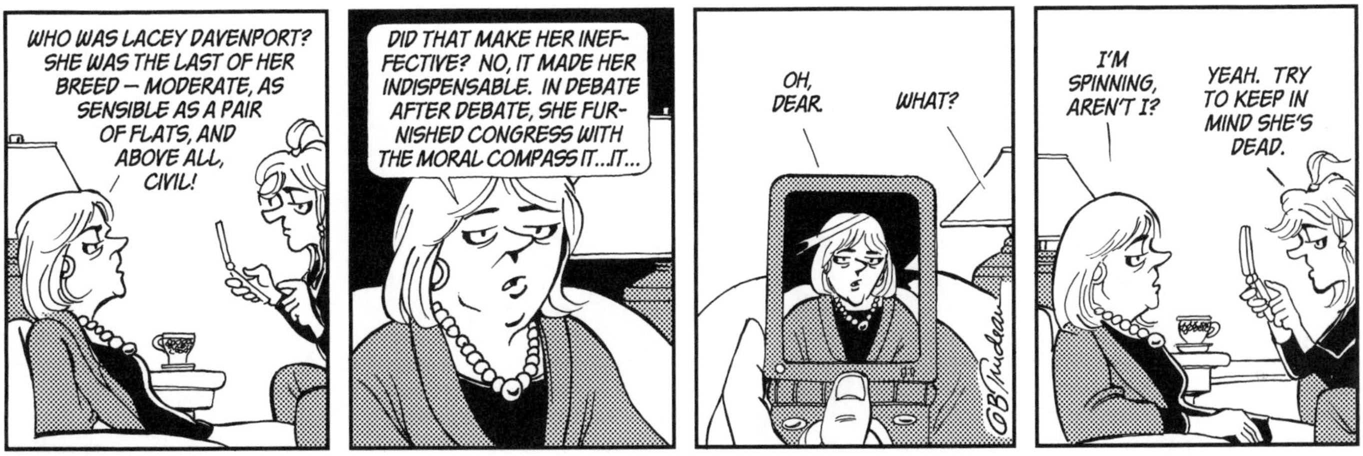
WHO WAS LACEY DAVENPORT? SHE WAS THE LAST OF HER BREED — MODERATE, AS SENSIBLE AS A PAIR OF FLATS, AND ABOVE ALL, CIVIL!
DID THAT MAKE HER INEFFECTIVE? NO, IT MADE HER INDISPENSABLE. IN DEBATE AFTER DEBATE, SHE FURNISHED CONGRESS WITH THE MORAL COMPASS IT...IT...
OH, DEAR.
WHAT?
©B Trudeau
I'M SPINNING, AREN'T I?
YEAH. TRY TO KEEP IN MIND SHE'S DEAD.

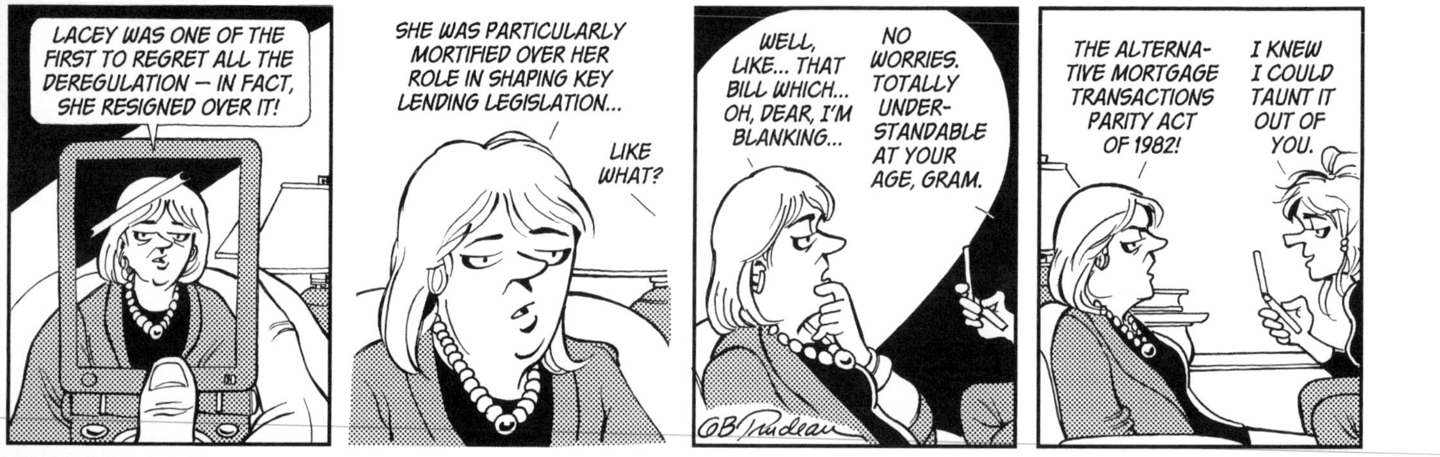
LACEY WAS ONE OF THE FIRST TO REGRET ALL THE DEREGULATION — IN FACT, SHE RESIGNED OVER IT!
SHE WAS PARTICULARLY MORTIFIED OVER HER ROLE IN SHAPING KEY LENDING LEGISLATION...
LIKE WHAT?
WELL, LIKE... THAT BILL WHICH... OH, DEAR, I'M BLANKING...
NO WORRIES. TOTALLY UNDER-STANDABLE AT YOUR AGE, GRAM.
THE ALTERNA-TIVE MORTGAGE TRANSACTIONS PARITY ACT OF 1982!
I KNEW I COULD TAUNT IT OUT OF YOU.

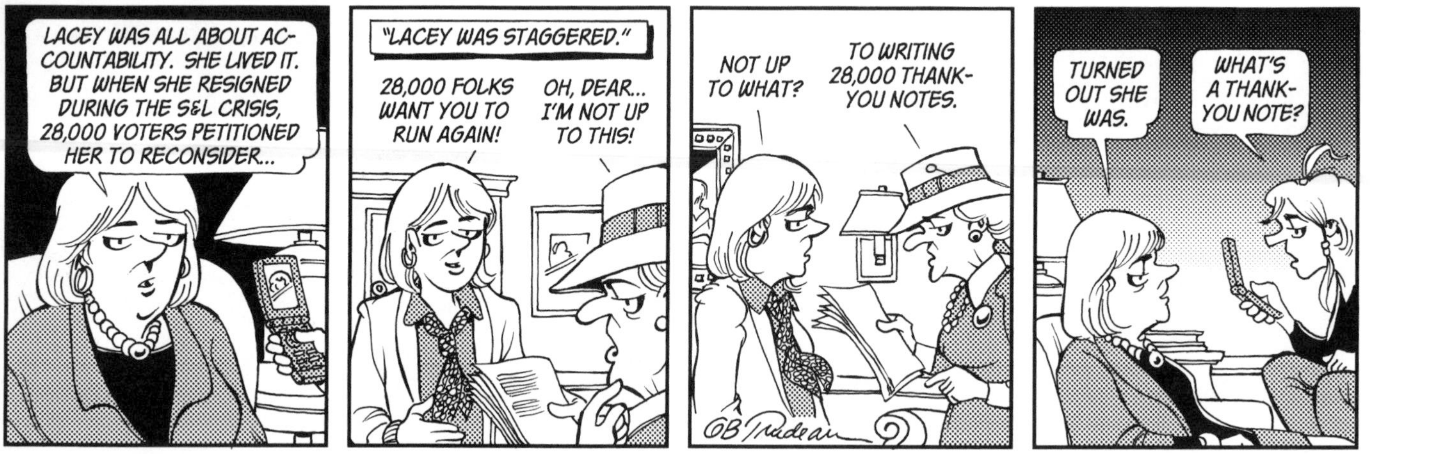
LACEY WAS ALL ABOUT AC-COUNTABILITY. SHE LIVED IT. BUT WHEN SHE RESIGNED DURING THE S&L CRISIS, 28,000 VOTERS PETITIONED HER TO RECONSIDER...
"LACEY WAS STAGGERED."
28,000 FOLKS WANT YOU TO RUN AGAIN!
OH, DEAR... I'M NOT UP TO THIS!
NOT UP TO WHAT?
TO WRITING 28,000 THANK-YOU NOTES.
TURNED OUT SHE WAS.
WHAT'S A THANK-YOU NOTE?

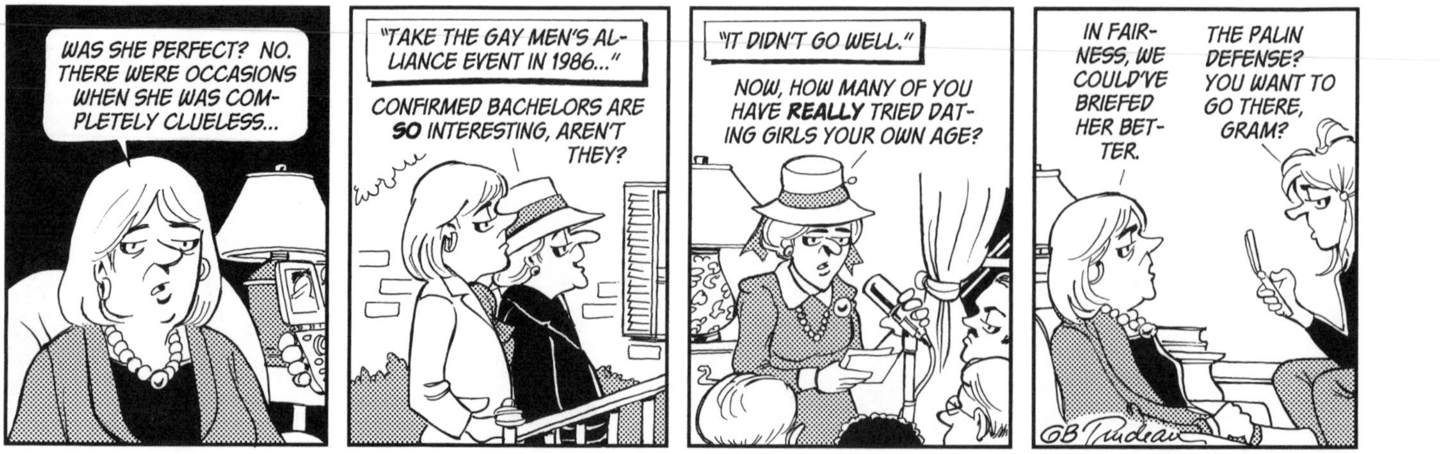
WAS SHE PERFECT? NO. THERE WERE OCCASIONS WHEN SHE WAS COM-PLETELY CLUELESS...
"TAKE THE GAY MEN'S AL-LIANCE EVENT IN 1986..."
CONFIRMED BACHELORS ARE SO INTERESTING, AREN'T THEY?
"IT DIDN'T GO WELL."
NOW, HOW MANY OF YOU HAVE REALLY TRIED DAT-ING GIRLS YOUR OWN AGE?
IN FAIR-NESS, WE COULD'VE BRIEFED HER BET-TER.
THE PALIN DEFENSE? YOU WANT TO GO THERE, GRAM?

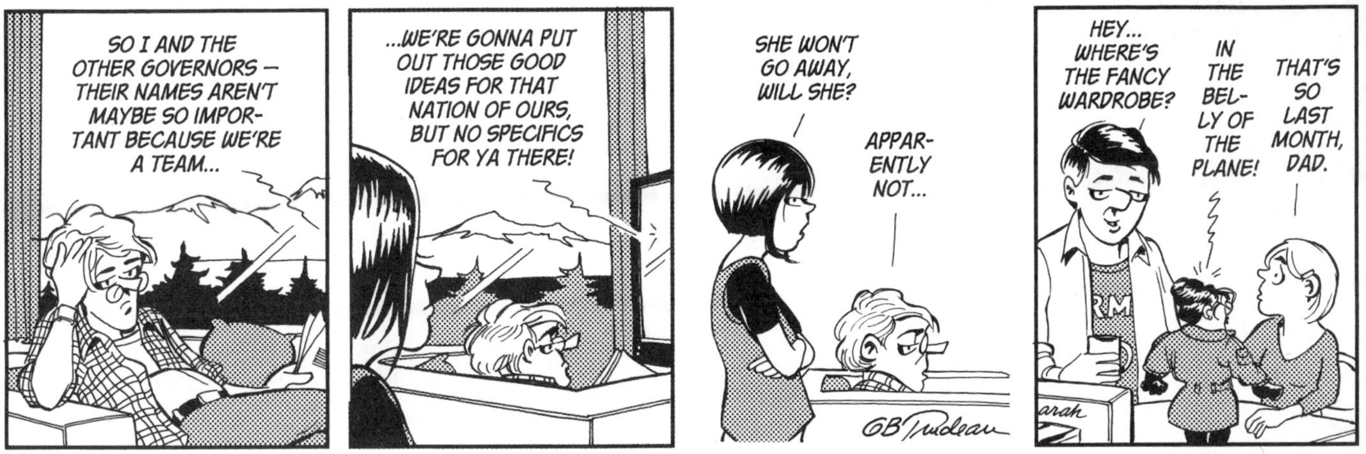
SO I AND THE OTHER GOVERNORS — THEIR NAMES AREN'T MAYBE SO IMPORTANT BECAUSE WE'RE A TEAM...
...WE'RE GONNA PUT OUT THOSE GOOD IDEAS FOR THAT NATION OF OURS, BUT NO SPECIFICS FOR YA THERE!
SHE WON'T GO AWAY, WILL SHE?
APPARENTLY NOT...
GB Trudeau
HEY... WHERE'S THE FANCY WARDROBE?
IN THE BELLY OF THE PLANE!
THAT'S SO LAST MONTH, DAD.

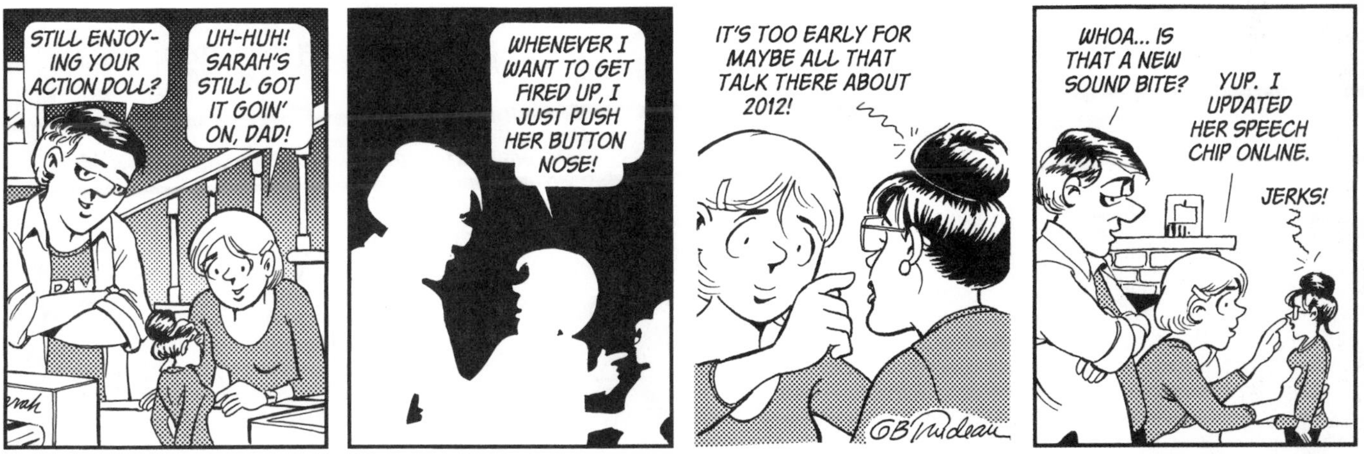
STILL ENJOYING YOUR ACTION DOLL?
UH-HUH! SARAH'S STILL GOT IT GOIN' ON, DAD!
WHENEVER I WANT TO GET FIRED UP, I JUST PUSH HER BUTTON NOSE!
IT'S TOO EARLY FOR MAYBE ALL THAT TALK THERE ABOUT 2012!
GB Trudeau
WHOA... IS THAT A NEW SOUND BITE?
YUP. I UPDATED HER SPEECH CHIP ONLINE.
JERKS!

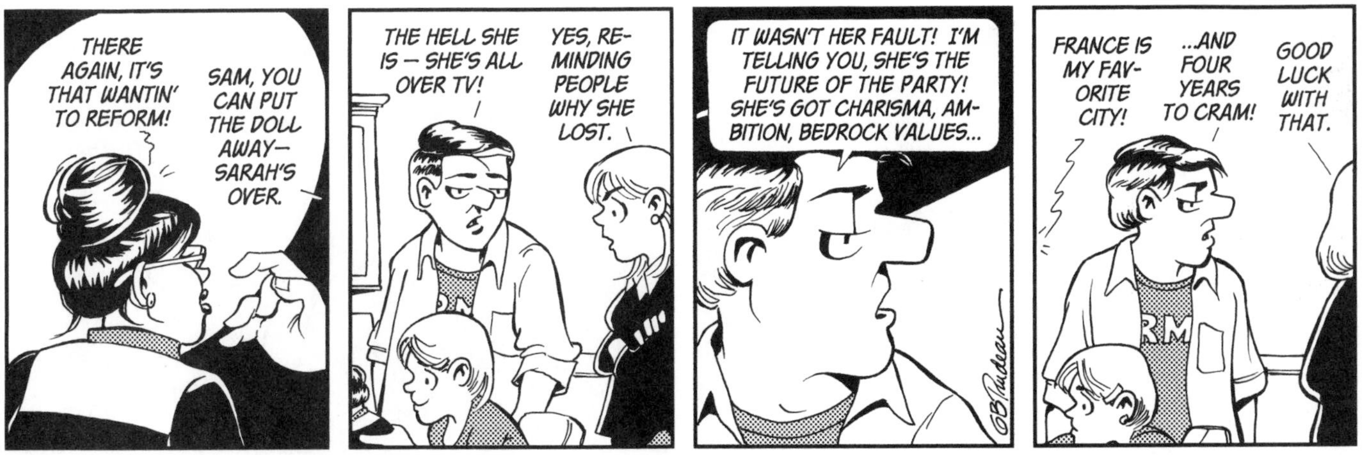
THERE AGAIN, IT'S THAT WANTIN' TO REFORM!
SAM, YOU CAN PUT THE DOLL AWAY— SARAH'S OVER.
THE HELL SHE IS — SHE'S ALL OVER TV!
YES, REMINDING PEOPLE WHY SHE LOST.
IT WASN'T HER FAULT! I'M TELLING YOU, SHE'S THE FUTURE OF THE PARTY! SHE'S GOT CHARISMA, AMBITION, BEDROCK VALUES...
GB Trudeau
FRANCE IS MY FAVORITE CITY!
...AND FOUR YEARS TO CRAM!
GOOD LUCK WITH THAT.

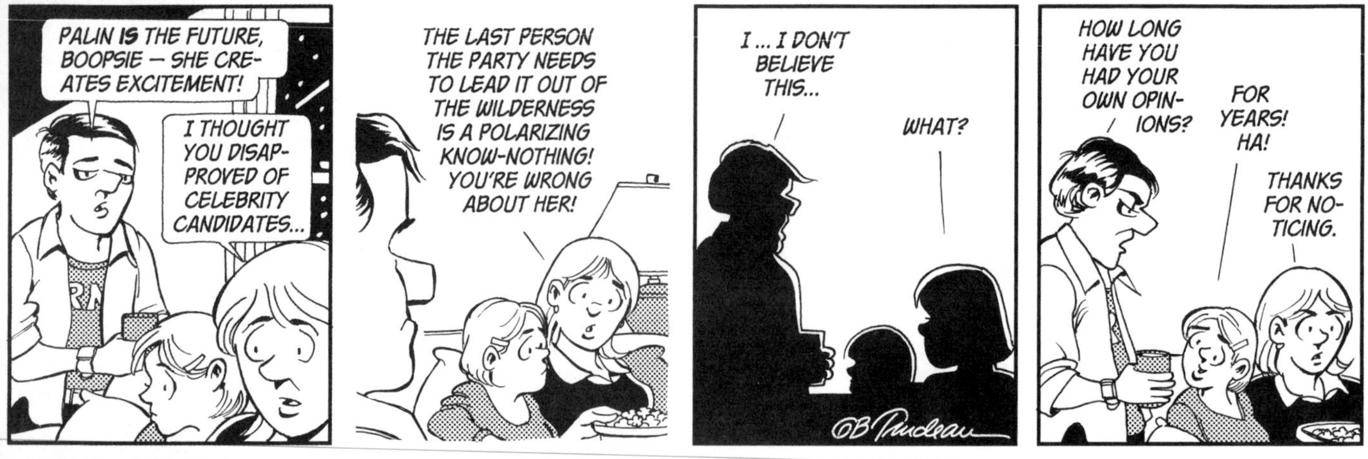
PALIN **IS** THE FUTURE, BOOPSIE — SHE CREATES EXCITEMENT!
I THOUGHT YOU DISAPPROVED OF CELEBRITY CANDIDATES...
THE LAST PERSON THE PARTY NEEDS TO LEAD IT OUT OF THE WILDERNESS IS A POLARIZING KNOW-NOTHING! YOU'RE WRONG ABOUT HER!
I ... I DON'T BELIEVE THIS...
WHAT?
G B Trudeau
HOW LONG HAVE YOU HAD YOUR OWN OPINIONS?
FOR YEARS! HA!
THANKS FOR NOTICING.

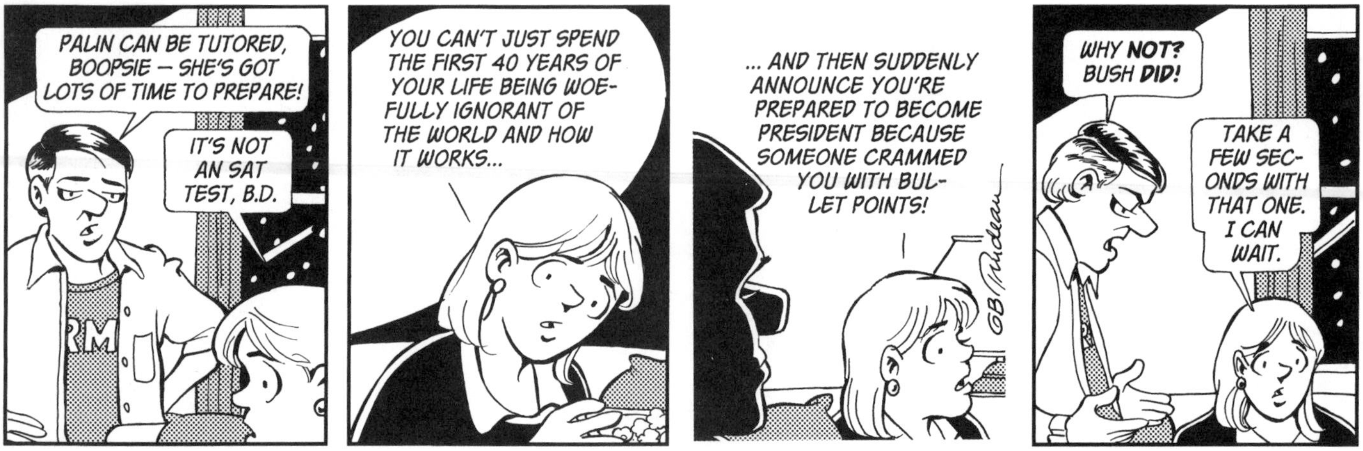
PALIN CAN BE TUTORED, BOOPSIE — SHE'S GOT LOTS OF TIME TO PREPARE!
IT'S NOT AN SAT TEST, B.D.
YOU CAN'T JUST SPEND THE FIRST 40 YEARS OF YOUR LIFE BEING WOEFULLY IGNORANT OF THE WORLD AND HOW IT WORKS...
... AND THEN SUDDENLY ANNOUNCE YOU'RE PREPARED TO BECOME PRESIDENT BECAUSE SOMEONE CRAMMED YOU WITH BULLET POINTS!
G B Trudeau
WHY **NOT?** BUSH **DID!**
TAKE A FEW SECONDS WITH THAT ONE. I CAN WAIT.

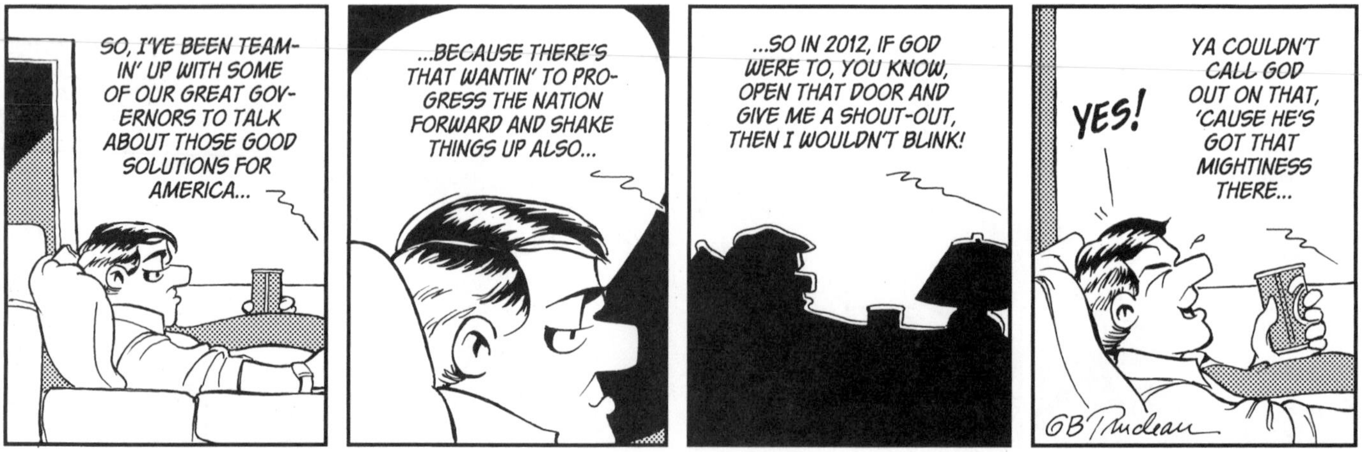
SO, I'VE BEEN TEAMIN' UP WITH SOME OF OUR GREAT GOVERNORS TO TALK ABOUT THOSE GOOD SOLUTIONS FOR AMERICA...
...BECAUSE THERE'S THAT WANTIN' TO PROGRESS THE NATION FORWARD AND SHAKE THINGS UP ALSO...
...SO IN 2012, IF GOD WERE TO, YOU KNOW, OPEN THAT DOOR AND GIVE ME A SHOUT-OUT, THEN I WOULDN'T BLINK!
YES!
YA COULDN'T CALL GOD OUT ON THAT, 'CAUSE HE'S GOT THAT MIGHTINESS THERE...
G B Trudeau

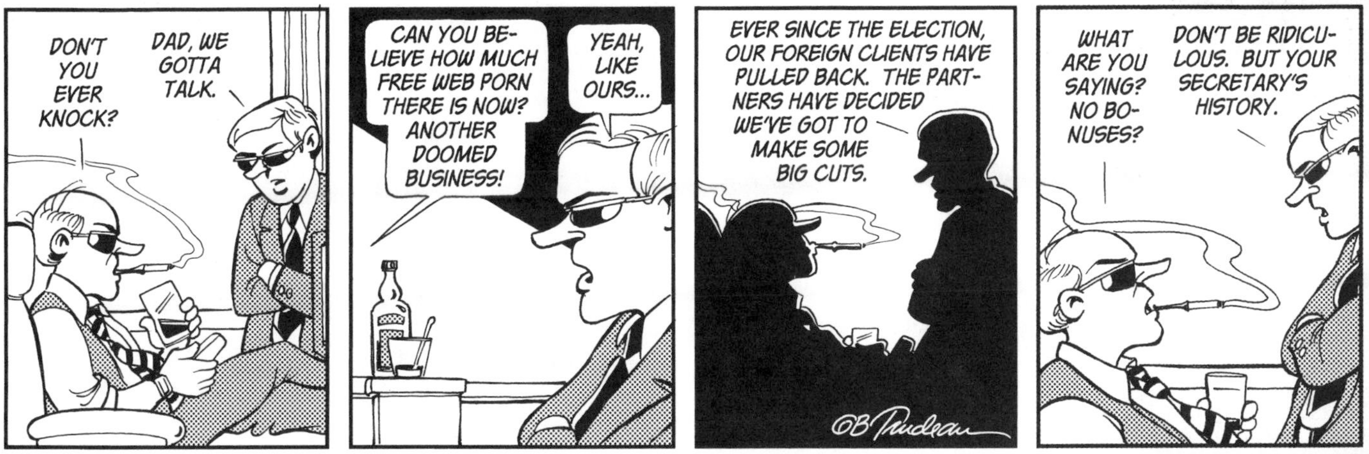
DON'T YOU EVER KNOCK?
DAD, WE GOTTA TALK.
CAN YOU BE-LIEVE HOW MUCH FREE WEB PORN THERE IS NOW? ANOTHER DOOMED BUSINESS!
YEAH, LIKE OURS...
EVER SINCE THE ELECTION, OUR FOREIGN CLIENTS HAVE PULLED BACK. THE PART-NERS HAVE DECIDED WE'VE GOT TO MAKE SOME BIG CUTS.
WHAT ARE YOU SAYING? NO BO-NUSES?
DON'T BE RIDICU-LOUS. BUT YOUR SECRETARY'S HISTORY.
GB Trudeau

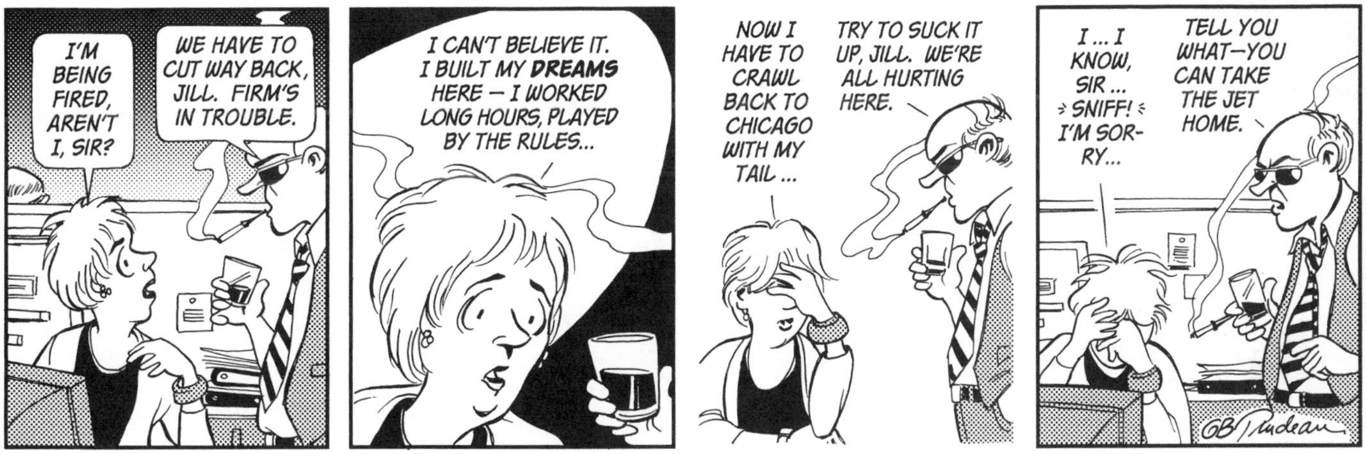
I'M BEING FIRED, AREN'T I, SIR?
WE HAVE TO CUT WAY BACK, JILL. FIRM'S IN TROUBLE.
I CAN'T BELIEVE IT. I BUILT MY **DREAMS** HERE — I WORKED LONG HOURS, PLAYED BY THE RULES...
NOW I HAVE TO CRAWL BACK TO CHICAGO WITH MY TAIL ...
TRY TO SUCK IT UP, JILL. WE'RE ALL HURTING HERE.
I ... I KNOW, SIR ... *SNIFF!* I'M SOR-RY...
TELL YOU WHAT—YOU CAN TAKE THE JET HOME.
GB Trudeau

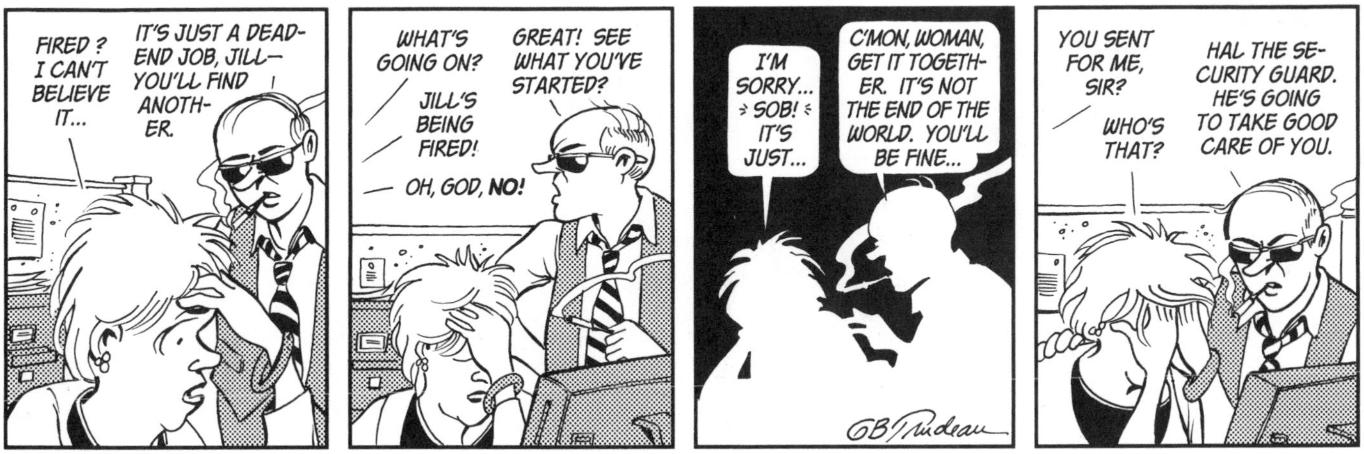
FIRED ? I CAN'T BELIEVE IT...
IT'S JUST A DEAD-END JOB, JILL— YOU'LL FIND ANOTH-ER.
WHAT'S GOING ON?
JILL'S BEING FIRED!
OH, GOD, **NO!**
GREAT! SEE WHAT YOU'VE STARTED?
I'M SORRY... *SOB!* IT'S JUST...
C'MON, WOMAN, GET IT TOGETH-ER. IT'S NOT THE END OF THE WORLD. YOU'LL BE FINE...
GB Trudeau
YOU SENT FOR ME, SIR?
WHO'S THAT?
HAL THE SE-CURITY GUARD. HE'S GOING TO TAKE GOOD CARE OF YOU.

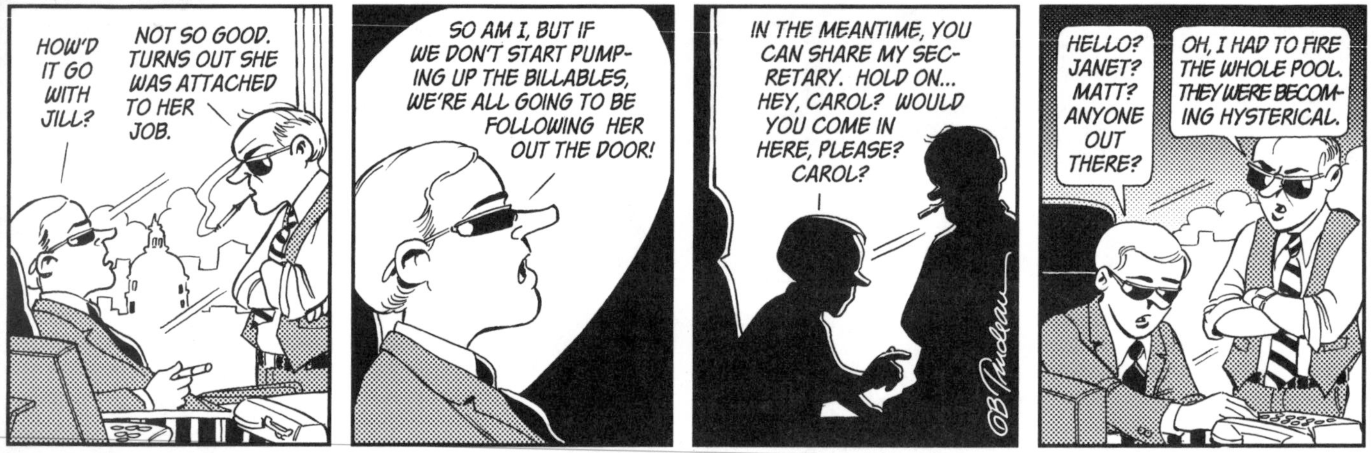
HOW'D IT GO WITH JILL?
NOT SO GOOD. TURNS OUT SHE WAS ATTACHED TO HER JOB.
SO AM I, BUT IF WE DON'T START PUMPING UP THE BILLABLES, WE'RE ALL GOING TO BE FOLLOWING HER OUT THE DOOR!
IN THE MEANTIME, YOU CAN SHARE MY SECRETARY. HOLD ON... HEY, CAROL? WOULD YOU COME IN HERE, PLEASE? CAROL?
GB Trudeau
HELLO? JANET? MATT? ANYONE OUT THERE?
OH, I HAD TO FIRE THE WHOLE POOL. THEY WERE BECOMING HYSTERICAL.

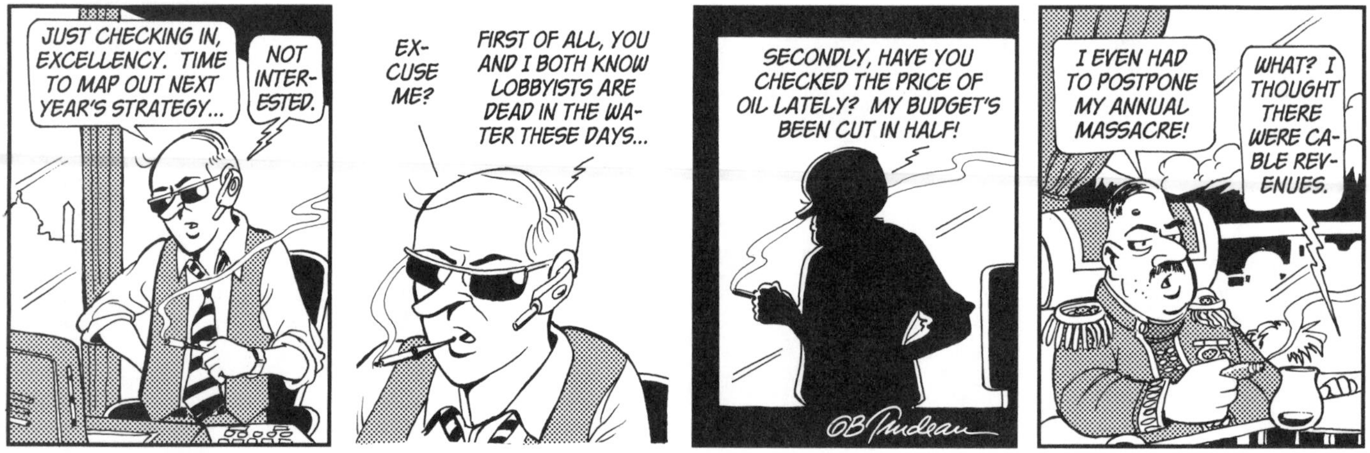
JUST CHECKING IN, EXCELLENCY. TIME TO MAP OUT NEXT YEAR'S STRATEGY...
NOT INTERESTED.
EXCUSE ME?
FIRST OF ALL, YOU AND I BOTH KNOW LOBBYISTS ARE DEAD IN THE WATER THESE DAYS...
SECONDLY, HAVE YOU CHECKED THE PRICE OF OIL LATELY? MY BUDGET'S BEEN CUT IN HALF!
GB Trudeau
I EVEN HAD TO POSTPONE MY ANNUAL MASSACRE!
WHAT? I THOUGHT THERE WERE CABLE REVENUES.

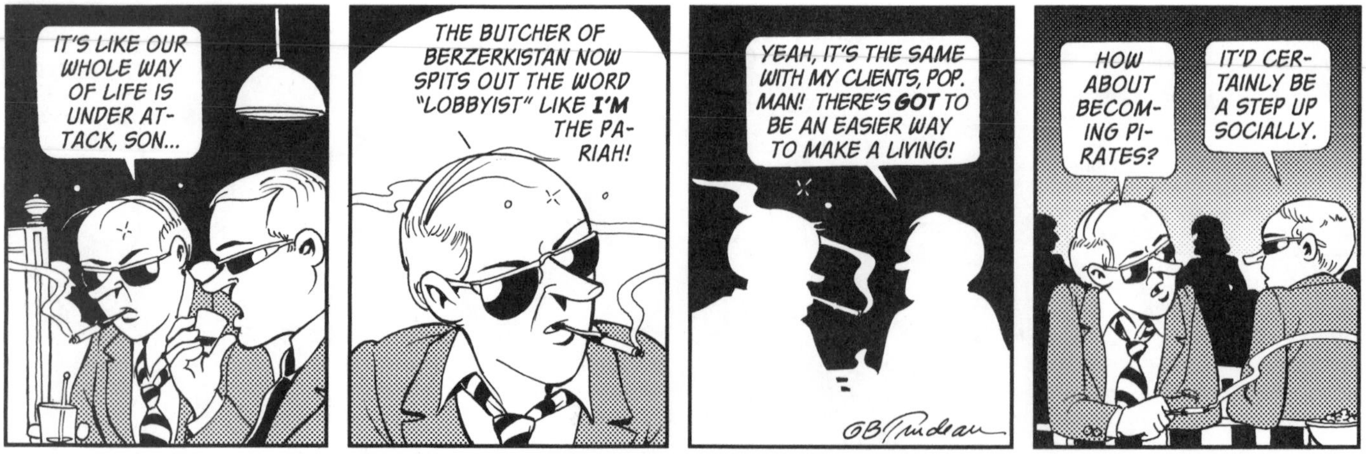
IT'S LIKE OUR WHOLE WAY OF LIFE IS UNDER ATTACK, SON...
THE BUTCHER OF BERZERKISTAN NOW SPITS OUT THE WORD "LOBBYIST" LIKE **I'M** THE PARIAH!
YEAH, IT'S THE SAME WITH MY CLIENTS, POP. MAN! THERE'S **GOT** TO BE AN EASIER WAY TO MAKE A LIVING!
GB Trudeau
HOW ABOUT BECOMING PIRATES?
IT'D CERTAINLY BE A STEP UP SOCIALLY.

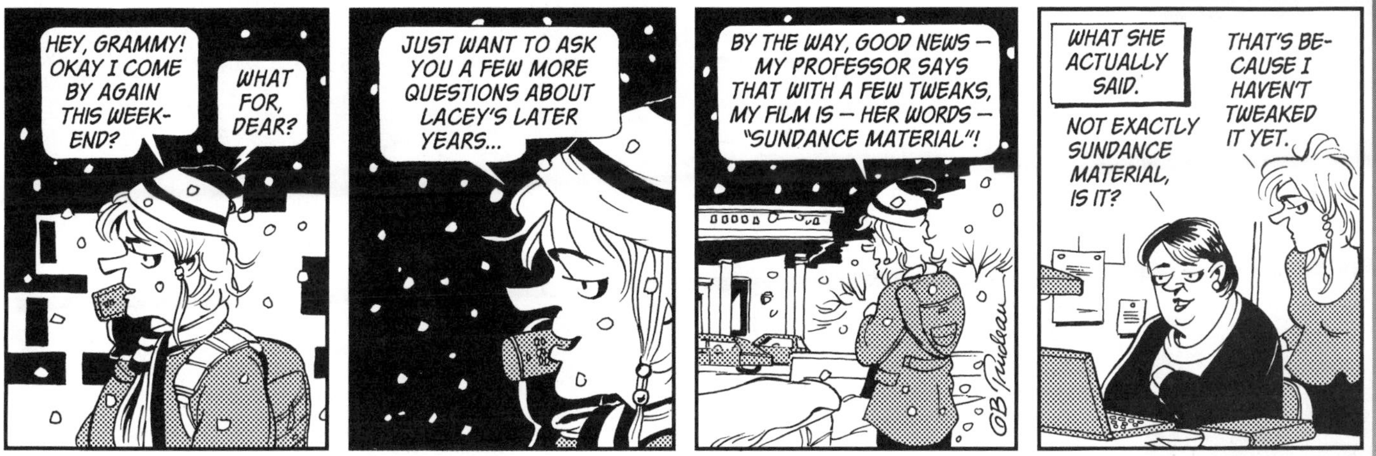
HEY, GRAMMY! OKAY I COME BY AGAIN THIS WEEK-END?
WHAT FOR, DEAR?
JUST WANT TO ASK YOU A FEW MORE QUESTIONS ABOUT LACEY'S LATER YEARS...
BY THE WAY, GOOD NEWS — MY PROFESSOR SAYS THAT WITH A FEW TWEAKS, MY FILM IS — HER WORDS — "SUNDANCE MATERIAL"!
WHAT SHE ACTUALLY SAID.
NOT EXACTLY SUNDANCE MATERIAL, IS IT?
THAT'S BE-CAUSE I HAVEN'T TWEAKED IT YET.

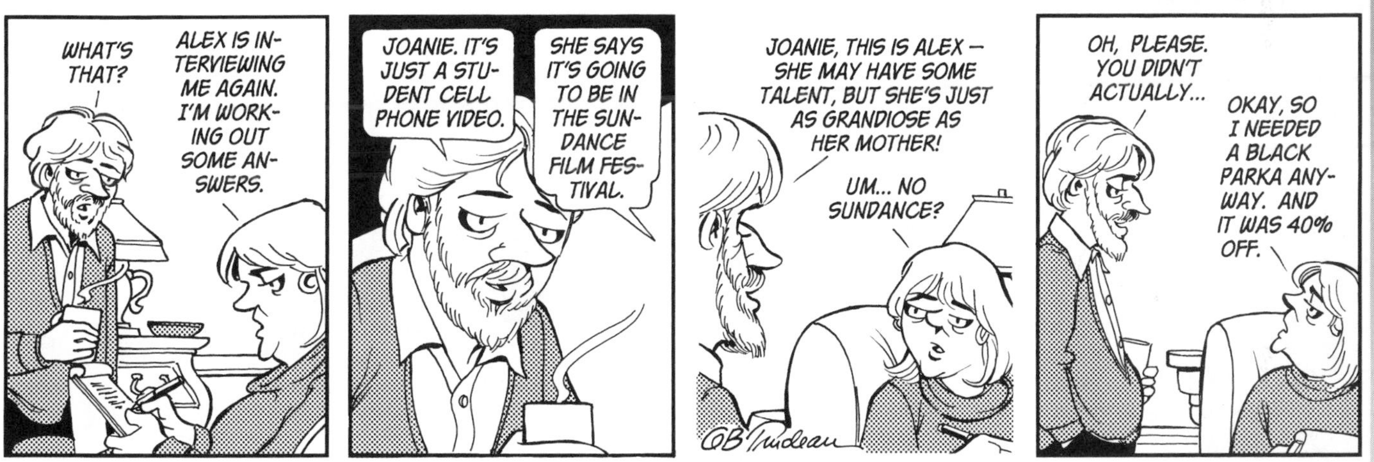
WHAT'S THAT?
ALEX IS IN-TERVIEWING ME AGAIN. I'M WORK-ING OUT SOME AN-SWERS.
JOANIE. IT'S JUST A STU-DENT CELL PHONE VIDEO.
SHE SAYS IT'S GOING TO BE IN THE SUN-DANCE FILM FES-TIVAL.
JOANIE, THIS IS ALEX — SHE MAY HAVE SOME TALENT, BUT SHE'S JUST AS GRANDIOSE AS HER MOTHER!
UM... NO SUNDANCE?
OH, PLEASE. YOU DIDN'T ACTUALLY...
OKAY, SO I NEEDED A BLACK PARKA ANY-WAY. AND IT WAS 40% OFF.

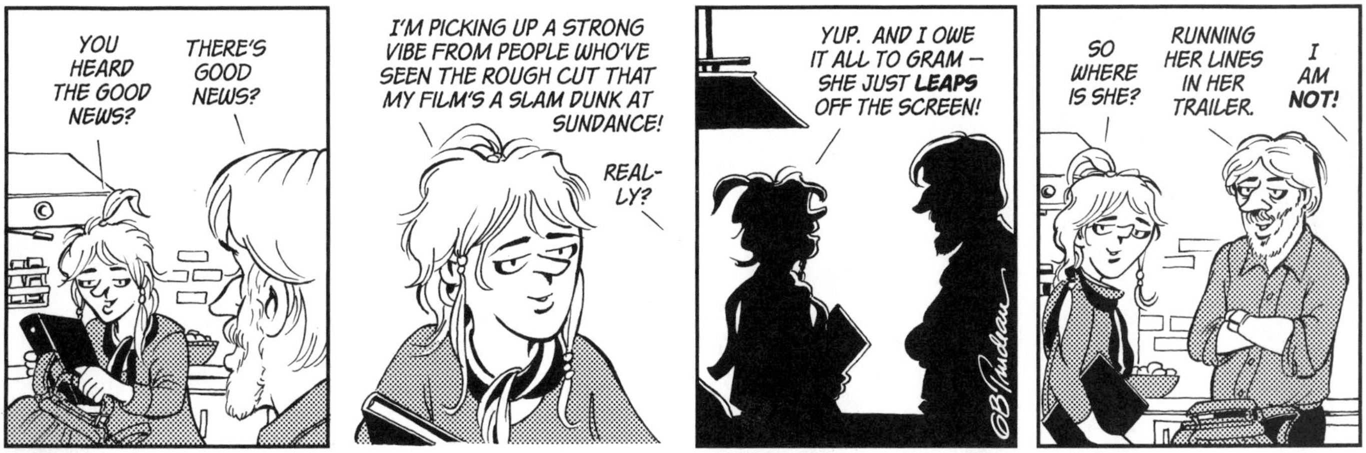
YOU HEARD THE GOOD NEWS?
THERE'S GOOD NEWS?
I'M PICKING UP A STRONG VIBE FROM PEOPLE WHO'VE SEEN THE ROUGH CUT THAT MY FILM'S A SLAM DUNK AT SUNDANCE!
REAL-LY?
YUP. AND I OWE IT ALL TO GRAM — SHE JUST LEAPS OFF THE SCREEN!
SO WHERE IS SHE?
RUNNING HER LINES IN HER TRAILER.
I AM NOT!

WHEN LACEY DEVELOPED ALZHEIMER'S AND HAD TO RETIRE, HER CARE FELL TO JEREMY CAVENDISH, AN OLD FAMILY FRIEND...

"IT WAS NOT AN IDEAL FIT..."

GOOD MORNING, MRS. D! RECOGNIZE ME TODAY? WHO AM I, MRS. D?

JUST TAKE THE STEREO AND SILVER AND LEAVE QUIETLY.

NO, NOT A BURGLAR. TRY TO CONCENTRATE.

OTHER DAYS SHE THOUGHT HE WAS MARIO THE PAPER BOY.

SO SHE HAD A VARIETY OF MEN IN HER LIFE!

AS LACEY'S DEMENTIA PROGRESSED, SHE BEFRIENDED ALICE, A HOMELESS WOMAN SHE THOUGHT WAS HER LONG-DEAD SISTER PEARL...

"THEY GOT TOGETHER FOR HOLIDAYS IN THE PARK."

HAPPY NEW YEAR, DUCKS!

AND TO YOU, TOO, PEARL! AND GOOD RIDDANCE, 1929!

1929?

I JUST HOPE MR. HOOVER KNOWS WHAT HE'S DOING.

WOW... SHE EXPERIENCED THE GREAT DEPRESSION **TWICE?**

IT'S A ROUGH DISEASE.

WHEN LACEY FINALLY DIED, SHE LEFT EVERYTHING TO HER "SISTER" PEARL. JEREMY FOUND THE WILL. HE WAS LIVID.

"I BEQUEATH EVERYTHING TO PEARL, IN GRATITUDE FOR THE PATIENCE, TENDERNESS AND COUNTLESS SMALL KINDNESSES MY SISTER HAS SHOWN ME IN MY DARKEST DAYS."

BUT SHE'S **NOT** HER SISTER!

NO, BUT ISN'T THAT WHAT YOU'D LIKE IN ONE?

THE JUDGE AGREED.

GET **OUT!** THAT IS **SO** MY NEXT MOVIE!

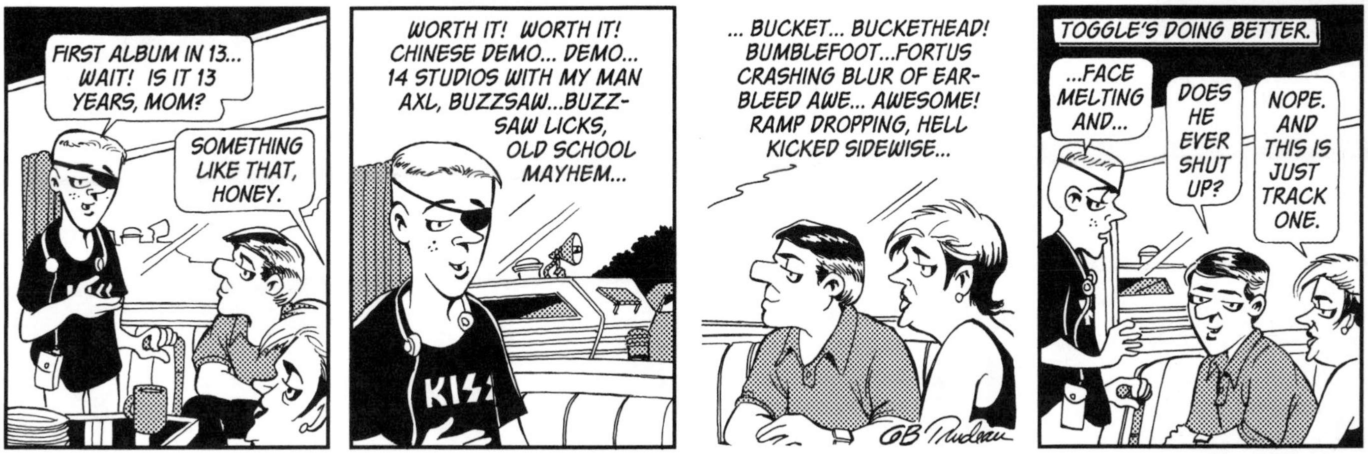
FIRST ALBUM IN 13... WAIT! IS IT 13 YEARS, MOM?
SOMETHING LIKE THAT, HONEY.
WORTH IT! WORTH IT! CHINESE DEMO... DEMO... 14 STUDIOS WITH MY MAN AXL, BUZZSAW...BUZZSAW LICKS, OLD SCHOOL MAYHEM...
KISS
... BUCKET... BUCKETHEAD! BUMBLEFOOT...FORTUS CRASHING BLUR OF EARBLEED AWE... AWESOME! RAMP DROPPING, HELL KICKED SIDEWISE...
TOGGLE'S DOING BETTER.
...FACE MELTING AND...
DOES HE EVER SHUT UP?
NOPE. AND THIS IS JUST TRACK ONE.

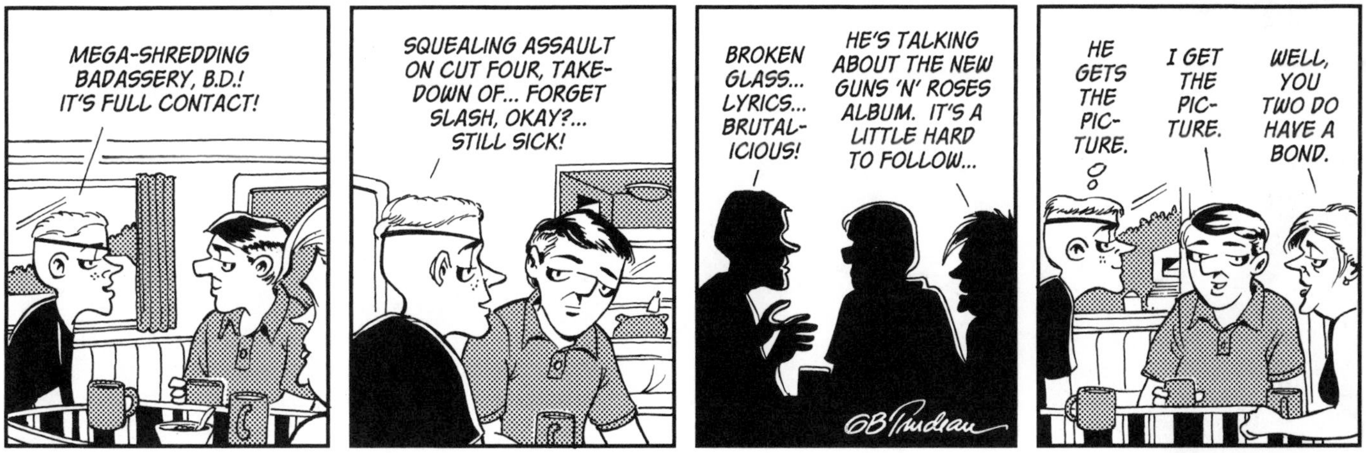
MEGA-SHREDDING BADASSERY, B.D.! IT'S FULL CONTACT!
SQUEALING ASSAULT ON CUT FOUR, TAKEDOWN OF... FORGET SLASH, OKAY?... STILL SICK!
BROKEN GLASS... LYRICS... BRUTALICIOUS!
HE'S TALKING ABOUT THE NEW GUNS 'N' ROSES ALBUM. IT'S A LITTLE HARD TO FOLLOW...
HE GETS THE PICTURE.
I GET THE PICTURE.
WELL, YOU TWO DO HAVE A BOND.

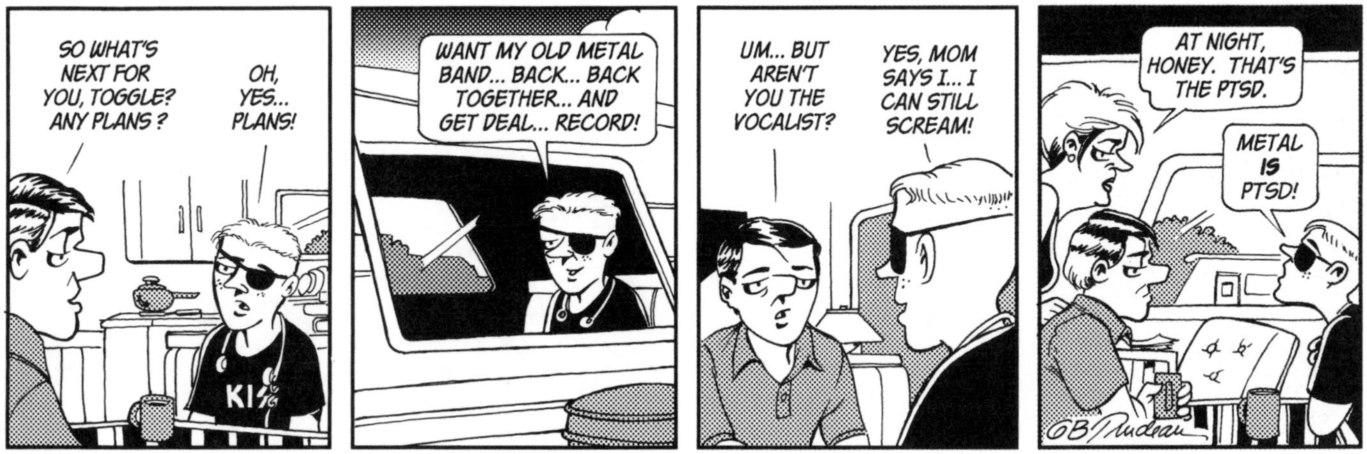
SO WHAT'S NEXT FOR YOU, TOGGLE? ANY PLANS ?
OH, YES... PLANS!
WANT MY OLD METAL BAND... BACK... BACK TOGETHER... AND GET DEAL... RECORD!
UM... BUT AREN'T YOU THE VOCALIST?
YES, MOM SAYS I... I CAN STILL SCREAM!
AT NIGHT, HONEY. THAT'S THE PTSD.
METAL IS PTSD!

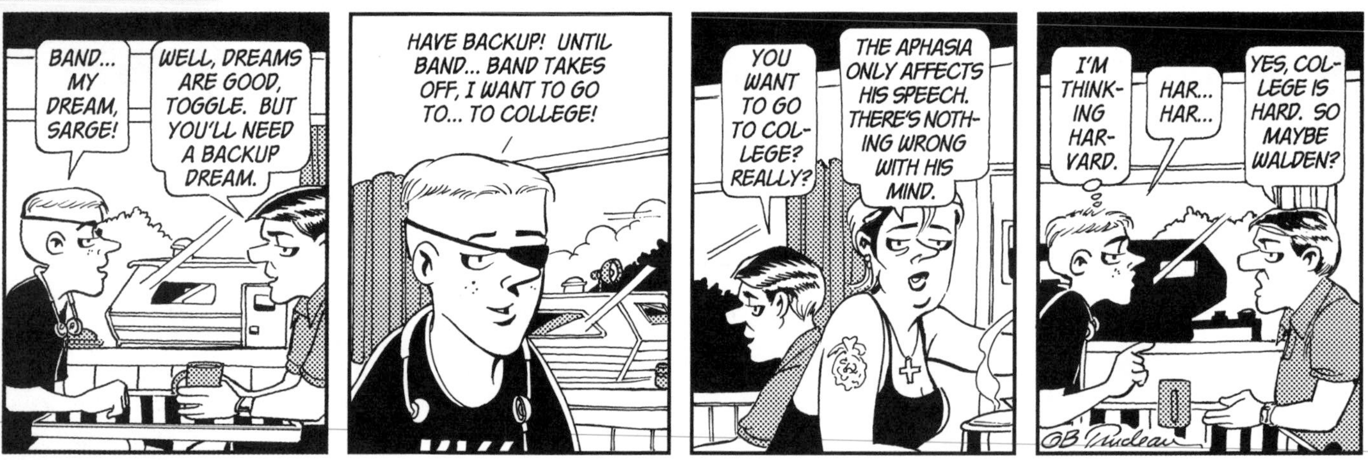
BAND... MY DREAM, SARGE!
WELL, DREAMS ARE GOOD, TOGGLE. BUT YOU'LL NEED A BACKUP DREAM.
HAVE BACKUP! UNTIL BAND... BAND TAKES OFF, I WANT TO GO TO... TO COLLEGE!
YOU WANT TO GO TO COLLEGE? REALLY?
THE APHASIA ONLY AFFECTS HIS SPEECH. THERE'S NOTHING WRONG WITH HIS MIND.
I'M THINKING HARVARD.
HAR... HAR...
YES, COLLEGE IS HARD. SO MAYBE WALDEN?

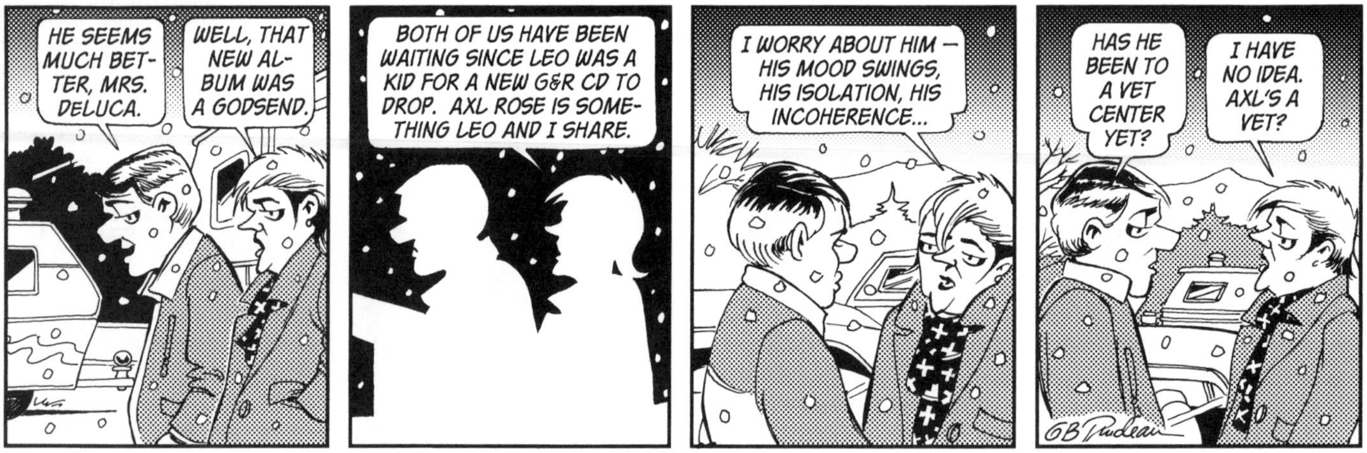
HE SEEMS MUCH BETTER, MRS. DELUCA.
WELL, THAT NEW ALBUM WAS A GODSEND.
BOTH OF US HAVE BEEN WAITING SINCE LEO WAS A KID FOR A NEW G&R CD TO DROP. AXL ROSE IS SOMETHING LEO AND I SHARE.
I WORRY ABOUT HIM — HIS MOOD SWINGS, HIS ISOLATION, HIS INCOHERENCE...
HAS HE BEEN TO A VET CENTER YET?
I HAVE NO IDEA. AXL'S A VET?

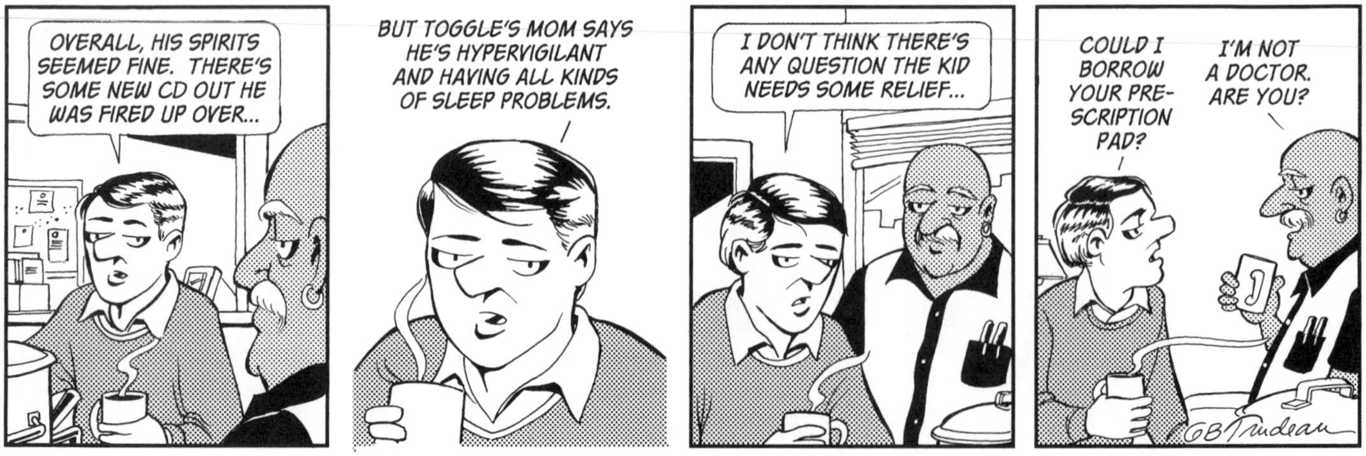
OVERALL, HIS SPIRITS SEEMED FINE. THERE'S SOME NEW CD OUT HE WAS FIRED UP OVER...
BUT TOGGLE'S MOM SAYS HE'S HYPERVIGILANT AND HAVING ALL KINDS OF SLEEP PROBLEMS.
I DON'T THINK THERE'S ANY QUESTION THE KID NEEDS SOME RELIEF...
COULD I BORROW YOUR PRESCRIPTION PAD?
I'M NOT A DOCTOR. ARE YOU?

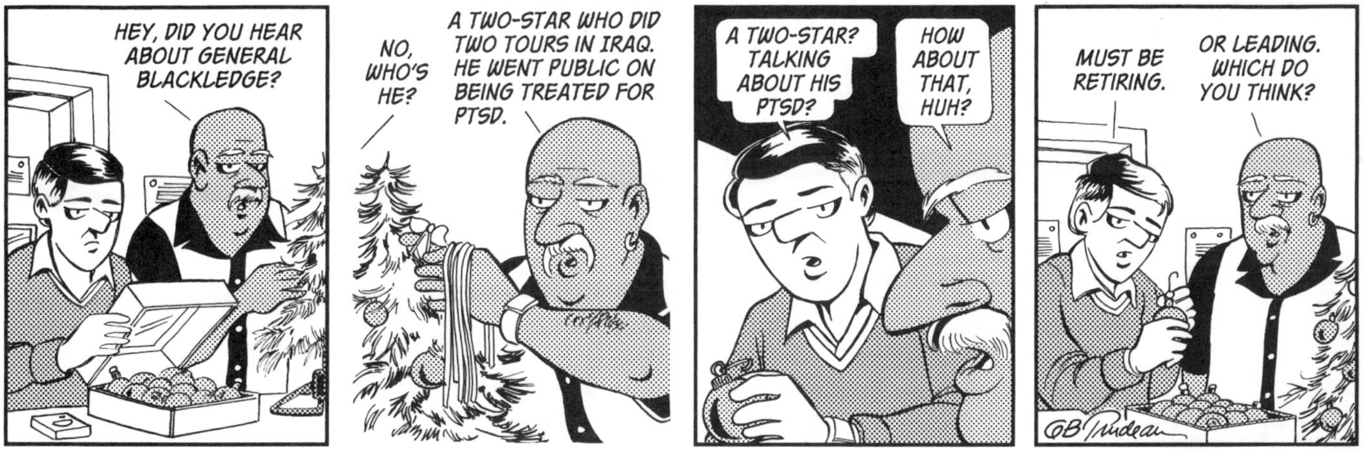
HEY, DID YOU HEAR ABOUT GENERAL BLACKLEDGE?
NO, WHO'S HE?
A TWO-STAR WHO DID TWO TOURS IN IRAQ. HE WENT PUBLIC ON BEING TREATED FOR PTSD.
A TWO-STAR? TALKING ABOUT HIS PTSD?
HOW ABOUT THAT, HUH?
MUST BE RETIRING.
OR LEADING. WHICH DO YOU THINK?
GB Trudeau

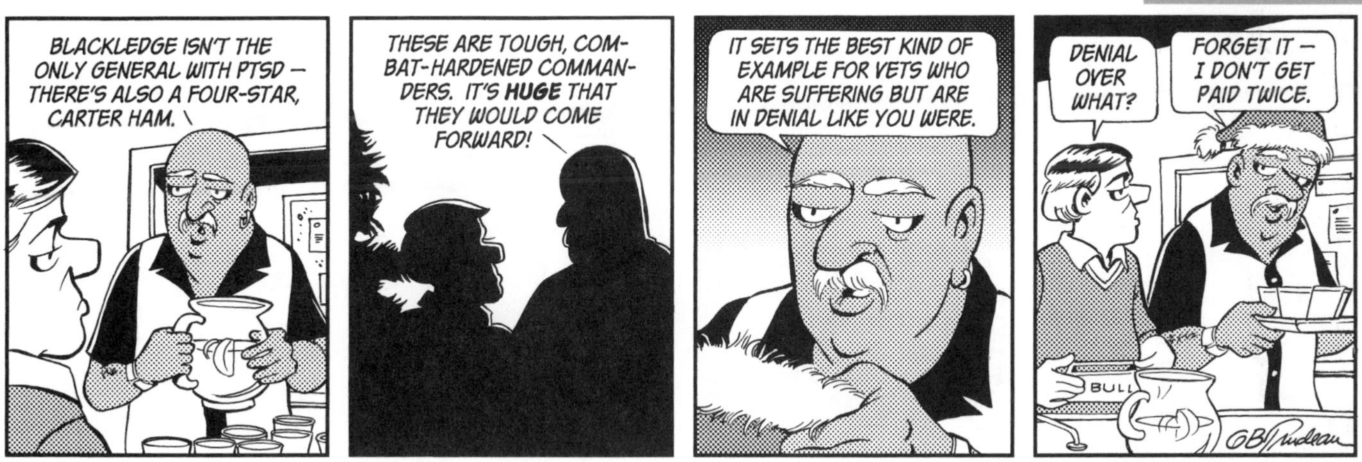
BLACKLEDGE ISN'T THE ONLY GENERAL WITH PTSD — THERE'S ALSO A FOUR-STAR, CARTER HAM.
THESE ARE TOUGH, COMBAT-HARDENED COMMANDERS. IT'S **HUGE** THAT THEY WOULD COME FORWARD!
IT SETS THE BEST KIND OF EXAMPLE FOR VETS WHO ARE SUFFERING BUT ARE IN DENIAL LIKE YOU WERE.
DENIAL OVER WHAT?
FORGET IT — I DON'T GET PAID TWICE.
BULL
GB Trudeau

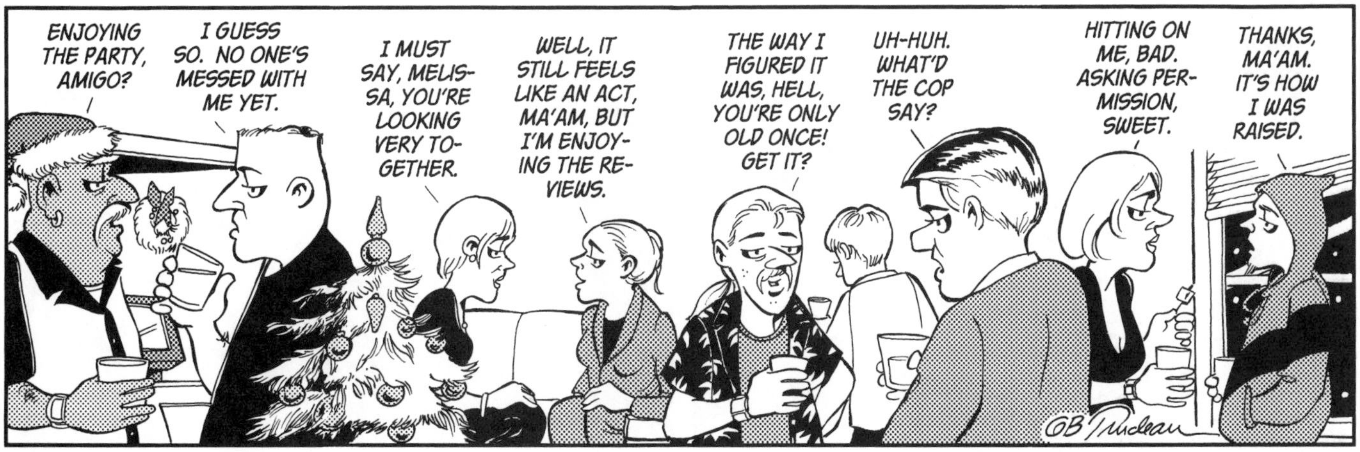
ENJOYING THE PARTY, AMIGO?
I GUESS SO. NO ONE'S MESSED WITH ME YET.
I MUST SAY, MELISSA, YOU'RE LOOKING VERY TOGETHER.
WELL, IT STILL FEELS LIKE AN ACT, MA'AM, BUT I'M ENJOYING THE REVIEWS.
THE WAY I FIGURED IT WAS, HELL, YOU'RE ONLY OLD ONCE! GET IT?
UH-HUH. WHAT'D THE COP SAY?
HITTING ON ME, BAD. ASKING PERMISSION, SWEET.
THANKS, MA'AM. IT'S HOW I WAS RAISED.
GB Trudeau

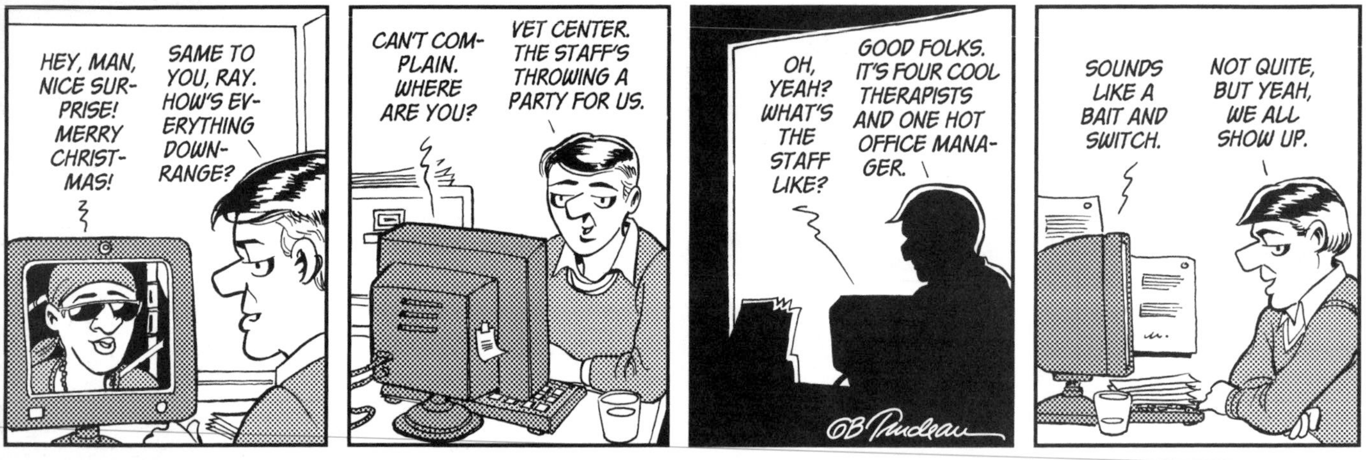
HEY, MAN, NICE SURPRISE! MERRY CHRISTMAS!
SAME TO YOU, RAY. HOW'S EVERYTHING DOWNRANGE?
CAN'T COMPLAIN. WHERE ARE YOU?
VET CENTER. THE STAFF'S THROWING A PARTY FOR US.
OH, YEAH? WHAT'S THE STAFF LIKE?
GOOD FOLKS. IT'S FOUR COOL THERAPISTS AND ONE HOT OFFICE MANAGER.
SOUNDS LIKE A BAIT AND SWITCH.
NOT QUITE, BUT YEAH, WE ALL SHOW UP.

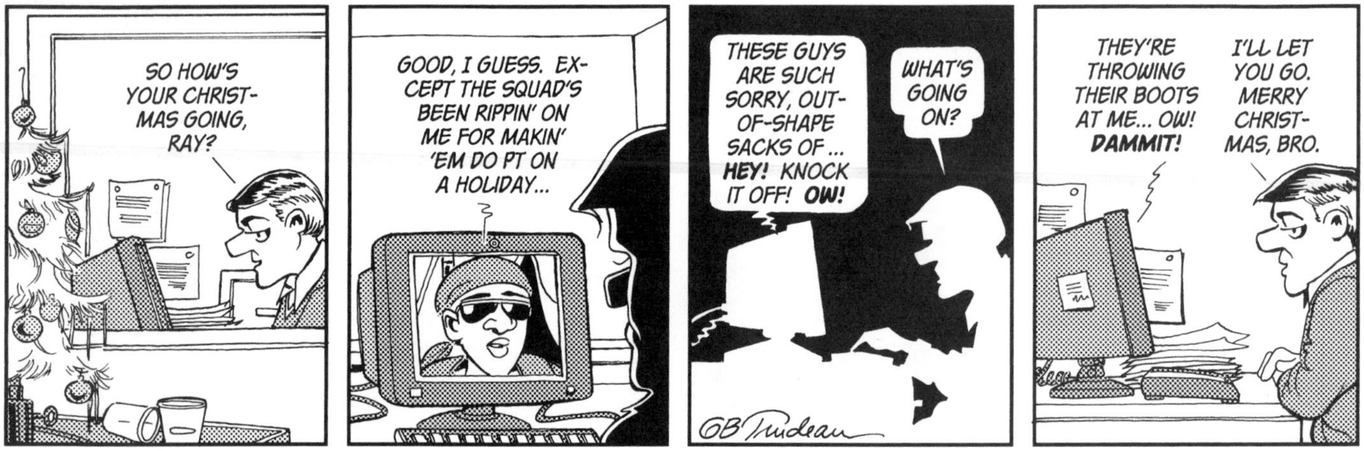
SO HOW'S YOUR CHRISTMAS GOING, RAY?
GOOD, I GUESS. EXCEPT THE SQUAD'S BEEN RIPPIN' ON ME FOR MAKIN' 'EM DO PT ON A HOLIDAY...
THESE GUYS ARE SUCH SORRY, OUT-OF-SHAPE SACKS OF ... **HEY!** KNOCK IT OFF! **OW!**
WHAT'S GOING ON?
THEY'RE THROWING THEIR BOOTS AT ME... OW! **DAMMIT!**
I'LL LET YOU GO. MERRY CHRISTMAS, BRO.

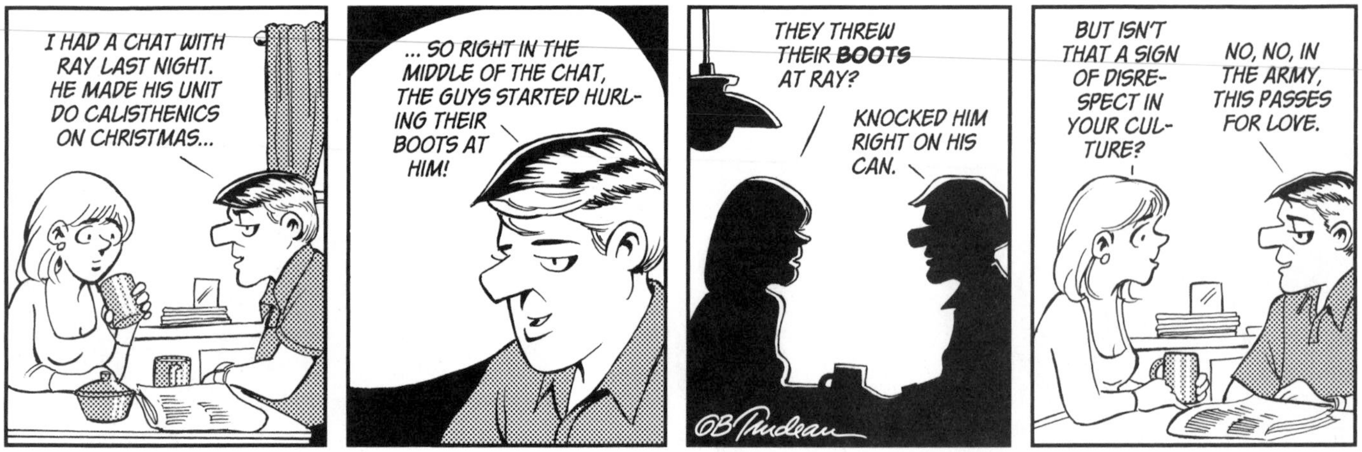
I HAD A CHAT WITH RAY LAST NIGHT. HE MADE HIS UNIT DO CALISTHENICS ON CHRISTMAS...
... SO RIGHT IN THE MIDDLE OF THE CHAT, THE GUYS STARTED HURLING THEIR BOOTS AT HIM!
THEY THREW THEIR **BOOTS** AT RAY?
KNOCKED HIM RIGHT ON HIS CAN.
BUT ISN'T THAT A SIGN OF DISRESPECT IN YOUR CULTURE?
NO, NO, IN THE ARMY, THIS PASSES FOR LOVE.

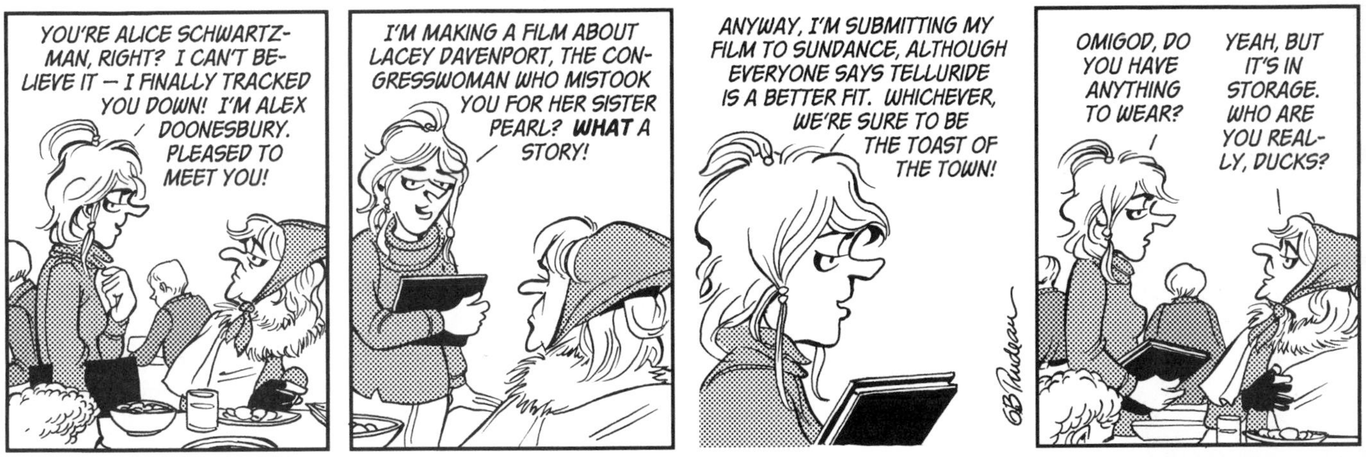
YOU'RE ALICE SCHWARTZMAN, RIGHT? I CAN'T BELIEVE IT — I FINALLY TRACKED YOU DOWN! I'M ALEX DOONESBURY. PLEASED TO MEET YOU!
I'M MAKING A FILM ABOUT LACEY DAVENPORT, THE CONGRESSWOMAN WHO MISTOOK YOU FOR HER SISTER PEARL? WHAT A STORY!
ANYWAY, I'M SUBMITTING MY FILM TO SUNDANCE, ALTHOUGH EVERYONE SAYS TELLURIDE IS A BETTER FIT. WHICHEVER, WE'RE SURE TO BE THE TOAST OF THE TOWN!
OMIGOD, DO YOU HAVE ANYTHING TO WEAR?
YEAH, BUT IT'S IN STORAGE. WHO ARE YOU REALLY, DUCKS?

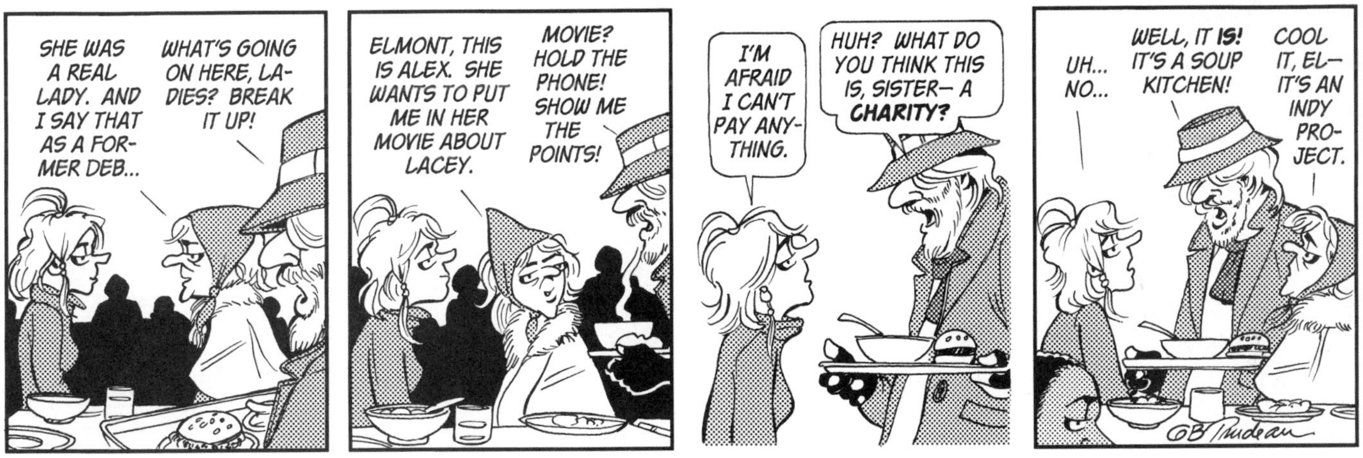
SHE WAS A REAL LADY. AND I SAY THAT AS A FORMER DEB...
WHAT'S GOING ON HERE, LADIES? BREAK IT UP!
ELMONT, THIS IS ALEX. SHE WANTS TO PUT ME IN HER MOVIE ABOUT LACEY.
MOVIE? HOLD THE PHONE! SHOW ME THE POINTS!
I'M AFRAID I CAN'T PAY ANYTHING.
HUH? WHAT DO YOU THINK THIS IS, SISTER— A CHARITY?
UH... NO...
WELL, IT IS! IT'S A SOUP KITCHEN!
COOL IT, EL— IT'S AN INDY PROJECT.

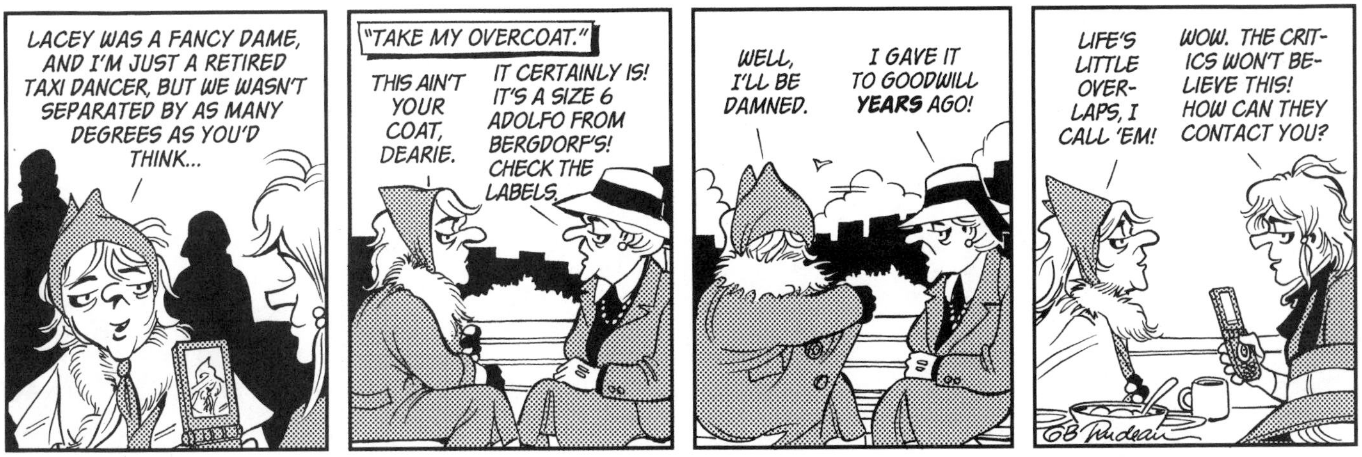
LACEY WAS A FANCY DAME, AND I'M JUST A RETIRED TAXI DANCER, BUT WE WASN'T SEPARATED BY AS MANY DEGREES AS YOU'D THINK...
"TAKE MY OVERCOAT."
THIS AIN'T YOUR COAT, DEARIE.
IT CERTAINLY IS! IT'S A SIZE 6 ADOLFO FROM BERGDORF'S! CHECK THE LABELS.
WELL, I'LL BE DAMNED.
I GAVE IT TO GOODWILL YEARS AGO!
LIFE'S LITTLE OVERLAPS, I CALL 'EM!
WOW. THE CRITICS WON'T BELIEVE THIS! HOW CAN THEY CONTACT YOU?

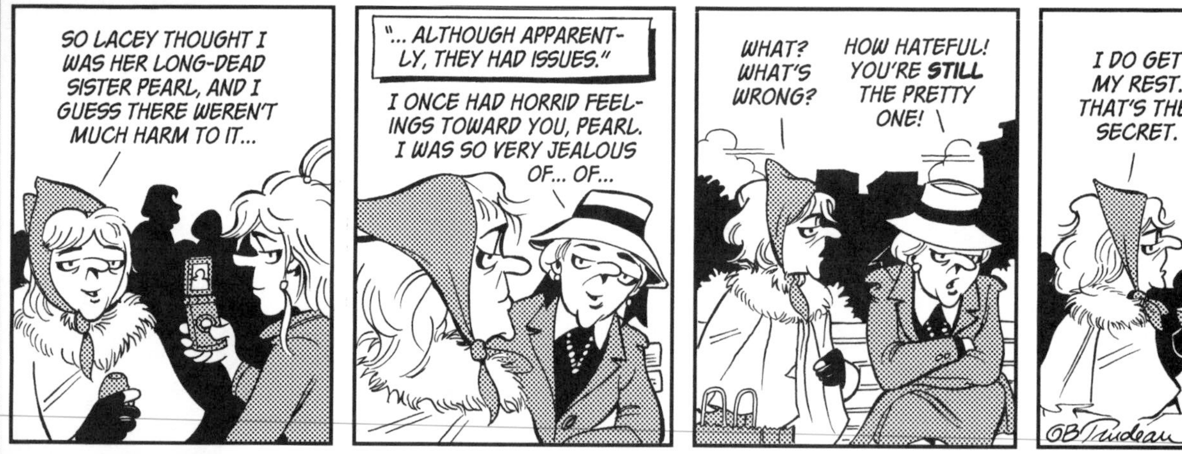
SO LACEY THOUGHT I WAS HER LONG-DEAD SISTER PEARL, AND I GUESS THERE WEREN'T MUCH HARM TO IT...
"... ALTHOUGH APPARENTLY, THEY HAD ISSUES."
I ONCE HAD HORRID FEELINGS TOWARD YOU, PEARL. I WAS SO VERY JEALOUS OF... OF...
WHAT? WHAT'S WRONG?
HOW HATEFUL! YOU'RE **STILL** THE PRETTY ONE!
I DO GET MY REST. THAT'S THE SECRET.
DID YOU SHARE THAT WITH HER?

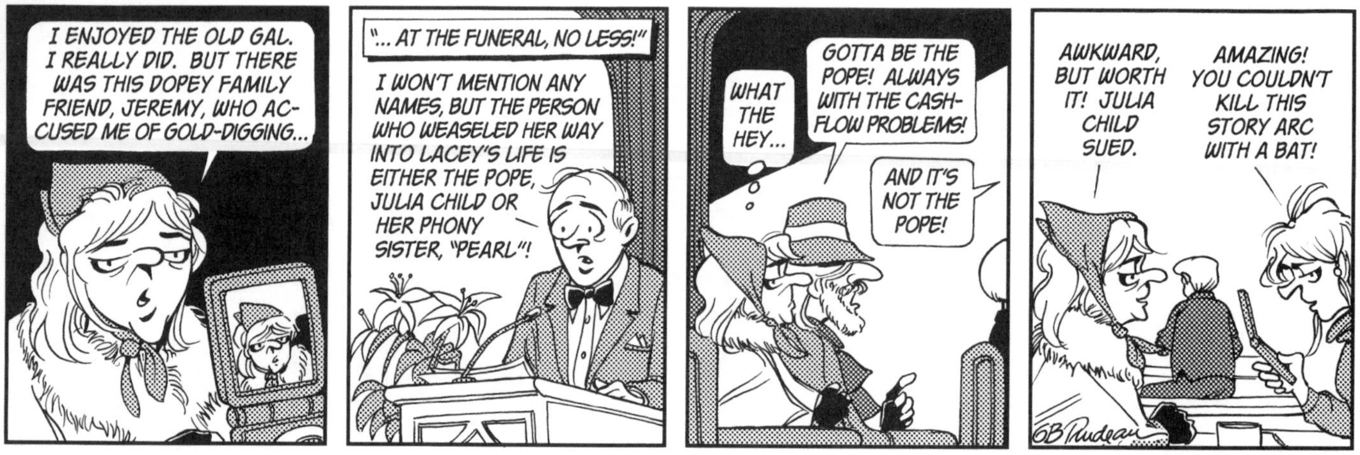
I ENJOYED THE OLD GAL. I REALLY DID. BUT THERE WAS THIS DOPEY FAMILY FRIEND, JEREMY, WHO ACCUSED ME OF GOLD-DIGGING...
"... AT THE FUNERAL, NO LESS!"
I WON'T MENTION ANY NAMES, BUT THE PERSON WHO WEASELED HER WAY INTO LACEY'S LIFE IS EITHER THE POPE, JULIA CHILD OR HER PHONY SISTER, "PEARL"!
WHAT THE HEY...
GOTTA BE THE POPE! ALWAYS WITH THE CASH-FLOW PROBLEMS!
AND IT'S NOT THE POPE!
AWKWARD, BUT WORTH IT! JULIA CHILD SUED.
AMAZING! YOU COULDN'T KILL THIS STORY ARC WITH A BAT!

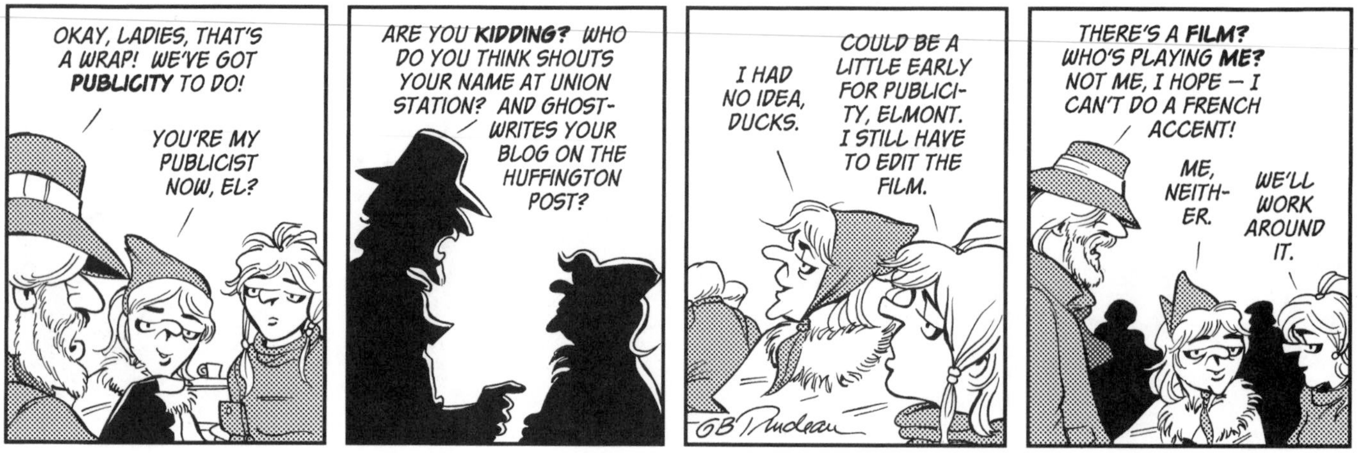
OKAY, LADIES, THAT'S A WRAP! WE'VE GOT **PUBLICITY** TO DO!
YOU'RE MY PUBLICIST NOW, EL?
ARE YOU **KIDDING?** WHO DO YOU THINK SHOUTS YOUR NAME AT UNION STATION? AND GHOST-WRITES YOUR BLOG ON THE HUFFINGTON POST?
I HAD NO IDEA, DUCKS.
COULD BE A LITTLE EARLY FOR PUBLICITY, ELMONT. I STILL HAVE TO EDIT THE FILM.
THERE'S A **FILM?** WHO'S PLAYING **ME?** NOT ME, I HOPE — I CAN'T DO A FRENCH ACCENT!
ME, NEITHER.
WE'LL WORK AROUND IT.

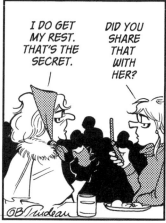

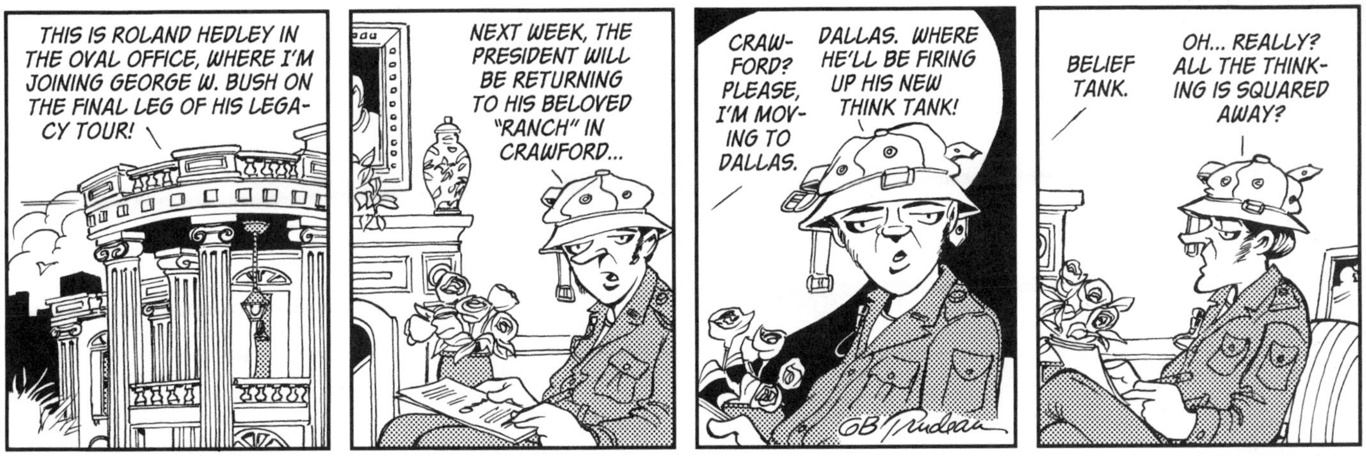
THIS IS ROLAND HEDLEY IN THE OVAL OFFICE, WHERE I'M JOINING GEORGE W. BUSH ON THE FINAL LEG OF HIS LEGACY TOUR!
NEXT WEEK, THE PRESIDENT WILL BE RETURNING TO HIS BELOVED "RANCH" IN CRAWFORD...
CRAWFORD? PLEASE, I'M MOVING TO DALLAS.
DALLAS. WHERE HE'LL BE FIRING UP HIS NEW THINK TANK!
GB Trudeau
BELIEF TANK.
OH... REALLY? ALL THE THINKING IS SQUARED AWAY?

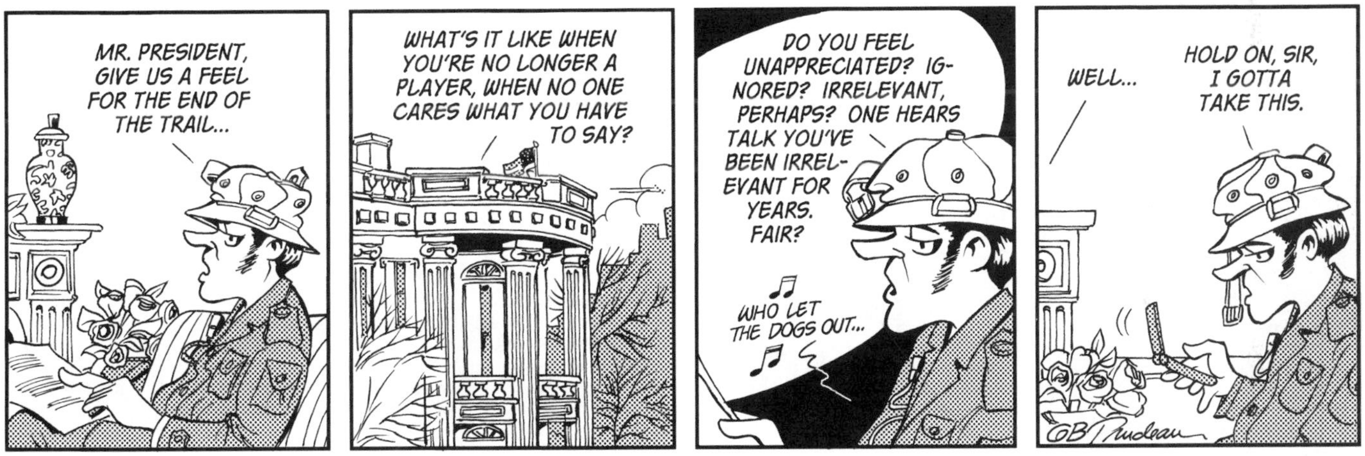
MR. PRESIDENT, GIVE US A FEEL FOR THE END OF THE TRAIL...
WHAT'S IT LIKE WHEN YOU'RE NO LONGER A PLAYER, WHEN NO ONE CARES WHAT YOU HAVE TO SAY?
DO YOU FEEL UNAPPRECIATED? IGNORED? IRRELEVANT, PERHAPS? ONE HEARS TALK YOU'VE BEEN IRRELEVANT FOR YEARS. FAIR?
WHO LET THE DOGS OUT...
WELL...
HOLD ON, SIR, I GOTTA TAKE THIS.
GB Trudeau

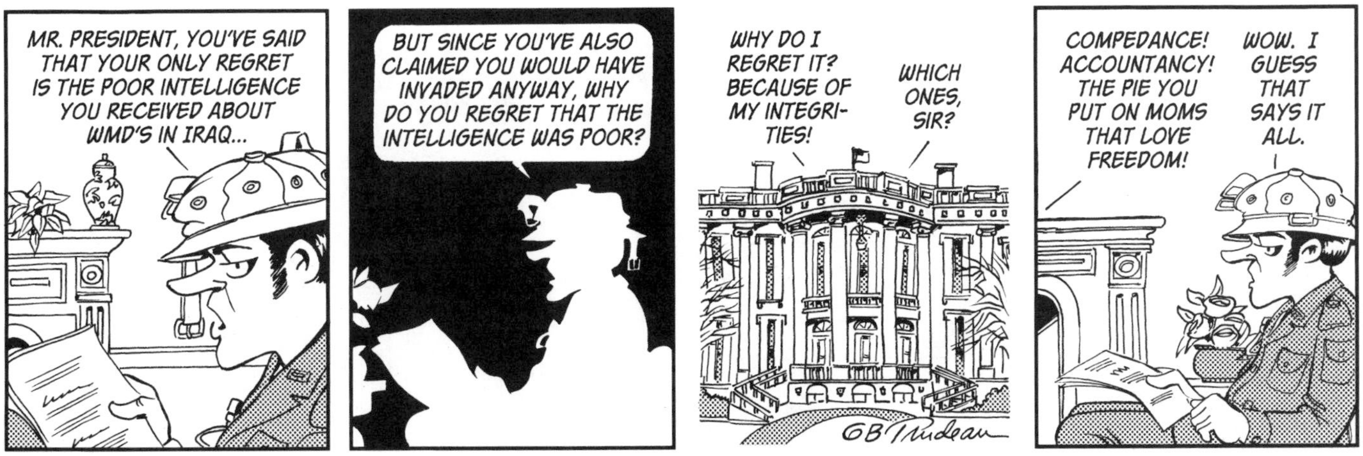
MR. PRESIDENT, YOU'VE SAID THAT YOUR ONLY REGRET IS THE POOR INTELLIGENCE YOU RECEIVED ABOUT WMD'S IN IRAQ...
BUT SINCE YOU'VE ALSO CLAIMED YOU WOULD HAVE INVADED ANYWAY, WHY DO YOU REGRET THAT THE INTELLIGENCE WAS POOR?
WHY DO I REGRET IT? BECAUSE OF MY INTEGRITIES!
WHICH ONES, SIR?
GB Trudeau
COMPEDANCE! ACCOUNTANCY! THE PIE YOU PUT ON MOMS THAT LOVE FREEDOM!
WOW. I GUESS THAT SAYS IT ALL.

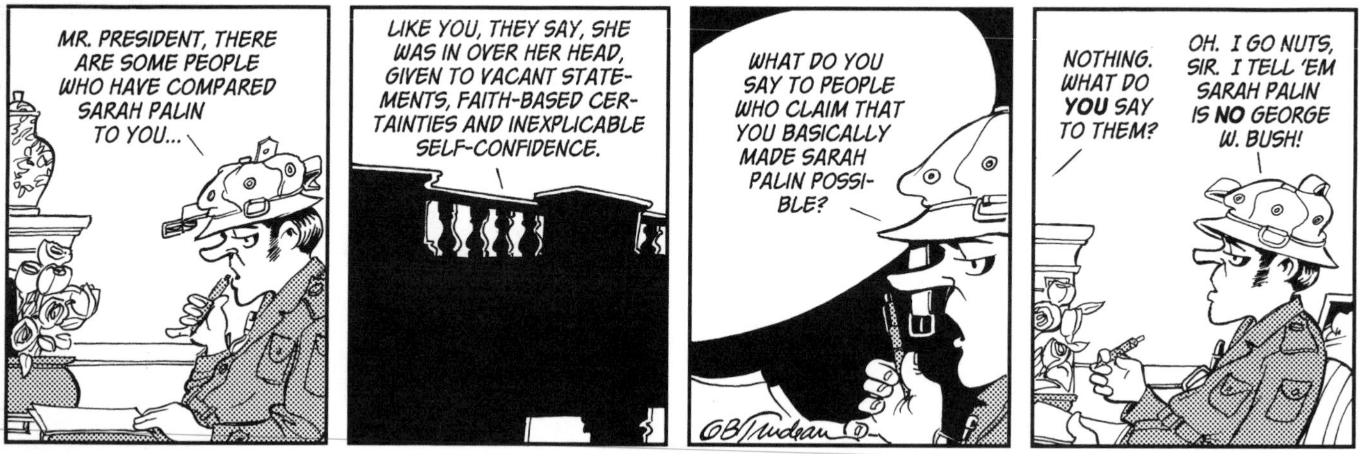
MR. PRESIDENT, THERE ARE SOME PEOPLE WHO HAVE COMPARED SARAH PALIN TO YOU...
LIKE YOU, THEY SAY, SHE WAS IN OVER HER HEAD, GIVEN TO VACANT STATEMENTS, FAITH-BASED CERTAINTIES AND INEXPLICABLE SELF-CONFIDENCE.
WHAT DO YOU SAY TO PEOPLE WHO CLAIM THAT YOU BASICALLY MADE SARAH PALIN POSSIBLE?
NOTHING. WHAT DO **YOU** SAY TO THEM?
OH. I GO NUTS, SIR. I TELL 'EM SARAH PALIN IS **NO** GEORGE W. BUSH!

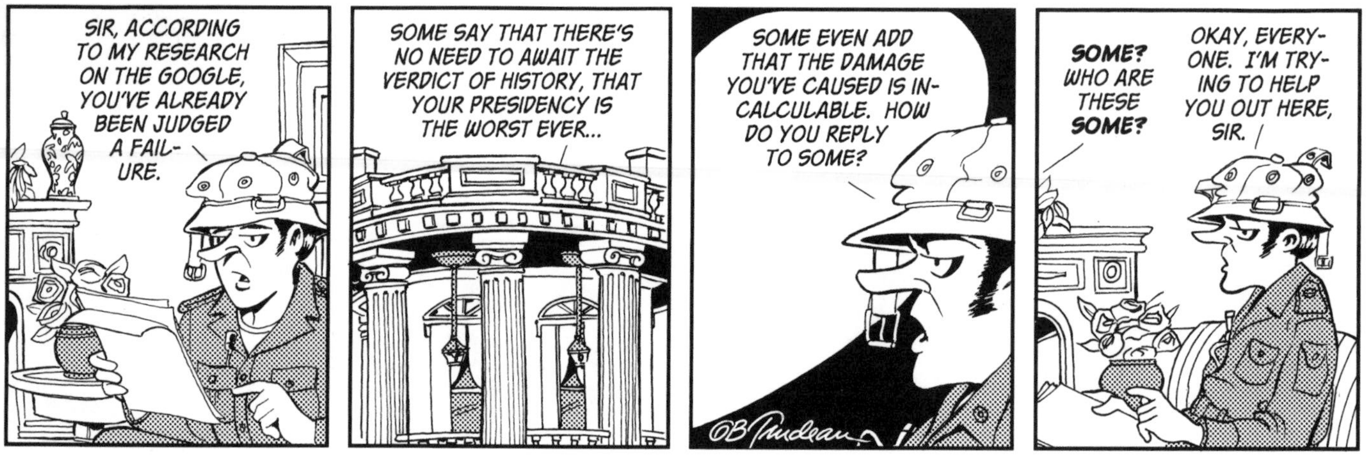
SIR, ACCORDING TO MY RESEARCH ON THE GOOGLE, YOU'VE ALREADY BEEN JUDGED A FAILURE.
SOME SAY THAT THERE'S NO NEED TO AWAIT THE VERDICT OF HISTORY, THAT YOUR PRESIDENCY IS THE WORST EVER...
SOME EVEN ADD THAT THE DAMAGE YOU'VE CAUSED IS INCALCULABLE. HOW DO YOU REPLY TO SOME?
SOME? WHO ARE THESE **SOME?**
OKAY, EVERYONE. I'M TRYING TO HELP YOU OUT HERE, SIR.

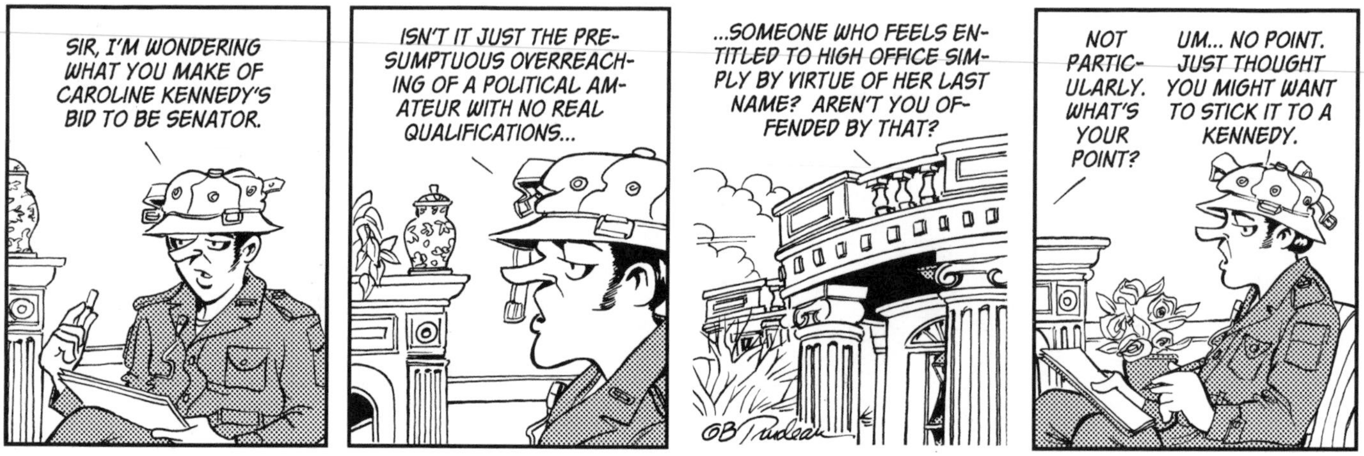
SIR, I'M WONDERING WHAT YOU MAKE OF CAROLINE KENNEDY'S BID TO BE SENATOR.
ISN'T IT JUST THE PRESUMPTUOUS OVERREACHING OF A POLITICAL AMATEUR WITH NO REAL QUALIFICATIONS...
...SOMEONE WHO FEELS ENTITLED TO HIGH OFFICE SIMPLY BY VIRTUE OF HER LAST NAME? AREN'T YOU OFFENDED BY THAT?
NOT PARTICULARLY. WHAT'S YOUR POINT?
UM... NO POINT. JUST THOUGHT YOU MIGHT WANT TO STICK IT TO A KENNEDY.

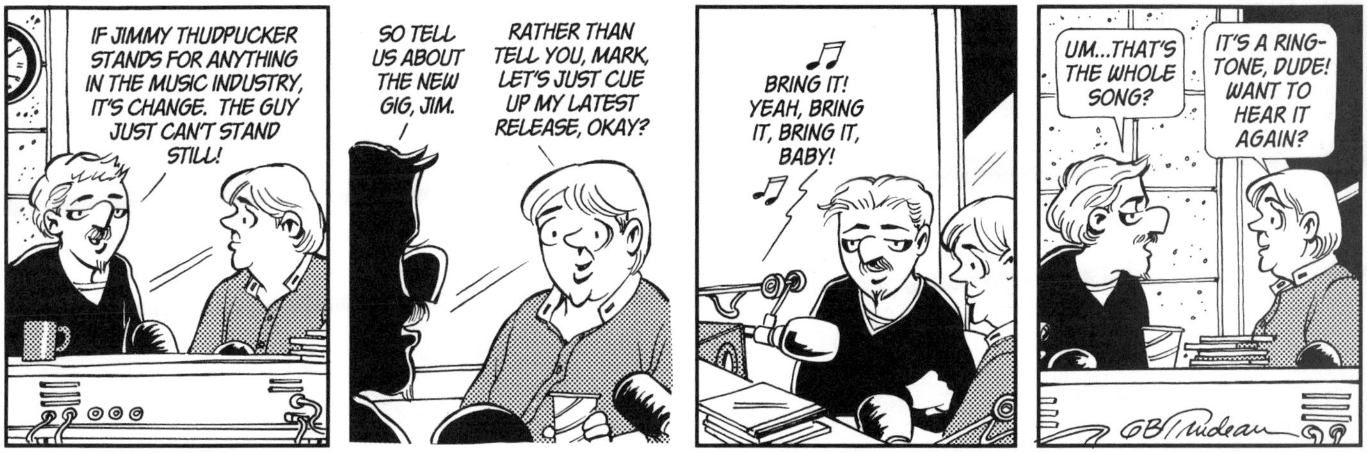
IF JIMMY THUDPUCKER STANDS FOR ANYTHING IN THE MUSIC INDUSTRY, IT'S CHANGE. THE GUY JUST CAN'T STAND STILL!
SO TELL US ABOUT THE NEW GIG, JIM.
RATHER THAN TELL YOU, MARK, LET'S JUST CUE UP MY LATEST RELEASE, OKAY?
BRING IT! YEAH, BRING IT, BRING IT, BABY!
UM...THAT'S THE WHOLE SONG?
IT'S A RING-TONE, DUDE! WANT TO HEAR IT AGAIN?
GB Trudeau

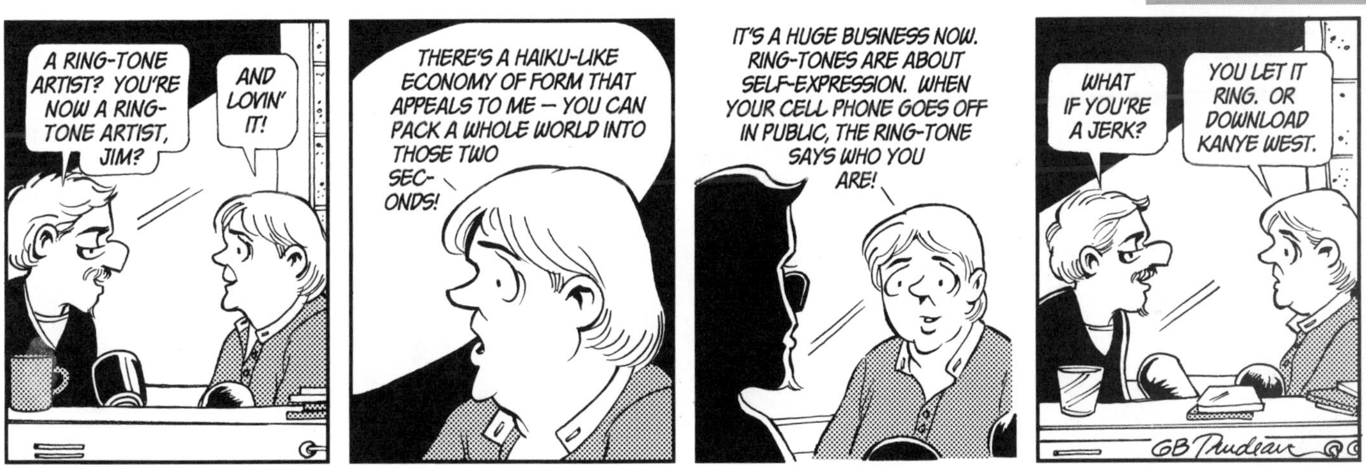
A RING-TONE ARTIST? YOU'RE NOW A RING-TONE ARTIST, JIM?
AND LOVIN' IT!
THERE'S A HAIKU-LIKE ECONOMY OF FORM THAT APPEALS TO ME — YOU CAN PACK A WHOLE WORLD INTO THOSE TWO SECONDS!
IT'S A HUGE BUSINESS NOW. RING-TONES ARE ABOUT SELF-EXPRESSION. WHEN YOUR CELL PHONE GOES OFF IN PUBLIC, THE RING-TONE SAYS WHO YOU ARE!
WHAT IF YOU'RE A JERK?
YOU LET IT RING. OR DOWNLOAD KANYE WEST.
GB Trudeau

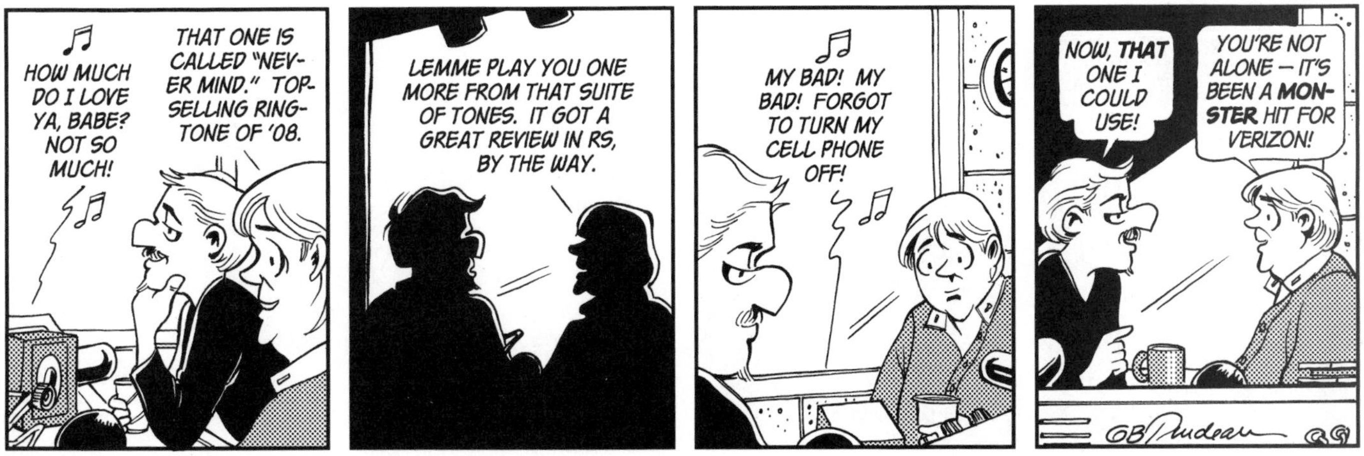
HOW MUCH DO I LOVE YA, BABE? NOT SO MUCH!
THAT ONE IS CALLED "NEVER MIND." TOP-SELLING RING-TONE OF '08.
LEMME PLAY YOU ONE MORE FROM THAT SUITE OF TONES. IT GOT A GREAT REVIEW IN RS, BY THE WAY.
MY BAD! MY BAD! FORGOT TO TURN MY CELL PHONE OFF!
NOW, **THAT** ONE I COULD USE!
YOU'RE NOT ALONE — IT'S BEEN A **MONSTER** HIT FOR VERIZON!
GB Trudeau

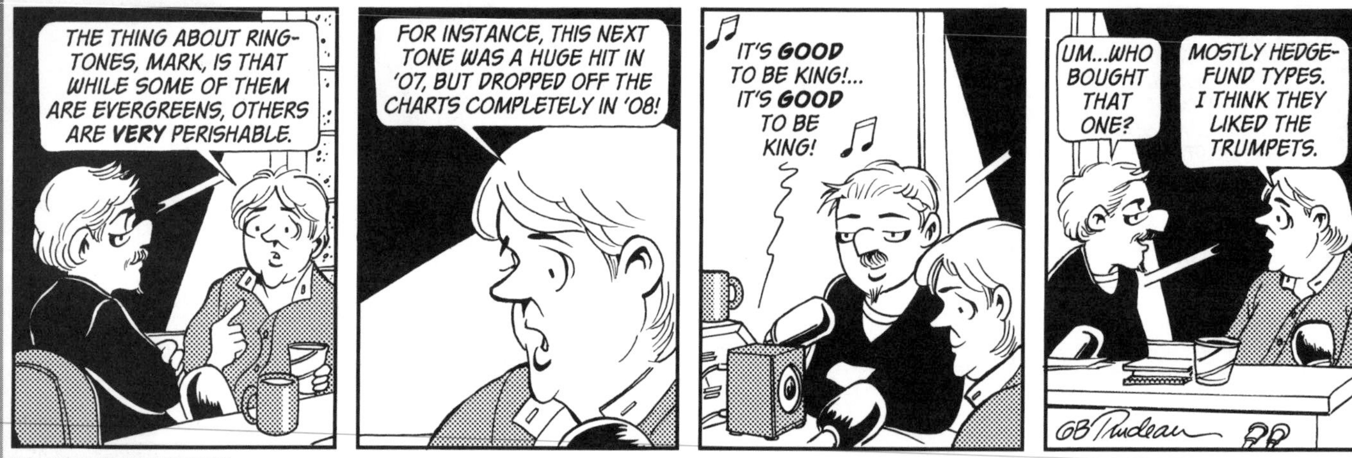
THE THING ABOUT RING-TONES, MARK, IS THAT WHILE SOME OF THEM ARE EVERGREENS, OTHERS ARE **VERY** PERISHABLE.
FOR INSTANCE, THIS NEXT TONE WAS A HUGE HIT IN '07, BUT DROPPED OFF THE CHARTS COMPLETELY IN '08!
IT'S **GOOD** TO BE KING!... IT'S **GOOD** TO BE KING!
UM...WHO BOUGHT THAT ONE?
MOSTLY HEDGE-FUND TYPES. I THINK THEY LIKED THE TRUMPETS.
GB Trudeau

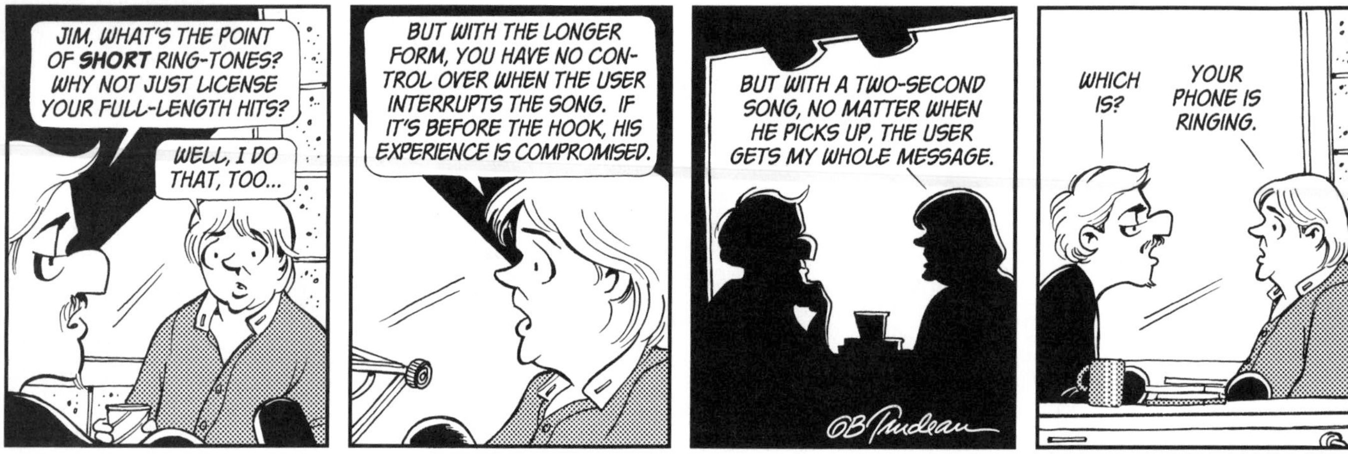
JIM, WHAT'S THE POINT OF **SHORT** RING-TONES? WHY NOT JUST LICENSE YOUR FULL-LENGTH HITS?
WELL, I DO THAT, TOO...
BUT WITH THE LONGER FORM, YOU HAVE NO CONTROL OVER WHEN THE USER INTERRUPTS THE SONG. IF IT'S BEFORE THE HOOK, HIS EXPERIENCE IS COMPROMISED.
BUT WITH A TWO-SECOND SONG, NO MATTER WHEN HE PICKS UP, THE USER GETS MY WHOLE MESSAGE.
GB Trudeau
WHICH IS?
YOUR PHONE IS RINGING.

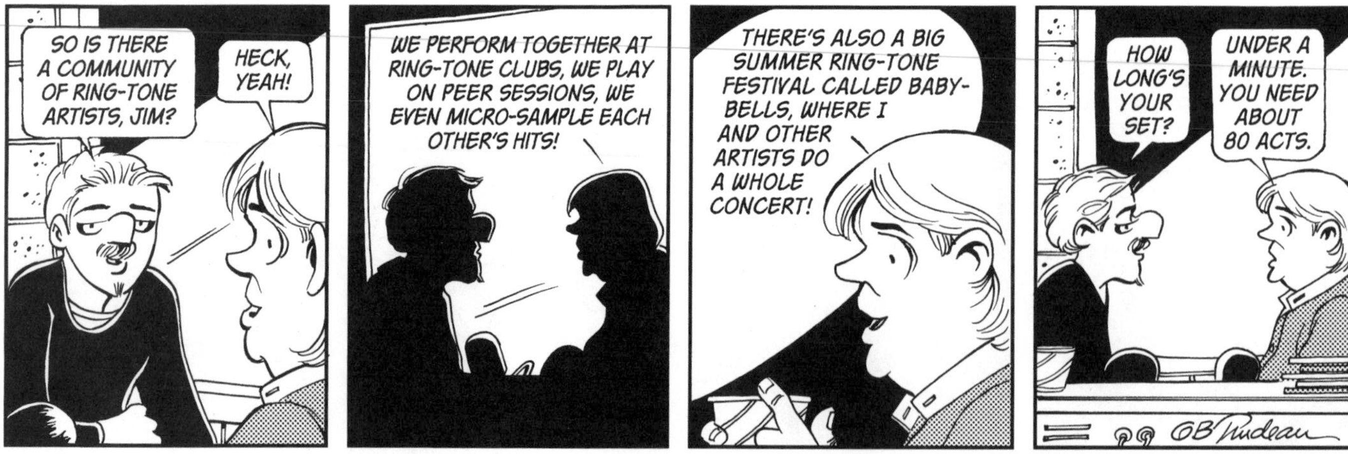
SO IS THERE A COMMUNITY OF RING-TONE ARTISTS, JIM?
HECK, YEAH!
WE PERFORM TOGETHER AT RING-TONE CLUBS, WE PLAY ON PEER SESSIONS, WE EVEN MICRO-SAMPLE EACH OTHER'S HITS!
THERE'S ALSO A BIG SUMMER RING-TONE FESTIVAL CALLED BABY-BELLS, WHERE I AND OTHER ARTISTS DO A WHOLE CONCERT!
HOW LONG'S YOUR SET?
UNDER A MINUTE. YOU NEED ABOUT 80 ACTS.
GB Trudeau

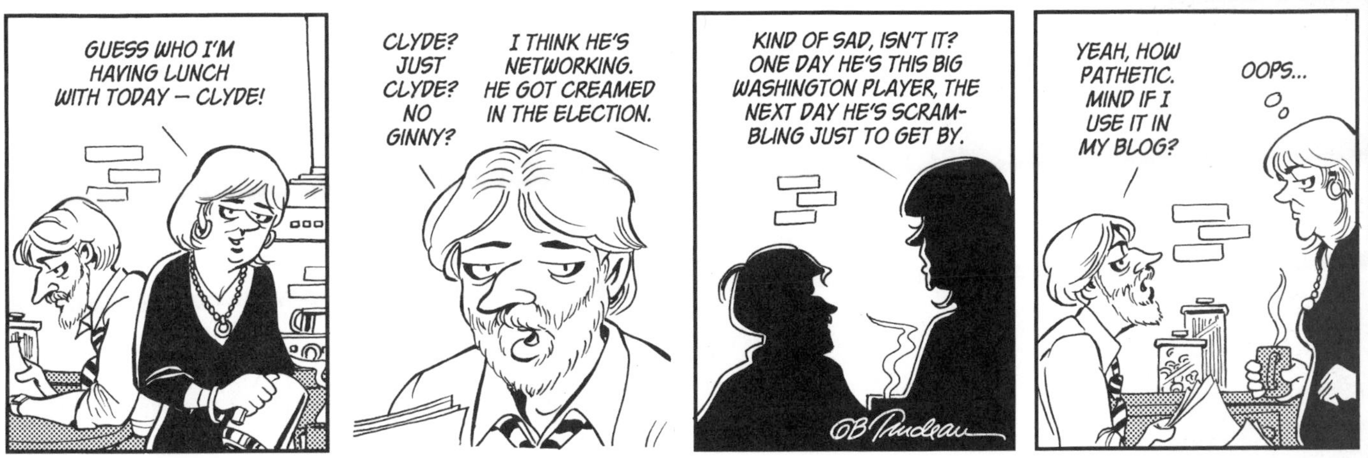
GUESS WHO I'M HAVING LUNCH WITH TODAY — CLYDE!
CLYDE? JUST CLYDE? NO GINNY?
I THINK HE'S NETWORKING. HE GOT CREAMED IN THE ELECTION.
KIND OF SAD, ISN'T IT? ONE DAY HE'S THIS BIG WASHINGTON PLAYER, THE NEXT DAY HE'S SCRAMBLING JUST TO GET BY.
GB Trudeau
YEAH, HOW PATHETIC. MIND IF I USE IT IN MY BLOG?
OOPS...

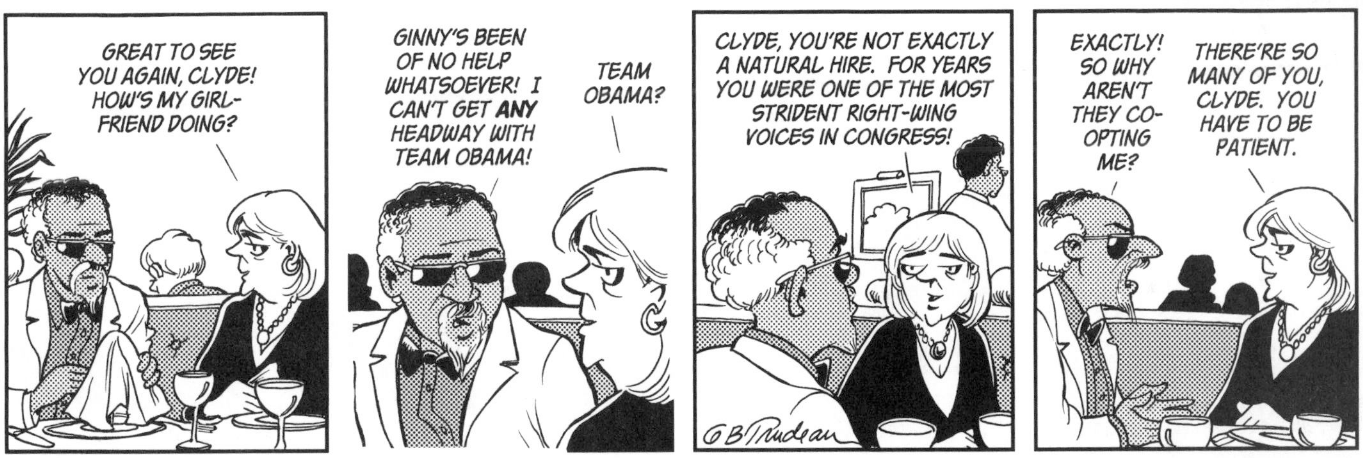
GREAT TO SEE YOU AGAIN, CLYDE! HOW'S MY GIRLFRIEND DOING?
GINNY'S BEEN OF NO HELP WHATSOEVER! I CAN'T GET **ANY** HEADWAY WITH TEAM OBAMA!
TEAM OBAMA?
CLYDE, YOU'RE NOT EXACTLY A NATURAL HIRE. FOR YEARS YOU WERE ONE OF THE MOST STRIDENT RIGHT-WING VOICES IN CONGRESS!
GB Trudeau
EXACTLY! SO WHY AREN'T THEY CO-OPTING ME?
THERE'RE SO MANY OF YOU, CLYDE. YOU HAVE TO BE PATIENT.

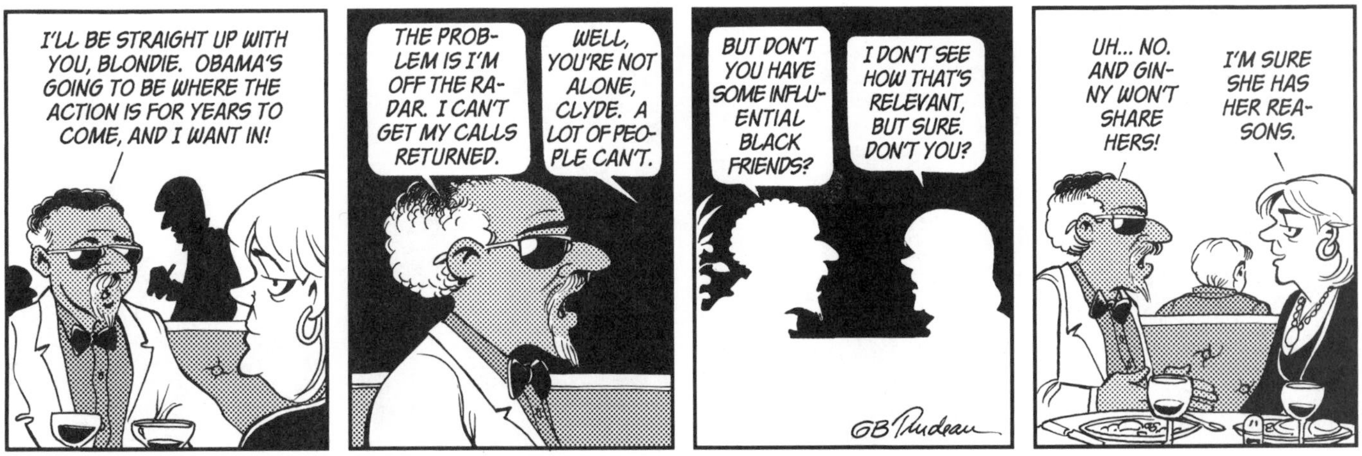
I'LL BE STRAIGHT UP WITH YOU, BLONDIE. OBAMA'S GOING TO BE WHERE THE ACTION IS FOR YEARS TO COME, AND I WANT IN!
THE PROBLEM IS I'M OFF THE RADAR. I CAN'T GET MY CALLS RETURNED.
WELL, YOU'RE NOT ALONE, CLYDE. A LOT OF PEOPLE CAN'T.
BUT DON'T YOU HAVE SOME INFLUENTIAL BLACK FRIENDS?
I DON'T SEE HOW THAT'S RELEVANT, BUT SURE. DON'T YOU?
GB Trudeau
UH... NO. AND GINNY WON'T SHARE HERS!
I'M SURE SHE HAS HER REASONS.

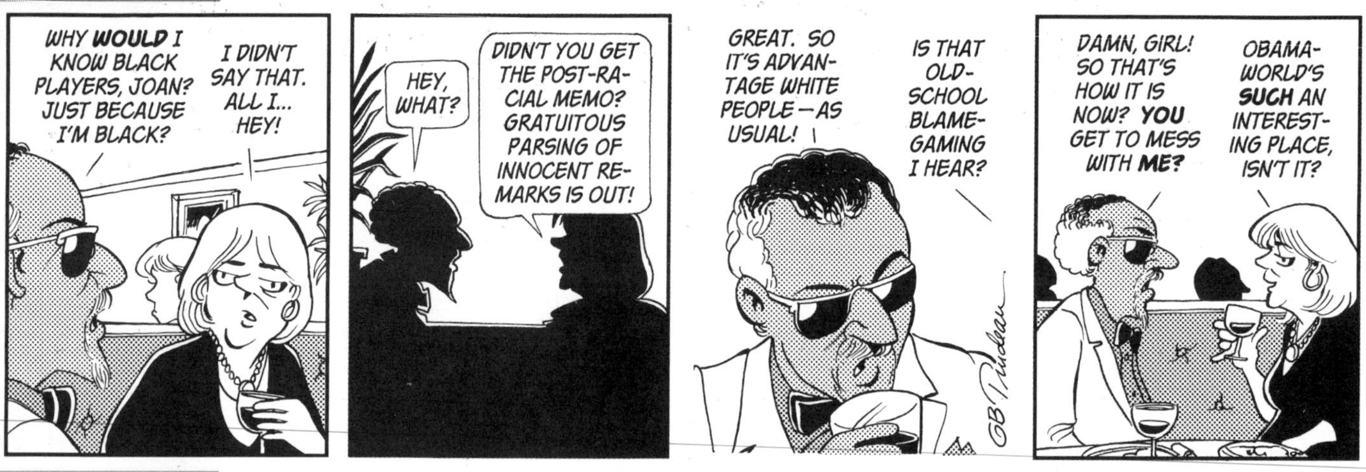
WHY **WOULD** I KNOW BLACK PLAYERS, JOAN? JUST BECAUSE I'M BLACK?
I DIDN'T SAY THAT. ALL I... HEY!
HEY, WHAT?
DIDN'T YOU GET THE POST-RACIAL MEMO? GRATUITOUS PARSING OF INNOCENT REMARKS IS OUT!
GREAT. SO IT'S ADVANTAGE WHITE PEOPLE—AS USUAL!
IS THAT OLD-SCHOOL BLAME-GAMING I HEAR?
DAMN, GIRL! SO THAT'S HOW IT IS NOW? **YOU** GET TO MESS WITH **ME?**
OBAMA-WORLD'S **SUCH** AN INTERESTING PLACE, ISN'T IT?

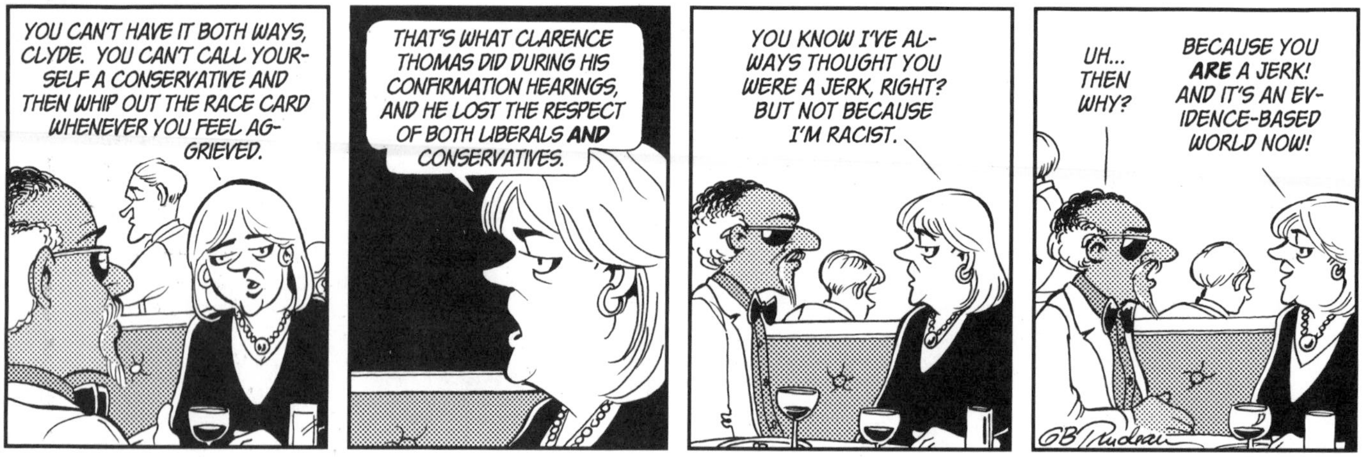
YOU CAN'T HAVE IT BOTH WAYS, CLYDE. YOU CAN'T CALL YOURSELF A CONSERVATIVE AND THEN WHIP OUT THE RACE CARD WHENEVER YOU FEEL AGGRIEVED.
THAT'S WHAT CLARENCE THOMAS DID DURING HIS CONFIRMATION HEARINGS, AND HE LOST THE RESPECT OF BOTH LIBERALS **AND** CONSERVATIVES.
YOU KNOW I'VE ALWAYS THOUGHT YOU WERE A JERK, RIGHT? BUT NOT BECAUSE I'M RACIST.
UH... THEN WHY?
BECAUSE YOU **ARE** A JERK! AND IT'S AN EVIDENCE-BASED WORLD NOW!

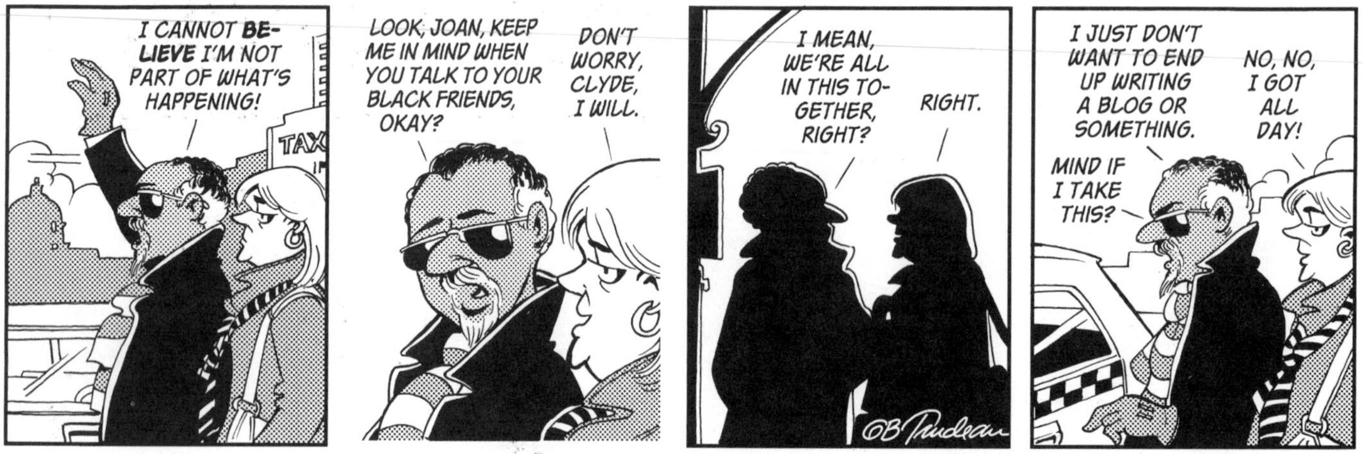
I CANNOT **BELIEVE** I'M NOT PART OF WHAT'S HAPPENING!
TAXI
LOOK, JOAN, KEEP ME IN MIND WHEN YOU TALK TO YOUR BLACK FRIENDS, OKAY?
DON'T WORRY, CLYDE, I WILL.
I MEAN, WE'RE ALL IN THIS TOGETHER, RIGHT?
RIGHT.
I JUST DON'T WANT TO END UP WRITING A BLOG OR SOMETHING.
NO, NO, I GOT ALL DAY!
MIND IF I TAKE THIS?

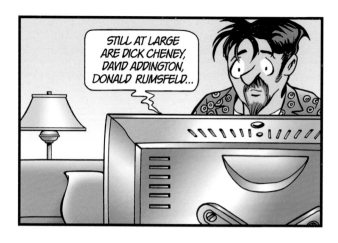

STILL AT LARGE ARE DICK CHENEY, DAVID ADDINGTON, DONALD RUMSFELD...

WOW... HOPE THEY CATCH 'EM!

JOHN YOO, DOUG FEITH...

LISTEN, DUDE, DO YOU STILL HAVE CONTACTS AT THE CIA?

SOME. WHY?

WELL, APPARENTLY, QUITE A FEW BUSHIES HAVE A SERIOUS WAR CRIMES PROBLEM...

CHENEY, ADDINGTON, RUMSFELD, GONZALES, FEITH, YOO—THE WHOLE TORTURE CROWD...

THEY'RE ALL VULNERABLE TO ARREST IF THEY TRAVEL ABROAD.

ANYWAY, IF YOU COULD SLEUTH OUT THEIR SCHEDULES, WE COULD TIP OFF LOCAL AUTHORITIES SO THEY'RE FINALLY BROUGHT TO JUSTICE.

NOW THERE'S AN IDEA.

THANK YOU.

WHERE'D IT COME FROM?

POLI SCI PROJECT. IF I DELIVER CHENEY TO THE HAGUE, NO WAY I DON'T GET AN "A."

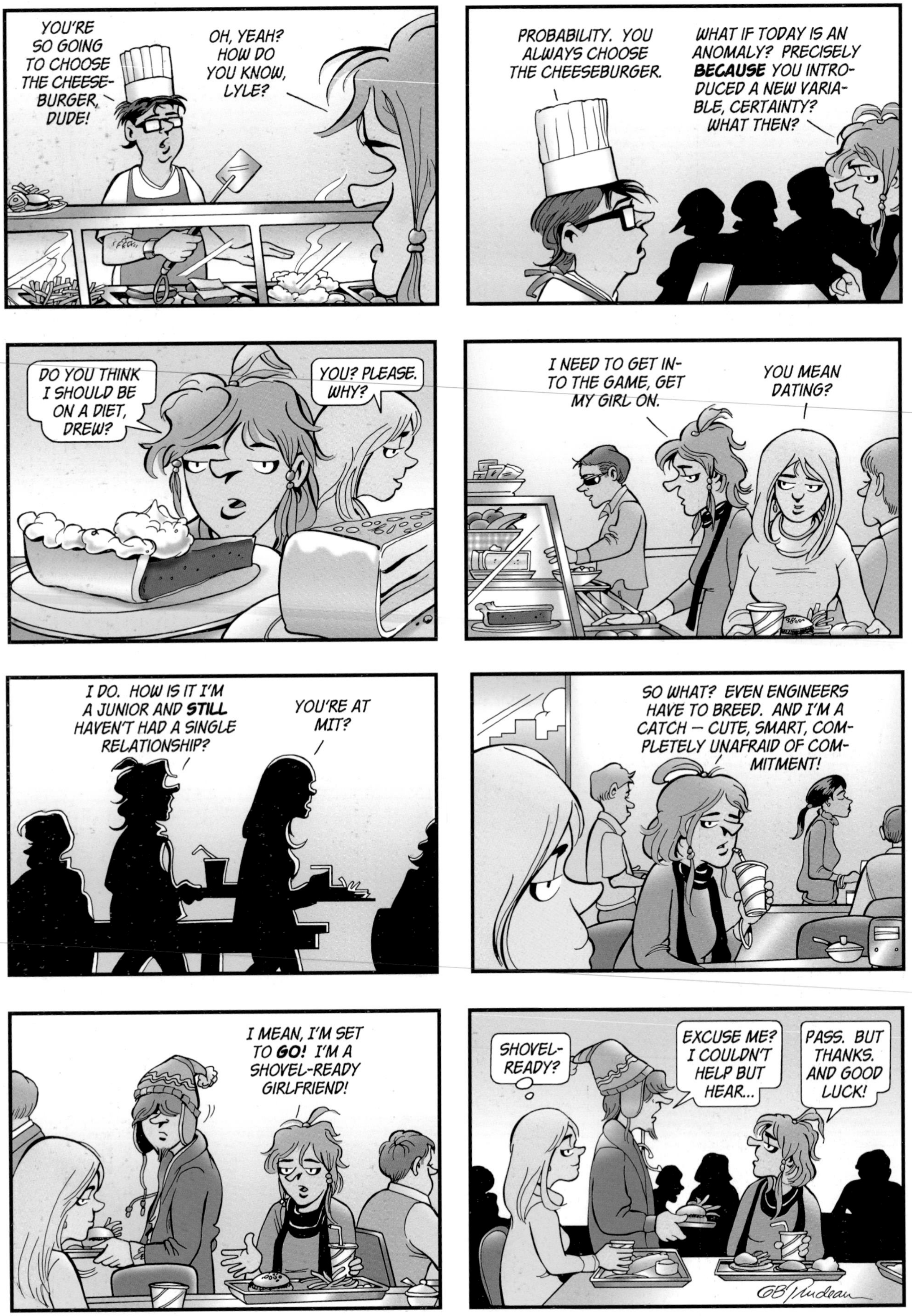

YOU'RE SO GOING TO CHOOSE THE CHEESE-BURGER, DUDE!
OH, YEAH? HOW DO YOU KNOW, LYLE?
PROBABILITY. YOU ALWAYS CHOOSE THE CHEESEBURGER.
WHAT IF TODAY IS AN ANOMALY? PRECISELY **BECAUSE** YOU INTRO-DUCED A NEW VARIA-BLE, CERTAINTY? WHAT THEN?
DO YOU THINK I SHOULD BE ON A DIET, DREW?
YOU? PLEASE. WHY?
I NEED TO GET IN-TO THE GAME, GET MY GIRL ON.
YOU MEAN DATING?
I DO. HOW IS IT I'M A JUNIOR AND **STILL** HAVEN'T HAD A SINGLE RELATIONSHIP?
YOU'RE AT MIT?
SO WHAT? EVEN ENGINEERS HAVE TO BREED. AND I'M A CATCH — CUTE, SMART, COM-PLETELY UNAFRAID OF COM-MITMENT!
I MEAN, I'M SET TO **GO!** I'M A SHOVEL-READY GIRLFRIEND!
SHOVEL-READY?
EXCUSE ME? I COULDN'T HELP BUT HEAR...
PASS. BUT THANKS. AND GOOD LUCK!
GB Trudeau

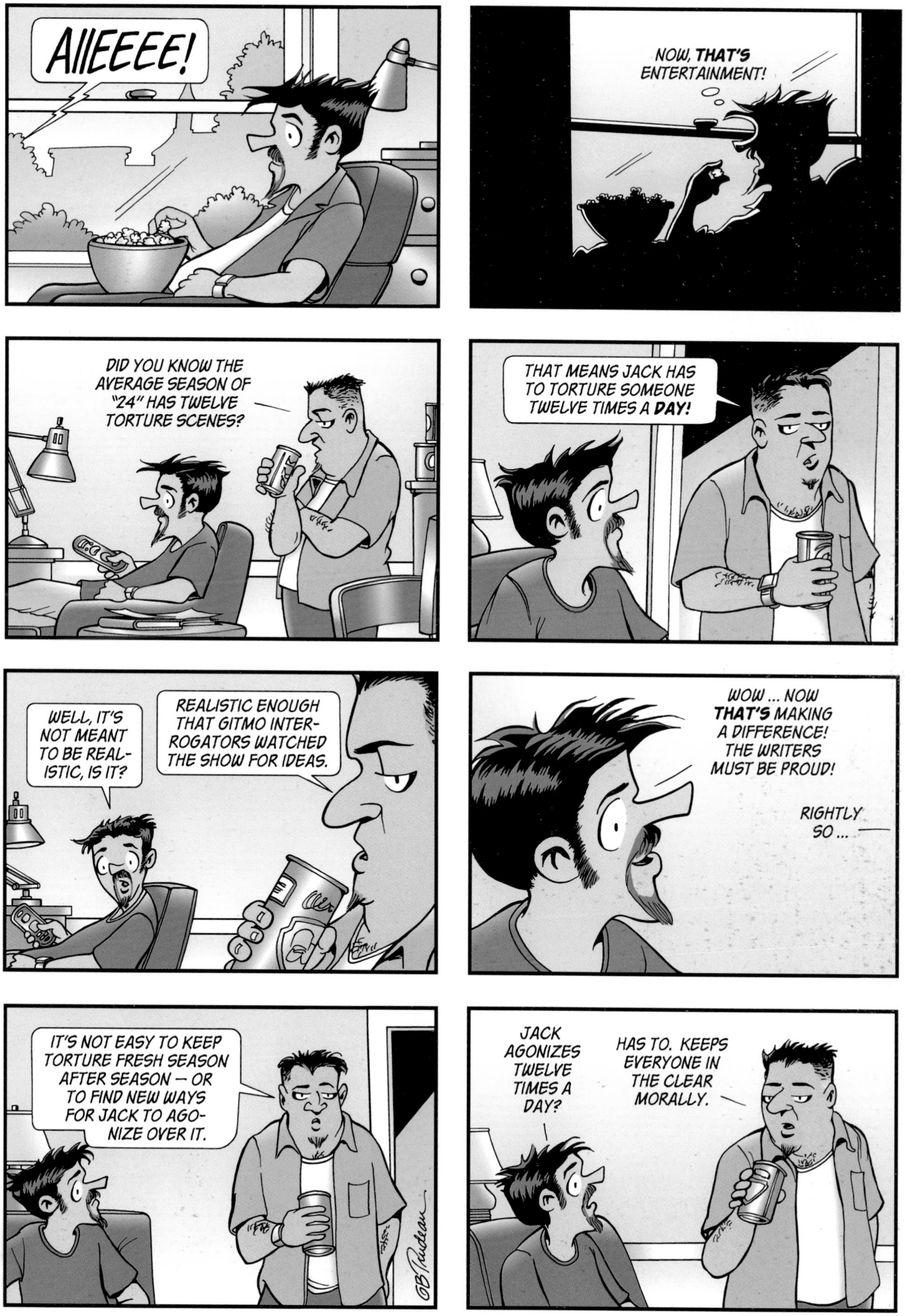
AIIEEEE!
NOW, **THAT'S** ENTERTAINMENT!
DID YOU KNOW THE AVERAGE SEASON OF "24" HAS TWELVE TORTURE SCENES?
THAT MEANS JACK HAS TO TORTURE SOMEONE TWELVE TIMES A **DAY!**
WELL, IT'S NOT MEANT TO BE REAL-ISTIC, IS IT?
REALISTIC ENOUGH THAT GITMO INTER-ROGATORS WATCHED THE SHOW FOR IDEAS.
WOW ... NOW **THAT'S** MAKING A DIFFERENCE! THE WRITERS MUST BE PROUD!
RIGHTLY SO ...
IT'S NOT EASY TO KEEP TORTURE FRESH SEASON AFTER SEASON — OR TO FIND NEW WAYS FOR JACK TO AGO-NIZE OVER IT.
©B Trudeau
JACK AGONIZES TWELVE TIMES A DAY?
HAS TO. KEEPS EVERYONE IN THE CLEAR MORALLY.

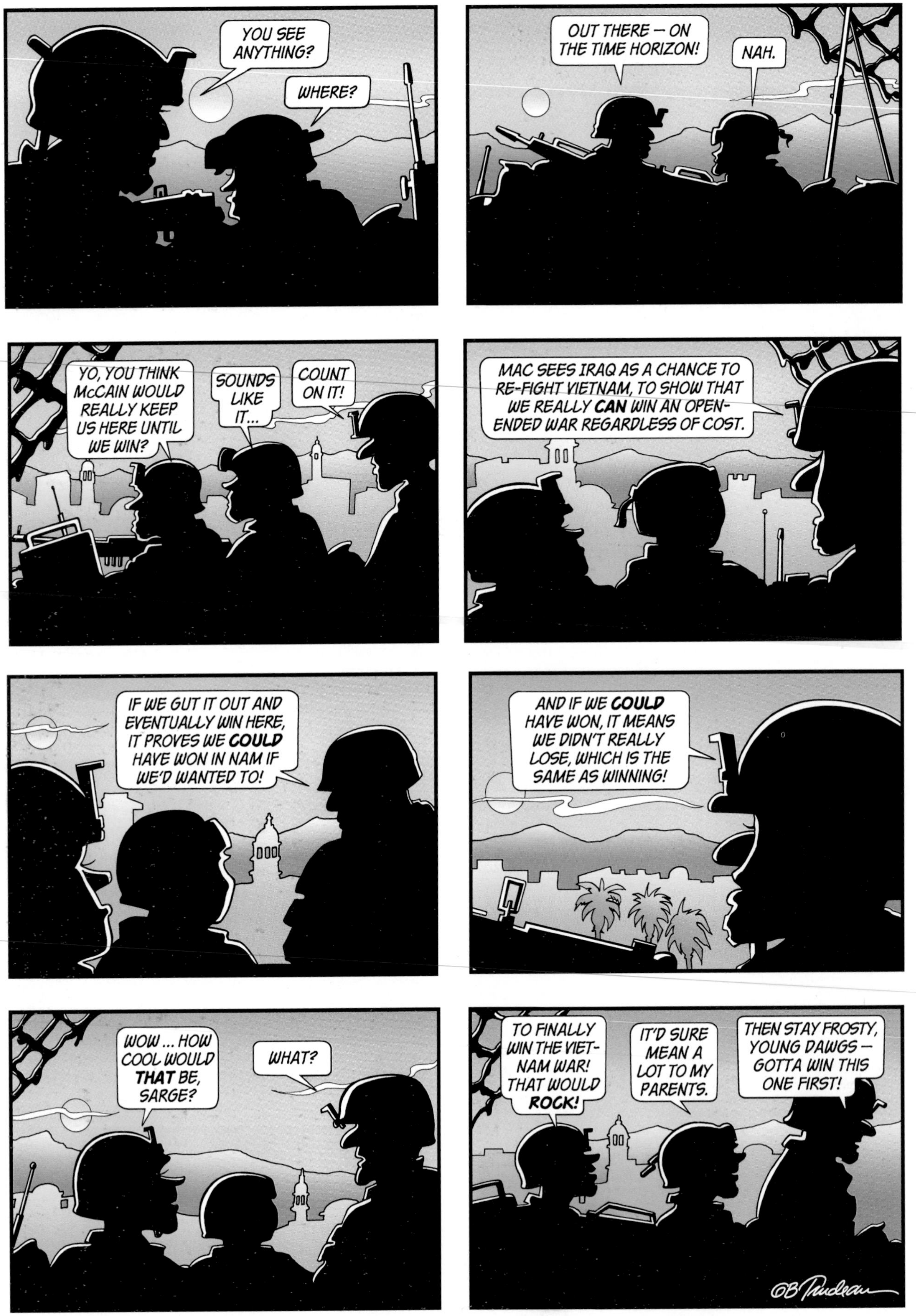
YOU SEE ANYTHING?
WHERE?
OUT THERE — ON THE TIME HORIZON!
NAH.
YO, YOU THINK McCAIN WOULD REALLY KEEP US HERE UNTIL WE WIN?
SOUNDS LIKE IT...
COUNT ON IT!
MAC SEES IRAQ AS A CHANCE TO RE-FIGHT VIETNAM, TO SHOW THAT WE REALLY CAN WIN AN OPEN-ENDED WAR REGARDLESS OF COST.
IF WE GUT IT OUT AND EVENTUALLY WIN HERE, IT PROVES WE COULD HAVE WON IN NAM IF WE'D WANTED TO!
AND IF WE COULD HAVE WON, IT MEANS WE DIDN'T REALLY LOSE, WHICH IS THE SAME AS WINNING!
WOW ... HOW COOL WOULD THAT BE, SARGE?
WHAT?
TO FINALLY WIN THE VIET-NAM WAR! THAT WOULD ROCK!
IT'D SURE MEAN A LOT TO MY PARENTS.
THEN STAY FROSTY, YOUNG DAWGS — GOTTA WIN THIS ONE FIRST!
©B Trudeau

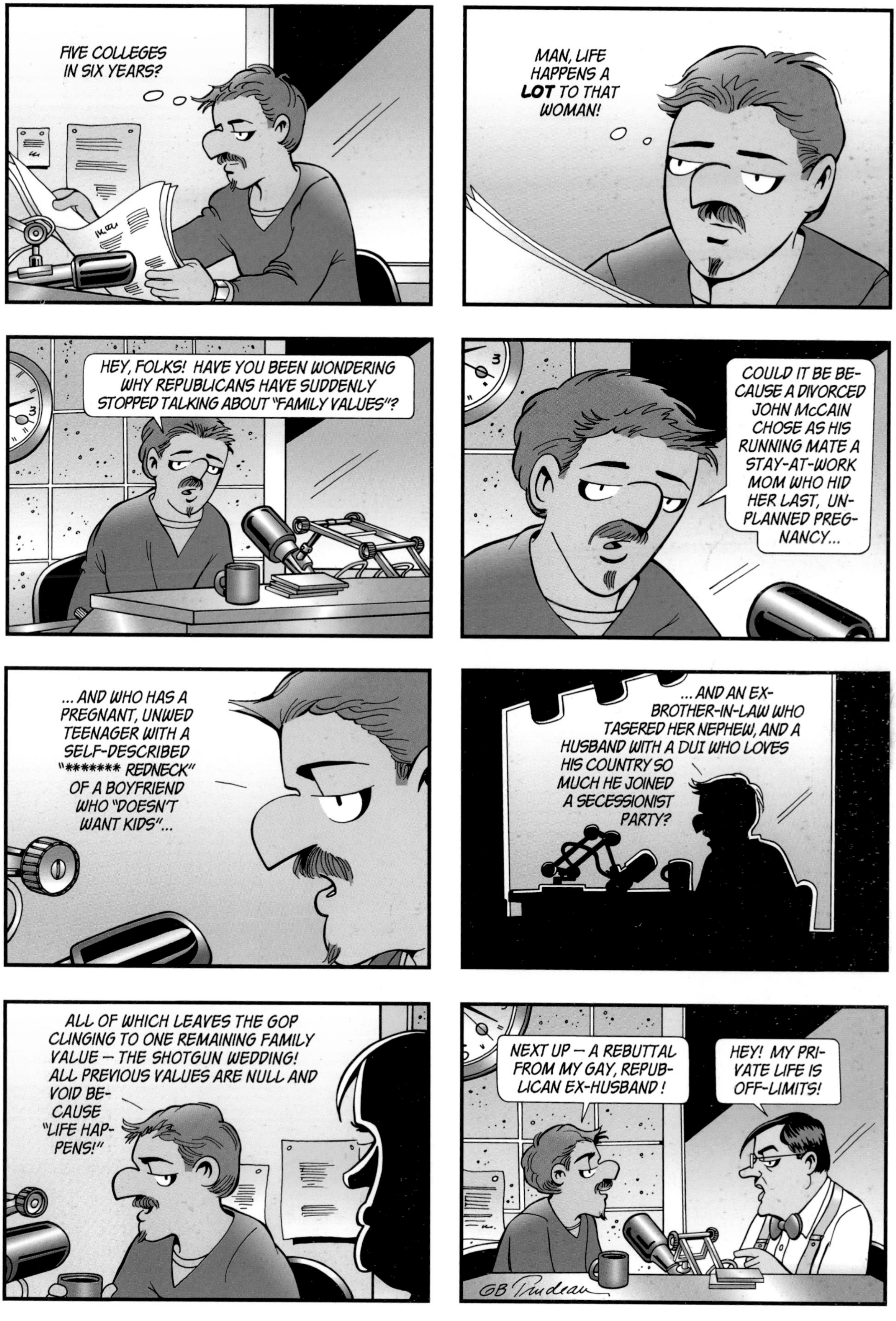
FIVE COLLEGES IN SIX YEARS?
MAN, LIFE HAPPENS A LOT TO THAT WOMAN!
HEY, FOLKS! HAVE YOU BEEN WONDERING WHY REPUBLICANS HAVE SUDDENLY STOPPED TALKING ABOUT "FAMILY VALUES"?
COULD IT BE BECAUSE A DIVORCED JOHN McCAIN CHOSE AS HIS RUNNING MATE A STAY-AT-WORK MOM WHO HID HER LAST, UNPLANNED PREGNANCY...
... AND WHO HAS A PREGNANT, UNWED TEENAGER WITH A SELF-DESCRIBED "******* REDNECK" OF A BOYFRIEND WHO "DOESN'T WANT KIDS"...
... AND AN EX-BROTHER-IN-LAW WHO TASERED HER NEPHEW, AND A HUSBAND WITH A DUI WHO LOVES HIS COUNTRY SO MUCH HE JOINED A SECESSIONIST PARTY?
ALL OF WHICH LEAVES THE GOP CLINGING TO ONE REMAINING FAMILY VALUE — THE SHOTGUN WEDDING! ALL PREVIOUS VALUES ARE NULL AND VOID BECAUSE "LIFE HAPPENS!"
NEXT UP — A REBUTTAL FROM MY GAY, REPUBLICAN EX-HUSBAND!
HEY! MY PRIVATE LIFE IS OFF-LIMITS!
GB Trudeau

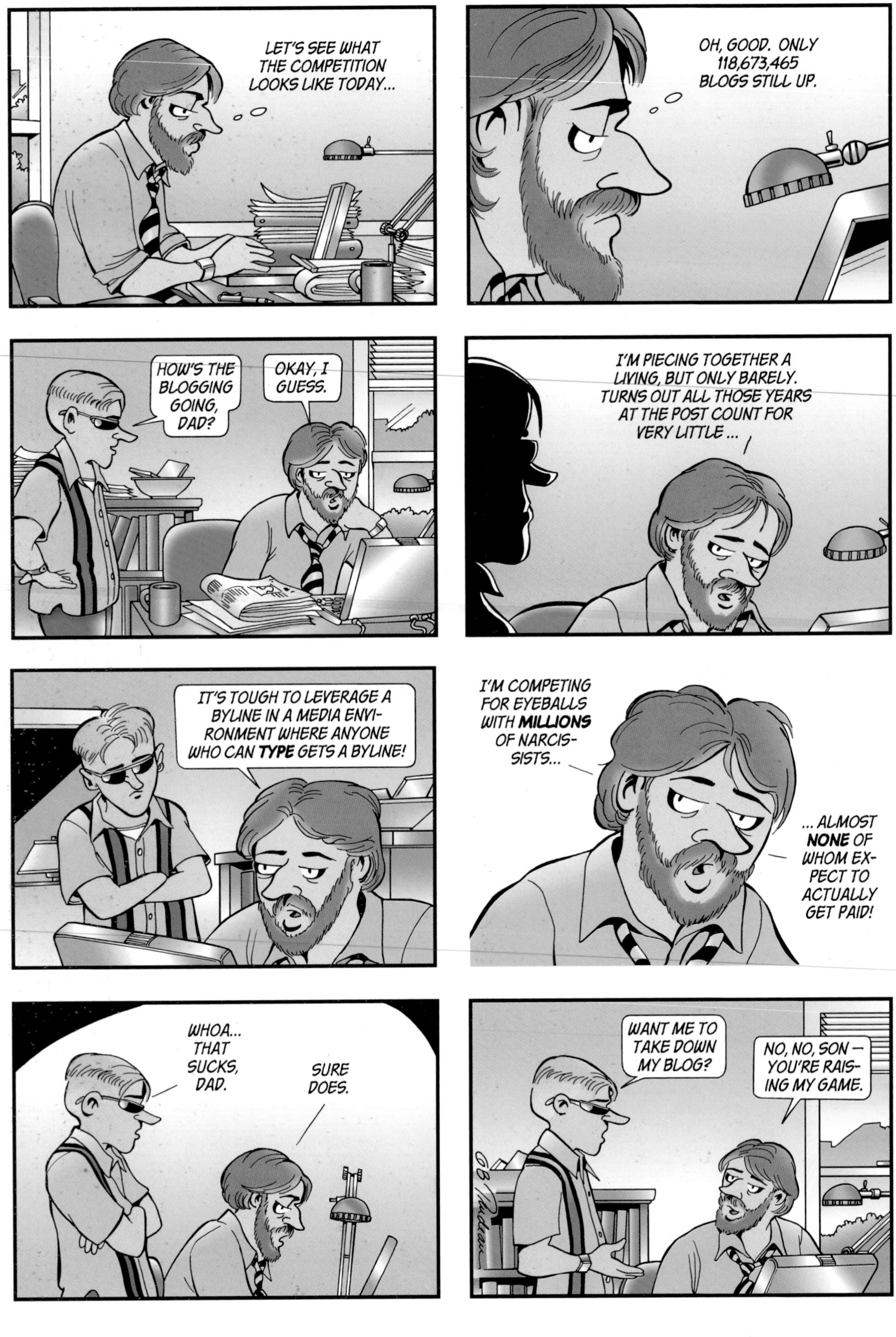
LET'S SEE WHAT THE COMPETITION LOOKS LIKE TODAY...
OH, GOOD. ONLY 118,673,465 BLOGS STILL UP.
HOW'S THE BLOGGING GOING, DAD?
OKAY, I GUESS.
I'M PIECING TOGETHER A LIVING, BUT ONLY BARELY. TURNS OUT ALL THOSE YEARS AT THE POST COUNT FOR VERY LITTLE ...
IT'S TOUGH TO LEVERAGE A BYLINE IN A MEDIA ENVIRONMENT WHERE ANYONE WHO CAN **TYPE** GETS A BYLINE!
I'M COMPETING FOR EYEBALLS WITH **MILLIONS** OF NARCISSISTS...
... ALMOST **NONE** OF WHOM EXPECT TO ACTUALLY GET PAID!
WHOA... THAT SUCKS, DAD.
SURE DOES.
WANT ME TO TAKE DOWN MY BLOG?
NO, NO, SON — YOU'RE RAISING MY GAME.

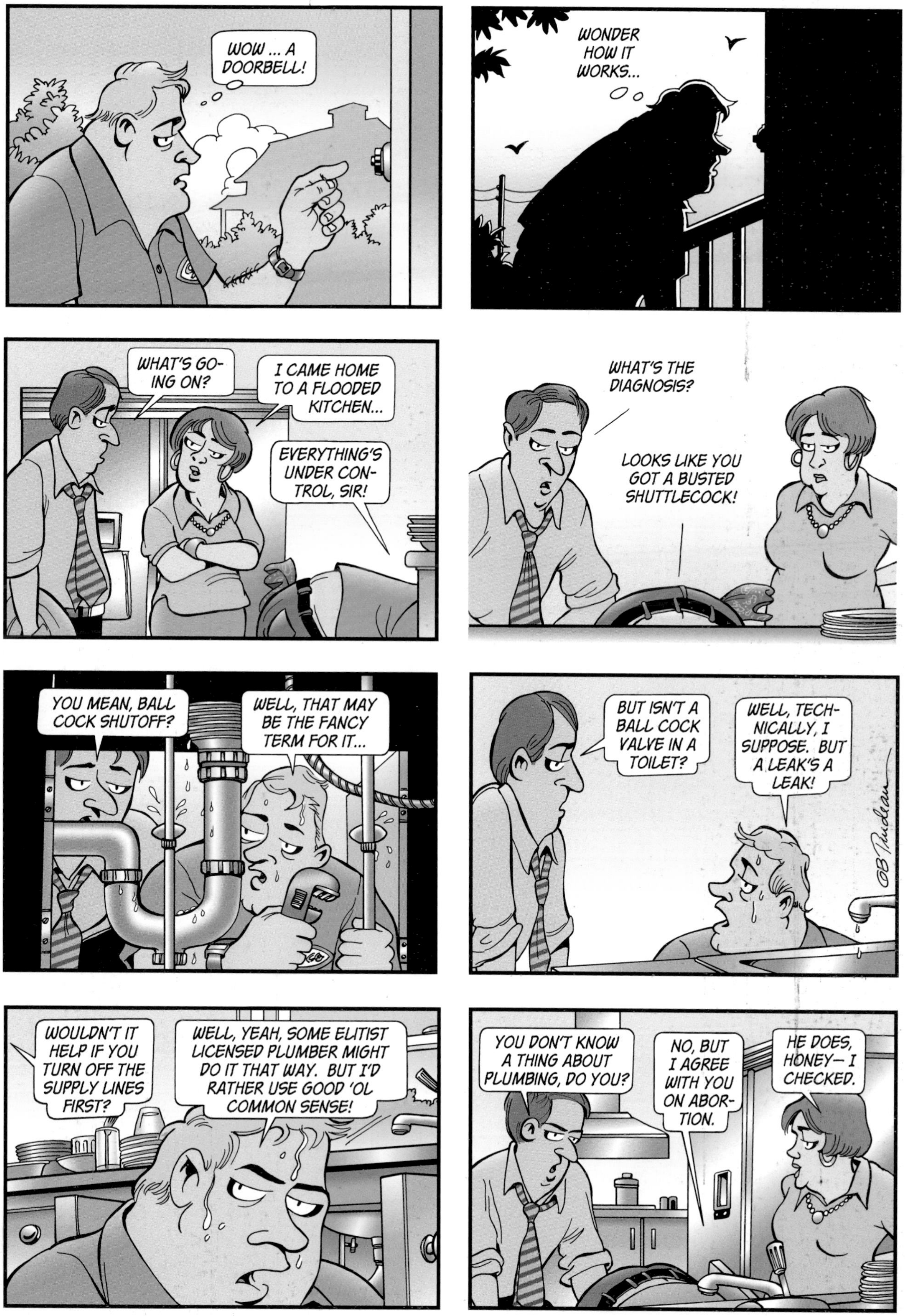
WOW ... A DOORBELL!
WONDER HOW IT WORKS...
WHAT'S GO-ING ON?
I CAME HOME TO A FLOODED KITCHEN...
EVERYTHING'S UNDER CON-TROL, SIR!
WHAT'S THE DIAGNOSIS?
LOOKS LIKE YOU GOT A BUSTED SHUTTLECOCK!
YOU MEAN, BALL COCK SHUTOFF?
WELL, THAT MAY BE THE FANCY TERM FOR IT...
BUT ISN'T A BALL COCK VALVE IN A TOILET?
WELL, TECH-NICALLY, I SUPPOSE. BUT A LEAK'S A LEAK!
WOULDN'T IT HELP IF YOU TURN OFF THE SUPPLY LINES FIRST?
WELL, YEAH, SOME ELITIST LICENSED PLUMBER MIGHT DO IT THAT WAY. BUT I'D RATHER USE GOOD 'OL COMMON SENSE!
YOU DON'T KNOW A THING ABOUT PLUMBING, DO YOU?
NO, BUT I AGREE WITH YOU ON ABOR-TION.
HE DOES, HONEY— I CHECKED.

I SHOULD BE OUT THERE CAMPAIGNING...
THEY MUST'VE LOST MY PRIVATE NUMBER.
ANY WORD FROM THE McCAIN PEOPLE YET?
ABOUT WHAT, SIR?
ABOUT USING ME TO CAMPAIGN, OF COURSE!
UM... IT DOESN'T SEEM TO BE PART OF THEIR STRATEGY, SIR.
WHAT, ARE THEY IDIOTS? A QUARTER OF THE COUNTRY STILL **LOVES** ME!
AND WHAT ABOUT ALL THOSE HUGS I PUT UP WITH IN '04? McCAIN **OWES** ME...
HELL, FORGET ME — YOU'D THINK THEY'D AT **LEAST** WANT TO LEVERAGE THE PRESIDENCY!
WHAT PART EXACTLY, SIR?
THE MAJESTY OF THE **OFFICE**, OBVIOUSLY!
I CAN SUGGEST IT.
GB Trudeau

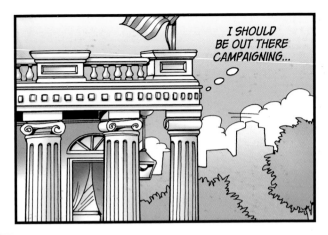

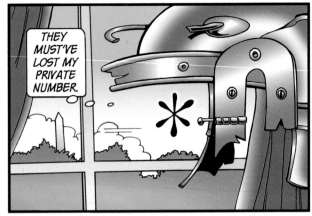

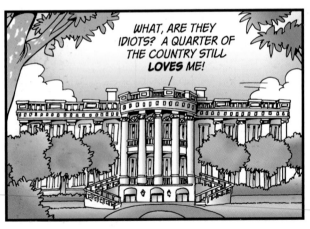

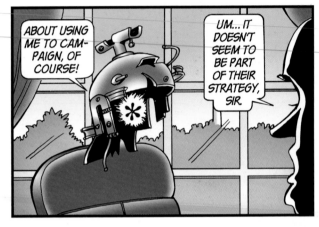

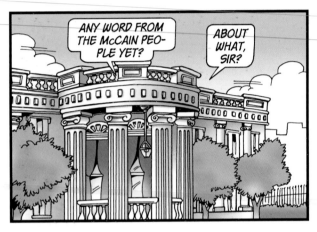

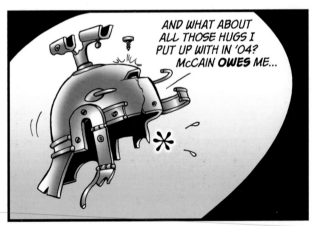

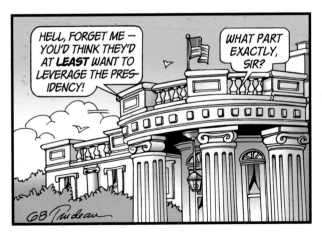

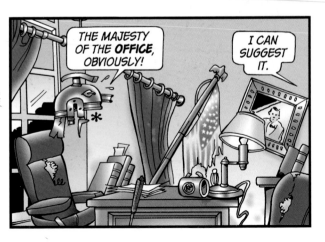

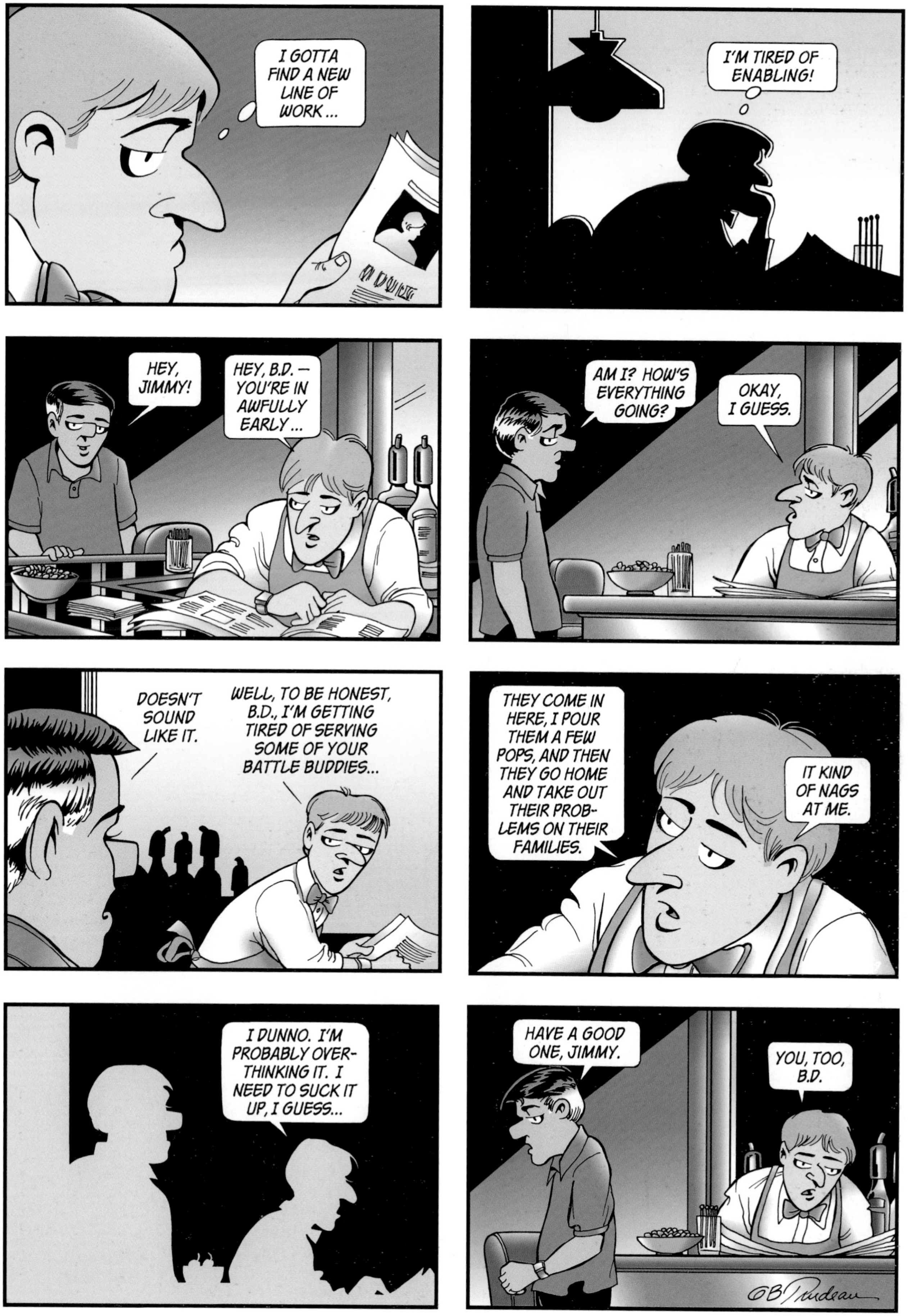
I GOTTA FIND A NEW LINE OF WORK...
I'M TIRED OF ENABLING!
HEY, JIMMY!
HEY, B.D. — YOU'RE IN AWFULLY EARLY...
AM I? HOW'S EVERYTHING GOING?
OKAY, I GUESS.
DOESN'T SOUND LIKE IT.
WELL, TO BE HONEST, B.D., I'M GETTING TIRED OF SERVING SOME OF YOUR BATTLE BUDDIES...
THEY COME IN HERE, I POUR THEM A FEW POPS, AND THEN THEY GO HOME AND TAKE OUT THEIR PROB-LEMS ON THEIR FAMILIES.
IT KIND OF NAGS AT ME.
I DUNNO. I'M PROBABLY OVER-THINKING IT. I NEED TO SUCK IT UP, I GUESS...
HAVE A GOOD ONE, JIMMY.
YOU, TOO, B.D.
GB Trudeau

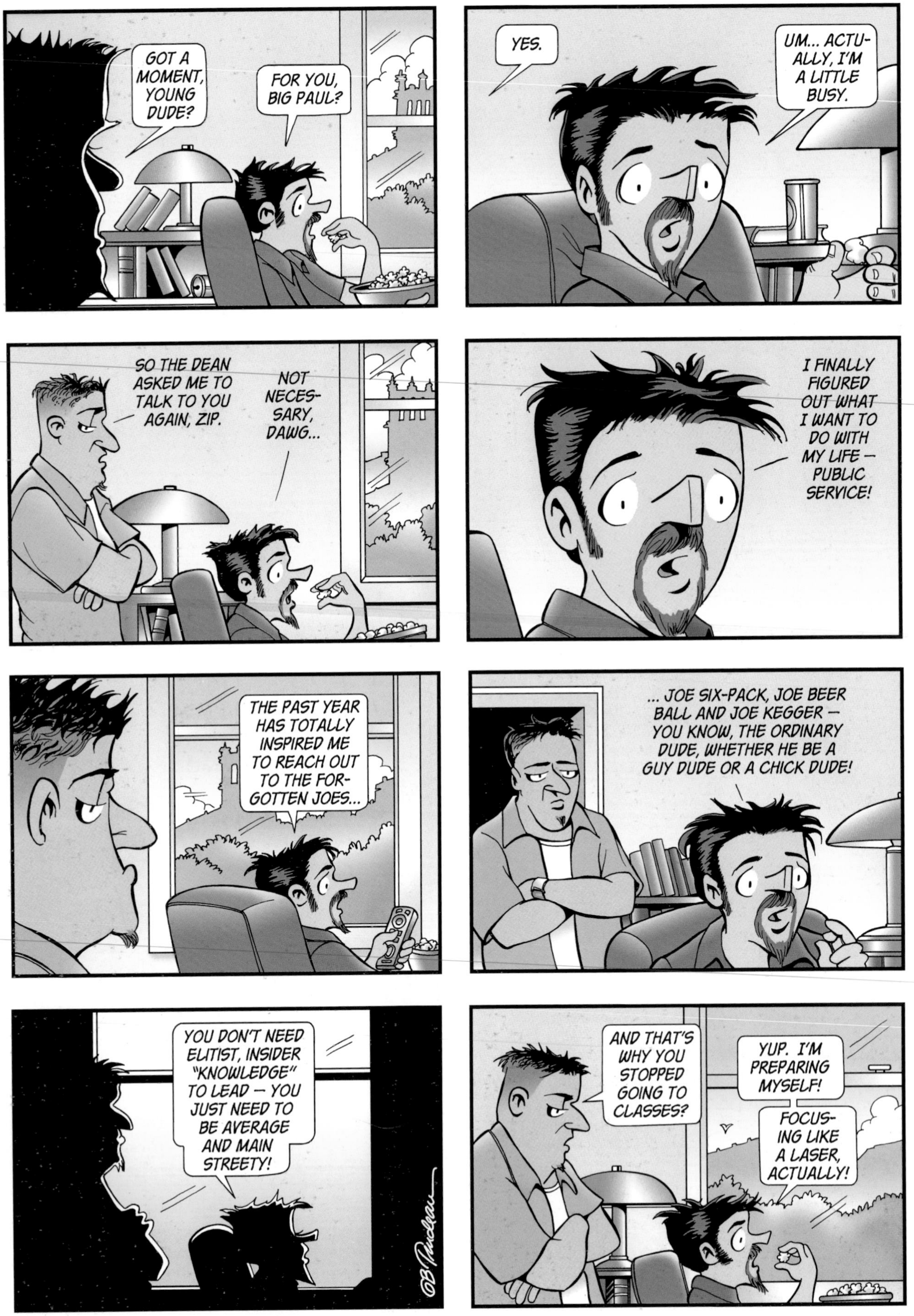
GOT A MOMENT, YOUNG DUDE?
FOR YOU, BIG PAUL?
YES.
UM... ACTUALLY, I'M A LITTLE BUSY.
SO THE DEAN ASKED ME TO TALK TO YOU AGAIN, ZIP.
NOT NECESSARY, DAWG...
I FINALLY FIGURED OUT WHAT I WANT TO DO WITH MY LIFE — PUBLIC SERVICE!
THE PAST YEAR HAS TOTALLY INSPIRED ME TO REACH OUT TO THE FORGOTTEN JOES...
... JOE SIX-PACK, JOE BEER BALL AND JOE KEGGER — YOU KNOW, THE ORDINARY DUDE, WHETHER HE BE A GUY DUDE OR A CHICK DUDE!
YOU DON'T NEED ELITIST, INSIDER "KNOWLEDGE" TO LEAD — YOU JUST NEED TO BE AVERAGE AND MAIN STREETY!
AND THAT'S WHY YOU STOPPED GOING TO CLASSES?
YUP. I'M PREPARING MYSELF!
FOCUSING LIKE A LASER, ACTUALLY!

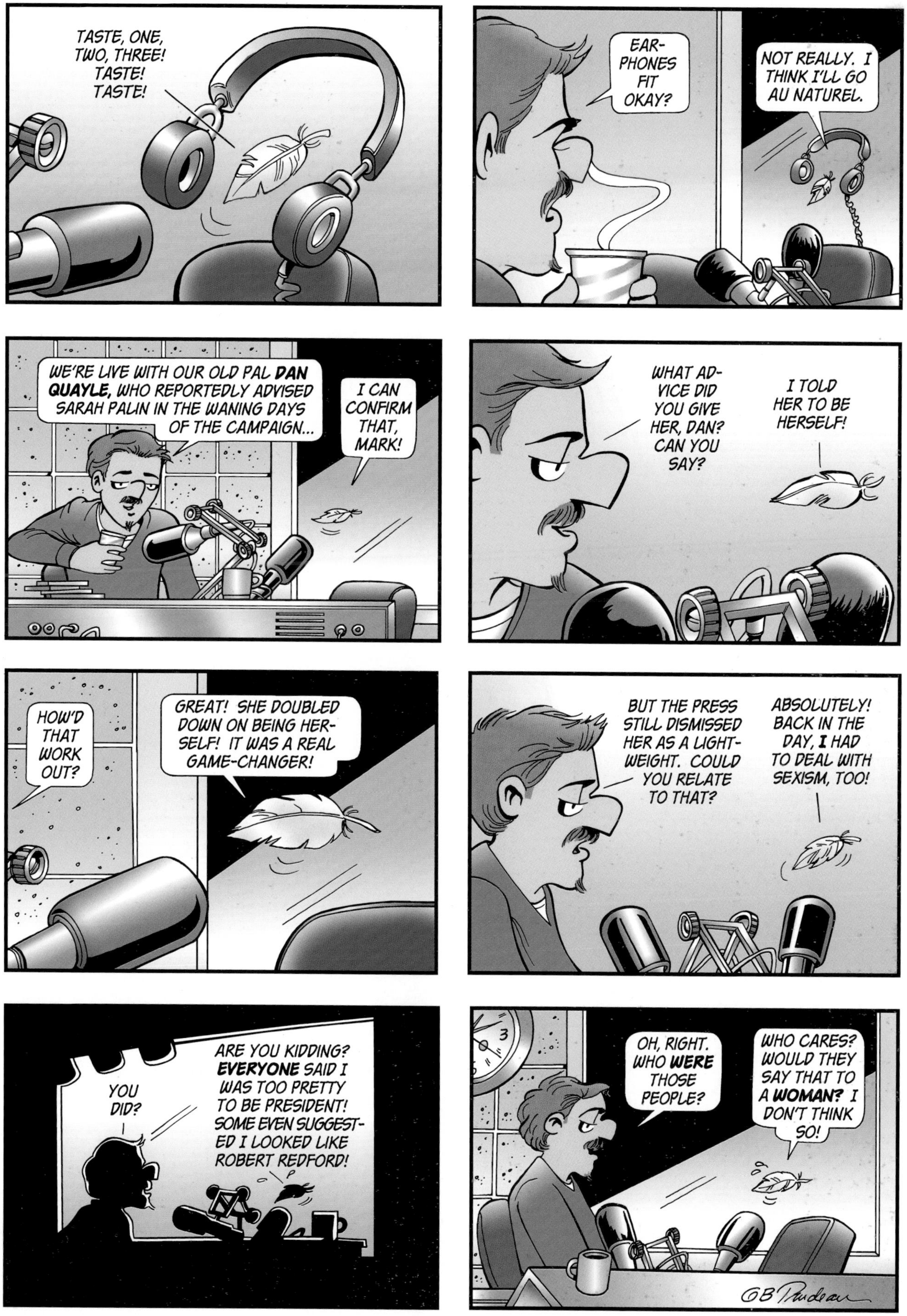
TASTE, ONE, TWO, THREE! TASTE! TASTE!
EAR-PHONES FIT OKAY?
NOT REALLY. I THINK I'LL GO AU NATUREL.
WE'RE LIVE WITH OUR OLD PAL DAN QUAYLE, WHO REPORTEDLY ADVISED SARAH PALIN IN THE WANING DAYS OF THE CAMPAIGN...
I CAN CONFIRM THAT, MARK!
WHAT AD-VICE DID YOU GIVE HER, DAN? CAN YOU SAY?
I TOLD HER TO BE HERSELF!
HOW'D THAT WORK OUT?
GREAT! SHE DOUBLED DOWN ON BEING HER-SELF! IT WAS A REAL GAME-CHANGER!
BUT THE PRESS STILL DISMISSED HER AS A LIGHT-WEIGHT. COULD YOU RELATE TO THAT?
ABSOLUTELY! BACK IN THE DAY, I HAD TO DEAL WITH SEXISM, TOO!
YOU DID?
ARE YOU KIDDING? EVERYONE SAID I WAS TOO PRETTY TO BE PRESIDENT! SOME EVEN SUGGEST-ED I LOOKED LIKE ROBERT REDFORD!
OH, RIGHT. WHO WERE THOSE PEOPLE?
WHO CARES? WOULD THEY SAY THAT TO A WOMAN? I DON'T THINK SO!
GB Trudeau

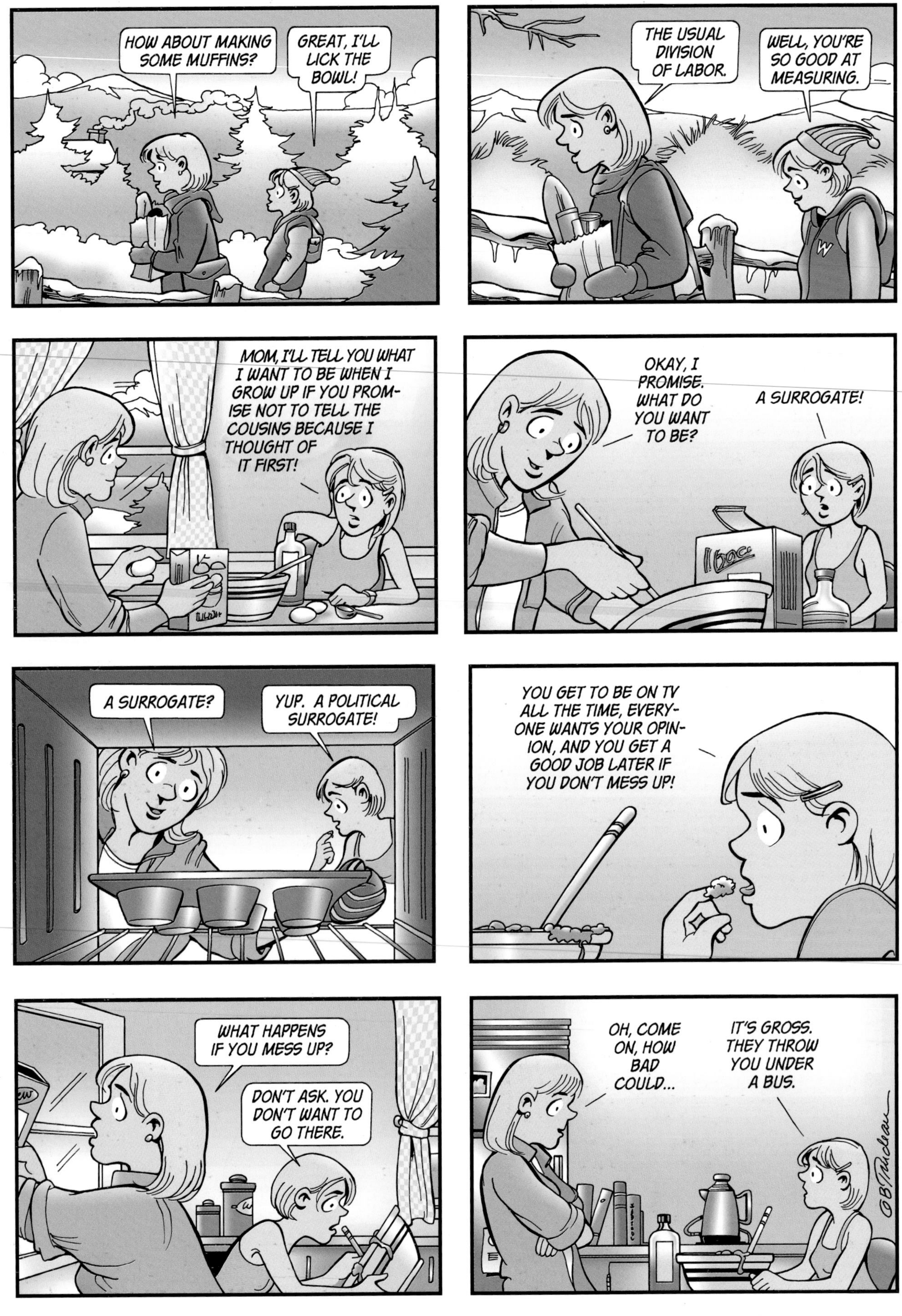
HOW ABOUT MAKING SOME MUFFINS?
GREAT, I'LL LICK THE BOWL!
THE USUAL DIVISION OF LABOR.
WELL, YOU'RE SO GOOD AT MEASURING.
MOM, I'LL TELL YOU WHAT I WANT TO BE WHEN I GROW UP IF YOU PROMISE NOT TO TELL THE COUSINS BECAUSE I THOUGHT OF IT FIRST!
OKAY, I PROMISE. WHAT DO YOU WANT TO BE?
A SURROGATE!
A SURROGATE?
YUP. A POLITICAL SURROGATE!
YOU GET TO BE ON TV ALL THE TIME, EVERYONE WANTS YOUR OPINION, AND YOU GET A GOOD JOB LATER IF YOU DON'T MESS UP!
WHAT HAPPENS IF YOU MESS UP?
DON'T ASK. YOU DON'T WANT TO GO THERE.
OH, COME ON, HOW BAD COULD...
IT'S GROSS. THEY THROW YOU UNDER A BUS.

HE'S HERE, SIR.
THAT ONE?
HE PREFERS THE ONE, SIR.
SO, BARACK, I GUESS YOU'RE WONDERING WHAT MY SECRET IS!
SIR?
YOU'RE WONDERING WHY I HAVEN'T AGED MUCH DURING MY PRESIDENCY — THE WAY CARTER AND CLINTON DID!
WELL, HERE'S THE DEAL. I GOT TWO RULES. FIRST, DON'T SWEAT THE SMALL STUFF! THAT'S WHAT STAFF IS FOR.
SECOND RULE: DON'T SWEAT THE BIG STUFF! THAT'S WHAT HISTORY IS FOR. AND BY THE TIME HISTORY GETS IT RIGHT, YOU'LL BE DEAD. LIKE LINCOLN AND THE OTHER GREATS!
WELL, YES, I GUESS THAT'S RIGHT, SIR.
ANYWAY, THAT'S MY SECRET.
IT'S SAFE WITH ME, SIR.

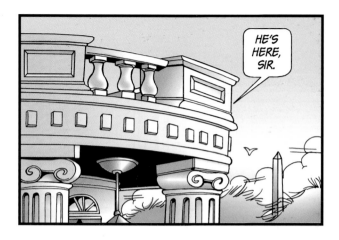

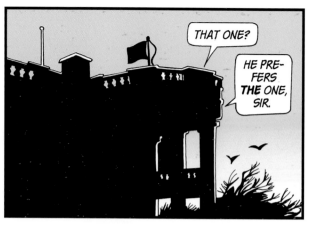

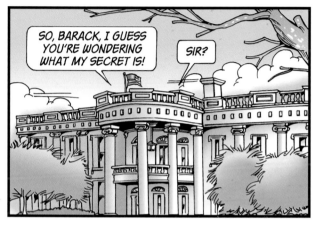

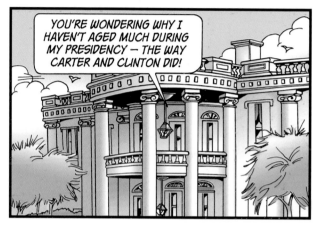

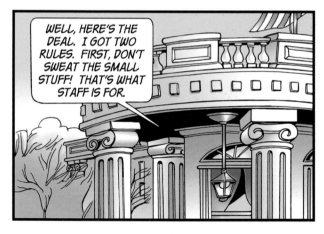

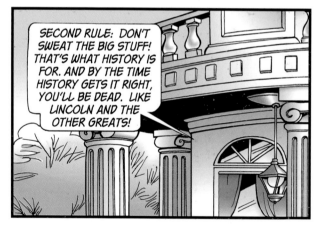

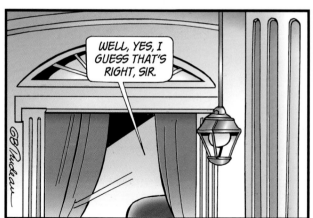

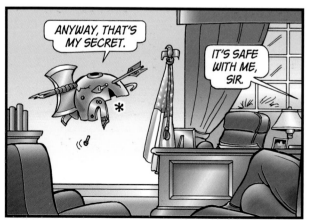

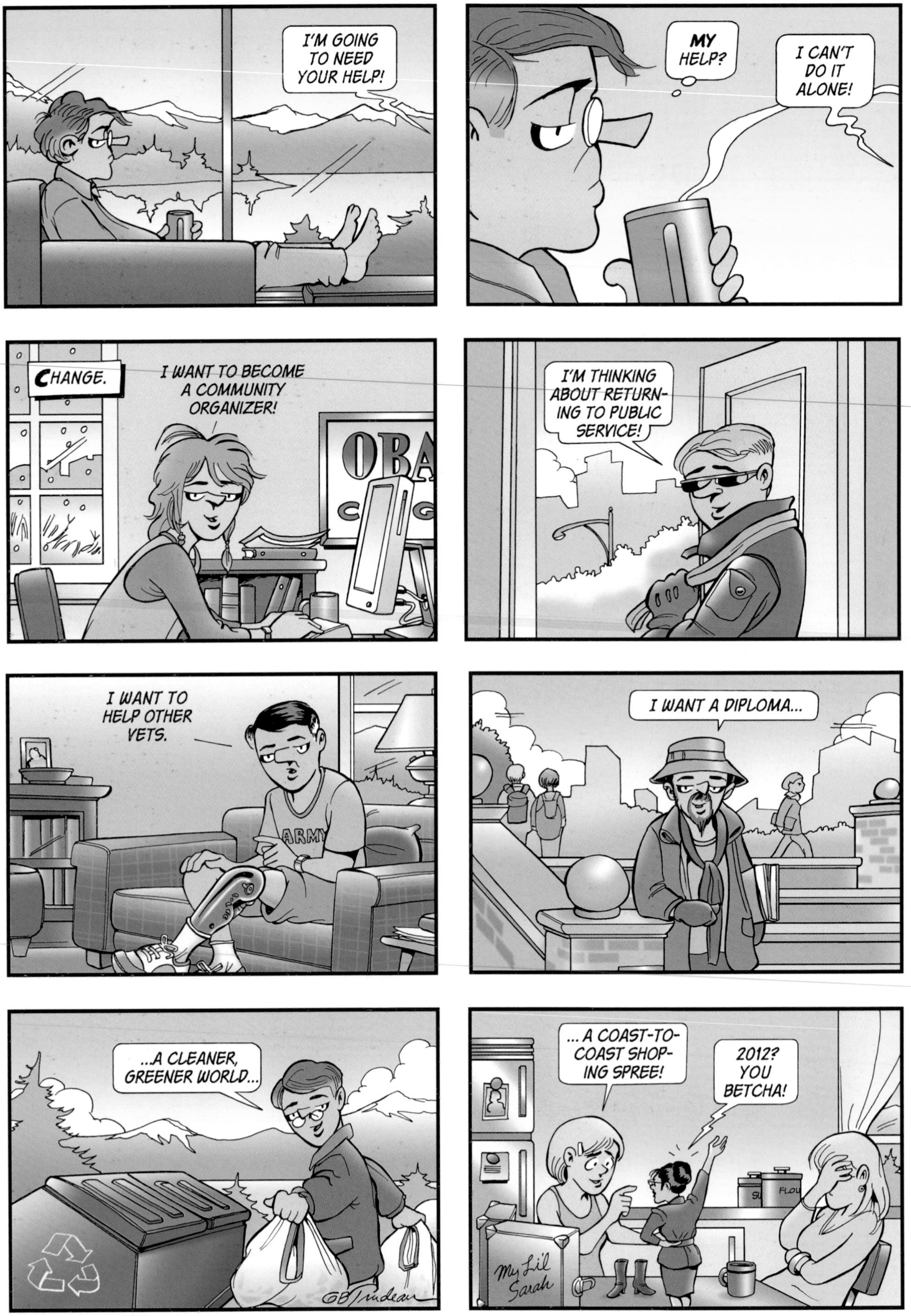
I'M GOING TO NEED YOUR HELP!
MY HELP?
I CAN'T DO IT ALONE!
CHANGE.
I WANT TO BECOME A COMMUNITY ORGANIZER!
I'M THINKING ABOUT RETURNING TO PUBLIC SERVICE!
I WANT TO HELP OTHER VETS.
ARMY
I WANT A DIPLOMA...
...A CLEANER, GREENER WORLD...
GB Trudeau
...A COAST-TO-COAST SHOPPING SPREE!
2012? YOU BETCHA!
My Lil Sarah

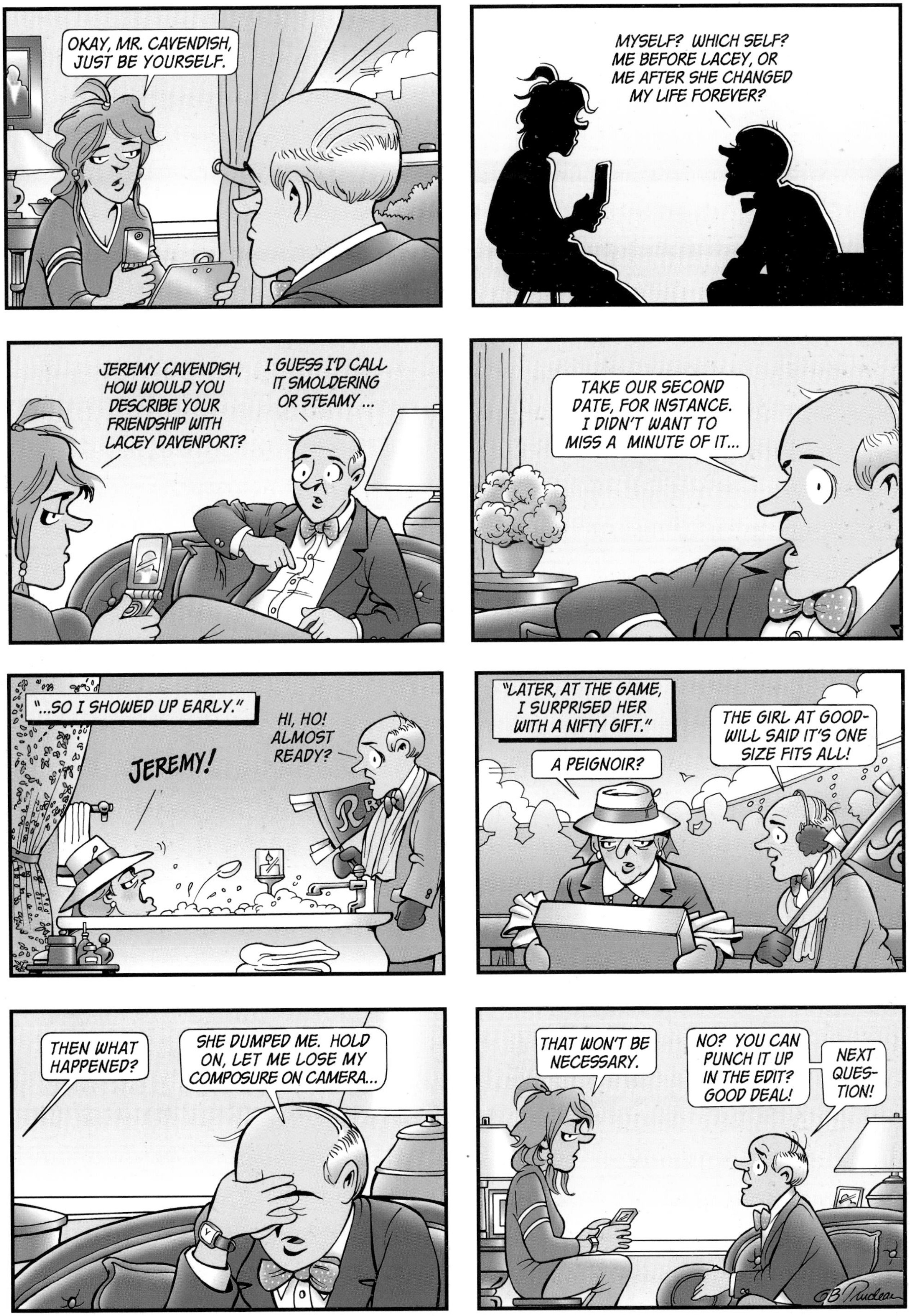
OKAY, MR. CAVENDISH, JUST BE YOURSELF.
MYSELF? WHICH SELF? ME BEFORE LACEY, OR ME AFTER SHE CHANGED MY LIFE FOREVER?
JEREMY CAVENDISH, HOW WOULD YOU DESCRIBE YOUR FRIENDSHIP WITH LACEY DAVENPORT?
I GUESS I'D CALL IT SMOLDERING OR STEAMY ...
TAKE OUR SECOND DATE, FOR INSTANCE. I DIDN'T WANT TO MISS A MINUTE OF IT...
"...SO I SHOWED UP EARLY."
JEREMY!
HI, HO! ALMOST READY?
"LATER, AT THE GAME, I SURPRISED HER WITH A NIFTY GIFT."
A PEIGNOIR?
THE GIRL AT GOOD-WILL SAID IT'S ONE SIZE FITS ALL!
THEN WHAT HAPPENED?
SHE DUMPED ME. HOLD ON, LET ME LOSE MY COMPOSURE ON CAMERA...
THAT WON'T BE NECESSARY.
NO? YOU CAN PUNCH IT UP IN THE EDIT? GOOD DEAL!
NEXT QUES-TION!
GB Trudeau

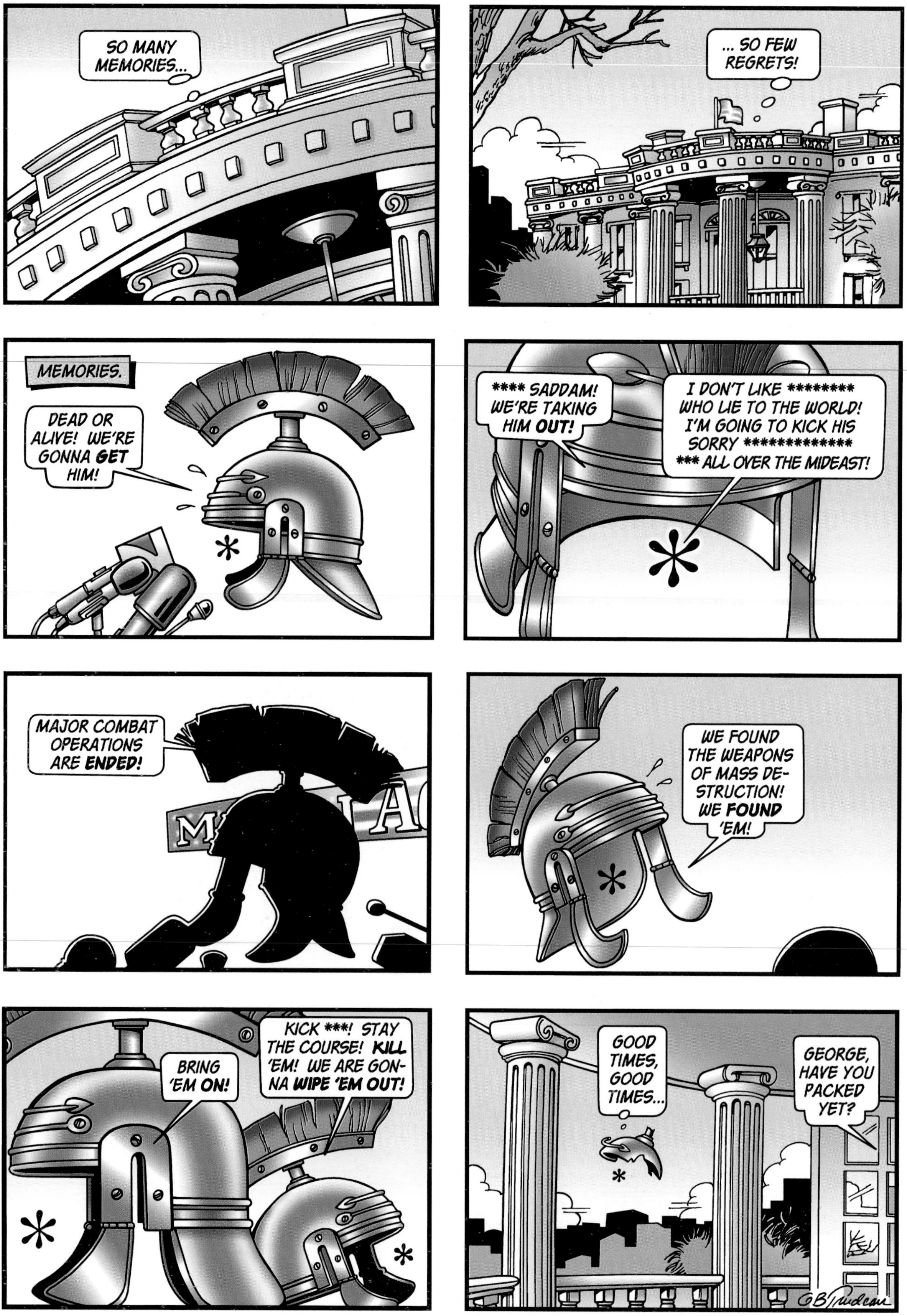
SO MANY MEMORIES...
... SO FEW REGRETS!
MEMORIES.
DEAD OR ALIVE! WE'RE GONNA GET HIM!
**** SADDAM! WE'RE TAKING HIM OUT!
I DON'T LIKE ******** WHO LIE TO THE WORLD! I'M GOING TO KICK HIS SORRY ************** *** ALL OVER THE MIDEAST!
MAJOR COMBAT OPERATIONS ARE ENDED!
WE FOUND THE WEAPONS OF MASS DESTRUCTION! WE FOUND 'EM!
BRING 'EM ON!
KICK ***! STAY THE COURSE! KILL 'EM! WE ARE GONNA WIPE 'EM OUT!
GOOD TIMES, GOOD TIMES...
GEORGE, HAVE YOU PACKED YET?
GBTrudeau

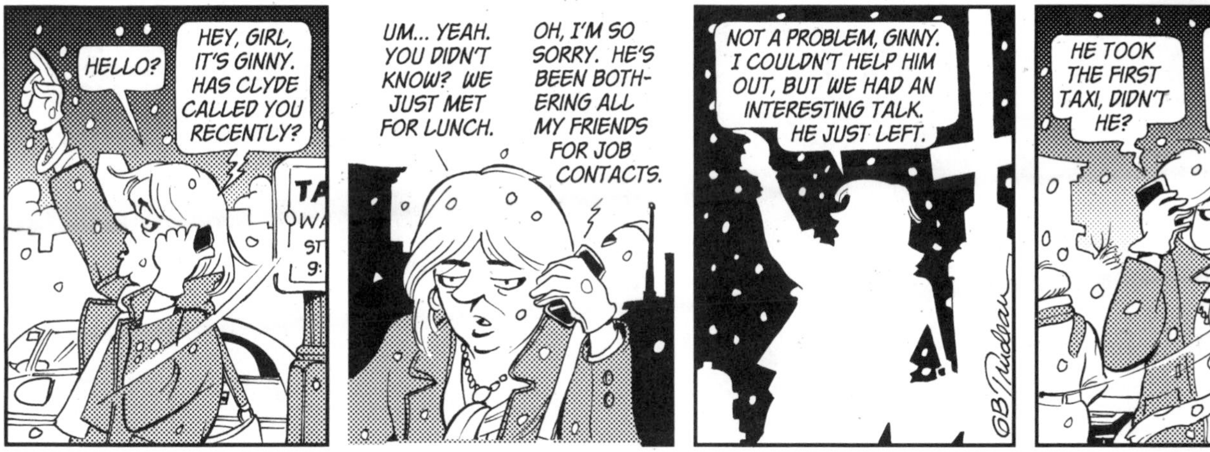
HELLO?
HEY, GIRL, IT'S GINNY. HAS CLYDE CALLED YOU RECENTLY?
UM... YEAH. YOU DIDN'T KNOW? WE JUST MET FOR LUNCH.
OH, I'M SO SORRY. HE'S BEEN BOTHERING ALL MY FRIENDS FOR JOB CONTACTS.
NOT A PROBLEM, GINNY. I COULDN'T HELP HIM OUT, BUT WE HAD AN INTERESTING TALK. HE JUST LEFT.
HE TOOK THE FIRST TAXI, DIDN'T HE?
WELL, IT SEEMED TO MEAN A LOT TO HIM.

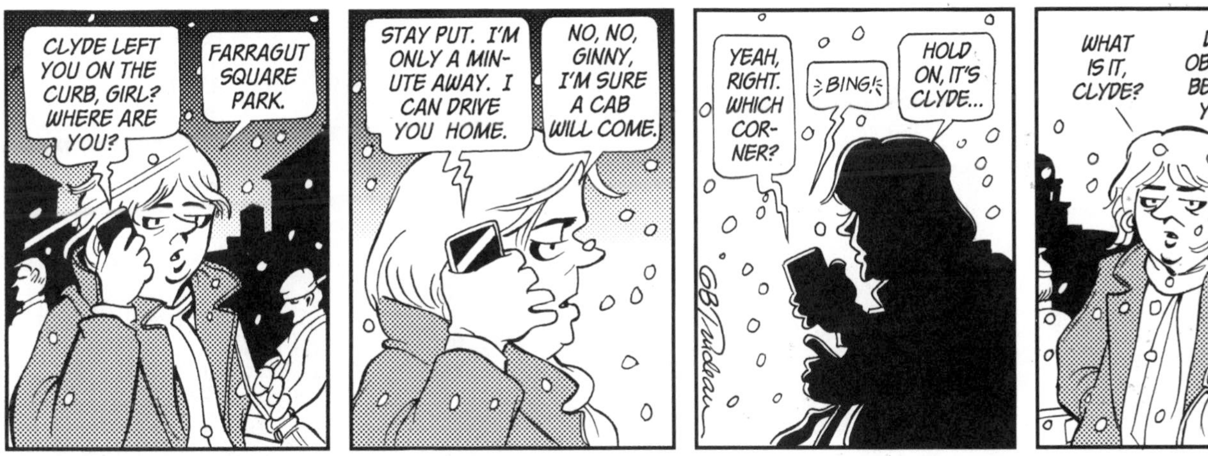
CLYDE LEFT YOU ON THE CURB, GIRL? WHERE ARE YOU?
FARRAGUT SQUARE PARK.
STAY PUT. I'M ONLY A MINUTE AWAY. I CAN DRIVE YOU HOME.
NO, NO, GINNY, I'M SURE A CAB WILL COME.
YEAH, RIGHT. WHICH CORNER?
BING!
HOLD ON, IT'S CLYDE...
WHAT IS IT, CLYDE?
DO YOU HAVE OBAMA'S BLACKBERRY NUMBER? YOU DO, DON'T YOU?

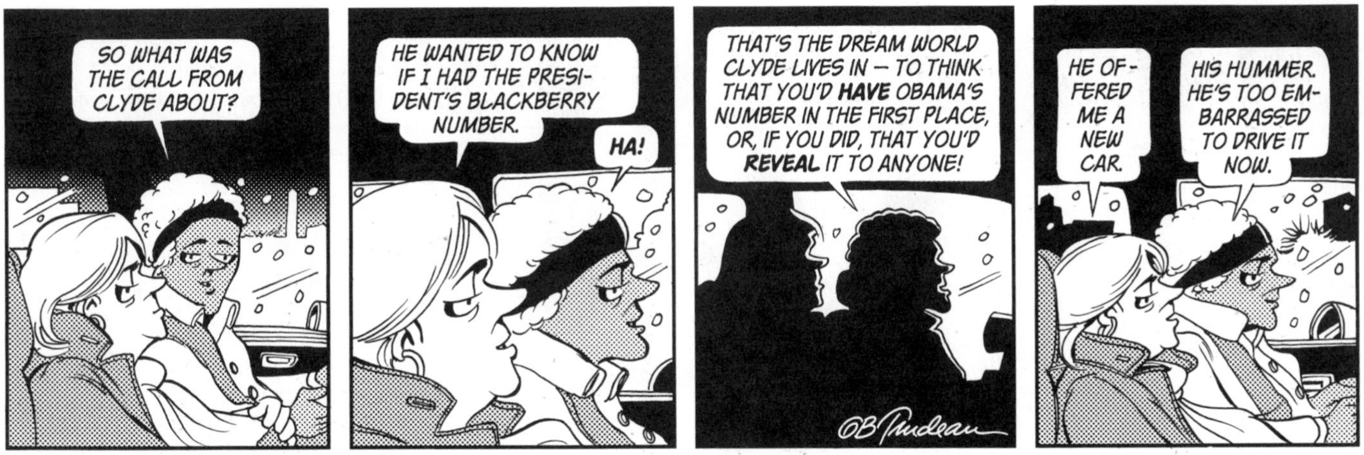
SO WHAT WAS THE CALL FROM CLYDE ABOUT?
HE WANTED TO KNOW IF I HAD THE PRESIDENT'S BLACKBERRY NUMBER.
HA!
THAT'S THE DREAM WORLD CLYDE LIVES IN — TO THINK THAT YOU'D **HAVE** OBAMA'S NUMBER IN THE FIRST PLACE, OR, IF YOU DID, THAT YOU'D **REVEAL** IT TO ANYONE!
HE OFFERED ME A NEW CAR.
HIS HUMMER. HE'S TOO EMBARRASSED TO DRIVE IT NOW.

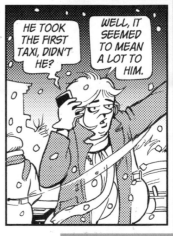

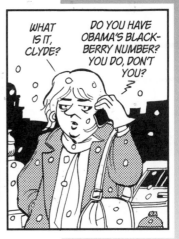

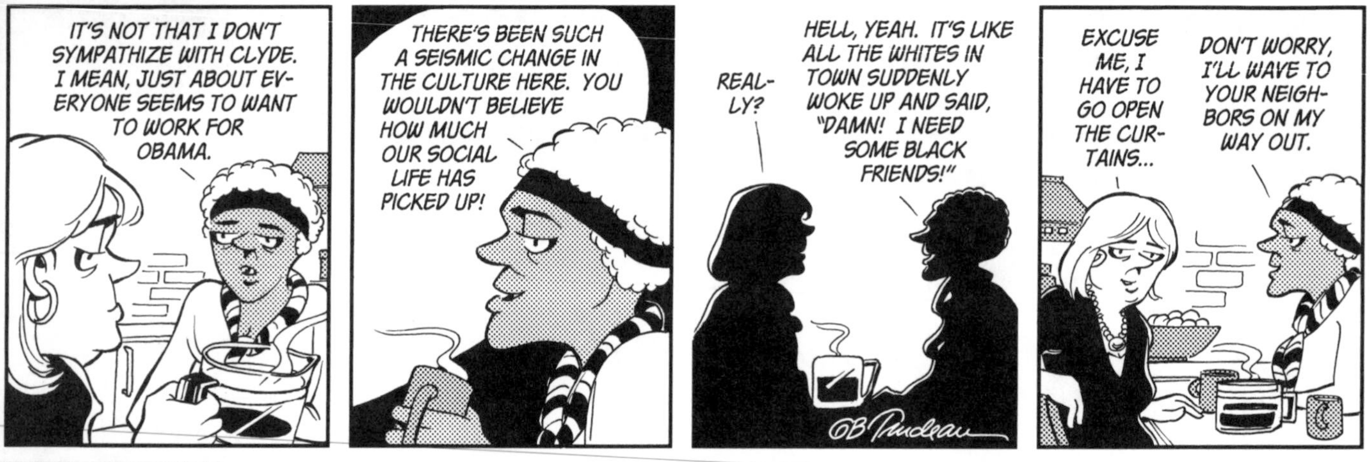
IT'S NOT THAT I DON'T SYMPATHIZE WITH CLYDE. I MEAN, JUST ABOUT EVERYONE SEEMS TO WANT TO WORK FOR OBAMA.
THERE'S BEEN SUCH A SEISMIC CHANGE IN THE CULTURE HERE. YOU WOULDN'T BELIEVE HOW MUCH OUR SOCIAL LIFE HAS PICKED UP!
REALLY?
HELL, YEAH. IT'S LIKE ALL THE WHITES IN TOWN SUDDENLY WOKE UP AND SAID, "DAMN! I NEED SOME BLACK FRIENDS!"
GB Trudeau
EXCUSE ME, I HAVE TO GO OPEN THE CURTAINS...
DON'T WORRY, I'LL WAVE TO YOUR NEIGHBORS ON MY WAY OUT.

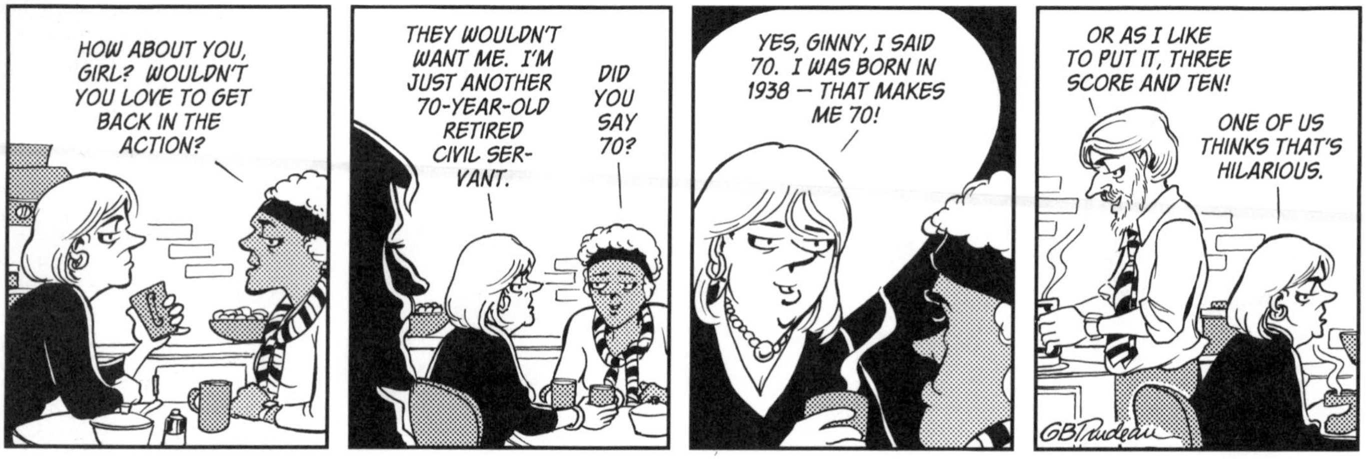
HOW ABOUT YOU, GIRL? WOULDN'T YOU LOVE TO GET BACK IN THE ACTION?
THEY WOULDN'T WANT ME. I'M JUST ANOTHER 70-YEAR-OLD RETIRED CIVIL SERVANT.
DID YOU SAY 70?
YES, GINNY, I SAID 70. I WAS BORN IN 1938 — THAT MAKES ME 70!
OR AS I LIKE TO PUT IT, THREE SCORE AND TEN!
ONE OF US THINKS THAT'S HILARIOUS.
GB Trudeau

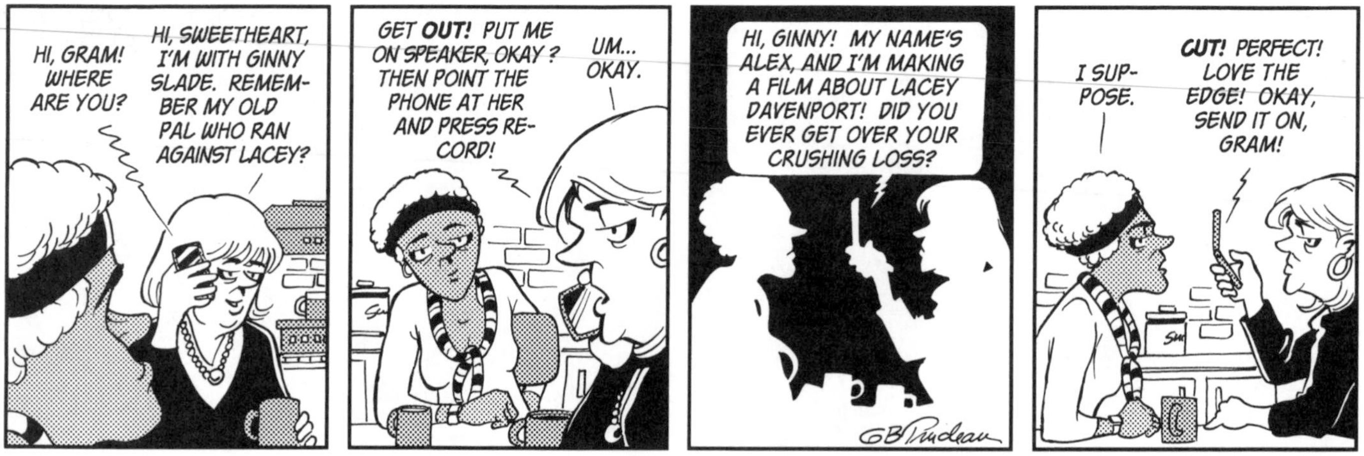
HI, GRAM! WHERE ARE YOU?
HI, SWEETHEART, I'M WITH GINNY SLADE. REMEMBER MY OLD PAL WHO RAN AGAINST LACEY?
GET OUT! PUT ME ON SPEAKER, OKAY? THEN POINT THE PHONE AT HER AND PRESS RECORD!
UM... OKAY.
HI, GINNY! MY NAME'S ALEX, AND I'M MAKING A FILM ABOUT LACEY DAVENPORT! DID YOU EVER GET OVER YOUR CRUSHING LOSS?
GB Trudeau
I SUPPOSE.
CUT! PERFECT! LOVE THE EDGE! OKAY, SEND IT ON, GRAM!

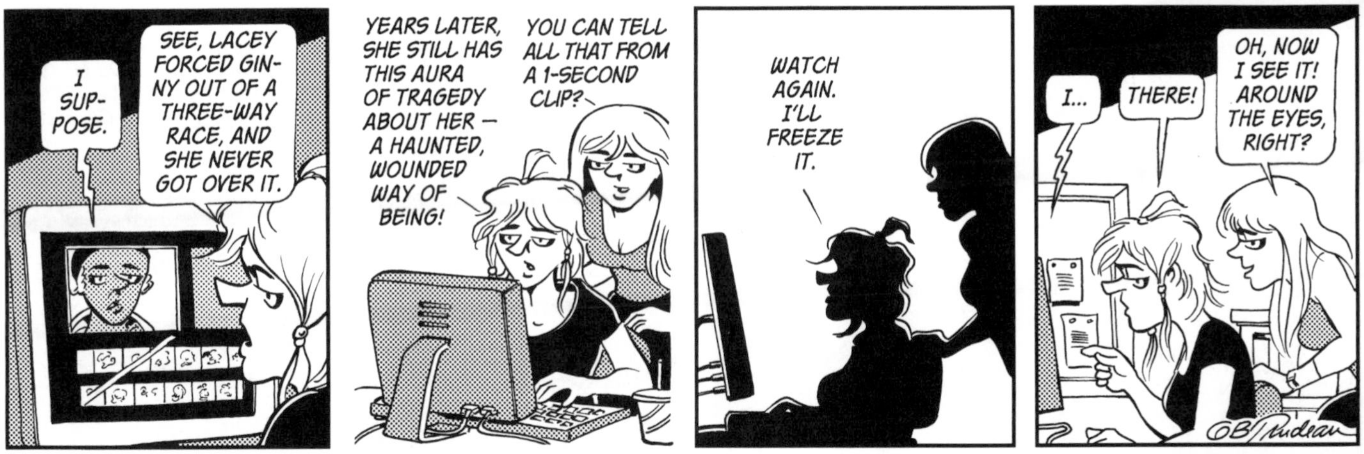
I SUPPOSE.
SEE, LACEY FORCED GINNY OUT OF A THREE-WAY RACE, AND SHE NEVER GOT OVER IT.
YEARS LATER, SHE STILL HAS THIS AURA OF TRAGEDY ABOUT HER — A HAUNTED, WOUNDED WAY OF BEING!
YOU CAN TELL ALL THAT FROM A 1-SECOND CLIP?
WATCH AGAIN. I'LL FREEZE IT.
I...
THERE!
OH, NOW I SEE IT! AROUND THE EYES, RIGHT?
GB Trudeau

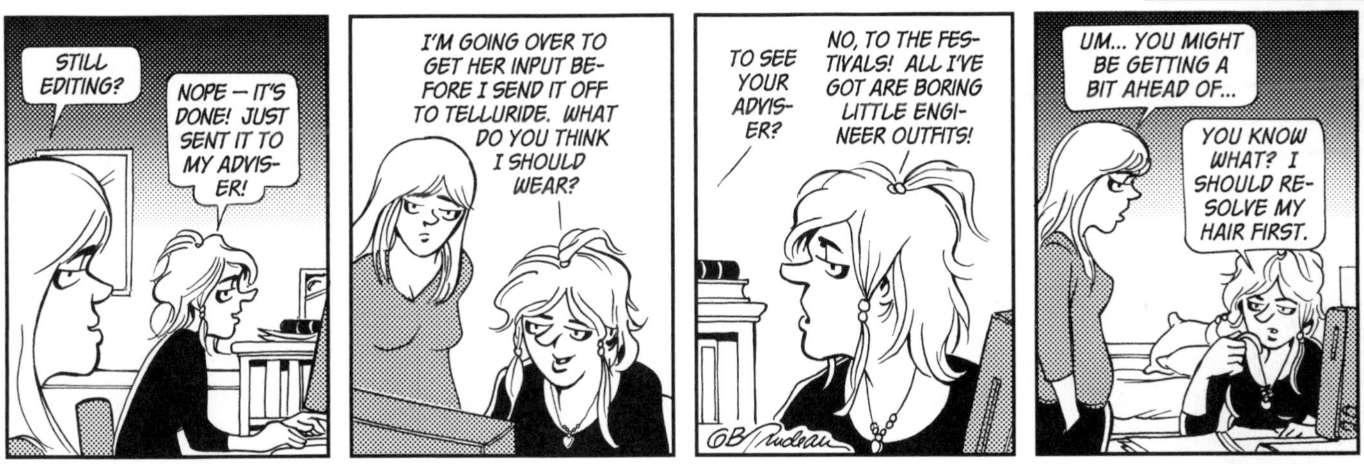
STILL EDITING?
NOPE — IT'S DONE! JUST SENT IT TO MY ADVISER!
I'M GOING OVER TO GET HER INPUT BEFORE I SEND IT OFF TO TELLURIDE. WHAT DO YOU THINK I SHOULD WEAR?
TO SEE YOUR ADVISER?
NO, TO THE FESTIVALS! ALL I'VE GOT ARE BORING LITTLE ENGINEER OUTFITS!
GB Trudeau
UM... YOU MIGHT BE GETTING A BIT AHEAD OF...
YOU KNOW WHAT? I SHOULD RESOLVE MY HAIR FIRST.

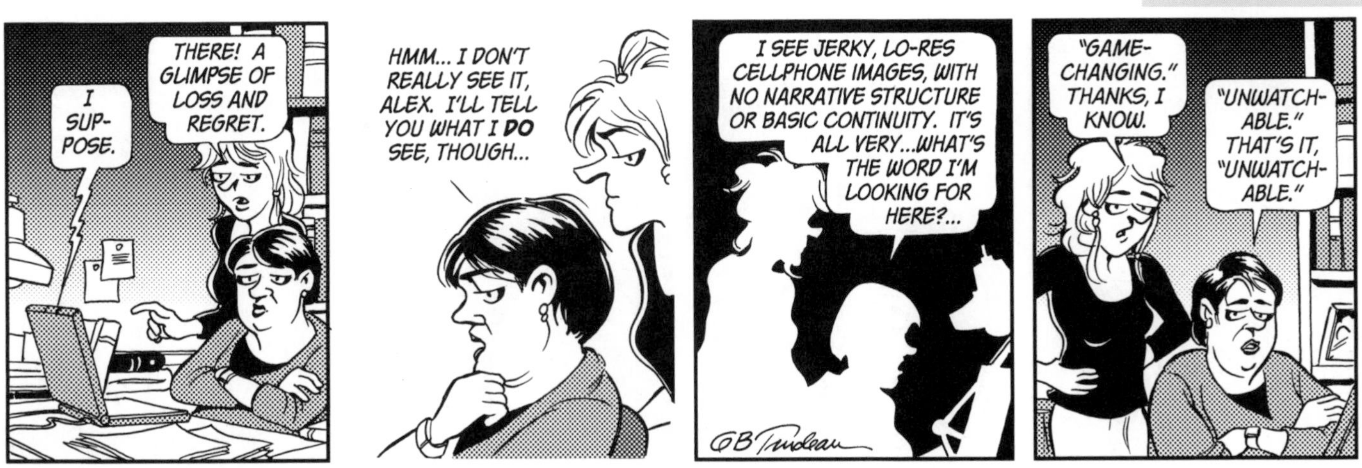
I SUPPOSE.
THERE! A GLIMPSE OF LOSS AND REGRET.
HMM... I DON'T REALLY SEE IT, ALEX. I'LL TELL YOU WHAT I **DO** SEE, THOUGH...
I SEE JERKY, LO-RES CELLPHONE IMAGES, WITH NO NARRATIVE STRUCTURE OR BASIC CONTINUITY. IT'S ALL VERY...WHAT'S THE WORD I'M LOOKING FOR HERE?...
GB Trudeau
"GAME-CHANGING." THANKS, I KNOW.
"UNWATCHABLE." THAT'S IT, "UNWATCHABLE."

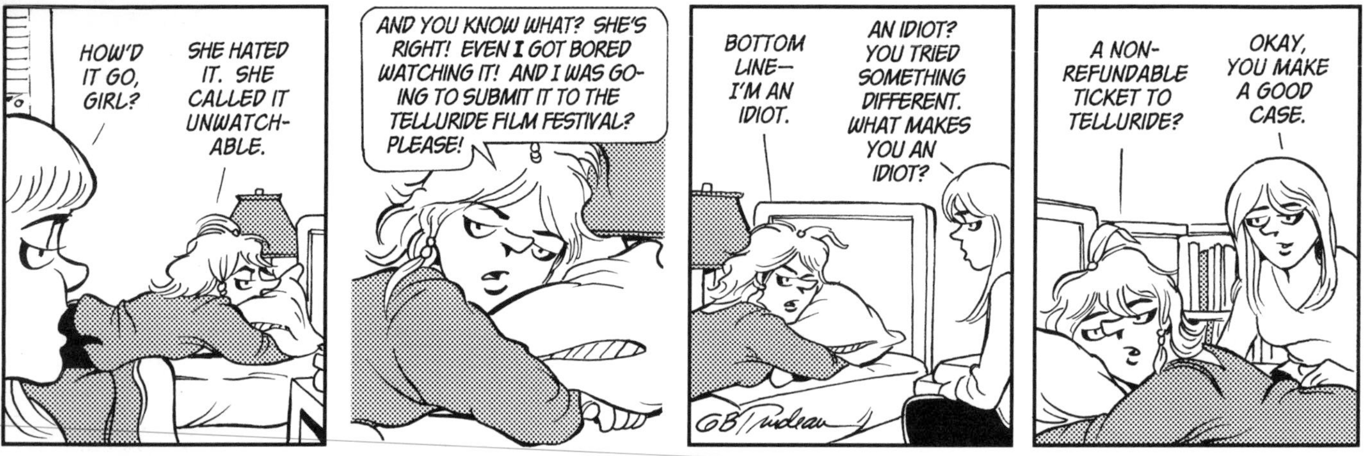
HOW'D IT GO, GIRL?
SHE HATED IT. SHE CALLED IT UNWATCHABLE.
AND YOU KNOW WHAT? SHE'S RIGHT! EVEN **I** GOT BORED WATCHING IT! AND I WAS GOING TO SUBMIT IT TO THE TELLURIDE FILM FESTIVAL? PLEASE!
BOTTOM LINE— I'M AN IDIOT.
AN IDIOT? YOU TRIED SOMETHING DIFFERENT. WHAT MAKES YOU AN IDIOT?
A NON-REFUNDABLE TICKET TO TELLURIDE?
OKAY, YOU MAKE A GOOD CASE.

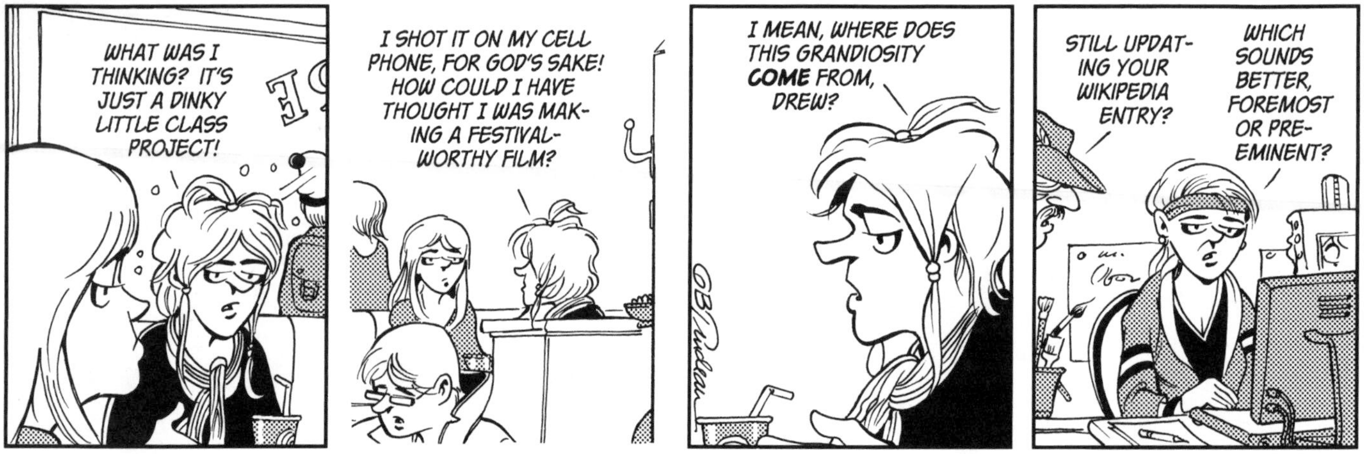
WHAT WAS I THINKING? IT'S JUST A DINKY LITTLE CLASS PROJECT!
I SHOT IT ON MY CELL PHONE, FOR GOD'S SAKE! HOW COULD I HAVE THOUGHT I WAS MAKING A FESTIVAL-WORTHY FILM?
I MEAN, WHERE DOES THIS GRANDIOSITY **COME** FROM, DREW?
STILL UPDATING YOUR WIKIPEDIA ENTRY?
WHICH SOUNDS BETTER, FOREMOST OR PRE-EMINENT?

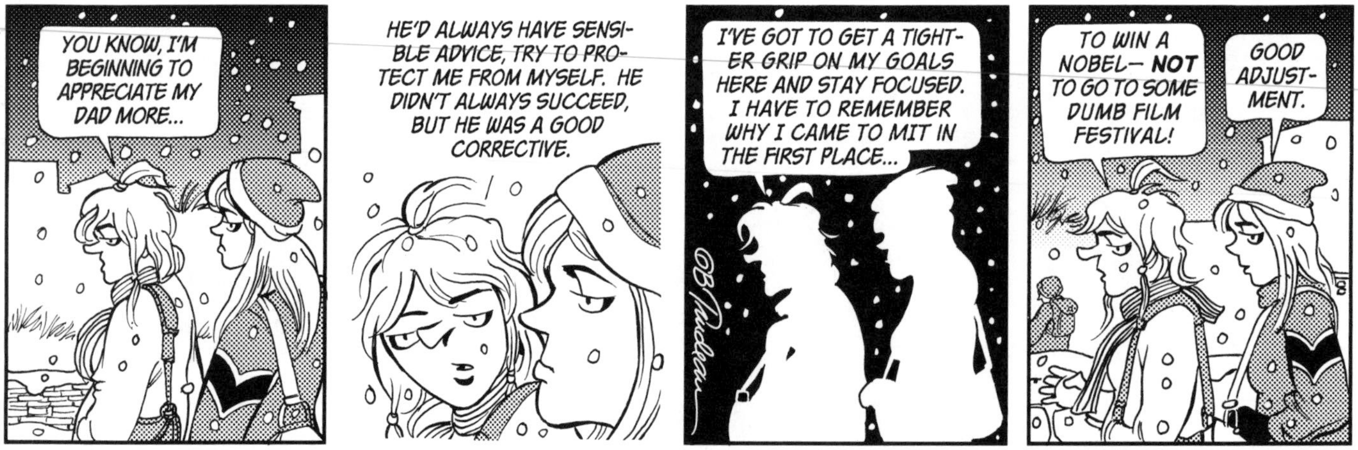
YOU KNOW, I'M BEGINNING TO APPRECIATE MY DAD MORE...
HE'D ALWAYS HAVE SENSIBLE ADVICE, TRY TO PROTECT ME FROM MYSELF. HE DIDN'T ALWAYS SUCCEED, BUT HE WAS A GOOD CORRECTIVE.
I'VE GOT TO GET A TIGHTER GRIP ON MY GOALS HERE AND STAY FOCUSED. I HAVE TO REMEMBER WHY I CAME TO MIT IN THE FIRST PLACE...
TO WIN A NOBEL— **NOT** TO GO TO SOME DUMB FILM FESTIVAL!
GOOD ADJUSTMENT.

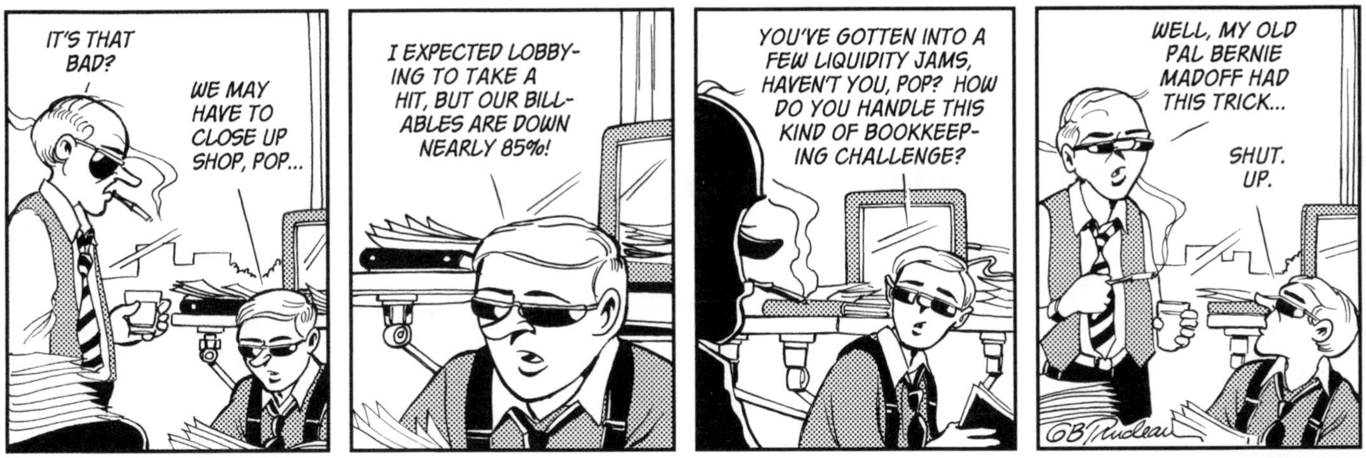
IT'S THAT BAD?
WE MAY HAVE TO CLOSE UP SHOP, POP...
I EXPECTED LOBBYING TO TAKE A HIT, BUT OUR BILLABLES ARE DOWN NEARLY 85%!
YOU'VE GOTTEN INTO A FEW LIQUIDITY JAMS, HAVEN'T YOU, POP? HOW DO YOU HANDLE THIS KIND OF BOOKKEEPING CHALLENGE?
WELL, MY OLD PAL BERNIE MADOFF HAD THIS TRICK...
SHUT. UP.
GB Trudeau

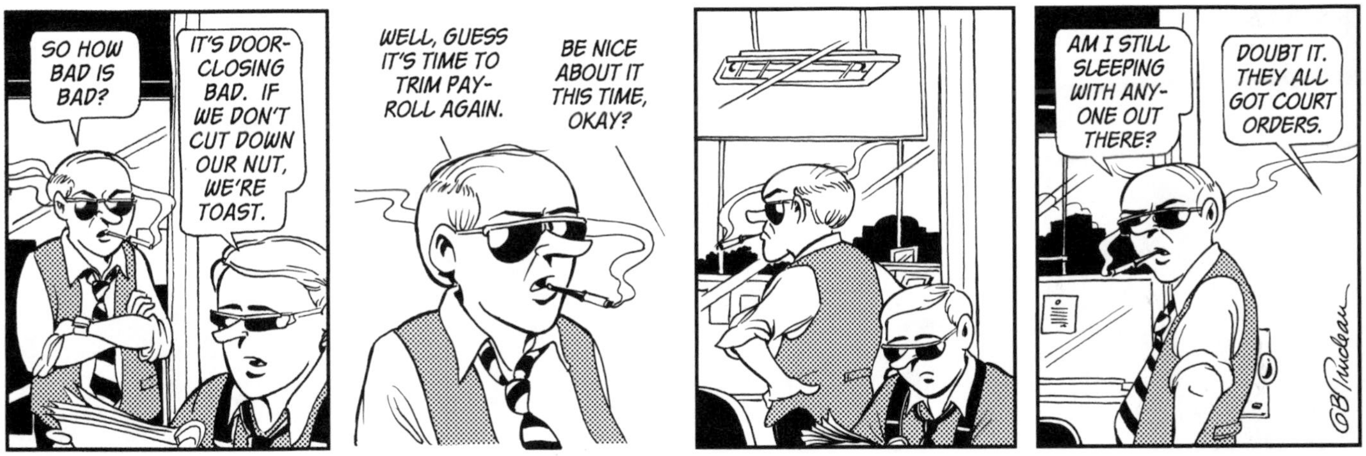
SO HOW BAD IS BAD?
IT'S DOOR-CLOSING BAD. IF WE DON'T CUT DOWN OUR NUT, WE'RE TOAST.
WELL, GUESS IT'S TIME TO TRIM PAYROLL AGAIN.
BE NICE ABOUT IT THIS TIME, OKAY?
AM I STILL SLEEPING WITH ANYONE OUT THERE?
DOUBT IT. THEY ALL GOT COURT ORDERS.
GB Trudeau

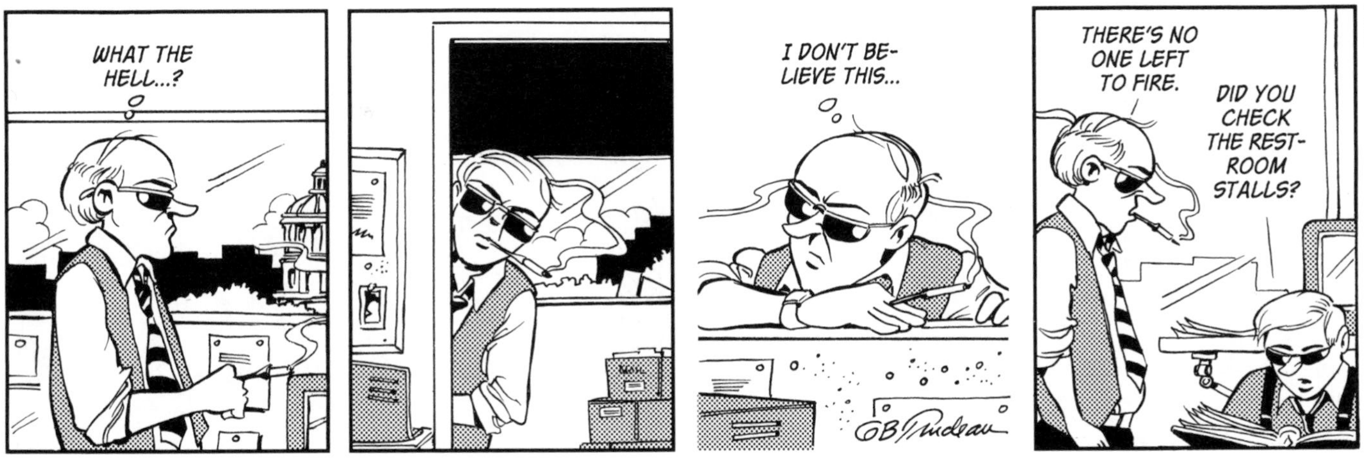
WHAT THE HELL...?
I DON'T BELIEVE THIS...
THERE'S NO ONE LEFT TO FIRE.
DID YOU CHECK THE RESTROOM STALLS?
GB Trudeau

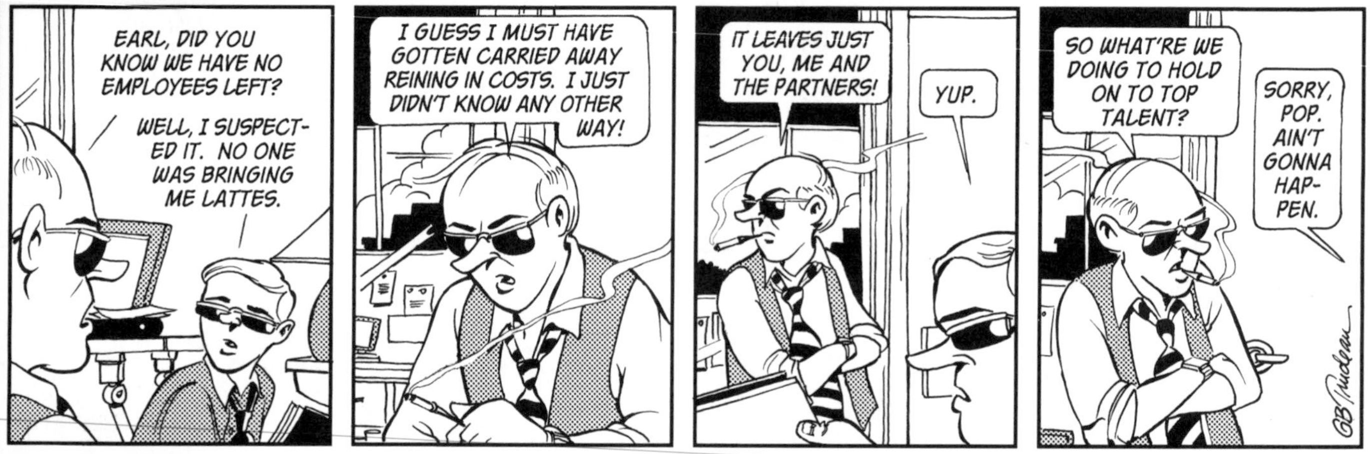
EARL, DID YOU KNOW WE HAVE NO EMPLOYEES LEFT?
WELL, I SUSPECTED IT. NO ONE WAS BRINGING ME LATTES.
I GUESS I MUST HAVE GOTTEN CARRIED AWAY REINING IN COSTS. I JUST DIDN'T KNOW ANY OTHER WAY!
IT LEAVES JUST YOU, ME AND THE PARTNERS!
YUP.
SO WHAT'RE WE DOING TO HOLD ON TO TOP TALENT?
SORRY, POP. AIN'T GONNA HAPPEN.
GB Trudeau

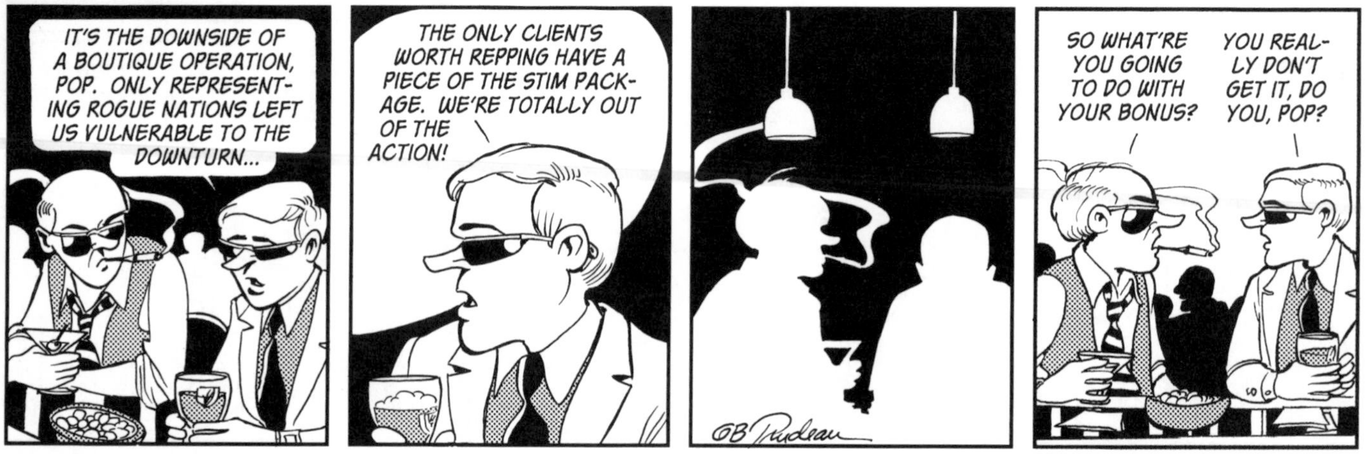
IT'S THE DOWNSIDE OF A BOUTIQUE OPERATION, POP. ONLY REPRESENTING ROGUE NATIONS LEFT US VULNERABLE TO THE DOWNTURN...
THE ONLY CLIENTS WORTH REPPING HAVE A PIECE OF THE STIM PACKAGE. WE'RE TOTALLY OUT OF THE ACTION!
GB Trudeau
SO WHAT'RE YOU GOING TO DO WITH YOUR BONUS?
YOU REALLY DON'T GET IT, DO YOU, POP?

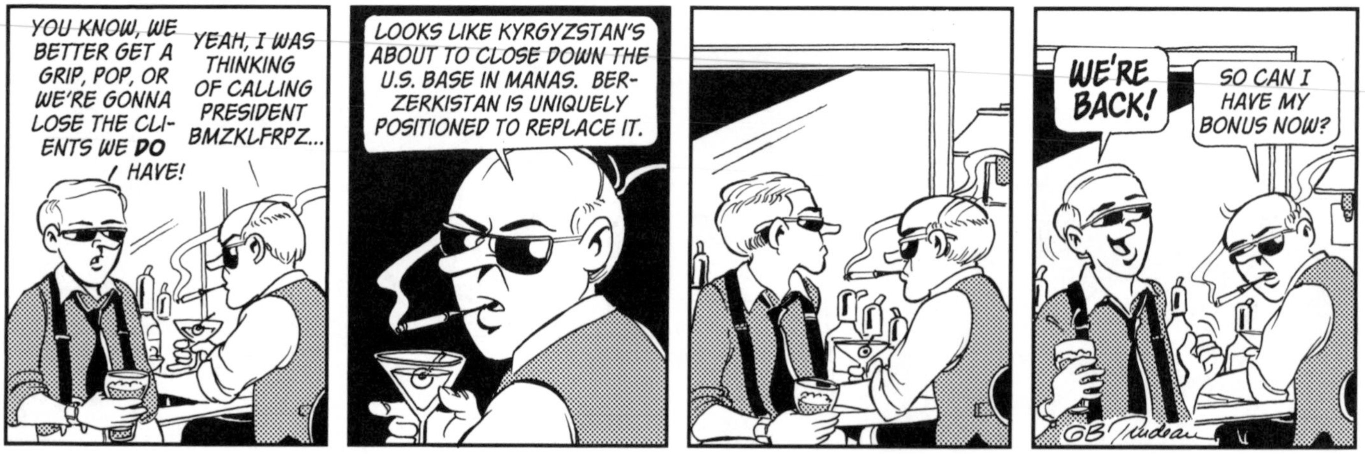
YOU KNOW, WE BETTER GET A GRIP, POP, OR WE'RE GONNA LOSE THE CLIENTS WE DO HAVE!
YEAH, I WAS THINKING OF CALLING PRESIDENT BMZKLFRPZ...
LOOKS LIKE KYRGYZSTAN'S ABOUT TO CLOSE DOWN THE U.S. BASE IN MANAS. BERZERKISTAN IS UNIQUELY POSITIONED TO REPLACE IT.
WE'RE BACK!
SO CAN I HAVE MY BONUS NOW?
GB Trudeau

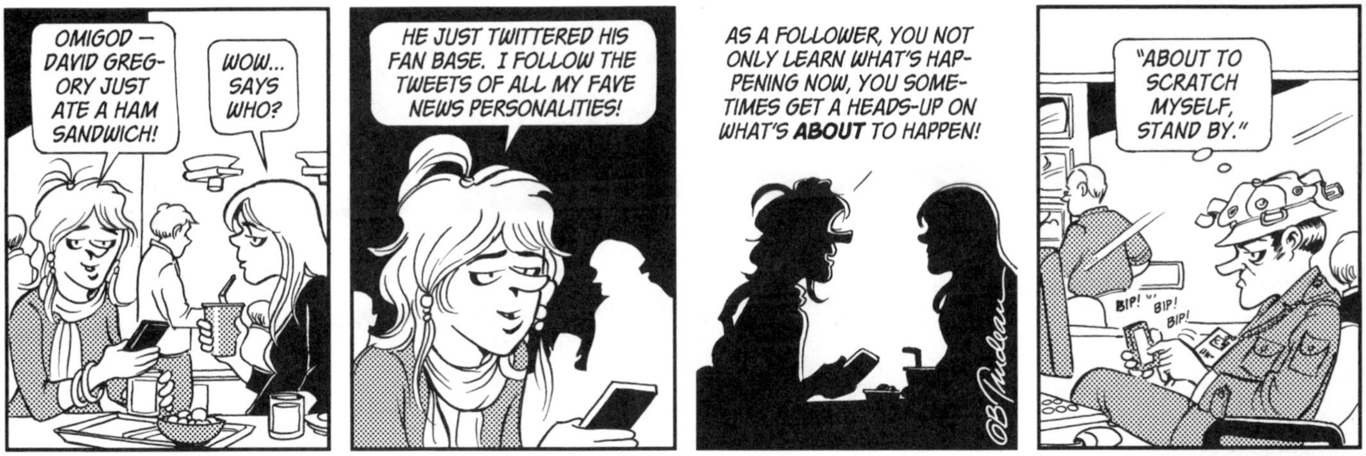
OMIGOD — DAVID GREGORY JUST ATE A HAM SANDWICH!
WOW... SAYS WHO?
HE JUST TWITTERED HIS FAN BASE. I FOLLOW THE TWEETS OF ALL MY FAVE NEWS PERSONALITIES!
AS A FOLLOWER, YOU NOT ONLY LEARN WHAT'S HAPPENING NOW, YOU SOMETIMES GET A HEADS-UP ON WHAT'S **ABOUT** TO HAPPEN!
"ABOUT TO SCRATCH MYSELF, STAND BY."
BIP! BIP! BIP!

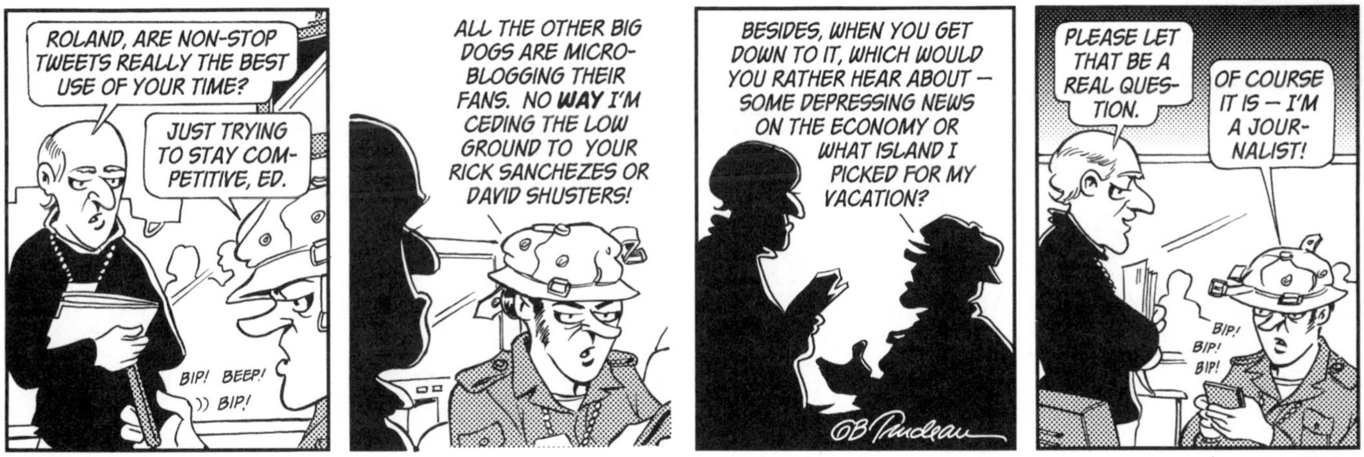
ROLAND, ARE NON-STOP TWEETS REALLY THE BEST USE OF YOUR TIME?
JUST TRYING TO STAY COMPETITIVE, ED.
BIP! BEEP! BIP!
ALL THE OTHER BIG DOGS ARE MICRO-BLOGGING THEIR FANS. NO **WAY** I'M CEDING THE LOW GROUND TO YOUR RICK SANCHEZES OR DAVID SHUSTERS!
BESIDES, WHEN YOU GET DOWN TO IT, WHICH WOULD YOU RATHER HEAR ABOUT — SOME DEPRESSING NEWS ON THE ECONOMY OR WHAT ISLAND I PICKED FOR MY VACATION?
PLEASE LET THAT BE A REAL QUESTION.
OF COURSE IT IS — I'M A JOURNALIST!
BIP! BIP! BIP!

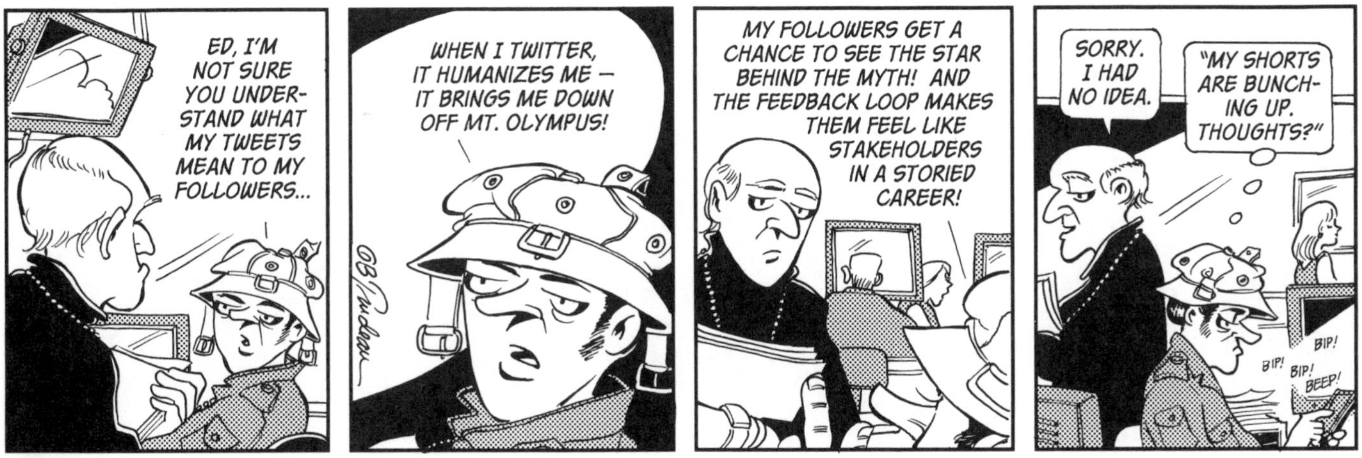
ED, I'M NOT SURE YOU UNDERSTAND WHAT MY TWEETS MEAN TO MY FOLLOWERS...
WHEN I TWITTER, IT HUMANIZES ME — IT BRINGS ME DOWN OFF MT. OLYMPUS!
MY FOLLOWERS GET A CHANCE TO SEE THE STAR BEHIND THE MYTH! AND THE FEEDBACK LOOP MAKES THEM FEEL LIKE STAKEHOLDERS IN A STORIED CAREER!
SORRY. I HAD NO IDEA.
"MY SHORTS ARE BUNCHING UP. THOUGHTS?"
BIP! BIP! BIP! BEEP!

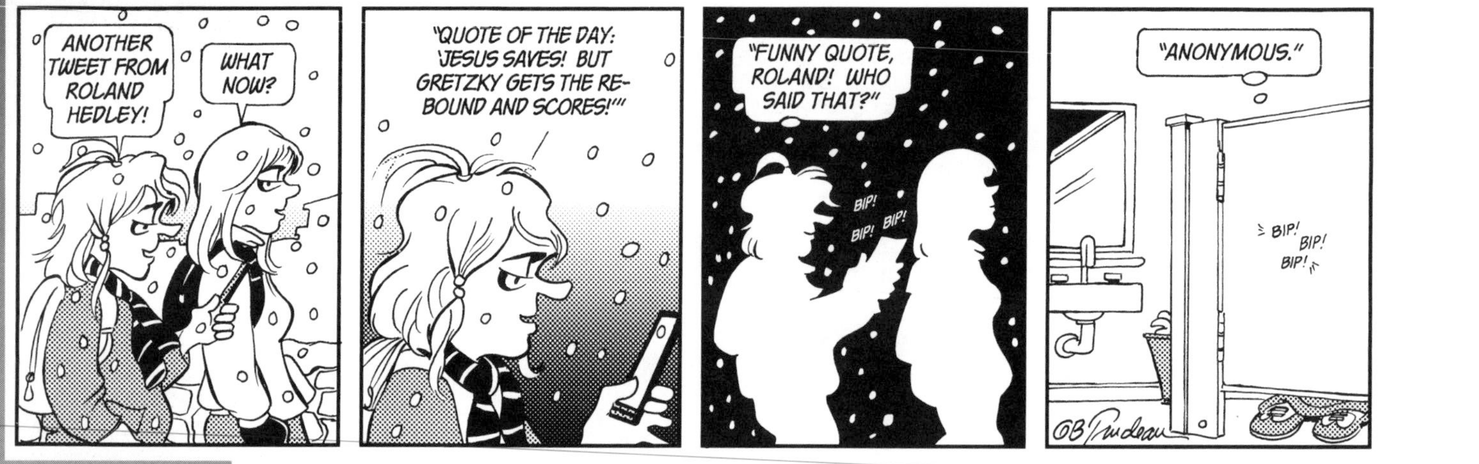
ANOTHER TWEET FROM ROLAND HEDLEY!
WHAT NOW?
"QUOTE OF THE DAY: 'JESUS SAVES! BUT GRETZKY GETS THE REBOUND AND SCORES!'"
"FUNNY QUOTE, ROLAND! WHO SAID THAT?"
BIP! BIP! BIP!
"ANONYMOUS."
BIP! BIP! BIP!

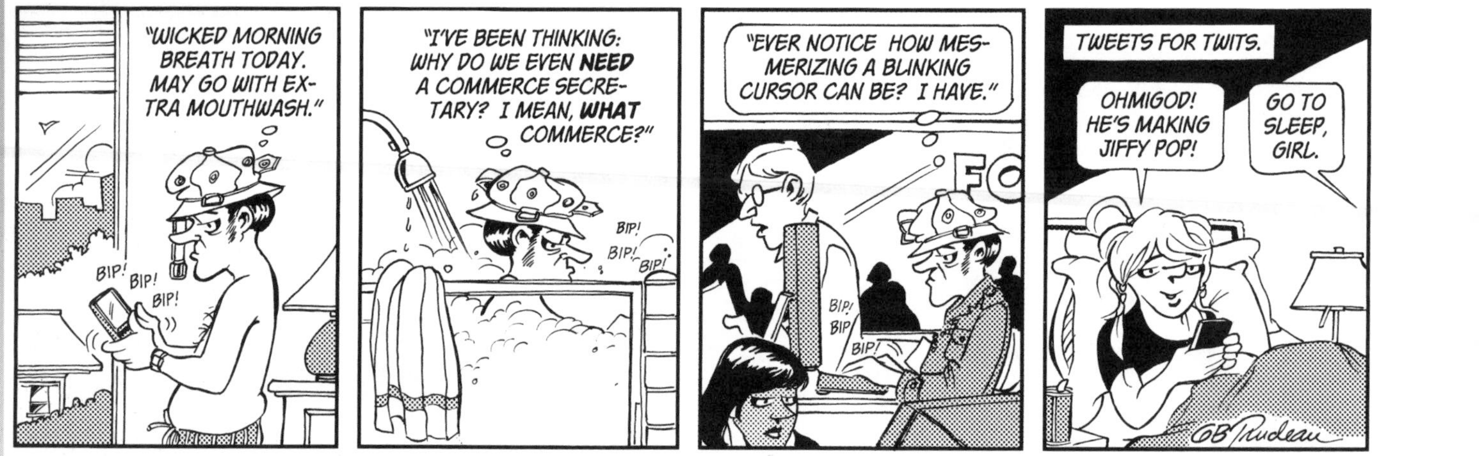
"WICKED MORNING BREATH TODAY. MAY GO WITH EXTRA MOUTHWASH."
BIP! BIP! BIP!
"I'VE BEEN THINKING: WHY DO WE EVEN **NEED** A COMMERCE SECRETARY? I MEAN, **WHAT** COMMERCE?"
BIP! BIP! BIP!
"EVER NOTICE HOW MESMERIZING A BLINKING CURSOR CAN BE? I HAVE."
BIP! BIP! BIP!
TWEETS FOR TWITS.
OHMIGOD! HE'S MAKING JIFFY POP!
GO TO SLEEP, GIRL.

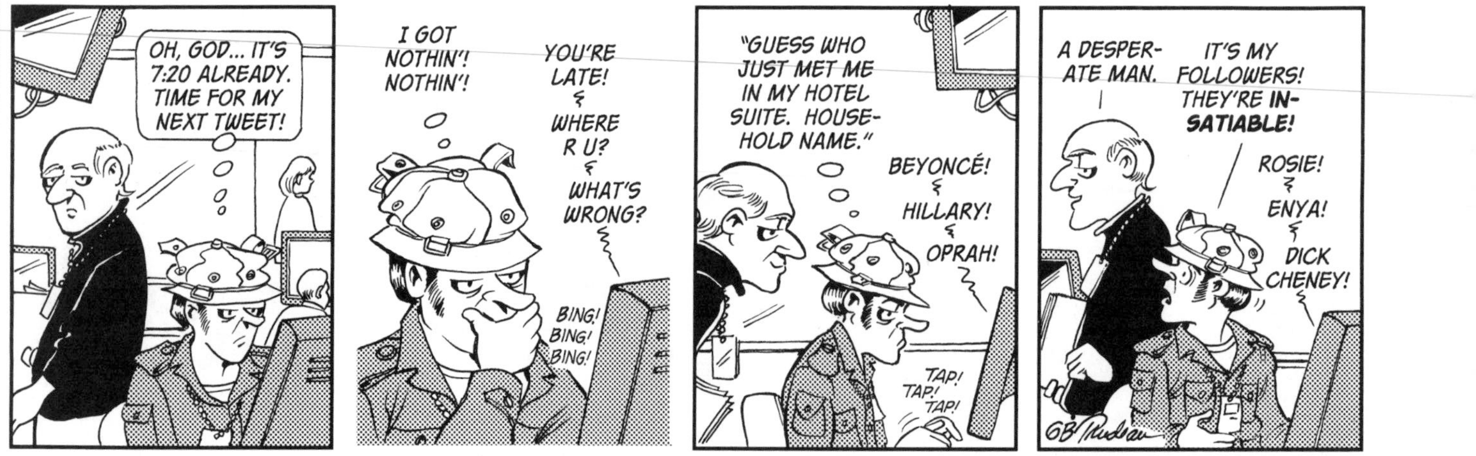
OH, GOD... IT'S 7:20 ALREADY. TIME FOR MY NEXT TWEET!
I GOT NOTHIN'! NOTHIN'!
YOU'RE LATE!
WHERE R U?
WHAT'S WRONG?
BING! BING! BING!
"GUESS WHO JUST MET ME IN MY HOTEL SUITE. HOUSEHOLD NAME."
BEYONCÉ!
HILLARY!
OPRAH!
TAP! TAP! TAP!
A DESPERATE MAN.
IT'S MY FOLLOWERS! THEY'RE **INSATIABLE!**
ROSIE!
ENYA!
DICK CHENEY!

SKULL & BONES, GEORGE W. BUSH'S YALE SECRET SOCIETY, IS BACK IN THE NEWS. ROLAND HEDLEY HAS MORE.

INDEED I DO, BRET, WHICH WILL COME AS NO SURPRISE TO READERS OF MY BLOG, "ROLLIN' WITH ROLAND," OR TO MY FOLLOWERS ON TWITTER...

... MY FRIENDS ON FACEBOOK OR MY FAN BASE AT MYSPACE! A BIG SHOUT-OUT TO ALL OF YOU! BRET?

UM ... WHAT ABOUT THE STORY, ROLAND?

WHOA! THIS JUST IN, BRET — I'M BEING CALLED OUT FOR MY SHOUT-OUT!

IN OTHER NEWS, THE HEIRS OF GERONIMO HAVE SUED A YALE SECRET SOCIETY TO RECOVER THE GREAT CHIEF'S SKULL. ROLAND HEDLEY HAS DETAILS.

BRET, HERE IN NEW HAVEN, MY FOLLOWERS, READERS, RECIPIENTS, CONTACTS, FANS AND FRIENDS HAVE ALL BEEN TRACKING MY EVERY MOVE AND THOUGHT!

WHAT A MIRACULOUS AGE WE LIVE IN WHEN ALL THESE PARTIES ARE EMPOWERED TO WATCH ME REPORT ON ... ON ...

WHAT WAS THE STORY AGAIN, BRET?

GERONIMO. THANKS FOR CHECKING.

SO DID GEORGE BUSH'S GRANDFATHER **REALLY** STEAL GERONIMO'S SKULL FOR HIS SECRET SOCIETY, AS THE SUIT ALLEGES?

REPEATED SEARCHES OF BLOGS AND AGGREGATOR SITES FAILED TO TURN UP ANY CORROBORATING EVIDENCE...

... AS DID REAL-TIME INQUIRIES TO MY FOLLOWERS, FANS AND FRIENDS! THIS STORY IS ICE COLD, BRET!

ROLAND, HAVE YOU TRIED REPORTING IT?

OLD SCHOOL? PLEASE, THAT'S FOR NEWSPAPERS.

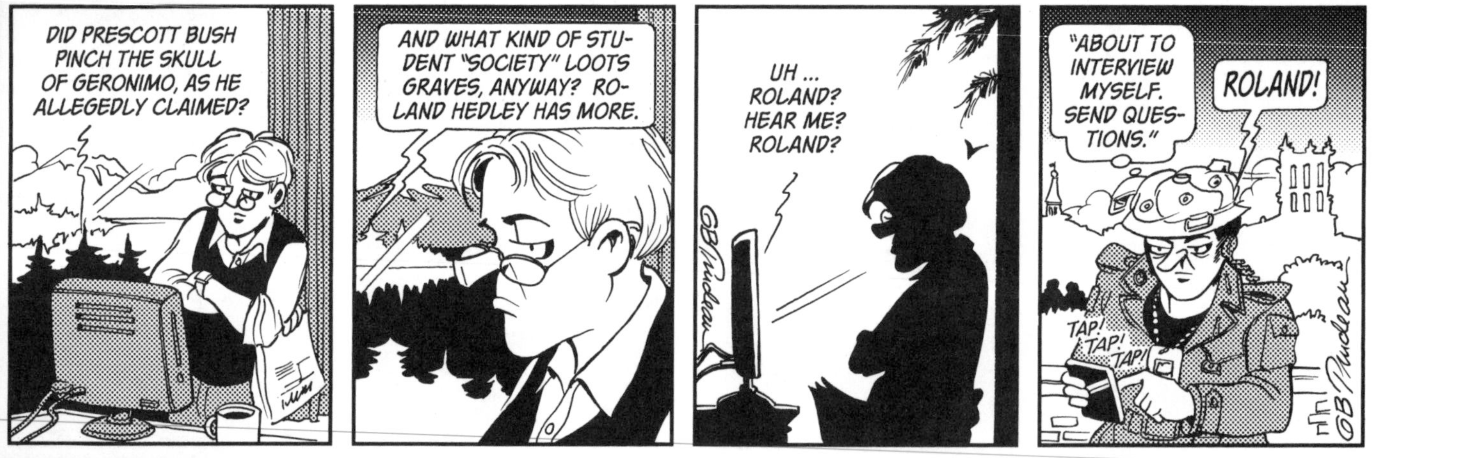
DID PRESCOTT BUSH PINCH THE SKULL OF GERONIMO, AS HE ALLEGEDLY CLAIMED?
AND WHAT KIND OF STUDENT "SOCIETY" LOOTS GRAVES, ANYWAY? ROLAND HEDLEY HAS MORE.
UH ... ROLAND? HEAR ME? ROLAND?
"ABOUT TO INTERVIEW MYSELF. SEND QUESTIONS."
ROLAND!
TAP! TAP! TAP!

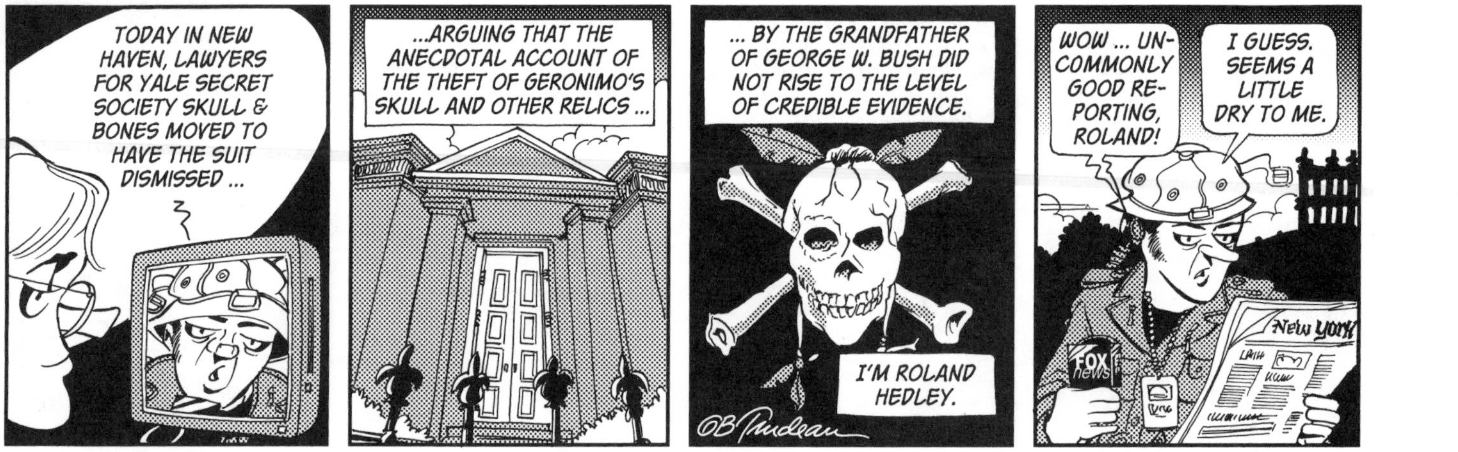
TODAY IN NEW HAVEN, LAWYERS FOR YALE SECRET SOCIETY SKULL & BONES MOVED TO HAVE THE SUIT DISMISSED ...
...ARGUING THAT THE ANECDOTAL ACCOUNT OF THE THEFT OF GERONIMO'S SKULL AND OTHER RELICS ...
... BY THE GRANDFATHER OF GEORGE W. BUSH DID NOT RISE TO THE LEVEL OF CREDIBLE EVIDENCE.
I'M ROLAND HEDLEY.
WOW ... UNCOMMONLY GOOD REPORTING, ROLAND!
I GUESS. SEEMS A LITTLE DRY TO ME.
FOX news
New York

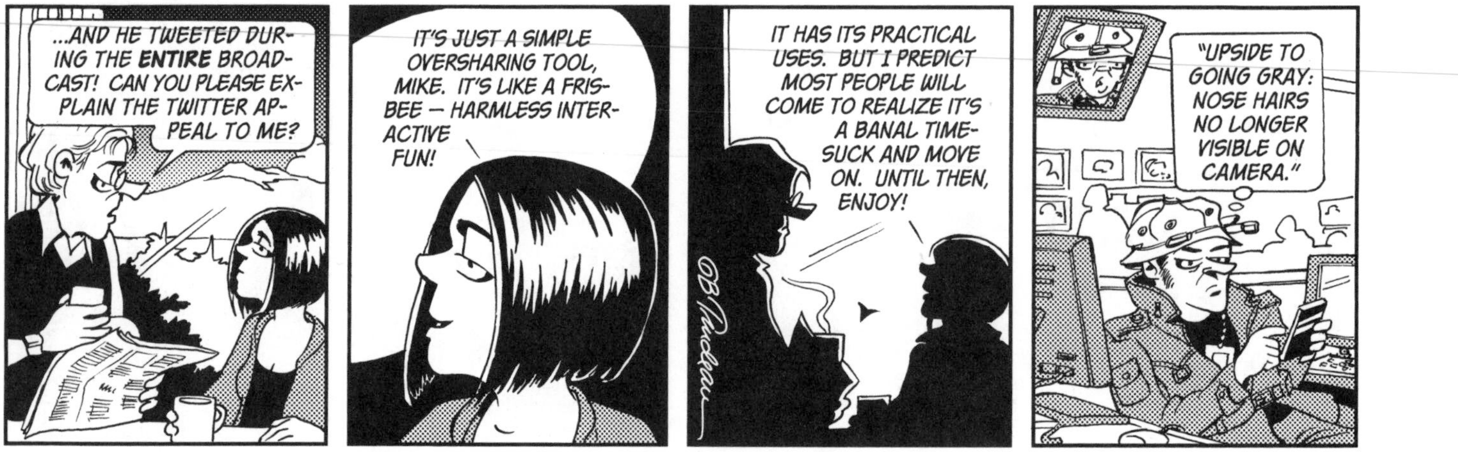
...AND HE TWEETED DURING THE **ENTIRE** BROADCAST! CAN YOU PLEASE EXPLAIN THE TWITTER APPEAL TO ME?
IT'S JUST A SIMPLE OVERSHARING TOOL, MIKE. IT'S LIKE A FRISBEE — HARMLESS INTERACTIVE FUN!
IT HAS ITS PRACTICAL USES. BUT I PREDICT MOST PEOPLE WILL COME TO REALIZE IT'S A BANAL TIME-SUCK AND MOVE ON. UNTIL THEN, ENJOY!
"UPSIDE TO GOING GRAY: NOSE HAIRS NO LONGER VISIBLE ON CAMERA."

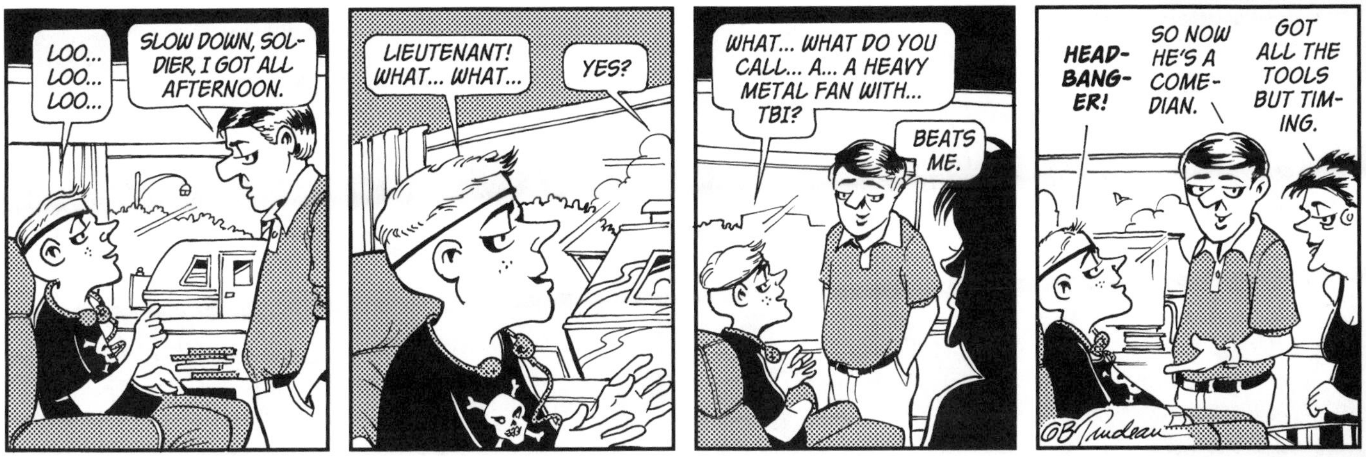
LOO... LOO... LOO...
SLOW DOWN, SOLDIER, I GOT ALL AFTERNOON.
LIEUTENANT! WHAT... WHAT...
YES?
WHAT... WHAT DO YOU CALL... A... A HEAVY METAL FAN WITH... TBI?
BEATS ME.
HEADBANGER!
SO NOW HE'S A COMEDIAN.
GOT ALL THE TOOLS BUT TIMING.
©B Trudeau

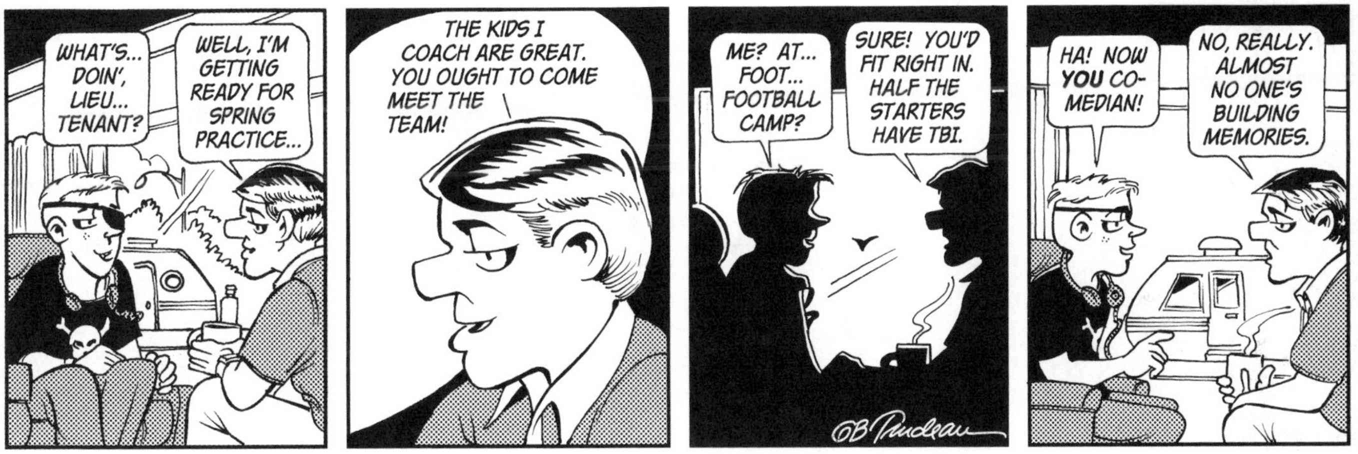
WHAT'S... DOIN', LIEU... TENANT?
WELL, I'M GETTING READY FOR SPRING PRACTICE...
THE KIDS I COACH ARE GREAT. YOU OUGHT TO COME MEET THE TEAM!
ME? AT... FOOT... FOOTBALL CAMP?
SURE! YOU'D FIT RIGHT IN. HALF THE STARTERS HAVE TBI.
©B Trudeau
HA! NOW YOU COMEDIAN!
NO, REALLY. ALMOST NO ONE'S BUILDING MEMORIES.

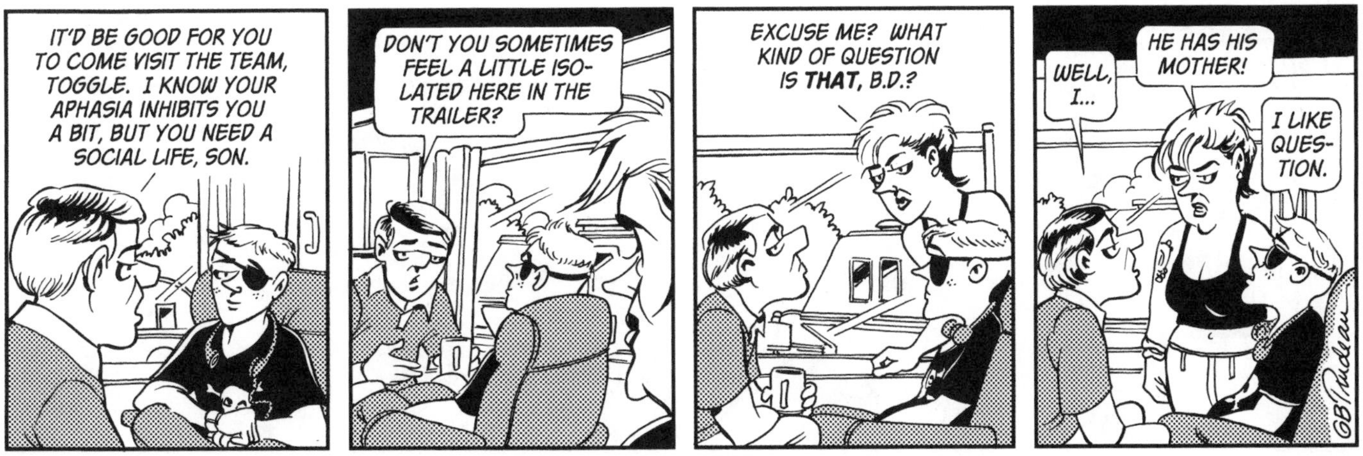
IT'D BE GOOD FOR YOU TO COME VISIT THE TEAM, TOGGLE. I KNOW YOUR APHASIA INHIBITS YOU A BIT, BUT YOU NEED A SOCIAL LIFE, SON.
DON'T YOU SOMETIMES FEEL A LITTLE ISOLATED HERE IN THE TRAILER?
EXCUSE ME? WHAT KIND OF QUESTION IS THAT, B.D.?
WELL, I...
HE HAS HIS MOTHER!
I LIKE QUESTION.
©B Trudeau

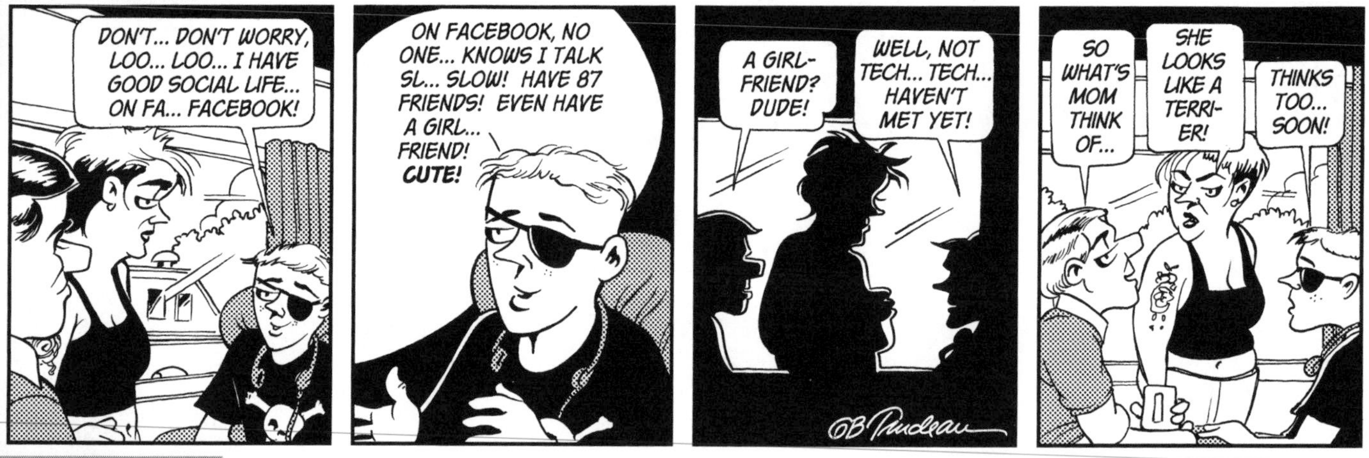
DON'T... DON'T WORRY, LOO... LOO... I HAVE GOOD SOCIAL LIFE... ON FA... FACEBOOK!
ON FACEBOOK, NO ONE... KNOWS I TALK SL... SLOW! HAVE 87 FRIENDS! EVEN HAVE A GIRL... FRIEND! **CUTE!**
A GIRL-FRIEND? DUDE!
WELL, NOT TECH... TECH... HAVEN'T MET YET!
SO WHAT'S MOM THINK OF...
SHE LOOKS LIKE A TERRI-ER!
THINKS TOO... SOON!
GB Trudeau

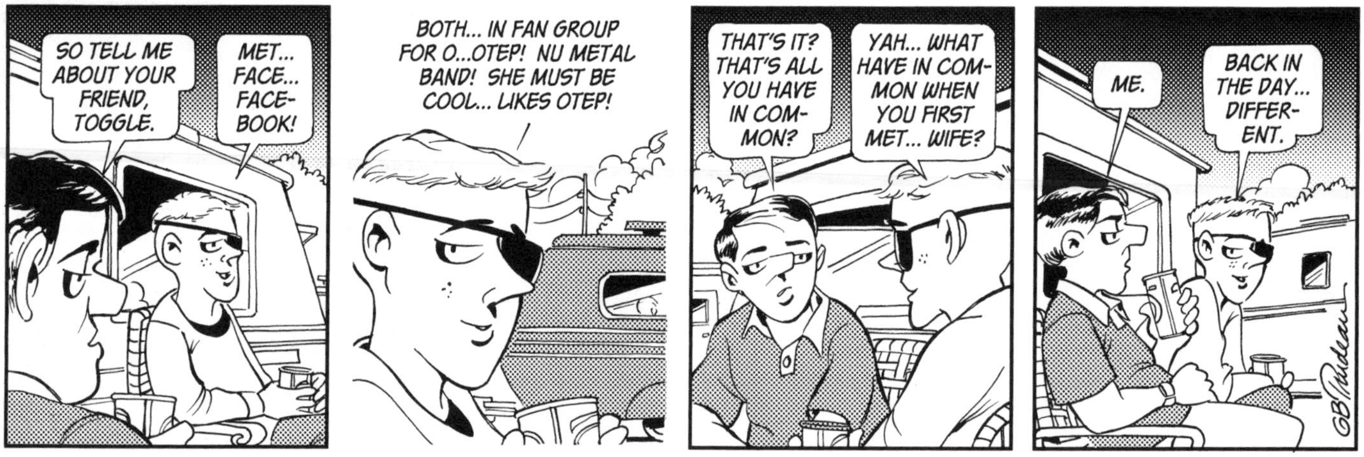
SO TELL ME ABOUT YOUR FRIEND, TOGGLE.
MET... FACE... FACE-BOOK!
BOTH... IN FAN GROUP FOR O...OTEP! NU METAL BAND! SHE MUST BE COOL... LIKES OTEP!
THAT'S IT? THAT'S ALL YOU HAVE IN COM-MON?
YAH... WHAT HAVE IN COM-MON WHEN YOU FIRST MET... WIFE?
ME.
BACK IN THE DAY... DIFFER-ENT.
GB Trudeau

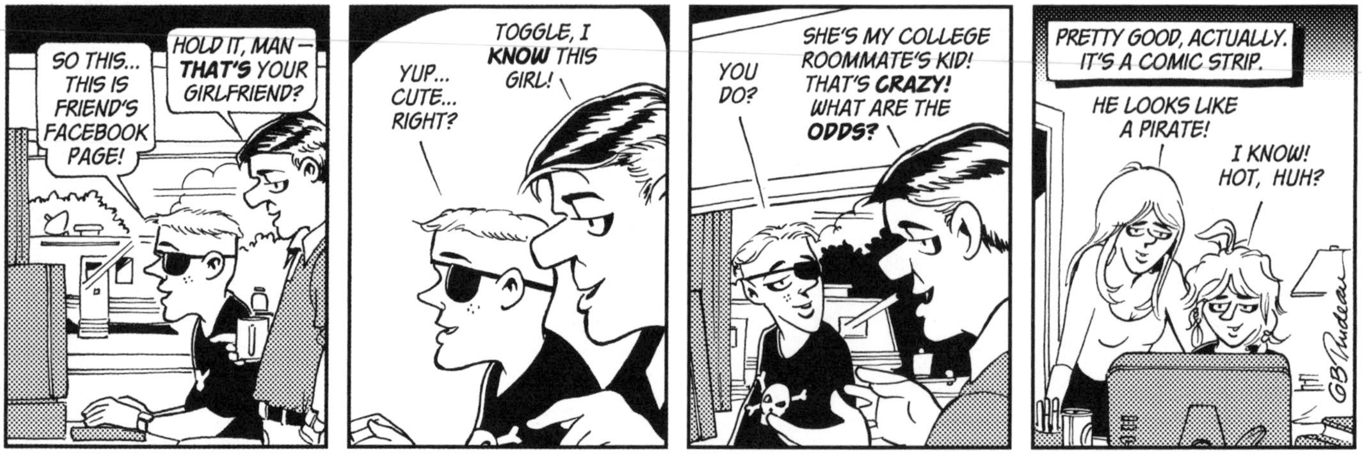
SO THIS... THIS IS FRIEND'S FACEBOOK PAGE!
HOLD IT, MAN – **THAT'S** YOUR GIRLFRIEND?
YUP... CUTE... RIGHT?
TOGGLE, I **KNOW** THIS GIRL!
YOU DO?
SHE'S MY COLLEGE ROOMMATE'S KID! THAT'S **CRAZY!** WHAT ARE THE **ODDS?**
PRETTY GOOD, ACTUALLY. IT'S A COMIC STRIP.
HE LOOKS LIKE A PIRATE!
I KNOW! HOT, HUH?
GB Trudeau

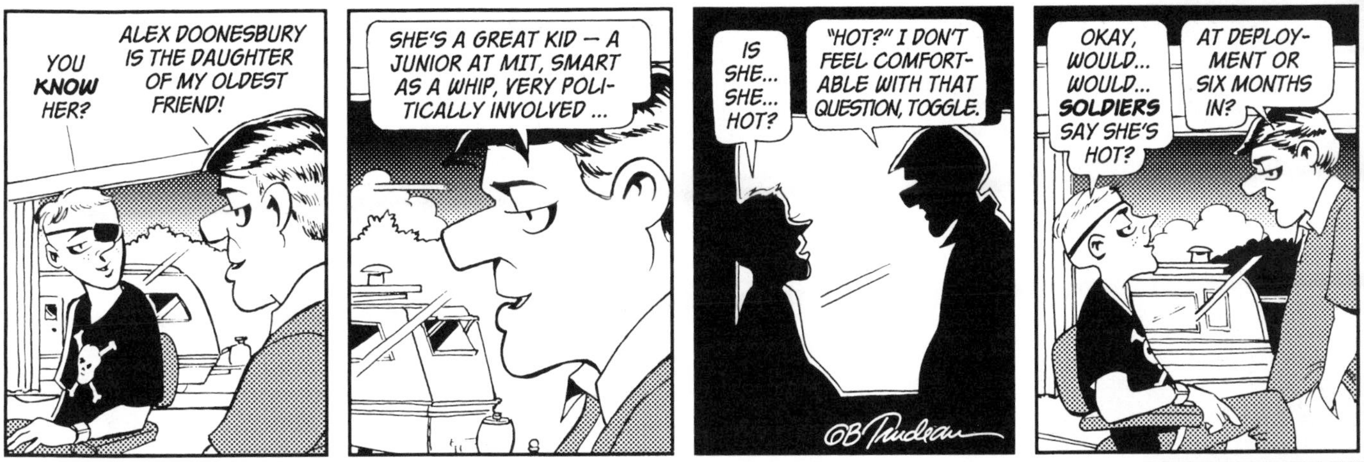
YOU KNOW HER?
ALEX DOONESBURY IS THE DAUGHTER OF MY OLDEST FRIEND!
SHE'S A GREAT KID — A JUNIOR AT MIT, SMART AS A WHIP, VERY POLITICALLY INVOLVED ...
IS SHE... SHE... HOT?
"HOT?" I DON'T FEEL COMFORTABLE WITH THAT QUESTION, TOGGLE.
©B Trudeau
OKAY, WOULD... WOULD... SOLDIERS SAY SHE'S HOT?
AT DEPLOYMENT OR SIX MONTHS IN?

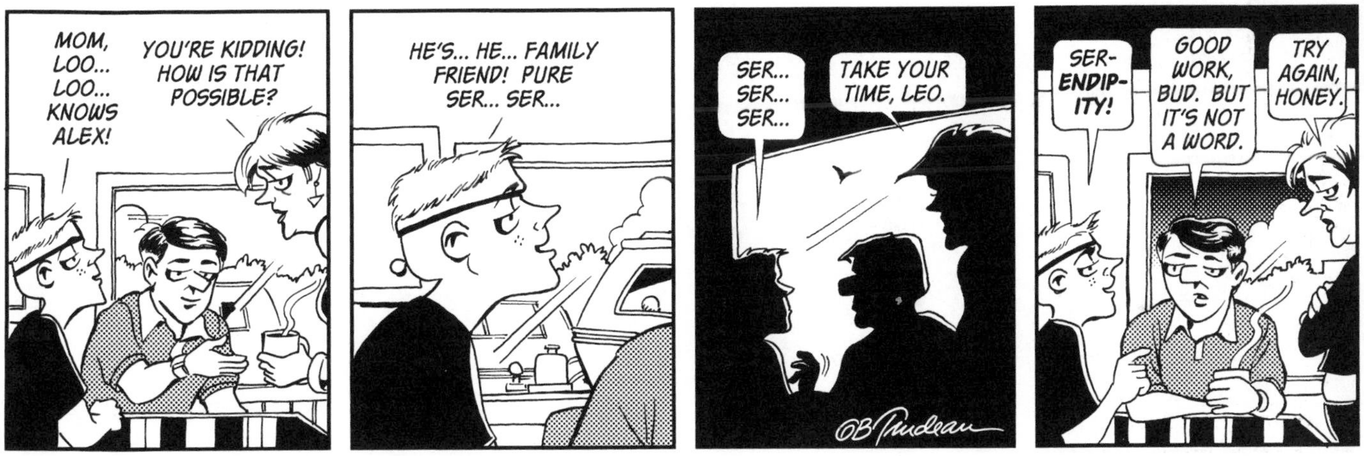
MOM, LOO... LOO... KNOWS ALEX!
YOU'RE KIDDING! HOW IS THAT POSSIBLE?
HE'S... HE... FAMILY FRIEND! PURE SER... SER...
SER... SER... SER...
TAKE YOUR TIME, LEO.
©B Trudeau
SER-ENDIP-ITY!
GOOD WORK, BUD. BUT IT'S NOT A WORD.
TRY AGAIN, HONEY.

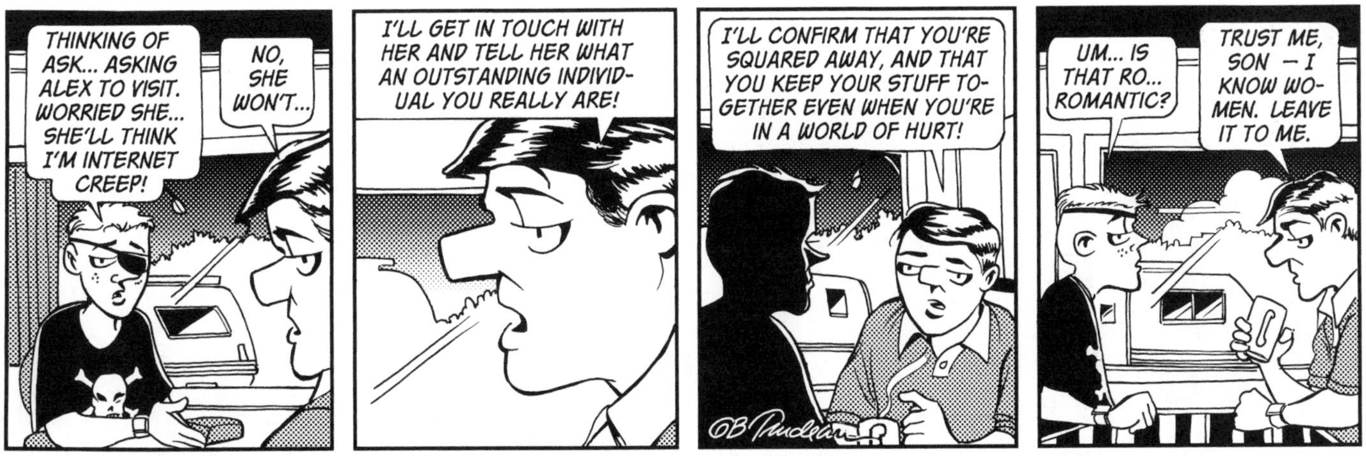
THINKING OF ASK... ASKING ALEX TO VISIT. WORRIED SHE... SHE'LL THINK I'M INTERNET CREEP!
NO, SHE WON'T...
I'LL GET IN TOUCH WITH HER AND TELL HER WHAT AN OUTSTANDING INDIVIDUAL YOU REALLY ARE!
I'LL CONFIRM THAT YOU'RE SQUARED AWAY, AND THAT YOU KEEP YOUR STUFF TOGETHER EVEN WHEN YOU'RE IN A WORLD OF HURT!
©B Trudeau
UM... IS THAT RO... ROMANTIC?
TRUST ME, SON — I KNOW WOMEN. LEAVE IT TO ME.

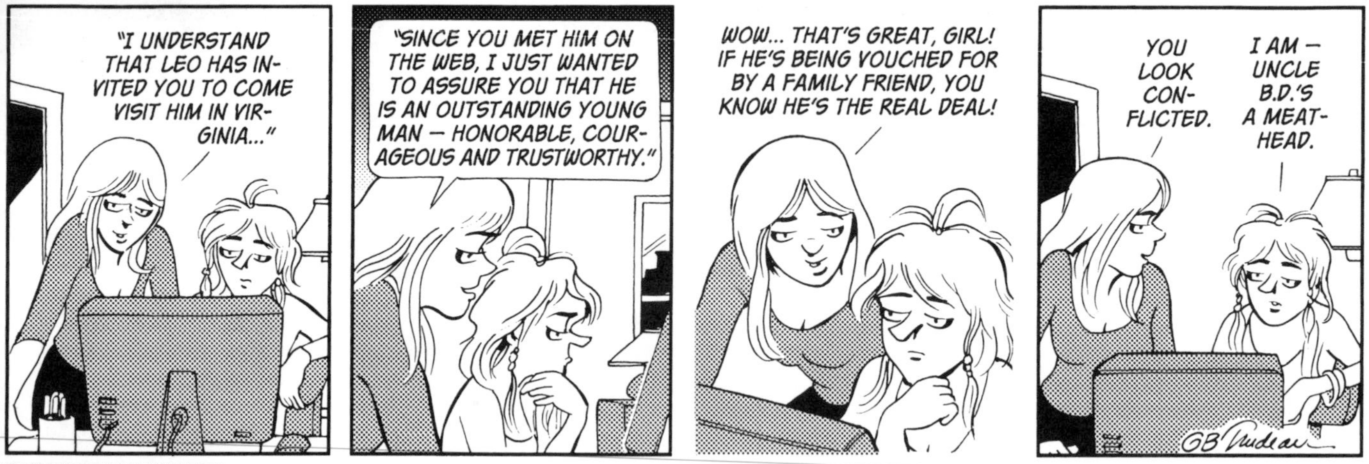
"I UNDERSTAND THAT LEO HAS INVITED YOU TO COME VISIT HIM IN VIRGINIA..."
"SINCE YOU MET HIM ON THE WEB, I JUST WANTED TO ASSURE YOU THAT HE IS AN OUTSTANDING YOUNG MAN — HONORABLE, COURAGEOUS AND TRUSTWORTHY."
WOW... THAT'S GREAT, GIRL! IF HE'S BEING VOUCHED FOR BY A FAMILY FRIEND, YOU KNOW HE'S THE REAL DEAL!
YOU LOOK CONFLICTED.
I AM — UNCLE B.D.'S A MEATHEAD.

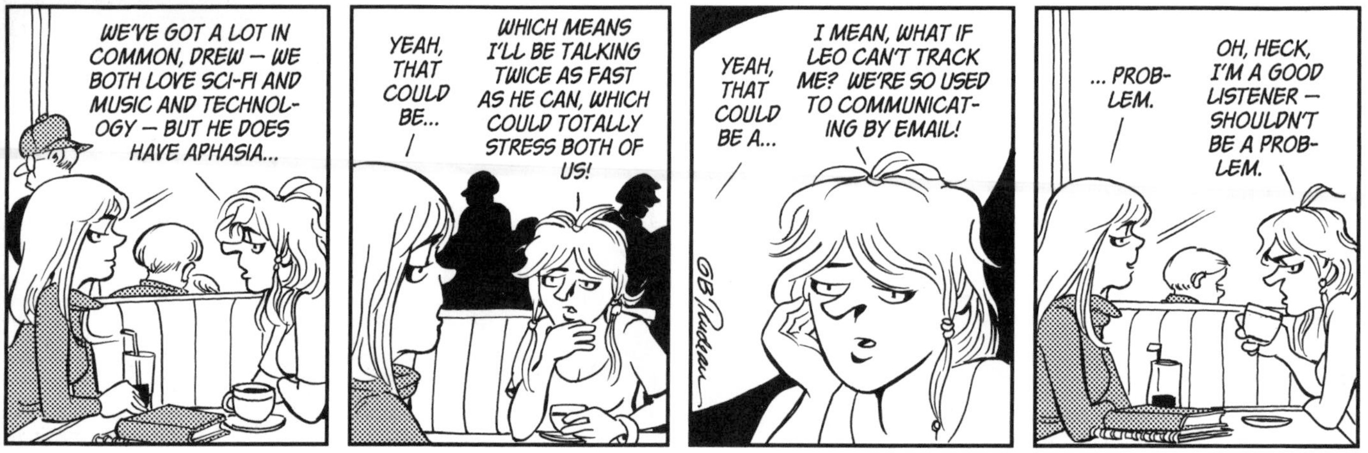
WE'VE GOT A LOT IN COMMON, DREW — WE BOTH LOVE SCI-FI AND MUSIC AND TECHNOLOGY — BUT HE DOES HAVE APHASIA...
YEAH, THAT COULD BE...
WHICH MEANS I'LL BE TALKING TWICE AS FAST AS HE CAN, WHICH COULD TOTALLY STRESS BOTH OF US!
YEAH, THAT COULD BE A...
I MEAN, WHAT IF LEO CAN'T TRACK ME? WE'RE SO USED TO COMMUNICATING BY EMAIL!
... PROBLEM.
OH, HECK, I'M A GOOD LISTENER — SHOULDN'T BE A PROBLEM.

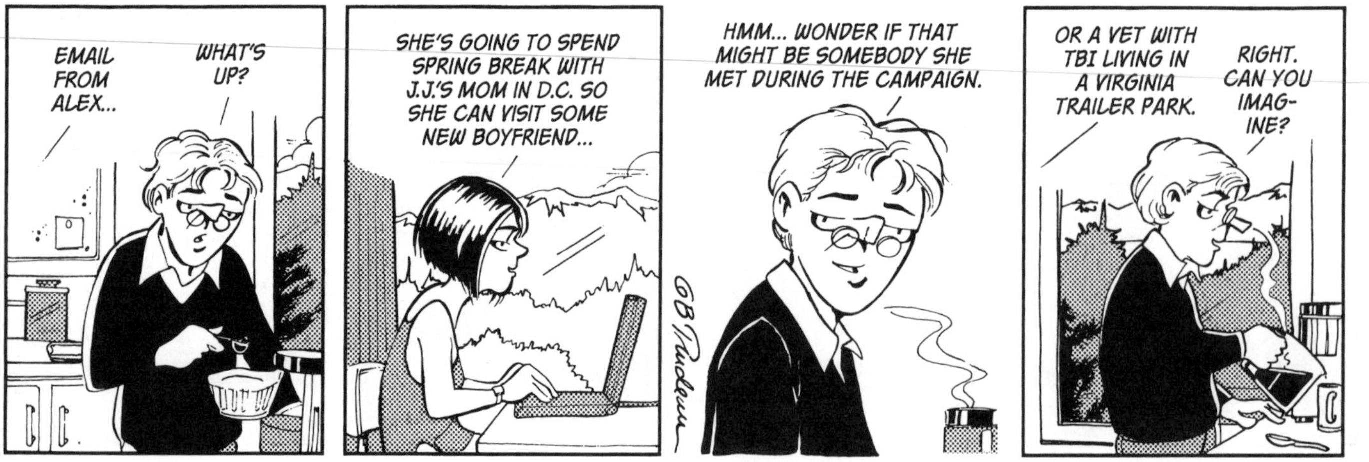
EMAIL FROM ALEX...
WHAT'S UP?
SHE'S GOING TO SPEND SPRING BREAK WITH J.J.'S MOM IN D.C. SO SHE CAN VISIT SOME NEW BOYFRIEND...
HMM... WONDER IF THAT MIGHT BE SOMEBODY SHE MET DURING THE CAMPAIGN.
OR A VET WITH TBI LIVING IN A VIRGINIA TRAILER PARK.
RIGHT. CAN YOU IMAGINE?

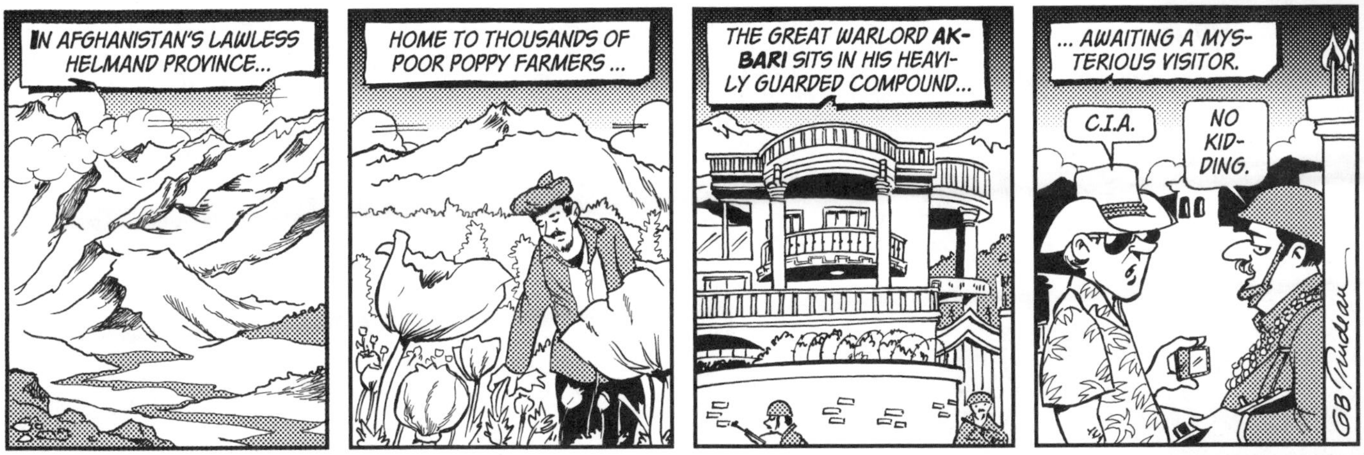
IN AFGHANISTAN'S LAWLESS HELMAND PROVINCE...
HOME TO THOUSANDS OF POOR POPPY FARMERS ...
THE GREAT WARLORD AKBARI SITS IN HIS HEAVILY GUARDED COMPOUND...
... AWAITING A MYSTERIOUS VISITOR.
C.I.A.
NO KIDDING.

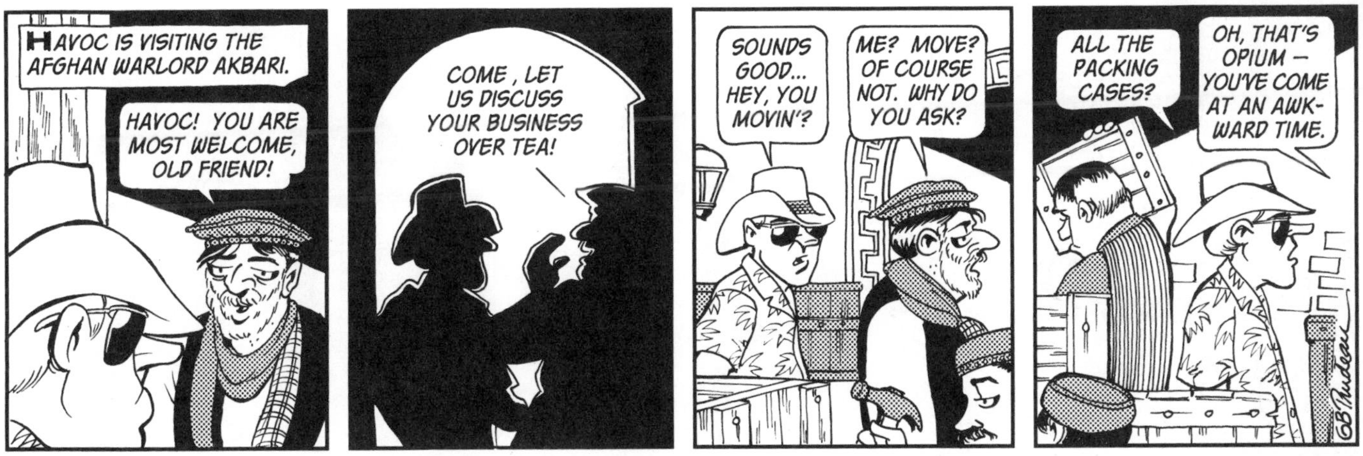
HAVOC IS VISITING THE AFGHAN WARLORD AKBARI.
HAVOC! YOU ARE MOST WELCOME, OLD FRIEND!
COME, LET US DISCUSS YOUR BUSINESS OVER TEA!
SOUNDS GOOD... HEY, YOU MOVIN'?
ME? MOVE? OF COURSE NOT. WHY DO YOU ASK?
ALL THE PACKING CASES?
OH, THAT'S OPIUM — YOU'VE COME AT AN AWKWARD TIME.

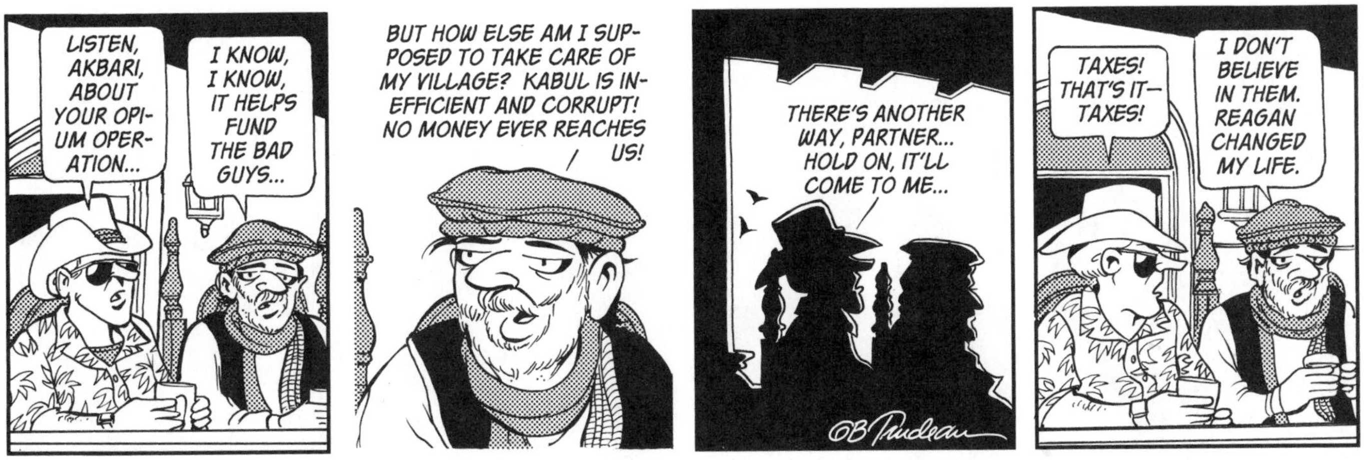
LISTEN, AKBARI, ABOUT YOUR OPIUM OPERATION...
I KNOW, I KNOW, IT HELPS FUND THE BAD GUYS...
BUT HOW ELSE AM I SUPPOSED TO TAKE CARE OF MY VILLAGE? KABUL IS INEFFICIENT AND CORRUPT! NO MONEY EVER REACHES US!
THERE'S ANOTHER WAY, PARTNER... HOLD ON, IT'LL COME TO ME...
TAXES! THAT'S IT — TAXES!
I DON'T BELIEVE IN THEM. REAGAN CHANGED MY LIFE.

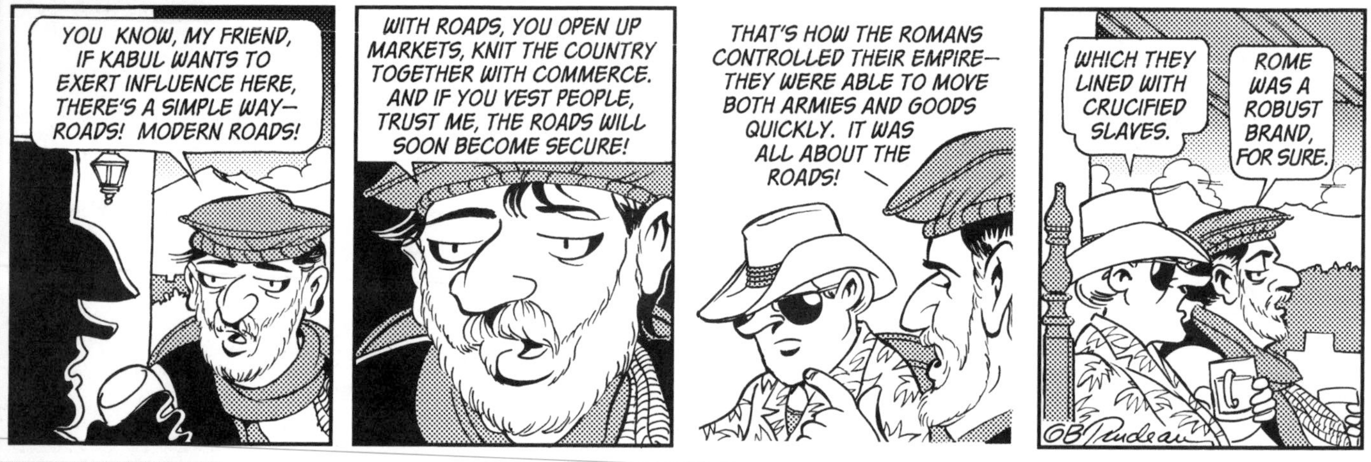
YOU KNOW, MY FRIEND, IF KABUL WANTS TO EXERT INFLUENCE HERE, THERE'S A SIMPLE WAY— ROADS! MODERN ROADS!
WITH ROADS, YOU OPEN UP MARKETS, KNIT THE COUNTRY TOGETHER WITH COMMERCE. AND IF YOU VEST PEOPLE, TRUST ME, THE ROADS WILL SOON BECOME SECURE!
THAT'S HOW THE ROMANS CONTROLLED THEIR EMPIRE— THEY WERE ABLE TO MOVE BOTH ARMIES AND GOODS QUICKLY. IT WAS ALL ABOUT THE ROADS!
WHICH THEY LINED WITH CRUCIFIED SLAVES.
ROME WAS A ROBUST BRAND, FOR SURE.
GB Trudeau

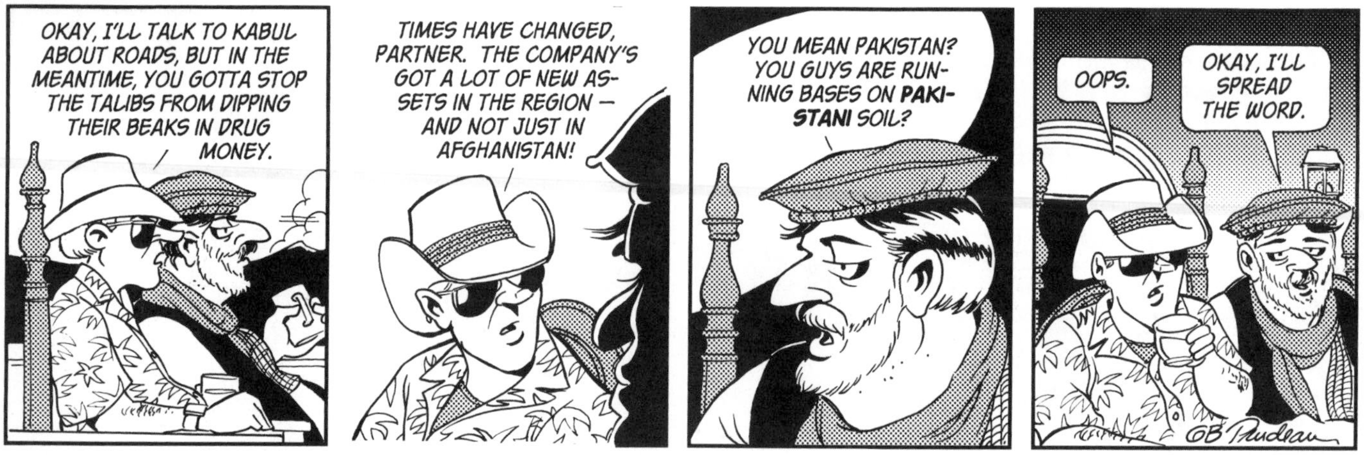
OKAY, I'LL TALK TO KABUL ABOUT ROADS, BUT IN THE MEANTIME, YOU GOTTA STOP THE TALIBS FROM DIPPING THEIR BEAKS IN DRUG MONEY.
TIMES HAVE CHANGED, PARTNER. THE COMPANY'S GOT A LOT OF NEW AS-SETS IN THE REGION — AND NOT JUST IN AFGHANISTAN!
YOU MEAN PAKISTAN? YOU GUYS ARE RUN-NING BASES ON **PAKI-STANI** SOIL?
OOPS.
OKAY, I'LL SPREAD THE WORD.
GB Trudeau

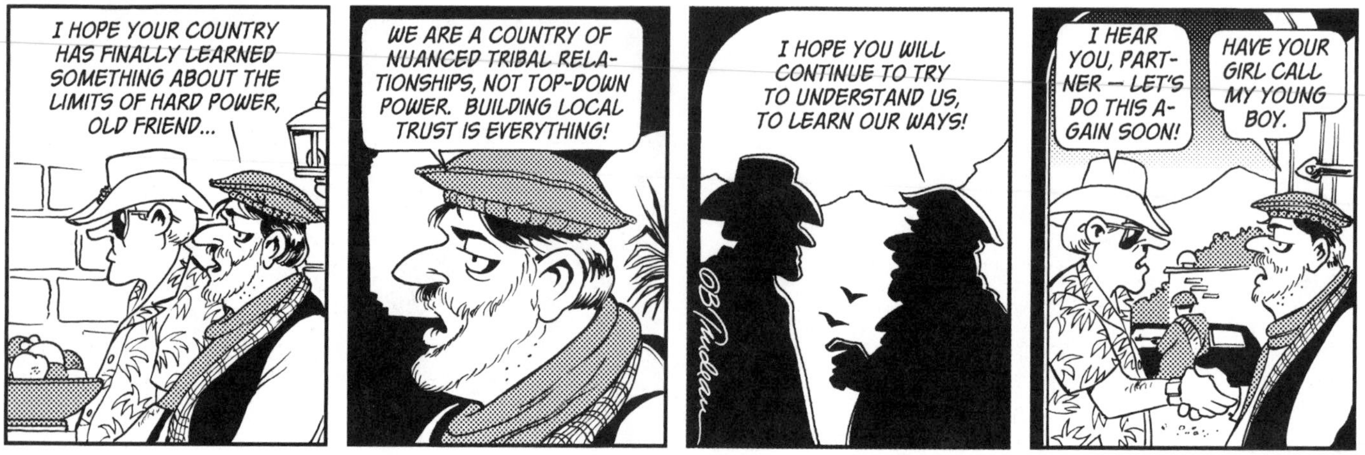
I HOPE YOUR COUNTRY HAS FINALLY LEARNED SOMETHING ABOUT THE LIMITS OF HARD POWER, OLD FRIEND...
WE ARE A COUNTRY OF NUANCED TRIBAL RELA-TIONSHIPS, NOT TOP-DOWN POWER. BUILDING LOCAL TRUST IS EVERYTHING!
I HOPE YOU WILL CONTINUE TO TRY TO UNDERSTAND US, TO LEARN OUR WAYS!
GB Trudeau
I HEAR YOU, PART-NER — LET'S DO THIS A-GAIN SOON!
HAVE YOUR GIRL CALL MY YOUNG BOY.

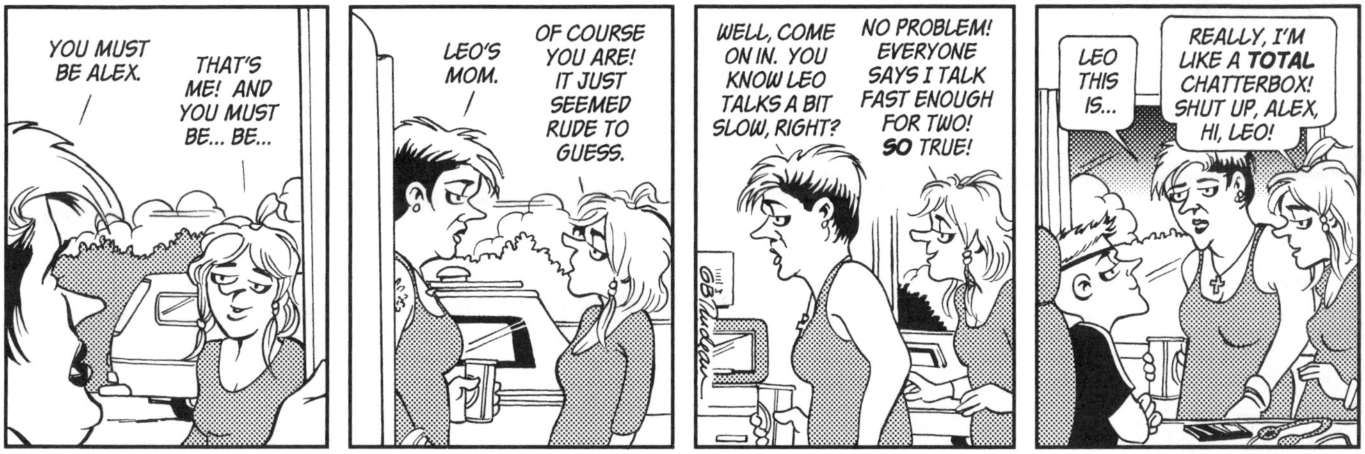
YOU MUST BE ALEX.
THAT'S ME! AND YOU MUST BE... BE...
LEO'S MOM.
OF COURSE YOU ARE! IT JUST SEEMED RUDE TO GUESS.
WELL, COME ON IN. YOU KNOW LEO TALKS A BIT SLOW, RIGHT?
NO PROBLEM! EVERYONE SAYS I TALK FAST ENOUGH FOR TWO! **SO** TRUE!
LEO THIS IS...
REALLY, I'M LIKE A **TOTAL** CHATTERBOX! SHUT UP, ALEX. HI, LEO!

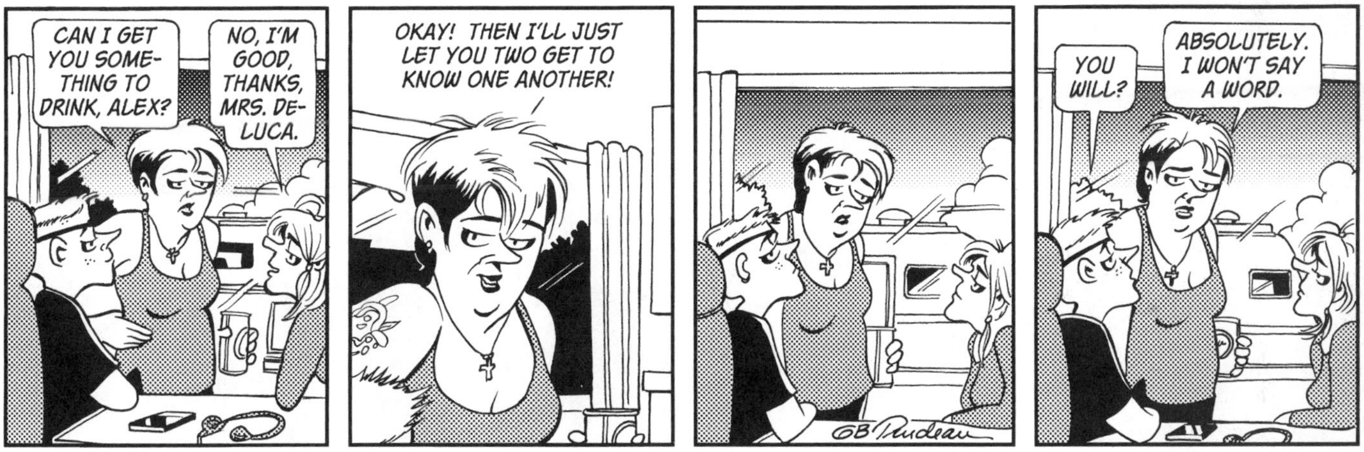
CAN I GET YOU SOME-THING TO DRINK, ALEX?
NO, I'M GOOD, THANKS, MRS. DE-LUCA.
OKAY! THEN I'LL JUST LET YOU TWO GET TO KNOW ONE ANOTHER!
YOU WILL?
ABSOLUTELY. I WON'T SAY A WORD.

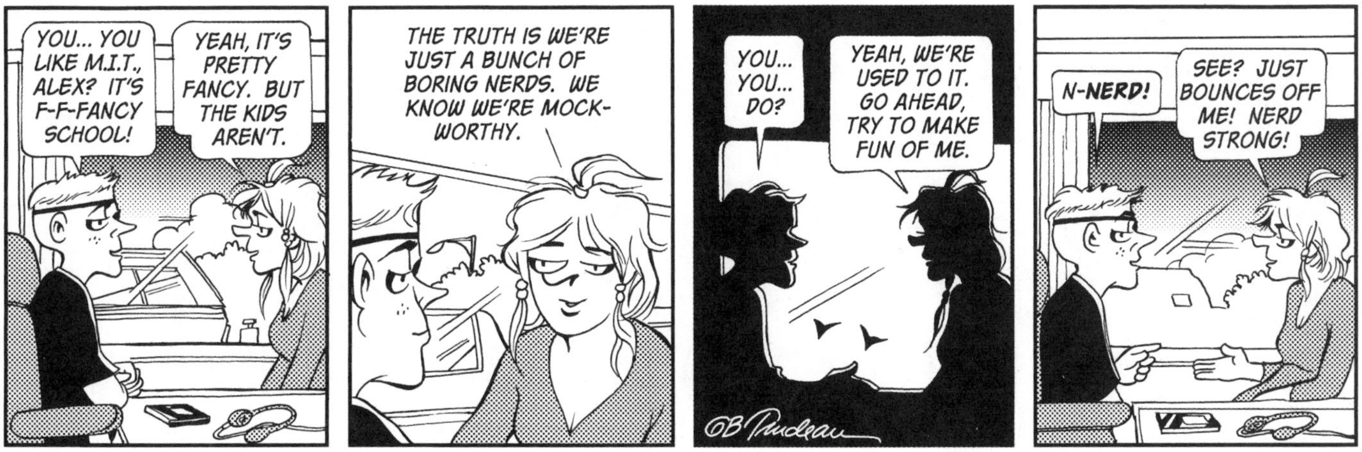
YOU... YOU LIKE M.I.T., ALEX? IT'S F-F-FANCY SCHOOL!
YEAH, IT'S PRETTY FANCY. BUT THE KIDS AREN'T.
THE TRUTH IS WE'RE JUST A BUNCH OF BORING NERDS. WE KNOW WE'RE MOCK-WORTHY.
YOU... YOU... DO?
YEAH, WE'RE USED TO IT. GO AHEAD, TRY TO MAKE FUN OF ME.
N-**NERD!**
SEE? JUST BOUNCES OFF ME! NERD STRONG!

SO, LEO, THERE ARE SOME GREAT DOCTORS AT M.I.T.! I COULD FIND OUT WHO'S THE TOP DOG IN APHASIA...
NO... NO... THANK YOU. HAPPY WITH CARE AT... V.A.
ALSO... B.D. GAVE ME ADVICE. NEV... NEVER...
NEVER WHAT?
ASK... ASK... FOR MEDICAL HELP ON A... D-D-DATE!
GOOD POINT. IT COULD COME OFF AS NEEDY.
GB Trudeau

SO YOU WANT TO GO GET SOME LUNCH OR SOMETHING, LEO?
L-L-LUNCH?
WHY NOT? WE'RE KIND OF HITTING IT OFF, AREN'T WE?
YES... BUT I... I'M WORRIED YOU'RE TOO... TOO...
TOO WHAT?
...TOO HOT FOR ME.
BUT I'M NOT, I'M NOT! YO, CHECK OUT MY NOSE!
GB Trudeau

ALEX... MY... MY FRIENDS C-C-CALL ME TOGGLE... NOT LEO.
TOGGLE? REALLY?
WHAT A **GREAT** NAME! I'M AN ENGINEER, SO I LOVE THE BINARY VIBE!
A TOGGLE SWITCH IS EITHER CLOSED OR IT'S NOT! THE JUICE IS FLOWING OR IT'S NOT! SO YOU LIKE ME, RIGHT?
R-R-ROGER THAT.
SEE? MOST GUYS WOULD EQUIVOCATE! NOT TOGGLE!
GB Trudeau

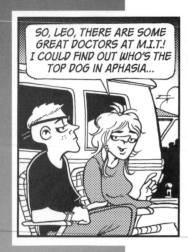

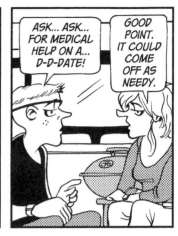

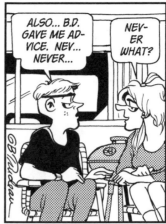

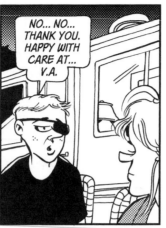

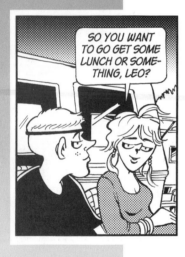

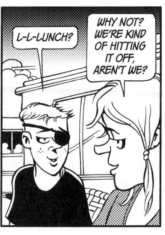

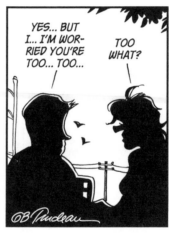

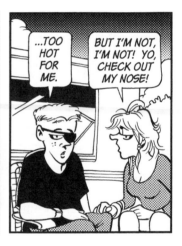

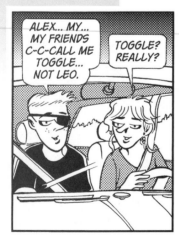

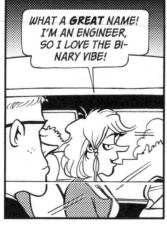

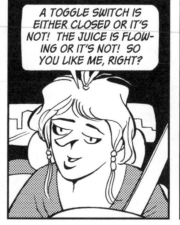

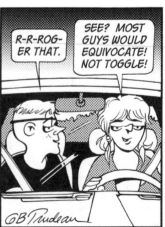

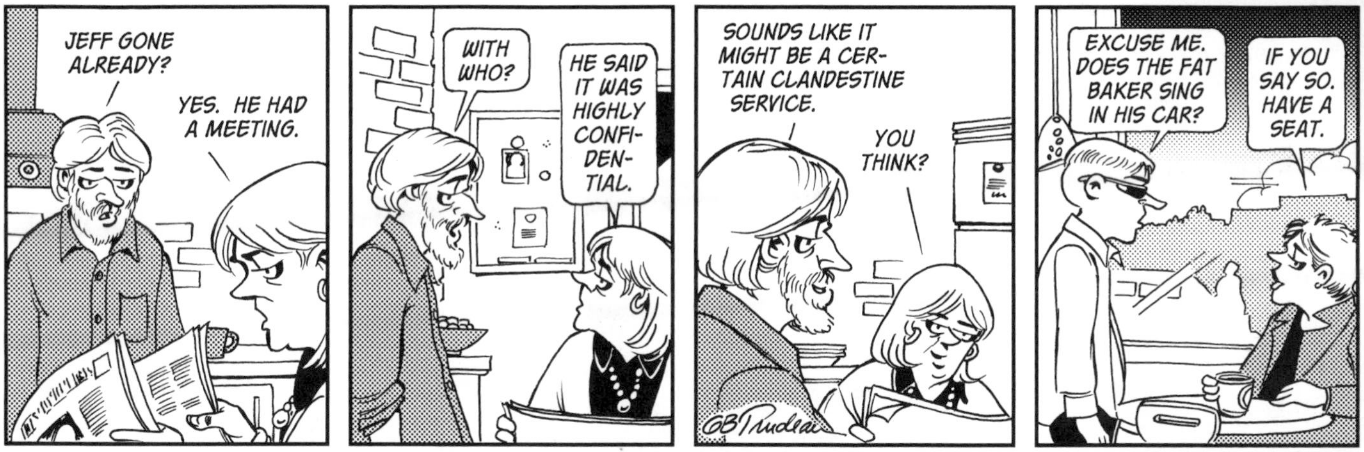
JEFF GONE ALREADY?
YES. HE HAD A MEETING.
WITH WHO?
HE SAID IT WAS HIGHLY CONFI-DEN-TIAL.
SOUNDS LIKE IT MIGHT BE A CER-TAIN CLANDESTINE SERVICE.
YOU THINK?
EXCUSE ME. DOES THE FAT BAKER SING IN HIS CAR?
IF YOU SAY SO. HAVE A SEAT.

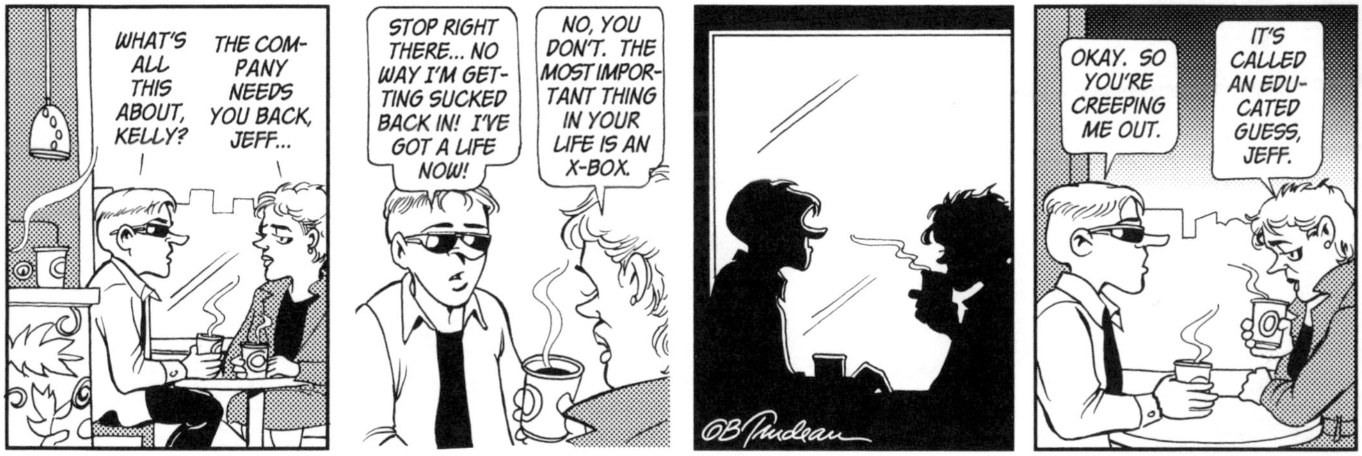
WHAT'S ALL THIS ABOUT, KELLY?
THE COM-PANY NEEDS YOU BACK, JEFF...
STOP RIGHT THERE... NO WAY I'M GET-TING SUCKED BACK IN! I'VE GOT A LIFE NOW!
NO, YOU DON'T. THE MOST IMPOR-TANT THING IN YOUR LIFE IS AN X-BOX.
OKAY. SO YOU'RE CREEPING ME OUT.
IT'S CALLED AN EDU-CATED GUESS, JEFF.

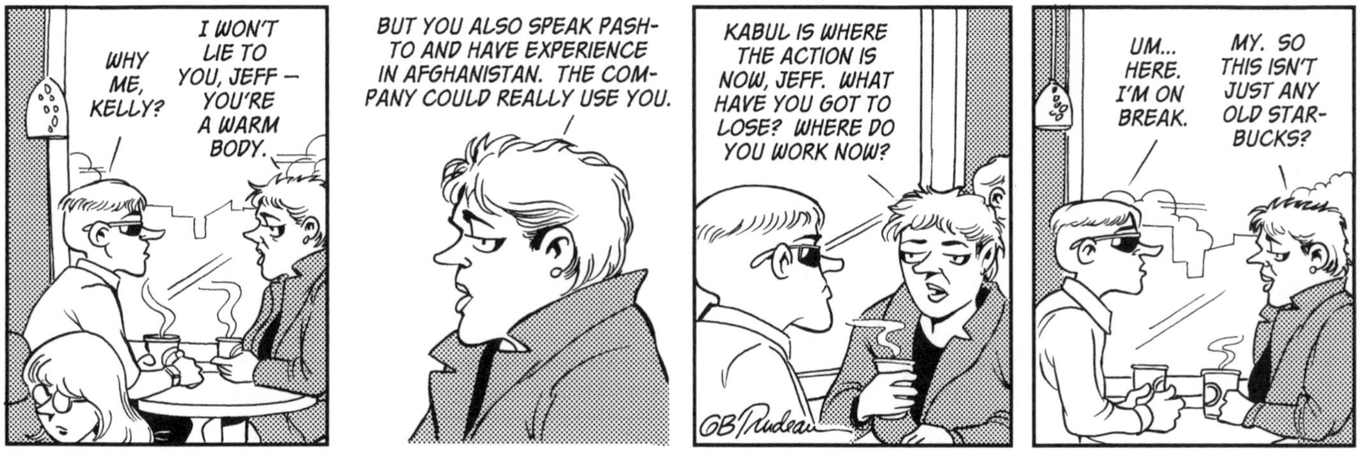
WHY ME, KELLY?
I WON'T LIE TO YOU, JEFF — YOU'RE A WARM BODY.
BUT YOU ALSO SPEAK PASH-TO AND HAVE EXPERIENCE IN AFGHANISTAN. THE COM-PANY COULD REALLY USE YOU.
KABUL IS WHERE THE ACTION IS NOW, JEFF. WHAT HAVE YOU GOT TO LOSE? WHERE DO YOU WORK NOW?
UM... HERE. I'M ON BREAK.
MY. SO THIS ISN'T JUST ANY OLD STAR-BUCKS?

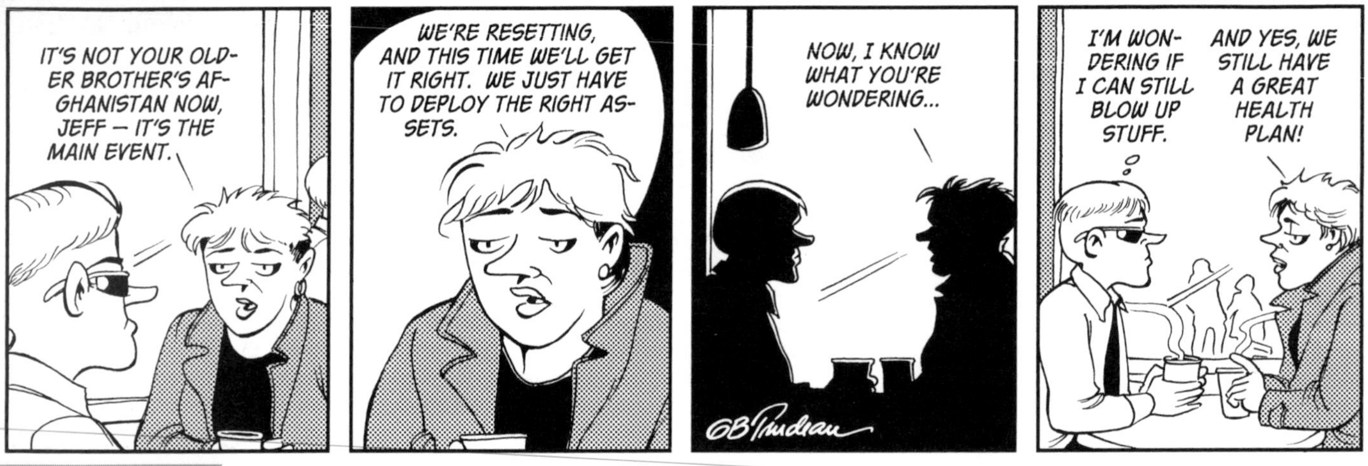
IT'S NOT YOUR OLDER BROTHER'S AFGHANISTAN NOW, JEFF — IT'S THE MAIN EVENT.
WE'RE RESETTING, AND THIS TIME WE'LL GET IT RIGHT. WE JUST HAVE TO DEPLOY THE RIGHT ASSETS.
NOW, I KNOW WHAT YOU'RE WONDERING...
I'M WONDERING IF I CAN STILL BLOW UP STUFF.
AND YES, WE STILL HAVE A GREAT HEALTH PLAN!

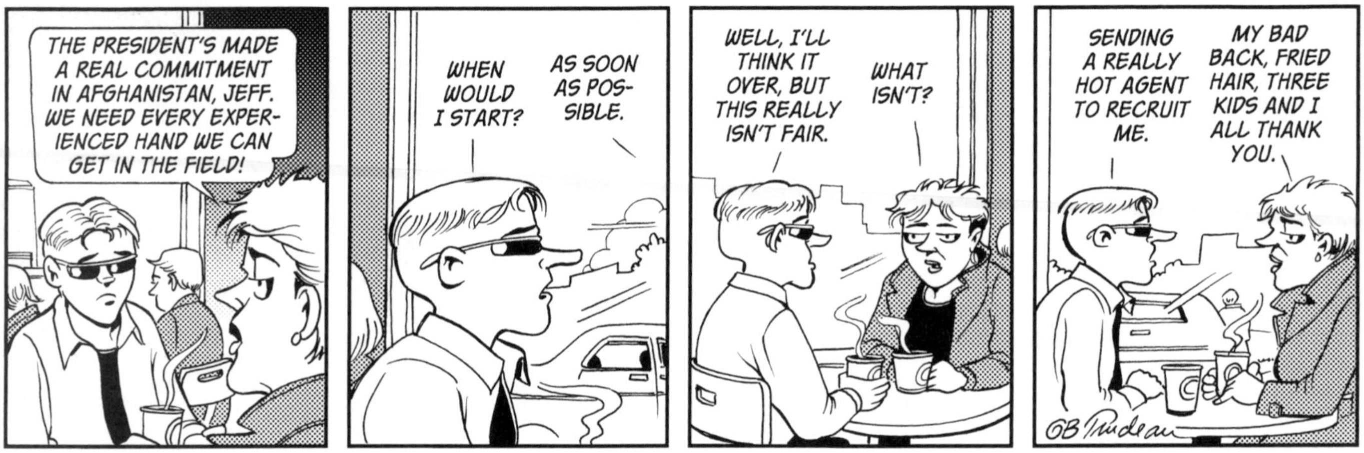
THE PRESIDENT'S MADE A REAL COMMITMENT IN AFGHANISTAN, JEFF. WE NEED EVERY EXPERIENCED HAND WE CAN GET IN THE FIELD!
WHEN WOULD I START?
AS SOON AS POSSIBLE.
WELL, I'LL THINK IT OVER, BUT THIS REALLY ISN'T FAIR.
WHAT ISN'T?
SENDING A REALLY HOT AGENT TO RECRUIT ME.
MY BAD BACK, FRIED HAIR, THREE KIDS AND I ALL THANK YOU.

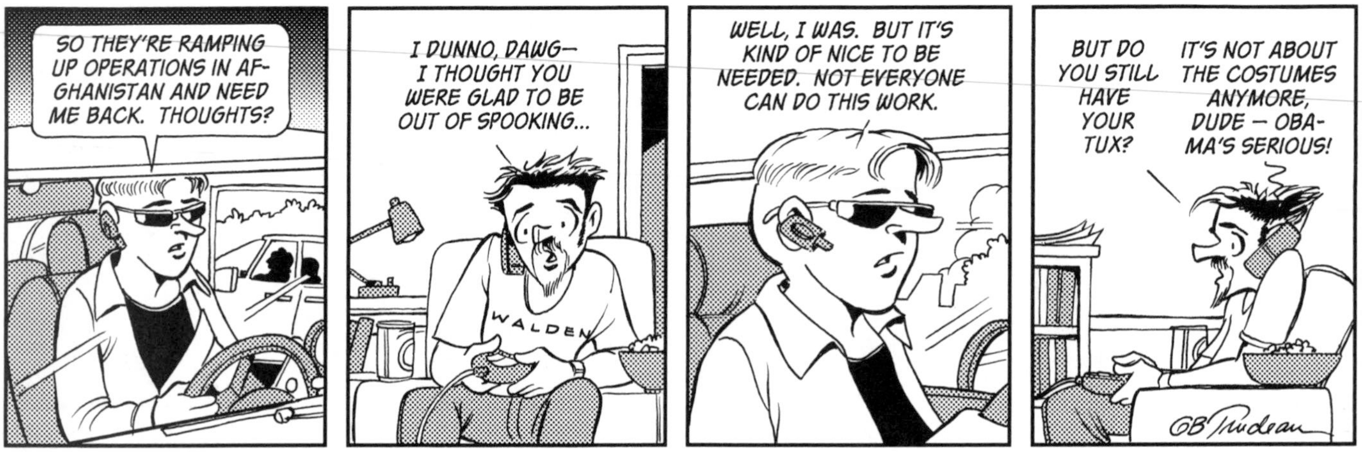
SO THEY'RE RAMPING UP OPERATIONS IN AFGHANISTAN AND NEED ME BACK. THOUGHTS?
I DUNNO, DAWG— I THOUGHT YOU WERE GLAD TO BE OUT OF SPOOKING...
WALDEN
WELL, I WAS. BUT IT'S KIND OF NICE TO BE NEEDED. NOT EVERYONE CAN DO THIS WORK.
BUT DO YOU STILL HAVE YOUR TUX?
IT'S NOT ABOUT THE COSTUMES ANYMORE, DUDE — OBAMA'S SERIOUS!

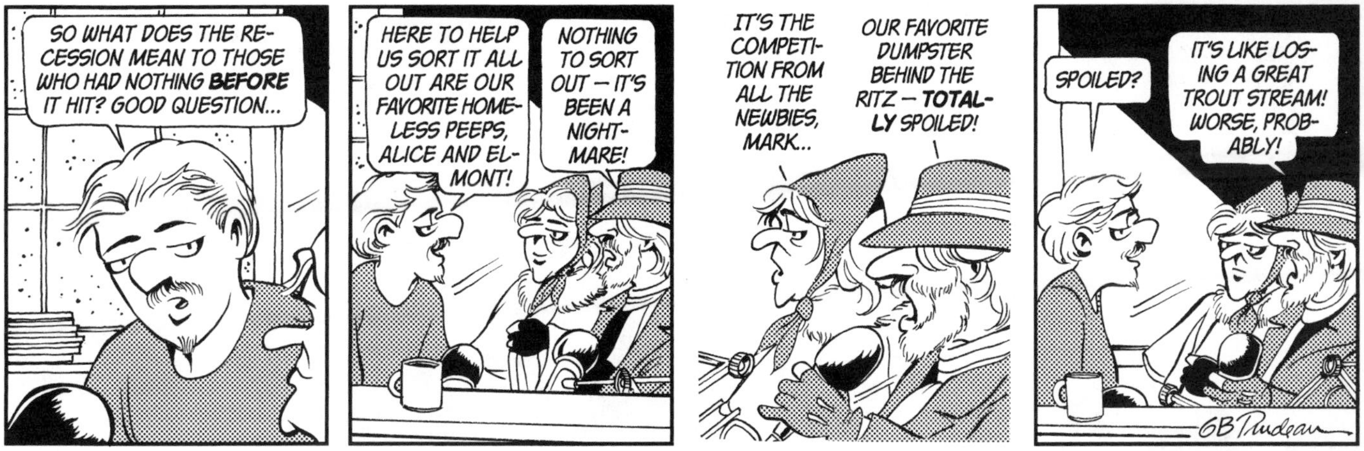
SO WHAT DOES THE RECESSION MEAN TO THOSE WHO HAD NOTHING **BEFORE** IT HIT? GOOD QUESTION...
HERE TO HELP US SORT IT ALL OUT ARE OUR FAVORITE HOMELESS PEEPS, ALICE AND ELMONT!
NOTHING TO SORT OUT — IT'S BEEN A NIGHTMARE!
IT'S THE COMPETITION FROM ALL THE NEWBIES, MARK...
OUR FAVORITE DUMPSTER BEHIND THE RITZ — **TOTALLY** SPOILED!
SPOILED?
IT'S LIKE LOSING A GREAT TROUT STREAM! WORSE, PROBABLY!
GB Trudeau

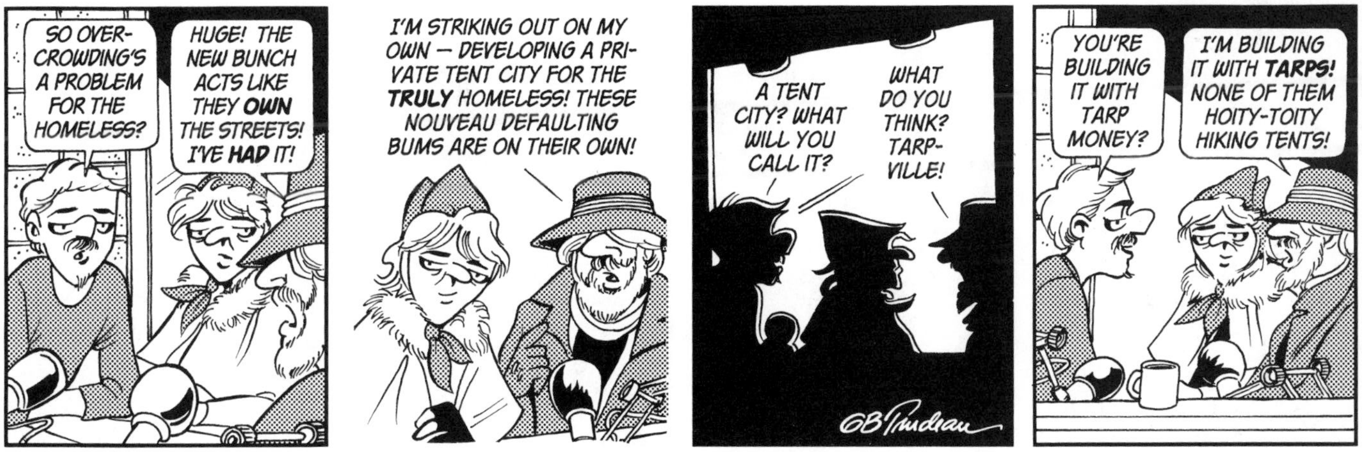
SO OVERCROWDING'S A PROBLEM FOR THE HOMELESS?
HUGE! THE NEW BUNCH ACTS LIKE THEY **OWN** THE STREETS! I'VE **HAD** IT!
I'M STRIKING OUT ON MY OWN — DEVELOPING A PRIVATE TENT CITY FOR THE **TRULY** HOMELESS! THESE NOUVEAU DEFAULTING BUMS ARE ON THEIR OWN!
A TENT CITY? WHAT WILL YOU CALL IT?
WHAT DO YOU THINK? TARPVILLE!
GB Trudeau
YOU'RE BUILDING IT WITH TARP MONEY?
I'M BUILDING IT WITH **TARPS!** NONE OF THEM HOITY-TOITY HIKING TENTS!

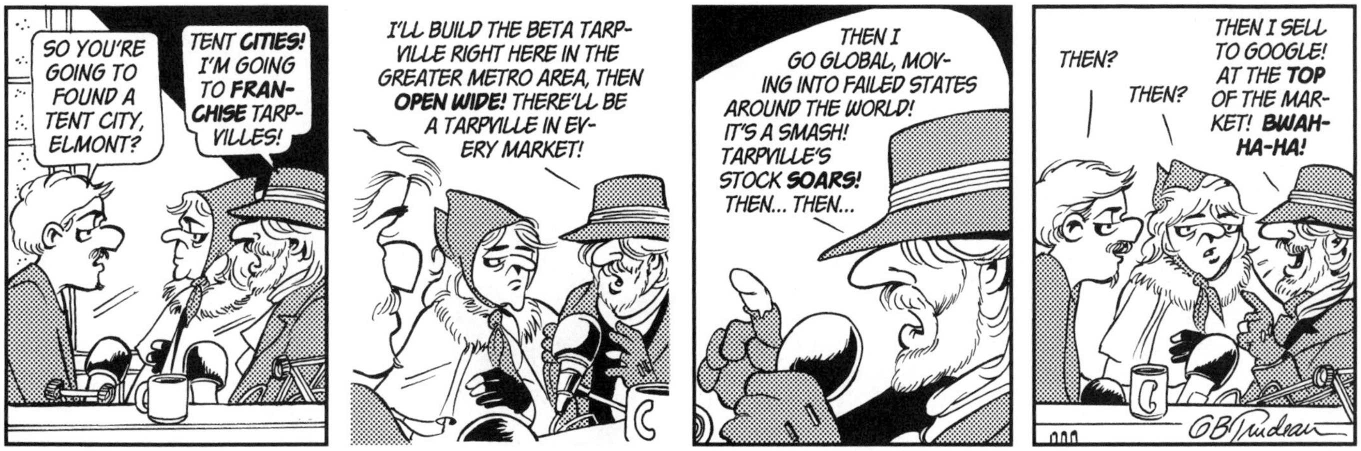
SO YOU'RE GOING TO FOUND A TENT CITY, ELMONT?
TENT **CITIES!** I'M GOING TO **FRANCHISE** TARPVILLES!
I'LL BUILD THE BETA TARPVILLE RIGHT HERE IN THE GREATER METRO AREA, THEN **OPEN WIDE!** THERE'LL BE A TARPVILLE IN EVERY MARKET!
THEN I GO GLOBAL, MOVING INTO FAILED STATES AROUND THE WORLD! IT'S A SMASH! TARPVILLE'S STOCK **SOARS!** THEN... THEN...
THEN?
THEN?
THEN I SELL TO GOOGLE! AT THE **TOP** OF THE MARKET! **BWAH-HA-HA!**
GB Trudeau

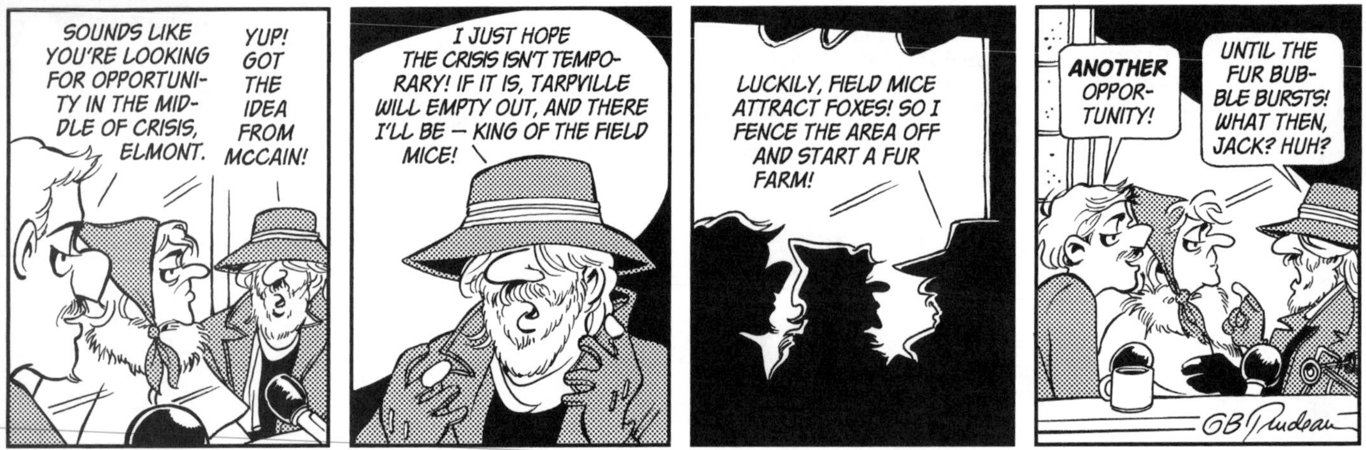
SOUNDS LIKE YOU'RE LOOKING FOR OPPORTUNITY IN THE MIDDLE OF CRISIS, ELMONT.
YUP! GOT THE IDEA FROM McCAIN!
I JUST HOPE THE CRISIS ISN'T TEMPORARY! IF IT IS, TARPVILLE WILL EMPTY OUT, AND THERE I'LL BE — KING OF THE FIELD MICE!
LUCKILY, FIELD MICE ATTRACT FOXES! SO I FENCE THE AREA OFF AND START A FUR FARM!
ANOTHER OPPORTUNITY!
UNTIL THE FUR BUBBLE BURSTS! WHAT THEN, JACK? HUH?
GB Trudeau

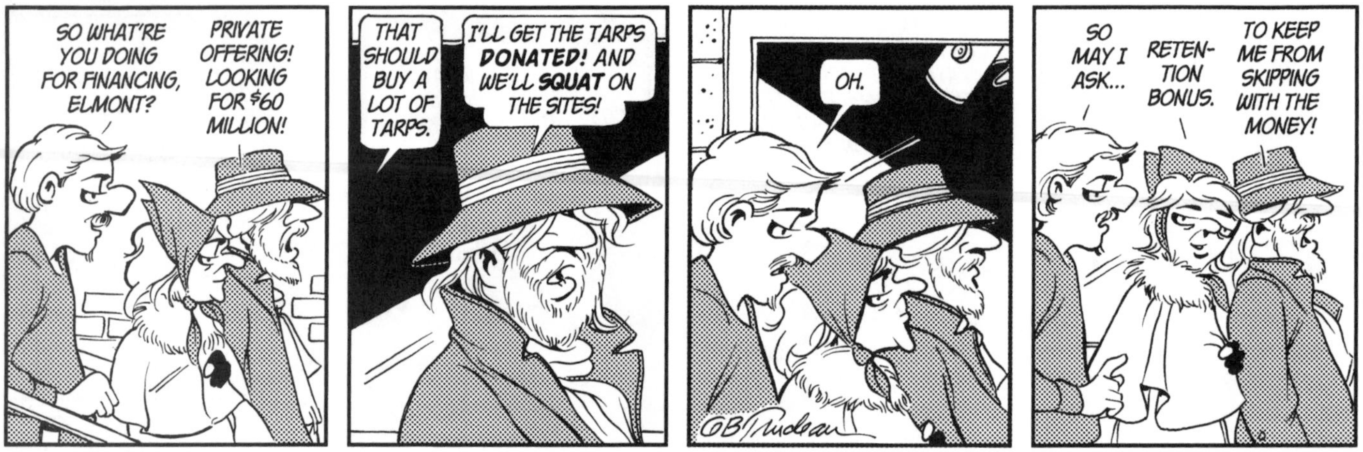
SO WHAT'RE YOU DOING FOR FINANCING, ELMONT?
PRIVATE OFFERING! LOOKING FOR $60 MILLION!
THAT SHOULD BUY A LOT OF TARPS.
I'LL GET THE TARPS **DONATED!** AND WE'LL **SQUAT** ON THE SITES!
OH.
GB Trudeau
SO MAY I ASK...
RETENTION BONUS.
TO KEEP ME FROM SKIPPING WITH THE MONEY!

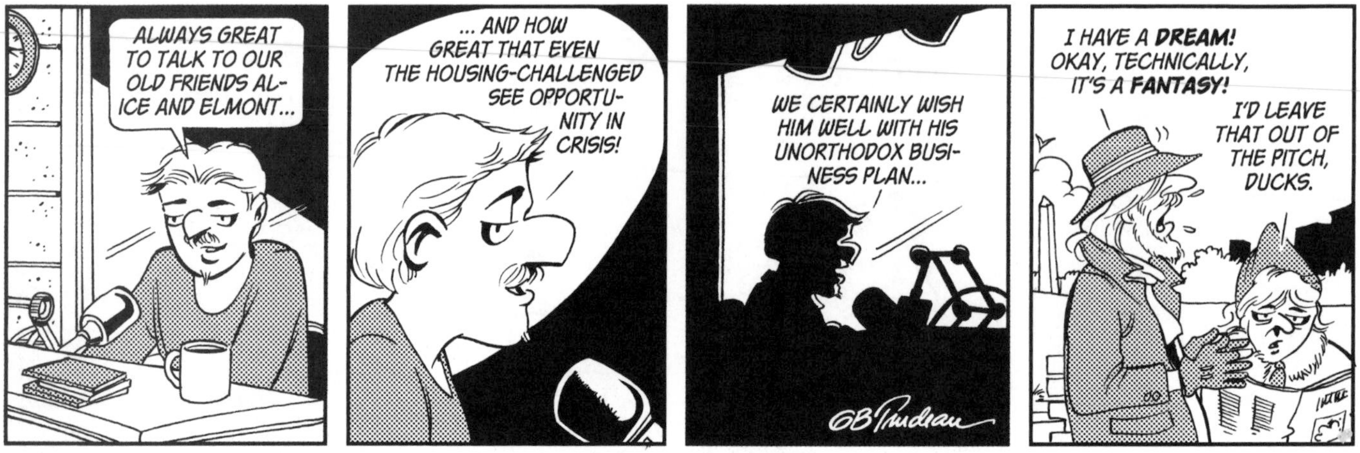
ALWAYS GREAT TO TALK TO OUR OLD FRIENDS ALICE AND ELMONT...
... AND HOW GREAT THAT EVEN THE HOUSING-CHALLENGED SEE OPPORTUNITY IN CRISIS!
WE CERTAINLY WISH HIM WELL WITH HIS UNORTHODOX BUSINESS PLAN...
GB Trudeau
I HAVE A **DREAM!** OKAY, TECHNICALLY, IT'S A **FANTASY!**
I'D LEAVE THAT OUT OF THE PITCH, DUCKS.

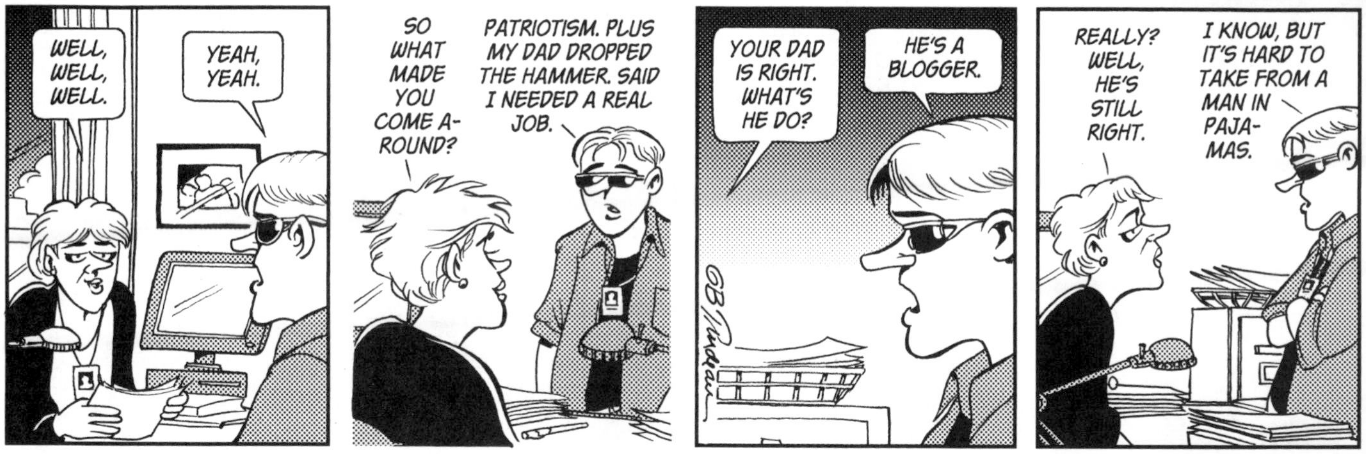
WELL, WELL, WELL.
YEAH, YEAH.
SO WHAT MADE YOU COME A-ROUND?
PATRIOTISM. PLUS MY DAD DROPPED THE HAMMER. SAID I NEEDED A REAL JOB.
YOUR DAD IS RIGHT. WHAT'S HE DO?
HE'S A BLOGGER.
REALLY? WELL, HE'S STILL RIGHT.
I KNOW, BUT IT'S HARD TO TAKE FROM A MAN IN PAJA-MAS.

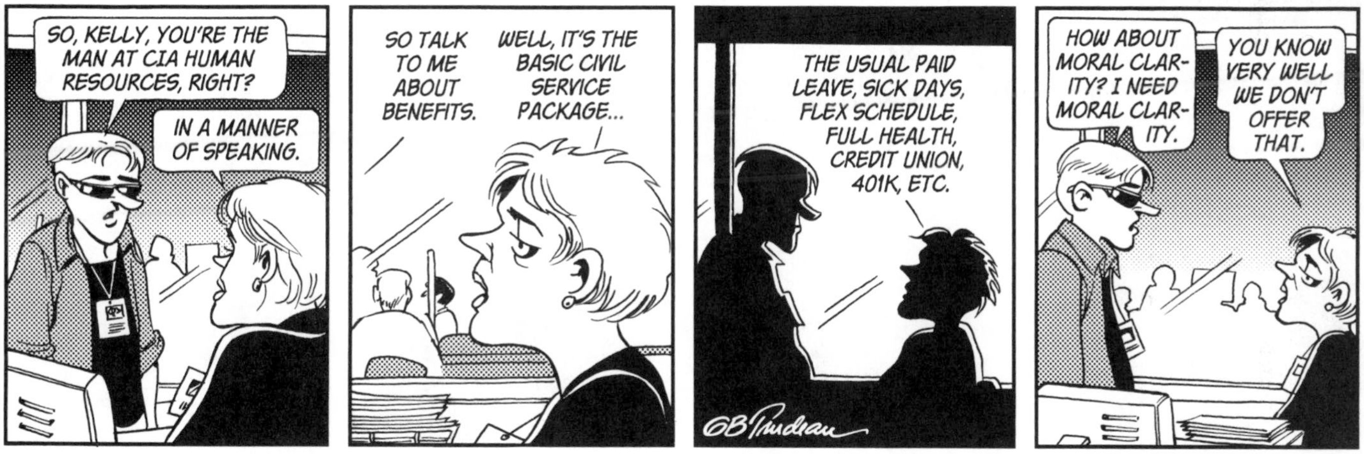
SO, KELLY, YOU'RE THE MAN AT CIA HUMAN RESOURCES, RIGHT?
IN A MANNER OF SPEAKING.
SO TALK TO ME ABOUT BENEFITS.
WELL, IT'S THE BASIC CIVIL SERVICE PACKAGE...
THE USUAL PAID LEAVE, SICK DAYS, FLEX SCHEDULE, FULL HEALTH, CREDIT UNION, 401K, ETC.
HOW ABOUT MORAL CLAR-ITY? I NEED MORAL CLAR-ITY.
YOU KNOW VERY WELL WE DON'T OFFER THAT.

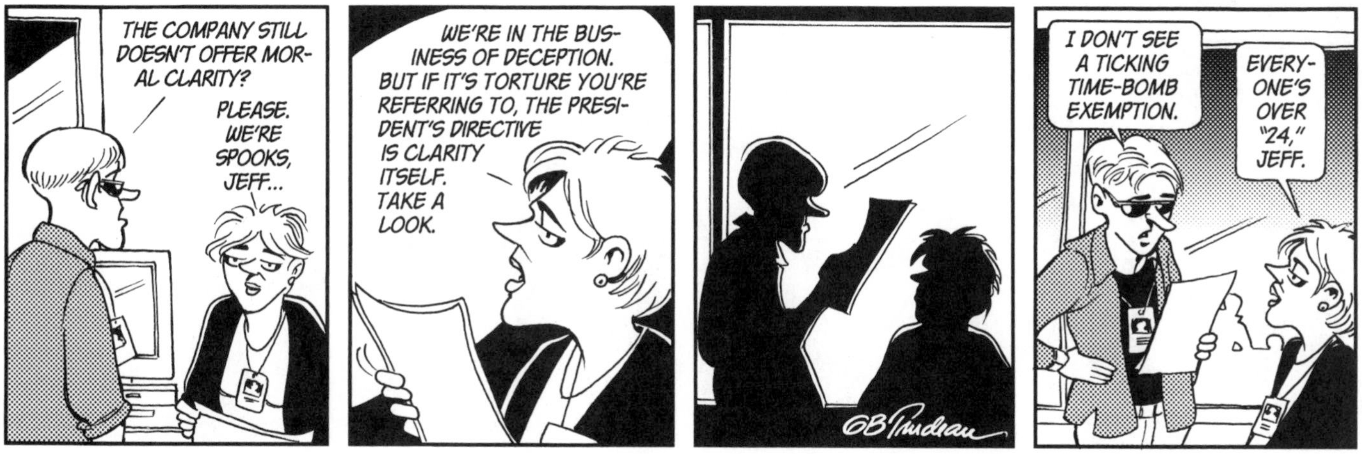
THE COMPANY STILL DOESN'T OFFER MOR-AL CLARITY?
PLEASE. WE'RE SPOOKS, JEFF...
WE'RE IN THE BUS-INESS OF DECEPTION. BUT IF IT'S TORTURE YOU'RE REFERRING TO, THE PRESI-DENT'S DIRECTIVE IS CLARITY ITSELF. TAKE A LOOK.
I DON'T SEE A TICKING TIME-BOMB EXEMPTION.
EVERY-ONE'S OVER "24," JEFF.

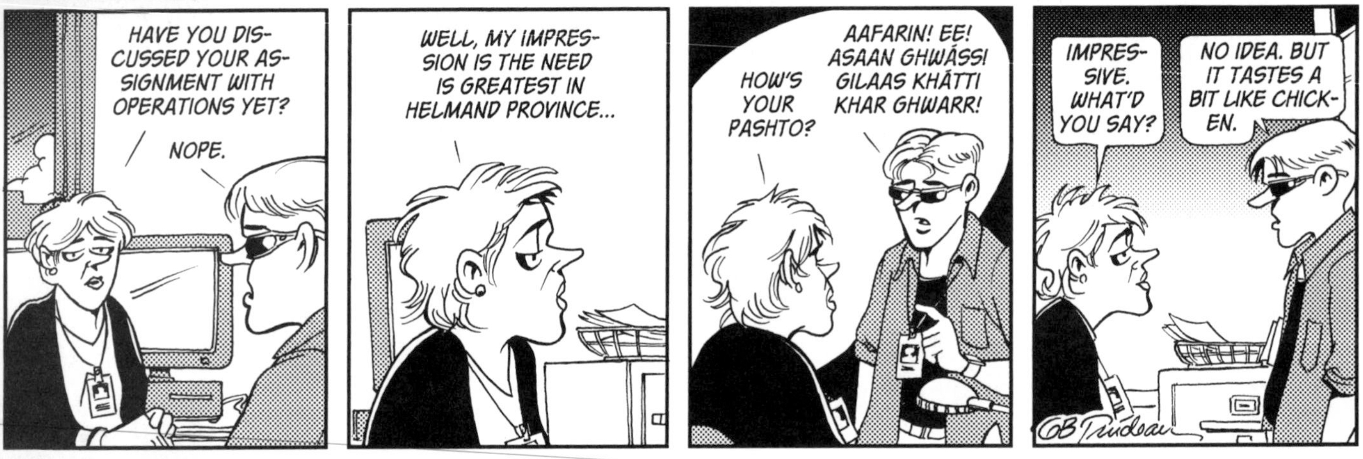
HAVE YOU DISCUSSED YOUR ASSIGNMENT WITH OPERATIONS YET?
NOPE.
WELL, MY IMPRESSION IS THE NEED IS GREATEST IN HELMAND PROVINCE...
HOW'S YOUR PASHTO?
AAFARIN! EE! ASAAN GHWÁSSI GILAAS KHÁTTI KHAR GHWARR!
IMPRESSIVE. WHAT'D YOU SAY?
NO IDEA. BUT IT TASTES A BIT LIKE CHICKEN.
GB Trudeau

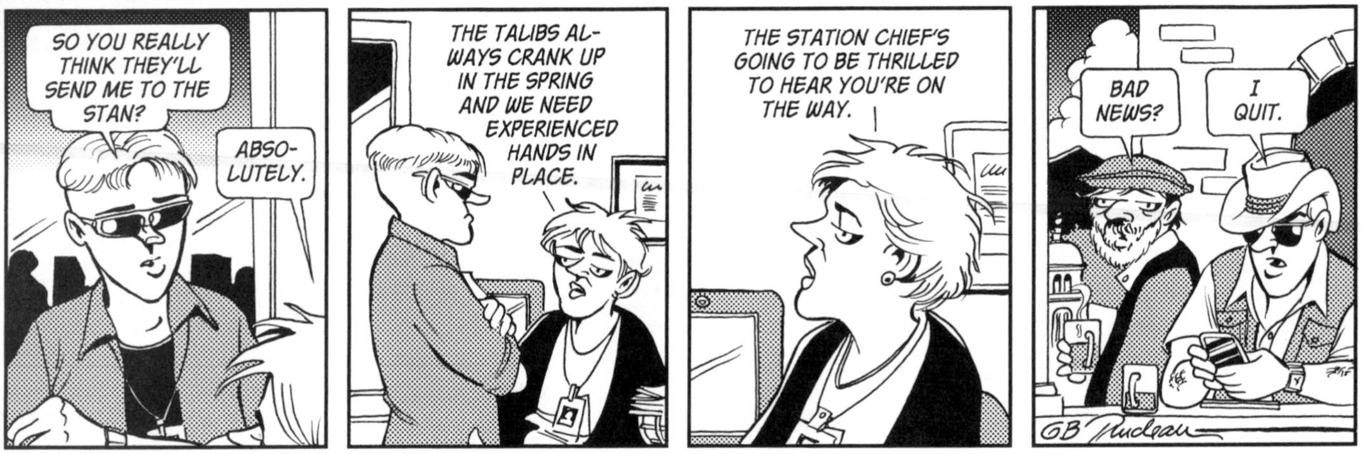
SO YOU REALLY THINK THEY'LL SEND ME TO THE STAN?
ABSOLUTELY.
THE TALIBS ALWAYS CRANK UP IN THE SPRING AND WE NEED EXPERIENCED HANDS IN PLACE.
THE STATION CHIEF'S GOING TO BE THRILLED TO HEAR YOU'RE ON THE WAY.
BAD NEWS?
I QUIT.
GB Trudeau

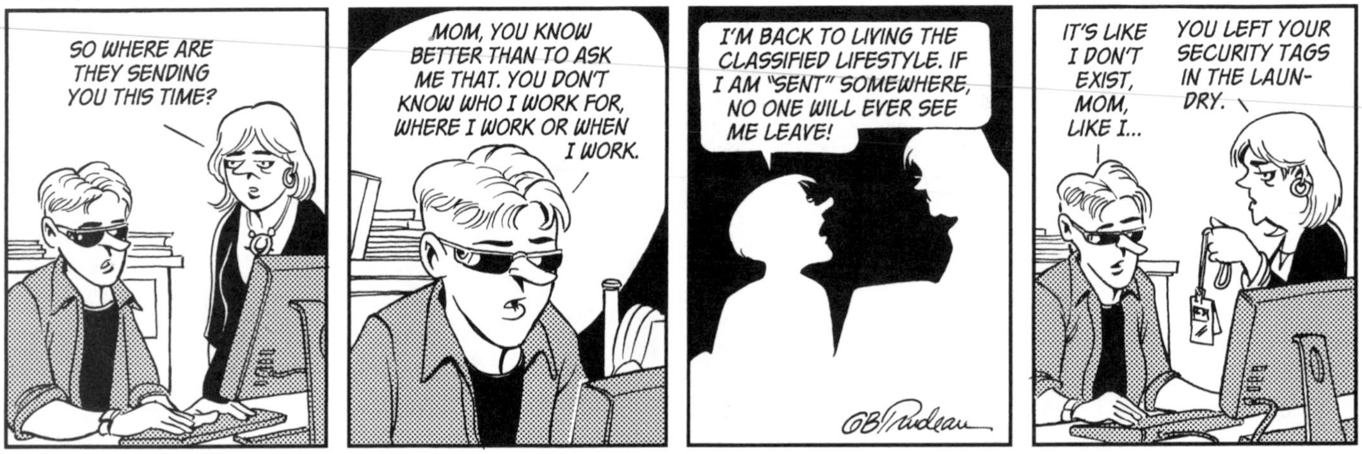
SO WHERE ARE THEY SENDING YOU THIS TIME?
MOM, YOU KNOW BETTER THAN TO ASK ME THAT. YOU DON'T KNOW WHO I WORK FOR, WHERE I WORK OR WHEN I WORK.
I'M BACK TO LIVING THE CLASSIFIED LIFESTYLE. IF I AM "SENT" SOMEWHERE, NO ONE WILL EVER SEE ME LEAVE!
IT'S LIKE I DON'T EXIST, MOM, LIKE I...
YOU LEFT YOUR SECURITY TAGS IN THE LAUNDRY.
GB Trudeau

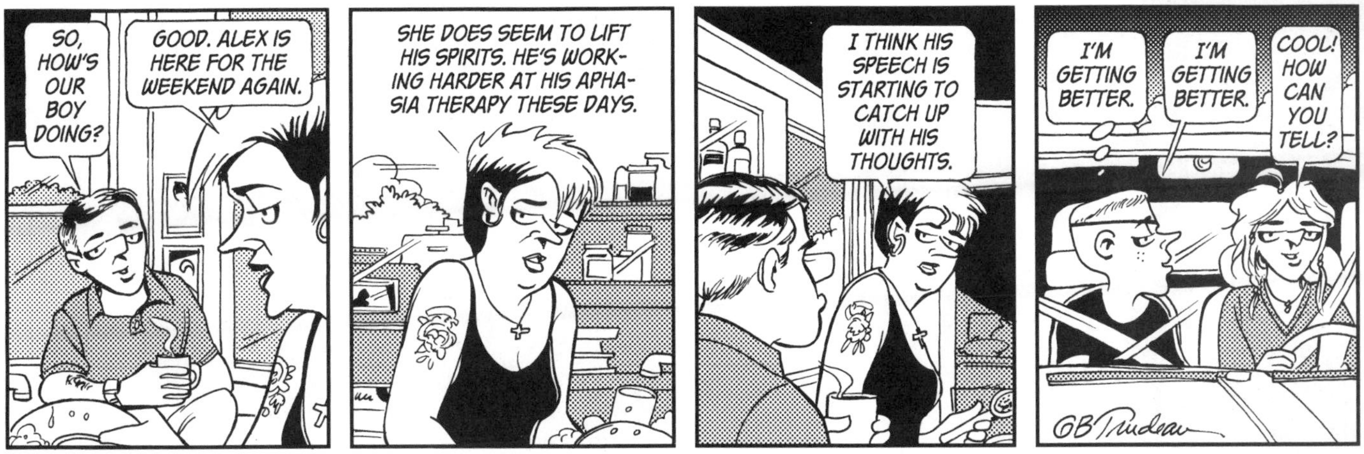
SO, HOW'S OUR BOY DOING?
GOOD. ALEX IS HERE FOR THE WEEKEND AGAIN.
SHE DOES SEEM TO LIFT HIS SPIRITS. HE'S WORK-ING HARDER AT HIS APHA-SIA THERAPY THESE DAYS.
I THINK HIS SPEECH IS STARTING TO CATCH UP WITH HIS THOUGHTS.
I'M GETTING BETTER.
I'M GETTING BETTER.
COOL! HOW CAN YOU TELL?
GB Trudeau

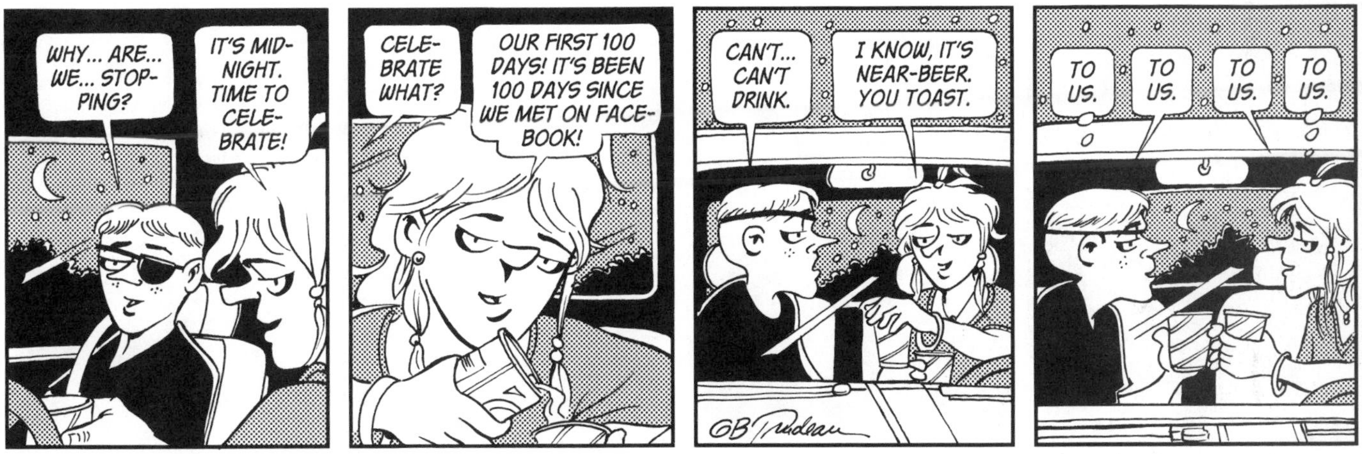
WHY... ARE... WE... STOP-PING?
IT'S MID-NIGHT. TIME TO CELE-BRATE!
CELE-BRATE WHAT?
OUR FIRST 100 DAYS! IT'S BEEN 100 DAYS SINCE WE MET ON FACE-BOOK!
CAN'T... CAN'T DRINK.
I KNOW, IT'S NEAR-BEER. YOU TOAST.
TO US.
TO US.
TO US.
TO US.
GB Trudeau

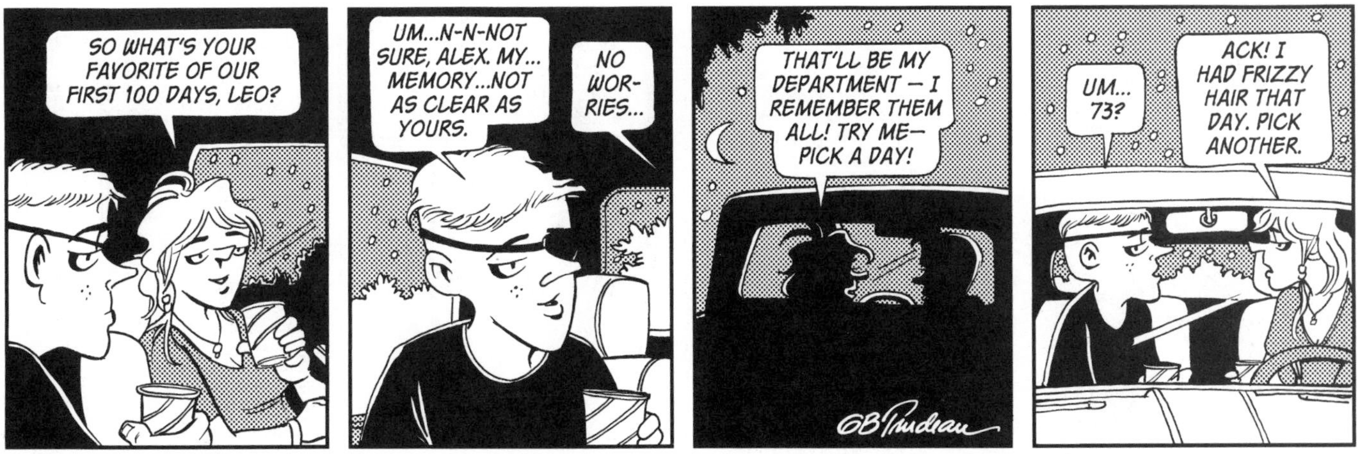
SO WHAT'S YOUR FAVORITE OF OUR FIRST 100 DAYS, LEO?
UM...N-N-NOT SURE, ALEX. MY... MEMORY...NOT AS CLEAR AS YOURS.
NO WOR-RIES...
THAT'LL BE MY DEPARTMENT — I REMEMBER THEM ALL! TRY ME-PICK A DAY!
UM... 73?
ACK! I HAD FRIZZY HAIR THAT DAY. PICK ANOTHER.
GB Trudeau

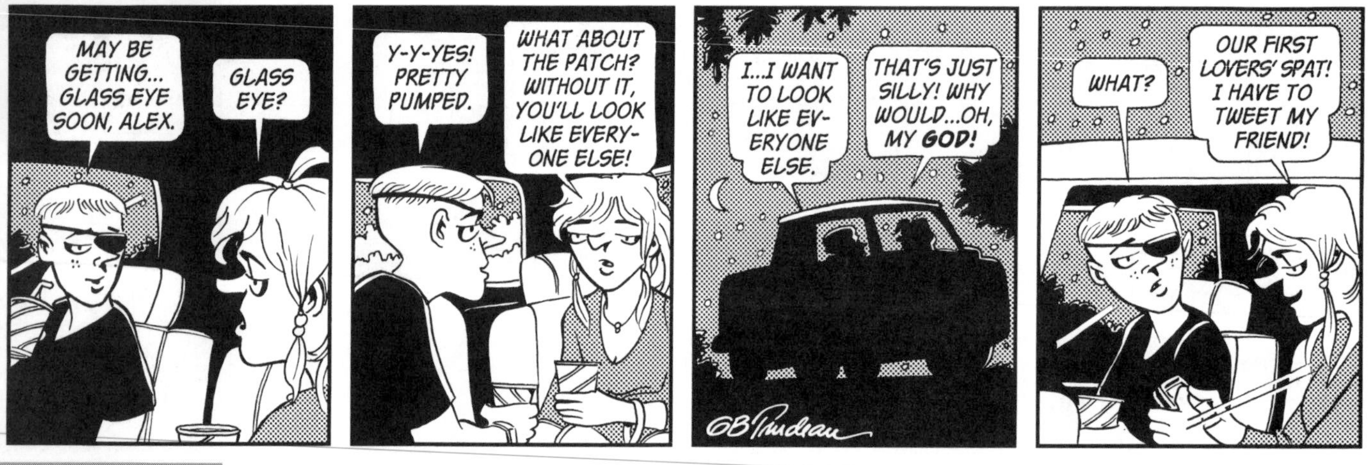
MAY BE GETTING... GLASS EYE SOON, ALEX.
GLASS EYE?
Y-Y-YES! PRETTY PUMPED.
WHAT ABOUT THE PATCH? WITHOUT IT, YOU'LL LOOK LIKE EVERY-ONE ELSE!
I...I WANT TO LOOK LIKE EV-ERYONE ELSE.
THAT'S JUST SILLY! WHY WOULD...OH, MY **GOD!**
WHAT?
OUR FIRST LOVERS' SPAT! I HAVE TO TWEET MY FRIEND!

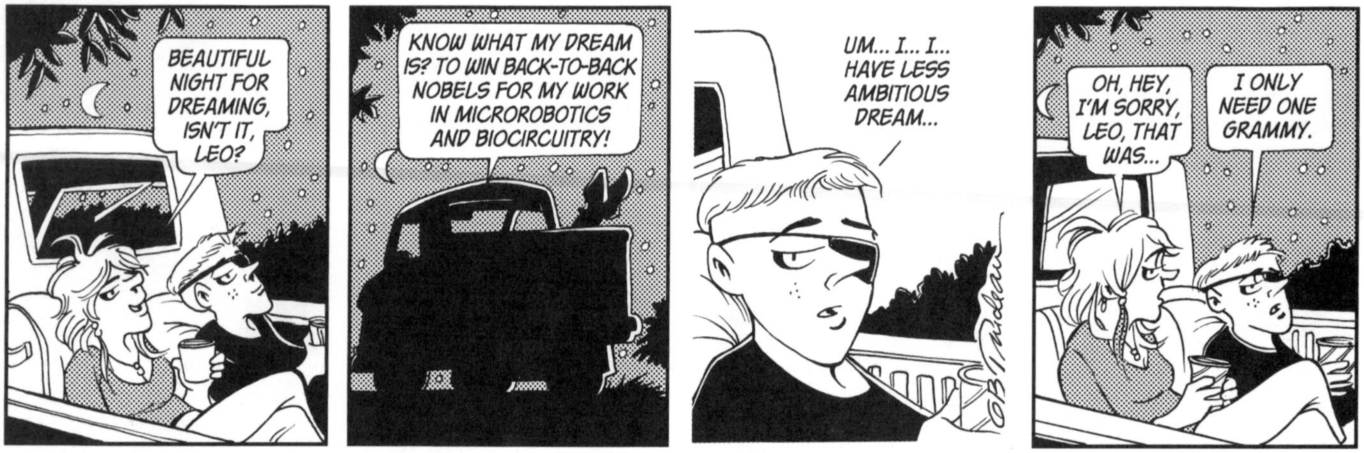
BEAUTIFUL NIGHT FOR DREAMING, ISN'T IT, LEO?
KNOW WHAT MY DREAM IS? TO WIN BACK-TO-BACK NOBELS FOR MY WORK IN MICROROBOTICS AND BIOCIRCUITRY!
UM... I... I... HAVE LESS AMBITIOUS DREAM...
OH, HEY, I'M SORRY, LEO, THAT WAS...
I ONLY NEED ONE GRAMMY.

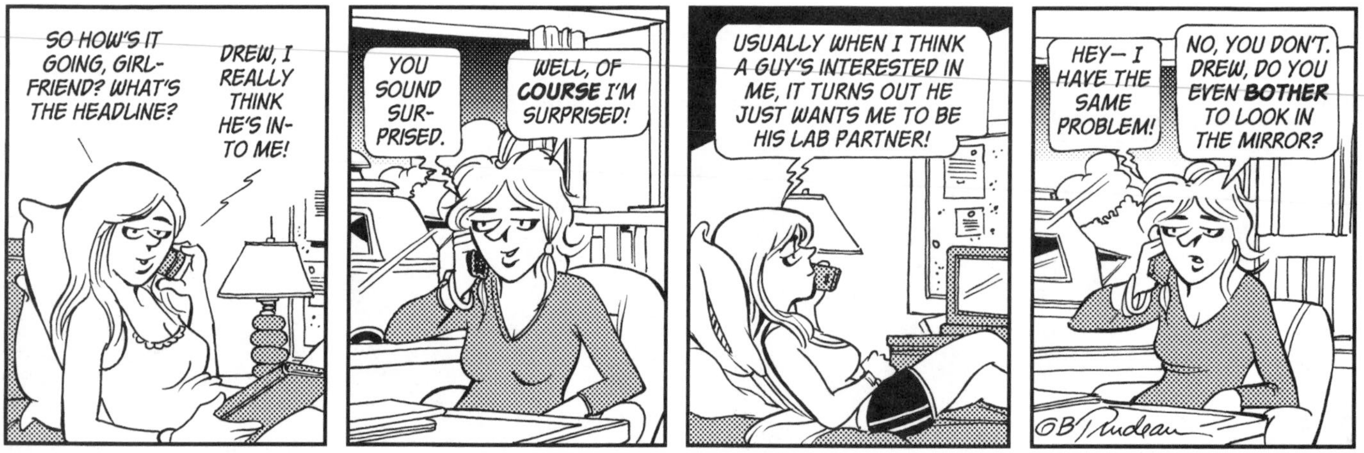
SO HOW'S IT GOING, GIRL-FRIEND? WHAT'S THE HEADLINE?
DREW, I REALLY THINK HE'S IN-TO ME!
YOU SOUND SUR-PRISED.
WELL, OF **COURSE** I'M SURPRISED!
USUALLY WHEN I THINK A GUY'S INTERESTED IN ME, IT TURNS OUT HE JUST WANTS ME TO BE HIS LAB PARTNER!
HEY— I HAVE THE SAME PROBLEM!
NO, YOU DON'T. DREW, DO YOU EVEN **BOTHER** TO LOOK IN THE MIRROR?

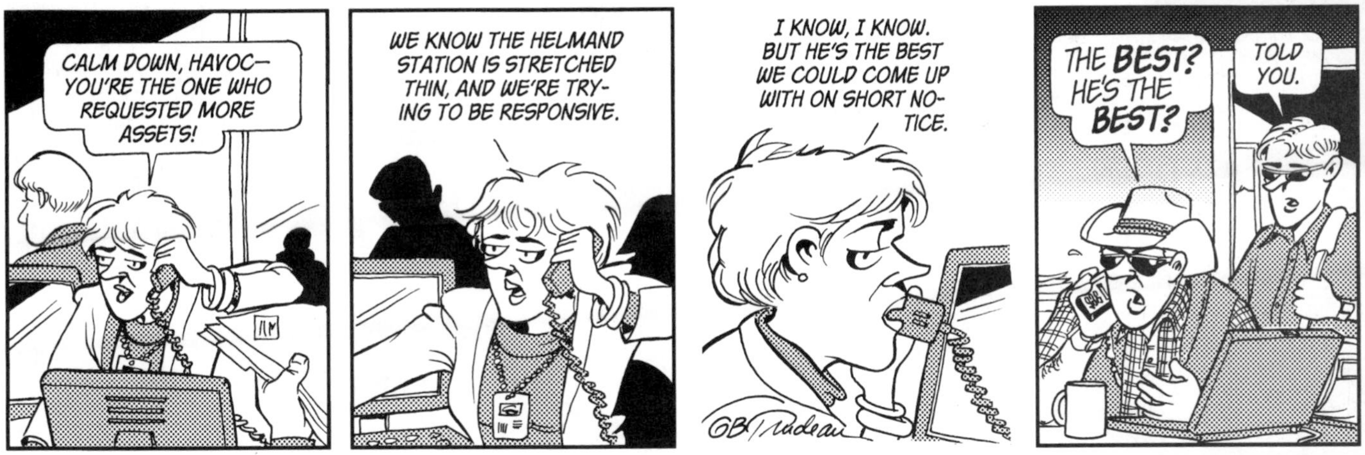
CALM DOWN, HAVOC— YOU'RE THE ONE WHO REQUESTED MORE ASSETS!
WE KNOW THE HELMAND STATION IS STRETCHED THIN, AND WE'RE TRY-ING TO BE RESPONSIVE.
I KNOW, I KNOW. BUT HE'S THE BEST WE COULD COME UP WITH ON SHORT NO-TICE.
GB Trudeau
THE BEST? HE'S THE BEST?
TOLD YOU.

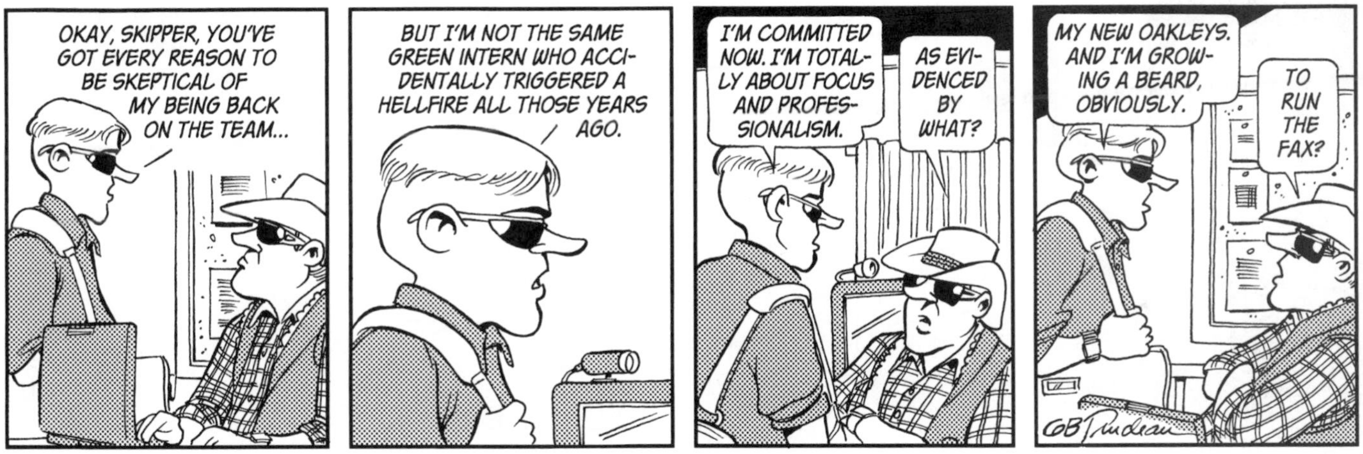
OKAY, SKIPPER, YOU'VE GOT EVERY REASON TO BE SKEPTICAL OF MY BEING BACK ON THE TEAM...
BUT I'M NOT THE SAME GREEN INTERN WHO ACCI-DENTALLY TRIGGERED A HELLFIRE ALL THOSE YEARS AGO.
I'M COMMITTED NOW. I'M TOTAL-LY ABOUT FOCUS AND PROFES-SIONALISM.
AS EVI-DENCED BY WHAT?
MY NEW OAKLEYS. AND I'M GROW-ING A BEARD, OBVIOUSLY.
TO RUN THE FAX?
GB Trudeau

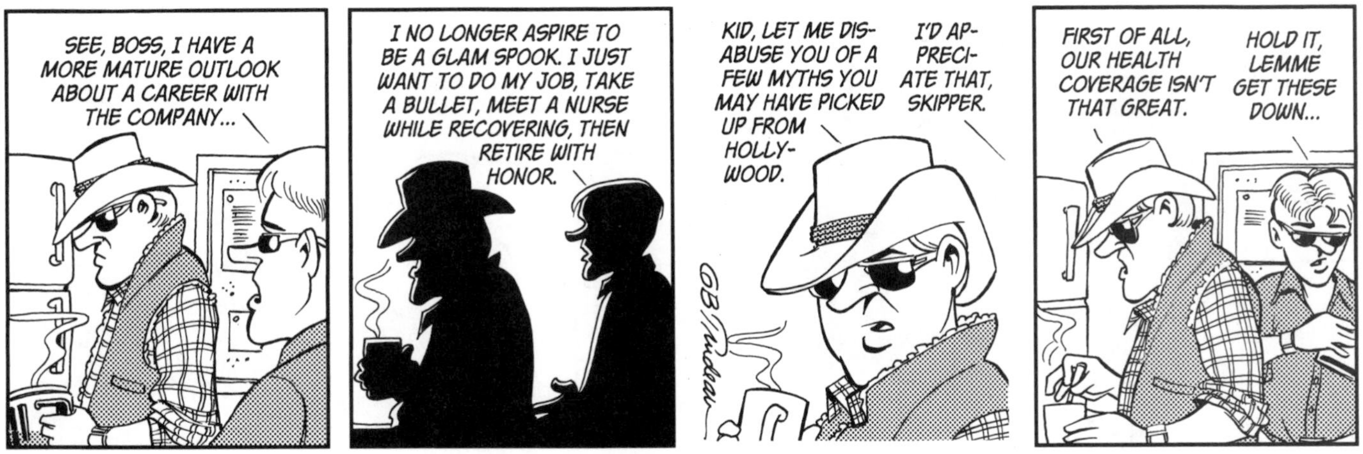
SEE, BOSS, I HAVE A MORE MATURE OUTLOOK ABOUT A CAREER WITH THE COMPANY...
I NO LONGER ASPIRE TO BE A GLAM SPOOK. I JUST WANT TO DO MY JOB, TAKE A BULLET, MEET A NURSE WHILE RECOVERING, THEN RETIRE WITH HONOR.
KID, LET ME DIS-ABUSE YOU OF A FEW MYTHS YOU MAY HAVE PICKED UP FROM HOLLY-WOOD.
I'D AP-PRECI-ATE THAT, SKIPPER.
GB Trudeau
FIRST OF ALL, OUR HEALTH COVERAGE ISN'T THAT GREAT.
HOLD IT, LEMME GET THESE DOWN...

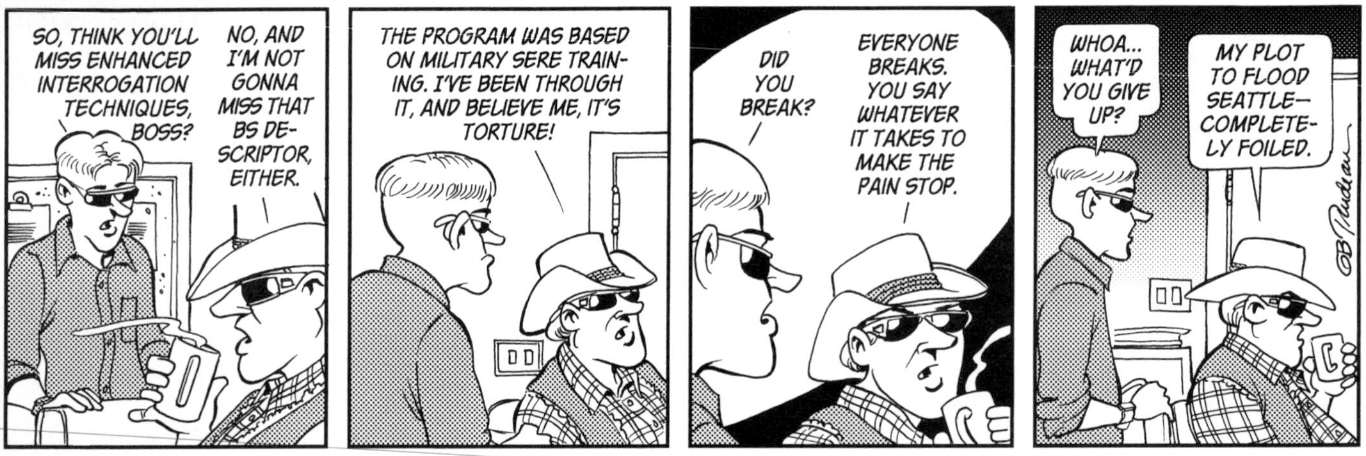
SO, THINK YOU'LL MISS ENHANCED INTERROGATION TECHNIQUES, BOSS?
NO, AND I'M NOT GONNA MISS THAT BS DESCRIPTOR, EITHER.
THE PROGRAM WAS BASED ON MILITARY SERE TRAINING. I'VE BEEN THROUGH IT, AND BELIEVE ME, IT'S TORTURE!
DID YOU BREAK?
EVERYONE BREAKS. YOU SAY WHATEVER IT TAKES TO MAKE THE PAIN STOP.
WHOA... WHAT'D YOU GIVE UP?
MY PLOT TO FLOOD SEATTLE— COMPLETELY FOILED.

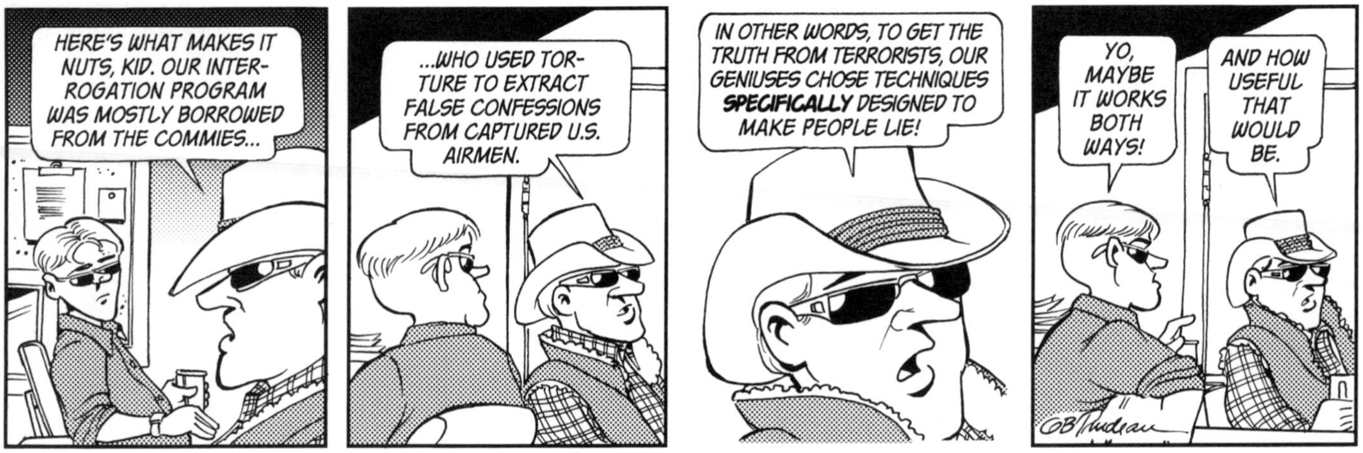
HERE'S WHAT MAKES IT NUTS, KID. OUR INTERROGATION PROGRAM WAS MOSTLY BORROWED FROM THE COMMIES...
...WHO USED TORTURE TO EXTRACT FALSE CONFESSIONS FROM CAPTURED U.S. AIRMEN.
IN OTHER WORDS, TO GET THE TRUTH FROM TERRORISTS, OUR GENIUSES CHOSE TECHNIQUES **SPECIFICALLY** DESIGNED TO MAKE PEOPLE LIE!
YO, MAYBE IT WORKS BOTH WAYS!
AND HOW USEFUL THAT WOULD BE.

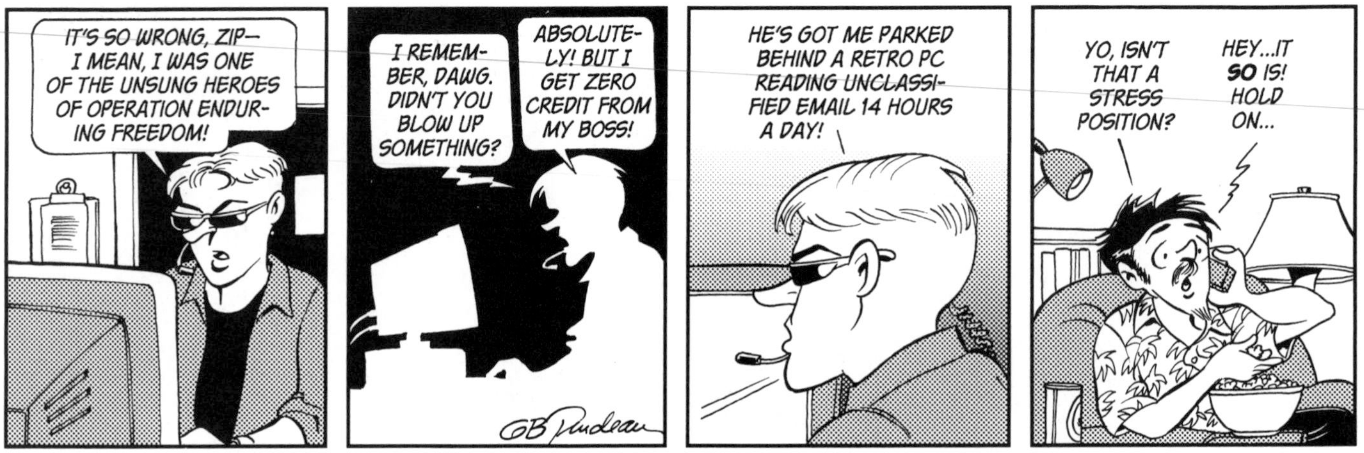
IT'S SO WRONG, ZIP— I MEAN, I WAS ONE OF THE UNSUNG HEROES OF OPERATION ENDURING FREEDOM!
I REMEMBER, DAWG. DIDN'T YOU BLOW UP SOMETHING?
ABSOLUTELY! BUT I GET ZERO CREDIT FROM MY BOSS!
HE'S GOT ME PARKED BEHIND A RETRO PC READING UNCLASSIFIED EMAIL 14 HOURS A DAY!
YO, ISN'T THAT A STRESS POSITION?
HEY...IT **SO** IS! HOLD ON...

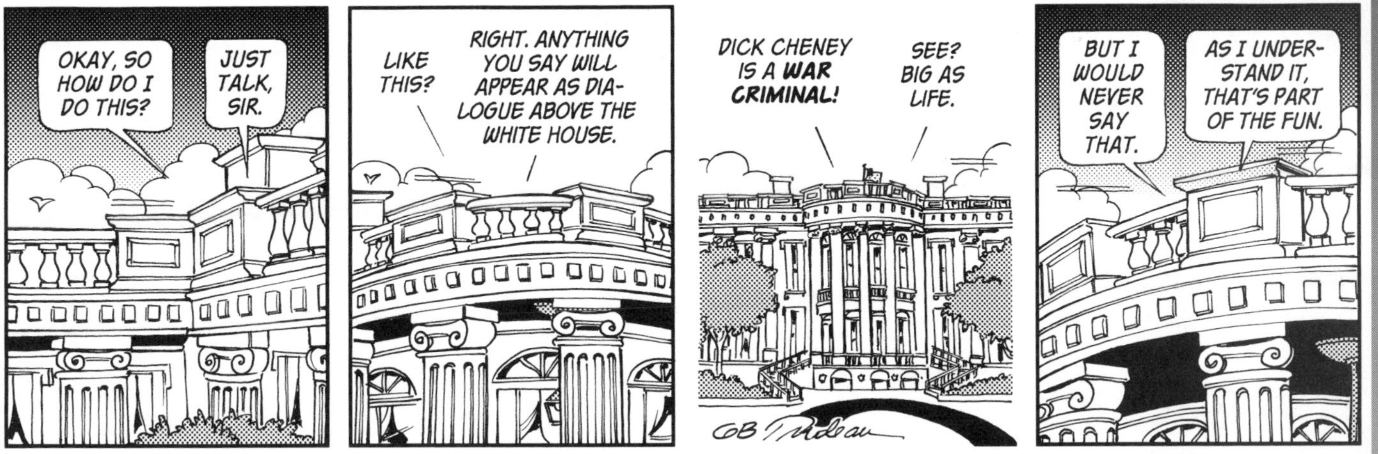
OKAY, SO HOW DO I DO THIS?
JUST TALK, SIR.
LIKE THIS?
RIGHT. ANYTHING YOU SAY WILL APPEAR AS DIALOGUE ABOVE THE WHITE HOUSE.
DICK CHENEY IS A WAR CRIMINAL!
SEE? BIG AS LIFE.
BUT I WOULD NEVER SAY THAT.
AS I UNDERSTAND IT, THAT'S PART OF THE FUN.
GB Trudeau

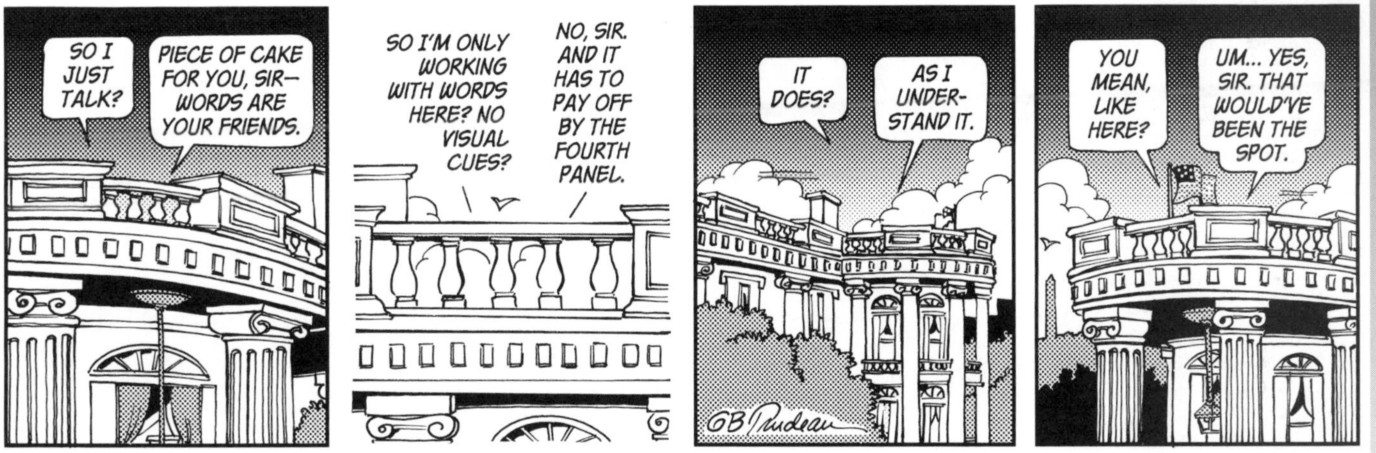
SO I JUST TALK?
PIECE OF CAKE FOR YOU, SIR— WORDS ARE YOUR FRIENDS.
SO I'M ONLY WORKING WITH WORDS HERE? NO VISUAL CUES?
NO, SIR. AND IT HAS TO PAY OFF BY THE FOURTH PANEL.
IT DOES?
AS I UNDERSTAND IT.
YOU MEAN, LIKE HERE?
UM... YES, SIR. THAT WOULD'VE BEEN THE SPOT.
GB Trudeau

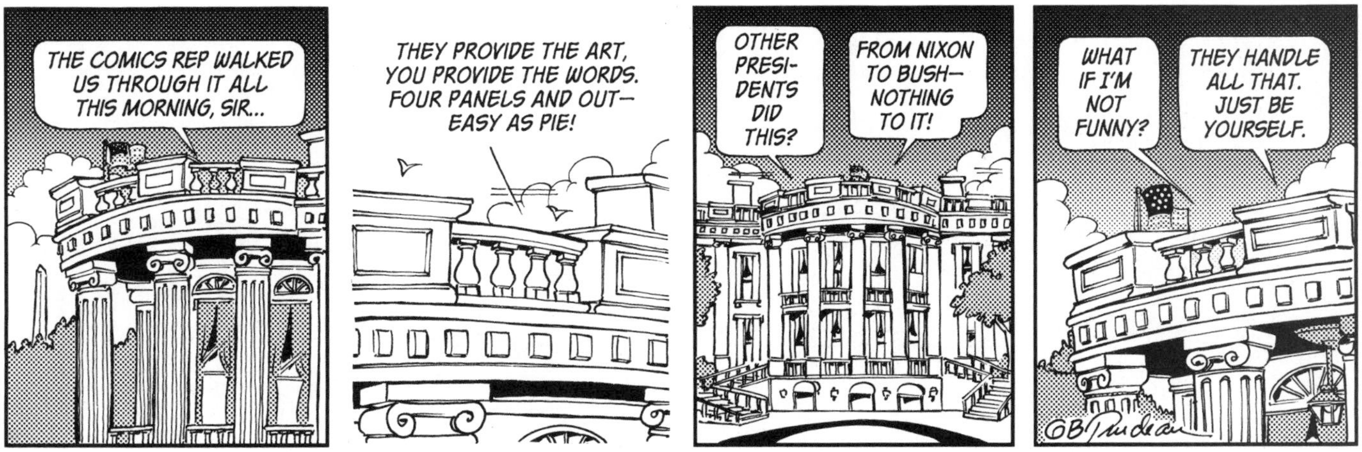
THE COMICS REP WALKED US THROUGH IT ALL THIS MORNING, SIR...
THEY PROVIDE THE ART, YOU PROVIDE THE WORDS. FOUR PANELS AND OUT— EASY AS PIE!
OTHER PRESIDENTS DID THIS?
FROM NIXON TO BUSH— NOTHING TO IT!
WHAT IF I'M NOT FUNNY?
THEY HANDLE ALL THAT. JUST BE YOURSELF.
GB Trudeau

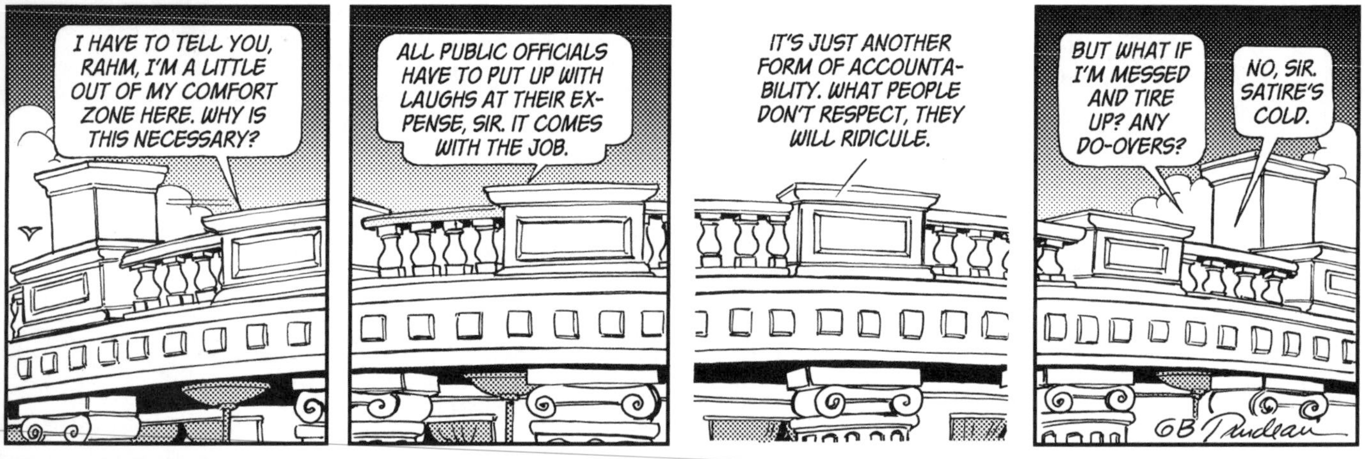
I HAVE TO TELL YOU, RAHM, I'M A LITTLE OUT OF MY COMFORT ZONE HERE. WHY IS THIS NECESSARY?
ALL PUBLIC OFFICIALS HAVE TO PUT UP WITH LAUGHS AT THEIR EXPENSE, SIR. IT COMES WITH THE JOB.
IT'S JUST ANOTHER FORM OF ACCOUNTABILITY. WHAT PEOPLE DON'T RESPECT, THEY WILL RIDICULE.
BUT WHAT IF I'M MESSED AND TIRE UP? ANY DO-OVERS?
NO, SIR. SATIRE'S COLD.
GB Trudeau

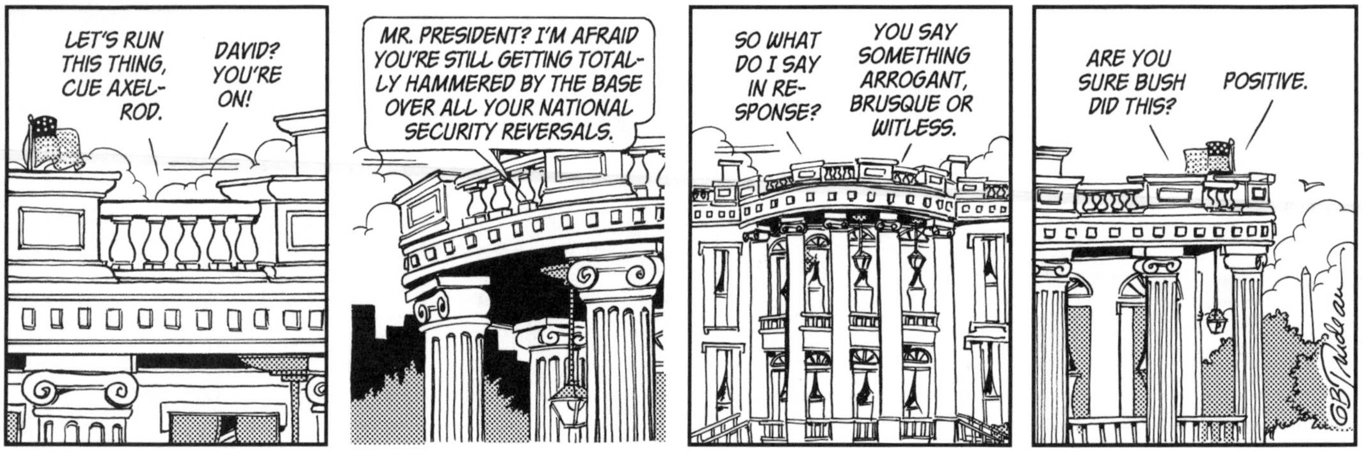
LET'S RUN THIS THING, CUE AXELROD.
DAVID? YOU'RE ON!
MR. PRESIDENT? I'M AFRAID YOU'RE STILL GETTING TOTALLY HAMMERED BY THE BASE OVER ALL YOUR NATIONAL SECURITY REVERSALS.
SO WHAT DO I SAY IN RESPONSE?
YOU SAY SOMETHING ARROGANT, BRUSQUE OR WITLESS.
ARE YOU SURE BUSH DID THIS?
POSITIVE.
GB Trudeau

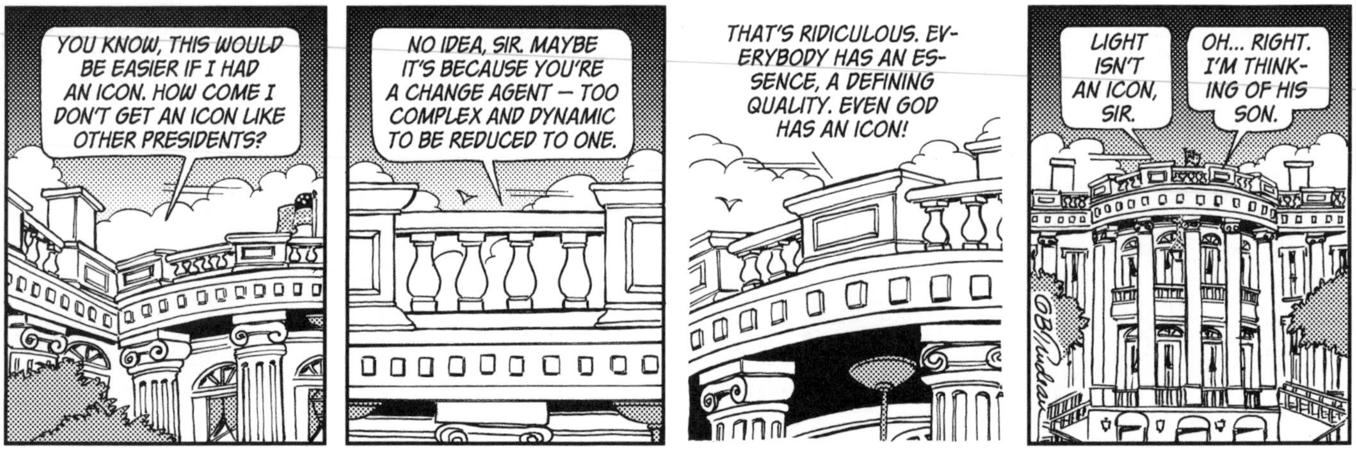
YOU KNOW, THIS WOULD BE EASIER IF I HAD AN ICON. HOW COME I DON'T GET AN ICON LIKE OTHER PRESIDENTS?
NO IDEA, SIR. MAYBE IT'S BECAUSE YOU'RE A CHANGE AGENT — TOO COMPLEX AND DYNAMIC TO BE REDUCED TO ONE.
THAT'S RIDICULOUS. EVERYBODY HAS AN ESSENCE, A DEFINING QUALITY. EVEN GOD HAS AN ICON!
LIGHT ISN'T AN ICON, SIR.
OH... RIGHT. I'M THINKING OF HIS SON.
GB Trudeau

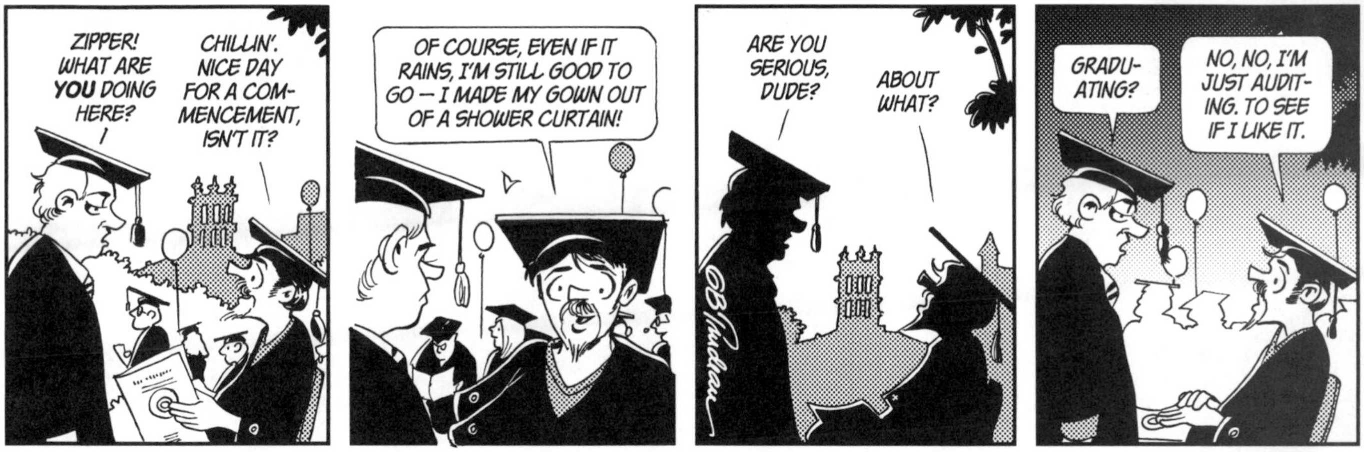
ZIPPER! WHAT ARE **YOU** DOING HERE?
CHILLIN'. NICE DAY FOR A COM-MENCEMENT, ISN'T IT?
OF COURSE, EVEN IF IT RAINS, I'M STILL GOOD TO GO — I MADE MY GOWN OUT OF A SHOWER CURTAIN!
ARE YOU SERIOUS, DUDE?
ABOUT WHAT?
GRADU-ATING?
NO, NO, I'M JUST AUDIT-ING. TO SEE IF I LIKE IT.
GB Trudeau

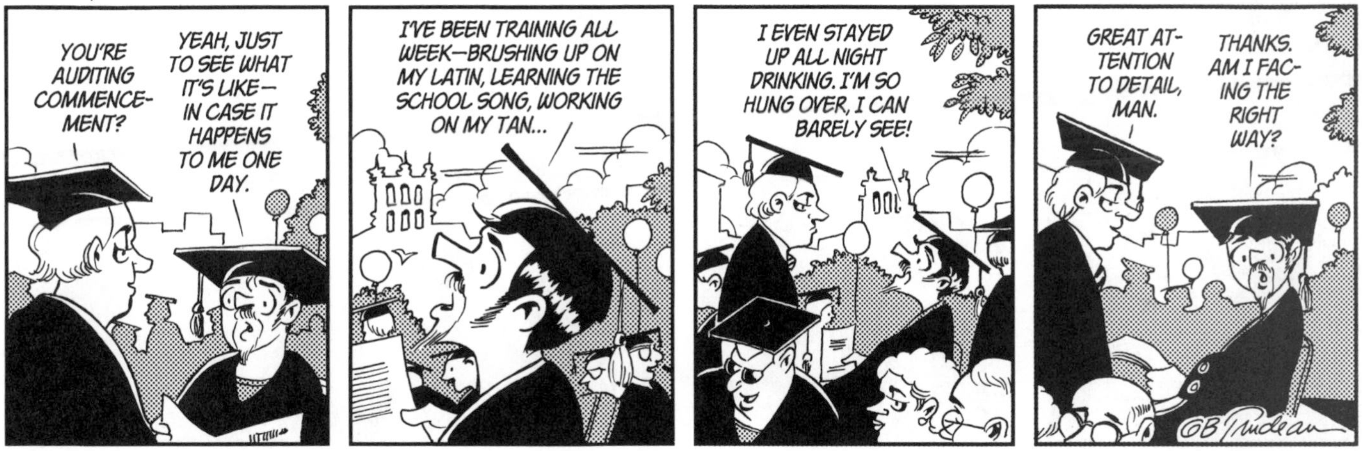
YOU'RE AUDITING COMMENCE-MENT?
YEAH, JUST TO SEE WHAT IT'S LIKE— IN CASE IT HAPPENS TO ME ONE DAY.
I'VE BEEN TRAINING ALL WEEK—BRUSHING UP ON MY LATIN, LEARNING THE SCHOOL SONG, WORKING ON MY TAN...
I EVEN STAYED UP ALL NIGHT DRINKING. I'M SO HUNG OVER, I CAN BARELY SEE!
GREAT AT-TENTION TO DETAIL, MAN.
THANKS. AM I FAC-ING THE RIGHT WAY?
GB Trudeau

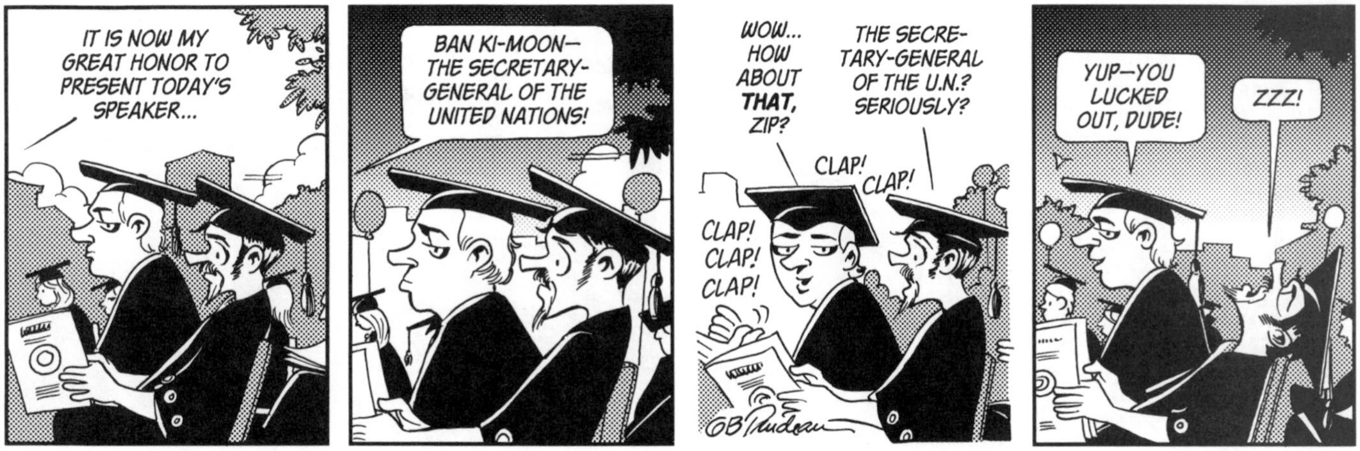
IT IS NOW MY GREAT HONOR TO PRESENT TODAY'S SPEAKER...
BAN KI-MOON— THE SECRETARY-GENERAL OF THE UNITED NATIONS!
WOW... HOW ABOUT **THAT,** ZIP?
THE SECRE-TARY-GENERAL OF THE U.N.? SERIOUSLY?
CLAP! CLAP!
CLAP! CLAP! CLAP!
GB Trudeau
YUP—YOU LUCKED OUT, DUDE!
ZZZ!

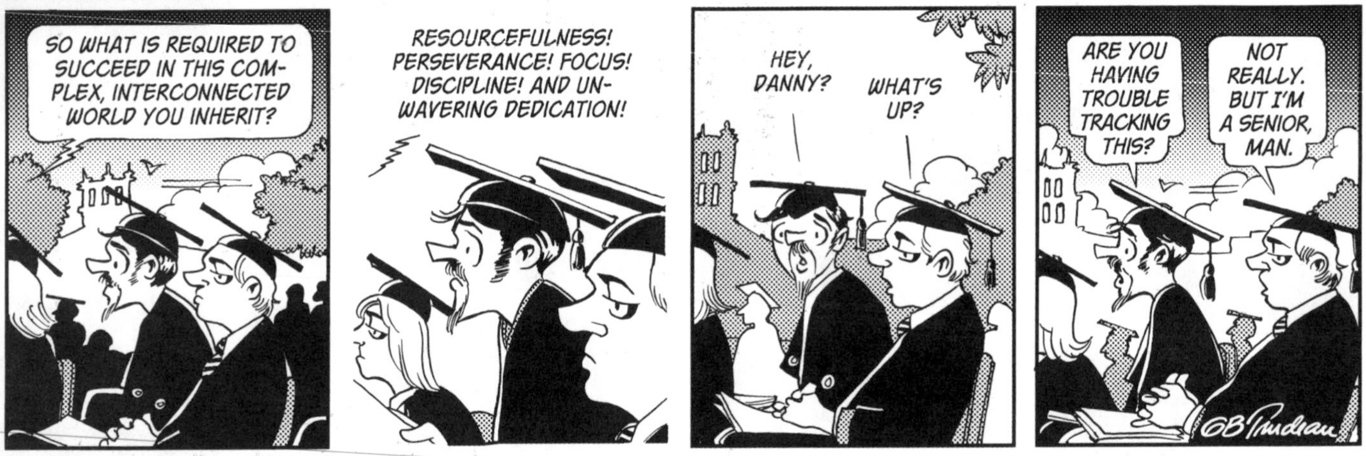
SO WHAT IS REQUIRED TO SUCCEED IN THIS COMPLEX, INTERCONNECTED WORLD YOU INHERIT?
RESOURCEFULNESS! PERSEVERANCE! FOCUS! DISCIPLINE! AND UNWAVERING DEDICATION!
HEY, DANNY?
WHAT'S UP?
ARE YOU HAVING TROUBLE TRACKING THIS?
NOT REALLY. BUT I'M A SENIOR, MAN.
GB Trudeau

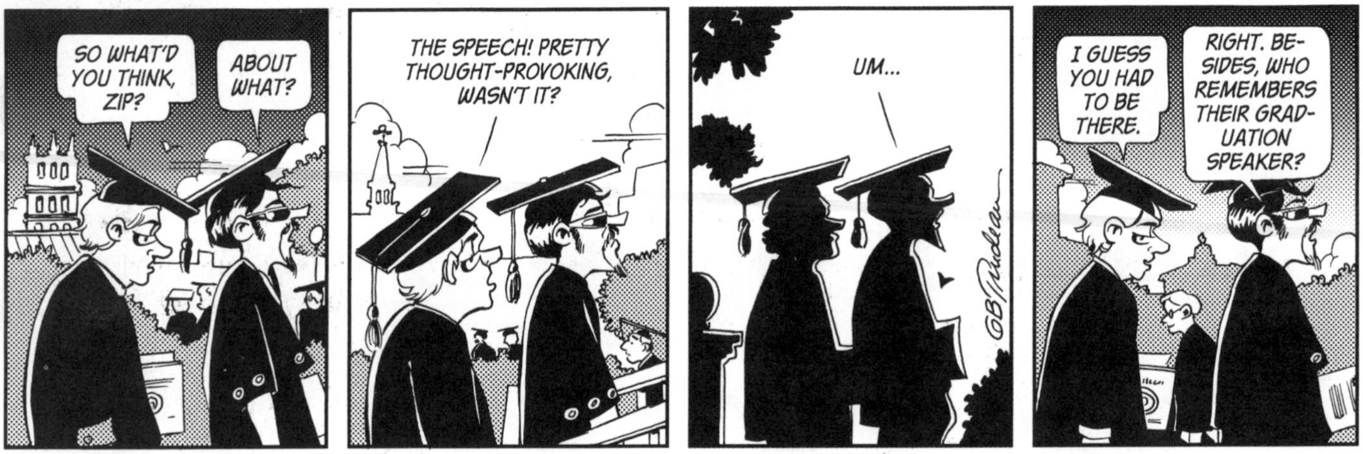
SO WHAT'D YOU THINK, ZIP?
ABOUT WHAT?
THE SPEECH! PRETTY THOUGHT-PROVOKING, WASN'T IT?
UM...
GB Trudeau
I GUESS YOU HAD TO BE THERE.
RIGHT. BESIDES, WHO REMEMBERS THEIR GRADUATION SPEAKER?

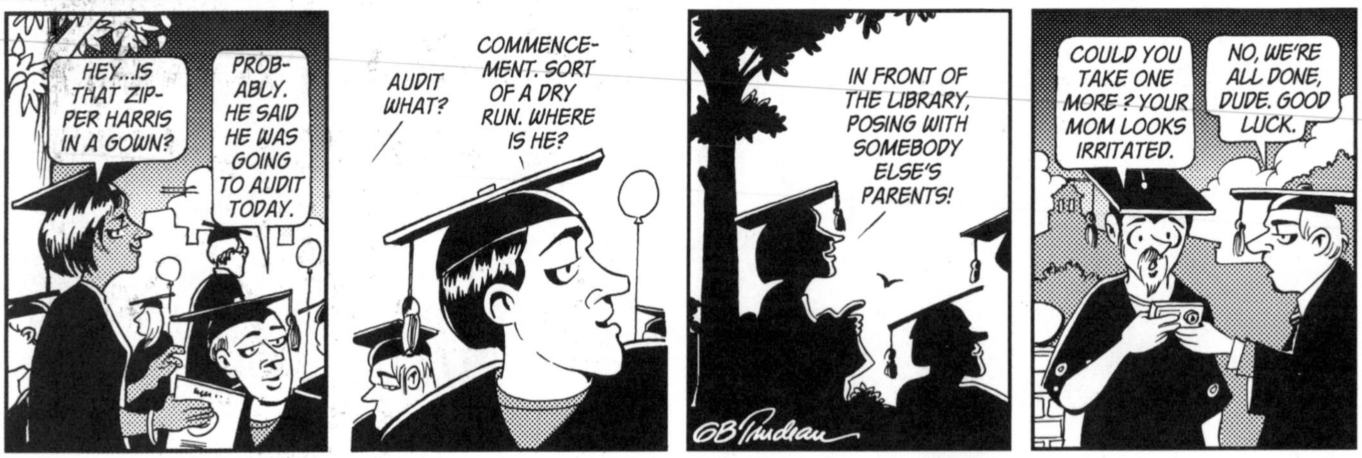
HEY...IS THAT ZIPPER HARRIS IN A GOWN?
PROBABLY. HE SAID HE WAS GOING TO AUDIT TODAY.
AUDIT WHAT?
COMMENCEMENT. SORT OF A DRY RUN. WHERE IS HE?
IN FRONT OF THE LIBRARY, POSING WITH SOMEBODY ELSE'S PARENTS!
GB Trudeau
COULD YOU TAKE ONE MORE? YOUR MOM LOOKS IRRITATED.
NO, WE'RE ALL DONE, DUDE. GOOD LUCK.

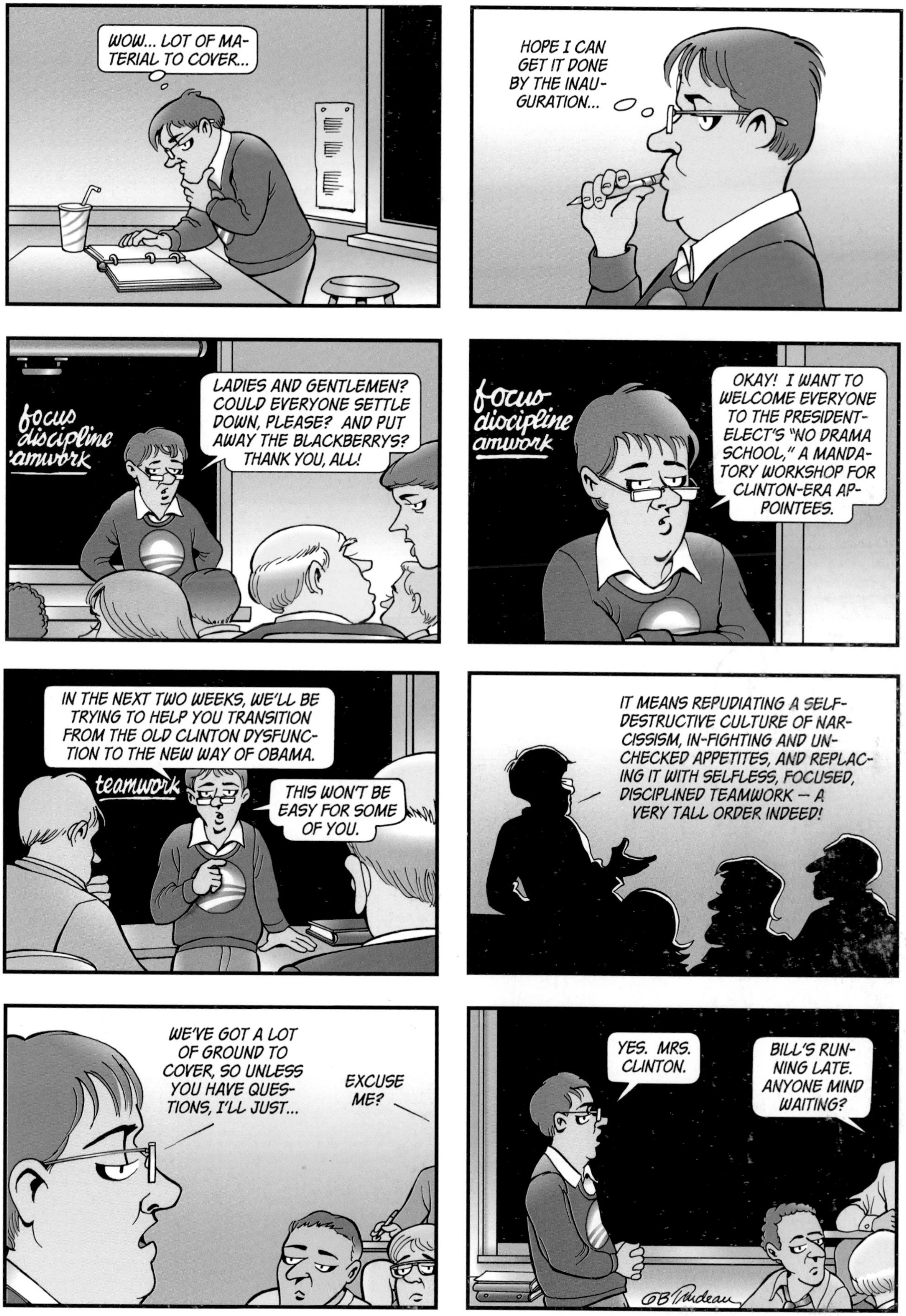
WOW... LOT OF MATERIAL TO COVER...
HOPE I CAN GET IT DONE BY THE INAUGURATION...
focus discipline teamwork
LADIES AND GENTLEMEN? COULD EVERYONE SETTLE DOWN, PLEASE? AND PUT AWAY THE BLACKBERRYS? THANK YOU, ALL!
OKAY! I WANT TO WELCOME EVERYONE TO THE PRESIDENT-ELECT'S "NO DRAMA SCHOOL," A MANDATORY WORKSHOP FOR CLINTON-ERA APPOINTEES.
IN THE NEXT TWO WEEKS, WE'LL BE TRYING TO HELP YOU TRANSITION FROM THE OLD CLINTON DYSFUNCTION TO THE NEW WAY OF OBAMA.
teamwork
THIS WON'T BE EASY FOR SOME OF YOU.
IT MEANS REPUDIATING A SELF-DESTRUCTIVE CULTURE OF NARCISSISM, IN-FIGHTING AND UNCHECKED APPETITES, AND REPLACING IT WITH SELFLESS, FOCUSED, DISCIPLINED TEAMWORK — A VERY TALL ORDER INDEED!
WE'VE GOT A LOT OF GROUND TO COVER, SO UNLESS YOU HAVE QUESTIONS, I'LL JUST...
EXCUSE ME?
YES. MRS. CLINTON.
BILL'S RUNNING LATE. ANYONE MIND WAITING?
GB Trudeau

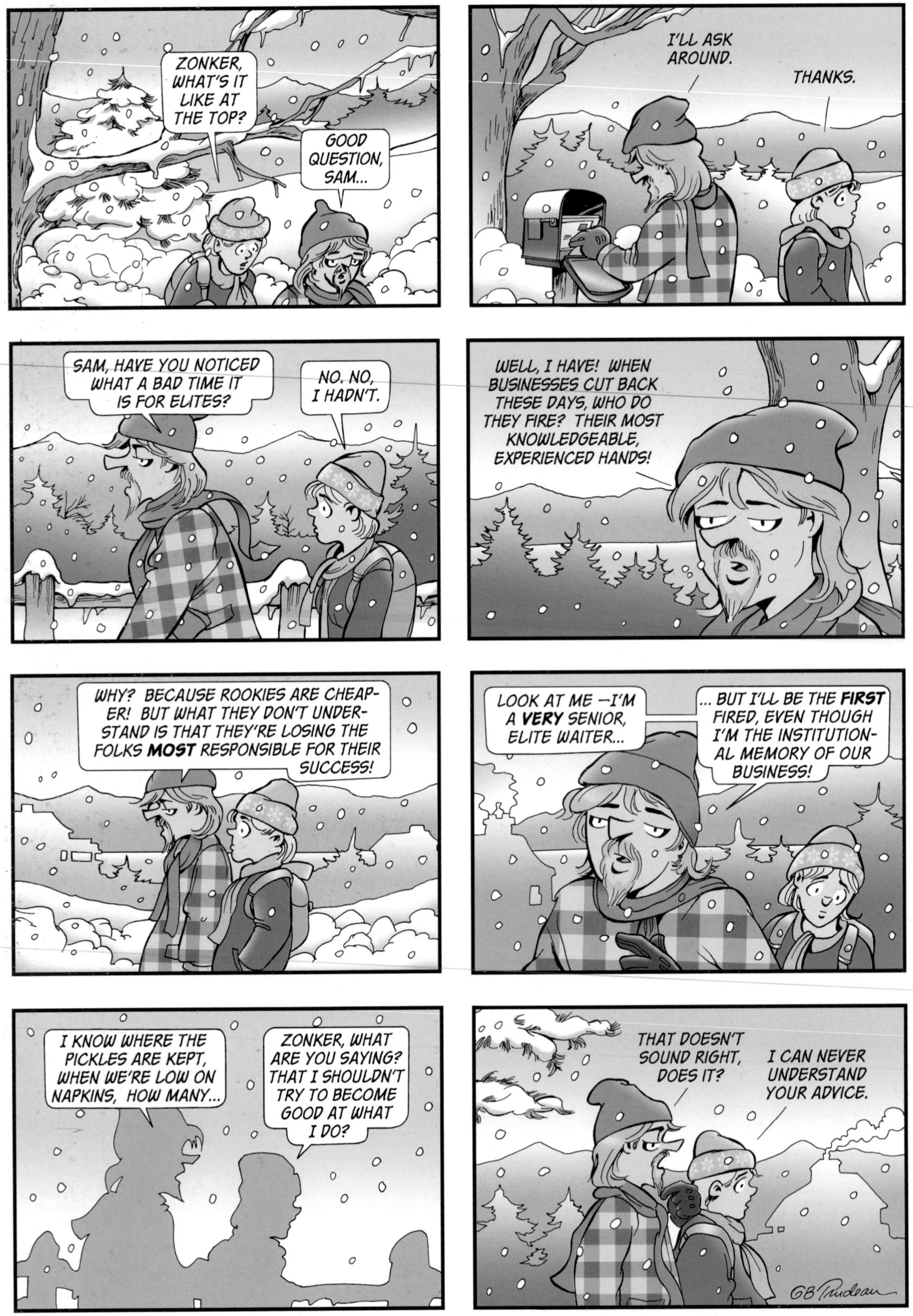
ZONKER, WHAT'S IT LIKE AT THE TOP?
GOOD QUESTION, SAM...
I'LL ASK AROUND.
THANKS.
SAM, HAVE YOU NOTICED WHAT A BAD TIME IT IS FOR ELITES?
NO. NO, I HADN'T.
WELL, I HAVE! WHEN BUSINESSES CUT BACK THESE DAYS, WHO DO THEY FIRE? THEIR MOST KNOWLEDGEABLE, EXPERIENCED HANDS!
WHY? BECAUSE ROOKIES ARE CHEAPER! BUT WHAT THEY DON'T UNDERSTAND IS THAT THEY'RE LOSING THE FOLKS **MOST** RESPONSIBLE FOR THEIR SUCCESS!
LOOK AT ME —I'M A **VERY** SENIOR, ELITE WAITER...
... BUT I'LL BE THE **FIRST** FIRED, EVEN THOUGH I'M THE INSTITUTIONAL MEMORY OF OUR BUSINESS!
I KNOW WHERE THE PICKLES ARE KEPT, WHEN WE'RE LOW ON NAPKINS, HOW MANY...
ZONKER, WHAT ARE YOU SAYING? THAT I SHOULDN'T TRY TO BECOME GOOD AT WHAT I DO?
THAT DOESN'T SOUND RIGHT, DOES IT?
I CAN NEVER UNDERSTAND YOUR ADVICE.
GB Trudeau

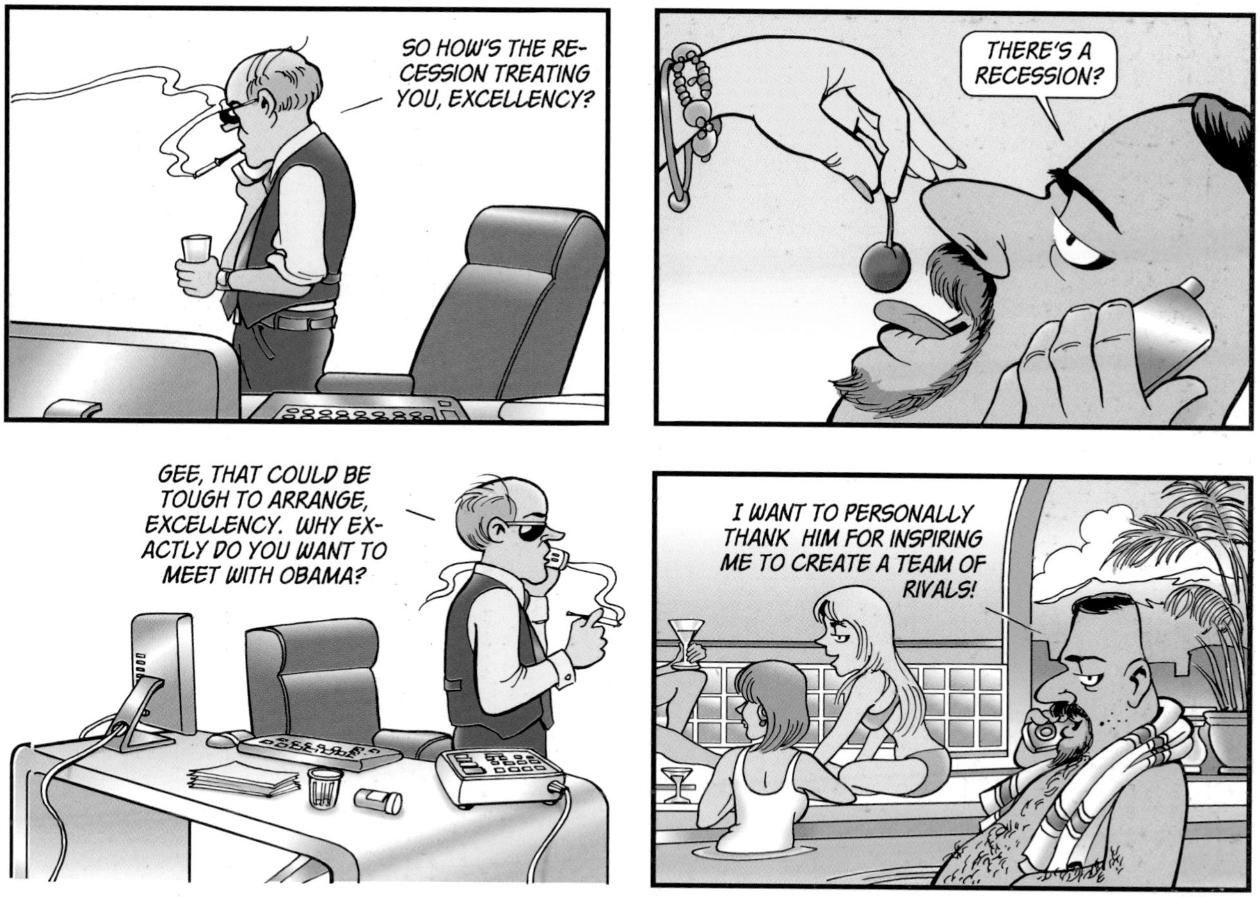
SO HOW'S THE RE-CESSION TREATING YOU, EXCELLENCY?
THERE'S A RECESSION?
GEE, THAT COULD BE TOUGH TO ARRANGE, EXCELLENCY. WHY EX-ACTLY DO YOU WANT TO MEET WITH OBAMA?
I WANT TO PERSONALLY THANK HIM FOR INSPIRING ME TO CREATE A TEAM OF RIVALS!

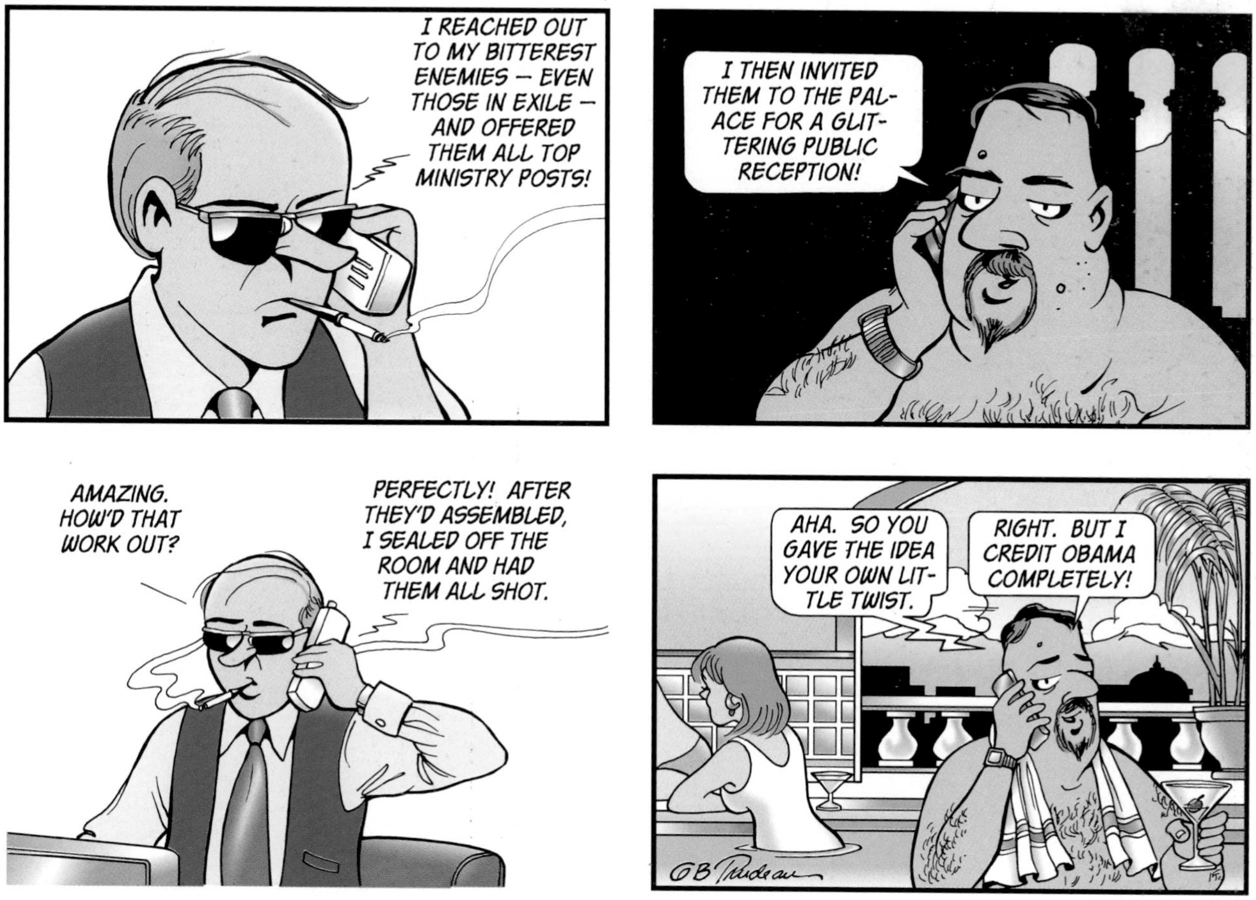
I REACHED OUT TO MY BITTEREST ENEMIES — EVEN THOSE IN EXILE — AND OFFERED THEM ALL TOP MINISTRY POSTS!
I THEN INVITED THEM TO THE PAL-ACE FOR A GLIT-TERING PUBLIC RECEPTION!
AMAZING. HOW'D THAT WORK OUT?
PERFECTLY! AFTER THEY'D ASSEMBLED, I SEALED OFF THE ROOM AND HAD THEM ALL SHOT.
AHA. SO YOU GAVE THE IDEA YOUR OWN LIT-TLE TWIST.
RIGHT. BUT I CREDIT OBAMA COMPLETELY!
GB Trudeau

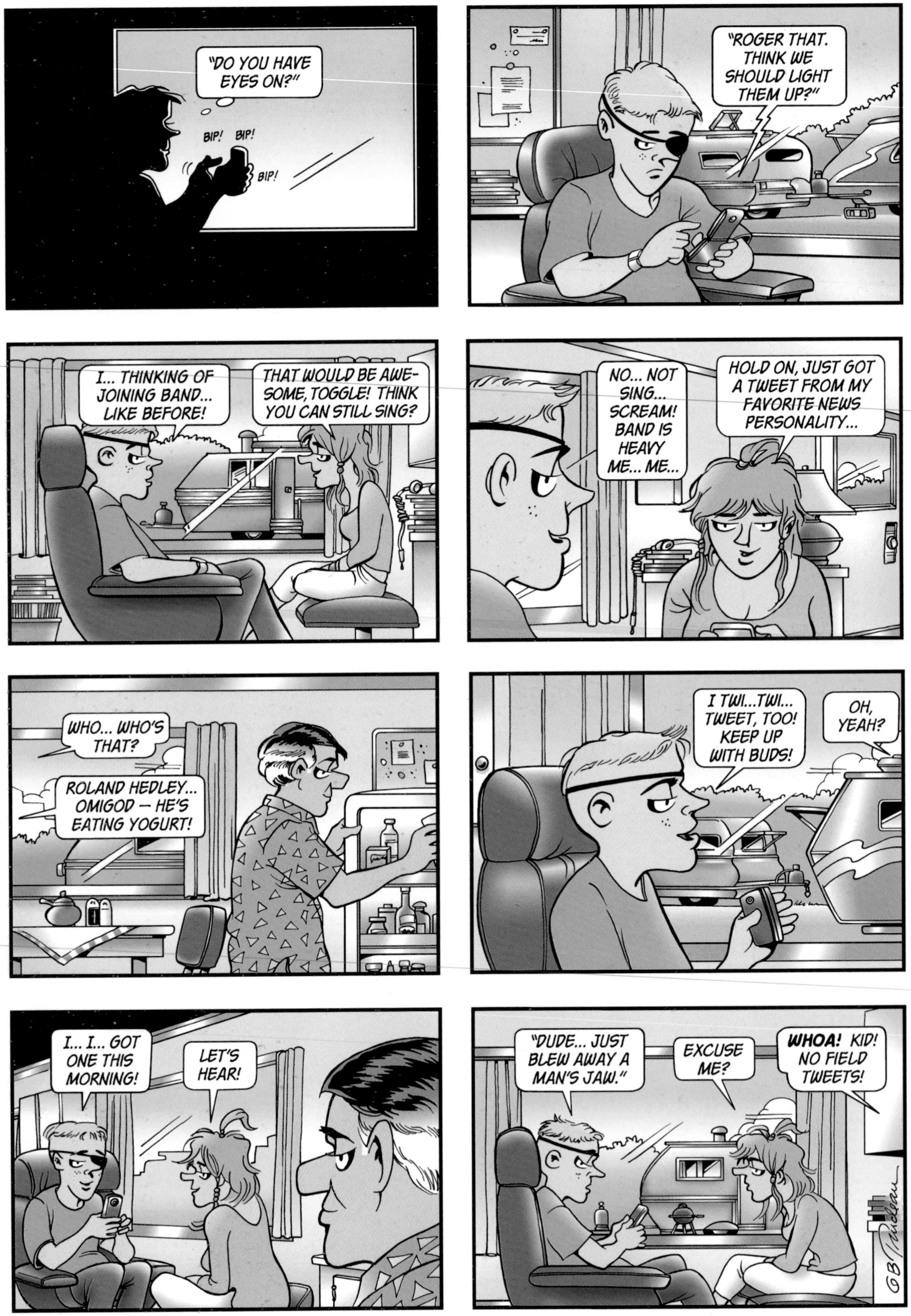
"DO YOU HAVE EYES ON?"
BIP! BIP!
BIP!
"ROGER THAT. THINK WE SHOULD LIGHT THEM UP?"
I... THINKING OF JOINING BAND... LIKE BEFORE!
THAT WOULD BE AWESOME, TOGGLE! THINK YOU CAN STILL SING?
NO... NOT SING... SCREAM! BAND IS HEAVY ME... ME...
HOLD ON, JUST GOT A TWEET FROM MY FAVORITE NEWS PERSONALITY...
WHO... WHO'S THAT?
ROLAND HEDLEY... OMIGOD — HE'S EATING YOGURT!
I TWI...TWI... TWEET, TOO! KEEP UP WITH BUDS!
OH, YEAH?
I... I... GOT ONE THIS MORNING!
LET'S HEAR!
"DUDE... JUST BLEW AWAY A MAN'S JAW."
EXCUSE ME?
WHOA! KID! NO FIELD TWEETS!
©B Trudeau

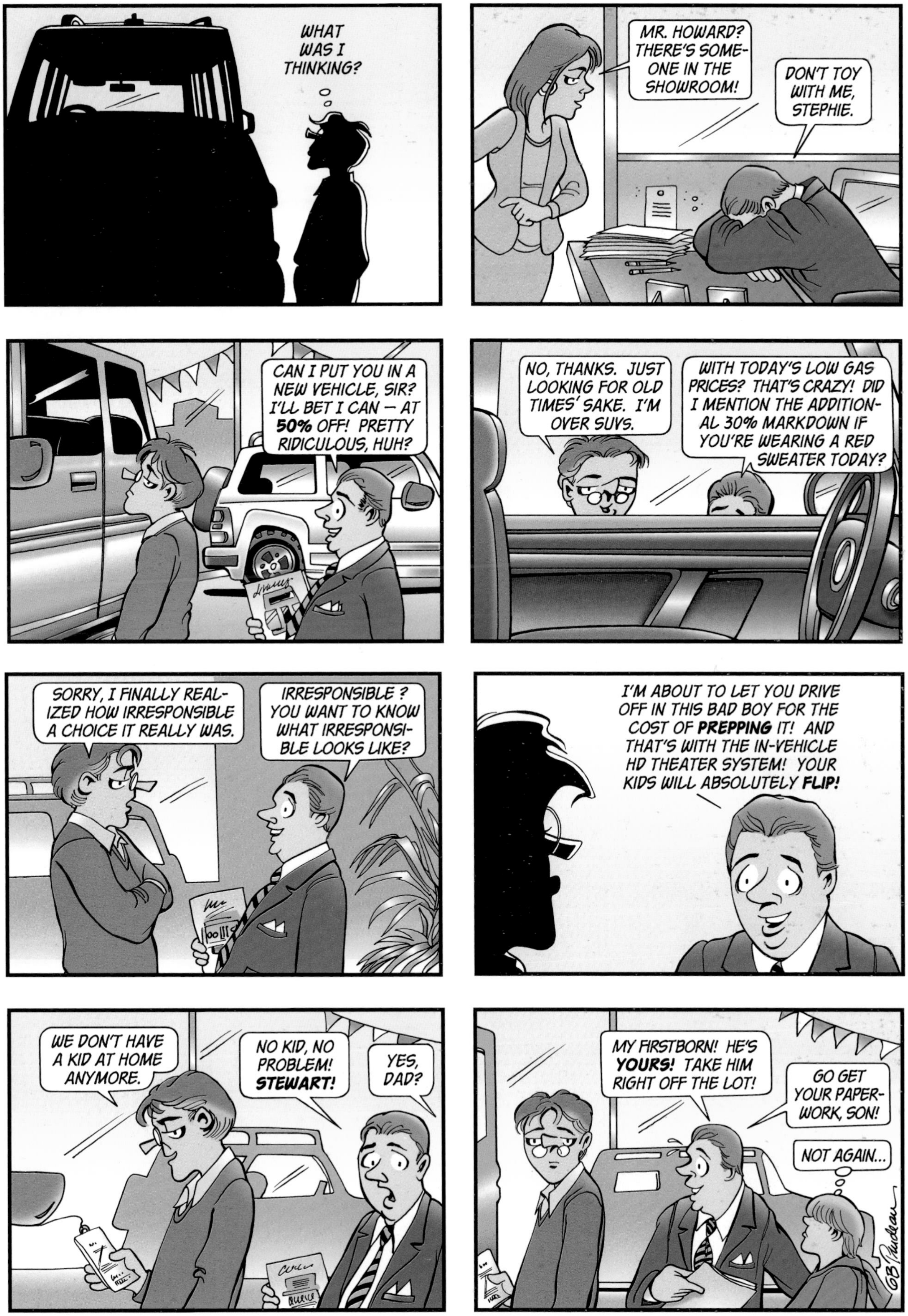
WHAT WAS I THINKING?
MR. HOWARD? THERE'S SOME-ONE IN THE SHOWROOM!
DON'T TOY WITH ME, STEPHIE.
CAN I PUT YOU IN A NEW VEHICLE, SIR? I'LL BET I CAN — AT 50% OFF! PRETTY RIDICULOUS, HUH?
NO, THANKS. JUST LOOKING FOR OLD TIMES' SAKE. I'M OVER SUVS.
WITH TODAY'S LOW GAS PRICES? THAT'S CRAZY! DID I MENTION THE ADDITION-AL 30% MARKDOWN IF YOU'RE WEARING A RED SWEATER TODAY?
SORRY, I FINALLY REAL-IZED HOW IRRESPONSIBLE A CHOICE IT REALLY WAS.
IRRESPONSIBLE ? YOU WANT TO KNOW WHAT IRRESPONSI-BLE LOOKS LIKE?
I'M ABOUT TO LET YOU DRIVE OFF IN THIS BAD BOY FOR THE COST OF PREPPING IT! AND THAT'S WITH THE IN-VEHICLE HD THEATER SYSTEM! YOUR KIDS WILL ABSOLUTELY FLIP!
WE DON'T HAVE A KID AT HOME ANYMORE.
NO KID, NO PROBLEM! STEWART!
YES, DAD?
MY FIRSTBORN! HE'S YOURS! TAKE HIM RIGHT OFF THE LOT!
GO GET YOUR PAPER-WORK, SON!
NOT AGAIN...

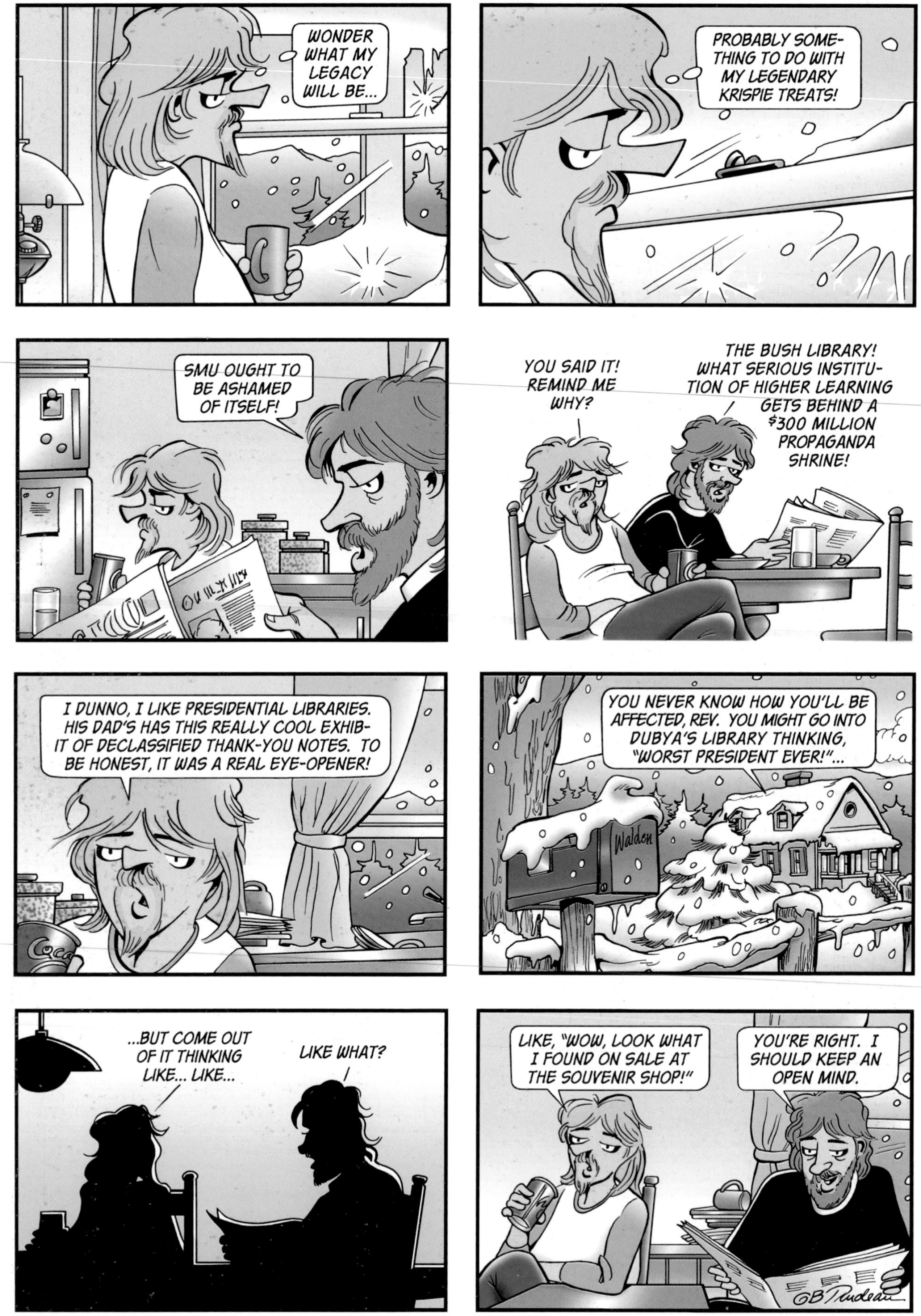
WONDER WHAT MY LEGACY WILL BE...
PROBABLY SOMETHING TO DO WITH MY LEGENDARY KRISPIE TREATS!
SMU OUGHT TO BE ASHAMED OF ITSELF!
YOU SAID IT! REMIND ME WHY?
THE BUSH LIBRARY! WHAT SERIOUS INSTITUTION OF HIGHER LEARNING GETS BEHIND A $300 MILLION PROPAGANDA SHRINE!
I DUNNO, I LIKE PRESIDENTIAL LIBRARIES. HIS DAD'S HAS THIS REALLY COOL EXHIBIT OF DECLASSIFIED THANK-YOU NOTES. TO BE HONEST, IT WAS A REAL EYE-OPENER!
YOU NEVER KNOW HOW YOU'LL BE AFFECTED, REV. YOU MIGHT GO INTO DUBYA'S LIBRARY THINKING, "WORST PRESIDENT EVER!"...
Walden
...BUT COME OUT OF IT THINKING LIKE... LIKE...
LIKE WHAT?
LIKE, "WOW, LOOK WHAT I FOUND ON SALE AT THE SOUVENIR SHOP!"
YOU'RE RIGHT. I SHOULD KEEP AN OPEN MIND.
GB Trudeau

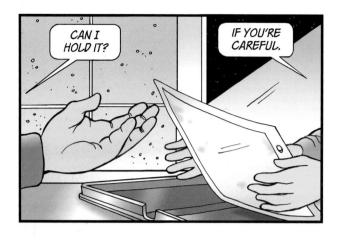

CAN I HOLD IT?

IF YOU'RE CAREFUL.

WOW... STILL WARM TO THE TOUCH!

REMARKABLE, ISN'T IT?

TIME FOR ANOTHER VISIT FROM LIBRARY OF CONGRESS ARCHIVIST VIOLET McPHEE! WHAT DO YOU HAVE FOR US TODAY, VIOLET?

AN EXCITING NEW ACQUISITION, MARK...

...THE FOUNDING DOCUMENT OF THE MODERN HATE-SPEECH MOVEMENT — NEWT GINGRICH'S FAMOUS GOPAC MEMO!

IN IT, THE SPEAKER INSTRUCTS REPUBLICAN CANDIDATES TO SMEAR OPPONENTS WITH WORDS LIKE "SICK, DISGRACE, CORRUPT, CHEAT, DECAY, PATHETIC, RADICAL, TRAITOR, GREED, ANTI-FAMILY" AND SO ON!

THE GOPAC MEMO IS THE MAGNA CARTA OF ATTACK POLITICS. IT CODIFIED THE TOXIC RHETORIC THAT CAME TO DEFINE AN ERA!

FASCINATING...

BY THE WAY, THAT'S THE SPEAKER'S ORIGINAL COPY — IT'S AN EXTREMELY VALUABLE ACQUISITION!

EVEN WITH THE DISCOLORATION?

WELL, THOSE ARE ORIGINAL MUD STAINS — MUCH PRIZED BY CURATORS!

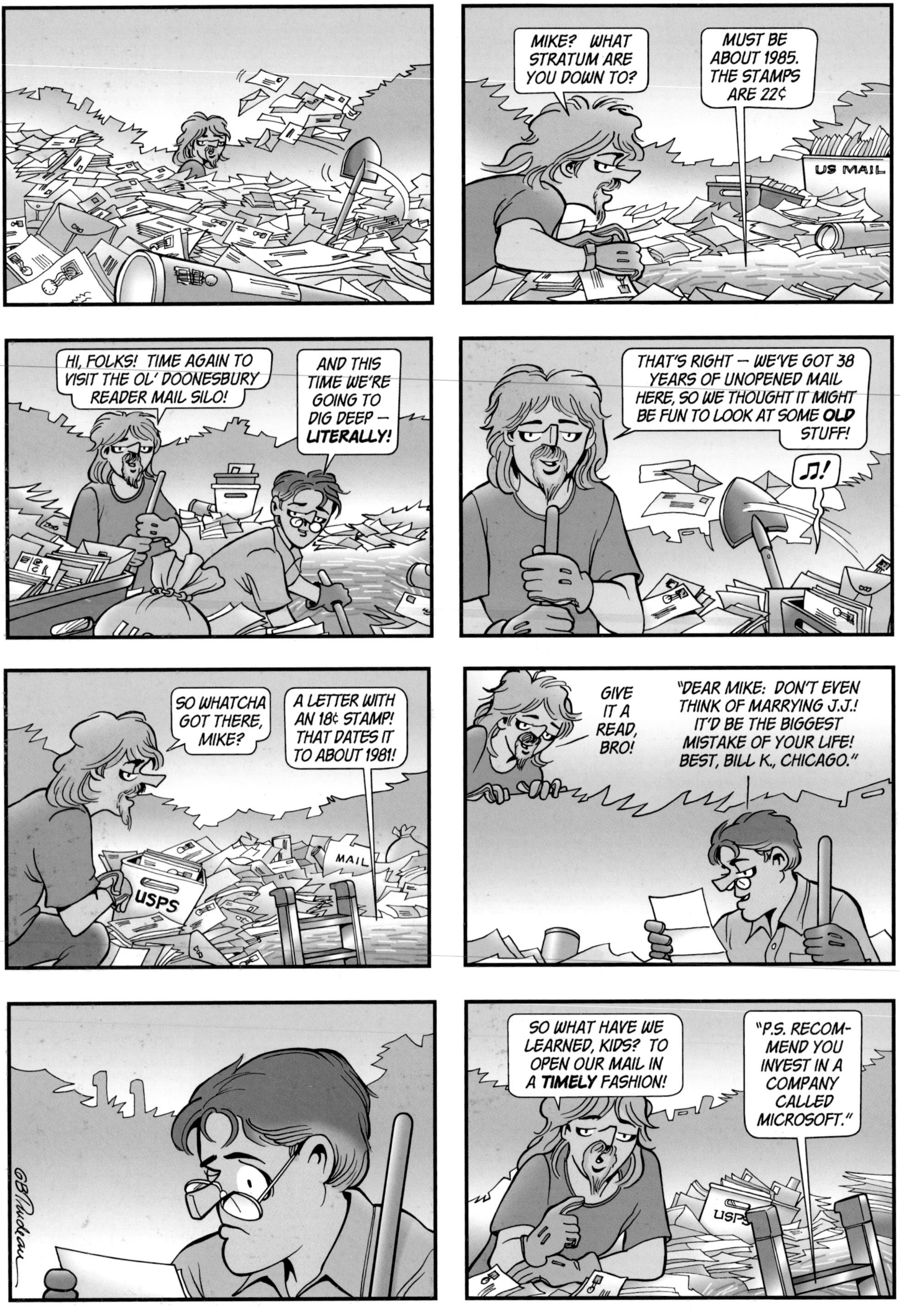
MIKE? WHAT STRATUM ARE YOU DOWN TO?
MUST BE ABOUT 1985. THE STAMPS ARE 22¢
US MAIL
HI, FOLKS! TIME AGAIN TO VISIT THE OL' DOONESBURY READER MAIL SILO!
AND THIS TIME WE'RE GOING TO DIG DEEP — LITERALLY!
THAT'S RIGHT — WE'VE GOT 38 YEARS OF UNOPENED MAIL HERE, SO WE THOUGHT IT MIGHT BE FUN TO LOOK AT SOME OLD STUFF!
♫!
SO WHATCHA GOT THERE, MIKE?
A LETTER WITH AN 18¢ STAMP! THAT DATES IT TO ABOUT 1981!
USPS
MAIL
GIVE IT A READ, BRO!
"DEAR MIKE: DON'T EVEN THINK OF MARRYING J.J.! IT'D BE THE BIGGEST MISTAKE OF YOUR LIFE! BEST, BILL K., CHICAGO."
©BTrudeau
SO WHAT HAVE WE LEARNED, KIDS? TO OPEN OUR MAIL IN A TIMELY FASHION!
"P.S. RECOMMEND YOU INVEST IN A COMPANY CALLED MICROSOFT."
USPS

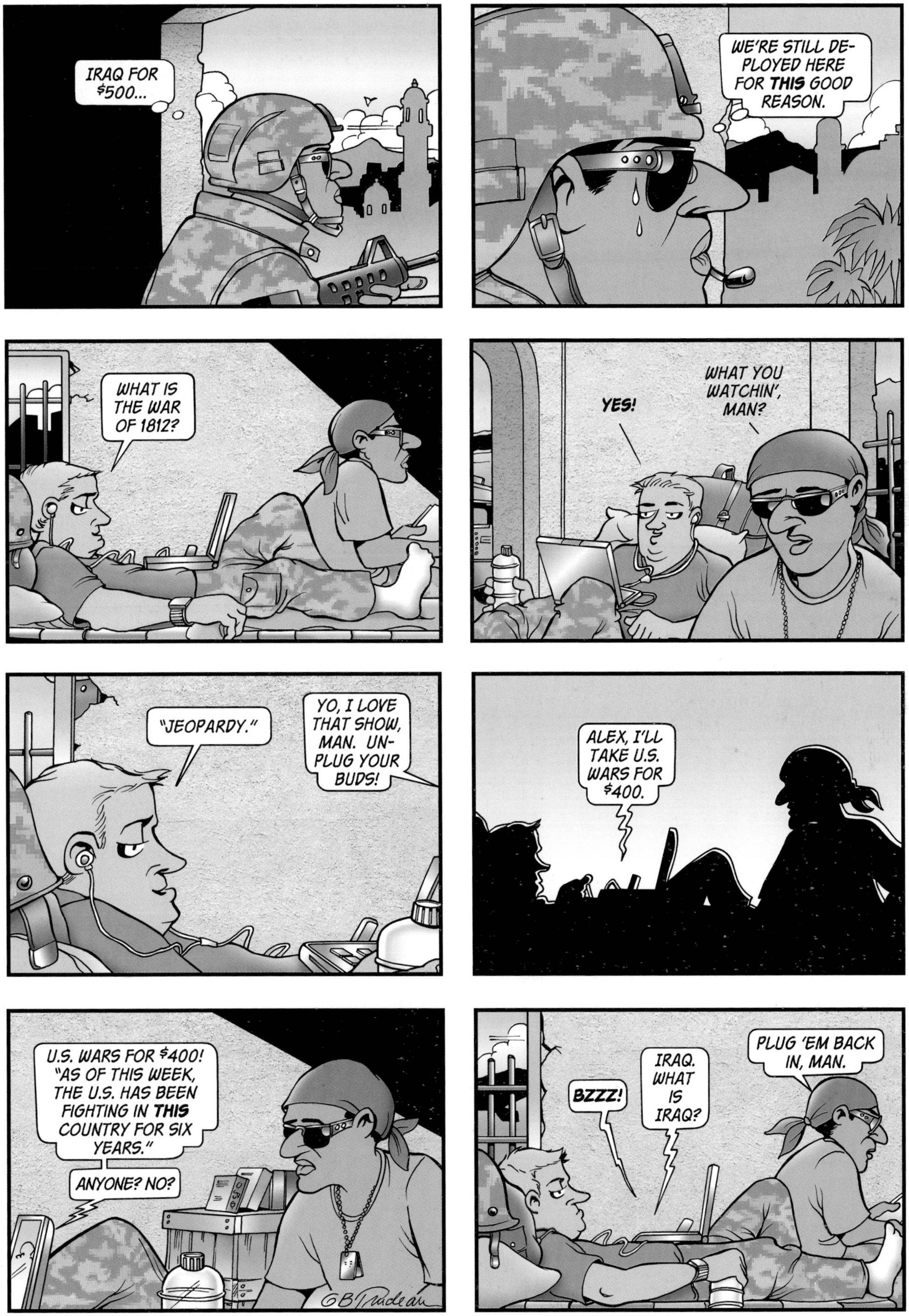
IRAQ FOR $500...
WE'RE STILL DE-PLOYED HERE FOR **THIS** GOOD REASON.
WHAT IS THE WAR OF 1812?
YES!
WHAT YOU WATCHIN', MAN?
"JEOPARDY."
YO, I LOVE THAT SHOW, MAN. UN-PLUG YOUR BUDS!
ALEX, I'LL TAKE U.S. WARS FOR $400.
U.S. WARS FOR $400! "AS OF THIS WEEK, THE U.S. HAS BEEN FIGHTING IN **THIS** COUNTRY FOR SIX YEARS."
ANYONE? NO?
GB Trudeau
BZZZ!
IRAQ. WHAT IS IRAQ?
PLUG 'EM BACK IN, MAN.

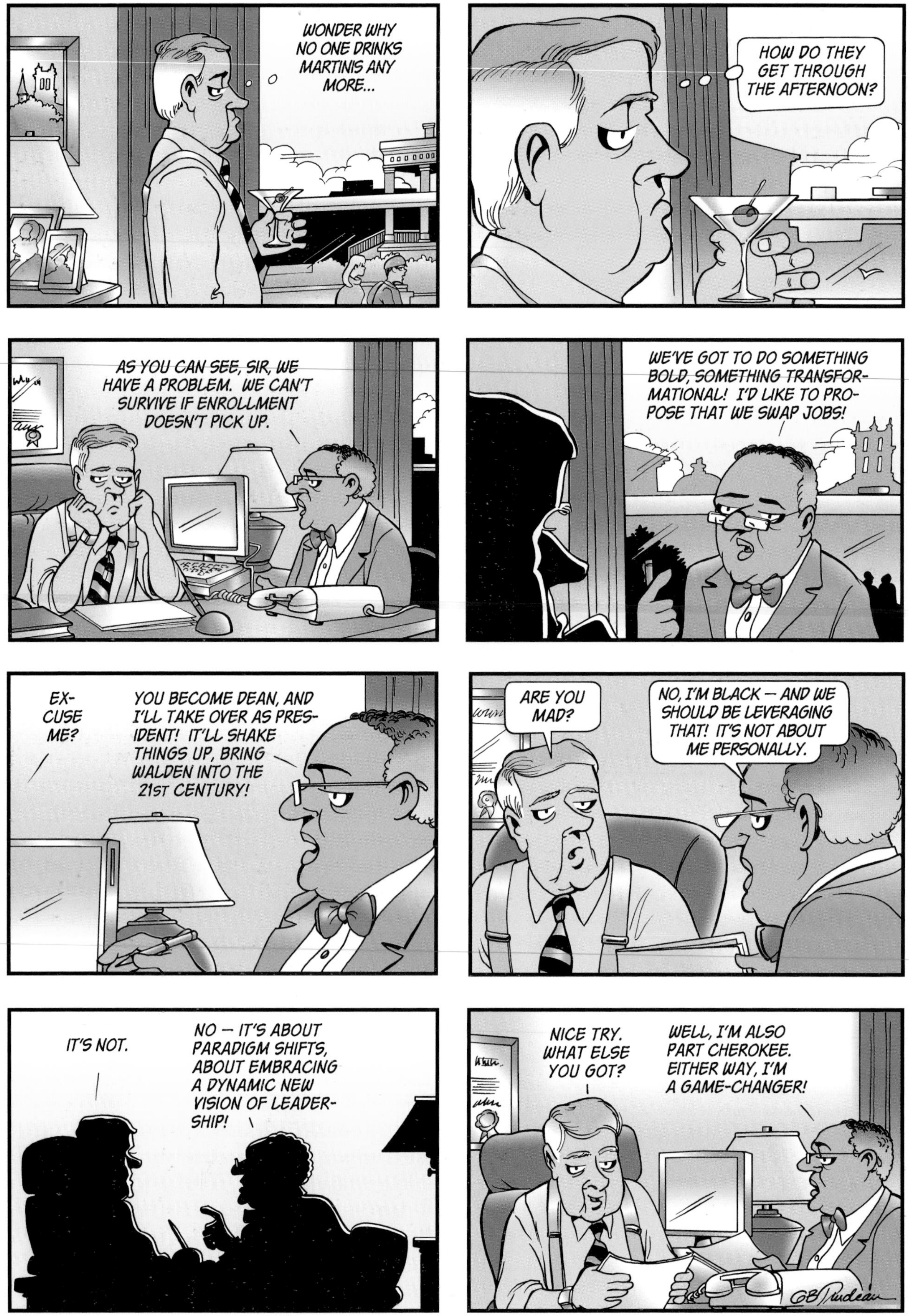
WONDER WHY NO ONE DRINKS MARTINIS ANY MORE...
HOW DO THEY GET THROUGH THE AFTERNOON?
AS YOU CAN SEE, SIR, WE HAVE A PROBLEM. WE CAN'T SURVIVE IF ENROLLMENT DOESN'T PICK UP.
WE'VE GOT TO DO SOMETHING BOLD, SOMETHING TRANSFORMATIONAL! I'D LIKE TO PROPOSE THAT WE SWAP JOBS!
YOU BECOME DEAN, AND I'LL TAKE OVER AS PRESIDENT! IT'LL SHAKE THINGS UP, BRING WALDEN INTO THE 21ST CENTURY!
EXCUSE ME?
ARE YOU MAD?
NO, I'M BLACK — AND WE SHOULD BE LEVERAGING THAT! IT'S NOT ABOUT ME PERSONALLY.
IT'S NOT.
NO — IT'S ABOUT PARADIGM SHIFTS, ABOUT EMBRACING A DYNAMIC NEW VISION OF LEADERSHIP!
NICE TRY. WHAT ELSE YOU GOT?
WELL, I'M ALSO PART CHEROKEE. EITHER WAY, I'M A GAME-CHANGER!
GB Trudeau

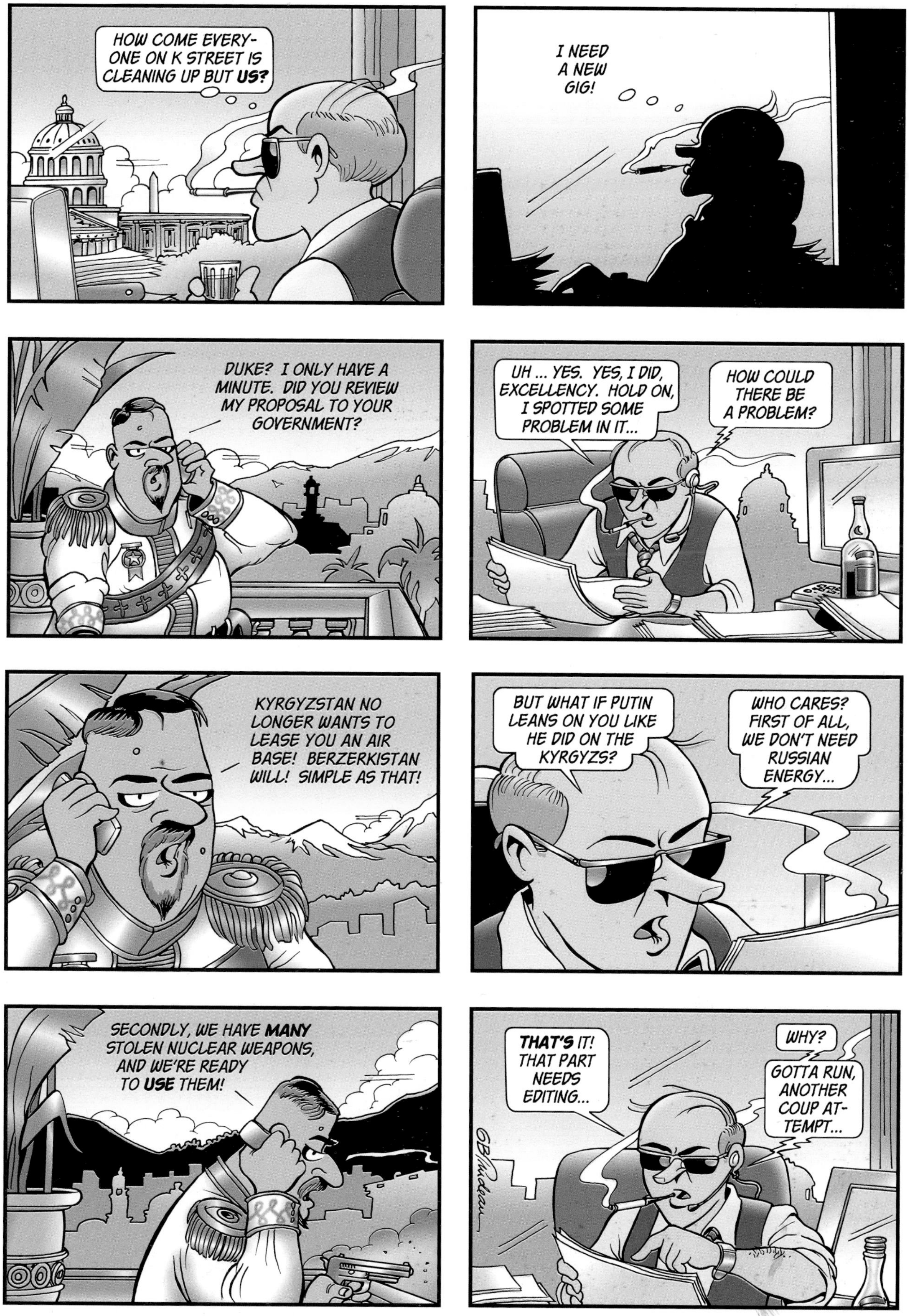
HOW COME EVERY-ONE ON K STREET IS CLEANING UP BUT US?
I NEED A NEW GIG!
DUKE? I ONLY HAVE A MINUTE. DID YOU REVIEW MY PROPOSAL TO YOUR GOVERNMENT?
UH ... YES. YES, I DID, EXCELLENCY. HOLD ON, I SPOTTED SOME PROBLEM IN IT...
HOW COULD THERE BE A PROBLEM?
KYRGYZSTAN NO LONGER WANTS TO LEASE YOU AN AIR BASE! BERZERKISTAN WILL! SIMPLE AS THAT!
BUT WHAT IF PUTIN LEANS ON YOU LIKE HE DID ON THE KYRGYZS?
WHO CARES? FIRST OF ALL, WE DON'T NEED RUSSIAN ENERGY...
SECONDLY, WE HAVE MANY STOLEN NUCLEAR WEAPONS, AND WE'RE READY TO USE THEM!
THAT'S IT! THAT PART NEEDS EDITING...
WHY?
GOTTA RUN, ANOTHER COUP AT-TEMPT...
©B Trudeau

I UNDERSTAND YOUR SUSPICIONS OF MODERNITY, AKBARI, I REALLY DO...
BUT COULDN'T YOU AT LEAST JOIN THE 16TH CENTURY?
SO, WHAT'VE YOU GOT FOR ME?
DRUG LORD. A MAJOR PLAYER.
HE'S CHALLENGING MY AUTHORITY HERE, BUT I CAN'T TOUCH HIM. HE HAS CONNECTIONS IN KABUL.
WHERE'S HE AT?
THAT GRAY HOUSE OVER THERE, JUST BEYOND THE MOSQUE.
BEEP! BEEP! BEEP!
WHOOM!
WHAT ELSE YOU GOT?
I DON'T GET IT — HOW COME YOU GUYS ARE LOSING?
©B. Trudeau

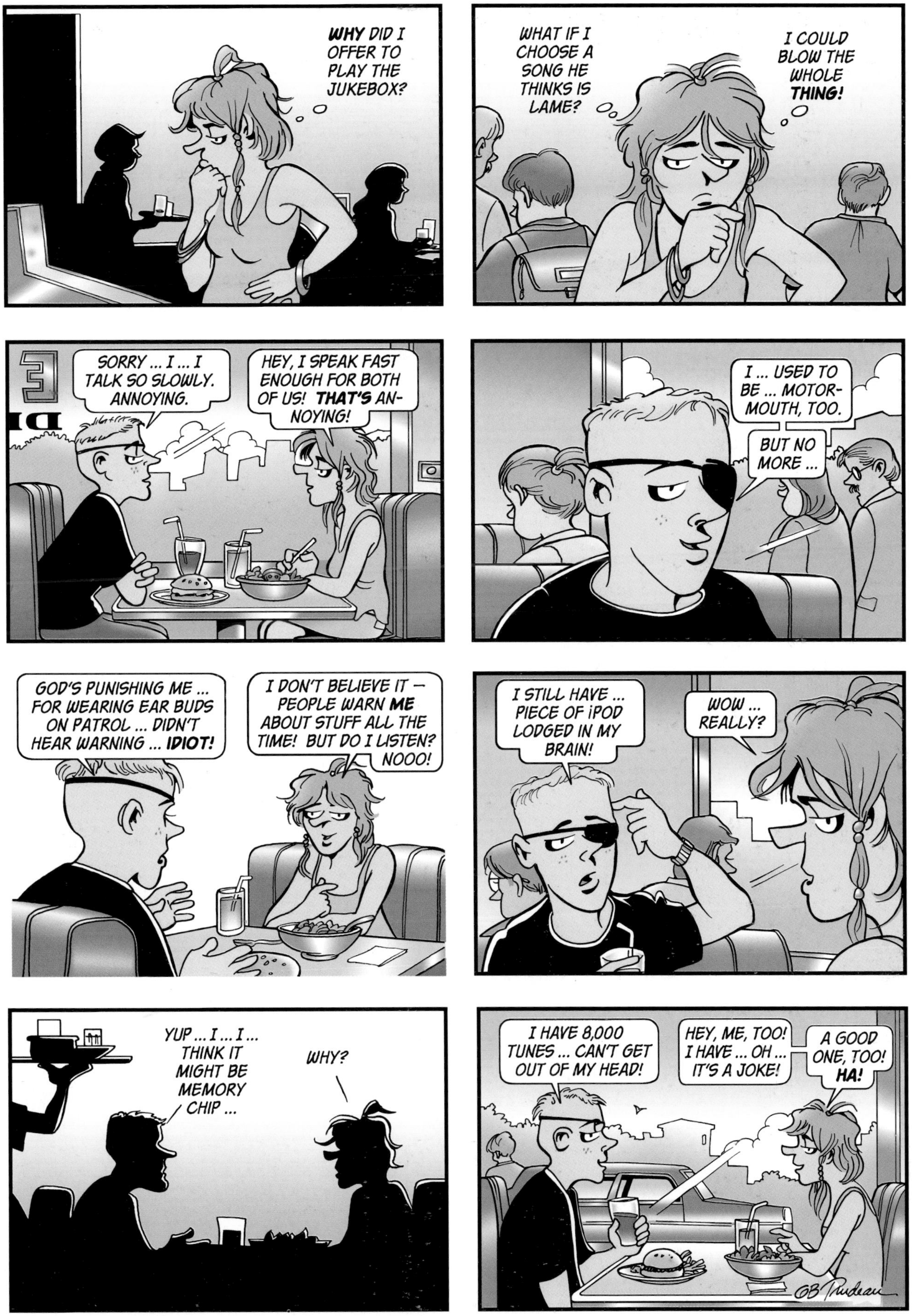
WHY DID I OFFER TO PLAY THE JUKEBOX?
WHAT IF I CHOOSE A SONG HE THINKS IS LAME?
I COULD BLOW THE WHOLE THING!
SORRY ... I ... I TALK SO SLOWLY. ANNOYING.
HEY, I SPEAK FAST ENOUGH FOR BOTH OF US! THAT'S ANNOYING!
I ... USED TO BE ... MOTOR-MOUTH, TOO.
BUT NO MORE ...
GOD'S PUNISHING ME ... FOR WEARING EAR BUDS ON PATROL ... DIDN'T HEAR WARNING ... IDIOT!
I DON'T BELIEVE IT — PEOPLE WARN ME ABOUT STUFF ALL THE TIME! BUT DO I LISTEN? NOOO!
I STILL HAVE ... PIECE OF iPOD LODGED IN MY BRAIN!
WOW ... REALLY?
YUP ... I ... I ... THINK IT MIGHT BE MEMORY CHIP ...
WHY?
I HAVE 8,000 TUNES ... CAN'T GET OUT OF MY HEAD!
HEY, ME, TOO! I HAVE ... OH ... IT'S A JOKE!
A GOOD ONE, TOO! HA!
GB Trudeau

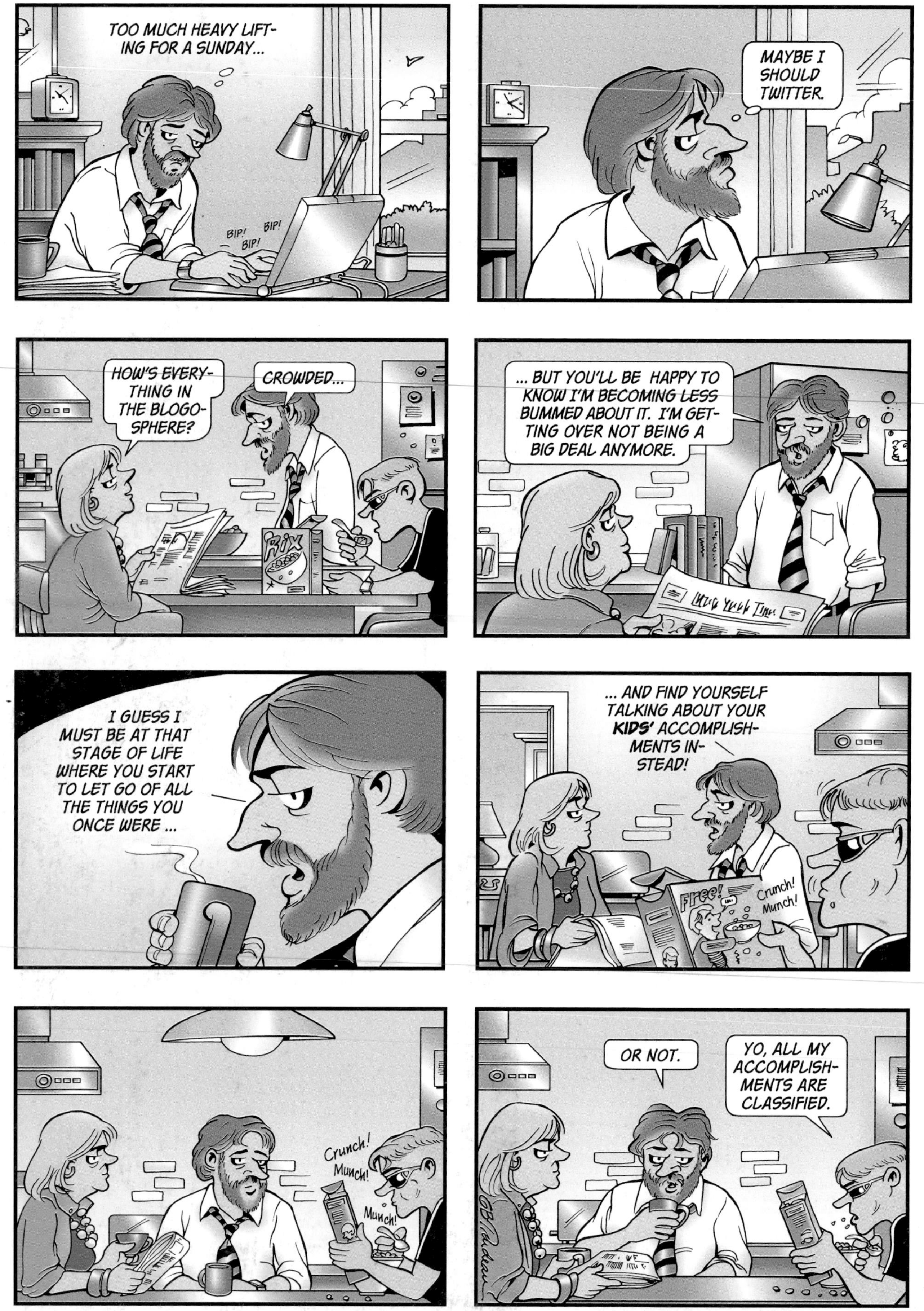
TOO MUCH HEAVY LIFT-ING FOR A SUNDAY...
BIP!
BIP!
BIP!
MAYBE I SHOULD TWITTER.
HOW'S EVERY-THING IN THE BLOGO-SPHERE?
CROWDED...
Rix
... BUT YOU'LL BE HAPPY TO KNOW I'M BECOMING LESS BUMMED ABOUT IT. I'M GET-TING OVER NOT BEING A BIG DEAL ANYMORE.
I GUESS I MUST BE AT THAT STAGE OF LIFE WHERE YOU START TO LET GO OF ALL THE THINGS YOU ONCE WERE ...
... AND FIND YOURSELF TALKING ABOUT YOUR **KIDS'** ACCOMPLISH-MENTS IN-STEAD!
Free!
Crunch! Munch!
Crunch! Munch!
Munch!
OR NOT.
YO, ALL MY ACCOMPLISH-MENTS ARE CLASSIFIED.

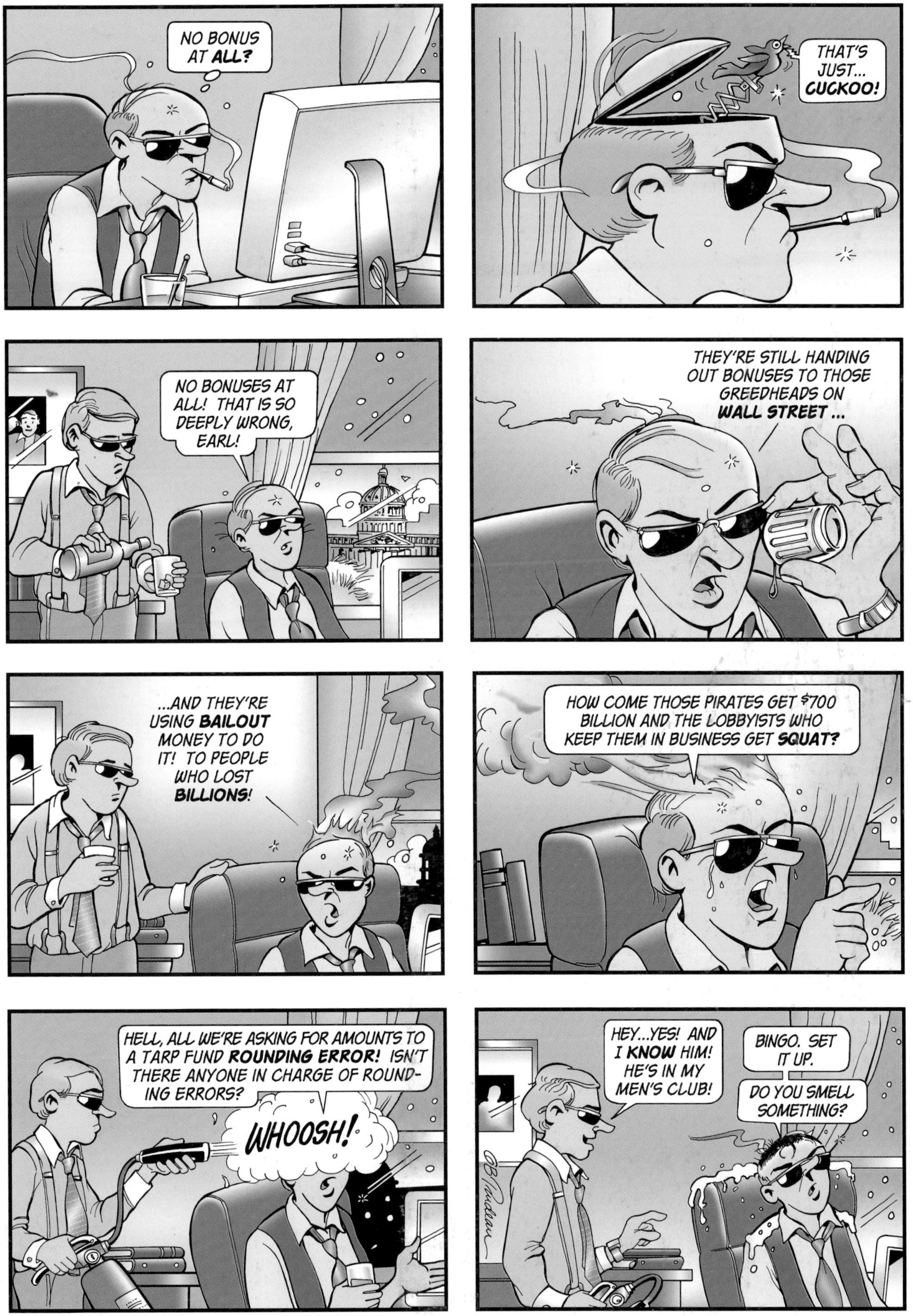
NO BONUS AT ALL?
THAT'S JUST... CUCKOO!
NO BONUSES AT ALL! THAT IS SO DEEPLY WRONG, EARL!
THEY'RE STILL HANDING OUT BONUSES TO THOSE GREEDHEADS ON WALL STREET ...
...AND THEY'RE USING BAILOUT MONEY TO DO IT! TO PEOPLE WHO LOST BILLIONS!
HOW COME THOSE PIRATES GET $700 BILLION AND THE LOBBYISTS WHO KEEP THEM IN BUSINESS GET SQUAT?
HELL, ALL WE'RE ASKING FOR AMOUNTS TO A TARP FUND ROUNDING ERROR! ISN'T THERE ANYONE IN CHARGE OF ROUNDING ERRORS?
WHOOSH!
HEY...YES! AND I KNOW HIM! HE'S IN MY MEN'S CLUB!
BINGO. SET IT UP.
DO YOU SMELL SOMETHING?

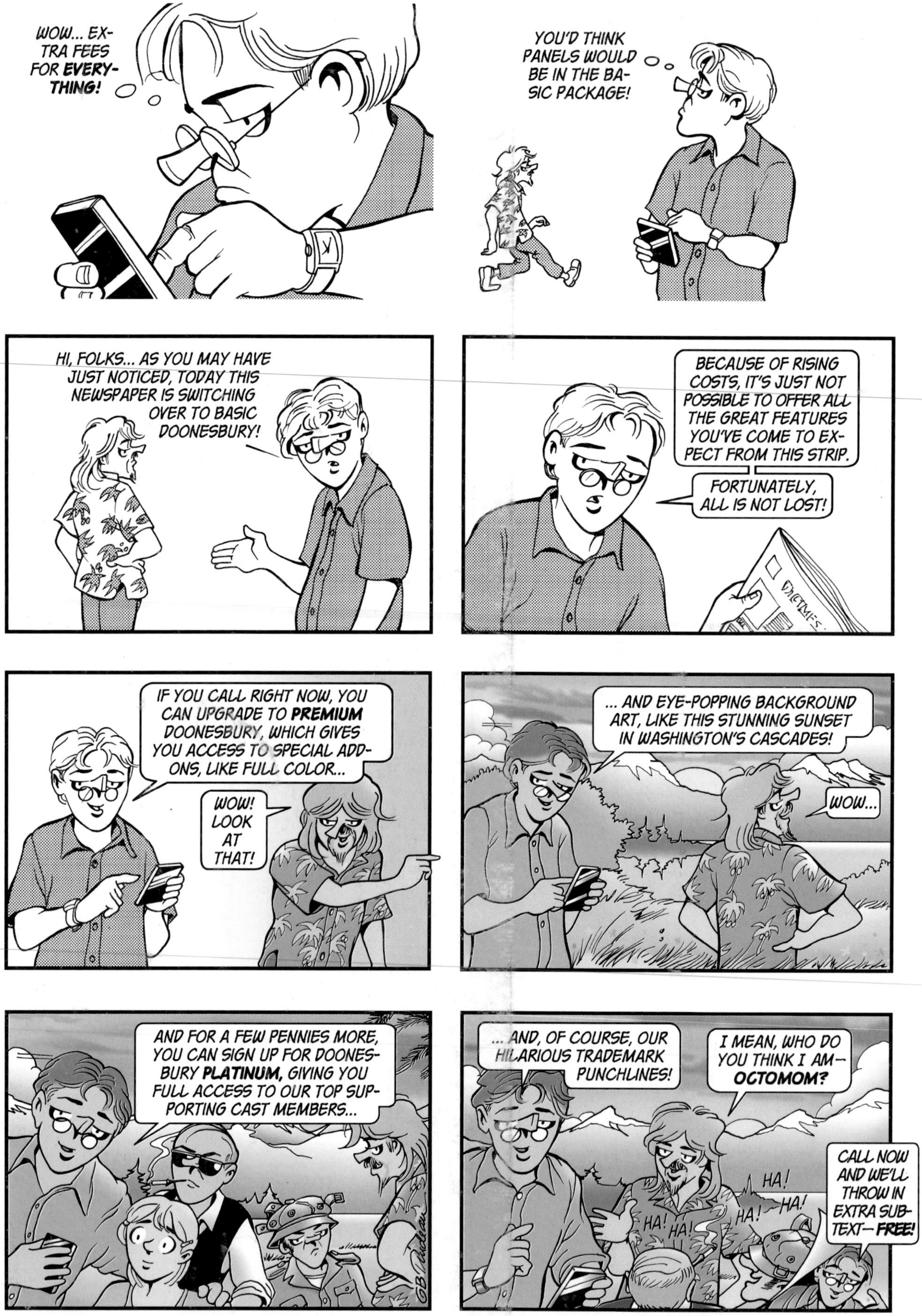
WOW... EXTRA FEES FOR **EVERYTHING!**
YOU'D THINK PANELS WOULD BE IN THE BASIC PACKAGE!
HI, FOLKS... AS YOU MAY HAVE JUST NOTICED, TODAY THIS NEWSPAPER IS SWITCHING OVER TO BASIC DOONESBURY!
BECAUSE OF RISING COSTS, IT'S JUST NOT POSSIBLE TO OFFER ALL THE GREAT FEATURES YOU'VE COME TO EXPECT FROM THIS STRIP.
FORTUNATELY, ALL IS NOT LOST!
IF YOU CALL RIGHT NOW, YOU CAN UPGRADE TO **PREMIUM** DOONESBURY, WHICH GIVES YOU ACCESS TO SPECIAL ADD-ONS, LIKE FULL COLOR...
WOW! LOOK AT THAT!
... AND EYE-POPPING BACKGROUND ART, LIKE THIS STUNNING SUNSET IN WASHINGTON'S CASCADES!
WOW...
AND FOR A FEW PENNIES MORE, YOU CAN SIGN UP FOR DOONESBURY **PLATINUM,** GIVING YOU FULL ACCESS TO OUR TOP SUPPORTING CAST MEMBERS...
... AND, OF COURSE, OUR HILARIOUS TRADEMARK PUNCHLINES!
I MEAN, WHO DO YOU THINK I AM— **OCTOMOM?**
HA! HA! HA! HA! HA!
CALL NOW AND WE'LL THROW IN EXTRA SUBTEXT— **FREE!**